THE WILLIAM STALLI ON COMPUTER AND DATA COMMUNICATIONS TECHNOLOGY

ISDN AND BROADBAND ISDN, with FRAME RELAY AND ATM, THIRD EDITION

An in-depth presentation of the technology and architecture of integrated services digital networks (ISDN). Covers the integrated digital network (IDN), ISDN services, architecture, signaling system no. 7 (SS7), and detailed coverage of the ITU-T standards. This new edition also provides detailed coverage of protocols and congestion control strategies for both frame relay and ATM.

BUSINESS DATA COMMUNICATIONS, SECOND EDITION

A comprehensive presentation of data communications and telecommunications from a business perspective. Covers voice, data, image, and video communications and applications technology and includes a number of case studies.

OPERATING SYSTEMS, SECOND EDITION

A state-of-the art survey of operating system principles. Covers fundamental technology as well as contemporary design issues, such as threads, real-time systems, multiprocessor scheduling, distributed systems, security, and object-oriented design.

PROTECT YOUR PRIVACY: A GUIDE FOR PGP USERS

Provides detailed step-by-step instructions on the use of PGP on the most important computer platforms. It explains the fundamentals of encryption and digital signatures so that the reader will know what PGP can do for him or her. Also provides explicit instructions on solving the all-important problem of obtaining trusted public keys of other users.

Local and Metropolitan Area Networks

FIFTH EDITION

William Stallings

Prentice Hall
Upper Saddle River, New Jersey 07458

Library of Congress Cataloging-in-Publication Data

Stallings, William
  Local and metropolitan area networks/William
Stallings.—5th ed.
    p. cm.
  Includes bibliographical references and index.
  ISBN 0-13-190737-9
  1. Local area networks (Computer networks)   2. Metropolitan area
networks (Computer networks)   I. Title.
TK5105.7.S77 1997   95-49213
004.6'8—dc20   CIP

Acquisitions editor: *Laura Steele/Alan Apt*
Editorial production supervision
 and interior design: *Barbara Marttine Cappuccio*
Managing Editor: *Bayani DeLeon*
Editor-in-chief: *Marcia Horton*
Director of production and manufacturing: *David W. Riccardi*
Cover design: *Heather Scott*
Cover illustrator: *Rolando E. Corujo*
Art director: *Amy Rosen*
Creative director: *Paula Maylahn*
Manufacturing buyer: *Donna Sullivan*
Editorial assistant: *Shirley McGuire*

©1997 by Prentice-Hall, Inc.
Simon & Schuster/A Viacom Company
Upper Saddle River, New Jersey 07458

Earlier edition copyrights © 1993 by Macmillan Publishing Company.
Earlier edition copyrights entitled *Local Networks*, © 1984, 1987, and 1990 by Macmillan
Publishing Company.

The author and publisher of this book have used their best efforts in preparing this book. These efforts include the development, research, and testing of the theories and programs to determine their effectiveness. The author and publisher make no warranty of any kind, expressed or implied, with regard to these programs or the documentation contained in this book. The author and publisher shall not be liable in any event for incidental or consequential damages in connection with, or arising out of, the furnishing, performance, or use of these programs.

Printed in the United States of America

10   9   8   7   6   5

ISBN   0-13-190737-9

Prentice-Hall International (UK) Limited, *London*
Prentice-Hall of Australia Pty. Limited, *Sydney*
Prentice-Hall Canada Inc., *Toronto*
Prentice-Hall Hispanoamericana, S.A., *Mexico*
Prentice-Hall of India Private Limited, *New Delhi*
Prentice-Hall of Japan, Inc., *Tokyo*
Simon & Schuster Asia Pte. Ltd., *Singapore*
Editora Prentice-Hall do Brasil, Ltda., *Rio de Janeiro*

For Tricia, the kindest and bravest

Contents

Part Three   **LAN/MAN SYSTEMS**

CHAPTER 6

Traditional LANs   174

CHAPTER 7

High-Speed Ethernet-Like LANs   221

CHAPTER 8

Fiber Distributed Data Interface   252

CHAPTER 9

Fibre Channel   287

Part Four   **DESIGN ISSUES**

CHAPTER 13

LAN/MAN Performance   426

Preface

Objectives

This book focuses on the broad and evolving field of local and metropolitan area networks. The aim of the text is to provide a reasoned balance among breadth, depth, and timeliness. The book emphasizes topics of fundamental importance concerning the technology and architecture of these networks. Certain key related areas, such as performance, internetworking, and network management, are also treated in some detail.

The book explores the key topics in the field in the following general categories:

- *Technology and architecture.* There is a small collection of ingredients that serves to characterize and differentiate local and metropolitan area networks, including transmission medium, topology, communication protocols, and switching technique.
- *Network type.* This book covers the important types of networks, including those defined in the IEEE 802 standards, plus FDDI, Fibre Channel, ATM LANs, and wireless LANs.
- *Design approaches.* The book examines alternative design choices and assesses their relative merits.

Plan of the Text

The book is organized into four parts:

I. *Background.* This part provides a preview and context for the remainder of the book.

II. *LAN/MAN Architecture.* This part examines technology areas common to all LAN and MAN systems. The various topologies and transmission media are discussed; this includes a consideration of cabling types and wiring layout. There is also a discussion of the communications protocol architecture within which LAN/MAN protocols are defined. Finally, logical link control (LLC), which is the common interface to upper-layer protocols, is described.

III. *LAN/MAN Systems.* The major types of LANs and MANS are covered. These include all of the LANs defined by the IEEE 802 committee, as well as FDDI, Fibre Channel, ATM LANs, and wireless LANs.

IV. *Design Issues.* This part looks at issues relating to the relative performance of various LAN/MAN approaches. It also covers the use of bridges and routers for network interconnection. Finally, network management and the use of SNMP is covered.

The book includes an extensive glossary, a list of frequently used acronyms, and a bibliography. Most chapters include problems and suggestions for further reading.

Throughout, there is an emphasis on both technology and on standards. The book provides a comprehensive guide to understanding specific LAN and MAN standards, such as IEEE 802 and FDDI, and the specifications issued by the ATM Forum and the Fibre Channel Association. This emphasis reflects the importance of such standards in defining the available products and future research directions in this field.

Internet Services

An internet mailing list has been set up so that instructors using this book can exchange information, suggestions, and questions with each other and with the author. To subscribe, send a message to majordomo@prenhall.com with a message body of subscribe ws-lan. To post a message, send to ws-lan@prenhall.com.

An errata list for the book is available via the web at http://www.shore.net/~ws/welcome.html.

What's New in the Fifth Edition

In the four years since the fourth edition of this book was published, the field has seen continued innovations and improvements. In this new edition, I try to capture these changes, while maintaining a broad and comprehensive coverage of the entire field. In addition, many users of the fourth edition have made constructive comments that have resulted in a substantial reorganization of the material.

The most obvious change in the fifth edition is the increased emphasis on high-speed networks. A number of trends dictate the rapid move to high-speed technology in the LAN/MAN field: the continued, relentless increase in the speed and capacity of computer systems; the evolution of applications to include greater emphasis on graphic and video; and the increased volume of data generated by the move to client–server computing. The result of these trends has been the introduction in recent years of a number of new schemes for moving large volumes of data at high rates within the local area. These schemes are both complementary and competing, making it difficult for the observer to assess their relative merits and areas of application. This new edition covers these alternative approaches to high-speed local networking and addresses the issues relating to interconnecting these networks with each other and with wide-area networks.

There is a number of new chapters in this edition. In addition, much of the material carried over from the fourth edition has been substantially revised. As an indication of the scope of the revision, over half of the figures (137 of 242) and two-thirds of the tables (46 of 69) are new, 58 references have been added, and 45 new homework problems have been included. Some of the most noteworthy changes are the following:

- Chapter 7 covers the two recent 100-Mbps LANs that have evolved from the original Ethernet: 100BASE-T and 100VG-AnyLAN.
- Chapter 9 covers the Fibre Channel, which operates at up to 800 Mbps and, unlike traditional LANs, uses a switched rather than a shared-medium configuration.
- Chapter 10 covers ATM LANs, which carry asynchronous transfer mode technology onto the local premises and provide a seamless integration with wide-area ATM networks.
- Chapter 11 covers the increasingly important area of wireless LANs.
- There is expanded coverage of transmission media, including the important category 5 unshielded twisted pair specification.
- Structure cabling systems are discussed, including a description of the new EIA-568 standard.
- The discussion of LLC, which is the "glue" that holds together the LAN/MAN protocol architecture, has been expanded significantly.
- TCP/IP, which is the near-universal communications architecture for LANs and MANs, is described.
- The chapter on network management has been completely revised and now includes a discussion of SNMP.

Acknowledgments

This new edition has benefited from review by a number of people, who gave generously of their time and expertise. A number of people reviewed the previous edition and made constructive comments for the new edition, including Kitel Albertson of the Trondheim College of Engineering, Greg Brewster of DePaul University, and Ravi Sankar of the University of South Florida. The chapter on ATM and ATM LANs was reviewed by Derya Cansever of GTE; Ken Christensen and Bill Ellington of IBM; and Mark McCutcheon, Alimudden Mohammad, and Darren Tsang of the University of British Columbia. Roger Cummings of StorageTek, Gary Stephens of FSI Consulting Services, and Jan Dedek of ANCOT Corporation reviewed the material on Fibre Channel. Bill Bunch of National Semiconductor, Daniel Dove of Hewlett Packard, and Ronald Cooper of IBM reviewed the chapter on 100BASE-T and 100VG-AnyLAN. Rajamani Ganesh of the David Sarnoff Research Center and Craig Mathias of Farpoint Group reviewed the material on wireless LANs.

CHAPTER

1

Introduction

The local area network (LAN) has come to play a central role in information distribution and office functioning within businesses and other organizations. The major factors driving the widespread use of LANs have been the proliferation of personal computers, workstations, and servers, coupled with the increasing reliance on the client–server computing model.

With the dropping price of LAN hardware and software, LANs have become more numerous and larger, and they have taken on more and more functions within the organization. The upshot is that the LAN, once installed, quickly becomes almost as essential as the telephone system. At the same time, there is a proliferation of LAN types and options and a need to interconnect a number of LANs at the same site and with LANs at other sites. This has led to the development of LANs of higher and higher data rates and the relatively recent introduction of the metropolitan area network (MAN).

Before defining the terms LAN and MAN, it is useful to look at the trends responsible for the importance of these networks, which we do in the first section. Next we contrast the differences among LANs, MANs, and wide-area networks (WANs). This is followed by a discussion of key application areas for LANs and MANs. This chapter also provides a preview of the remainder of the book and pointers to Internet resources relating to LANs and MANs.

1.1

THE NEED FOR LOCAL NETWORKS

Perhaps the driving force behind the widespread use of LANs and MANs is the dramatic and continuing decrease in computer hardware costs, accompanied by an increase in computer hardware capability. Year by year, the cost of computer systems continues to drop dramatically while the performance and capacity of those systems continue to rise equally dramatically. At a local warehouse club, you can pick up a personal computer for less than $1000 that packs the wallop of an IBM mainframe from 10 years ago. Inside that personal computer, including the microprocessor and memory and other chips, you get roughly 100 million transistors. You can't buy 100 million of anything else for so little. That many sheets of toilet paper would run more than $100,000.

Thus we have virtually "free" computer power. And this ongoing technological revolution has enabled the development of applications of astounding complexity and power. For example, desktop applications that require the great power of today's microprocessor-based systems include:

- Image processing
- Speech recognition
- Videoconferencing
- Multimedia authoring
- Voice and video annotation of files

Workstation systems now support highly sophisticated engineering and scientific applications, as well as simulation systems, and the ability to apply workgroup principles to image and video applications. In addition, businesses are relying on increasingly powerful servers to handle transaction and database processing and to support massive client–server networks that have replace the huge mainframe computer centers of yesteryear.

All of these factors lead to an increased number of systems, with increased power, at a single site: office building, factory, operations center, and so on. At the same time, there is an absolute requirement to interconnect these systems to:

- Share and exchange data among systems
- Share expensive resources

The need to share data is a compelling reason for interconnection. Individual users of computer resources do not work in isolation. They need facilities to exchange messages with other users, to access data from several sources in the preparation of a document or for an analysis, and to share project-related information with other members of a work group.

The need to share expensive resources is another driving factor in the development of networks. The cost of processor hardware has dropped far more rapidly than the cost of mass storage devices, video equipment, printers, and other peripheral devices. The result is a need to share these expensive devices among a number of users to justify the cost of the equipment. This sharing requires some sort of client–server architecture operating over a network that interconnects users and resources.

1.2

LANs, MANs, AND WANs

Local area networks (LANs), metropolitan area networks (MANs), and wide-area networks (WANs) are all examples of communications networks. A communications network is a facility that interconnects a number of devices and provides a means for transmitting data from one attached device to another.

There are a number of ways of classifying communications networks. One way is in terms of the technology used: specifically, in terms of topology and transmission medium. That approach is explored in Chapter 3. Perhaps the most commonly used means of classification is on the basis of geographical scope. Traditionally, networks have been classified as either local area networks (LANs) or wide-area networks (WANs). A category that recently began to receive much attention is the metropolitan area network (MAN). Figure 1.1 illustrates these categories in addition to some special cases. By way of contrast, the typical range of parameters for a multiple-processor computer is also depicted.

Wide-Area Network

Wide-area networks have traditionally been considered to be those that cover a large geographical area, require the crossing of public rights-of-way, and rely at least in part on circuits provided by a common carrier. Typically, a WAN consists of a number of interconnected switching nodes. A transmission from any one device is routed through these internal nodes to the specified destination device.

Traditionally, WANs have provided only relatively modest capacity to subscribers. For data attachment, either to a data network or to a telephone network by means of a modem, data rates of 9600 bps or even less have been common. Business subscribers have been able to obtain higher rates, with a service known as T-1, which operates at 1.544 Mbps, being common. The most important recent development in WANs in this range of performance has been the development of the integrated services digital network

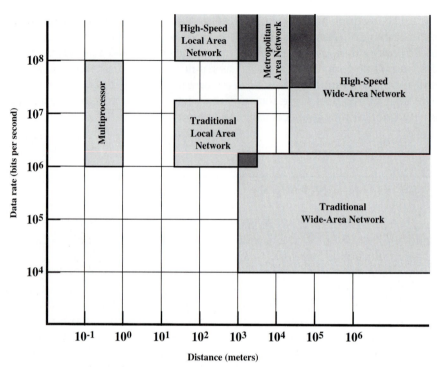

FIGURE 1.1 Comparison of Multiprocessor Systems, LANs, MANs, and WANs

(ISDN), which provides circuit-switching and packet-switching services at rates up to 1.544 Mbps (2.048 Mbps in Europe).

The continuing development of practical optical fiber facilities has led to the standardization of much higher data rates for WANs, and these services are becoming more widely available. These high-speed WANs provide user connections in the tens and hundreds of Mbps, using transmission techniques known as frame relay and asynchronous transfer mode (ATM).

Local Area Network

As with wide-area networks, a local area network is a communications network that interconnects a variety of devices and provides a means for information exchange among those devices. There are several key distinctions between LANs and WANs:

1. The scope of the LAN is small, typically a single building or a cluster of buildings. This difference in geographic scope leads to different technical solutions, as we shall see.

2. It is usually the case that the LAN is owned by the same organization that owns the attached devices. For WANs, this is less often the case, or at least a significant fraction of the network assets are not owned.

This has two implications. First, care must be taken in the choice of LAN, since there may be a substantial capital investment (compared to dial-up or leased charges for wide-area networks) for both purchase and maintenance. Second, the network management responsibility for a local network falls solely on the user.

3. The internal data rates of LANs are typically much greater than those of wide-area networks.

LANs have been the focus of a standardization effort by the IEEE 802 committee, and it is perhaps useful to quote their definition of a LAN[1]:

> The LANs described herein are distinguished from other types of data networks in that they are optimized for a moderate size geographic area such as a single office building, a warehouse, or a campus. The IEEE 802 LAN is a shared medium peer-to-peer communications network that broadcasts information for all stations to receive. As a consequence, it does not inherently provide privacy. The LAN enables stations to communicate directly using a common physical medium on a point-to-point basis without any intermediate switching node being required. There is always need for an access sublayer in order to arbitrate the access to the shared medium. The network is generally owned, used, and operated by a single organization. This is in contrast to Wide Area Networks (WANs) that interconnect communication facilities in different parts of a country or are used as a public utility. These LANs are also different from networks, such as backplane buses, that are optimized for the interconnection of devices on a desk top or components within a single piece of equipment.

Simple LAN.   A simple example of a LAN that highlights some of its characteristics is shown in Figure 1.2. All of the devices are attached to a shared transmission medium. A transmission from any device can be received by all other devices attached to the same network.

What is not apparent in Figure 1.2 is that each device attaches to the LAN through a hardware/software module that handles the transmission and medium access functions associated with the LAN. Typically, this module is implemented as a physically distinct network interface card (NIC) in each attached device. The NIC contains the logic for accessing the LAN and for sending and receiving blocks of data on the LAN.

An important function of the NIC is that it uses a buffered transmission technique to accommodate the difference in the data rate between the LAN medium and the NIC–processor link, as illustrated in Figure 1.3. The NIC captures transmissions intended for the attached device, which arrive at the data rate of the LAN, which may be, for example, 10 Mbps. When a block of data is captured, it is stored temporarily in an input buffer. It is then delivered to the host processor, often over some sort of backplane bus, at the data rate of that bus. This data rate is typically different from the LAN data rate.

[1]From IEEE 802 Standard, *Local and Metropolitan Area Networks: Overview and Architecture,* 1990.

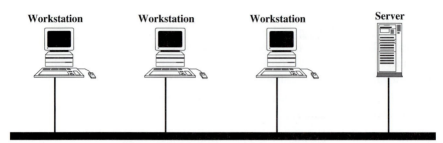

Shared transmission medium
FIGURE 1.2   Simple Local Area Network

For example, it may be 50 or 100 Mbps. Thus the LAN acts as an adapter between the data rate on the host system bus and the data rate on the LAN.

High-Speed LANs.   Traditional LANs, typified by those standardized by the IEEE 802 committee, have provided data rates in a range from about 1 to 20 Mbps. These data rates, although substantial, have become increasingly inadequate with the proliferation of devices, the growth in multimedia applications, and the increased use of the client–server architecture. As a result, much of the effort in LAN development has been in the development of high-speed LANs, with data rates of 100 Mbps or more. In later chapters we will see a number of examples of high-speed LANs.

Metropolitan Area Networks

As the name suggests, a MAN occupies a middle ground between LANs and WANs. Interest in MANs has come about as a result of a recognition that the traditional point-to-point and switched network techniques used in WANs may be inadequate for the growing needs of organizations. While frame relay and ATM promise to meet a wide range of high-speed needs, there is a requirement now for both private and public networks that provide high capacity at low costs over a large area. The high-speed shared-medium approach of the LAN standards provides a number of benefits that can be realized on a metropolitan scale.

After many years of research on MANs, a number of alternatives have been explored and rejected. One approach has emerged that has received widespread support from providers and users, and has been standardized by the IEEE 802 committee as IEEE 802.6. Again, it is useful to look at their definition:

> A MAN is optimized for a larger geographical area than a LAN, ranging from several blocks of buildings to entire cities. As with local networks, MANs can also depend on communications channels of moderate-to-high data rates. Error rates and delay may be slightly higher than might be obtained on a LAN. A MAN might be owned and operated by a single organization, but usually will

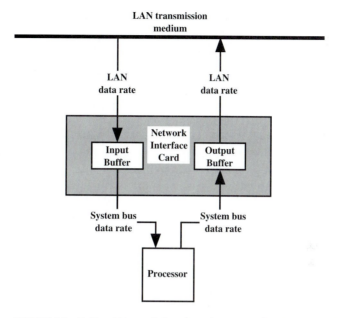

FIGURE 1.3   Buffered Transmission through a Network Interface Card

be used by many individuals and organizations. MANs might also be owned and operated as public utilities. They will often provide means for inter-networking of local networks. Although not a requirement for all LANs, the capability to perform local networking of integrated voice and data (IVD) devices is considered an optional function for a LAN. Likewise, such capabilities in a network covering a metropolitan area are optional functions of a MAN.

Whereas the LANs defined by IEEE 802 are typically used only to support data traffic, the 802.6 MAN is intended for the support of both data and voice traffic. As Figure 1.1 indicates, MANs cover greater distances at higher data rates than LANs, although there is some overlap in geographical coverage. The primary market for MANs is the customer that has high-capacity needs in a metropolitan area. A MAN is intended to provide the required capacity at lower cost and greater efficiency than can be obtained from an equivalent service from the local telephone company.

1.3

APPLICATIONS OF LANs AND MANs

The variety of applications for LANs and MANs is wide. To provide some insight into the types of requirements that LANs and MANs are intended to meet, this section provides a brief discussion of some of the most important general application areas for these networks.

Personal Computer Local Networks

We start at one extreme, a system designed to support personal computers. With the relatively low cost of such systems, individual managers within organizations are independently procuring personal computers for stand-alone applications, such as spreadsheet and project management tools. Today's personal computers put processor, file storage, high-level languages, and problem-solving tools in an inexpensive, user-friendly package. The reasons for acquiring such a system are compelling.

But a collection of stand-alone processors will not meet all of an organization's needs: Central processing facilities are still required. Some programs, such as econometric forecasting models, are too big to run on a small computer. Corporate-wide data files, such as accounting and payroll, require a centralized facility but should be accessible to a number of users. In addition, there are other kinds of files that, although specialized, must be shared by a number of users. Further, there are sound reasons for connecting individual intelligent workstations not only to a central facility but to each other as well. Members of a project or organization team need to share work and information. By far the most efficient way to do so is electronically.

Certain expensive resources, such as a disk or a laser printer, can be shared by all users of the departmental local network. In addition, the network can tie into larger corporate network facilities. For example, the corporation may have a building-wide local network and a wide-area private network. A communications server can provide controlled access to these resources.

Local networks for the support of personal computers and workstations have become nearly universal in organizations of all sizes. Even those sites that still depend heavily on the mainframe have transferred much of the processing load to networks of personal computers. Perhaps the prime example of the way in which personal computers are being used is to implement client–server applications.

For personal computer networks, a key requirement is low cost. In particular, the cost of attachment to the network must be significantly less than the cost of the attached device. Thus for the ordinary personal computer, an attachment cost in the hundreds of dollars is desirable. For more expensive, high-performance workstations, higher attachment costs can be tolerated. In any case, this suggests that the data rate of the network may be limited; in general, the higher the data rate, the higher the cost.

Backend Networks

Backend networks are used to interconnect large systems such as mainframes, supercomputers, and mass storage devices. The key requirement here is for bulk data transfer among a limited number of devices in a small area. High reliability is generally also a requirement. Typical characteristics include:

- *High data rate.* To satisfy the high-volume demand, data rates of 100 Mbps or more are required.
- *High-speed interface.* Data transfer operations between a large host system and a mass storage device are typically performed through high-speed parallel I/O interfaces rather than slower communications interfaces. Thus the physical link between station and network must be high speed.
- *Distributed access.* Some sort of distributed medium access control (MAC) technique is needed to enable a number of devices to share the medium with efficient and reliable access.
- *Limited distance.* Typically, a backend network will be employed in a computer room or a small number of contiguous rooms.
- *Limited number of devices.* The number of expensive mainframes and mass storage devices found in the computer room generally is in the tens of devices.

Typically, backend networks are found at sites of large companies or research installations with large data processing budgets. Because of the scale involved, a small difference in productivity can mean millions of dollars. Consider a site that uses a dedicated mainframe computer. This implies a fairly large application or set of applications. As the load at the site grows, the existing mainframe may be replaced by a more powerful one, perhaps a multiprocessor system. At some sites, a single-system replacement will not be able to keep up; equipment performance growth rates will be exceeded by demand growth rates. The facility will eventually require multiple independent computers. Again, there are compelling reasons for interconnecting these systems. The cost of system interrupt is high, so it should be possible, easily and quickly, to shift applications to backup systems. It must be possible to test new procedures and applications without degrading the production system. Large bulk storage files must be accessible from more than one computer. Load leveling should be possible to maximize utilization and performance. To get some idea of the top end of requirements for backend networks, consider Table 1.1, which is a list of the world's most powerful computing sites.

It can be seen that some key requirements for computer room networks are the opposite of those for personal computer local networks. High data rates are required to keep up with the work, which typically involves the transfer of large blocks of data. The electronics for achieving high speeds are expensive, on the order of tens of thousands of dollars per attachment. Fortunately, given the much higher cost of the attached devices, such costs are reasonable.

TABLE 1.1 World's Most Powerful Computing Sites[a]

1. 845.1—National Aerospace Laboratories, Chofushi, Tokyo, Japan
NAL NWT 2/140	827.05	
Intel Paragon-330	18.05	(7 @ 128 nodes)

2. 603.6—National Security Agency, Headquarters, Fort Meade, Maryland
Cray T3D MC1024-8	220.16	(3.44 @ 16 cpus)
4 * Cray C916/161024	183.04	(2.86 @ 1 cpu)
5 * Cray J932/32512	105.6	(0.66 @ 1 cpu)
TMC CM-5/256-128	22.4	(2.8 @ 32 cpus)
6 * Cray Y-MP8E/81024	48	(1 @ 1 cpu)
Cray T94/4256	16.4	(4.1 @ 1 cpu)
SRC Terasys	8	

3. 461.12—National Security Agency, Dallas, Texas
8 * Cray C916/16512	366.08	(2.86 @ 1 cpu)
9 * Cray J916/16256	95.04	(0.66 @ 1 cpu)

4. 307.12—Los Alamos National Laboratories, Los Alamos, New Mexico
Cray T3D MC512-8/4-256	126.48	(3.44 @ 16 cpus + 4.1 @ 1 cpu)
TMC CM-5/1024-32	89.6	(2.8 @ 32 cpus)
Cray T3D SC256-8/4-64	59.04	(3.44 @ 16 cpus + 1 @ 1 cpu)
Cray Y-MP8/8128	8	(1 @ 1 cpu)
Cray Y-MP8/8128	8	(1 @ 1 cpu)
Cray Y-MP8/864	8	(1 @ 1 cpu)
Cray Y-MP8/832	8	(1 @ 1 cpu)

5. 273.44—Cray Research, Eagan, Minnesota
Cray T3D MCA128-2/16-512		
	73.28	(3.44 @ 16 cpus + 2.86 @ 1 cpu)
Cray T3D MC256-2/8-64		
	63.04	(3.44 @ 16 cpus + 1 @ 1 cpu)
Cray T3D MCA128-2/2E-16		
	29.52	(3.44 @ 16 cpus + 1 @ 1 cpu)
Cray C98/8512	22.88	(2.86 @ 1 cpu)
Cray T916/4128	16.4	(4.1 @ 1 cpu)
Cray C94/4128	11.44	(2.86 @ 1 cpu)
Cray T3D MCA32-2/2E-32		
	8.88	(3.44 @ 16 cpus + 1 @ 1 cpu)
Cray Y-MP8E/8128	8	(1 @ 1 cpu)
Cray Y-MP8D/8128	8	(1 @ 1 cpu)
Cray Y-MP8D/864	8	(1 @ 1 cpu)
Cray Y-MP8D/864	8	(1 @ 1 cpu)
Cray Y-MP8D/864	8	(1 @ 1 cpu)
Cray Y-MP8D/864	8	(1 @ 1 cpu)

6. 245.12—Cornell University, Ithaca, New York
IBM RS/6000 SP2/512	245.12	(3.83 @ 8 cpus)

7. 229.8—Maui High Performance Computing Center, Maui, Hawaii
IBM RS/6000 SP2/400	191.5	(3.83 @ 8 cpus)
IBM RS/6000 SP2/64	30.64	(3.83 @ 8 cpus)
IBM RS/6000 SP2/16	7.66	(3.83 @ 8 cpus)

TABLE 1.1 World's Most Powerful Computing Sites[a] (continued)

8. 188.4—Angstrom Technology Partnership, Tsukuba, Ibaraki, Japan

Fujitsu VPP500/30	166.8	(5.56 @ 1 cpu)
TMC CM-5E/128-128	21.6	(5.4 @ 32 cpus)

9. 177.42—NASA Ames Research Center, Mountain View, California

IBM RS/6000 SP2/160	76.6	(3.83 @ 8 cpus)
Cray C916/161024	45.76	(2.86 @ 1 cpu)

Cray C916/8256	22.88	(2.86 @ 1 cpu)
Intel Paragon-208	11.38	(7 @ 128 nodes)
TMC CM-5/128-32	11.2	(2.8 @ 32 cpus)
SGI POWER CHALLENGEarray-75 L/16		
	9.6	(0.6 @ 1 cpu)

10. 176.37—University of Tsukuba, Tsukuba, Ibaraki, Japan

Fujitsu VPP500/30	166.8	(5.56 @ 1 cpu)
Tsukuba QCDPAX-480		9.57

[a]Ratings are ratios to a Cray Y-MP1 based on NASA NPB BT Size A benchmark reports (1 BT ≈ 1.46 GFlops). This list is updated regularly by Gunter Ahrendt and is available at http://yarrow.wt.com.au/~gunter. This table is based on the report of July 4, 1995.

High-Speed Office Networks

Traditionally, the office environment has included a variety of devices with low- to medium-speed data transfer requirements. However, new applications in the office environment are being developed for which the limited speeds (up to 10 Mbps) of the typical LAN are inadequate. Desktop image processors could soon increase network data flow by an unprecedented amount. Examples of these applications include fax machines, document image processors, and graphics programs on personal computers and workstations. Resolutions as high as 400 × 400 per page are standard for these applications. Even with compression techniques, this will generate a tremendous load. In addition, optical disks are beginning to reach technical maturity and are being developed toward realistic desktop capacities exceeding 1 Gbyte. These new demands will require LANs with high speed that can support the larger numbers and greater geographic extent of office systems than those of computer room systems.

Backbone Local Networks

The increasing use of distributed processing applications and personal computers has led to a need for a flexible strategy for local networking. Support of premises-wide data communications requires a networking service that is capable of spanning the distances involved and that interconnects equipment in a single (perhaps large) building or a cluster of buildings. Although it is possible to develop a single LAN to interconnect all the data processing equipment of a premise, this is probably not a practical alternative in most cases. There are several drawbacks to a single-LAN strategy:

- *Reliability.* With a single LAN, a service interruption, even of short duration, could result in a major disruption for users.
- *Capacity.* A single LAN could be saturated as the number of devices attached to the network grows over time.
- *Cost.* A single LAN technology is not optimized for the diverse requirements of interconnection and communication. The presence of large numbers of low-cost microcomputers dictates that network support for these devices be provided at low cost. LANs that support very low cost attachment will not be suitable for meeting the overall requirement.

A more attractive alternative is to employ lower-cost, lower-capacity LANs within buildings or departments and to interconnect these networks with a higher-capacity network. This latter network is referred to as a backbone network. If confined to a single building or cluster of buildings, a high-capacity LAN can perform the backbone function. For greater distances, a metropolitan area network (MAN) is needed for the backbone.

Factory Local Networks

The factory environment is increasingly being dominated by automated equipment: programmable controllers, automated materials handling devices, time and attendance stations, machine vision devices, and various forms of robots. To manage the production or manufacturing process, it is essential to tie this equipment together, and indeed, the very nature of the equipment facilitates this. Microprocessor devices have the potential to collect information from the shop floor and accept commands. With proper use of the information and commands, it is possible to improve the manufacturing process and to provide detailed machine control.

The more that a factory is automated, the greater the need for communications. Only by interconnecting all of the devices and by providing mechanisms for their cooperation can the automated factory be made to work. The means for interconnection is the factory local network. Key characteristics of a factory local network include:

- High capacity
- Ability to handle a variety of data traffic
- Large geographic extent
- High reliability
- Ability to specify and control transmission delays

Factory local networks are a niche market requiring, in general, more flexible and reliable local networks than are found in the typical office environment.

1.4

LOCAL NETWORK ARCHITECTURE

Information Distribution

In determining the requirements for local networking, it is important to examine the traffic patterns that it is reasonable to expect. Figure 1.4 illustrates the distribution of nonvoice information that has consistently been reported in a number of studies. About half of the information generated within a small unit of an organization (such as a department) remains within that unit. Typically, only summary-type information or consolidated data are disseminated beyond the basic unit of an organization. Another 25 percent is normally shared with peer departments within a somewhat larger grouping (e.g., a division) and the immediate superior of the department. In a typical office layout, this would translate to a radius of about 600 feet. Another 15 percent goes elsewhere within the organization, such as to

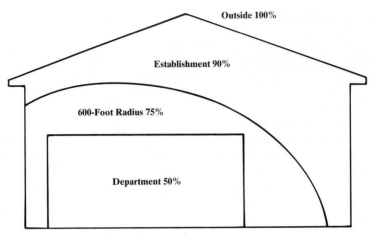

FIGURE 1.4 **Information Distribution**

other departments within other divisions, central staff organizations, and top management. Finally, only about 10 percent of the total information generated is distributed beyond the confines of a single building or cluster of buildings. Example destinations include remote corporate headquarters, customers, suppliers, and government agencies.

This pattern of information communications suggests that a single LAN might not be the most cost-effective means of linking together all of the equipment within an organization. Before suggesting a way of designing a LAN strategy to meet these information distribution requirements, let us consider another way of looking at the requirement.

Tiered Local Area Networks

Consider the kinds of data processing equipment to be supported in a typical organization. In rough terms, we can group this equipment into three categories:

- *Personal computers and workstations.* The workhorse in most office environments is the microcomputer, including personal computers and workstations. Most of this equipment is found at the departmental level, used by individual professionals and secretarial personnel. When used for network applications, the load generated tends to be rather modest.

- *Servers.* Servers, used within a department or shared by users in a number of departments, can perform a variety of functions. Generic examples include support of expensive peripherals such as mass storage devices, providing applications that require large amounts of processor resources, and maintaining databases accessible by many users. Because of this shared use, these machines may generate sub-stantial traffic.

- *Mainframes.* For large database and scientific applications, the main-frame is still the machine of choice. When the machines are net-worked, bulk data transfers dictate that a high-capacity network be used.

The requirements indicated by this spectrum suggest that a single local network will not, in many cases, be the most cost-effective solution. A single network would have to be rather high speed to support the aggregate demand. However, the cost of attachment to a local network tends to increase as a function of the network data rate. Accordingly, a high-speed local network would be very expensive for attachment of low-cost personal computers.

An alternative approach, which is becoming increasingly common, is to employ two or three tiers of local networks (Figure 1.5). Within a depart-ment, a low-cost, moderate-speed LAN supports a cluster of personal com-puters and workstations. These departmental LANs are lashed together with a backbone local network of higher capacity. In addition, shared sys-tems are also supported off this backbone. If mainframes are also part of the office equipment suite, a separate high-speed LAN supports these devices and may be linked, as a whole, to the backbone local network to support traffic between the mainframes and other office equipment. We will see that LAN standards and products address the need for all three types of local networks.

Applications and Tiers

The use of a tiered local area network strategy fits well not only with the hardware attached to the networks but to the applications to be performed. As the cost of an application (hardware, software) grows, we can expect that the cost of the communications facilities to support that application will also grow. However, experience has shown that end users are willing to pay no more than 10 to 15 percent of their system cost to obtain data communi-cation capability; this percentage constrains the kind of local area network-ing solution that can be achieved. Fortunately, we can map application requirements into our three-tiered model easily.

At the very high end is the database and scientific applications. These are generally supported on mainframes or supercomputers and involve the production and communications of large amounts of data. Thus high data rates are required. By the same token, because of the cost of the system and the importance of the application, the user is willing to pay the high net-work costs needed to support the high data rate. Average connection costs in the tens of thousands of dollars are typical for tier 1 types of LANs.

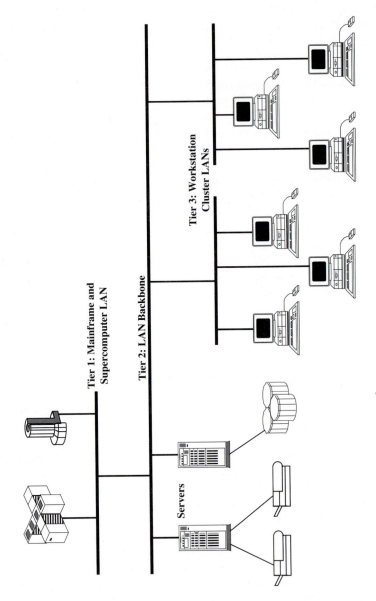

Tier 1: Mainframe and Supercomputer LAN

Tier 2: LAN Backbone

Tier 3: Workstation Cluster LANs

Servers

FIGURE 1.5   Tiered Local Area Networks

Tier 2 corresponds to resource sharing and server applications that are of general use to many users. Because of the number of users involved, moderately high data rates are needed. In addition, applications such as CAD/CAM, which require very expensive peripherals such as electrostatic plotters and large disks, need a networking solution that allows sharing of these devices at reasonable response times. Connection costs in the thousands of dollars are tolerable, and this is what is available with tier 2 types of LANs.

At the lowest end of the performance spectrum are terminal and personal computer requirements. This application category spans a wide range of performance requirements. At the low end, data entry can tolerate very low data rates with not much performance degradation and consequently, is the most cost sensitive. At the higher end, resource sharing and graphics requirements for personal computers require at least 1 Mbps for adequate performance, and perhaps more. But because of the increased cost of the systems and the need for high productivity, users are willing to pay more for the increased data rate.

The wide range of personal computer and terminal data rate requirements make the selection of tier 3 LANs challenging. It is possible for a user to spend too much for performance that will not be used. On the other hand, it is easy to get locked into a LAN that will not grow gracefully to match performance requirements growth.

Evolution Scenario

One final aspect of the tiered architecture should be mentioned: the way in which such a networking implementation comes about in an organization. This will vary widely from one organization to the next, but two general scenarios can be defined. It is useful to be aware of these scenarios because of their implications for the selection and management of local area networks.

In the first scenario, the LAN decisions are made from the bottom up, with each department making decisions more or less in isolation. In this scenario, the particular application requirements of a department are typically well known. For example, an engineering department has very high data rate requirements to support its CAD environment; whereas the sale department has low data rate requirements for their order entry and order inquiry needs. Because the applications are well known, a decision can be made quickly on which network to purchase. Departmental budgets usually can cover the costs of these networks, so approval of a higher authority is not required. The result is that each department will develop its own cluster network (tier 3). In the meantime, if this is a large organization, the central data processing organization may acquire a high-speed (tier 1) LAN to interconnect mainframes.

Over time, many departments will develop their own cluster tier; each department will realize they have a need to interconnect among each other. For example, the marketing department may have to access cost information from the finance department as will as last month's order rate from sales. When cluster-to-cluster communication requirements become important, the company will make a conscious decision to provide interconnect capability. This interconnect capability is realized through the LAN backbone (tier 2).

The advantage of this scenario is that since the department manager is closest to the department's needs, local interconnect strategies can be responsive to the specific applications of the department, and acquisition can be timely. There are several disadvantages to this approach. First, there is the problem of suboptimization. If procurement is made on a company-wide basis, perhaps less total equipment will be acquired to satisfy the total need. In addition, larger-volume purchases may result in more favorable terms. Second, the company is eventually faced with the need to interconnect all of these departmental LANs. If there are a wide variety of such LANs from many different vendors, the interconnection problem becomes more difficult.

For these reasons, an alternative scenario is becoming increasingly common: a top-down design of a LAN strategy. In this case the company decides to map out a total local networking strategy. The decision is centralized because it affects the entire operation or company. The advantage of this approach is built-in compatibility to interconnect the users. The difficulty with this approach is, of course, the need to be responsive and timely in meeting needs at the departmental level.

1.5

OUTLINE OF THE BOOK

This chapter serves as an introduction to the entire book. A brief synopsis of the remaining chapters follows.

Topics in Data Communications and Computer Networking

This book focuses on a specific aspect of data communications and computer networking. To provide a context and to make the book as self-contained as possible, Chapter 2 provides a basic overview of the entire field. The chapter begins with a look at some data communications concepts, including techniques for encoding analog and digital data for both analog and digital signaling and the concept of multiplexing; the concepts of asynchronous and synchronous transmission are also discussed. The chapter then examines the properties of circuit switching and packet switching. Finally, communications architecture is discussed using the TCP/IP and the OSI model as a basis for discussion.

Topologies and Transmission Media

The essential technology underlying all forms of LANs and MANs comprises topology, transmission medium, and medium access control technique. The first two of these elements is examined in Chapter 3. Four topologies are in common use: bus, tree, ring, and star. The most common transmission media for local networking are twisted pair (unshielded and shielded), coaxial cable (baseband and broadband), and optical fiber. These topologies and transmission media are discussed and the most promising combinations described. The chapter closes with a discussion of structured cabling systems.

Protocol Architecture

Chapter 4 introduces the protocols needed for stations attached to a LAN to cooperate with each other in the exchange of data. Specifically, the chapter provides an overview of link control and medium access control protocols. The use of bridges and routers to interconnect LANs is also introduced.

Logical Link Control

Logical link control (LLC) is the highest layer that is specifically part of the LAN/MAN protocol architecture. It is used above all of the medium access control (MAC) standards. The primary purpose of this layer is to provide a means of exchanging data between end users across a link or a collection of LANs interconnected by bridges. Different forms of the LLC service are specified to meet specific reliability and efficiency needs. After a discussion of these services, Chapter 5 deals with some of the key mechanisms of link control protocols. Finally, the specific LLC protocols are examined.

Traditional LANs

Traditional LANs are operate in a range 1 to 20 Mbps. The most important of these are LANs standardized by the IEEE 802 committee. These include CSMA/CD, token ring, and token bus medium access control (MAC) techniques. Chapter 6 looks in detail at the topologies, transmission media, and MAC protocols of traditional LANs.

High-Speed Ethernet-Like LANs

The most widely used LANs are a family of related schemes based on the Ethernet specification. With the need to develop higher-speed LANs to accommodate growing demand, one area of intense interest has been in developing LANs compatible with Ethernet but operating at higher data rates. Two standards have emerged: 100BASE-T and 100VG-AnyLAN. Both of these specify LANs using twisted pair wiring and operating at 100 Mbps. Chapter 7 examines both in detail.

Fiber Distributed Data Interface

Fiber distributed data interface (FDDI) was one of the first specifications for a high-speed local network. FDDI can be configured as either a LAN or a MAN and is in widespread use. Chapter 8 examines the medium access control and physical layer aspects of FDDI.

Fiber Channel

Fiber Channel is designed to combine the best features of two technologies: the simplicity and speed of I/O channel communications with the flexibility and interconnectivity that characterize protocol-based local network communications. This fusion of approaches allows system designers to combine traditional peripheral connections, host-to-host internetworking, loosely coupled processor clustering, and multimedia applications in a single multiprotocol interface. Chapter 9 introduces the Fiber Channel architecture and then examines the details of the topologies, transmission media, and protocols of this network.

ATM LANs

The asynchronous transfer mode (ATM) has become the standard means of providing high-speed wide-area networking. ATM is capable of very high speeds and has the flexibility to carry all types of information, including voice, video, and ordinary data. In recent years, there has been interest in extending this technology to LANs. Chapter 10 provides an overview of ATM technology and protocols, and then approaches to the implementation of ATM LANs are examined.

Wireless LANs

In just the past few years, an entirely new class of local area networks have arrived to provide an alternative to LANs based on twisted pair, coaxial cable, and optical fiber—wireless LANs. The principal advantages of the wireless LAN are that it eliminates the wiring cost, which is often the most costly component of a LAN, and that it accommodates mobile workstations. Wireless LANS use one of three transmission techniques: spread spectrum, narrowband microwave, and infrared. Each of these techniques is examined in Chapter 11.

Distributed Queue Dual Bus

The distributed queue dual bus (DQDB) specification is the only standard developed specifically for the MAN application. The details of DQDB, including topology, protocols, and physical layer aspects, are examined in Chapter 12.

LAN/MAN Performance

In a LAN or MAN, the data rate, length, and medium access control technique of the network are the key factors in determining the effective capacity of the network. Chapter 13 examines performance on LANs and MANs and introduces a key parameter, a, that provides a concise but powerful means of characterizing network performance.

Bridges and Routers

The increasing deployment of LANs has led to an increased need to interconnect LANs with each other and with wide-area networks. Chapters 14 and 15 focus on the two most important devices used in internetworking involving LANs: bridges and routers. In both cases, two types of protocols are involved: protocols for forwarding packets and protocols for exchanging routing information.

Network Management

The final chapter, Chapter 16, looks at the important issue of network management. Following a general discussion of network management requirements and systems, the SNMP standards for network management are introduced. The remainder of the chapter covers network management functions and services that are specific to LANs and MANs.

1.6

RECOMMENDED READING

[MART94] and [MADR94] are book-length treatments of LANs. [SADI95] and [KESS92] cover MANs.

KESS92   Kessler, G., and Train, D. *Metropolitan Area Networks: Concepts, Standards, and Services.* New York: McGraw-Hill, 1992.

MADR94   Madron, T. *Local Area Networks: New Technologies, Emerging Standards.* New York: Wiley, 1994.

MART94   Martin, J., Chapman, K., and Leben, J. *Local Area Networks: Architectures and Implementations.* Englewood Cliffs, NJ: Prentice Hall, 1994.

SADI95   Sadiku, M. *Metropolitan Area Networks.* Boca Raton, FL: CRC Press, 1995.

1.7

PROBLEMS

1.1 A computer network is an interconnected set of computers and other devices (terminals, printers, etc.) that can communicate and cooperate with each other to support certain applications. A subset of a computer network is a communications network, which provides the necessary functions for transferring data between devices attached to the network. List functions that should be part of the communications network and those that should be part of the computer network but not part of the communications network.

1.2 Consider a collection of terminals and workstations connected by point-to-point links to a central UNIX server, all in the same building. Would you consider this an example of a local area network?

1.3 What are the key factors that determine the response time and through-put of a local area network such as that of Figure 1.2? Of a centralized system such as that of Problem 1.2?

APPENDIX 1A

INTERNET RESOURCES

There are a number of resources available on the Internet for keeping up with developments in this field.

USENET Newsgroups

A number of USENET newsgroups are devoted to some aspect of LANs and MANs. Good ones to track:

- *comp.dcom.lans, comp.dcom.lans.misc:* general discussions of LANs
- *comp.dcom.lans.ethernet:* covers Ethernet, Ethernet-like systems, and the IEEE 802.3 CSMA/CD standards
- *comp.dcom.lans.fddi:* discussion of fiber distributed data interface (FDDI)
- *comp.dcom.lans.token-ring:* discussion of token ring products and the IEEE 802.5 token ring standards
- *comp.std.wireless:* general discussion of wireless networks including wireless LANs

Web Sites

- *http://web.syr.edu/~jmwobus/lans:* has links to most important source of LAN information on the Internet, including all of the related FAQs
- *http://www.racal.com/networking.html:* information and links to resources about data communications and networking
- *http://wwwhost.ots.utexas.edu/ethernet:* provides general Ethernet information, technical specifications, an Ethernet reading list, and an image of inventor Robert Metcalf's original 1976 Ethernet drawing

Errata

As soon as any typos or other errors are discovered, an errata list for this book will be available at http://www.shore.net/~ws/welcome.html. The file will be updated as needed. Errata sheets for all of my other books are in the same directory at this web site. The file Order-Form in the same directory contains a discount order form for all my books.

CHAPTER

2

Topics in Data Communications and Computer Networking

The purpose of this chapter is to make this book self-contained for the reader with little or no background in data communications. For the reader with greater interest, references for further study are supplied at the end of the chapter.

2.1

DATA COMMUNICATIONS CONCEPTS

Analog and Digital Data Communications

The terms *analog* and *digital* correspond, roughly, to continuous and discrete, respectively. These two terms are used frequently in data communications in at least three contexts:

- Data
- Signaling
- Transmission

Very briefly, we define *data* as entities that convey meaning. A useful distinction is that data have to do with the form of something; *information* has to do with the content or interpretation of those data. *Signals* are electric or electromagnetic encoding of data. *Signaling* is the act of propagating the signal along a suitable medium. Finally, *transmission* is the communication of data by the propagation and processing of signals. In what follows we try to make these abstract concepts clear by discussing the terms *analog* and *digital* in these three contexts.

The concepts of analog and digital data are simple enough. *Analog data* take on continuous values on some interval. For example, voice and video are continuously varying patterns of intensity. Most data collected by sensors, such as temperature and pressure, are continuous valued. *Digital data* take on discrete values; examples are text and integers.

In a communications system, data are propagated from one point to another by means of electric signals. An *analog signal* is a continuously varying electromagnetic wave that may be transmitted over a variety of media, depending on frequency; examples are wire media, such as twisted pair and coaxial cable, fiber optic cable, and atmosphere or space propagation. A *digital signal* is a sequence of voltage pulses that may be transmitted over a wire medium; for example, a constant positive voltage level may represent binary 1 and a constant negative voltage level may represent binary 0.

The principal advantages of digital signaling are that it is generally cheaper than analog signaling and is less susceptible to noise interference. The principal disadvantage is that digital signals suffer more from attenuation than do analog signals. Figure 2.1 shows a sequence of voltage pulses, generated by a source using two voltage levels, and the received voltage some distance down a conducting medium. Because of the attenuation or reduction of signal strength at higher frequencies, the pulses become rounded and smaller. It should be clear that this attenuation can rather quickly lead to the loss of the information contained in the propagated signal.

Both analog and digital data can be represented, and hence propagated, by either analog or digital signals. This is illustrated in Figure 2.2. Generally, analog data are a function of time and occupy a limited frequency spectrum. Such data can be directly represented by an electromagnetic signal occupying the same spectrum. The best example of this is voice data. As sound waves, voice data have frequency components in the range 20 Hz to 20 kHz. However, most of the speech energy is in a much narrower range. The standard spectrum of voice signals is 300 to 3400 Hz, and this is

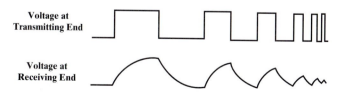

FIGURE 2.1   Attenuation of Digital Signals

quite adequate to propagate speech intelligibly and clearly. The telephone instrument does just that. For all sound input in the range 300 to 3400 Hz, an electromagnetic signal with the same frequency–amplitude pattern is produced. The process is performed in reverse to convert the electromagnetic energy back into sound.

Digital data can also be represented by analog signals by use of a *modem* (modulator/demodulator). The modem converts a series of binary (two-valued) voltage pulses into an analog signal by modulating a *carrier frequency.* The resulting signal occupies a certain spectrum of frequency centered about the carrier and may be propagated across a medium suitable for that carrier. The most common modems represent digital data in the voice spectrum and hence allow those data to be propagated over ordinary voice-grade telephone lines. At the other end of the line, a modem demodulates the signal to recover the original data. Various modulation techniques are discussed below.

In an operation very similar to that performed by a modem, analog data can be represented by digital signals. The device that performs this function for voice data is a *codec* (coder/decoder). In essence, the codec takes an analog signal that directly represents the voice data and approximates that signal by a bit stream. At the other end of a line, the bit stream is used to reconstruct the analog data.

Analog Signals - Represent data with continuously varying electromagnetic wave

Digital Data

Digital Signals - Represent data with sequence of voltage pulses

Digital Data

    Direct representation or coded

FIGURE 2.2 **Analog and Digital Signaling for Analog and Digital Data**

Finally, digital data can be represented directly, in binary form, by two voltage levels. To improve propagation characteristics, however, the binary data are often encoded, as explained below.

A final distinction remains to be made. Both analog and digital signals may be transmitted on suitable transmission media. The way these signals are treated is a function of the transmission system. Table 2.1 summarizes the methods of data transmission. Analog transmission is a means of transmitting analog signals without regard to their content; the signals may represent analog data (e.g., voice) or digital data (e.g., data that pass through a modem). In either case, the analog signal will attenuate after a certain distance. To achieve longer distances, the analog transmission system includes amplifiers that boost the energy in the signal. Unfortunately, the amplifier also boosts the noise components. With amplifiers cascaded to achieve long distances, the signal becomes more and more distorted. For analog data, such as voice, quite a bit of distortion can be tolerated and the data remain intelligible. However, for digital data, cascaded amplifiers will introduce errors.

Digital transmission, in contrast, is concerned with the content of the signal. We have mentioned that a digital signal can be transmitted only a limited distance before attenuation endangers the integrity of the data. To achieve greater distances, repeaters are used. A repeater receives the digital signal, recovers the pattern of ones and zeros, and retransmits a new signal. Thus the attenuation is overcome.

The same technique may be used with an analog signal if it is assumed that the signal carries digital data. At appropriately spaced points, the transmission system has retransmission devices rather than amplifiers. The retransmission device recovers the digital data from the analog signal and generates a new, clean analog signal. Thus noise is not cumulative.

For long-haul communications, digital signaling is not as versatile and practical as analog signaling. For example, digital signaling is impossible for satellite and microwave systems. However, digital transmission is superior to analog, both in terms of cost and quality, and wide-area communications systems are gradually converting to digital transmission for both voice and digital data.

We will see that in local networks the trade-offs do not always lead to the same solutions as for wide-area communications. It is still true, within the local context, that digital techniques tend to be cheaper because of the declining cost of digital circuitry. However, the limited distances of local networks limit the severity of the noise and attenuation problems, and the cost and quality of analog techniques approach those of digital. Consequently, there is a secure place for analog signaling and analog transmission in local networks.

Data Encoding Techniques

As we have pointed out, data, either analog or digital, must be converted into a signal for purposes of transmission.

TABLE 2.1   Analog and Digital Transmission

(a) Data and Signals

	Analog signal	**Digital signal**
Analog data	Two alternatives: (1) signal occupies the same spectrum as the analog data; (2) analog data are encoded to occupy a different portion of spectrum.	Analog data are encoded using a codec to produce a digital bit stream.
Digital data	Digital data are encoded using a modem to produce analog signal.	Two alternatives: (1) signal consists of a two voltage levels to represent the two binary values; (2) digital data are encoded to produce a digital signal with desired properties.

(b) Treatment of Signals

	Analog transmission	**Digital transmission**
Analog signal	Is propagated through amplifiers; same treatment whether signal is used to represent analog data or digital data.	Assumes that the analog signal represents digital data. Signal is propagated through repeaters; at each repeater, digital data are recovered from inbound signal and used to generate a new analog outbound signal.
Digital signal	Not used.	Digital signal represents a stream of ones and zeros, which may represent digital data or may be an encoding of analog data. Signal is propagated through repeaters; at each repeater, stream of ones and zeros is recovered from inbound signal and used to generate a new digital outbound signal.

In the case of **digital data,** different signal elements are used to represent binary 1 and binary 0. The mapping from binary digits to signal elements is the *encoding scheme* used for transmission. To understand the significance of the encoding scheme, consider that there are two important tasks in interpreting signals (analog or digital) that carry digital data at the receiver. First, the receiver must know when a bit begins and ends, so that the receiver may sample the incoming signal once per bit time. Second, the receiver must recognize the value of each bit. A number of factors determines how successful the receiver will be in interpreting the incoming signal. For example, the greater the strength of the signal, the more it will withstand attenuation and the more it will stand out from any noise that is present. Also, the higher the data rate, the more difficult the receiver's task is, since each bit occupies a smaller amount of time: the receiver must be more careful about sampling properly and will have less time to make decisions. Finally, the encoding scheme will affect receiver performance. We will describe a number of different encoding techniques for converting digital data to both analog and digital signals.

In the case of **analog data,** the encoding scheme will also affect transmission performance. In this case, we are concerned about the quality, or fidelity, of the transmission. That is, we would like the received data to be as close as possible to the transmitted data. For the purposes of this book, we are concerned about the encoding of analog data in digital form, and techniques for this encoding are presented below.

Digital Data, Analog Signals.   The basis for analog signaling is a continuous constant-frequency signal known as the *carrier signal.* Digital data are encoded by modulating one of the three characteristics of the carrier: amplitude, frequency, or phase, or some combination of these. Figure 2.3 illustrates the three basic forms of modulation of analog signals for digital data:

- Amplitude-shift keying (ASK)
- Frequency-shift keying (FSK)
- Phase-shift keying (PSK)

In all these cases, the resulting signal contains a range of frequencies on both sides of the carrier frequency. That range is referred to as the *bandwidth* of the signal.

In ASK, the two binary values are represented by two different amplitudes of the carrier frequency. In some cases, one of the amplitudes is zero; that is, one binary digit is represented by the presence, at constant amplitude, of the carrier, and the other is represented by the absence of the carrier. ASK is susceptible to sudden gain changes and is a rather inefficient modulation technique. On voice-grade lines, it is typically used up to only 1200 bps.

In FSK, the two binary values are represented by two different frequencies near the carrier frequency. This scheme is less susceptible to error than ASK. On voice-grade lines, it is typically used up to 1200 bps. It is also commonly used for high-frequency (3 to 30 MHz) radio transmission. It can also be used at even higher frequencies on local networks that use coaxial cable.

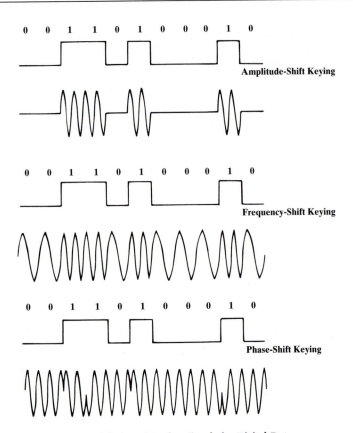

FIGURE 2.3   Modulation of Analog Signals for Digital Data

Figure 2.4 shows an example of the use of FSK for full-duplex operation over a voice-grade line. *Full duplex* means that data can be transmitted in both directions at the same time. To accomplish this, one bandwidth is used for sending, another for receiving. The figure is a specification for the Bell System 108 series modems. In one direction (transmit or receive), the modem passes frequencies in the range 300 to 1700 Hz. The two frequencies used to represent 1 and 0 are centered on 1170 Hz, with a shift of 100 Hz on either side. Similarly, for the other direction (receive or transmit) the modem passes 1700 to 3000 Hz and uses a center frequency of 2125 Hz. The shaded area around each pair of frequencies indicates the actual bandwidth of each signal. Note that there is little overlap and thus little interference.

In PSK, the phase of the carrier signal is shifted to represent data. Figure 2.3 shows an example of a two-phase system. In this system, a 0 is represented by sending a signal burst of the same phase as the previous signal burst sent. A 1 is represented by sending a signal burst of opposite phase to the previous one. PSK can use more than two phase shifts. A four-phase sys-

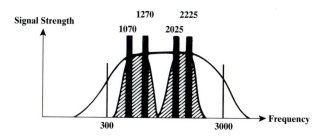

FIGURE 2.4   Full-Duplex FSK Transmission on a Voice-Grade Line

tem would encode 2 bits with each signal burst. The PSK technique is more noise resistant and efficient than FSK; on a voice-grade line, rates up to 9600 bps are achieved.

Finally, the techniques discussed above may be combined. A common combination is PSK and ASK, where some or all of the phase shifts may occur at one of two amplitudes.

Digital Data, Digital Signals.   Although a common means of transmitting digital data is to pass them through a modem and transmit them as an analog signal, we will see that the transmission of digital data as digital signals is the technique used in a number of local networks. The use of digital signals may be less expensive and, under some circumstances, provide better performance than analog signaling. In this subsection we consider two families of coding techniques: NRZ codes and biphase codes.

With **nonreturn-to-zero** (NRZ) **codes,** two different voltage levels, one positive and one negative, are used as the signal elements for the two binary digits. The name refers to the fact that the voltage level never returns to zero, but is always positive or negative. NRZ is the most common and easiest way to transmit digital signals. However, we shall see that its use is not appropriate for local networks.

Figure 2.5a shows the use of a constant negative voltage to represent binary 1 and a constant positive voltage to represent binary 0. This code is known as **NRZ-L** (NRZ level). This code is often used for very short connections, such as between a terminal and a modem or a terminal and a nearby computer.

A variation on NRZ is **NRZI** (NRZ, invert on ones). As with NRZ-L, NRZI maintains a constant-voltage pulse for the duration of a bit time. The data themselves are encoded as the presence or absence of a signal transition at the beginning of the bit time. A transition (low-to-high or high-to-low) at the beginning of a bit time denotes a binary 1 for that bit time; no transition indicates a binary 0 (Figure 2.5b).

NRZI is an example of differential encoding. In differential encoding, the signal is decoded by comparing the polarity of adjacent signal elements

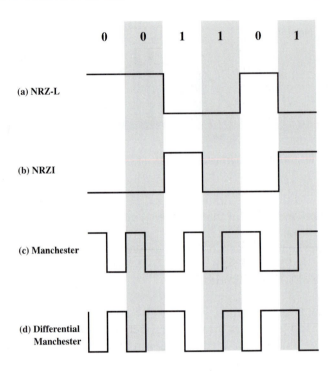

FIGURE 2.5   Digital Signal Encoding

rather than determining the absolute value of a signal element. One benefit of this scheme is that it may be more reliable to detect a transition in the presence of noise than to compare a value to a threshold. Another benefit is that with a complex transmission layout, it is easy to lose the sense of the polarity of the signal. For example, on a twisted-pair medium, if the leads from an attached device to the twisted pair are accidentally inverted, all ones and zeros will be inverted. This cannot happen with differential encoding.

There are several disadvantages to NRZ transmission. It is difficult to determine where one bit ends and another begins. To picture the problem, consider that with a long string of 1's or 0's for NRZ-L, the output is a constant voltage over a long period of time. Under these circumstances, any drift between the timing of transmitter and receiver will result in the loss of synchronization between the two. Also, there is a direct-current (dc) component during each bit time that may accumulate if positive or negative pulses predominate. Thus, alternating-current (ac) coupling, which uses a transformer and provides excellent electrical isolation between data communicating devices and their environment, is not possible. Furthermore, the dc component can cause plating or other deterioration at attachment contacts.

There is a set of alternative coding techniques, grouped under the term **biphase codes,** which overcomes these problems. Two of these techniques, Manchester and Differential Manchester, are in common use for local networks. All of the biphase techniques require at least one transition per bit time and may have as many as two transitions. Thus, the maximum modulation rate is twice that for NRZ; this means that the bandwidth or transmission capacity required is correspondingly greater. To compensate for this, the biphase schemes have several advantages:

- *Synchronization.* Because there is a predictable transition during each bit time, the receiver can synchronize on that transition. For this reason, the biphase codes are known as self-clocking codes.
- *No dc component.* Because of the transition in each bit time, biphase codes have no dc component, yielding the benefits just described.
- *Error detection.* The absence of an expected transition can be used to detect errors. Noise on the line would have to invert both the signal before and after the expected transition to cause an undetected error.

In the **Manchester** code (Figure 2.5c), there is a transition at the middle of each bit period. The mid-bit transition serves as a clock and also as data: a low-to-high transition represents a 1, and a high-to-low transition represents a 0. In **Differential Manchester** (Figure 2.5d), the midbit transition is used only to provide clocking. The encoding of a 0 is represented by the presence of a transition at the beginning of a bit period, and a 1 is represented by the absence of a transition at the beginning of a bit period. Differential Manchester exhibits the further advantage of being a differential encoding technique.

Analog Data, Digital Signals.   The most common example of the use of digital signals to encode analog data is *pulse code modulation* (PCM), which is used to encode voice signals. This section describes PCM and then looks briefly at a similar, less used scheme, *delta modulation* (DM).

PCM is based on the sampling theorem, which states [VALK93]:

> If a signal *f(t)* is sampled at regular intervals of time and at a rate higher than twice the highest significant signal frequency, then the samples contain all the information of the original signal. The function *f(t)* may be reconstructed from these samples by the use of a low-pass filter.

If voice data are limited to frequencies below 4000 Hz, a conservative procedure for intelligibility, then 8000 samples per second would be sufficient to characterize the voice signal completely. Note, however, that these are analog samples. To convert to digital, each of these analog samples must be assigned a binary code. Figure 2.6 shows an example in which each sample is approximated by being "quantized" into one of 16 different levels.

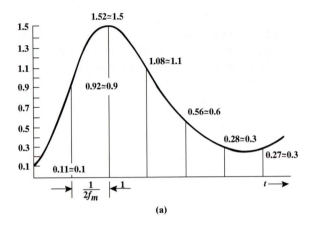

(a)

Digit	Binary equivalent	Pulse-code waveform
0	0000	
1	0001	
2	0010	
3	0011	
4	0100	
5	0101	
6	0110	
7	0111	
8	1000	
9	1001	
10	1010	
11	1011	
12	1100	
13	1101	
14	1110	
15	1111	

(b)

FIGURE 2.6   Pulse Code Modulation

Each sample can then be represented by 4 bits. Of course, it is now impossible to recover the original signal exactly. By using a 7-bit sample, which allows 128 quantizing levels, the quality of the recovered voice signal is comparable to that achieved via analog transmission. Note that this implies that a data rate of 8000 samples per second × 7 bits per sample = 56 kbps is needed for a single voice signal.

Typically, the PCM scheme is refined using a technique known as *non-linear encoding*, which means, in effect, that the 128 quantization levels are not equally spaced. The problem with equal spacing is that the mean absolute error for each sample is the same, regardless of signal level. Consequently, lower-amplitude values are relatively more distorted. By using a greater number of quantizing steps for signals of low amplitude, and a small number of quantizing steps for signals of large amplitude, a marked reduction in overall signal distortion is achieved.

PCM can, of course, be used for other than voice signals. For example, a color TV signal has a useful bandwidth of 4.6 MHz, and reasonable quality can be achieved with 10-bit samples, for a data rate of 92 Mbps.

With DM, a bit stream is produced by approximating the derivative of an analog signal rather than its amplitude. A 1 is generated if the current sample is greater in amplitude than the immediately preceding sample; a 0 is generated otherwise. For equal data rates, DM is comparable to PCM in terms of signal quality. Note that for equal data rates, DM requires a higher sampling rate: a 56-kbps voice signal is generated from 8000 PCM samples per second but 56,000 DM samples per second. In general, DM systems are less complex and less expensive than are comparable PCM systems.

Multiplexing

In both local and long-haul communications, it is almost always the case that the capacity of the transmission medium exceeds that required for the transmission of a single signal. To make cost-effective use of the transmission system, it is desirable to use the medium efficiently by having it carry multiple signals simultaneously. This is referred to as *multiplexing*, and two techniques are in common use: frequency-division multiplexing (FDM) and time-division multiplexing (TDM).

FDM takes advantage of the fact that the useful bandwidth of the medium exceeds the required bandwidth of a given signal. A number of signals can be carried simultaneously if each signal is modulated onto a different carrier frequency, and the carrier frequencies are sufficiently separated so that the bandwidths of the signals do not overlap. A simple example of FDM is full-duplex FSK transmission (Figure 2.4). A general case of FDM is shown in Figure 2.7a. Six signal sources are fed into a multiplexer that modulates each signal onto a different frequency ($f_1, \ldots . f_6$). Each signal requires a certain bandwidth centered around its carrier frequency, referred to as a *channel*. To prevent interference, the channels are separated by guard bands, which are unused portions of the spectrum.

An example is the multiplexing of voice signals. We mentioned that the useful spectrum for voice is 300 to 3400 Hz. Thus a bandwidth of 4 kHz is adequate to carry the voice signal and provide a guard band. For both North America (Bell System standard) and internationally [Consultative Committee on International Telegraphy and Telephony (CCITT) standard], a standard voice multiplexing scheme is twelve 4-kHz voice channels from 60 to 108 kHz. For higher-capacity links, both Bell and CCITT define larger groupings of 4-kHz channels.

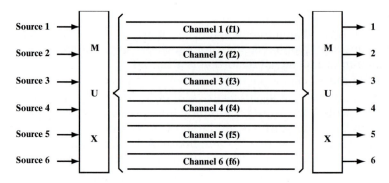

(a) Frequency-Division Multiplexing

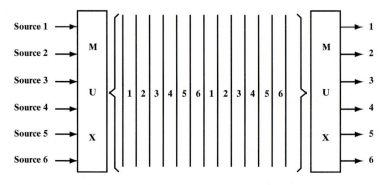

(b) Time-Division Multiplexing

FIGURE 2.7   Multiplexing

TDM takes advantage of the fact that the achievable bit rate (sometimes, unfortunately, called bandwidth) of the medium exceeds the required data rate of a digital signal. Multiple digital signals can be carried on a single transmission path by interleaving portions of each signal in time. The interleaving can be at the bit level or in blocks of bytes or larger quantities. For example, the multiplexer in Figure 2.7b has six inputs that might each be, say, 9.6 kbps. A single line with a capacity of 57.6 kbps could accommodate all six sources. Analogously to FDM, the sequence of time slots dedicated to a particular source is called a *channel*. One cycle of time slots (one per source) is called a *frame*.

The TDM scheme depicted in Figure 2.7 is also known as *synchronous TDM*, referring to the fact that time slots are preassigned and fixed. Hence the timing of transmission from the various sources is synchronized. In contrast, asynchronous TDM allows time on the medium to be allocated dynamically. Examples of this will be given later. Unless otherwise noted, the term TDM will be used to mean synchronous TDM only.

One example of TDM is the standard scheme used for transmitting PCM voice data, known in Bell parlance as *T1 carrier*. Data are taken from each source, one sample (7 bits) at a time. An eighth bit is added for signaling and supervisory functions. For T1, 24 sources are multiplexed, so there are $8 \times 24 = 192$ bits of data and control signals per frame. One final bit is added for establishing and maintaining synchronization. Thus a frame consists of 193 bits and contains one 7-bit sample per source. Since sources must be sampled 8000 times per second, the required data rate is $8000 \times 193 = 1.544$ Mbps. As with voice FDM, higher data rates are defined for larger groupings.

TDM is not limited to digital signals. Analog signals can also be interleaved in time. Also, with analog signals, a combination of TDM and FDM is possible. A transmission system can be frequency-divided into a number of channels, each of which is further divided via TDM. This technique is possible with broadband local networks, discussed in Chapter 3.

2.2

TRANSMISSION MEDIA

The transmission medium is the physical path between transmitter and receiver in a data transmission system. Transmission media can be classified as guided or unguided. In both cases, communication is in the form of electromagnetic waves. With guided media, the waves are guided along a solid medium, such as copper twisted pair, copper coaxial cable, and optical fiber, all of which are used in LANs. The atmosphere and outer space are examples of unguided media, which provide a means of transmitting electromagnetic signals but do not guide them. Various forms of transmission through the atmosphere are employed for implementing wireless LANs.

The characteristics and quality of a data transmission are determined both by the characteristics of the medium and the characteristics of the signal. In the case of guided media, the medium itself is more important in determining the limitations of transmission. For unguided media, the bandwidth of the signal produced by the transmitting antenna is more important than the medium in determining transmission characteristics. One key property of signals transmitted by the antenna is directionality. In general, signals at lower frequencies are omnidirectional; that is, the signal propagates in all directions from the antenna. At higher frequencies, it is possible to focus the signal into a directional beam.

In considering the design of LAN and MAN transmission systems, our primary concern is generally data rate and distance: The greater the data rate and distance, the better. A number of design factors relating to the transmission medium and the signal determine the data rate and distance:

- *Bandwidth.* All other factors remaining constant, the greater the bandwidth of a signal, the higher the data rate that can be achieved.
- *Transmission impairments.* Impairments, such as attenuation, limit the distance. For guided media, twisted pair generally suffer more impairment than coaxial cable, which in turn suffers more than optical fiber.
- *Interference.* Interference from competing signals in overlapping frequency bands can distort or wipe out a signal. Interference is of particular concern for unguided media but is also a problem with guided media. For guided media, interference can be caused by emanations from nearby cables. For example, twisted pair are often bundled together and conduits often carry multiple cables. Interference can also be experienced from unguided transmissions. Proper shielding of a guided medium can minimize this problem.
- *Number of receivers.* A guided medium can be used to construct a point-to-point link or a shared link with multiple attachments. In the latter case, each attachment introduces some attenuation and distortion on the line, limiting distance and/or data rate.

Before turning to a description of the various media, we say a few words about transmission impairments.

Twisted Pair

A twisted pair consists of two insulated copper wires arranged in a regular spiral pattern (Figure 2.8a). A wire pair acts as a single communication link. Typically, a number of these pairs are bundled together into a cable by wrapping them in a tough protective sheath. Over longer distances, cables may contain hundreds of pairs.

Twisted pair is much less expensive than the other commonly used guided transmission media (coaxial cable, optical fiber) and is easier to work with. Compared to other transmission media, twisted pair is limited in distance, bandwidth, and data rate. The medium is quite susceptible to interference and noise because of its easy coupling with electromagnetic fields. For example, a wire run parallel to an ac power line will pick up 60-Hz energy. Impulse noise also easily intrudes into twisted pair. Several measures are taken to reduce impairments. Shielding the wire with metallic braid or sheathing reduces interference. The twisting of the wire reduces low-frequency interference, and the use of different twist lengths in adjacent pairs reduces crosstalk.

Unshielded and Shielded Twisted Pair.   Twisted pair comes in two varieties: unshielded and shielded. Unshielded twisted pair (UTP) is ordinary telephone wire. Office buildings, by universal practice, are prewired with a lot of excess unshielded twisted pair, more than is needed for simple tele-

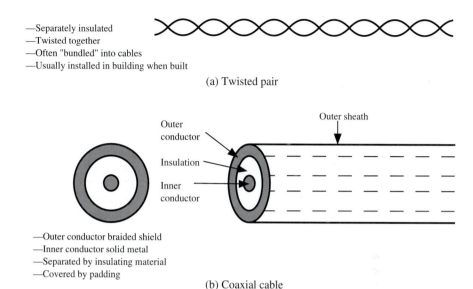

—Separately insulated
—Twisted together
—Often "bundled" into cables
—Usually installed in building when built

(a) Twisted pair

Outer sheath

Outer
conductor

Insulation

Inner
conductor

—Outer conductor braided shield
—Inner conductor solid metal
—Separated by insulating material
—Covered by padding

(b) Coaxial cable

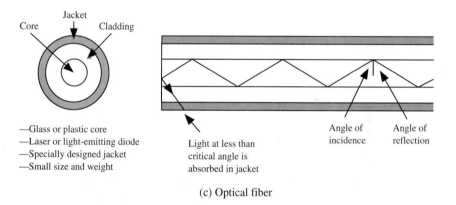

Jacket

Core   Cladding

—Glass or plastic core
—Laser or light-emitting diode
—Specially designed jacket
—Small size and weight

Light at less than
critical angle is
absorbed in jacket

Angle of   Angle of
incidence   reflection

(c) Optical fiber

FIGURE 2.8   Guided Transmission Media

phone support. This is the least expensive of all the transmission media commonly used for local area networks and is easy to work with and easy to install.

Unshielded twisted pair is subject to external electromagnetic interference, including interference from nearby twisted pair and from noise generated in the environment. A way to improve the characteristics of this medium is to shield the twisted pair with a metallic braid or sheathing that reduces interference. This shielded twisted pair (STP) provides better performance at lower data rates. However, it is more expensive and more difficult to work with than unshielded twisted pair.

Category 3 and Category 5 UTP.   Most office buildings are prewired with a type of 100-ohm twisted pair cable commonly referred to as voice-grade. Because voice-grade twisted pair is already installed, it is an attractive alternative for use as a LAN medium. Unfortunately, the data rates and distances achievable with voice-grade twisted pair are limited.

In 1991, the Electronic Industries Association published standard EIA-568, *Commercial Building Telecommunications Cabling Standard*, that specified the use of voice-grade unshielded twisted pair as well as shielded twisted pair for in-building data applications. At that time, the specification was felt to be adequate for the range of frequencies and data rates found in office environments. Up to that time, the principal interest for LAN designs was in the range of data rates from 1 to 16 Mbps. Subsequently, as users migrated to higher-performance workstations and applications, there was increasing interest in providing LANs that could operate up to 100 Mbps over inexpensive cable. In response to this need, EIA-568-A was issued in 1995. The new standard reflects advances in cable and connector design and test methods. It covers 150-ohm shielded twisted pair and 100-ohm unshielded twisted pair.

EIA-568-A recognizes three categories of UTP cabling:

- *Category 3*. UTP cables and associated connecting hardware whose transmission characteristics are specified up to 16 MHz
- *Category 4*. UTP cables and associated connecting hardware whose transmission characteristics are specified up to 20 MHz
- *Category 5*. UTP cables and associated connecting hardware whose transmission characteristics are specified up to 100 MHz

Of these, it is category 3 and category 5 cable that have received the most attention for LAN applications. Category 3 corresponds to the voice-grade cable found in abundance in most office buildings. Over limited distances, and with proper design, data rates of up to 16 Mbps should be achievable with category 3. Category 5 is a data-grade cable that is becoming increasingly common for preinstallation in new office buildings. Over limited distances, and with proper design, data rates of up to 100 Mbps should be achievable with category 5. Details of how these two cable types are used to implement high-speed LANs are covered in Chapters 7 and 8.

A key difference between category 3 and category 5 cable is the number of twists in the cable per unit distance. Category 5 is much more tightly twisted, typically three to four twists per inch compared to three to four twists per foot for category 3. The tighter twisting is more expensive but provides much better performance than category 3.

Table 2.2 summarizes the performance of category 3 and 5 UTP, as well as the STP specified in EIA-568-A. The first parameter used for comparison, attenuation, is fairly straightforward. The strength of a signal falls

TABLE 2.2 Comparison of Unshielded and Shielded Twisted Pair

Frequency (MHz)	Attenuation (dB per 100 m)			Near-End Crosstalk (dB)		
	Category 3 UTP	Category 5 UTP	150 Ω STP	Category 3 UTP	Category 5 UTP	150 Ω STP
1	2.6	2.0	1.1	41	62	58
4	5.6	4.1	2.2	32	53	58
16	13.1	8.2	4.4	23	44	50.4
25	—	10.4	6.2	—	32	47.5
100	—	22.0	12.3	—	—	38.5
300	—	—	21.4	—	—	31.3

off with distance over any transmission medium. For guided media, attenuation is generally logarithmic and therefore is typically expressed as a constant number of decibels per unit distance. Attenuation introduces three considerations for the designer. First, a received signal must have sufficient magnitude so that the electronic circuitry in the receiver can detect and interpret the signal. Second, the signal must maintain a level sufficiently higher than noise to be received without error. Third, attenuation is an increasing function of frequency.

Near-end crosstalk as it applies to twisted-pair wiring systems is the coupling of the signal from one pair of conductors to another pair. These conductors may be the metal pins in a connector or wire pairs in a cable. The near end refers to coupling that takes place when the transmit signal entering the link couples back to the receive conductor pair at that same end of the link (i.e., the near transmitted signal is picked up by the near receive pair).

Coaxial Cable

Like twisted pair, coaxial cable consists of two conductors but is constructed differently, to permit it to operate over a wider range of frequencies. It consists of a hollow outer cylindrical conductor which surrounds a single inner wire conductor (Figure 2.8b). The inner conductor is held in place by either regularly spaced insulating rings or a solid dielectric material. The outer conductor is covered with a jacket or shield. A single coaxial cable has a diameter of from 0.4 to about 1 inch. Because of its shielded, concentric construction, coaxial cable in much less susceptible to interference and crosstalk than is twisted pair. Coaxial cable can be used over longer distances than twisted pair and support more stations on a shared line.

For local area networks, we can classify coaxial cable into three categories, depending on the type of signaling used. A **baseband** coaxial cable uses digital signaling. In this case the signal occupies the entire frequency spectrum of the cable and therefore only one channel is allowed on the cable. Baseband coaxial LANs use a special-purpose 50-ohm cable. This is usually referred to as Ethernet cable, since it was originally used in the Ethernet LAN.

The remaining two types of coaxial cable used for LANs are broadband and carrierband. With **broadband** coaxial cable, analog signaling is used. That is, the digital data to be transmitted onto the LAN are first passed through a modem to produce an analog signal. As a result, it is possible to have multiple signals on the cable at the same time, each at its own frequency band. This is, in fact, the way that cable television is implemented. A single coaxial cable comes into the home of the subscriber; on the cable, multiple channels are carried, each occupying a separate frequency. The subscriber can receive any of these channels by tuning the television set attached to the cable appropriately. Similarly, with multiple data channels on a single cable, a number of devices can be attached to the cable and tuned to one of the various channels.

Carrierband transmission on a coaxial cable also makes use of a modem and analog signaling. However, in this case very inexpensive modems are used, which spill energy across the entire frequency spectrum. The result is that like baseband, carrierband only allows the use of a single data channel on the cable. Both broadband and carrierband make use of standard cable-television cable.

Coaxial cable, like shielded twisted pair, provides good immunity from electromagnetic interference. Coaxial cable is more expensive than shielded twisted pair but provides greater capacity. Traditionally, coaxial cable has been an important transmission medium for LANs, beginning with the early popularity of Ethernet. However, in recent years, the emphasis has been on low-cost limited-distance LANs using twisted pair, and high-performance LANs using optical fiber. The effect is the gradual but steady decline in the use of coaxial cable for LAN implementation.

Optical Fiber

An optical fiber is a thin (2 to 125 μm), flexible medium capable of conducting an optical ray. Various glasses and plastics can be used to make optical fibers. The lowest losses have been obtained using fibers of ultra-pure fused silica. Ultrapure fiber is difficult to manufacture; higher-loss multicomponent glass fibers are more economical and still provide good performance. Plastic fiber is even less costly and can be used for short-haul links, for which moderately high losses are acceptable.

An optical fiber cable has a cylindrical shape and consists of three concentric sections: the core, the cladding, and the jacket (Figure 2.8c). The *core* is the innermost section and consists of one or more very thin strands, or fibers, made of glass or plastic. Each fiber is surrounded by its own *cladding,* a glass or plastic coating that has optical properties different from those of the core. The outermost layer, surrounding one or a bundle of cladded fibers, is the *jacket.* The jacket is composed of plastic and other material layered to protect against moisture, abrasion, crushing, and other environmental dangers.

One of the most significant technological breakthroughs in information transmission has been the development of practical fiber optic communications systems. Optical fiber already enjoys considerable use in long-distance telecommunications, and its use in military applications is growing. The continuing improvements in performance and decline in prices, together with the inherent advantages of optical fiber, have made it increasingly attractive for local area networking. The following characteristics distinguish optical fiber from twisted pair or coaxial cable:

- *Greater capacity.* The potential bandwidth, and hence data rate, of optical fiber is immense; data rates of 2 Gbps over tens of kilometers have been demonstrated. Compare this to the practical maximum of hundreds of Mbps over about 1 km for coaxial cable and just a few Mbps over 1 km or up to 100 Mbps over a few tens of meters for twisted pair.
- *Smaller size and lighter weight.* Optical fibers are considerably thinner than coaxial cable or bundled twisted-pair cable—at least an order of magnitude thinner for comparable information transmission capacity. For cramped conduits in buildings and underground along public rights-of-way, the advantage of small size is considerable. The corresponding reduction in weight reduces structural support requirements.
- *Lower attenuation.* Attenuation is significantly lower for optical fiber than for coaxial cable or twisted pair and is constant over a wide range.
- *Electromagnetic isolation.* Optical fiber systems are not affected by external electromagnetic fields. Thus the system is not vulnerable to interference, impulse noise, or crosstalk. By the same token, fibers do not radiate energy, causing little interference with other equipment and providing a high degree of security from eavesdropping. In addition, fiber is inherently difficult to tap.

Optical fiber systems operate in the range of about 10^{14} to 10^{15} Hz; this covers portions of the infrared and visible spectrums. The principle of optical fiber transmission is as follows. Light from a source enters the cylindrical glass or plastic core. Rays at shallow angles are reflected and propagated along the fiber; other rays are absorbed by the surrounding material. This form of propagation is called *multimode*, referring to the variety of angles that will reflect. When the fiber core radius is reduced, fewer angles will reflect. By reducing the radius of the core to the order of a wavelength, only a single angle or mode can pass: the axial ray. This single-mode propagation provides superior performance for the following reason. With multimode transmission, multiple propagation paths exist, each with a different path length and hence time to traverse the fiber. This causes signal elements to spread out in time, which limits the rate at which data can be accurately received. Since there is a single transmission path with single-mode transmission, such distortion cannot occur. Finally, by varying the index of refraction of the core, a third type of transmission, known as multimode graded index, is possible. This type is intermediate between the other two in characteristics. The variable refraction has the effect of focusing the rays more efficiently than ordinary multimode, also known as multimode step index. Table 2.3 compares the three fiber transmission modes.

TABLE 2.3 Typical Fiber Characteristics [STER93]

Fiber Type	Core Diameter (μm)	Cladding Diameter (μm)	Attenuation (dB/km) (max)			Bandwidth (MHz/km) (max.)
			850 nm	1300 nm	1500 nm	
Single mode	5.0 8.1	85 or 125 125	2.3	0.5	0.25	5000 @ 850 nm
Graded-index	50	125	2.4	0.6	0.5	600 @ 850 nm 1500 @ 1300 nm
	62.5	125	3.0	0.7	0.3	200 @ 850 nm 1000 @ 1300 nm
	100	140	3.5	1.5	0.9	300 @ 850 nm 500 @ 1300 nm
Step-index	200 or 300	380 or 440	6.0			6

Two different types of light source are used in fiber optic systems: the light-emitting diode (LED) and the injection laser diode (ILD). Both are semiconductor devices that emit a beam of light when a voltage is applied. The LED is less costly, operates over a greater temperature range, and has a longer operational life. The ILD, which operates on the laser principle, is more efficient and can sustain greater data rates.

There is a relationship among the wavelength employed, the type of transmission, and the achievable data rate. Both single mode and multi-mode can support several different wavelengths of light and can employ laser or LED light source. In optical fiber, light propagates best in three distinct wavelength "windows," centered on 850, 1300, and 1550 nanometers (nm). These are all in the infrared portion of the frequency spectrum, below the visible-light portion, which is 400 to 700 nm. The loss is lower at higher wavelengths, allowing greater data rates over longer distances (Table 2.3). Most local applications today use 850-nm LED light sources. Although this combination is relatively inexpensive, it is generally limited to data rates under 100 Mbps and distances of a few kilometers. To achieve higher data rates and longer distances, a 1300-nm LED or laser source is needed. The highest data rates and longest distances require 1500-nm laser sources.

Unguided Media

In this section we introduce two unguided transmission techniques that have found application for LANs: microwave and infrared. These topics are covered in more detail in Chapter 11.

Microwave.   Microwave refers to the high end of the radio-frequency spectrum, from about 1 to 30 GHz. Microwave antennas can produce either highly directional or broader beams to cover larger areas. Microwave transmission presents three challenges to the LAN designer:

- *Frequency allocation.* High-speed data communications is a relatively recent application that must make use of frequency bands that preexisting applications are not already using. For LAN applications, the following microwave frequency ranges have been used:
  - 902 to 928 MHz
  - 2.4 to 2.4835 GHz
  - 5.725 to 5.825 GHz
  - 18.825 to 19.205 GHz

  The first three are known as the industrial, scientific, and medical bands. In the United States and in some other countries, these bands have been reserved for unlicensed local use.
- *Interference.* One important characteristic of microwave signals is that they can penetrate walls. This has the advantage that a microwave-

based LAN need not be confined to a single room. However, if several wireless LANs are operating in the same building, there is the potential for interference. Interference can be avoided by prior agreements about frequency bands or by using spread spectrum techniques, which are discussed in Chapter 11.

- *Security.* Because microwave signals penetrate walls, security becomes a consideration. One technique to increase security is to encrypt all transmissions and carefully control the distribution of the encryption keys. Also, spread spectrum transmission can provide security if properly implemented.

Infrared.   Infrared communication is achieved using transmitters/receivers (transceivers) that modulate noncoherent infrared light. Transceivers must be with line of sight of each other either directly or via reflection from a light-colored surface such as the ceiling of a room. One important difference between infrared and microwave transmission is that the former does not penetrate walls. Thus the security and interference problems encountered in microwave systems are not present. Furthermore, there is no frequency allocation issue with infrared, since no licensing is required.

2.3

DATA COMMUNICATIONS NETWORKS

For transmission of data[1] beyond a local area, communication is typically achieved by transmitting data from source to destination through a network of intermediate switching nodes; this switched network design is sometimes used to implement LANs and MANs as well. The switching nodes are not concerned with the content of the data; rather, their purpose is to provide a switching facility that will move the data from node to node until they reach their destination. Figure 2.9 illustrates a simple network. The end devices that wish to communicate may be referred to as *stations*. The stations may be computers, terminals, telephones, or other communicating devices. We will refer to the switching devices whose purpose is to provide communication as *nodes*. The nodes are connected to each other in some topology by transmission links. Each station attaches to a node, and the collection of nodes is referred to as a *communications network*.

Figure 2.10 describes a spectrum of switching techniques available to transport information across a network. The two extreme ends of the spectrum represent the two traditional switching techniques: circuit switching

---

[1]We use this term here in a very general sense, to include voice, image, and video as well as ordinary data (e.g., numerical, text).

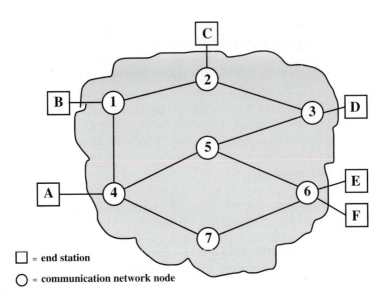

= end station

= communication network node

FIGURE 2.9   Simple Switching Network

and packet switching; the remaining techniques are of more recent vintage. In general, the techniques toward the left end of the line provide transmission with little or no variability and with minimal processing demands on attached stations, while techniques toward the right end provide increased flexibility to handle varying bit rates and unpredictable traffic at the expense of increasing processing complexity. In the remainder of this section, we provide a somewhat detailed look at circuit and packet switching and briefly examine the other techniques.

Circuit Switching

Communication via circuit switching implies that there is a dedicated communication path between two stations. That path is a connected sequence of links between nodes. On each physical link, a channel is dedicated to the connection. The most common example of circuit switching is the telephone network.

Communication via circuit switching involves three phases, which can be explained with reference to Figure 2.9.

1. *Circuit establishment.* Before any data can be transmitted, an end-to-end (station-to-station) circuit must be established. For example, station A sends a request to node 4 requesting a connection to station E. Typically, the circuit from A to 4 is a dedicated line, so that part of the connection already exists. Node 4 must find the next leg in a route

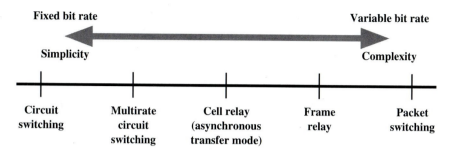

FIGURE 2.10   Spectrum of Switching Techniques (based on [PRYC93])

leading to node 6. Based on routing information and measures of availability and perhaps cost, node 4 selects the circuit to node 5, allocates a free channel (using TDM or FDM) on that circuit, and sends a message requesting connection to E. So far, a dedicated path has been established from A through 4 to 5. Since a number of stations may attach to 4, it must be able to establish internal paths from multiple stations to multiple nodes. How this is done is explained in Chapter 7. The remainder of the process proceeds similarly. Node 5 dedicates a channel to node 6 and internally ties that channel to the channel from node 4. Node 6 completes the connection to E. In completing the connection, a test is made to determine if E is busy or is prepared to accept the connection.

2. *Data transfer.* Signals can now be transmitted from A through the network to E. The data may be digital (e.g., terminal to host) or analog (e.g., voice). The signaling and transmission may each be either digital or analog. In any case, the path is: A-4 circuit, internal switching through 4, 4-5 channel, internal switching through 5, 5-6 channel, internal switching through 6, 6-E circuit. Generally, the connection is full duplex, and data may be transmitted in both directions.

3. *Circuit disconnect.* After some period of data transfer, the connection is terminated, usually by the action of one of the two stations. Signals must be propagated to 4, 5, and 6 to deallocate the dedicated resources.

Note that the connection path is established before data transmission begins. Thus channel capacity must be available and reserved between each pair of nodes in the path, and each node must have internal switching capacity to handle the connection. The switches must have the intelligence to make these allocations and to devise a route through the network.

Circuit switching can be rather inefficient. Channel capacity is dedicated for the duration of a connection, even if no data are being transferred. For a voice connection, utilization may be rather high, but it still does not approach 100 percent. For a terminal-to-computer connection, the capacity may be idle during most of the time of the connection. In terms of performance, there is a delay prior to data transfer for call establishment. However, once the circuit is established, the network is effectively transparent to the users. Data are transmitted at a fixed data rate with no delay other than the propagation delay through the transmission links. The delay at each node is negligible.

Packet Switching

Long-haul circuit-switching telecommunications networks were originally designed to handle voice traffic, and the majority of traffic on these networks continues to be voice. A key characteristic of circuit-switching networks is that resources within the network are dedicated to a particular call. For voice connections, the resulting circuit will enjoy a high percentage of utilization since, most of the time, one party or the other is talking. However, as the circuit-switching network began to be used increasingly for data connections, two shortcomings became apparent:

1. In a typical terminal-to-host data connection, much of the time the line is idle. Thus, with data connections, a circuit-switching approach is inefficient.

2. In a circuit-switching network, the connection provides for transmission at constant data rate. Thus each of the two devices that are connected must transmit and receive at the same data rate as the other, which limits the utility of the network in interconnecting a variety of host computers and terminals.

To understand how packet switching addresses these problems, let us briefly summarize packet-switching operation. Data are transmitted in blocks, called *packets*. A typical upper bound on packet length is 1000 octets (bytes). If a source has a longer message to send, the message is broken up into a series of packets (Figure 2.11). Each packet consists of a portion of the data (or all of the data for a short message) that a station wants to transmit, plus a packet header that contains control information. The control information, at a minimum, includes the information that the network requires in order to be able to route the packet through the network and deliver it to the intended destination. At each node en route, the packet is received, stored briefly, and passed on to the next node.

Figure 2.12 illustrates the basic operation. A transmitting computer or other device sends a message as a sequence of packets (a). Each packet includes control information indicating the destination station (computer, terminal, etc.). The packets are initially sent to the node to which the sending station attaches. As each packet arrives at this node, it stores the packet briefly, determines the next leg of the route, and queues the packet to go out

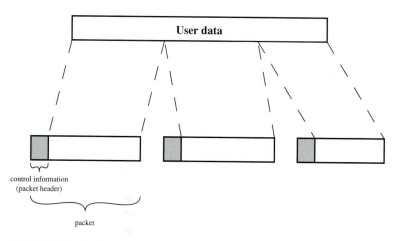

FIGURE 2.11   Packets

on that link. Each packet is transmitted to the next node (b) when the link is available. All of the packets eventually work their way through the network and are delivered to the intended destination.

The packet-switching approach has a number of advantages over circuit switching:

1. Line efficiency is greater, since a single node-to-node link can be dynamically shared by many packets over time. The packets are queued up and transmitted as rapidly as possible over the link. By contrast, with circuit switching, time on a node-to-node link is preallocated using synchronous time-division multiplexing. Much of the time, such a link may be idle because a portion of its time is dedicated to a connection that is idle.

2. A packet-switching network can carry out data-rate conversion. Two stations of different data rates can exchange packets, since each connects to its node at its proper data rate.

3. When traffic becomes heavy on a circuit-switching network, some calls are blocked; that is, the network refuses to accept additional connection requests until the load on the network decreases. On a packet-switching network, packets are still accepted, but delivery delay increases.

4. Priorities can be used. Thus, if a node has a number of packets queued for transmission, it can transmit the higher-priority packets first. These packets will therefore experience less delay than lower-priority packets.

Let us now consider the operation of a packet-switching network. Consider that a station has a message to send through a packet-switching network that is of greater length than the maximum packet size. It there-

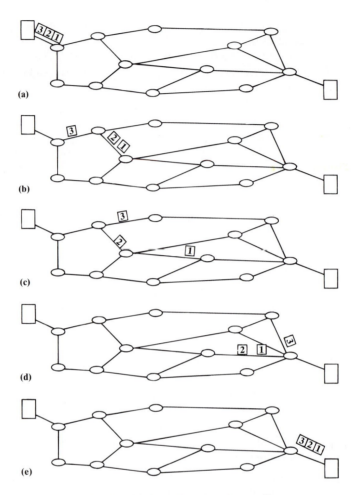

FIGURE 2.12   Packet Switching (Datagram Approach)

fore breaks up the message into packets and sends these packets, one at a time, to the network. A question arises as to how the network will handle this stream of packets as it attempts to route them through the network and deliver them to the intended destination. There are two approaches that are used in contemporary networks: datagram and virtual circuit.

In the **datagram** approach, each packet is treated independently, with no reference to packets that have gone before. This approach is illustrated in Figure 2.12. Each node chooses the next node on a packet's path, taking into account information received from neighboring nodes on traffic, line failures, and so on. So the packets, each with the same destination address, may not all follow the same route (c), and they may arrive out of sequence at the exit point. In this example, the exit node restores the packets to their original order before delivering them to the destination. In some datagram networks, it is up to the destination rather than the exit node to do the reordering. Also, it is possible for a packet to be destroyed in the network. For example, if a packet-switching node crashes momentarily, all of its queued packets may be lost. Again, it is up to either the exit node or the destination to detect the loss of a packet and to decide how to recover it. In this technique, each packet, treated independently, is referred to as a *datagram*.

In the **virtual circuit** approach, a preplanned route is established before any packets are sent; this route serves to support a logical connection between the end systems. Once the route is established, all of the packets between a pair of communicating parties follow this same route through the network, as illustrated in Figure 2.13. Because the route is fixed for the duration of the logical connection, it is somewhat similar to a circuit in a circuit-

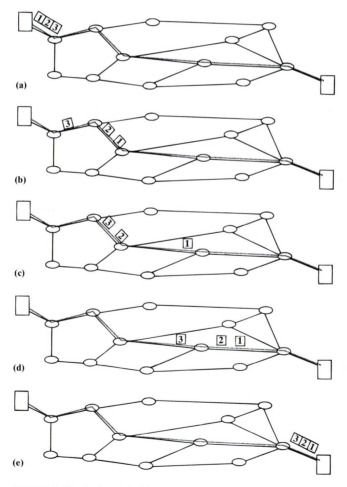

FIGURE 2.13   Packet Switching (Virtual Circuit Approach)

switching network and is referred to as a *virtual circuit.* Each packet now contains a virtual circuit identifier as well as data. Each node on the preestablished route knows where to direct such packets; no routing decisions are required. At any time, each station can have more than one virtual circuit to any other station and can have virtual circuits to more than one station.

So the main characteristic of the virtual circuit technique is that a route between stations is set up prior to data transfer. Note that this setup does not mean that the route is a dedicated path, as in circuit switching. A packet is still buffered at each node and queued for output over a line. The difference from the datagram approach is that, with virtual circuits, the node need not make a routing decision for each packet. It is made only once for all packets using that virtual circuit.

If two stations wish to exchange data over an extended period of time, there are certain advantages to virtual circuits. First, the network may provide services related to the virtual circuit, including sequencing, error control, and flow control. *Sequencing* is provided since all packets follow the same route; and therefore they arrive in the original order. *Error control* is a service assuring not only that packets arrive in proper sequence, but that all packets arrive correctly. For example, if a packet in a sequence from node 4 to node 6 fails to arrive at node 6, or arrives with an error, node 6 can request a retransmission of that packet from node 4. *Flow control* is a technique for assuring that a sender does not overwhelm a receiver with data. For example, if station E is buffering data from station A and perceives that it is about to run out of buffer space, it can request, via the virtual circuit facility, that station A suspend transmission until further notice. Another advantage is that packets should transit the network more rapidly with a virtual circuit; it is not necessary to make a routing decision for each packet at each node.

One advantage of the datagram approach is that the call setup phase is avoided. Thus, if a station wishes to send only one or a few packets, datagram delivery will be quicker. Another advantage of the datagram service is that because it is more primitive it is more flexible. For example, if congestion develops in one part of the network, incoming datagrams can be routed away from the congestion. With the use of virtual circuits, packets follow a predefined route, and thus it is more difficult for the network to adapt to congestion. A third advantage is that datagram delivery is inherently more reliable. With the use of virtual circuits, if a node fails, all virtual circuits that pass through that node are lost. With datagram delivery, if a node fails, subsequent packets may find an alternate route that bypasses that node.

Multirate Circuit Switching

One of the drawbacks of circuit switching is its inflexibility with respect to data rate. If a station attaches to an ordinary circuit-switching network, it is committed to operating at a particular data rate. This data rate must be used regardless of the application, whether it is digitized voice or some data application. Thus, an application with a low data rate requirement would make inefficient use of the network link.

To overcome this inflexibility, an enhanced service known as *multirate circuit switching* was developed. This technique combines circuit switching with multiplexing. The station attaches to the network by means of a single physical link. That link is used to carry multiple fixed-data-rate channels between the station and a network node. The traffic on each channel can be switched independently through the network to various destinations.

For this technique, it is possible to develop a scheme in which all of the available channels operate at the same data rate, or a scheme that uses various data rates. For example, integrated services digital network (ISDN) is a standardized digital telecommunications specification. It defines a variety of station-network interfaces, all of which employ multirate circuit switching. The simplest ISDN interface consists of two 64-kbps channels and one 16-kbps channel.

Although this technique is more flexible than simple circuit switching, the same fundamental limitation exists. The user now has the choice of a number of data rates, but each rate remains fixed and the likelihood of inefficient use of a particular channel remains.

Frame Relay

Packet switching was developed at a time when digital long-distance transmission facilities exhibited a relatively high error rate compared to today's facilities. As a result, there is a considerable amount of overhead built into packet-switching schemes to compensate for errors. The overhead includes additional bits added to each packet to enhance redundancy, and additional processing at the end stations and the intermediate network nodes to detect and recover from errors.

With modern, high-speed telecommunications systems, this overhead is unnecessary and counterproductive. It is unnecessary because the rate of errors has been dramatically lowered and any remaining errors can easily be caught by logic in the end systems that operates above the level of the packet-switching logic. It is counterproductive because the overhead involved soaks up a significant fraction of the high capacity provided by the network.

To take advantage of the high data rates and low error rates of contemporary networking facilities, frame relay was developed. Whereas the original packet-switching networks were designed with a data rate to the end user of about 64 kbps, frame relay networks are designed to operate at user data rates of up to 2 Mbps. The key to achieving these high data rates is to strip out most of the overhead involved with error control.

Cell Relay

Cell relay, also known as *asynchronous transfer mode*, is in a sense a culmination of all of the developments in circuit switching and packet switching over the past 20 years. One useful way to view cell relay is as an evolution from frame relay. The most obvious difference between cell relay and frame relay is that frame relay uses variable-length packets and cell relay uses fixed-length packets, called cells. As with frame relay, cell relay provides minimum overhead for error control, depending on the inherent reliability of the transmission system and on higher layers of logic to catch and correct remaining errors. By using a fixed packet length, the processing overhead is reduced even further for cell relay compared to frame relay. The result is that cell relay is designed to work in the range of tens and hundreds of Mbps, compared to the 2 Mbps of frame relay.

Another way to view cell relay is as an evolution from multirate circuit switching. With multirate circuit switching, only fixed-data-rate channels are available to the end system. Cell relay allows the definition of virtual channels with data rates that are dynamically defined at the time that the virtual channel is created. By using small, fixed-size cells, cell relay is so efficient that it can offer a constant-data-rate channel even though it is using a packet-switching technique. Thus cell relay extends multirate circuit switching to allow multiple channels with the data rate of each channel dynamically set on demand.

2.4

TCP/IP AND OSI

When communication is desired among computers from different vendors, the software development effort can be a nightmare. Different vendors use different data formats and data exchange protocols. Even within one vendor's product line, different model computers may communicate in unique ways.

As the use of computer communications and computer networking proliferates, a one-at-a-time special-purpose approach to communications software development is too costly to be acceptable. The only alternative is for computer vendors to adopt and implement a common set of conventions. For this to happen, standards are needed. Such standards would have two benefits:

- Vendors feel encouraged to implement the standards because of an expectation that because of wide use of the standards, their products would be less marketable without them.

- Customers are in a position to require that the standards be implemented by any vendor wishing to propose equipment to them.

It should become clear from the ensuing discussion that no single standard will suffice. Any distributed application, such as electronic mail or client–server interaction, requires a complex set of communications functions for proper operation. Many of these functions, such as reliability mechanisms, are common across many or even all applications. Thus the communications task is best viewed as consisting of a modular architecture, in which the various elements of the architecture perform the various required functions. Hence, before one can develop standards, there should be a structure, or *protocol architecture,* that defines the communications tasks.

Two protocol architectures have served as the basis for the development of interoperable communications standards: the TCP/IP protocol suite and the OSI reference model. TCP/IP is the most widely used interoperable architecture, especially in the context of local area networks. In this section we provide a brief overview of the two architectures.

TCP/IP Protocol Architecture

This architecture is a result of protocol research and development conducted on the experimental packet-switched network, ARPANET, funded by the Defense Advanced Research Projects Agency (DARPA), and is generally referred to as the TCP/IP protocol suite. This protocol suite consists of a large collection of protocols that have been issued as Internet standards by the Internet Activities Board (IAB).

TCP/IP Layers.   In general terms, communications can be said to involve three agents: applications, computers, and networks. Examples of applications include file transfer and electronic mail. The applications that we are concerned with here are distributed applications that involve the exchange of data between two computer systems. These applications, and others, execute on computers that can often support multiple simultaneous applications. Computers are connected to networks, and the data to be exchanged are transferred by the network from one computer to another. Thus the transfer of data from one application to another involves first getting the data to the computer in which the application resides and then getting it to the intended application within the computer.

With these concepts in mind, it appears natural to organize the communication task into four relatively independent layers:

- Network access layer
- Internet layer
- Host-to-host layer
- Process layer

The **network access layer** is concerned with the exchange of data between an end system (server, workstation, etc.) and the network to which it is attached. The sending computer must provide the network with the address of the destination computer, so that the network may route the data to the appropriate destination. The sending computer may wish to invoke certain services, such as priority, that might be provided by the network. The specific software used at this layer depends on the type of network to be used; different standards have been developed for circuit switching, packet switching (e.g., X.25), local area networks (e.g., Ethernet), and others. Thus it makes sense to separate those functions having to do with network access into a separate layer. By doing this, the remainder of the communications software, above the network access layer, need not be concerned about the specifics of the network to be used. The same higher-layer software should function properly regardless of the particular network to which the computer is attached.

The network access layer is concerned with access to and routing data across a network for two end systems attached to the same network. In those cases where two devices are attached to different networks, procedures are needed to allow data to traverse multiple interconnected networks. This is the function of the **internet layer.** The internet protocol (IP) is used at this layer to provide the routing function across multiple networks. This protocol is implemented not only in the end systems but also in routers. A router is a processor that connects tow networks and whose primary function is to relay data from one network to the other on its route from the source to the destination end system.

Regardless of the nature of the applications that are exchanging data, there is usually a requirement that data be exchanged reliably. That is, we would like to be assured that all of the data arrive at the destination application and that the data arrive in the same order in which they were sent. As we shall see, the mechanisms for providing reliability are essentially independent of the nature of the applications. Thus it makes sense to collect those mechanisms in a common layer shared by all applications; this is referred to as the **host-to-host layer.** The transmission control protocol (TCP) provides this functionality.

Finally, the **process layer** contains the logic needed to support the various user applications. For each type of application, such as file transfer, a separate module is needed that is peculiar to that application.

Operation of TCP and IP.   Figure 2.14 indicates how these protocols are configured for communications. To make clear that the total communications facility may consist of multiple networks, the constituent networks are usually referred to as *subnetworks.* Some sort of network access protocol, such as the Ethernet logic, is used to connect a computer to a subnetwork. This protocol enables the host to send data across the subnetwork to another host or, in the case of a host on another subnetwork, to a router. IP is implemented in all of the end systems and the routers. It acts as a relay to move a block of data from one host, through one or more routers, to another host. TCP is implemented only in the end systems; it keeps track of the blocks of data to assure that all are delivered reliably to the appropriate application.

For successful communication, every entity in the overall system must have a unique address. Actually, two levels of addressing are needed. Each host on a subnetwork must have a unique global internet address; this allows the data to be delivered to the proper host. Each process with a host must have an address that is unique within the host; this allows the host-to-host protocol (TCP) to deliver data to the proper process. The latter addresses are known as ports.

Let us trace a simple operation. Suppose that a process associated with port 1 at host A wishes to send a message to another process, associated with port 2 at host B. The process at A hands the message down to TCP with instructions to send it to host B, port 2. TCP hands the message down to IP with instructions to send it to host B. Note that IP need not be told the identity of the destination port. All it needs to know is that the data are intended for host B. Next, IP hands the message down to the network access layer (e.g., Ethernet logic) with instructions to send it to router X (the first hop on the way to B).

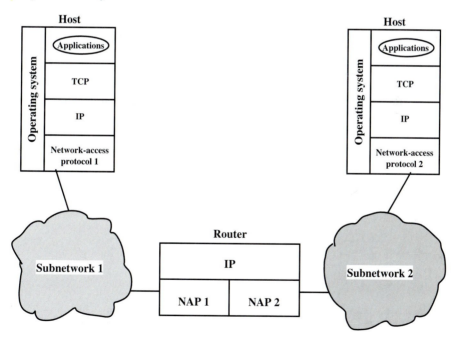

FIGURE 2.14   Communications Using the TCP/IP Protocol Architecture

To control this operation, control information as well as user data must be transmitted, as suggested in Figure 2.15. Let us say that the sending process generates a block of data and passes this to TCP. TCP may break this block into smaller pieces to make it more manageable. To each of these pieces, TCP appends control information known as the TCP header, forming a *TCP segment.* The control information is to be used by the peer TCP protocol entity at host B. Examples of items that are included in this header include:

- *Destination port.* When the TCP entity at B receives the segment, it must know to whom the data are to be delivered.
- *Sequence number.* TCP numbers the segments that it sends to a particular destination port sequentially, so that if they arrive out of order, the TCP entity at B can reorder them.
- *Checksum.* The sending TCP includes a code that is a function of the contents of the remainder of the segment. The receiving TCP performs the same calculation and compares the result with the incoming code. A discrepancy results if there has been some error in transmission.

Next, TCP hands each segment over to IP, with instructions to transmit it to B. These segments must be transmitted across one or more subnetworks and relayed through one or more intermediate routers. This operation, too, requires the use of control information. Thus IP appends a header of control information to each segment to form an *IP datagram.* An example of an item stored in the IP header is the destination host address (in this example, B).

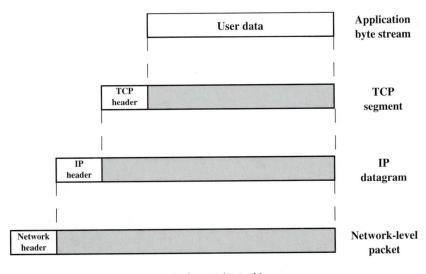

FIGURE 2.15 Protocol Data Units in the TCP/IP Architecture

Finally, each IP datagram is presented to the network access layer for transmission across the first subnetwork in its journey to the destination. The network access layer appends its own header, creating a packet, or frame. The packet is transmitted across the subnetwork to router X. The packet header contains the information that the subnetwork needs to transfer the data across the subnetwork. Examples of items that may be contained in this header include:

- *Destination subnetwork address.* The subnetwork must know to which attached device the packet is to be delivered.
- *Facilities requests.* The network access protocol might request the use of certain subnetwork facilities, such as priority.

At router X, the packet header is stripped off and the IP header examined. On the basis of the destination address information in the IP header, the IP module in the router directs the datagram out across subnetwork 2 to B. To do this, the datagram is again augmented with a network access header.

When the data are received at B, the reverse process occurs. At each layer the corresponding header is removed, and the remainder is passed on to the next-higher layer, until the original user data are delivered to the destination process.

TCP/IP Applications.   A number of applications have been standardized to operate on top of TCP. We mention three of the most common here.

The **simple mail transfer protocol** (SMTP) provides a basic electronic mail facility. It provides a mechanism for transferring messages among separate hosts. Features of SMTP include mailing lists, return receipts, and forwarding. The SMTP protocol does not specify the way in which messages are to be created; some local editing or native electronic mail facility is required. Once a message is created, SMTP accepts the message and makes use of TCP to send it to an SMTP module on another host. The target SMTP module will make use of a local electronic mail package to store the incoming message in a user's mailbox.

The **file transfer protocol** (FTP) is used to send files from one system to another under user command. Both text and binary files are accommodated, and the protocol provides features for controlling user access. When a user wishes to engage in file transfer, FTP sets up a TCP connection to the target system for the exchange of control messages. These allow user ID and password to be transmitted and allow the user to specify the file and file actions desired. Once a file transfer is approved, a second TCP connection is set up for the data transfer. The file is transferred over the data connection, without the overhead of any headers or control information at the application level. When the transfer is complete, the control connection is used to signal the completion and to accept new file transfer commands.

TELNET provides a remote logon capability, which enables a user at a terminal or personal computer to logon to a remote computer and function as if directly connected to that computer. The protocol was designed to work with simple scroll-mode terminals. TELNET is actually implemented in two modules: User TELNET interacts with the terminal I/O module to communicate with a local terminal. It converts the characteristics of real terminals to the network standard, and vice versa. Server TELNET interacts with an application, acting as a surrogate terminal handler so that remote terminals appear as local to the application. Terminal traffic between User and Server TELNET is carried on a TCP connection.

OSI Model

The Open Systems Interconnection (OSI) reference model was developed by the International Organization for Standardization (ISO) to serve as a framework for the development of communications protocol standards.

Overall Architecture.   A widely accepted structuring technique, and the one chosen by ISO, is layering. The communications functions are partitioned into a hierarchical set of layers. Each layer performs a related subset of the functions required to communicate with another system. It relies on the next-lower layer to perform more primitive functions and to conceal the details of those functions. It provides services to the next-higher layer. Ideally, the layers should be defined so that changes in one layer do not require changes in the other layers. Thus we have decomposed one problem into a number of more manageable subproblems.

The task of ISO was to define a set of layers and the services performed by each layer. The partitioning should group functions logically, and should have enough layers to make each layer manageably small, but should not have so many layers that the processing overhead imposed by the collection of layers is burdensome. The resulting OSI architecture has seven layers, which are listed with a brief definition in Table 2.4.

Figure 2.16 illustrates the OSI architecture, and Figure 2.17 compares it to the TCP/IP architecture. Each computer contains the seven layers. Communication is between applications in the two computers, labeled application X and application Y in Figure 2.16. If application X wishes to send a message to application Y, it invokes the application layer (layer 7). Layer 7 establishes a peer relationship with layer 7 of the target computer, using a layer 7 protocol (application protocol). This protocol requires services from layer 6, so the two layer 6 entities use a protocol of their own, and so on down to the physical layer, which actually transmits bits over a transmission medium.

The figure also illustrates the way in which the protocols at each layer are realized. When application X has a message to send to application Y, it

TABLE 2.4   OSI Layers

Layer	Definition
1 Physical	Concerned with transmission of unstructured bit stream over physical link; involves such parameters as signal voltage swing and bit duration; deals with the mechanical, electrical, and procedural characteristics to establish, maintain, and deactivate the physical link
2 Data link	Provides for the reliable transfer of data across the physical link; sends blocks of data (frames) with the necessary synchronization, error control, and flow control
3 Network	Provides upper layers with independence from the data transmission and switching technologies used to connect systems; responsible for establishing, maintaining, and termination connections across networks
4 Transport	Provides reliable, transparent transfer of data between end points; provides end-to-end error recovery and flow control
5 Session	Provides the control structure for communication between applications; establishes, manages, and terminates connections (sessions) between cooperating applications
6 Presentation	Performs generally useful transformations on data to provide a standardized application interface and to provide common communications services; examples: encryption, text compression, reformatting
7 Application	Provides services to the users of the OSI environment; examples: transaction server, file transfer protocol, network management

transfers those data to an application layer module. That module appends an application header to the data; the header contains the control information needed by the peer layer on the other side. The original data plus the header, referred to as an application PDU, is passed as a unit to layer 6. The presentation module treats the whole unit as data and appends its own header. This process continues down through layer 2, which generally adds both a header and a trailer. This layer-2 protocol data unit, usually called a *frame*, is then transmitted by the physical layer onto the transmission medium. When the frame is received by the target computer, the reverse process occurs. As we ascend the layers, each layer strips off the outermost header, acts on the protocol information contained therein, and passes the remainder up to the next layer.

The principal motivation for the development of the OSI model was to provide a framework for standardization. Within the model, one or more protocol standards can be developed at each layer. The model defines in general terms the functions to be performed at that layer and facilitates the standards-making process in two ways:

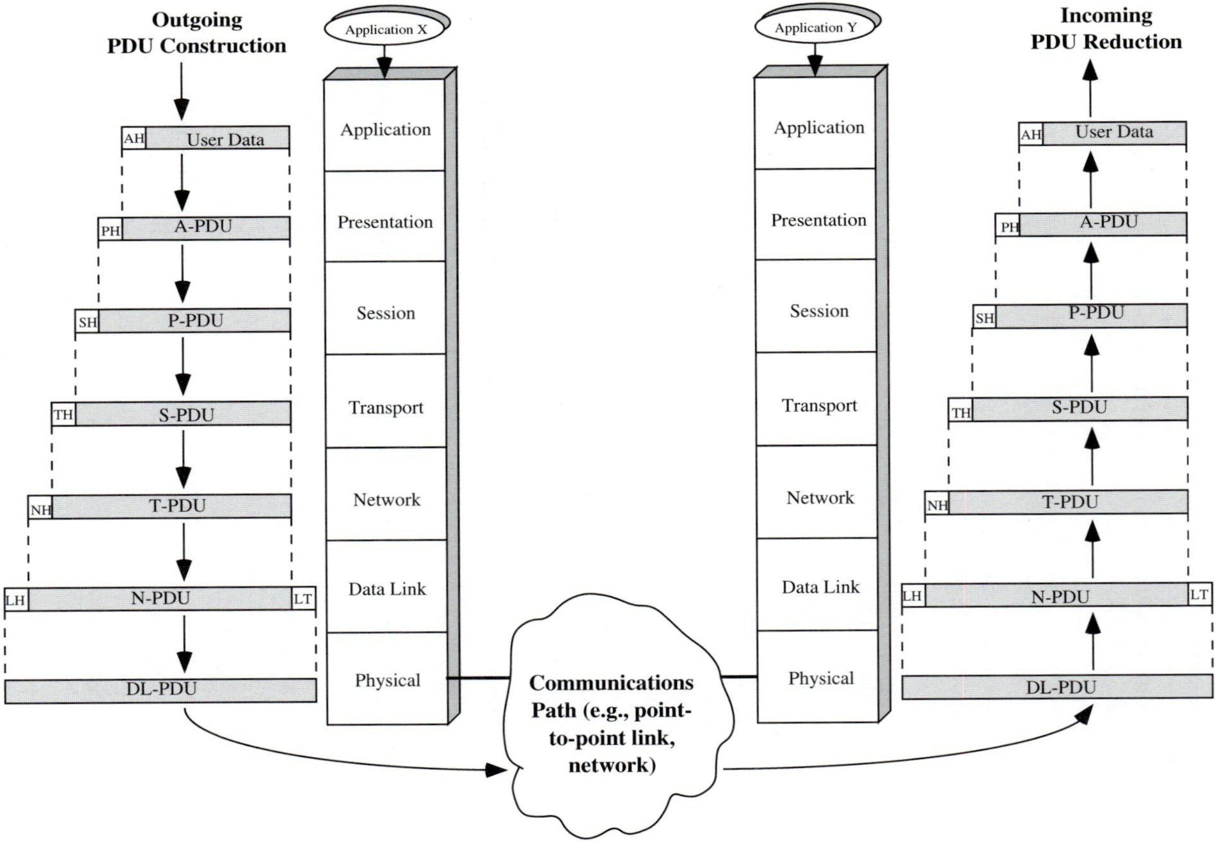

FIGURE 2.16 OSI Environment

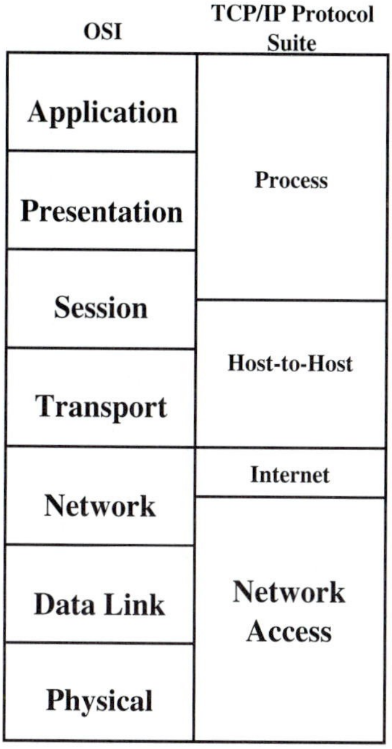

OSI	TCP/IP Protocol Suite
Application	Process
Presentation	
Session	Host-to-Host
Transport	
Network	Internet
Data Link	Network Access
Physical	

FIGURE 2.17   Comparison of the OSI and TCP/IP Communications Architectures

- Since the functions of each layer are well defined, standards can be developed independently and simultaneously for each layer. This speeds up the standards-making process.
- Since the boundaries between layers are well defined, changes in standards in one layer need not affect software already existing in another layer. This makes it easier to introduce new standards.

We now turn to a brief description of each layer and discuss some of the standards that have been developed for each layer.

Physical Layer.   The physical layer covers the physical interface between a data transmission device and a transmission medium and the rules by which bits are passed from one to another. A well-known physical layer standard is RS-232-C.

Data Link Layer.   The physical layer provides only a raw bit stream service. The data link layer attempts to make the physical link reliable and provides the means to activate, maintain, and deactivate the link. The principal service provided by the data link layer to higher layers is that of error detection and control. Thus with a fully functional data link layer protocol, the next-higher layer may assume error-free transmission over the link.

A well-known data link layer standard is HDLC. For LANs, the functionality of the data link layer is generally split into two sublayers: logical link control (LLC) and medium access control (MAC).

Network Layer.   The network layer provides for the transfer of information between computers across some sort of communications network. It relieves higher layers of the need to know anything about the underlying data transmission and switching technologies used to connect systems. The network service is responsible for establishing, maintaining, and terminating connections across the intervening network. At this layer, the computer system engages in a dialogue with the network to specify the destination address and to request certain network facilities, such as priority.

There is a spectrum of possibilities for intervening communications facilities to be managed by the network layer. At one extreme, there is a direct point-to-point link between stations. In this case there may be no need for a network layer because the data link layer can perform the necessary function of managing the link.

Next, the systems could be connected across a single network, such as a circuit- or packet-switching network. Figure 2.18 shows how the presence of a network affects the OSI architecture. The lower three layers are concerned with attaching to and communicating with the network; a well-known example is the X.25 standard. The packets that are created by the end system pass through one or more network nodes that act as relays between the two end systems. The network nodes implement layers 1 to 3 of the architecture. In the figure, two end systems are connected through a single network node. Layer 3 in the node performs a switching and routing function. Within the node, there are two data link layers and two physical layers, corresponding to the links to the two end systems. Each data link (and physical) layer operates independently to provide service to the network layer over its respective link. The upper four layers are "end-to-end" protocols between the attached computers.

At the other extreme, two stations might wish to communicate but are not even connected to the same network. Rather, they are connected to networks that, directly or indirectly, are connected to each other. This case requires the use of some sort of internetworking technique; we explore this approach in Chapter 15.

Transport Layer.   The transport layer provides a reliable mechanism for the exchange of data between computers. It ensures that data are delivered error-free, in sequence, with no losses or duplications. The transport layer may also be concerned with optimizing the use of network services and providing a requested quality of service. For example, the session layer may specify acceptable error rates, maximum delay, priority, and security features.

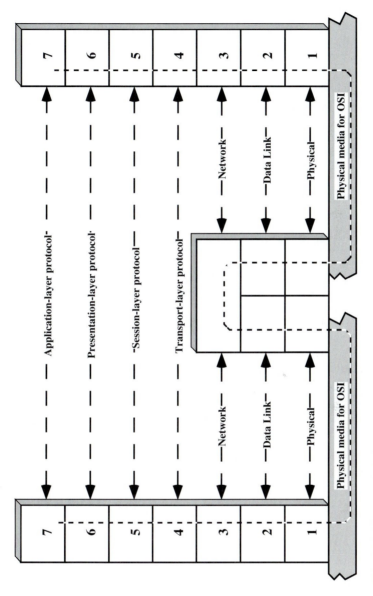

FIGURE 2.18   Use of a Relay

67

The mechanisms used by the transport protocol to provide reliability are very similar to those used by data link control protocols such as HDLC: the use of sequence numbers, error-detecting codes, and retransmission after timeout. The reason for this apparent duplication of effort is that the data link layer only deals with a single, direct link, whereas the transport layer deals with a chain of network nodes and links. Although each link in that chain is reliable because of the use of HDLC, a node along that chain may fail at a critical time. Such a failure will affect data delivery, and it is the transport protocol that addresses this problem.

The size and complexity of a transport protocol depend on how reliable or unreliable the underlying network and network layer services are. Accordingly, ISO has developed a family of five transport protocol standards, each oriented toward a different underlying service.

Session Layer.   The session layer provides the mechanism for controlling the dialogue between the two end systems. In many cases there will be little or no need for session-layer services, but for some applications, such services are used. The key services provided by the session layer include:

- *Dialogue discipline.* This can be two-way simultaneous (full duplex) or two-way alternate (half duplex).
- *Grouping.* The flow of data can be marked to define groups of data. For example, if a retail store is transmitting sales data to a regional office, the data can be marked to indicate the end of the sales data for each department. This would signal the host computer to finalize running totals for that department and start new running counts for the next department.
- *Recovery.* The session layer can provide a checkpointing mechanism, so that if a failure of some sort occurs between checkpoints, the session entity can retransmit all data since the last checkpoint.

ISO has issued a standard for the session layer that includes as options services such as those just described.

Presentation Layer.   The presentation layer defines the format of the data to be exchanged between applications and offers application programs a set of data transformation services. For example, data compression or data encryption could occur at this level.

Application Layer.   The application layer provides a means for application programs to access the OSI environment. This layer contains management functions and generally useful mechanisms to support distributed applications. In addition, general-purpose applications such as file transfer, electronic mail, and terminal access to remote computers are considered to reside at this layer.

2.5

RECOMMENDED READING

[STAL97] covers all of the topics in this chapter. A thorough treatment of both analog and digital communications can be found in [COUC95]. A thorough discussion of the OSI model can be found in [TANE88], which averages about one chapter per layer. [STAL93b] covers the standards at each layer of the OSI model, emphasizing the more recent, leading-edge standards.

COUC95   Couch, L. *Modern Communication Systems: Principles and Applications.* Englewood Cliffs, NJ: Prentice Hall, 1994.

STAL93b   Stallings, W. *Networking Standards: A Guide to OSI, ISDN, LAN, and MAN Standards.* Reading, MA: Addison-Wesley, 1993.

STAL97   Stallings, W. *Data and Computer Communications,* 5th ed. Englewood Cliffs, NJ: Prentice Hall, 1994.

TANE88   Tanenbaum, A. *Computer Networks.* Englewood Cliffs, NJ: Prentice Hall, 1994.

2.6

PROBLEMS

2.1   Are the modem and the codec functional inverses (i.e., could an inverted modem function as a codec, and vice versa)?

2.2   Another form of digital encoding of digital data is known as delay modulation or Miller coding. In this scheme, a logic 1 is represented by a midbit transition (in either direction) and a logic 0 is represented by a transition at the end of the bit period if the next bit is 0, and is represented by the absence of transition if the next bit is a 1. Draw a Miller code waveform for the bit stream of Figure 2.5. Why might this technique be preferable to NRZ? To Manchester?

2.3   A modified NRZ code known as enhanced NRZ (E-NRZ) is sometimes used for high-density magnetic tape recording. E-NRZ encoding entails separating the NRZ-L data stream into 7-bit words; inverting bits 2, 3, 6, and 7; and adding one parity bit to each word. The parity bit is chosen to make the total number of 1's in the 8-bit word an odd count. What are the advantages of E-NRZ over NRZ-L? Are there any disadvantages?

2.4   For the bit stream 0101110, sketch the waveforms for NRZ, NRZI, Manchester, and Differential Manchester as well as for Miller coding and E-NRZ.

2.5 The waveform of Figure 2.19 belongs to a Manchester encoded binary data stream. Determine the beginning and end of bit periods (i.e., extract clock information) and give the data sequence.

FIGURE 2.19   Manchester Stream

2.6 If digital data are passed through a modem to produce an analog signal in the voice band (0 to 4000 Hz), the resulting analog signal has more high-frequency components than a voice signal in the same band. With this fact in mind, why should PCM be preferable to DM for encoding analog signals that represent digital data?

2.7 What is the percentage of overhead in a T1 carrier?

2.8 Define the following parameters for a switching network:

> N = number of hops between two given end systems
> L = message length, in bits
> B = data rate, in bits per second (bps), on all links
> P = packet size
> H = overhead (header) bits per packet
> S = call setup time (circuit switching or virtual circuit), in seconds
> D = propagation delay per hop, in seconds

a. For $N = 4$, $1 = 3200$, $b = 9600$, $P = 1024$, $H = 16$, $S = 0.2$, $D = 0.001$, compute the end-to-end delay for circuit switching, virtual circuit packet switching, and datagram packet switching. Assume that there are no acknowledgments.

b. Derive general expressions for the three techniques of part (a), taken two at a time (six expressions in all), showing the conditions under which the delays are equal.

2.9 What value of P, as a function of N, B, and H, results in minimum end-to-end delay on a datagram network? Assume that L is much larger than P and that D is zero.

2.10 Among the principles used by ISO to define the OSI layers were:

- The number of layers should be small enough to avoid unwieldy design and implementation, but large enough so that separate layers handle functions that are different in process or technology.
- Layer boundaries should be chosen to minimize the number and size of interactions across boundaries.

Based on these principles, design an architecture with eight layers and make a case for it. Design one with six layers and make a case for that.

2.11 In Figure 2.16, exactly one protocol data unit (PDU) in layer N is encapsulated in a PDU at layer $(N - 1)$. It is also possible to break one N-level PDU into multiple $(N - 1)$-level PDUs (segmentation) or to group multiple N-level PDUs into one $(N - 1)$-level PDU (blocking).

    a. In the case of segmentation, is it necessary that each $(N - 1)$-level segment contain a copy of the N-level header?

    b. In the case of blocking, is it necessary that each N-level PDU retain its own header, or can the data be consolidated into a single N-level PDU with a single N-level header?

Topologies and Transmission Media

The key technology ingredients that determine the nature of a LAN or MAN are:

- Topology
- Transmission medium
- Medium access control technique

The topologies and transmission media that are most commonly used for LANs and MANs are surveyed in this chapter. The issue of access control is raised briefly but is covered in more detail in Chapter 4 and Part II. The chapter begins with an overview of the principal topologies. Then one section is devoted to providing more detail for each of these topologies (bus/tree, ring, star). Finally, the concept of structured cabling systems is introduced.

3.1

TOPOLOGY OVERVIEW

In the context of a communication network, the term *topology* refers to the way in which the end systems, or stations, attached to the network are interconnected. The common topologies for LANs are bus, tree, ring, and

72

star (Figure 3.1). The bus is a special case of the tree, with only one trunk and no branches; we shall use the term *bus/tree* when the distinction is unimportant.

Bus and Tree Topologies

With the bus topology, the communications network is simply the transmission medium; there are no switches or repeaters. All stations attach, through appropriate hardware interfacing known as a tap, directly to the bus. Full-duplex operation between the station and the tap allows data to be transmitted onto the bus and received from the bus. A transmission from any station propagates the length of the medium in both directions and can be received by all other stations. At each end of the bus is a terminator, which absorbs any signal, removing it from the bus.

Two problems present themselves in this arrangement. First, because a transmission from any one station can be received by all other stations, there needs to be some way of indicating for whom the transmission is intended. Second, a mechanism is needed to regulate transmission. To see the reason for this, consider that if two stations on the bus attempt to transmit at the same time, their signals will overlap and become garbled. Or, consider that one station decides to transmit continuously for a long period of time.

To solve these problems, stations transmit data in small blocks, known as frames. Each frame consists of a portion of the data that a station wishes to transmit, plus a frame header that contains control information. Each station on the bus is assigned a unique address, or identifier, and the destination address for a frame is included in its header.

Figure 3.2 illustrates the scheme. In this example, station *C* wishes to transmit a frame of data to *A*. The frame header includes *A*'s address. As the frame propagates along the bus, it passes *B*. *B* observes the address and ignores the frame. *A*, on the other hand, sees that the frame is addressed to itself and therefore copies the data from the frame as it goes by.

So the frame structure solves the first problem mentioned above: It provides a mechanism for indicating the intended recipient of data. It also provides the basic tool for solving the second problem, the regulation of access. In particular, the stations take turns sending frames in some cooperative fashion. This involves putting additional control information into the frame header. We defer a discussion of this regulation until Chapter 4.

The tree topology is a generalization of the bus topology. The transmission medium is a branching cable with no closed loops. The tree layout begins at a point known as the *headend*. One or more cables start at the headend, and each of these may have branches. The branches in turn may have additional branches to allow quite complex layouts. Again, a transmission from any station propagates throughout the medium and can be received by all other stations.

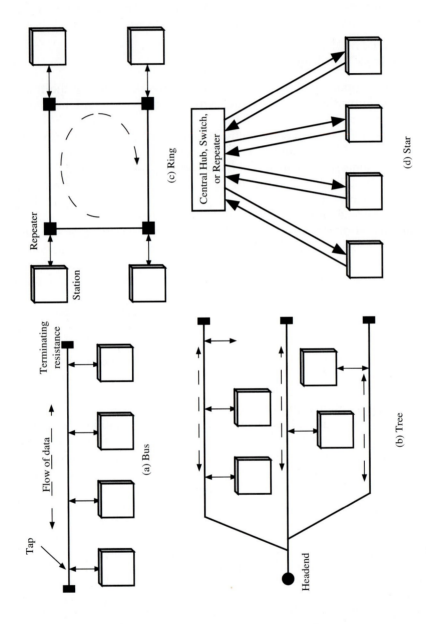

FIGURE 3.1 LAN/MAN Topologies

74

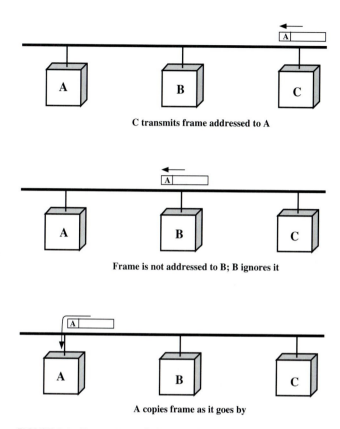

FIGURE 3.2   Frame Transmission on a Bus LAN

With the bus or tree, no special action needs to be taken to remove frames from the medium. When a signal reaches the end of the medium, it is absorbed by the terminator.

Ring Topology

In the ring topology, the LAN or MAN consists of a set of *repeaters* joined by point-to-point links in a closed loop. The repeater is a comparatively simple device, capable of receiving data on one link and transmitting them, bit by bit, on the other link as fast as they are received, with no buffering at the repeater. The links are unidirectional; that is, data are transmitted in one direction only and all oriented in the same way. Thus data circulate around the ring in one direction (clockwise or counterclockwise).

Each station attaches to the network at a repeater and can transmit data onto the network through the repeater. As with the bus and tree, data are transmitted in frames. As a frame circulates past all the other stations, the destination station recognizes its address and copies the frame into a local buffer as it goes by. The frame continues to circulate until it returns to the source station, where it is removed (Figure 3.3). Because multiple stations share the ring, medium access control is needed to determine at what time each station may insert frames.

Star Topology

In the star LAN topology, each station is connected directly to a common central node. Typically, each station attaches to a central node, referred to as the star coupler, via two point-to-point links, one for transmission in each direction. In general, there are two alternatives for operation of the central node. One approach is for the central node to operate in a broadcast fash-

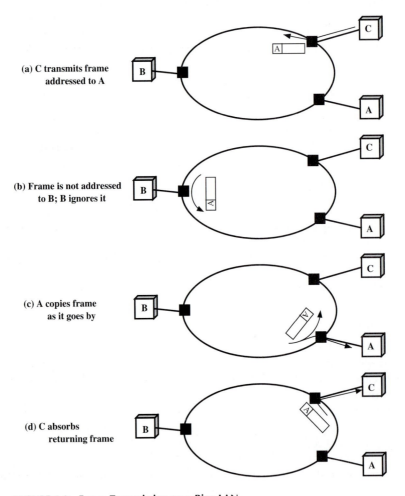

(a) C transmits frame
addressed to A

(b) Frame is not addressed
to B; B ignores it

(c) A copies frame
as it goes by

(d) C absorbs
returning frame

FIGURE 3.3   **Frame Transmission on a Ring LAN**

ion. A transmission of a frame from one station to the node is retransmitted on all the outgoing links. In this case, although the arrangement is physically a star, it is logically a bus: A transmission from any station is received by all other stations, and only one station at a time may transmit successfully. Another approach is for the central node to act as a frame switching device. An incoming frame is buffered in the node and then retransmitted on an the outgoing link to the destination station.

Choice of Topology

The choice of topology depends on a variety of factors, including reliability, expandability, and performance. This choice is part of the overall task of designing a LAN. Accordingly, this choice cannot be made in isolation, independent of the choice of transmission medium, wiring layout, and access control technique. However, a few general remarks can be made at this point.

The bus/tree topology appears to be the most flexible. It is able to handle a wide range of devices in terms of number of devices, data rates, and data types. The tree topology has the advantage that it is relatively easy to lay out, regardless of the physical configuration of the building and the location of wiring ducts or other cable pathways. Any time that an intersection is reached, the cable can simply be branched in all desired directions.

Very high speed links over considerable distances can be used for the ring topology. Hence the ring has the potential of providing the best throughput of any topology. One disadvantage of the ring is that a single link or repeater failure could disable the entire network.

The star topology takes advantage of the natural layout of wiring in a building, as we will explore in Section 3.5. It is generally best for short distances and can support a small number of devices at high data rates.

Choice of Transmission Medium

The choice of transmission medium is determined by a number of factors. It is, we shall see, constrained by the topology of the LAN. Other factors come into play, including:

- *Capacity:* to support the expected network traffic
- *Reliability:* to meet requirements for availability
- *Types of data supported:* tailored to the application
- *Environmental scope:* to provide service over the range of environments required

The choice is part of the overall task of designing a local network, which is addressed in later chapters. Here we can make a few general observations.

Unshielded twisted pair is an inexpensive, well-understood medium. Typically, office buildings are wired to meet the anticipated telephone system demand plus a healthy margin; thus there are no cable installation costs in the use of unshielded twisted pair. However, the data rate that can be supported is generally quite limited, with the exception of very small LAN. Unshielded twisted pair is likely to be the most cost-effective for a single-building, low-traffic LAN installation.

Shielded twisted pair and baseband coaxial cable are more expensive than unshielded twisted pair but provide greater capacity. Broadband cable is even more expensive but provides even greater capacity. For the broad range of LAN requirements, these media are quite attractive. For most requirements, a system based on one of these media can be designed to meet current demand with plenty of room for expansion, at reasonable cost. Broadband coaxial cable systems excel when there are a lot of devices and a considerable amount of traffic. Examples include large data processing installations and sophisticated office automation systems, which may support facsimile machines, image processing systems, and graphics-intensive computing.

Optical fiber has a number of attractive features, such as electromagnetic isolation, high capacity, and small size, which have attracted a great deal of interest. As yet the market penetration of fiber LANs is low; this is due primarily to the high cost of fiber components and the lack of skilled personnel to install and maintain fiber systems. This situation is beginning to change rapidly as more products using fiber are introduced.

Relationship between Medium and Topology

The choices of transmission medium and topology are not independent. Table 3.1 shows the preferred combinations. The ring topology requires point-to-point links between repeaters. Twisted-pair wire, baseband coaxial cable, and optical fiber can all be used to provide the links. However, broadband coaxial cable would not work well in this topology. Each repeater would have to be capable of receiving and transmitting data simultaneously on multiple channels. It is doubtful that the expense of such devices could be justified. Table 3.2 summarizes representative parameters for transmission media for commercially available ring LANs.

For the bus topology, twisted pair and both baseband and broadband coaxial cable are appropriate, and numerous products exist for each of these media. Until recently, optical fiber cable has not been considered feasible; the multipoint configuration was considered not cost-effective, due to the difficulty in constructing low-loss optical taps. However, recent advances have made the optical fiber bus practical, even at quite high data rates.

TABLE 3.1   Medium versus Topology for LANs

Medium	Topology			
	Ring	Bus	Tree	Star
Twisted pair	✳	✳		✳
Baseband coaxial cable	✳	✳		
Broadband coaxial cable		✳	✳	
Optical fiber	✳	✳		✳
Wireless	✳	✳		✳

TABLE 3.2   Transmission Media for Local Area Networks: Ring

Transmission Medium	Data Rate (Mbps)	Repeater Spacing (km)	Number of Taps
Unshielded twisted pair	4	0.1	70
Shielded twisted pair	16	0.3	250
Baseband coaxial cable	16	1.0	250
Optical fiber	100	2.0	250
Wireless	100	0.1	10's

The tree topology can be employed with broadband coaxial cable. The unidirectional nature of broadband signaling allows the construction of a tree architecture. On the other hand, the bidirectional nature of baseband signaling, on either twisted pair or coaxial cable, is not suited to the tree topology. Table 3.3 summarizes representative parameters for transmission media for commercially available bus and tree LANs.

The reader will note that the performance for a given medium is considerably better for the ring topology than for the bus/tree topology. In the bus/tree topology, each station is attached to the medium by a tap, and each tap introduces some attenuation and distortion to the signal as it passes by. In the ring, each station is attached to the medium by a repeater, and each repeater generates a new signal to compensate for effects of attenuation and distortion.

The star topology requires a point-to-point link between each device and the central node. Most recent activity for this topology has focused on the use of twisted pair over short distances; optical fiber can also be used. Table 3.4 summarizes representative parameters for transmission media for commercially available star LANs.

TABLE 3.3   Transmission Media for Local Area Networks: Bus/Tree

Transmission Medium	Data Rate (Mbps)	Range (km)	Number of Taps
Unshielded twisted pair	1	<2	10s
Baseband coaxial cable	10; 50 with limitations	<3/<1	100s/10s
Broadband coaxial cable	50; 20 per channel	<30	100s–1000s
Optical fiber	45	<150	500
Wireless	10	<1	10s

TABLE 3.4   Transmission Media for Local Area Networks: Star

Transmission Medium	Data Rate (Mbps)	Distance from Station to Central Node (km)	Number of Stations
Unshielded twisted pair	10–100	0.1	10s
Shielded twisted pair	100	0.1	10s
Optical fiber	100	0.1	10s
Wireless	10	<1	10s

3.2

BUS/TREE TOPOLOGY

This section covers some technical details on bus/tree topology LANs and MANs. The section begins with an overview of the general characteristics of this topology. In the remainder of the section the use of coaxial cable and optical fiber for implementing this topology is examined.

Characteristics of the Bus/Tree Topology

The bus/tree topology is a multipoint configuration. That is, there are more than two devices connected to the medium and capable of transmitting on the medium. This gives rise to several design issues.

If more than one device at a time on a bus or tree network transmits at the same time, the signals will interfere. Thus there is a requirement to regulate which station on the medium may transmit at any point in time. Historically, the most common multipoint access scheme has been the multidrop line, in which access is determined by polling from a controlling station. The controlling station may send data to any other station, or it may issue a poll to a specific station, asking for an immediate response. This method, however, negates some of the advantages of a distributed system and is awkward for communication between two noncontroller stations. A variety of distributed strategies, referred to as distributed medium access control (MAC) protocols, have been developed for bus and tree topologies. These are discussed in Part III.

Another design issue has to do with signal balancing. When two stations exchange data over a link, the signal strength of the transmitter must be adjusted to be within certain limits. The signal must be strong enough so that after attenuation across the medium, it meets the receiver's minimum signal strength requirements. It must also be strong enough to maintain an adequate signal/noise ratio. On the other hand, the signal must not be so strong that it overloads the circuitry of the transmitter, which distorts the signal. Although easily done for a point-to-point link, signal balancing is no easy task for a multipoint line. If any station can transmit to any other station, the signal balancing must be performed for all permutations of stations taken two at a time. For n stations, that works out to $n \times (n - 1)$ permutations. So for a 200-station network (not a particularly large system), 39,800 signal strength constraints must be satisfied simultaneously. With interdevice distances ranging from tens to thousands of meters, this would be an extremely difficult task for any but small networks. In systems that use radio-frequency (RF) signals, the problem is compounded because of the possibility of RF signal interference across frequencies. A common solution is to divide the medium into smaller segments within which pairwise balancing is possible, using amplifiers or repeaters between segments.

Baseband Coaxial Cable

For bus/tree LANs, the most popular medium is coaxial cable. The two common transmission techniques that are used on coaxial cable are baseband and broadband, which are compared in Table 3.5. This subsection is devoted to baseband systems; broadband LANs are discussed in the next section.

A baseband LAN or MAN is defined as one that uses digital signaling; that is, the binary data to be transmitted are inserted onto the cable as a sequence of voltage pulses, usually using Manchester or Differential Manchester encoding (see Figure 2.5). The nature of digital signals is such that the entire frequency spectrum of the cable is consumed. Hence it is not possible to have multiple channels (frequency-division multiplexing) on the

TABLE 3.5   Bus/Tree Transmission Techniques

Baseband	Broadband
Digital signaling	Analog signaling (requires RF modem)
Entire bandwidth consumed by signal; — no FDM	FDM possible; —multiple data channels, video, audio
Bidirectional	Unidirectional
Bus topology	Bus or tree topology
Distance: up to a few kilometers	Distance: up to 10s of kilometers

cable. Transmission is bidirectional. That is, a signal inserted at any point on the medium propagates in both directions to the ends, where it is absorbed (Figure 3.4a). The digital signaling requires a bus topology. Unlike analog signals, digital signals cannot easily be propagated through the branching points required for a tree topology. Baseband bus LAN systems can extend only a limited distance, about 1 km at most. This is because the attenuation of the signal, which is most pronounced at higher frequencies, causes a blurring of the pulses and a weakening of the signal to the extent that communication over larger distances is impractical. The original use of baseband coaxial cable for a bus LAN was the Ethernet system, which operates at 10 Mbps. Ethernet became the basis of the IEEE 802.3 standard.

Most baseband coaxial cable systems use a special 50-ohm cable rather than the standard CATV 75-ohm cable. These values refer to the impedance of the cable. Roughly speaking, impedance is a measure of how much voltage must be applied to the cable to achieve a given signal strength (see Appendix 3A). For digital signals, the 50-ohm cable suffers less intense reflections from the insertion capacitance of the taps and provides better immunity against low-frequency electromagnetic noise.

As with any transmission system, there are engineering trade-offs involving data rate, cable length, number of taps, and the electrical characteristics of the cable and the transmit/receive components. For example, the lower the data rate, the longer the cable can be. That statement is true for the following reason: When a signal is propagated along a transmission medium, the integrity of the signal suffers due to attenuation, noise, and other impairments. The longer the length of propagation, the greater the effect, increasing the probability of error. However, at a lower data rate, the individual pulses of a digital signal last longer and can be recovered in the presence of impairments more easily than can higher-rate, shorter pulses.

Here is one example that illustrates some of the trade-offs. The Ethernet specification and the original IEEE 802.3 standard specified the use of 50-ohm cable with a 0.4-inch diameter and a data rate of 10 Mbps. With these parameters, the maximum length of the cable is set at 500 meters. Stations attach to the cable by means of a tap, with the distance between any two taps being a multiple of 2.5 meters; this is to ensure that reflections from adjacent taps do not

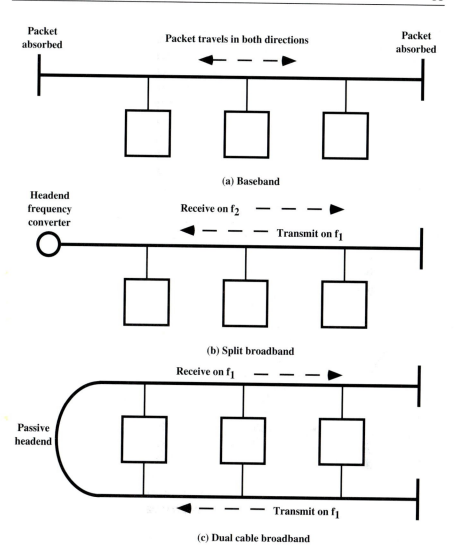

(a) Baseband

(b) Split broadband

(c) Dual cable broadband

FIGURE 3.4   Baseband and Broadband Transmission Techniques

add in phase [YEN83]. A maximum of 100 taps is allowed. In IEEE jargon, this system is referred to as 10BASE5 (*10* Mbps, *base*band, *500*-meter cable length).

To provide a lower-cost system for personal computer LANs, IEEE 802.3 later added a 10BASE2 specification. Table 3.6 compares this scheme, dubbed Cheapernet, with 10BASE5. The key change is the use of a thinner (0.25 inch) cable of the type employed in products such as public address systems. The thinner cable is more flexible; thus it is easier to bend around corners and bring to a workstation rather than installing a cable in the wall and having to provide a drop cable between the main cable and the workstation. The cable is easier to install and uses cheaper electronics than the

TABLE 3.6   IEEE 802.3 Specifications for 10-Mbps Baseband Coaxial Cable Bus LANs

	10BASE5	10BASE2
Data rate	10 Mbps	10 Mbps
Maximum segment length	500 m	185 m
Network span	2500 m	1000 m
Nodes per segment	100	30
Node spacing	2.5 m	0.5 m
Cable diameter	0.4 in.	0.25 in.

thicker cable. On the other hand, the thinner cable suffers greater attenuation and lower noise resistance than the thicker cable. Thus it supports fewer taps over a shorter distance.

To extend the length of the network, repeaters may be used. This device works in a somewhat different fashion than the repeater on the ring. The bus repeater is not used as a device attachment point and is capable of transmitting in both directions. A repeater joins two segments of cable and passes digital signals in both directions between the two segments. A repeater is transparent to the rest of the system; as it does no buffering, it does not logically isolate one segment from another. For example, if two stations on different segments attempt to transmit at the same time, their packets will interfere with each other (collide). To avoid multipath interference, only one path of segments and repeaters is allowed between any two stations. Figure 3.5 illustrates a multiple-segment baseband bus LAN.

Broadband Coaxial Cable

In the local network context, the term refers to coaxial cable on which analog signaling is used. Table 3.5 summarizes the key characteristics of broadband systems. As mentioned, broadband implies the use of analog signaling. FDM is possible: the frequency spectrum of the cable can be divided into channels or sections of bandwidth. Separate channels can support data traffic, television, and radio signals. Broadband components allow splitting and joining operations; hence both bus and tree topologies are possible. Much greater distances—tens of kilometers—are possible with broadband compared to baseband. This is because the analog signals that carry the digital data can propagate greater distances before the noise and attenuation damage the data.

Dual and Split Configurations.   As with baseband, stations on a broadband LAN attach to the cable by means of a tap. Unlike baseband, however, broadband is inherently a unidirectional medium; the taps that are used allow signals inserted onto the medium to propagate in only one direction. The primary reason for this is that it is unfeasible to build amplifiers that

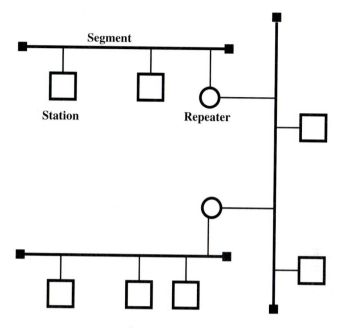

FIGURE 3.5   Baseband Configuration

will pass signals of one frequency in both directions. This unidimensional property means that only those stations "downstream" from a transmitting station can receive its signals. How, then, to achieve full connectivity?

Clearly, two data paths are needed. These paths are joined at a point on the network known as the **headend.** For a bus topology, the headend is simply one end of the bus. For a tree topology, the headend is the root of the branching tree. All stations transmit on one path toward the headend (inbound). Signals arriving at the headend are then propagated along a second data path away from the headend (outbound). All stations receive on the outbound path.

Physically, two different configurations are used to implement the inbound and outbound paths (Figure 3.4b and c). On a **dual-cable** configuration, the inbound and outbound paths are separate cables, with the headend simply a passive connector between the two. Stations send and receive on the same frequency.

By contrast, on a **split** configuration, the inbound and outbound paths are different frequency bands on the same cable. Bidirectional amplifiers[1]

---

[1]Unfortunately, this terminology is confusing, since we have said that broadband is inherently a unidirectional medium. At a given frequency, broadband is unidirectional. However, there is no difficulty in having signals in nonoverlapping frequency bands traveling in opposite directions on the cable.

pass lower frequencies inbound and higher frequencies outbound. Between the inbound and outbound frequency bands is a guardband, which carries no signals and serves merely as a separator. The headend contains a device for converting inbound frequencies to outbound frequencies.

The frequency-conversion device at the headend can be either an analog or a digital device. An analog device, known as a **frequency translator,** converts a block of frequencies from one range to another. A digital device, known as a **remodulator,** recovers the digital data from the inbound analog signal and then retransmits the data on the outbound frequency. Thus a remodulator provides better signal quality by removing all of the accumulated noise and attenuation and transmitting a cleaned-up signal.

Split systems are categorized by the frequency allocation of the two paths, as shown in Table 3.7. *Subsplit,* commonly used by the cable television industry, was designed for metropolitan area television distribution, with limited subscriber-to-central office communication. It provides the easiest way to upgrade existing one-way cable systems to two-way operation. Subsplit has limited usefulness for local area networking because a bandwidth of only 25 MHz is available for two-way communication. *Midsplit* is more suitable for LANs, since it provides a more equitable distribution of bandwidth. However, midsplit was developed at a time when the practical spectrum of a cable-TV cable was 300 MHz, whereas a spectrum of 400 to 450 MHz is now available. Accordingly, a highsplit specification has been developed to provide greater two-way bandwidth for a split cable system.

The differences between split and dual configurations are minor. The split system is useful when a single-cable plant is already installed in a building. If a large amount of bandwidth is needed or such a need is anticipated, a dual-cable system is indicated. Beyond these considerations, it is a matter of a trade-off between cost and size. The single-cable system has the fixed cost of the headend remodulator or frequency translator. The dual-cable system makes use of more cable, taps, splitters, and amplifiers. Thus dual cable is cheaper for smaller systems, where the fixed cost of the headend is noticeable, and single cable is cheaper for larger systems, where incremental costs dominate.

TABLE 3.7   Common Cable Frequency Splits (MHz)

Format	Inbound Frequency Band	Outbound Frequency Band	Maximum Two-Way Bandwidth
Subsplit	5–30	54–400	25
Midsplit	5–116	168–400	111
Highsplit	5–174	232–400	168
Dual cable	40–400	40–400	360

Broadband Components.   Broadband systems use standard off-the-shelf cable television components, including 75-ohm coaxial cable. All endpoints are terminated with a 75-ohm terminator to absorb signals (see Appendix 3A). Broadband is suitable for tens of kilometers radius from the headend and hundreds or even thousands of devices. The main components of the system are:

- Cable
- Terminators
- Amplifiers
- Directional couplers
- Modems

Cables used in broadband networks are of three types. Trunk cable forms the spine of a large LAN system. **Trunk cables** use a semirigid construction. As the name implies, semirigid cable is not flexible. The outer portion of the cable is made of solid aluminum. The cable can be bent but not too many times and not very easily. Trunk lines come in six sizes, ranging from 0.412 to 1 inch in diameter. The greater the diameter of the cable, the lower the attenuation. Semirigid cable has excellent noise rejection characteristics and can be used indoors and outdoors. Typically, a trunk cable will extend from a few kilometers to tens of kilometers.

Distribution cables, or **feeder cables,** are used for shorter distances and for branch cables. They may be semirigid or flexible and are typically 0.4 to 0.5 inch in diameter. Whereas trunk cables may be used indoors or outdoors, feeder cables are generally limited to indoor use. The choice of cable depends on a number of criteria:

- The physical constraints of the route: Smaller-diameter cables are easier to install.
- The required signal level for the distribution network: Larger-diameter cables have less signal loss.
- Local and national building codes.

The flexible cable most commonly used for feeder cable has the designation RG-11. With a diameter of 0.405 inch and with poorer noise resistance than semirigid cable, distance is limited to about 800 meters.

Drop cables are used to connect outlets and stations to distribution cables. These are short (10 to 50 feet) and therefore need not be very large in diameter; although attenuation per unit length is greater for narrower cable, the short distance means that the total attenuation will be small even with a narrow cable. The cables used are flexible and include RG-59 (0.242 inch in diameter), RG-6 (0.332 inch), and RG-11 (0.405 inch) cables.

Amplifiers may be used on trunk and distribution cables to compensate for cable attenuation. As Figure 3.6 indicates, attenuation on a cable is an increasing function of frequency. Therefore, amplifiers must have a slope to account for the variability of attenuation. For split systems, amplifiers must be bidirectional, passing and amplifying lower frequencies in one direction and higher frequencies in the other.

Directional couplers provide a means for dividing one input into two outputs and combining two inputs into one output. **Splitters,** used to branch the cable, provide roughly equal attenuation along the split branches. **Taps,** used to connect drop cable and hence station to the LAN, provide more attenuation to the drop cable. Figure 3.7 illustrates these concepts.

Modems are needed to convert between the digital data of the attached stations and the analog signal on the medium. A variety of modulation techniques are in use. A characteristic common to virtually all broadband LAN modems is the use of scrambling. This gives the data a pseudorandom nature that helps the receiver extract bit-timing information. It also improves the spectral characteristics of the signal, giving it a more uniform power distribution, than that of the potentially strong discrete spectral lines

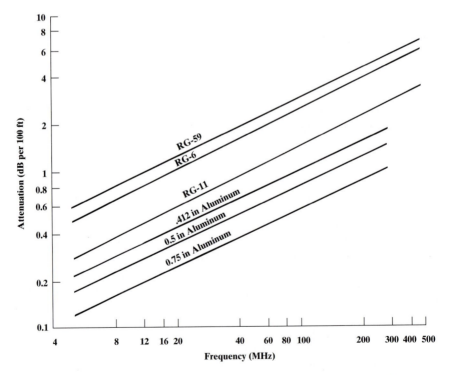

FIGURE 3.6   Cable Attenuation versus Frequency for Various Sizes of Coaxial Cable

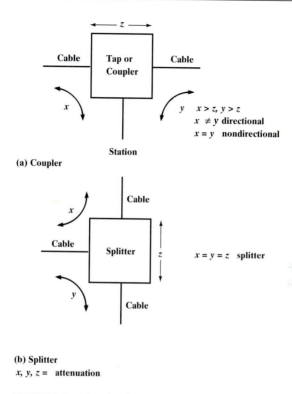

FIGURE 3.7   Directional Couplers and Splitters

in nonscrambled data. This gives the signal better noise resistance. The scrambling process is explained in Appendix 3C.

Carrierband.   There is another application of analog signaling on a LAN, known as carrierband or single-channel broadband. In this case the entire spectrum of the cable is devoted to a single transmission path for the analog signals; frequency-division multiplexing is not possible.

Typically, a carrierband LAN has the following characteristics. Bidirectional transmission, using a bus topology, is employed. Hence there can be no amplifiers and there is no need for a headend. Although the entire spectrum is used, most of the signal energy is concentrated at relatively low frequencies. This is an advantage, because attenuation is less at lower frequencies. Because the cable is dedicated to a single task, it is not necessary to take care that the modem output be confined to a narrow bandwidth. Energy can spread over the entire spectrum. As a result, the electronics are simple and relatively inexpensive. Typically, some form of frequency-shift keying (FSK) is used. Carrierband would appear to provide performance comparable to that of baseband at a comparable price.

Optical Fiber Bus

Several approaches can be taken in the design of a fiber bus topology LAN or MAN. The differences have to do with the nature of the taps into the bus and the detailed topology.

Optical Fiber Taps.   With an optical fiber bus, either an active or a passive tap can be used. In the case of an active tap (Figure 3.8a), the following steps occur:

1. Optical signal energy enters the tap from the bus.
2. Clocking information is recovered from the signal and the signal is converted to an electrical signal.
3. The converted signal is presented to the node and perhaps modified by the latter.
4. The optical output (a light beam) is modulated according to the electrical signal and launched into the bus.

In effect, the bus consists of a chain of point-to-point links, and each node acts as a repeater. Each tap actually consists of two of these active couplers and requires two fibers. This is because of the inherently unidirectional nature of the device of Figure 3.8a.

In the case of a passive tap (Figure 3.8b), the tap extracts a portion of the optical energy from the bus for reception and it injects optical energy directly into the medium for transmission. Thus there is a single run of cable rather than a chain of point-to-point links. This passive approach is equivalent to the type of tap typically used for twisted pair and coaxial cable. Each tap must connect to the bus twice, once for transmit and once for receive.

The electronic complexity and interface cost are drawbacks for implementation of the active tap. Also, each tap will add some increment of delay, just as in the case of a ring. For passive taps, the lossy nature of pure optical taps limits the number of devices and the length of the medium. However, the performance of such taps has improved sufficiently in recent years to make fiber bus networks practical.

Optical Fiber Bus Configurations.   A variety of configurations for the optical fiber bus have been proposed. All of these fall into two categories: those that use a single bus and those that use two buses. Figure 3.9a shows a typical single-bus configuration, referred to as a loop bus. The operation of this bus is essentially the same as that of the dual-bus broadband coaxial system described earlier. Each station transmits on the bus in the direction toward the headend and receives on the bus in the direction away from the headend. In addition to the two connections shown, some MAC protocols require that each station have an additional *sense tap* on the inbound

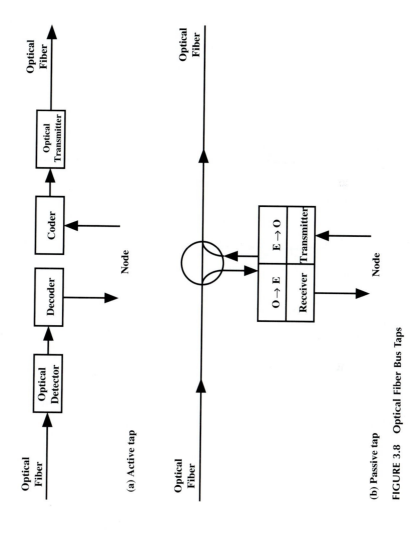

(a) Active tap

(b) Passive tap

FIGURE 3.8   Optical Fiber Bus Taps

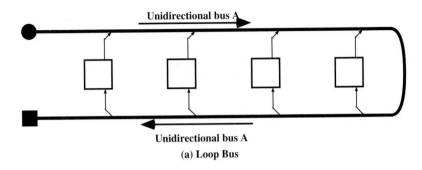

Unidirectional bus A

Unidirectional bus A

(a) Loop Bus

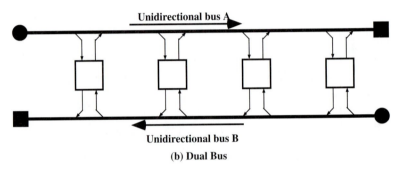

Unidirectional bus A

Unidirectional bus B

(b) Dual Bus

FIGURE 3.9   **Optical Fiber Bus Configurations**

(toward the headend) portion of the bus. The sense tap is able to sense the presence or absence of light on the fiber but is not able to recover data.

Figure 3.9b shows the two-bus configuration. Each station attaches to both buses and has both transmit and receive taps on both buses. On each bus, a station may transmit only to stations downstream from it. By using both buses, a station may transmit to and receive from all other stations. A given node, however, must know which bus to use to transmit to another node; if not, all data would have to be sent out on both buses. This is the configuration used in the IEEE 802.6 MAN and is described in Chapter 12.

3.3

RING TOPOLOGY

Description

The ring consists of a number of repeaters, each connected to two others by unidirectional transmission links to form a single closed path (Figure 3.10). Data are transferred sequentially, bit by bit, around the ring from one repeater to the next. Each repeater regenerates and retransmits each bit.

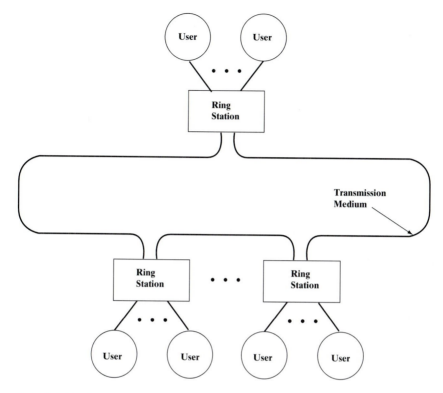

FIGURE 3.10   Ring System

For a ring to operate as a communications network, three functions are required: data insertion, data reception, and data removal. These functions are provided by the repeaters. Each repeater, in addition to serving as an active element on the ring, serves as a device attachment point for data insertion. Data are transmitted in packets, each of which contains a destination address field. As a packet circulates past a repeater, the address field is copied to the attached station. If the station recognizes the address, the remainder of the packet is copied.

A variety of strategies can be used for determining how and when packets are added to and removed from the ring. The strategy can be viewed, at least conceptually, as residing in a medium access control layer, discussed in Chapter 4.

Repeaters perform the data insertion and reception functions in a manner not unlike that of taps, which serve as device attachment points on a bus or tree. Data removal, however, is more difficult on a ring. For a bus or tree, signals inserted onto the line propagate to the end points and are absorbed by terminators. Hence, shortly after transmission ceases, the bus or tree is clear of data. However, because the ring is a closed loop, data will circulate indefinitely unless removed. A packet may be removed by the addressed repeater. Alternatively, each packet could be removed by the transmitting repeater after it has made one trip around the loop. The latter approach is more desirable because (1) it permits automatic acknowledgement, and (2) it permits multicast addressing: one packet sent simultaneously to multiple stations.

The repeater, then, can be seen to have two main purposes: (1) to contribute to the proper functioning of the ring by passing on all the data that come its way, and (2) to provide an access point for attached stations to send and receive data. Corresponding to these two purposes are two states (Figure 3.11): the listen state and the transmit state.

In the *listen state*, each bit that is received is retransmitted with a small delay, required to allow the repeater to perform necessary functions. Ideally, the delay should be on the order of 1 bit time (the time it takes for a repeater to transmit 1 complete bit onto the outgoing line). These functions are:

- Scan passing bit stream for pertinent patterns. Chief among these is the address or addresses of attached devices. Another pattern, used in the token control strategy explained later, indicates permission to

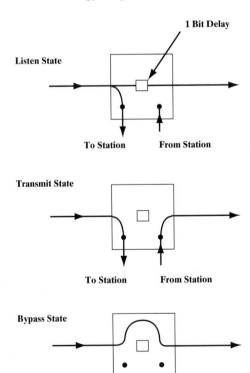

FIGURE 3.11   Ring Repeater States

transmit. Note that to perform the scanning function, the repeater must have some knowledge of packet format.

- Copy each incoming bit and send it to the attached station, while continuing to retransmit each bit. This will be done for each bit of each packet addressed to this station.
- Modify a bit as it passes by. In certain control strategies, bits may be modified to, for example, indicate that the packet has been copied. This would serve as an acknowledgment.

When a repeater's station has data to send and when the repeater, based on the control strategy, has permission to send, the repeater enters the *transmit state*. In this state, the repeater receives bits from the station and retransmits them on its outgoing link. During the period of transmission, bits may appear on the incoming ring link. There are two possibilities, and they are treated differently:

1. The bits could be from the same packet that the repeater is still sending. This will occur if the bit length of the ring is shorter than the packet. In this case, the repeater passes the bits back to the station, which can check them as a form of acknowledgment.
2. For some control strategies, more than one packet could be on the ring at the same time. If the repeater, while transmitting, receives bits from a packet it did not originate, it must buffer them to be transmitted later.

These two states, listen and transmit, are sufficient for proper ring operation. A third state, the *bypass state,* is also useful. In this state, a bypass relay is activated, so that signals propagate past the repeater with no delay other than medium propagation. The bypass relay affords two benefits: (1) it provides a partial solution to the reliability problem, discussed later, and (2) it improves performance by eliminating repeater delay for those stations that are not active on the network.

Ring Benefits

Like the bus and tree, the ring is a shared-access or multiaccess network (although the medium itself is a collection of point-to-point links). Hence the ring shares the same benefits as the bus/tree, including ability to broadcast and incremental cost growth. There are other benefits provided by the ring that are not shared by the bus/tree topology.

The most important benefit or strength of the ring is that it uses point-to-point communication links. There are a number of implications of this fact. First, because the transmitted signal is regenerated at each node, greater distances can be covered than with baseband bus. Broadband bus/tree can cover a similar range, but cascaded amplifiers can result in loss of data integrity at high data rates. Second, the ring can accommodate optical fiber links that provide very high data rates and excellent electromagnetic interference (EMI) characteristics. Finally, the electronics and maintenance of point-to-point lines are simpler than for multipoint lines.

Another benefit of the ring is that fault isolation and recovery are simpler than for bus/tree. This is discussed in more detail later in this section. With the ring, the duplicate address problem is easily solved. If, on a bus or tree, two stations are by accident assigned the same address, there is no easy way to sort this out. A relatively complex algorithm must be incorporated into the LAN protocol. On a ring, the first station with an address match that is encountered by a packet can modify a bit in the packet to acknowledge reception. Subsequent stations with the same address will easily recognize the problem.

Finally, there is the potential throughput of the ring. Under certain conditions, the ring has greater throughput than a comparable bus or tree LAN. This topic is explored in Chapter 13.

Potential Ring Problems

The potential problems of a ring are, at first blush, more obvious than the benefits:

1. *Cable vulnerability.* A break on any of the links between repeaters disables the entire network until the problem can be isolated and a new cable installed. The ring may range widely throughout a building and is vulnerable at every point to accidents.

2. *Repeater failure.* As with the links, a failure of a single repeater disables the entire network. In many networks, it will be common for many of the stations not to be in operation at any time; yet all repeaters must always operate properly.

3. *Perambulation.* When either a repeater or a link fails, locating the failure requires perambulation of the ring, and thus access to all rooms containing repeaters and cable. This is known as the "pocket full of keys" problem.

4. *Installation headaches.* Installation of a new repeater to support new devices requires the identification of two nearby, topologically adjacent repeaters. It must be verified that they are in fact adjacent (documentation could be faulty or out of date), and cable must be run from the new repeater to both of the old repeaters. There are several unfortunate consequences. The length of cable driven by the source repeater may change, possibly requiring retuning. Old cable, if not removed, accumulates. In addition, the geometry of the ring may become highly irregular, exacerbating the perambulation problem.

5. *Size limitations.* There is a practical limit to the number of repeaters on a ring. This limit is suggested by the reliability and maintenance problems cited earlier, the timing jitter discussed below, and the accumulating delay of large numbers of repeaters. A limit of a few hundred repeaters seems reasonable.

6. *Initialization and recovery.* To avoid designating one ring node as a controller (negating the benefit of distributed control), a strategy is required to assure that all stations can cooperate smoothly when initialization and recovery are required. This need arises, for example, when a packet is garbled by a transient line error; in that case, no repeater may wish to assume the responsibility of removing the circulating packet.

7. *Timing jitter.* This is a subtle problem having to do with the clocking or timing of a signal in a distributed network. It is discussed below.

Problems 1 and 2 are reliability problems. However, these two problems, together with problems 3 to 5 can be ameliorated by a refinement in the ring architecture, explained in the next section. Problem 6 is a software problem, to be dealt with by the MAC protocols discussed in Chapter 6. Problem 7 is discussed next.

Timing Jitter.   On a twisted-pair or coaxial-cable ring LAN, digital signaling is generally used with biphase encoding, typically Differential Manchester. As data circulate around the ring, each receiver must recover the binary data from the received signal. To do this, the receiver must know the starting and ending times of each bit, so that it can sample the received signal properly. This requires that all the repeaters on the ring be synchronized, or clocked, together. Recall from Chapter 2 that biphase codes are self-clocking; the signal includes a transition in the middle of each bit time. Thus each repeater recovers clocking as well as data from the received signal. This clock recovery will deviate in a random fashion from the mid-bit transitions of the received signal for several reasons, including noise during transmission and imperfections in the receiver circuitry. The predominant reason, however, is delay distortion. Delay distortion is caused by the fact that the velocity of propagation of a signal through a guided medium varies with frequency. The effect is that some of the signal components of one pulse will spill over into other pulse positions; this is known as *intersymbol interference*. The deviation of clock recovery is known as *timing jitter*.

As each repeater receives data, it recovers the clocking for two purposes: first to know when to sample the incoming signal to recover the data, and second, to use the clocking for transmitting the Differential Manchester signal to the next repeater. The repeater issues a clean signal with no distortion. However, since the clocking is recovered from the incoming signal, the timing error is not eliminated. Thus the digital pulse width will expand and contract in a random fashion as the signal travels around the ring and the timing jitter accumulates. The cumulative effect of the jitter is to cause the bit latency, or bit length, of the ring to vary. However, unless the latency of the ring remains constant, bits will be dropped (not retransmitted) as the latency of the ring decreases or added as the latency increases.

Thus timing jitter places a limitation on the number of repeaters in a ring. Although this limitation cannot be entirely overcome, several measures can be taken to improve matters; these are illustrated in Figure 3.12. First, each repeater can include a phase-locked loop (PLL). This is a device that uses feedback to minimize the deviation from one bit time to the next. Although the use of phase-locked loops reduces the jitter, there is still an accumulation around the ring. A supplementary measure is to include a buffer in one of the repeaters, usually designated as the monitor repeater or station. Bits are written in using the recovered clock and are read out using a crystal master clock. The buffer is initialized to hold a certain number of bits and expands and contracts as needed. For example, the IEEE standard specifies a 6-bit buffer, which is initialized to hold 3 bits. That is, as bits come in, they are placed in the buffer for 3 bit times before being retransmitted. If the received signal at the monitor station is slightly faster than the master clock, the buffer will expand, as required, to 4, 5, or 6 bits to avoid dropping bits. If the received signal is slow, the buffer will contract to 2, 1, or 0 bits to avoid adding bits to the repeated bit stream. Thus the cleaned-up signals that are retransmitted are purged of the timing jitter. This combination of PLLs and a buffer significantly increases maximum feasible ring size. The actual limit will depend on the characteristics of the transmission medium, which determine the amount of delay distortion and therefore the amount of accumulated jitter. For example, the IBM ring product specifies a

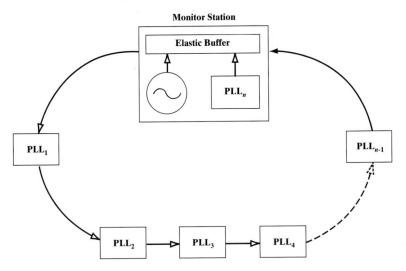

FIGURE 3.12   Ring Synchronization

maximum of 72 repeaters in a ring using unshielded twisted pair, and a maximum of 260 repeaters in a ring using shielded twisted pair.

Star-Ring Architecture

Two observations can be made about the basic ring architecture described above. First, there is a practical limit to the number of repeaters on a ring. As was mentioned above, a number of factors combine to limit the practical size of a ring LAN to a few hundred repeaters. Second, the cited benefits of the ring do not depend on the actual routing of the cables that link the repeaters.

These observations have led to the development of a refined ring architecture, the star ring, which overcomes some of the problems of the ring and allows the construction of large local networks. This architecture uses the star wiring strategy discussed in Section 3.5.

As a first step, consider the rearrangement of a ring into a star. This is achieved by having the interrepeater link all threads through a single site (Figure 3.13). This ring wiring concentrator has a number of advantages. Because there is access to the signal on every link, it is a simple matter to

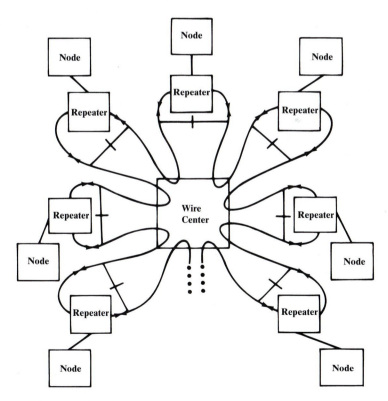

FIGURE 3.13   Ring Wiring Concentrator

isolate a fault. A message can be launched into the ring and tracked to see how far it gets without mishap. A faulty segment can be disconnected—no pocket full of keys needed—and repaired at a later time. New repeaters can easily be added to the ring: simply run two cables from the new repeater to the site of ring wiring concentration and splice into the ring.

The bypass relay associated with each repeater can be moved into the ring wiring concentrator. The relay can automatically bypass its repeater and two links for any malfunction. A nice effect of this feature is that the transmission path from one working repeater to the next is approximately constant; thus the range of signal levels to which the transmission system must automatically adapt is much smaller.

The ring wiring concentrator greatly alleviates the perambulation and installation problems mentioned earlier. It also permits rapid recovery from a cable or repeater failure. Nevertheless, a single failure could, at least temporarily, disable the entire network. Furthermore, throughput and jitter considerations still place a practical upper limit on the number of repeaters in a ring. Finally, in a spread-out network, a single wire concentration site dictates a lot of cable.

To attack these remaining problems, consider a local network consisting of multiple rings. Each ring consists of a connected sequence of wiring concentrators, and the set of rings is connected by a bridge (Figure 3.14). The bridge routes data packets from one ring subnetwork to another, based on addressing information in the packet so routed. From a physical point of view, each ring operates independently of the other rings attached to the bridge. From a logical point of view, the bridge provides transparent routing among the rings.

The bridge must perform five functions:

1. *Input filtering.* For each ring, the bridge monitors the traffic on the ring and copies all packets addressed to other rings on the bridge. This function can be performed by a bridge programmed to recognize a family of addresses rather than a single address.

2. *Input buffering.* Received packets may need to be buffered, either because the inter-ring traffic is peaking, or because the target output buffer is temporarily full.

3. *Switching.* Each packet must be routed through the bridge to its appropriate destination ring.

4. *Output buffering.* A packet may need to be buffered at the threshold of the destination ring, waiting for an opportunity to be inserted.

5. *Output transmission.* This function can be performed by an ordinary repeater.

For a small number of rings, a bridge can be a reasonably simple device. As the number of rings on a bridge grows, the switching complexity and load on the bridge also grow. For very large installations, multiple

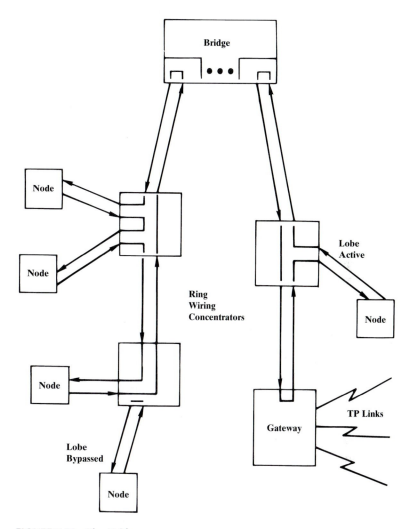

FIGURE 3.14   Ring Bridge

bridges, interconnected by high-speed trunks, may be needed (Figure 3.15).

Three principal advantages accrue from the use of a bridge. First, the timing jitter problem, which becomes more difficult as the number of repeaters on a ring grows, is bounded by restricting the size of the ring. Second, the failure of a ring, for whatever reason, will disable only a portion of the network; failure of the bridge does not prevent intra-ring traffic. Finally, multiple rings may be employed to obtain a satisfactory level of performance when the throughput capability of a single ring is exceeded.

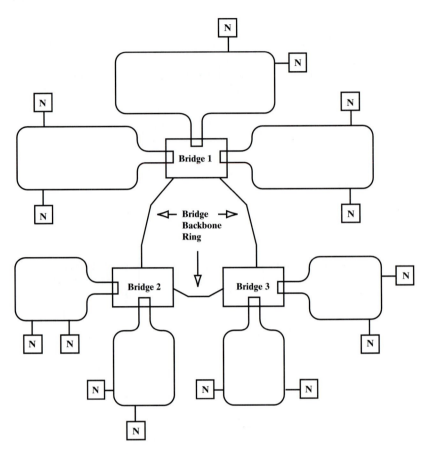

FIGURE 3.15   Multiple Bridges

There are several pitfalls to be noted. First, the automatic acknowledgment feature of the ring is lost; higher-level protocols must provide acknowledgment. Second, performance may not significantly improve if there is a high percentage of inter-ring traffic. If it is possible to do so, network devices should be judiciously allocated to rings to minimize inter-ring traffic.

3.4

STAR TOPOLOGY

Twisted-Pair Star LANs

In recent years there has been increasing interest in the use of twisted pair as a transmission medium for LANs. From the earliest days of commercial LAN availability, twisted-pair bus LANs have been popular. However, such

LANs suffer in comparison with a coaxial cable LAN. First, when a linear bus layout is used, the apparent cost advantage of twisted pair is not as great as it might seem. True, twisted-pair cable is less expensive than coaxial cable. On the other hand, much of the cost of LAN wiring is the labor cost of installing the cable, which is no greater for coaxial cable than for twisted pair. Second, coaxial cable provides superior signal quality and therefore can support more devices over longer distances at higher data rates than can twisted pair.

The renewed interest in twisted pair, at least in the context of bus/tree LANs, is in the use of unshielded twisted pair in a star wiring arrangement. The reason for the interest is that unshielded twisted pair is simply telephone wire, and virtually all office buildings are equipped with spare twisted pairs running from wiring closets to each office. This yields several benefits when deploying a LAN:

1. There is essentially no installation cost with unshielded twisted pair, since the wire is already there. Coaxial cable has to be pulled. In older buildings, this may be difficult since existing conduits may be crowded.

2. In most office building, it is impossible to anticipate all the locations where network access will be needed. Since it is extravagantly expensive to run coaxial cable to every office, a coaxial cable–based LAN will typically only cover a portion of a building. If equipment subsequently has to be moved to an office not covered by the LAN, significant expense is involved in extending the LAN coverage. With telephone wire, this problem does not arise since all offices are covered.

The most popular approach to the use of unshielded twisted pair for a LAN is therefore a star-wiring approach. The products on the market use a scheme suggested by Figure 3.16, in which the central element of the star is an active element, referred to as the **hub.** Each station is connected to the hub by two twisted pairs (transmit and receive). The hub acts as a repeater: When a single station transmits, the hub repeats the signal, on the outgoing line to each station.

Note that although this scheme is physically a star, it is logically a bus: A transmission from any one station is received by all other stations, and if two stations transmit at the same time there will be a collision.

Multiple levels of hubs can be cascaded in a hierarchical configuration. Figure 3.17 illustrates a two-level configuration. There is one **header hub** (HHUB) and one or more **intermediate hubs** (IHUBs). Each hub may have a mixture of stations and other hubs attached to it from below. This layout fits well with building wiring practices. Typically, there is a wiring closet on each floor of an office building, and a hub can be placed in each. Each hub could service the stations on its floor.

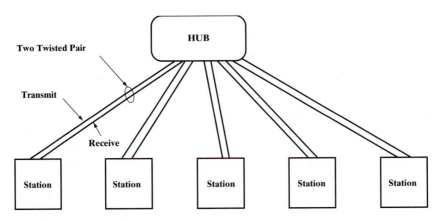

FIGURE 3.16   Twisted-Pair, Star-Wiring, Logical-Bus Arrangement

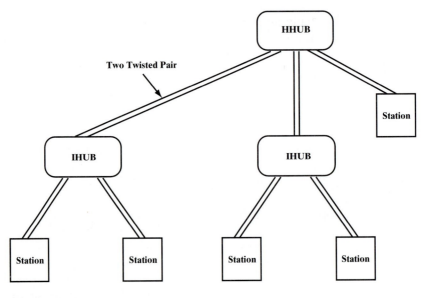

HHUB = Header Hub
IHUB = Intermediate Hub

FIGURE 3.17   Two-Level Hierarchy

Figure 3.18 shows an abstract representation of intermediate and header hubs. The header hub performs all the functions described previously for a single-hub configuration. In the case of an intermediate hub, any incoming signal from below is repeated upward to the next-higher level. Any signal from above is repeated on all lower-level outgoing lines. Thus the logical bus characteristic is retained: A transmission from any station is received by all other stations, and if two stations transmit at the same time, there will be a collision.

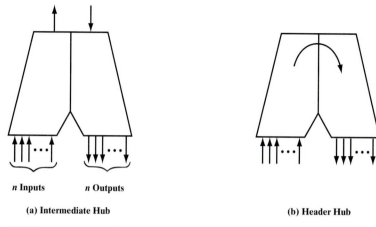

(a) Intermediate Hub   **(b) Header Hub**

FIGURE 3.18   Intermediate and Header Hubs

The initial version of the scheme described above employed a data rate of 1 Mbps and was dubbed StarLAN. These were quickly followed by products operating at 10 Mbps. These are intended to be compatible with 10-Mbps baseband coaxial cable bus systems such as Ethernet, requiring only a change of transceiver. Some details of such schemes are covered in Chapter 6. More recently there has been great interest in twisted-pair star LANs that operate at 100 Mbps; these are discussed in Chapter 7. For both the 10- and 100-Mbps cases, serious technical problems must be confronted, including the following:

- Existing telephone wire in buildings can be inadequate for data transmission. Problems include twisted pair that is not twisted, splicing and other connections, and other faults that are not noticeable for voice transmission but that would produce very high error rates at 10 and 100 Mbps.
- Twisted-pair cables are rather tightly packed together in conduits. The mutual capacitance from adjacent pairs adversely affects attenuation, crosstalk, and velocity of propagation. The effects on data transmission may not be noticeable at 1 Mbps but become a problem at 10 and 100 Mbps.

These problems can to some extent be overcome by the use of signal processing techniques and by careful design of the transceiver. The problems are also alleviated by going to category 5 twisted pair, which was described in Chapter 2. However, just as we saw with the 10-Mbps coaxial cable bus, there are trade-offs to be made. In this case, typical distances between hubs and stations are limited to a few hundred meters.

Optical Fiber Star

One of the first commercially available approaches for fiber LANs was the *passive-star coupler,* which is fabricated by fusing together a number of optical fibers. Any light input to one of the fibers on one side of the coupler will be divided equally among, and output through, all the fibers on the other side. To form a network, each device is connected to the coupler with two fibers, one for transmit and one for receive (Figure 3.19). All of the transmit fibers enter the coupler on one side, and all of the receive fibers exit on the other side. Thus although the arrangement is physically a star, it acts like a bus: A transmission from any device is received by all other devices, and if two devices transmit simultaneously, there will be a collision.

Two methods of fabrication of the star coupler have been pursued: the biconic fused coupler and the mixing rod coupler. In the *biconic fused* coupler, the fibers are bundled together. The bundled fibers are heated with an oxyhydrogen flame and pulled into a biconical tapered shape. That is, the rods come together into a fused mass that tapers into a conical shape and then expands back out again. The *mixing rod* approach begins in the same fashion. Then the biconical taper is cut at the waist and a cylindrical rod is inserted between the tapers and fused to the two cut ends. The latter technique allows the use of a less narrow waist and is easier to fabricate.

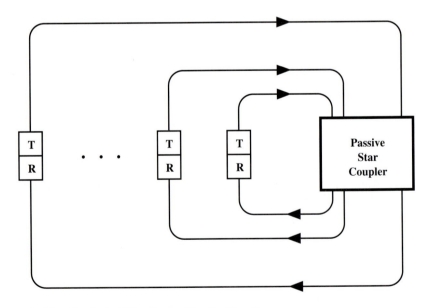

FIGURE 3.19 Optical Fiber Passive Star Configuration

Commercially available passive star couplers can support a few tens of stations at a radial distance of up to 1 km or more. Figure 3.20 shows the operating range of the two types of couplers. The limitations on number of stations and distances are imposed by the losses in the network. With today's equipment, the optical power loss between transmitter and receiver that can be tolerated is on the order of 25 to 30 dB. In the figure, the outer edge of each region is defined by a maximum end-to-end attenuation of 30 dB. The attenuation that will occur in the network consists of the following components:

- *Optical connector losses.* Connectors are used to splice together cable segments for increased length. Typical connector losses are 1.0 to 1.5 dB per connector. A typical passive star network will have from zero to four connectors in a path from transmitter to receiver, for a total maximum attenuation of 4 to 6 dB.
- *Optical cable attenuation.* Typical cable attenuation for the cable that has been used in these systems ranges from 3 to 6 dB per kilometer.
- *Optical power division in the coupler.* The coupler divides the optical power from one transmission path equally among all reception paths. Expressed in decibels, the loss seen by any node is 10 log N, where N is the number of nodes. For example, the effective loss in a 16-port coupler is about 12 dB.

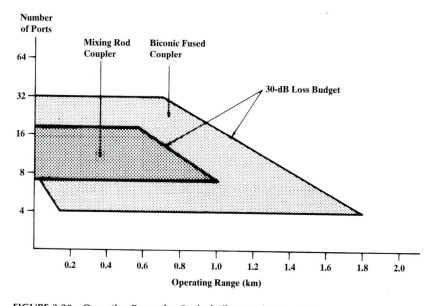

FIGURE 3.20   Operating Range for Optical Fiber Passive-Star LAN

3.5

STRUCTURED CABLING SYSTEMS

In Part III we discuss a wide variety of medium- and high-speed LANs, which can be supported by a variety of transmission media and topologies. As a practical matter, the network manager needs a cabling plan that deals with the selection of cable and the layout of the cable in a building. The cabling plan should be easy to implement and accommodate future growth.

To aid in the development of cabling plans, standards have been issued that specify the cabling types and layout for commercial buildings. These standards are referred to as structured cabling systems. A structured cabling system is a generic wiring scheme with the following characteristics:

1. The scheme refers to the wiring within a commercial building.
2. The scope of the system includes cabling to support of all types of information transfer, including voice, LANs, video and image transmission, and other forms of data transmission.
3. The cabling layout and cable selection is independent of vendor and end-user equipment.
4. The cable layout is designed to encompass distribution to all work areas within the building, so that relocation of equipment does not require rewiring but simply requires plugging the equipment into a preexisting outlet in the new location.

One advantage of such standards is that it provides guidance for pre-installation of cable in new buildings so that future voice and data networking needs can be met without the need to rewire the building. The standards also simplify cable layout design for network managers.

Two standards for structured cabling systems have been issued: EIA/TIA-568,[2] issued jointly by the Electronic Industries Association and the Telecommunications Industry Association, and ISO 11801 issued by the International Organization for Standardization. The two standards are quite similar; the details in this section are from the EIA/TIA-568 document.

A structured cabling strategy is based on the use of a hierarchical, star-wired cable layout. Figure 3.21 illustrates the key elements for a typical commercial building. External cables, from the local telephone company and from wide-area networks, terminate in an equipment room that is generally on the ground floor or a basement level. Patch panel and cross-connect equipment in the equipment room connect the external cables to internal distribution cable. Typically, the first level of distribution consists of backbone cables. In the simplest implementation, a single backbone cable or set of cables runs from the equipment room to telecommunications closets (called wiring closets) on each floor. A telecommunications closet differs

---

[2]*Commercial Building Telecommunications Cabling Standard*, EIA/TIA-568A, 1995.

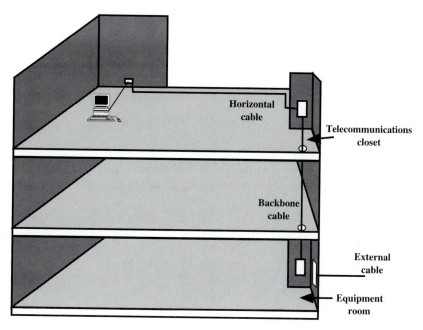

FIGURE 3.21   Elements of a Structured Cabling Layout

from the equipment room only in that it is less complex; the telecommunications closet generally contains cross-connect equipment for interconnecting cable on a single floor to the backbone.

The cable distributed on a single floor is referred to as *horizontal cabling.* This cabling connects the backbone to wall outlets that service individual telephone and data equipment. Figure 3.22 shows a more general depiction of the structured cabling hierarchy, using the terminology of EIA-568; the terms are defined in Table 3.8. Note that the backbone cabling system may itself be hierarchical. This will occur in large commercial buildings where there is a need to have multiple telecommunications closets on a single floor to achieve complete coverage.

The use of a structured cabling plan enables an enterprise to use the transmission media appropriate for its requirements in a systematic and standardized fashion. Figure 3.23 indicates the media recommended for each portion of the structured cabling hierarchy. For horizontal cabling, a maximum distance of 90 meters is recommended independent of media type. This distance is adequate to provide coverage for an entire floor for many commercial buildings. For buildings with a very large floor space, backbone cable may be required to interconnect multiple telecommunications closets on a single floor. For backbone cabling, distances range from 90 to 3000 meters, depending on cable type and position in the hierarchy.

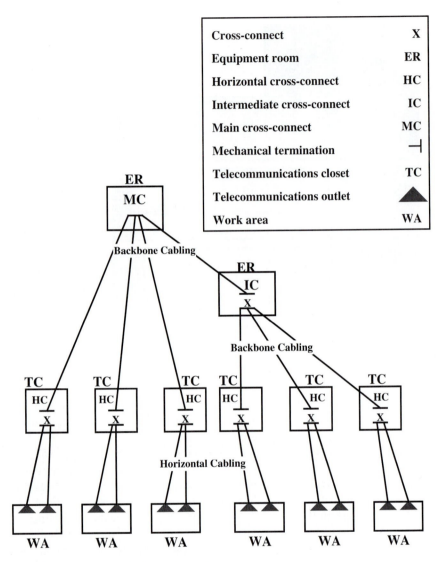

FIGURE 3.22   Structured Cabling Hierarchy

3.6

RECOMMENDED READING

For other treatments of the material in this chapter, see [MART94] and [MADR94]. A thorough explanation of structured cabling systems is provided in [MCEL93].

TABLE 3.8 Structured Cabling Terminology

EIA-568 Term	Definition	Equivalent ISO 11801 Term
Backbone	A facility between telecommunications closets, or floor distribution terminals, the entrance facilities, and the equipment rooms within or between buildings	Backbone
Horizontal cabling	The wiring/cabling between the telecommunications outlet and the horizontal cross-connect	Horizontal cabling
Cross-connect	A facility enabling the termination of cable elements and their interconnection, and/or cross-connection, primarily by means of a patch cord or jumper	Cross-connect
Equipment room	A centralized space for telecommunications equipment that serves the occupants of the building	Campus distributor, building distributor
Telecommunications closet	An enclosed space for housing telecommunications equipment, cable terminations, and cross-connect cabling; the location for cross-connection between the backbone and horizontal facilities	Telecommunications closet, floor distributor
Work area	A building space where the occupants interact with telecommunications terminal equipment	Work area
Main cross-connect	A cross-connect for first-level backbone cables, entrance cables, and equipment cables	
Intermediate cross-connect	A cross-connect between first- and second-level backbone cabling	
Horizontal cross-connect	A cross-connect of horizontal cabling to other cabling (e.g., horizontal, backbone, or equipment)	
Telecommunications outlet	A connecting device in the work area on which horizontal cable terminates	Telecommunications outlet

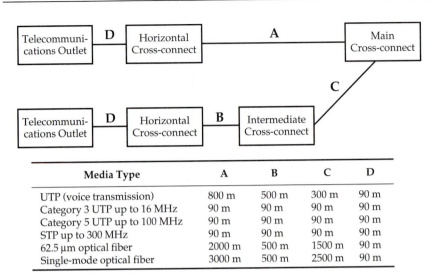

FIGURE 3.23   Cable Distances Specified in EIA-568-A

MADR94   Madron, T. *Local Area Networks: New Technologies, Emerging Standards.* New York: Wiley, 1994.

MART94   Martin, J., Chapman, K., and Leben, J. *Local Area Networks: Architectures and Implementations.* Englewood Cliffs, NJ: Prentice Hall, 1994.

MCEL93   McElroy, M. *The Corporate Cabling Guide.* Boston: Artech House, 1993.

3.7

PROBLEMS

3.1   An asynchronous device such as a teletype transmits characters one at a time with unpredictable delays between characters. What problems, if any, do you foresee if such a device is connected to a local network and allowed to transmit at will (subject to gaining access to the medium)? How might such problems be resolved? Answer for ring, bus, and star.

3.2   Which combination or combinations of medium and topology would be appropriate for the following applications, and why?

a. Terminal intensive: many terminals throughout an office: one or a few shared central computers

b. Small network: fewer than 50 devices, all low speed (<56 kbps)

c. Office automation: a few hundred devices, mostly terminals and minicomputers

3.3   Consider the transfer of a file containing one million characters from one section to another. What is the total elapsed time and effective throughput for the following cases?

    a. A circuit-switched, star topology local network. Call setup time is negligible, and the data rate on the medium is 64 kbps.

    b. A bus topology local network with two stations a distance D apart, a data rate of B bps, and a packet size P with 80 bits of overhead. Each packet is acknowledged with an 88-bit packet before the text is sent. The propagation speed on the bus is 200 m/γs. Solve for:

        (1) $D = 1$ km, $B = 1$ Mbps, $P = 256$ bits

        (2) $D = 1$ km, $B = 10$ Mbps, $P = 256$ bits

        (3) $D = 10$ km, $B = 1$ Mbps, $P = 256$ bits

        (4) $D = 1$ km, $B = 50$ Mbps, $P = 10{,}000$ bits

    c. A ring topology with a total circular length of $2D$, with the two stations a distance D apart. Acknowledgment is achieved by allowing a packet to circulate past the destination station, back to the source station. There are N repeaters on the ring, each of which introduces a delay of 1 bit time. Repeat the calculation for each of b1 through b4 for $N = 10$; 100; 1000.

3.4 A 10-story office building has the floor plan of Figure 3.24 for each floor. A local network is to be installed that will allow attachment of a device from each office on each floor. Attachment is to take place along the outside wall at the baseboard. Cable or wire can be run vertically through the indicated closet and horizontally along the baseboards. The height of each story is 10 feet. What is the minimum total length of cable or wire required for bus, tree, ring, and star topologies?

3.5 A tree-topology local network is to be provided that spans two buildings. If permission can be obtained to string cable between the two buildings, then one continuous tree layout will be used. Otherwise, each building will have an independent tree topology network and a point-to-point link will connect a special communications station on one network with a communications station on the other network. What functions must the communications stations perform? Repeat for ring and star.

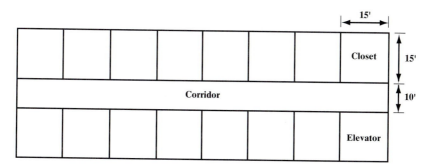

FIGURE 3.24   Building Layout for a Local Network

3.6 Consider a baseband bus with a number of equally spaced stations. As a fraction of the end-to-end propagation delay, what is the mean delay between stations? What is it for broadband bus? Now, rearrange the broadband bus into a tree with N equal-length branches emanating from the headend; what is the mean delay?

3.7 Consider a baseband bus with a number of equally spaced stations with a data rate of 10 Mbps and a bus length of 1 km. What is the average time to send a packet of 1000 bits to another station, measured from the beginning of transmission to the end of reception? Assume a propagation speed of 200 m/μs. If two stations begin to transmit at exactly the same time, their packets will interfere with each other. If each transmitting station monitors the bus during transmission, how long before it notices an interference, in seconds? In bit times?

3.8 Repeat Problem 3.7 for a data rate of 1 Mbps.

3.9 Repeat Problems 3.7 and 3.8 for broadband bus.

3.10 Repeat Problems 3.7 and 3.8 for a broadband tree consisting of 10 cables of length 100 m emanating from a headend.

3.11 Reconsider Problem 3.4. Can a baseband bus following the IEEE 802 rules (500-meter segments, maximum of four repeaters in a path) span the building? If so, what is the total cable length?

3.12 Reconsider Problem 3.4 for a broadband tree. Can the total length be reduced compared to the broadband bus?

3.13 Reconsider Problem 3.4, but now assume that there are two rings, with a bridge on floor 5 and a ring wiring concentrator on each floor. The bridge and concentrators are located in closets along the vertical shaft.

3.14 At a propagation speed of 200 m/μs, what is the effective length added to a ring by a bit delay at each repeater:
   a. At 1 Mbps?
   b. At 40 Mbps?

3.15 System A consists of a single ring with 300 stations, one per repeater. System B consists of three 100-station rings linked by a bridge. If the probability of a link failure is P_l, a repeater failure is p_r, and a bridge failure is P_b, derive an expression for parts (a) to (d):
   a. Probability of failure of system A.
   b. Probability of complete failure of system B.
   c. Probability that a particular station will find the network unavailable, for systems A and B.
   d. Probability that any two stations, selected at random, will be unable to communicate, for systems A and B.
   e. Compare values of parts (a) to (d) for $P_l = P_b = P_r = 10^{-2}$.

3.16 Consider two rings of 100 stations each joined by a bridge. The data rate on each link is 10 Mbps. Each station generates data at a rate of 10 packets of 2000 bits each per second. Let F be the fraction of packets on each ring destined for the other. What is the minimum throughput of the bridge required to keep up?

Appendix 3A

CHARACTERISTIC IMPEDANCE

An important parameter associated with any transmission line is its characteristic impedance. To understand its significance, we need to consider the electrical properties of a transmission line. Any transmission line has both inductance and capacitance, which are distributed along the entire length of the line. These quantities can be expressed in terms of inductance and capacitance per unit length.

An infinite transmission line has similar electrical properties to the circuit depicted in Figure 3.25. Of course, the actual inductance and capacitance is distributed uniformly along the line and not lumped as shown in the figure, but the equivalent circuit is good enough to explain the behavior of an actual line. Figure 3.25a shows a section of an infinite line connected to a voltage source. Closing the switch (Figure 3.25b) will cause current to flow. Now, in a finite line, at steady state, the inductors will behave as short circuits (zero resistance) and the capacitors as open circuits (infinite resistance). However, in the instance that the switch is closed, current will flow and be resisted by the inductance and capacitance. The process will continue indefinitely because there are an infinite number of capacitors to be charged. There will be a definite relationship between the applied voltage and the amount of current that will flow. The relationship will depend only on the value of L and C, which in turn depend on the physical dimensions of the line. In our example, an applied voltage of 100 volts causes a current of 2 amperes to flow into the line when the switch is closed. As far as the source is concerned, it has no way of knowing whether it is connected to a transmission line that is infinitely long or to a 50-ohm resistor, as shown in Figure 3.25. In both cases, a current of 2 amperes would flow. For this reason, we say that this particular line has a characteristic impedance, or surge, of 50 ohms.

The characteristic is given by the equation

$$Z_0 = \sqrt{\frac{L}{C}}$$

where

Z = characteristic of the line, in ohms

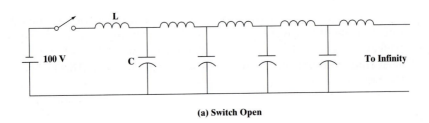

(a) Switch Open

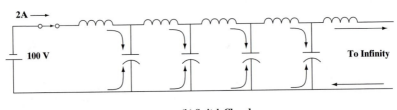

(b) Switch Closed

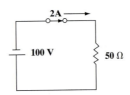

FIGURE 3.25   Characteristic Impedance

L = inductance, in henrys per unit length
C = capacitance, in farads per unit length

Since the inductance and capacitance depend on the construction of the line, the characteristic can also be determined from the physical dimensions of the line. In particular, for coaxial cable,

$$Z_0 = \frac{138}{\sqrt{\epsilon}} \log \frac{D}{d}$$

where

log = logarithm to the base 10
D = diameter of outside conductor
d = diameter of inside conductor
ϵ = dielectric constant of the insulating material between the two conductors; for air, the value is 1

For a dielectric constant of 1 and an impedance of 50 ohms, the ratio D/d is 2.3, and for an impedance of 75 ohms, the ratio is 3.5.

It is important to realize that the characteristic impedance of a transmission line is a function of the construction of the line itself; it does not depend on the signal carried or on what is connected to the line. The significance of characteristic impedance is this: When a line is terminated in its characteristic impedance, any signal on the line is absorbed when it reaches the terminating resistance. There are no reflections. Obviously, such reflections are to be avoided since they would interfere with the signal being transmitted.

Appendix 3B

DECIBELS

An important parameter in any transmission system is the strength of the signal being transmitted. As a signal propagates along a transmission medium, there will be a loss, or attenuation, of signal strength. Additional losses occur at taps and splitters. To compensate, amplifiers may be inserted at various points to impart a gain in signal strength. It is customary to express gains, losses, and relative levels in decibels, because:

- Signal strength often falls off logarithmically, so loss is easily expressed in terms of the decibel, which is a logarithmic unit.
- The net gain or loss in a cascaded transmission path can be calculated with simple addition and subtraction.

The decibel is a measure of the difference in two signal levels:

$$N_{dB} = 10 \log \frac{P_1}{P_2}$$

where

N_{dB} = number of decibels
$P_{1,2}$ = power values

For example, if a signal with a power level of 10 mW is inserted onto a transmission line and the measured power some distance away is 5 mW, the loss can be expressed as

$$\text{loss} = 10 \log(5/10) = 10(-0.3) = -3 \text{ dB}$$

Note that the decibel is a measure of relative, not absolute difference. A loss from 1000 mW to 500 mW is also a −3 dB loss. Thus a loss of 3 dB halves the voltage level; a gain of 3 dB doubles the magnitude.

The decibel is also used to measure the difference in voltage, taking into account that power is proportional to the square of the voltage:

$$P = \frac{V^2}{R}$$

where

P = power dissipated across resistance R
V = voltage across resistance R

Thus

$$N_{dB} = 10 \log \frac{P_1}{P_2} = 10 \log \frac{V_1^2/R}{V_2^2/R} = 20 \log \frac{V_1}{V_2}$$

Decibel values refer to relative magnitudes or changes in magnitude, not to an absolute level. It is convenient to be able to refer to an absolute level of voltage in decibels, so that gains and losses with reference to an initial signal level may easily be calculated. One unit in common use in cable television and broadband LAN applications is the dBmV (decibel-millivolt). This is an absolute unit with 0 dBmV equivalent to 1 mV. Thus

$$\text{voltage(dBmV)} = 20 \log \frac{\text{voltage(mv)}}{1 \text{ mV}}$$

The voltage levels are assumed to be across a 75-ohm resistance.

The decibel is convenient for determining overall gain or loss in a signal path. The amplifier gain and the losses due to the cables, tap, and splitter are expressed in decibels. By using simple addition and subtraction, the signal level at the outlet is easily calculated.

Appendix 3C

SCRAMBLING AND DESCRAMBLING

For some digital data encoding techniques, a long string of binary zeros or ones in a transmission can degrade system performance. For example, in the differential phase-shift keying (DPSK) scheme used in broadband LAN modems, a phase shift occurs only when the input is a zero bit. If there is a long string of ones, it is difficult for the receiver to maintain synchronization with the transmitter. A similar problem arises with the other common broadband LAN modulation scheme, duobinary AM/PSK. Also, other transmission properties are enhanced if the data are more nearly of a random nature rather than constant or repetitive. A technique commonly used with modems to improve signal quality is scrambling and descrambling. The scrambling process tends to make the data appear more random.

The scrambling process consists of a feedback shift register, and the matching descrambler consists of a feedforward shift register. An example

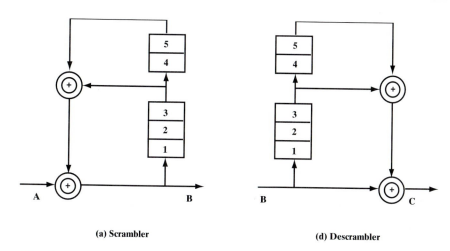

(a) Scrambler   (d) Descrambler

FIGURE 3.26   Scrambler and Descrambler

is shown in Figure 3.26. In this example the scrambled data sequence may be expressed as follows:

$$B_m = A_m \oplus B_{m-3} \oplus B_{m-5}$$

where $\oplus$ indicates the exclusive or operation. The descrambled sequence is

$$\begin{aligned} C_m &= B_m \oplus B_{m-3} \oplus B_{m-5} \\ &= (A_m \oplus B_{m-3} \oplus B_{m-5}) \oplus B_{m-3} \oplus B_{m-5} \\ &= A_m \end{aligned}$$

As can be seen, the descrambled output is the original sequence.

We can represent this process with the use of polynomials. Thus, for this example, the polynomial is $P = 1 + X^{-3} + X^{-5}$. The input is divided by this polynomial to produce the scrambled sequence. At the receiver the received scrambled signal is multiplied by the same polynomial to reproduce the original input. Figure 3.27 is an example using the polynomial P and an input of 101010100000111. The scrambled transmission, produced by dividing by P (100101), is 101110001101001. When this number is multiplied by P, we get the original input. Note that the input sequence contains the periodic sequence 10101010 as well as a long string of zeros. The scrambler effectively removes both patterns.

```
                              1 0 1 1 1 0 0 0 1 1 0 1 0 0 1  ←——— B
                  ─────────────────────────────────────────
P ──→ 1 0 0 1 0 1 1 0 1 0 1 0 1 0 0 0 0 0 1 1 1- - - - -  ←——— A
        1 0 0 1 0 1
        ─────────
          1 1 1 1 1 0
          1 0 0 1 0 1
          ─────────
            1 1 0 1 1 0
            1 0 0 1 0 1
            ─────────
              1 0 0 1 1 0
              1 0 0 1 0 1
              ─────────
                1 1 0 0 1 1
                1 0 0 1 0 1
                ─────────
                  1 0 1 1 0 1
                  1 0 0 1 0 1
                  ─────────
                    1 0 0 0 0 0
                    1 0 0 1 0 1
                    ─────────
                      1 0 1 0 0 0
```

(a) Scrambling

```
    1 0 1 1 1 0 0 0 1 1 0 1 0 0 1  ←——— B
                  1 0 0 1 0 1  ←——— P
    ─────────────────────────────
    1 0 1 1 1 0 0 0 1 1 0 1 0 0 1
    1 0 1 1 1 0 0 0 1 1 0 1 0 0 1
    1 0 1 1 1 0 0 0 1 1 0 1 0 0 1
    ─────────────────────────────
C = A ──→ 1 0 1 0 1 0 1 0 0 0 0 0 1 1 1 - - - - -
```

(b) Descrambling

FIGURE 3.27   Example of Scrambling with $P(X) = 1 + X^{-3} + X^{-5}$

CHAPTER

4

Protocol Architecture

This chapter begins our discussion of LAN[1] architecture with a description of the protocol architecture that is in common use for implementing LANs. This architecture is also the basis of standardization efforts. The chapter then presents the general principles of the medium access control (MAC) protocol layer, which is central to the definition of different types of LANs. This is followed by an introduction to the logical link control (LLC) protocol layer. Next, the concepts of bridge and router, which play a critical role in extending LAN coverage, are introduced. Finally, the chapter provides an overview of the LAN standardization effort. Most of the important standards have been drafted by the IEEE 802 committee, and the structure of this committee and the scope of its work are discussed in this chapter.

---

[1]For the sake of brevity, the book often uses LAN when referring to LAN and MAN concerns. The context should clarify when only LAN or both LAN and MAN is meant.

4.1

PROTOCOL REFERENCE MODEL

Protocols defined specifically to deal with LAN and MAN transmission deal with issues relating to the transmission of blocks of data over the network. In OSI terms, higher-layer protocols (layer 3 or 4 and above) are independent of network architecture and are applicable to LANs, MANs, and WANs. Thus a discussion of a protocol reference model is concerned principally with lower layers of the OSI model.

Figure 4.1 relates the LAN standards to the OSI architecture. This architecture was developed by the IEEE 802 committee and has been adopted by all organizations working on the specification of LAN standards. It is generally referred to as the IEEE 802 reference model.

Working from the bottom up, the lowest layer of the IEEE 802 reference model corresponds to the **physical layer** of the OSI model and includes such functions as:

- Encoding/decoding of signals
- Preamble generation/removal (for synchronization)
- Bit transmission/reception

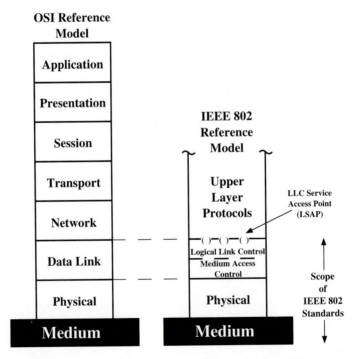

FIGURE 4.1   IEEE 802 Protocol Layers Compared to OSI Model

In addition, the physical layer of the 802 model includes a specification of the transmission medium. Generally, this is considered "below" the lowest layer of the OSI model. However, the choice of transmission medium is critical in LAN design, so a specification of the medium is included.

Above the physical layer are the functions associated providing service to LAN users. These include:

- Provide one or more service access points (SAPs).
- On transmission, assemble the data into a frame with address and error-detection fields.
- On reception, disassemble the frame and perform address recognition and error detection.
- Govern access to the LAN transmission medium.

These are functions typically associated with OSI layer 2. The first function, and related functions, are grouped into a **logical link control** (LLC) layer. The last three functions are treated as a separate layer, called **medium access control** (MAC). This is done for the following reasons:

- The logic required to manage access to a shared-access medium is not found in traditional layer 2 data link control.
- For the same LLC, several MAC options may be provided.

In the next two sections we introduce the fundamental principles of the MAC and LLC layers. This overview is useful in setting the various LAN and MAN options in context. MAC layer protocols specific to particular networks are discussed in detail in the appropriate chapter. LLC is treated in detail in Chapter 5. Finally, as with MAC, physical layer details of each network type are provided in the appropriate chapter.

4.2

LOGICAL LINK CONTROL

In this section we look first at the general link-level requirements for a LAN, then examine the issue of addressing and protocol data unit format.

Principles

The LLC layer for LANs is similar in many respects to other link layers in common use. Like all link layers, LLC is concerned with the transmission of a link-level protocol data unit (PDU) between two stations, without the necessity of an intermediate switching node. LLC has two characteristics not shared by most other link control protocols:

1. It must support the multiaccess, shared-medium nature of the link (this differs from a multidrop line in that there is no primary node).
2. It is relieved of some details of link access by the MAC layer.

Figure 4.2 will help clarify the requirements for the link layer. Consider two stations that communicate via a shared-medium LAN. Higher layers, above LLC, provide end-to-end services between the stations. The LLC layer is also end to end, providing the service of OSI layer 2. Below the LLC layer, the MAC provides the necessary logic for gaining access to the network. Typically, the protocol data units at the MAC level, called MAC frames, are communicated end to end with no alteration. However, conceptually, the MAC layer of a station interacts with the network medium to perform the access control protocol.

As an end-to-end protocol, there are three fundamental services that can be provided by LLC:

- *Connectionless service:* a service that does not require the overhead of establishing a logical connection is needed for support of highly interactive traffic
- *Connection-oriented:* a connection-oriented service is also convenient to support certain types of traffic
- *Multiplexing:* generally, a single physical link attaches a station to a LAN; it should be possible to provide data transfer with multiple logical endpoints over that link

The connectionless service is easily supported by supplying the proper addressing information. Because a transmitted LLC PDU may be sent to one of many stations on the medium, and because a received LLC PDU may come from one of many stations on the medium, both source and destination addresses are required.

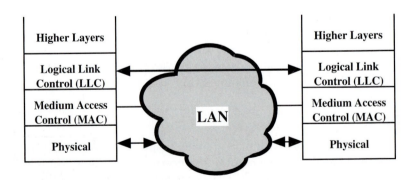

FIGURE 4.2   Scope of LAN Protocols

Both the connection-oriented and multiplexing capabilities can be supported with the concept of the service access point (SAP), introduced in Chapter 2. An example may make this clear. Figure 4.3 shows three stations attached to a LAN. Each station has a unique address. Further, LLC supports multiple SAPs, each with its own LSAP address. LLC provides communication between LSAPs. Assume that a process or application X in station A wishes to send a message to a process in station C. X may be a report generator program in a workstation; C may be a printer or a simple printer driver. X attaches itself to LSAP 1 and request a connection to station C, LSAP 1 (C may have only one LSAP if it is a single printer). The LLC in A sends to the LAN a connection-request PDU that includes the source address (A, 1), the destination address (C, 1), and some control bits indicating that this is a connection request. The LAN delivers this frame to C, which, if it is free, returns a connection-accepted PDU. Henceforth, all data from X will be transmitted in PDUs that include the source (A, 1) and destination (C, 1) addresses. Any data from the printer (e.g., acknowledgments, reports) will be transmitted in PDUs that include (A, 1) and (C, 1) as destination and source addresses.

At the same time, process Y could attach to (A, 2) and exchange data with (B, 1). This is an example of multiplexing. In addition, another process in A could use (A, 3) to send connectionless PDUs to various destinations.

One final function of the link layer should be included in our list, to take advantage of the shared access nature of the LAN:

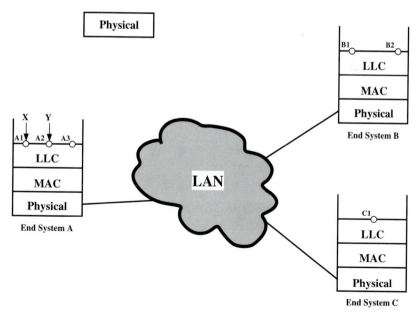

FIGURE 4.3   LLC Scenario

- *Multicast, broadcast.* The link layer should provide the service of sending a message to multiple stations or all stations.

Addressing

The preceding discussion referred to both station and LLC addresses. A further elaboration of this point is warranted. To understand the function of addressing, we need to consider the requirements for exchanging data.

In general terms, communication can be said to involve three agents: processes, stations, and networks. The processes that we are concerned with here are distributed applications that involve the exchange of data between two computer systems. These processes, and others, execute on stations that can often support multiple simultaneous applications. One example is a file transfer operation, which involves a file transfer process in one station exchanging data with a file transfer process in another station. Another example is remote terminal access, in which a terminal emulation process on a workstation connects that workstation to a remote server. Stations are connected by a network, and the data to be exchanged are transferred by the network from one station to another. Thus the transfer of data from one process to another involves first getting the data to the station in which the destination process resides and then getting it to the intended process within the computer.

These concepts suggest the need for two levels of addressing. Consider Figure 4.4, which shows the relationship between LLC PDUs and MAC frames (compare Figure 2.15). LLC user data (e.g., an IP datagram) to be sent are passed down to LLC, which appends a header. This header contains the control information that is used to manage the protocol between

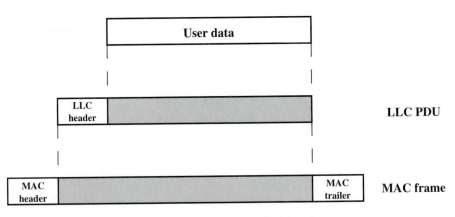

FIGURE 4.4   User Data and LAN/MAN Protocol Control Information

the local LLC entity and the remote LLC entity. The combination of user data and LLC header is referred to as an LLC PDU. After the source LLC has prepared a PDU, the PDU is passed as a block of data down to the MAC entity. The MAC entity appends both a header and trailer, to manage the MAC protocol. The result is a MAC-level PDU. To avoid confusion with an LLC-level PDU, the MAC-level PDU is typically referred to as a frame.

The MAC header must contain a destination address that uniquely identifies a station on the LAN. This is needed because each station on the LAN will read the destination address field to determine if it should capture the MAC frame. When a MAC frame is captured, the destination MAC entity strips off the MAC header and trailer and passes the resulting LLC PDU up to the LLC entity. The LLC header must contain a destination SAP address so the LLC can determine to whom the data are to be delivered. Hence two levels of addressing are needed:

- *MAC address:* identifies a physical interface from the station to the LAN. In most cases there is a one-to-one relationship between stations and physical addresses. In other cases a single station may have multiple attachments to the same medium for reasons of performance or reliability. In other cases, such as a bridge or router (discussed in Section 4.4), a station may have physical interfaces to more than one LAN.

- *LLC address:* identifies an LLC user. The LLC address is associated with a particular user within a station. In some cases the SAP refers to a process executing on the station. In other cases the SAP may refer to a hardware port. For example, a terminal concentration device might provide attachment to a LAN for multiple terminals, each connected to the concentrator through a different physical port.

So far, we have discussed the use of addresses that identify unique entities. In addition to these individual addresses, group addresses are also employed. A group address specifies a set of one or more entities. For example, one might wish to send a message to all terminal users attached to a particular concentrator or to all terminal and workstation users on the entire LAN. Two types of group addresses are used. A broadcast address refers to all entities within some context; each entity in that context would interpret the broadcast address as indicating a PDU addressed to itself. A multistation address refers to some subset of entities within some context; each entity in that subset would interpret the corresponding multicast address as indicating a PDU addressed to itself.

Figure 4.5 illustrates the possible combinations. The first three combinations are straightforward: a specific user can be addressed, or a group of users or all users at a specific station can be addressed. Alternatives (f) and (i) are also easily understood: One may wish to address all users on some stations or all users on all stations.

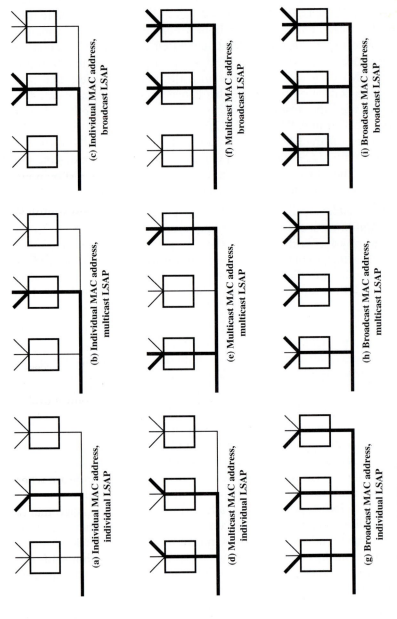

(a) Individual MAC address, individual LSAP

(b) Individual MAC address, multicast LSAP

(c) Individual MAC address, broadcast LSAP

(d) Multicast MAC address, individual LSAP

(e) Multicast MAC address, multicast LSAP

(f) Multicast MAC address, broadcast LSAP

(g) Broadcast MAC address, individual LSAP

(h) Broadcast MAC address, multicast LSAP

(i) Broadcast MAC address, broadcast LSAP

FIGURE 4.5 LAN Addressing

The remaining four alternatives in the figure are perhaps less easily understood. To understand their use, you need to recognize that LSAPs are unique only within a single station. It is only the LLC entity within a station that examines the LLC header and determines the user. However, it is possible to assign LSAPs uniquely across all stations. This is undesirable for the following reasons:

1. The total number of LLC users on all stations would be limited by the LSAP field length in the LLC header.

2. Central management of LSAP assignment would be required, no matter how large and heterogeneous the user population.

On the other hand, it is useful to have certain dedicated LSAP addresses that are the same in all stations. For example, a station management entity in a station may always be given an LSAP value of 1, to facilitate network management. Or a group of management and control entities within a station may always be given the same multicast LSAP address. When such a convention is followed, it becomes possible to address data to one LSAP or a multicast LSAP in a group of stations or all stations.

4.3

MEDIUM ACCESS CONTROL

All LANs and MANs consist of collections of devices that must share the network's transmission capacity. Some means of controlling access to the transmission medium is needed to provide for an orderly and efficient use of that capacity. This is the function of a medium access control (MAC) protocol.

MAC Techniques

The key parameters in any medium access control technique are where and how. *Where* refers to whether control is exercised in a centralized or distributed fashion. In a centralized scheme a controller is designated that has the authority to grant access to the network. A station wishing to transmit must wait until it receives permission from the controller. In a decentralized network the stations collectively perform a medium access control function to determine the order in which stations transmit. A centralized scheme has certain advantages, including:

- It may afford greater control over access for providing such things as priorities, overrides, and guaranteed capacity.
- It enables the use of relatively simple access logic at each station.
- It avoids problems of distributed coordination among peer entities.

The principal disadvantages of centralized schemes are:

- It creates a single point of failure; that is, there is a point in the network that, if it fails, causes the entire network to fail.
- It may act as a bottleneck, reducing performance.

The pros and cons of distributed schemes are mirror images of the points made above.

The second parameter, *how,* is constrained by the topology and is a trade-off among competing factors, including cost, performance, and complexity. In general, we can categorize access control techniques as being either synchronous or asynchronous. With synchronous techniques, a specific capacity is dedicated to a connection. This is the same approach used in circuit switching, frequency-division multiplexing (FDM), and synchronous time-division multiplexing (TDM). Such techniques are generally not optimal in LANs and MANs because the needs of the stations are unpredictable. It is preferable to be able to allocate capacity in an asynchronous (dynamic) fashion, more or less in response to immediate demand. The asynchronous approach can be further subdivided into three categories: round robin, reservation, and contention.

Round Robin.   With round robin, each station in turn is given the opportunity to transmit. During that opportunity, the station may decline to transmit or may transmit subject to a specified upper bound, usually expressed as a maximum amount of data transmitted or time for this opportunity. In any case, the station, when it is finished, relinquishes its turn, and the right to transmit passes to the next station in logical sequence. Control of sequence may be centralized or distributed. Polling is an example of a centralized technique.

When many stations have data to transmit over an extended period of time, round-robin techniques can be very efficient. If only a few stations have data to transmit over an extended period of time, there is a considerable overhead in passing the turn from station to station, since most of the stations will not transmit but simply pass their turns. Under such circumstances other techniques may be preferable, largely depending on whether the data traffic has a stream or bursty characteristic. Stream traffic is characterized by lengthy and fairly continuous transmissions; examples are voice communication, telemetry, and bulk file transfer. Bursty traffic is characterized by short, sporadic transmissions; interactive terminal–host traffic fits this description.

Reservation.   For stream traffic, reservation techniques are well suited. In general, for these techniques, time on the medium is divided into slots, much as with synchronous TDM. A station wishing to transmit reserves future slots for an extended or even an indefinite period. Again, reservations may be made in a centralized or distributed fashion.

Contention.   For bursty traffic, contention techniques are usually appropriate. With these techniques, no control is exercised to determine whose turn it is; all stations contend for time in a way that can be, as we shall see, rather rough and tumble. These techniques are of necessity distributed in nature. Their principal advantage is that they are simple to implement and, under light to moderate load, efficient. For some of these techniques, however, performance tends to collapse under heavy load. Although both centralized and distributed reservation techniques have been implemented in some LAN products, round-robin and contention techniques are the most common.

The discussion above has been somewhat abstract and should become clearer as specific techniques are discussed in Part III. For future reference, Table 4.1 lists the MAC protocols that are defined in LAN and MAN standards.

MAC Frame Format

The MAC layer receives a block of data from the LLC layer and is responsible for performing functions related to medium access and for transmitting the data. As with other protocol layers, MAC implements these functions making use of a protocol data unit at its layer. In this case the PDU is referred to as a MAC frame.

The exact format of the MAC frame differs somewhat for the various MAC protocols in use. In general, all of the MAC frames have a format similar to that of Figure 4.6. The fields of this frame are:

- *MAC control:* contains any protocol control information needed for the functioning of the MAC protocol. For example, a priority level could be indicated here.
- *Destination MAC address:* the destination physical attachment point on the LAN for this frame.
- *Source MAC address:* the source physical attachment point on the LAN for this frame.
- *LLC:* the LLC data from the next-higher layer.
- *CRC:* the cyclic redundancy check field [also known as the frame check sequence (FCS) field]. The CRC field is a function of the contents of the control, address, and LLC fields. It is generated by the sender and again by the receiver. If the receiver's result differs from the received value of the CRC field, a transmission error has occurred (see Appendix 4A).

In most data link control protocols, the data link protocol entity is responsible not only for detecting errors using the CRC, but for recovering from those errors by retransmitting damaged frames. In the LAN protocol

TABLE 4.1   Standardized Medium Access Control Techniques

	Bus Topology	Ring Topology	Switched Topology
Round robin	Token bus (IEEE 802.4) Polling (IEEE 802.11)	Token Ring (IEEE 802.5; FDDI)	Request/priority (IEEE 802.12)
Reservation	DQDB (IEEE 802.6)		
Contention	CSMA/CD (IEEE 802.3) CSMA (IEEE 802.11)		CSMA/CD (IEEE 802.3)

MAC Control	Destination MAC Address	Source MAC Address	LLC	CRC

FIGURE 4.6   Generic MAC Frame Format

architecture, these two functions are split between the MAC and LLC layers. The MAC layer is responsible for detecting errors and discarding any frames that are in error. Optionally, the LLC layer keeps track of which frames have been received successfully and retransmits unsuccessful frames. Figure 4.7 puts the LLC PDU and MAC frame in the context of a TCP/IP transmission. Each layer adds fields that are needed for the operation of the protocol at that layer.

4.4

BRIDGES AND ROUTERS

In virtually all cases, there is a need to expand beyond the confines of a single LAN, to provide interconnection to other LANs and to wide-area networks. Two general approaches are used for this purpose: bridges and routers. In this section we provide a brief overview of these two topics; a general understanding of bridges and routers is needed to discuss some of the issues in Part III. Bridges and routers are covered in more detail in Chapters 14 and 15, respectively.

Bridges

The bridge is designed for interconnection of local area networks (LANs) that use identical protocols at the MAC layer (e.g., all conforming to IEEE 802.3 or all conforming to FDDI). Because the devices all use the same protocols, the amount of processing required at the bridge is minimal.[2]

Since the bridge is used in a situation in which all of the LANs have the same characteristics, the reader may ask, why not simply have one large LAN? Depending on circumstance, there are several reasons for the use of multiple LANs connected by bridges:

- *Reliability.* The danger in connecting all data processing devices in an organization to one network is that a fault on the network may disable communication for all devices. By using bridges, the network can be partitioned into self-contained units.

---

[2]In fact, some bridges are capable of mapping between different MAC protocols; we defer examination of this detail to Chapter 14.

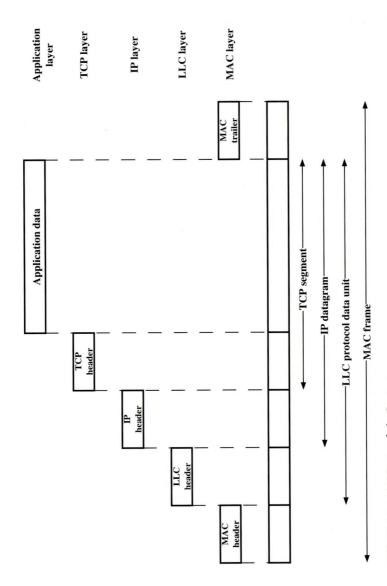

FIGURE 4.7 LAN Protocols in Context

- *Performance.* In general, performance on a LAN declines with an increase in the number of devices or the length of the wire. A number of smaller LANs will often give improved performance if devices can be clustered so that intranetwork traffic significantly exceeds internetwork traffic.

- *Security.* The establishment of multiple LANs may improve security of communications. It is desirable to keep different types of traffic (e.g., accounting, personnel, strategic planning) that have different security needs on physically separate media. At the same time, the different types of users with different levels of security need to communicate through controlled and monitored mechanisms.

- *Geography.* Clearly, two separate LANs are needed to support devices clustered in two geographically distant locations. Even in the case of two buildings separated by a highway, it may be far easier to use a microwave bridge link than to attempt to string coaxial cable between the two buildings.

Figure 4.8 illustrates the action of a bridge connecting two LANs, *A* and *B*, using the same MAC protocol. In this example, a single bridge attaches to both LANs; frequently, the bridge function is performed by two "half-bridges," one on each LAN. The functions of the bridge are few and simple:

- Read all frames transmitted on *A* and accept those addressed to any station on *B*.

- Using the medium access control protocol for *B*, retransmit each frame on *B*.

- Do the same for *B*-to-*A* traffic.

Several design aspects of a bridge are worth highlighting:

1. The bridge makes no modification to the content or format of the frames it receives, nor does it encapsulate them with an additional header. Each frame to be transferred is simply copied from one LAN and repeated with exactly the same bit pattern as the other LAN. Since the two LANs use the same LAN protocols, it is permissible to do this.

2. The bridge must contain addressing and routing intelligence. At a minimum, the bridge must know which addresses are on each network in order to know which frames to pass. Further, there may be more than two LANs interconnected by a number of bridges. In that case, a frame may have to be routed through several bridges in its journey from source to destination.

3. A bridge may connect more than two LANs.

In summary, the bridge provides an extension to the LAN that requires no modification to the communications software in the stations

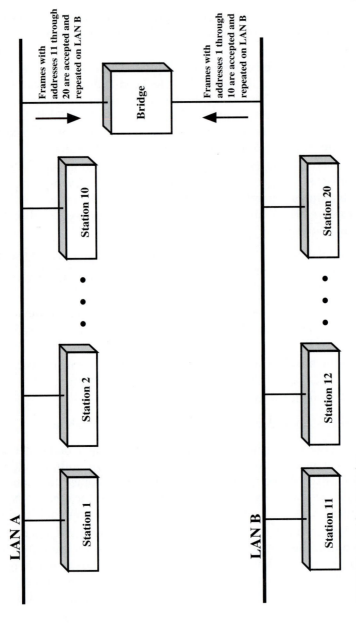

FIGURE 4.8 Bridge Operation

attached to the LANs. It appears to all stations on the two (or more) LANs that there is a single LAN on which each station has a unique address. The station uses that unique address and need not explicitly discriminate between stations on the same LAN and stations on other LANs; the bridge takes care of that.

Figure 4.9a suggests the protocol architecture of a bridge; in this case, end systems use TCP/IP above the LLC layer. Note that the bridge encompasses only the MAC and physical layers for interfacing to the LAN. For interfacing to the intermediate network or link, the bridge uses the appropriate protocols for that network (indicated by the shaded area in the figure). In effect, the bridge operates as a MAC-level relay. The LLC layer and above must be identical in the two end systems for successful end-to-end communications.

Routers

The bridge is only applicable to a configuration involving a single type of LAN. Of course, in many cases, an organization will need access to devices on a variety of networks. For example, an organization may have a tiered LAN architecture, with different types of LANs used for different purposes within an organization. There may also need to be access to devices on a wide-area network.

A general-purpose device that can be used to connect dissimilar networks and that operates at layer 3 of the OSI model is known as a router.[3] The router must be able to cope with a variety of differences among networks, including:

- *Addressing schemes.* The networks may use different schemes for assigning addresses to devices. For example, an IEEE 802 LAN uses either 16- or 48-bit binary addresses for each attached device; an X.25 public frame-switching network uses 12-digit decimal addresses (encoded as four bits per digit for a 48-bit address). Some form of global network addressing must be provided, as well as a directory service.

- *Maximum frame sizes.* Frames from one network may have to be broken into smaller pieces to be transmitted on another network, a process known as *segmentation.* For example, Ethernet imposes a maximum frame size of 1500 bytes; a maximum frame size of 1000 bytes is common on X.25 networks. A frame that is transmitted on an Ethernet system and picked up by a router for retransmission on an X.25 network may have to segment the incoming frame into two smaller ones.

---

[3]A router is also referred to as an intermediate system (IS), interworking unit (IWU), network relay, or gateway. We will generally use the term *router*.

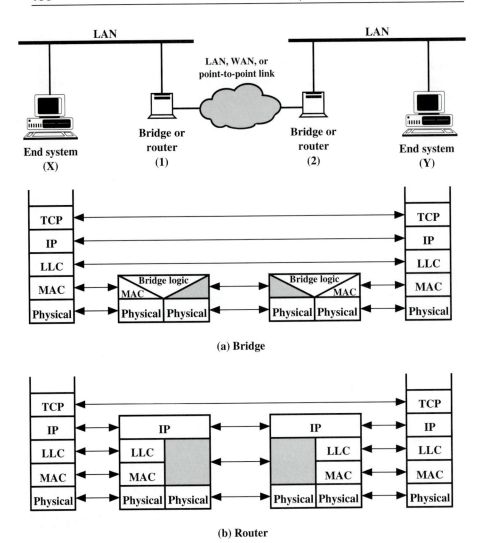

FIGURE 4.9   Protocol Architectures for Bridge and Router

- *Interfaces.* The hardware and software interfaces to various networks differ. The concept of a router must be independent of these differences.
- *Reliability.* Various network services may provide anything from a reliable end-to-end virtual circuit to an unreliable service. The operation of the routers should not depend on an assumption of network reliability.

As Figure 4.9b indicates, operation of the router depends on a protocol at OSI layer 3 (network layer). In this example. the internet protocol (IP) of the TCP/IP protocol suite performs that function. IP must be implemented in all stations on all LANs as well as on the routers. In addition, as with the bridge configuration, each station must have compatible protocols above IP to communicate successfully. The intermediate routers need only have up through IP.

Consider the transfer of a block of data from station X to station Y in Figure 4.9. The IP layer at X receives blocks of data to be sent to Y from TCP in X. The IP layer attaches a header that specifies the global internet address of Y. That address is in two parts: network identifier and station identifier. Let us refer to this block as the IP data unit. Next, IP recognizes that the destination (Y) is on another subnetwork. So the first step is to send the data to a router, in this case router 1. To accomplish this, IP hands its data unit down to LLC with the appropriate addressing information. LLC creates an LLC PDU, which is handed down to the MAC layer. The MAC layer constructs a MAC frame whose header contains the address of router 1.

Next, the frame travels through LAN to router 1. The router removes the frame and LLC headers and trailers and analyzes the IP header to determine the ultimate destination of the data, in this case Y. The router must now make a routing decision. There are two possibilities:

1. The destination station Y is connected directly to one of the subnetworks to which the router is attached.
2. To reach the destination, one or more additional routers must be traversed.

In this example, the data must be routed through router 2 before reaching the destination. So router 1 passes the IP data unit to router 2 via the intermediate network. For this purpose, the protocols of that network are used. For example, if the intermediate network is an X.25 network, the IP data unit is wrapped in an X.25 packet with appropriate addressing information to reach router 2. When this packet arrives at router 2, the packet header is stripped off. The router determines that this IP data unit is destined for Y, which is connected directly to a subnetwork to which the router is attached. The router therefore creates a frame with a destination address of Y and sends it out onto the LAN. The data finally arrive at Y, where the frame, LLC, and internet headers and trailers can be stripped off.

This service offered by IP is an unreliable one. That is, IP does not guarantee that all data will be delivered or that the data that are delivered will arrive in the proper order. It is the responsibility of the next-higher layer, in this case TCP, to recover from any errors that occur. This approach provides for a great deal of flexibility. The IP approach means that each unit of data is passed from router to router in an attempt to get from source to destination. Since delivery is not guaranteed, there is no particular reliability requirement on any of the subnetworks. Thus the protocol will work with any combination of subnetwork types. Since the sequence of delivery is not guaranteed, successive data units can follow different paths through the internet. This allows the protocol to react to congestion and failure in the internet by changing routes.

There is a place for both bridges and routers in planning the development of an internet. Bridges are simple, easy to configure, and have no impact on the host software. In an environment where all of the communicating devices are on similar LANs, this is the appropriate solution. In a mixed environment, the more complex routers are needed. However, even then, bridges may be used to interconnect some of the LANs.

4.5

IEEE 802 STANDARDS

The key to the development of the LAN market is the availability of a low-cost interface. The cost to connect equipment to a LAN must be much less than the cost of the equipment alone. This requirement, plus the complexity of the LAN logic, dictates a solution based on the use of chips and very-large-scale integration (VLSI). However, chip manufacturers will be reluctant to commit the necessary resources unless there is a high-volume market. A widely accepted LAN standard assures that volume and also enables equipment from a variety of manufacturers to intercommunicate. This is the rationale of the IEEE 802 committee.

The committee issued a set of standards, which were subsequently adopted in 1985 by the American National Standards Institute (ANSI) as American National Standards. These standards were subsequently revised and reissued as international standards by the International Organization for Standardization (ISO) in 1987, with the designation ISO 8802. Since then, the IEEE 802 committee has continued to revise and extend the standards, which are ultimately adopted by ISO.

Two conclusions were quickly reached by the committee. First, the task of communication across the local network is sufficiently complex that it needs to be broken up into more manageable subtasks. This resulted in the IEEE 802 reference model introduced earlier in this chapter (Figure 4.1).

Second, no single technical approach will satisfy all requirements. The second conclusion was reached reluctantly when it became apparent that no single standard would satisfy all committee participants. There was support for various topologies, access methods, and transmission media. The response of the committee was to standardize all serious proposals rather than to attempt to settle on just one. Figure 4.10 summarizes the current state of standardization. The figure also includes the fiber distributed data interface (FDDI) standard, which was developed by the American National Standards Institute (ANSI). Although FDDI is not an IEEE 802 standard, it was developed to conform to the IEEE 802 reference model.

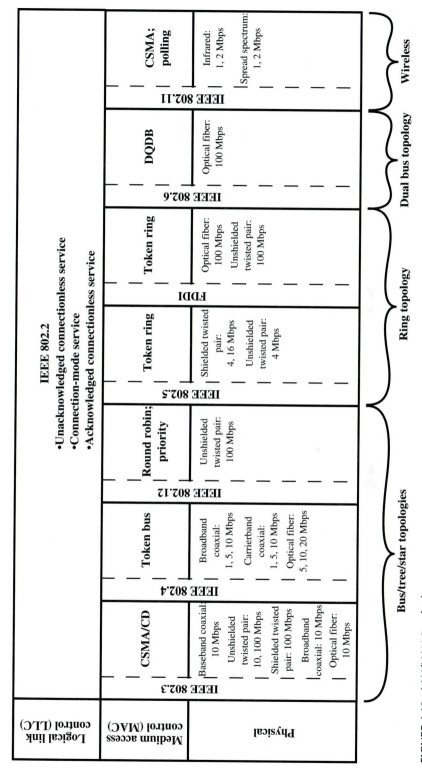

FIGURE 4.10 LAN/MAN Standards

Logical link control (LLC)	Medium access control (MAC)	Physical
IEEE 802.2 • Unacknowledged connectionless service • Connection-mode service • Acknowledged connectionless service	**IEEE 802.3** CSMA/CD	Baseband coaxial: 10 Mbps Unshielded twisted pair: 10, 100 Mbps Shielded twisted pair: 100 Mbps Broadband coaxial: 10 Mbps Optical fiber: 10 Mbps
	IEEE 802.4 Token bus	Broadband coaxial: 1, 5, 10 Mbps Carrierband coaxial: 1, 5, 10 Mbps Optical fiber: 5, 10, 20 Mbps
	IEEE 802.12 Round robin; priority	Unshielded twisted pair: 100 Mbps
	IEEE 802.5 Token ring	Shielded twisted pair: 4, 16 Mbps Unshielded twisted pair: 4 Mbps
	FDDI Token ring	Optical fiber: 100 Mbps Unshielded twisted pair: 100 Mbps
	IEEE 802.6 DQDB	Optical fiber: 100 Mbps
	IEEE 802.11 CSMA; polling	Infrared: 1, 2 Mbps Spread spectrum: 1, 2 Mbps

Bus/tree/star topologies — Ring topology — Dual bus topology — Wireless

LAN Implementation Model

In addition to developing a protocol reference model to structure the work of the committee, the committee also introduced an implementation model to guide the development of specific standards. The two models are compared in Figure 4.11. The difference is that the implementation model highlights the complexity of physical layer standardization. As we will see in Part III, for a given MAC layer, a number of different physical medium options are available. In most cases there is a medium-independent portion of the physical layer specification, which deals with signal encoding, synchronization, and other design issues that are common across multiple media. There is in addition a medium-dependent portion that deals with electrical and mechanical issues specific to a particular medium. Depending on implementation, these two parts may be implemented separately with an interface in between.

Organization of IEEE 802

The work of the IEEE 802 committee is currently organized into the following working groups (for material covered in this book, chapter references are provided):

- 802.1: Higher Level Interface (HILI)
- 802.2: Logical Link Control (LLC) (Chapter 5)
- 802.3: CSMA/CD (Chapters 6 and 7)
- 802.4: Token Bus (Chapter 6)
- 802.5: Token Ring (Chapter 6)
- 802.6: Metropolitan Area Network (MAN) (Chapter 12)
- 802.7: Broadband Technical Advisory Group (BBTAG)
- 802.8: Fiber Optic Technical Advisory Group (FOTAG)
- 802.9: Integrated Services LAN (ISLAN) Interface
- 802.10: Standard for Interoperable LAN Security (SILS)
- 802.11: Wireless LAN (WLAN) (Chapter 11)
- 802.12: Demand Priority (Chapter 7)
- 802.14: Cable-TV Based Broadband Communication Network

The Higher Level Interface working group deals with issues related to network architecture, internetworking, and network management for LANs. Standards have been issued for LLC, CSMA/CD, token bus, token ring, MAN, WLAN, and demand priority. Work on new options and features continues in each working group.

The purpose of 802.7 and 802.8 is to provide technical guidance to the other subcommittees on broadband and optical fiber technology, respec-

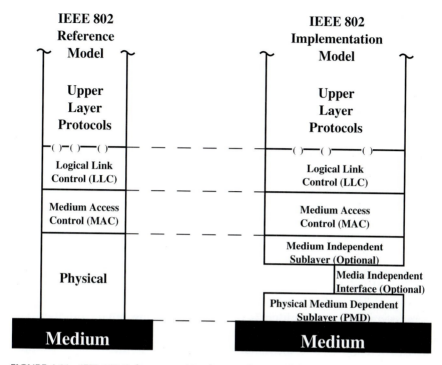

FIGURE 4.11   IEEE 802 Reference and Implementation Models

tively. The Broadband Technical Advisory Group has produced a recommended practices document for broadband cabling systems. The Fiber Optic Technical Advisory Group is investigating the use of optical fiber as an alternative transmission medium for 802.3, 802.4, and 802.5. It is also considering installation recommendations and a tutorial on fiber optic standards and related information.

The Integrated Services LAN (ISLAN) Interface working group was chartered in 1986. It is developing an architecture and an interface standard for desktop devices to 802 LANs and to Integrated Services Digital Networks (ISDNs), utilizing twisted-pair wiring to carry both voice and data (see [KESS94] for a description).

The Standard for Interoperable LAN Security working group was formed in 1988. It addresses such issues as secure data exchange, encryption key management, security aspects of network management, and the application of the OSI security architecture to LANs.

The Cable-TV Based Broadband Communication Network working group was established in 1994 to develop standards for data, voice, and video over cable television systems. The group is studying the introduction of new multiservice capabilities over CATV systems, such as remote data access and LAN interconnection, allowing users to transit two-way information (see [ENG95] for a description).

CYCLIC REDUNDANCY CHECK

Most data link control protocols include an error detection capability so that the receiver can detect any bit errors in received frames and request that the sender retransmit those frames. This technique requires the addition of a **frame check sequence** (FCS), or **error-detecting code,** to each frame. On transmission, a calculation is performed on the bits of the frame to be transmitted; the result is inserted as an additional field in the frame. On reception, the same calculation is performed on the received bits and the calculated result is compared to the value found in the incoming frame. If there is a discrepancy, the receiver assumes that an error has occurred.

One of the most common, and one of the most powerful, of the error-detecting codes is the cyclic redundancy check (CRC). For this technique, the message to be transmitted is treated as one long binary number. This number is divided by a unique prime binary number (a number divisible only by itself and 1), and the remainder is attached to the frame to be transmitted. When the frame is received, the receiver performs the same division, using the same divisor, and compares the calculated remainder with the remainder received in the frame. The most commonly used divisors are a 17-bit divisor, which produces a 16-bit remainder, and a 33-bit divisor, which produces a 32-bit remainder.

The measure of effectiveness of any error-detecting code is what percentage of errors it detects. It can be shown that all of the following errors are not divisible by a prime divisor and hence are detectable [STAL97]:

- All single-bit errors
- All double-bit errors, as long as the divisor has at least three ones
- Any odd number of errors, as long as the divisor contains a factor 11
- Any burst error for which the length of the burst is less than the length of the divisor polynomial, that is, less than or equal to the length of the FCS
- Most larger burst errors

These results are summarized in Table 4.2. As you can see, this is a very powerful means of error detection and requires very little overhead. As an example, if a 16-bit FCS is used with frames of 1000 bits, the overhead is only 1.6 percent. With a 32-bit FCS, the overhead is 3.2 percent. All of the IEEE 802 MAC frame formats use a 32-bit CRC.

TABLE 4.2   Effectiveness of the Cyclic Redundancy Check

Type of Error	Probability of Detection	
	16-bit CRC	32-bit CRC
Single bit error	1.0	1.0
Two bits in error (separate or not)	1.0	1.0
Odd number of bits in error	1.0	1.0
Error burst of length less than the length of the CRC (16 or 32 bits)	1.0	1.0
Error burst of length equal to the length of the CRC	$1 - \dfrac{1}{2^{15}}$	$1 - \dfrac{1}{2^{31}}$
Error burst of length greater than the length of the CRC	$1 - \dfrac{1}{2^{16}}$	$1 - \dfrac{1}{2^{32}}$

CHAPTER
5

Logical Link Control

Logical link control (LLC) is the highest layer of the IEEE 802 protocol reference model. It is used above all of the medium access control (MAC) standards specified by IEEE 802 and ANSI. The primary purpose of this layer is to provide a means of exchanging data between end users across a MAC-controlled link or a collection of LANs interconnected by MAC-level bridges. Different forms of the LLC service are specified to meet specific reliability and efficiency needs.

This chapter begins with a description of the LLC service. Each of the three forms of service is described. The next section deals with some of the key mechanisms of link control protocols. We are then in a position to examine the LLC protocols that support the various LLC services.

5.1

LLC SERVICES

This section provides an overview of the three types of LLC services that have been standardized.

146

Forms of LLC Service

Logical link control provides services to users through LLC service access points (LSAPs). The LLC standard specifies three forms of service to LLC users:

- Unacknowledged connectionless service
- Connection-mode service
- Acknowledged connectionless service

These services are specified in terms of primitives that can be viewed as commands or procedure calls with parameters.[1] Table 5.1 summarizes the LLC service primitives.

Unacknowledged Connectionless Service.   The unacknowledged connectionless service is a datagram style of service that simply allows for sending and receiving LLC PDUs, with no form of acknowledgment to assure delivery, and no flow control or error control mechanisms. This service supports individual, multicast, and broadcast addressing.

This service provides for only two primitives across the interface between the next-higher layer and LLC. DL-UNITDATA.request is used to pass a block of data down to LLC for transmission. DL-UNITDATA.indication is used to pass a block of data up to the destination user from LLC upon reception. The *source-address* and *destination-address* parameters specify the local and remote LLC users, respectively. Each of these parameters actually is a combination of LLC service access point and the MAC address. The *data* parameter is the block of data transmitted from one LLC user to another. The *priority* parameter specifies the desired priority. This parameter (together with the MAC portion of the address) is passed down through the LLC entity to the MAC entity, which has the responsibility of implementing a priority mechanism. Token bus (IEEE 802.4) and token ring (IEEE 802.5, FDDI) are capable of enforcing priority, but the 802.3 CSMA/CD system is not.

Connection-Mode Service.   The connection-mode LLC service enables two communicating LLC users to set up a logical connection for data transfer. It provides a means by which a user can request or be notified of the establishment or termination of a logical connection. It also provides flow control, sequencing, and error recovery. This service supports individual addressing only (no multicast or broadcast). Figure 5.1 shows the key service primitive sequences that define this service.

The first four primitives listed for the service in Table 5.1 deal with connection establishment. In addition to specifying the source and destination

---

[1]These primitives always include one of four modifiers: request, indication, response, and confirm. The interpretation of these primitives is discussed in Appendix 5A.

TABLE 5.1 Logical Link Control Primitives

Service Primitive	Parameters
Unacknowledged Connectionless Service	
DL-UNITDATA.request	source-address, destination-address, data, priority
DL-UNITDATA.indication	source-address, destination-address, data, priority
Connection-Mode Service	
DL-CONNECT.request	source-address, destination-address, priority
DL-CONNECT.indication	source-address, destination-address, priority
DL-CONNECT.response	source-address, destination-address, priority
DL-CONNECT.confirm	source-address, destination-address, priority
DL-DATA.request	source-address, destination-address, data
DL-DATA.indication	
DL-DISCONNECT.request	source-address, destination-address
DL-DISCONNECT.indication	source-address, destination-address, reason
DL-RESET.request	source-address, destination-address
DL-RESET.indication	source-address, destination-address, reason
DL-RESET.response	source-address, destination-address
DL-RESET.confirm	
DL-CONNECTION-FLOWCONTROL.request	source-address, destination-address, amount
DL-CONNECTION-FLOWCONTROL.indication	source-address, destination-address, amount

TABLE 5.1   Logical Link Control Primitives (continued)

Service Primitive	Parameters
Acknowledged Connectionless Service	
DL-DATA-ACK.request	source-address, destination-address, data, priority, service-class
DL-DATA-ACK.indication	source-address, destination-address, data, priority, service-class
DL-DATA-ACK-STATUS.indication	source-address, destination-address, priority, service-class, status
DL-REPLY.request	source-address, destination-address, data, priority, service-class
DL-REPLY.indication	source-address, destination-address, data, priority, service-class
DL-REPLY-STATUS.indication	source-address, destination-address, data, priority, service-class, status
DL-REPLY-UPDATE.request	source-address, data
DL-REPLY-UPDATE-STATUS.indication	source-address, status

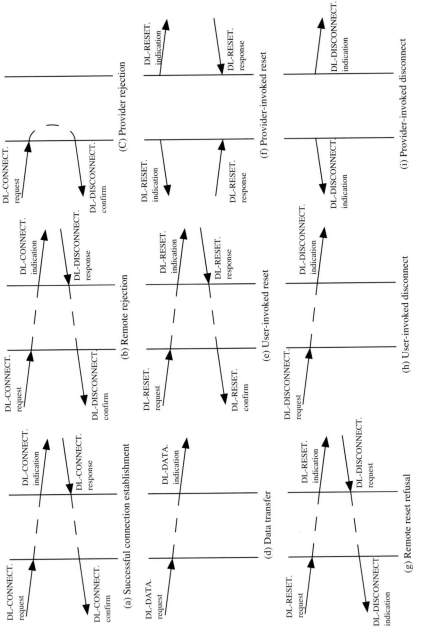

FIGURE 5.1 LLC Connection-Mode Service: Primitive Sequences

150

addresses, the user can request a priority level to be provided for the requested connection. If the connection is established, the priority is assigned to the connection as a whole and may be used to determine the relative resources allocated by the LLC entity to each active connection. In addition, the priority is passed down to the MAC entity for each data unit transferred over the logical connection.

Figure 5.1 indicates two ways in which a connection request may be rejected. The remote user may refuse the connection by issuing a DL-DISCONNECT.request in response to a DL-CONNECT.indication. This is reported to the requesting user as a DL-DISCONNECT.indication. Also, the connection may be refused by the LLC service. Examples of reasons for the latter event:

- The remote LLC entity never replied to the connection request. The local LLC entity will attempt to set up the connection a number of times before giving up and reporting failure.
- The local LLC entity is unable to set up the connection (e.g., inadequate buffer space available, LAN malfunction).

Once a connection is established, blocks of data are exchanged using DL-DATA.request and DL-DATA.indication. Note that there are no response and confirm primitives to provide acknowledgment. The reason is that this service guarantees to deliver all data in the proper order, with no losses. Thus, normally, the user needs no form of acknowledgment. If something goes wrong, the user is informed by means of the reset or disconnect functions.

At any point, either side may terminate the connection with a DL-DISCONNECT.request; the other side is informed with a DL-DISCON-NECT.indication. A service provider may need to perform a disconnect if for some reason it experiences an unrecoverable failure.

The LLC entities on both sides of the connection keep track of the data units flowing in both directions so that they can assure that each data unit is delivered successfully in the proper order. At any time, the LLC service provider or either of the LLC users may reset the logical connection. This means that the connection is reinitialized and some data units may be lost. That is, some data units may have been sent by one LLC entity but have not yet been acknowledged by the other LLC entity, and these data units may not be delivered. A service provider may need to perform a reset if for some reason it becomes out of synchronization with the other side. A user may need to perform a reset because it wishes to abort the current exchange without losing the connection.

The DL-RESET primitives may be used by the LLC service user to resynchronize the use of an LLC connection or by the LLC service provider to report the loss of user data that cannot be recovered by the LLC service provider. In either case, outstanding service data units on the LLC connection may be lost; it is up to higher layers to recover the lost data. A reset attempt may fail leading to a termination of the connection. This can happen either because the remote user refused the reset request (Figure 5.1g) or because the remote LLC entity did not respond.

Finally, the two flow control primitives regulate the flow of data across the LSAP. The flow can be controlled in either direction. This is a local flow control mechanism which specifies the amount of data that may be passed across the LSAP.

Acknowledged Connectionless Service.   The acknowledged connectionless service provides a mechanism by which a user can send a unit of data and receive an acknowledgment that the data was delivered, without the necessity of setting up a connection. There are actually two related but independent services. The DL-DATA-ACK service is a guaranteed delivery service, in which data are sent from an originating LLC user, and acknowledged. The DL-REPLY service is essentially a poll with a guaranteed response; it enables a user to request a previously prepared data unit from another user or to exchange data units with another user.

The DL-DATA-ACK service includes DL-DATA-ACK.request and DL-DATA-ACK.indication, with meanings analogous to those for the Unacknowledged Connectionless Service. The service-class parameter specifies whether or not an acknowledgment capability in the MAC layer is to be used for the data unit transmission. So far, only the 802.4 standard supports this capability. The DL-DATA-ACK-STATUS.indication provides acknowledgment to the sending user; it includes a status parameter that indicates whether or not the data unit was received successfully by the peer LLC entity.

The DL-REPLY primitives provide a data exchange service. It allows a user to request that data be returned from a remote station or that data units be exchanged with a remote station. Associated with these primitives are the DL-REPLY-UPDATE primitives. These primitives allow a user to pass data to LLC to be held and sent out at a later time when requested to do so (by a DL-REPLY primitive) by some other station.

5.2

LINK CONTROL PROTOCOL MECHANISMS

Before examining the particular protocols defined for the LLC standard, it will be useful to describe two of the most important mechanisms used in link control protocols: flow control and error control. These mechanisms are found in most data link control protocols. Flow control and error control mechanisms are used in both the connection-oriented and acknowledged connectionless LLC protocols.

Flow Control

Flow control is a technique for assuring that a transmitting entity does not overwhelm a receiving entity with data. The receiving entity typically allocates a data buffer of some maximum length for a transfer. When data are received, the receiver must do a certain amount of processing (e.g., examine the header and strip it off the PDU) before passing the data to the higher-level software. In the absence of flow control, the receiver's buffer may fill up and overflow while it is processing old data.

To begin, we examine mechanisms for flow control in the absence of errors. The model we will use is depicted in Figure 5.2a, which is a vertical-time sequence diagram. It has the advantages of showing time dependencies and illustrating the correct send–receive relationship. Each arrow represents a single PDU transiting a data link between two stations. The data are sent in a sequence of PDUs, with each PDU containing a portion of the data and some control information. For now, we assume that all PDUs that are transmitted are received successfully; no PDUs are lost and none arrive with errors. Furthermore, PDUs arrive in the same order in which they are sent. However, each PDU transmitted suffers an arbitrary and variable amount of delay before reception.

Stop-and-Wait Flow Control.   The simplest form of flow control, known as stop-and-wait flow control, supports the acknowledged connectionless LLC service and works as follows. A source entity transmits a PDU. After reception, the destination entity indicates its willingness to accept another PDU by sending back an acknowledgment to the PDU just received. The source must wait until it receives the acknowledgment before sending the next PDU. The destination can thus stop the flow of data simply by withholding acknowledgment. This procedure works fine and, indeed, can hardly be improved upon when a message is sent in a few large PDUs. However, it is often the case that a source will break up a large block of data into smaller blocks and transmit the data in many PDUs. This is done for the following reasons:

- The buffer size of the receiver may be limited.
- The longer the transmission, the more likely that there will be an error, necessitating retransmission of the entire PDU. With smaller PDUs, errors are detected sooner, and a smaller amount of data needs to be retransmitted.
- On a shared medium such as a LAN, it is usually desirable not to permit one station to occupy the medium for an extended period, thus causing long delays at the other sending stations.

With the use of multiple PDUs for a single message, the stop-and-wait procedure may be inadequate. The essence of the problem is that only one PDU at a time can be in transit. In situations where the bit length of the link

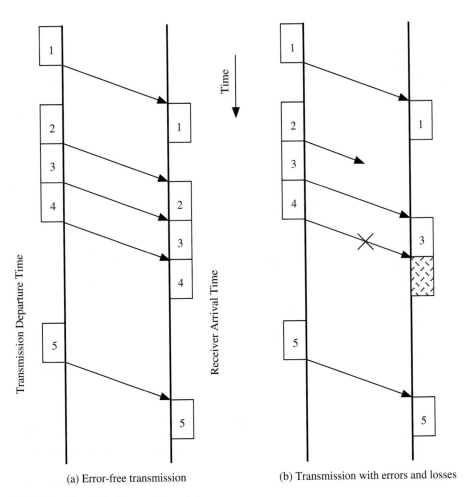

(a) Error-free transmission   (b) Transmission with errors and losses

FIGURE 5.2   Model of Frame Transmission

is greater than the PDU length, serious inefficiencies result. This is illustrated in Figure 5.3. In the figure, the transmission time (the time it takes for a station to transmit a PDU) is normalized to 1, and the propagation delay (the time it takes for a bit to travel from sender to receiver) is expressed as the variable a. Note that most of the time the line is idle.

Sliding-Window Flow Control.   Efficiency can be greatly improved by allowing multiple PDUs to be in transit at the same time. Let us examine how this might work for two stations, A and B, connected via a full-duplex link. Station B allocates buffer space for n PDUs instead of the one just discussed. Thus B can accept n PDUs, and A is allowed to send n PDUs without waiting for any acknowledgments. To keep track of which PDUs have

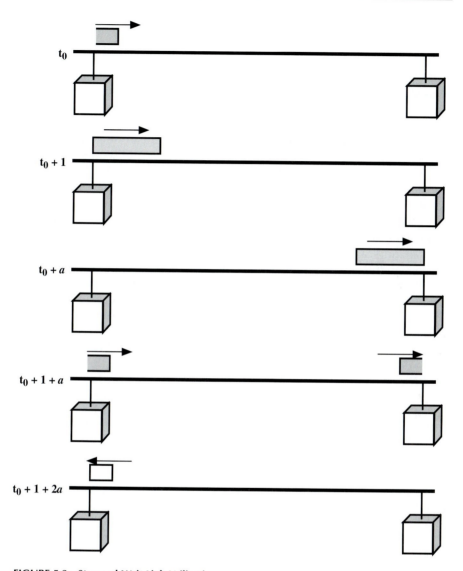

FIGURE 5.3   Stop-and-Wait Link Utilization

been acknowledged, each is labeled with a sequence number. *B* acknowledges a PDU by sending an acknowledgment that includes the sequence number of the next PDU expected. This acknowledgment also implicitly announces that *B* is prepared to receive the next *n* PDUs, beginning with the number specified. This scheme can also be used to acknowledge multiple PDUs. For example, *B* could receive PDUs 2, 3, and 4 but withhold acknowledgment until PDU 4 has arrived. By then returning an acknowledgment with sequence number 5, *B* acknowledges PDUs 2, 3, and 4 at one time. *A* maintains a list of sequence numbers that it is allowed to send, and *B* maintains a list of sequence numbers that it is prepared to receive. Each of these lists can be thought of as a *window* of PDUs. The operation is referred to as sliding-window flow control.

Several additional comments need to be made. Since the sequence number to be used occupies a field in the PDU, it is clearly of bounded size. For example, for a 3-bit field, the sequence number can range from 0 to 7. Accordingly, PDUs are numbered modulo 8; that is, after sequence number 7, the next number is 0. With this in mind, Figure 5.4 is a useful way of depicting the sliding-window process. It assumes the use of a 3-bit sequence number, so that PDUs are numbered sequentially from 0 through 7, and then the same numbers are reused for subsequent PDUs. The shaded rectangle indicates that the sender may transmit 7 PDUs, beginning with PDU 6. Each time a PDU is sent, the shaded window shrinks; each time an acknowledgment is received, the shaded window grows.

The window size need not be the maximum possible size for a given sequence number length. For example, using a 3-bit sequence number, a window size of four PDUs could be configured. The example in Figure 5.5 assumes a 3-bit sequence number field and a maximum window size of seven PDUs. Initially, *A* and *B* have windows indicating that *A* may transmit seven PDUs, beginning with PDU 0 (P0). After transmitting three PDUs (P0, P1, P2) without acknowledgment, *A* has shrunk its window to indicate that *A* may transmit four PDUs, beginning with PDU number 3. *B* then transmits an RR (receive ready) 3, which means: "I have received all PDUs up through PDU number 2 and am ready to receive seven PDUs, beginning with PDU number 3." With this acknowledgment, *A* is back up to permission to transmit seven PDUs, still beginning with PDU 3. *A* proceeds to transmit PDUs 3, 4, 5, and 6. *B* returns RR 4, which acknowledges P3, and allows transmission of P4 through P2. But, by the time this reaches *A*, *A* has already transmitted P4, P5, and P6. Thus *A* may only open its window to permit sending 4 PDUs, beginning with P7.

This mechanism does indeed provide a form of flow control: The receiver need only accommodate 7 PDUs beyond the one it has last acknowledged. To supplement this, most protocols also allow a station to cut off the flow of PDUs from the other side completely by sending a receive not ready (RNR) message, which acknowledges former PDUs but forbids transfer of future PDUs. Thus RNR 5 means: "I have received all PDUs up through number 4 but am unable to accept any more." At a subsequent point, the station must send a normal acknowledgment to reopen the window.

So far, we have discussed transmission in one direction only. If two stations exchange data, each needs to maintain two windows, one for transmit and one for receive, and each side needs to send the data and acknowl-

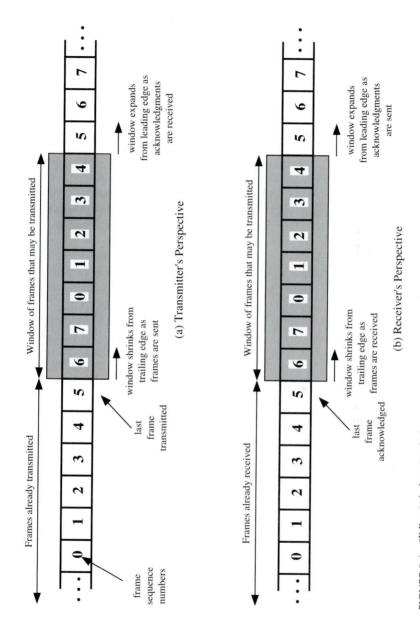

FIGURE 5.4 Sliding-Window Depiction

157

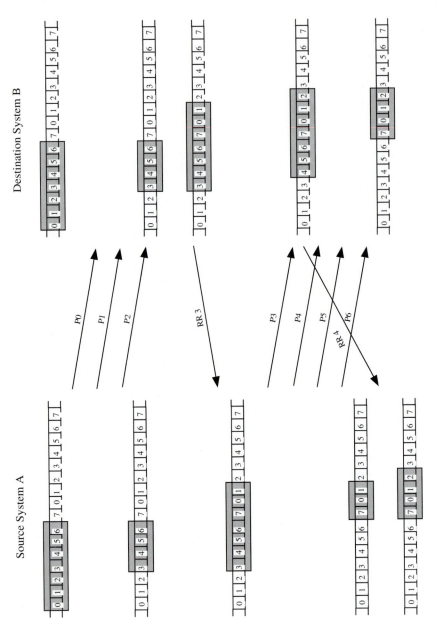

FIGURE 5.5 Example of a Sliding-Window Protocol

158

edgments to the other. To provide efficient support for this requirement, a feature known as *piggybacking* is typically provided. Each *data PDU* includes a field that holds the sequence number of that PDU plus a field that holds the sequence number used for acknowledgment. Thus, if a station has data to send and an acknowledgment to send, it sends both together in one PDU, saving communication capacity. Of course, if a station has an acknowledgment but no data to send, it sends a separate *acknowledgment PDU*. If a station has data to send but no new acknowledgment to send, it must repeat the last acknowledgment that it sent. This is because the data PDU includes a field for the acknowledgment number, and some value must be put into that field. When a station receives a duplicate acknowledgment, it simply ignores it.

Error Control

Error control refers to mechanisms to detect and correct errors that occur in the transmission of PDUs. The model that we will use, which covers the typical case, is illustrated in Figure 5.2b. As before, data are sent as a sequence of PDUs; PDUs arrive in the same order in which they are sent; and each transmitted PDU suffers an arbitrary and variable amount of delay before reception. In addition, we admit the possibility of two types of errors:

- *Lost PDU.* A PDU fails to arrive at the other side. For example, a noise burst may damage a PDU to the extent that the receiver is not aware that a PDU has been transmitted.
- *Damaged PDU.* A recognizable PDU does arrive, but some of the bits are in error (have been altered during transmission).

The most common techniques for error control are based on some or all of the following ingredients:

- *Error detection.* The receiver detects errors and discards PDUs that are in error. This function is actually performed by the MAC layer and is described in Chapter 4.
- *Positive acknowledgment.* The destination returns a positive acknowledgment to successfully received, error-free PDUs.
- *Retransmission after timeout.* The source retransmits a PDU that has not been acknowledged after a predetermined amount of time.
- *Negative acknowledgment and retransmission.* The destination returns a negative acknowledgment to PDUs in which an error is detected. The source retransmits such PDUs.

Collectively, these mechanisms are all referred to as **automatic repeat request** (ARQ); the effect of ARQ is to turn an unreliable data link into a reliable one. Two versions of ARQ are employed in the LLC standard: stop-and-wait ARQ, used to support the acknowledged connectionless service, and go-back-N ARQ, used to support the connection mode service. ARQ is based on the use of the flow control techniques described in the preceding subsection.

Stop-and-Wait ARQ.   Stop-and-wait ARQ is based on the stop-and-wait flow control technique outlined previously and is depicted in Figure 5.6. The source station transmits a single PDU and then must await an acknowledgment. No other data PDUs can be sent until the destination station's reply arrives at the source station.

Two sorts of errors could occur. First, the PDU that arrives at the destination could be damaged. The receiver detects this by using the error detection technique referred to earlier and simply discards the PDU. To account for this possibility, the source station is equipped with a timer. After a PDU is transmitted, the source station waits for an acknowledgment. If no acknowledgment is received by the time the timer expires, the same PDU is sent again. Note that this method requires that the transmitter maintain a copy of a transmitted PDU until an acknowledgment is received for that PDU.

The second sort of error is a damaged acknowledgment. Consider the following situation. Station *A* sends a PDU. The PDU is received correctly by station *B*, which responds with an acknowledgment (ACK). The ACK is damaged in transit and is not recognizable by *A*, which will therefore time out and resend the same PDU. This duplicate PDU arrives and is accepted by *B*. *B* has therefore accepted two copies of the same PDU as if they were separate. To avoid this problem, PDUs are alternately labeled with 0 or 1, and positive acknowledgments are of the form ACK0 and ACK1. In keeping with the sliding-window convention, an ACK0 acknowledges receipt of a PDU numbered 1 and indicates that the receiver is ready for a PDU numbered 0.

Go-Back-N ARQ.   The principal advantage of stop-and-wait ARQ is its simplicity. Its principal disadvantage is that of the underlying stop-and-wait flow control technique: It is inefficient. However, just as the stop-and-wait flow control technique can be used as the basis for error control, so can the sliding-window flow control technique be adapted. The form of error control based on sliding-window flow control that is most commonly used is called go-back-N ARQ.

In go-back-N ARQ, a station may send a series of PDUs sequentially numbered modulo some maximum value. The number of unacknowledged PDUs outstanding is determined by window size, using the sliding-window flow control technique. While no errors occur, the destination will acknowledge (RR = receive ready) incoming PDUs as usual. If the destina-

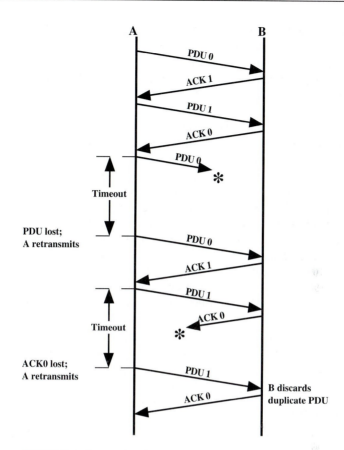

FIGURE 5.6   Stop-and-Wait ARQ

tion station detects an error in a PDU, it sends a negative acknowledgment (REJ = reject) for that PDU. The destination station will discard that PDU and all future incoming PDUs until the PDU in error is correctly received. Thus the source station, when it receives a REJ, must retransmit the PDU in error plus all succeeding PDUs that had been transmitted in the interim.

Consider that station A is sending PDUs to station B. After each transmission, A sets an acknowledgment timer for the PDU just transmitted. The go-back-N technique takes into account the following contingencies:

1. *Damaged PDU.* There are two subcases:
   a. A transmits PDU i, which is lost or damaged in transit. A subsequently sends PDU $(i + 1)$. B receives PDU $(i + 1)$ out of order and sends a REJ i. A must retransmit PDU i and all subsequent PDUs.
   b. PDU i is lost or damaged in transit and A does not soon send additional PDUs. B receives nothing and returns neither an RR nor an

REJ. When *A's* timer expires, it transmits an RR PDU that includes a bit known as the P bit, which is set to 1. *B* interprets the RR PDU with a P bit of 1 as a command that must be acknowledged by sending an RR indicating the next PDU that it expects. When *A* receives the RR, it retransmits PDU *i*.

2. *Damaged RR.* There are two subcases:
   a. *B* receives PDU *i* and sends RR $(i + 1)$, which is lost in transit. Since acknowledgments are cumulative (e.g., RR 6 means that all PDUs through 5 are acknowledged), it may be that *A* will receive a subsequent RR to a subsequent PDU that will arrive before the timer associated with PDU *i* expires.
   b. If *A's* timer expires, it transmits an RR command as in case 1b. It sets another timer, called the P-bit timer. If *B* fails to respond to the RR command, or if its response is damaged, *A's* P-bit timer will expire. At this point *A* will try again by issuing a new RR command and restarting the P-bit timer. This procedure is tried for a number of iterations. If *A* fails to obtain an acknowledgment after a maximum number of attempts, it initiates a reset procedure.

Figure 5.7 is an example of the PDU flow for go-back-N ARQ. Because of the propagation delay on the line, by the time that an acknowledgment (positive or negative) arrives back at the sending station, it has already sent two additional PDUs beyond the one being acknowledged. Thus, when a REJ is received to PDU 5, not only PDU 5 but PDUs 6 and 7 must be retransmitted. Thus the transmitter must keep a copy of all unacknowledged PDUs.

5.3

LLC PROTOCOLS

The basic LLC protocols are modeled after HDLC and have similar functions and formats. The reader should be able to see how these protocols support the LLC services defined in Section 5.1.

LLC Types and Classes

There are three LLC protocols (referred to as types of operation) defined in the standard, one for each of the three forms of service:

- Type 1 operation supports unacknowledged connectionless service.
- Type 2 operation supports connection-mode service.
- Type 3 operation supports acknowledged connectionless service.

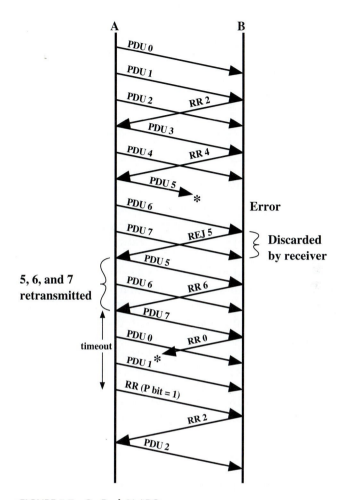

FIGURE 5.7   Go-Back-N ARQ

It is possible for a single station to support more than one form of service and hence employ more than one of the types of protocols. The combination of services supported is given by the station class. Table 5.2 indicates the allowable station classes. Note that all allowable classes support type 1. This ensures that all stations on a LAN will have a common service mode that can be used for management operations. Beyond that, each station supports only those services needed by its users, and thus the implementation size is minimized.

If a station supports more than one mode of service, individual LSAPs may be activated for one or more of the available services. This is a configuration function beyond the scope of the standard.

TABLE 5.2 LLC Classes

		Class of LLC			
		I	II	III	IV
Types of	1	×	×	×	×
operation	2		×		×
supported	3			×	×

LLC Protocol Data Units

All three LLC protocols employ the same PDU format (Figure 5.8), which consists of four fields. The DSAP and SSAP fields each contain a 7-bit address. The eighth bit of the DSAP field indicates whether this is an individual or a group address. The eighth bit of the SSAP field indicates whether this is a command or response PDU.

The control field identifies the particular PDU and specifies various control functions. It is 8 or 16 bits long, depending on the identity of the PDU. A PDU is a command if it is issued with the expectation of a response; correspondingly, some PDUs are responses. Some PDUs can be used as either a command or a response. The P/F (poll/final) bit used in all three control field formats has to do with the linking of commands and responses. In command PDUs, it is referred to as the P bit and is set to 1 to force a response. In a response PDU, it is referred to as the F bit and is set to 1 to indicate the response transmitted as a result of a soliciting command.

There are three types of PDU, each with a different control field format:

- *Information:* used to carry user data. The control field includes a 7-bit sequence number, N(S), associated with this PDU; it also includes a piggybacked acknowledgment sequence number, N(R).
- *Supervisory:* used for flow and error control. It includes an acknowledgment sequence number and a 2-bit S field to distinguish three different PDUs: receive ready (RR), receive not ready (RNR), and reject (REJ).
- *Unnumbered:* various protocol control PDUs. The 5-bit M field indicates which PDU.

Table 5.3 lists the PDUs used in all three LLC protocols.

Type 1 Operation

Type 1 operation supports the unacknowledged connectionless service. The UI PDU is used to transfer user data. There is no acknowledgment, flow control, or error control. However, there is error detection and discard at the MAC level.

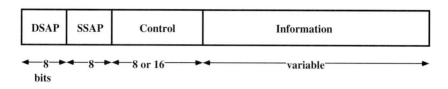

(a) Frame format

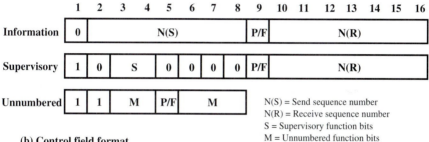

N(S) = Send sequence number
N(R) = Receive sequence number
S = Supervisory function bits
M = Unnumbered function bits
P/F = Poll/final bit

(b) Control field format

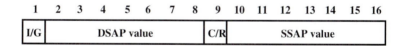

I/G: 0 = individual DSAP; 1 = group DSAP
C/R: 0 = command; 1 = response

(c) LLC address fields

FIGURE 5.8 LLC Protocol Data Unit Formats

The remaining two type 1 PDUs are intended to support management functions associated with all three types of operation. Both PDUs are used in the following fashion. An LLC entity may issue a command (C/R bit = 0) XID or TEST. The receiving LLC entity issues a corresponding XID or TEST in response.

The XID PDU is used to exchange two types of information: types of operation supported and window size. If the DSAP and SSAP fields are null (all zeros), the information field indicates which LLC class (Table 5.2) is provided by the sending LLC entity.[2] If the XID includes specific DSAP and SSAP addresses, the information field indicates which types of operation

---

[2]The identity of the sending end system is known because its MAC address is included in the MAC frame.

TABLE 5.3   LLC Protocol Data Units

Name	Function	Description
(a) Unacknowledged Connectionless Service		
Unnumbered (U)		
UI Unnumbered information	C	Exchange user data
XID Exchange identification	C/R	Type of operation and window size information
TEST	C/R	Loopback test
(b) Connection-Mode Service		
Information (I)	C/R	Exchange user data
Supervisory (S)		
RR Receive ready	C/R	Positive acknowledgment; ready to receive I PDU
RNR Receive not ready	C/R	Positive acknowledgment; not ready to receive
REJ Reject	C/R	Negative acknowledgment; go back N
Unnumbered		
SABME Set asynchronous balanced mode extended	C	Connection request
DISC Disconnect	C	Terminate connection
UA Unnumbered acknowledgement	R	Acknowledge unnumbered command
DM Disconnected mode	R	Connection rejection
FRMR Frame reject	R	Reports receipt of unacceptable frame
(c) Acknowledged Connectionless Service		
Unnumbered		
AC Acknowledged connectionless information	C/R	Exchange user information

may be provided for that particular SSAP. For a SAP that supports type 2 operation, and for a particular connection (identified by the SSAP, DSAP pair), the information field also includes the receive window size used in the sliding-window flow control mechanism.

The TEST PDU is used to conduct a loopback test of the transmission path between two LLC entities. Upon receipt of a TEST command PDU, the addressed LLC entity issues a TEST response PDU as soon as possible.

Type 2 Operation

Type 2 operation supports the connection-mode service. It makes use of all three PDU formats. Type 2 operation involves three phases: connection establishment, data transfer, and connection termination.

Connection Establishment.   With type 2 operation, a data link connection is established between two LLC SAPs prior to data exchange. Connection establishment is attempted by the type 2 protocol in response to a DL-CONNECT.request from a user. The LLC entity issues a SABME PDU[3] to request a logical connection with the other LLC entity. If the connection is accepted by the LLC user designated by the DSAP, the destination LLC entity returns a UA PDU. The connection is henceforth uniquely identified by the pair of user SAPs. If the destination LLC user rejects the connection request, its LLC entity returns a DM PDU.

Data Transfer.   When connection request has been accepted and confirmed, the connection is established. Both sides may begin to send user data in I-PDUs, starting with sequence number 0. The N(S) and N(R) fields of the I-PDU are sequence numbers that support flow control and error control. An LLC entity sending a sequence of I-PDUs will number them sequentially, modulo 128, and place the sequence number in N(S). N(R) is the acknowledgment for I-PDUs received; it enables the LLC entity to indicate which number I-PDU it expects to receive next.

S-PDUs are also used for flow control and error control. The receive ready (RR) PDU is used to acknowledge the last I-PDU received by indicating the next I-PDU expected. The RR is used when there is no reverse user data traffic (I-PDUs) to carry an acknowledgment. Receive not ready (RNR) acknowledges an I-PDU, as with RR, but also asks the peer entity to suspend transmission of I-PDUs. When the entity that issued RNR is again ready, it sends an RR. REJ initiates the go-back-N ARQ. It indicates that the last I-PDU received has been rejected and that retransmission of all I-PDUs beginning with number N(R) is required.

Either LLC entity can request a reset, either on its own initiative or in response to a user's DL-RESET.request. An LLC entity requests a reset on a particular connection simply by issuing a SABME using the appropriate SSAP and DSAP. The remote LLC user has the choice of accepting the reset, which causes its LLC entity to reply with a UA, or rejecting it, which causes its LLC entity to reply with a DM. When a reset occurs, both LLC entities reset their send and receive sequence numbers to zero.

---

[3]This stands for "set asynchronous balanced mode extended." It is used in HDLC to choose ABM and to select extended sequence numbers of 7 bits. Both ABM and 7-bit sequence numbers are mandatory in type 2 operation.

Disconnect.   Either LLC entity can terminate a logical LLC connection, either on its own initiative or in response to a user's DL-DISCONNECT.request. The entity initiates a disconnect on a particular connection by issuing a DISC PDU to the other LLC entity on the connection. The remote entity must accept the disconnect by replying with a UA and issuing a DL-DISCONNECT.indication to its user. No assumption can be made about outstanding I PDUs.

Examples of Operation.   To better understand LLC type 2 operation, several examples are presented in Figure 5.9. In the example diagrams, each arrow includes a legend that specifies the PDU name, the setting of the P/F bit, and, where appropriate, the values of N(R) and N(S). The setting of the P or F bit is 1 if the designation is present and 0 if absent.

Figure 5.9a shows the PDUs involved in link setup and disconnect. The LLC entity for one side issues an SABME command to the other side and starts a timer. The other side, upon receiving the SABME, returns a UA response and sets local variables and counters to their initial values. The initiating entity receives the UA response, sets its variables and counters, and stops the timer. The logical connection is now active, and both sides may begin transmitting PDUs. Should the timer expire without a response, the originator will repeat the SABME, as illustrated. This would be repeated until a UA or DM is received or until, after a given number of tries, the entity attempting initiation gives up and reports failure to a management entity. In such a case, higher-layer intervention is necessary. The same diagram shows the disconnect procedure. One side issues a DISC command, and the other responds with a UA response.

Figure 5.9b illustrates the full-duplex exchange of I-PDUs. When an entity sends a number of I-PDUs in a row with no incoming data, the receive sequence number is simply repeated (e.g., I,1,1; I,2,1 in the *A*-to-*B* direction). When an entity receives a number of I-PDUs in a row with no outgoing PDUs, the receive sequence number in the next outgoing PDU must reflect the cumulative activity (e.g., I,1,3 in the *B*-to-*A* direction). Note that in addition to I-PDUs, data exchange may involve supervisory PDUs.

Figure 5.9c shows an operation involving a busy condition. Such a condition may arise because an LLC entity is not able to process I-PDUs as fast as they are arriving, or the intended user is not able to accept data as fast as they arrive in I-PDUs. In either case, the entity's receive buffer fills up and it must halt the incoming flow of I-PDUs, using an RNR command. In this example, the station issues an RNR, which requires the other side to halt transmission of I-PDUs. The station receiving the RNR will usually poll the busy station at a periodic interval by sending an RR with the P-bit set. This requires the other side to respond with either an RR or an RNR. When the busy condition has cleared, *A* returns an RR, and I-PDU transmission from *B* can resume.

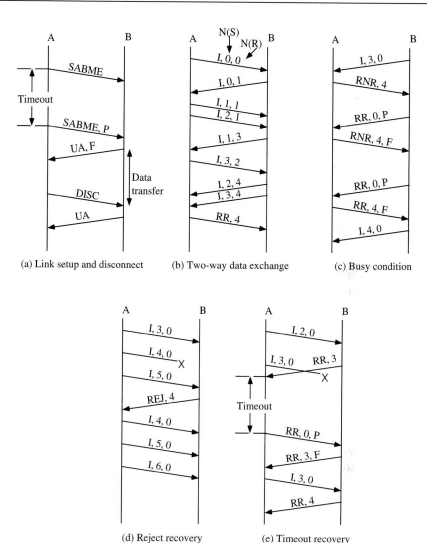

FIGURE 5.9   Examples of LLC Type 2 Operation

An example of error recovery using the REJ command is shown in Figure 5.9d. In this example, A transmits I-PDUs 3, 4, and 5. Number 4 suffers an error. B detects the error and discards the PDU. When B receives I-PDU 5, it discards this PDU because it is out of order and sends an REJ with an N(R) of 4. This causes A to initiate retransmission of all I-PDUs sent, beginning with PDU 4. It may continue to send additional PDUs after the retransmitted PDUs.

An example of error recovery using a timeout is shown in Figure 5.9e. In this example, A transmits I-PDU 3 as the last in a sequence of I-PDUs.

The PDU suffers an error. *B* detects the error and discards it. However, *B* cannot send an REJ. This is because there is no way to know if this was an I-PDU. If an error is detected in a PDU, all the bits of that PDU are suspect, and the receiver has no way to act upon it. *A*, however, started a timer as the PDU was transmitted. This timer has a duration long enough to span the expected response time. When the timer expires, *A* initiates recovery action. This is usually done by polling the other side with an RR command with the P-bit set, to determine the status of the other side. Since the poll demands a response, the entity will receive a PDU containing an N(R) field and be able to proceed. In this case, the response indicates that PDU 3 was lost, which *A* retransmits.

These examples are not exhaustive. However, they should give the reader a good feel for the behavior of LLC.

Type 3 Operation

With type 3 operation, each PDU transmitted is acknowledged. A new (not found in HDLC) unnumbered PDU, the Acknowledged Connectionless (AC) Information PDU is defined. User data are sent in AC command PDUs and must be acknowledged using an AC response PDU. To guard against lost PDUs, a 1-bit sequence number is used. The sender alternates the use of 0 and 1 in its AC command PDU, and the receiver responds with an AC PDU with the opposite number of the corresponding command. Only one PDU in each direction may be outstanding at any time.

For the DL-DATA-ACK service, the P/F bit is always set to 0. The AC command PDU contains user data and the AC response PDU does not. For the DL-REPLY service, the P/F bit is always set to 1. The AC command may or may not contain user data. The AC response contains user data if they are available; otherwise, it does not, which signals the other side that the reply has failed.

5.4

PROBLEMS

5.1 For each of the service primitive sequences of Figure 5.1, show the exchange of LLC PDUs that implements the corresponding service.

5.2 With stop-and-wait ARQ, there is a loss of time due to the discard of a PDU in error and the timeout operation. Suppose that *B* receives a damaged PDU from *A* and immediately returns a negative acknowledgment (NAK0 or NAK1), indicating that the last PDU was received in error. Could this technique be used to speed things up?

5.3 A LAN has a data rate of 4 Mbps and a propagation delay between two stations at opposite ends of 20 μs. For what range of PDU sizes does stop-and-wait give an efficiency of at least 50 percent?

5.4 Two communicating stations (A and B) use go-back-N ARQ with a 3-bit sequence number. As the ARQ mechanism, go-back-N is used with a window size of 4. Assuming that A is transmitting and B is receiving, show the window positions for the following succession of events:

a. Before A sends any PDUs

b. After A sends PDUs 0, 1, 2 and receives acknowledgment from B for 0 and 1

c. After A sends 3, 4, 5 and B acknowledges 4

5.5 In go-back-N, for a k-bit sequence number field, which provides a sequence number range of 2^k, the maximum window size is limited to $2^k - 1$. Explain why the maximum window size is not 2^k.

5.6 What parameters are essential for each of the LLC primitives in Table 5.1?

5.7 Why is there not an LLC primitive L-CONNECTION-FLOWCON-TROL.confirm?

APPENDIX 5A

SERVICE PRIMITIVES AND PARAMETERS

In a communications architecture such as the OSI model or the LAN architecture (Figure 4.1), each layer is defined in two parts: the protocol between peer (at the same level) entities in different systems and the services provided by one layer to the next-higher layer in the same system. The services between adjacent layers in the OSI architecture are expressed in terms of primitives and parameters. A primitive specifies the function to be performed, and the parameters are used to pass data and control information. The actual form of a primitive is implementation dependent. An example is a procedure call.

Four types of primitives are used in standards to define the interaction between adjacent layers in the architecture (X.210). These are defined in Table 5.4. The layout of Figure 5.10a suggests the time ordering of these events. For example, consider the transfer of a connection request from LLC user A to a peer entity B in another system. The following steps occur:

1. A invokes the services of LLC with a DL-CONNECT.request primitive. Associated with the primitive are the parameters needed, such as the destination address.

2. The LLC entity in A's system prepares an LLC PDU to be sent to its peer LLC entity in B.

3. The destination LLC entity delivers the data to *B* via a DL-CON-NECT.indication, which includes the source address and other parameters.

4. *B* issues a DL-CONNECT.response to its LLC entity.

5. *B*'s LLC entity conveys the acknowledgment to *A*'s LLC entity in a PDU.

6. The acknowledgment is delivered to *A* via a DL-CONNECT.confirm.

TABLE 5.4   **Primitive Types**

Type	Definition
X.request	A primitive issued by a service user to invoke some service and to pass the parameters needed to fully specify the requested service
X.indication	A primitive issued by a service provider to either: 1. Indicate that a procedure has been invoked by the peer service user on the connection and to provide the associated parameters, or 2. Notify the service user of a provider-initiated action
X.response	A primitive issued by a service user to acknowledge or complete some procedure previously invoked by an indication to that user
X.confirm	A primitive issued by a service provider to acknowledge or complete some procedure previously invoked by a request by the service user

This sequence of events is referred to as a **confirmed service,** as the initiator receives confirmation that the service requested has had the desired effect at the other end. If only request and indication primitives are involved (corresponding to steps 1 through 3), the service dialogue is a **nonconfirmed service;** the initiator receives no confirmation that the action requested has taken place (Figure 5.10b).

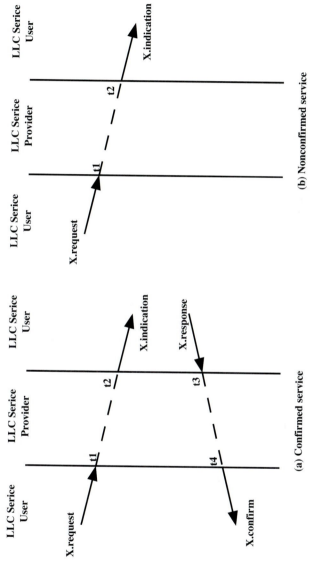

(a) Confirmed service

(b) Nonconfirmed service

FIGURE 5.10   **Relationship among LLC Service Primitives**

173

CHAPTER

6

Traditional LANs

Although there has been much interest recently in the design and implementation of high-speed LANs (in the area of 100 Mbps) and of wireless LANs, the bulk of the installed base of LANs operate at speeds of 10 Mbps or less using guided media. Of these "traditional" LANs, the most important are those that have been standardized by the IEEE 802 committee. The three standards are identified by the medium access control technique that is used:

- *Carrier-sense multiple access with collision detection* (CSMA/CD): popularized as the Ethernet product and standardized as IEEE 802.3
- *Token bus:* developed primarily for use in industrial and factory environments; standardized as IEEE 802.4
- *Token ring:* popularized as an IBM product; standardized as IEEE 802.5

6.1

CSMA/CD (ETHERNET)

The IEEE 802.3 standard is based on the Ethernet specification. The standard states that it is intended for use in commercial and light industrial environments. Use in home or heavy industrial environments, although not precluded, is not considered within the scope of the standard. The IEEE 802.3 standard, as with 802.4 and 802.5, defines both a medium access control layer and a physical layer.

IEEE 802.3 Medium Access Control

The most commonly used medium access control technique for bus/tree and star topologies is carrier-sense multiple access with collision detection (CSMA/CD). The original baseband version of this technique was developed by Xerox as part of the Ethernet LAN. The original broadband version was developed by MITRE as part of its MITREnet LAN. Before examining this technique, we look at some earlier schemes from which CSMA/CD evolved.

Precursors.   CSMA/CD and its precursors can be termed *random access*, or *contention*, techniques. They are random access in the sense that there is no predictable or scheduled time for any station to transmit; station transmissions are ordered randomly. The term *contention* is used in the sense that stations contend for time on the medium.

The earliest of these techniques, known as ALOHA, was developed for packet radio networks. However, it is applicable to any shared transmission medium. ALOHA, or pure ALOHA as it is sometimes called, is a true free-for-all. Whenever a station has a frame to send, it does so. The station then listens for an amount of time equal to the maximum possible round-trip propagation delay on the network (twice the time it takes to send a frame between the two most widely separated stations) plus a small fixed time increment. If the station hears an acknowledgment during that time, fine; otherwise, it resends the frame. If the station fails to receive an acknowledgment after repeated transmissions, it gives up. A receiving station determines the correctness of an incoming frame by examining a frame-check-sequence field, as in HDLC. If the frame is valid and if the destination address in the frame header matches the receiver's address, the station immediately sends an acknowledgment. The frame may be invalid due to noise on the channel or because another station transmitted a frame at about the same time. In the latter case, the two frames may interfere with each other at the receiver so that neither gets through; this is known as a *collision*. If a received frame is determined to be invalid, the receiving station simply ignores the frame.

ALOHA is as simple as can be and pays a penalty for it. Because the number of collisions rise rapidly with increased load, the maximum utilization of the channel is only about 18 percent (see Chapter 13). To improve efficiency, a modification of ALOHA, known as slotted ALOHA, was developed. In this scheme, time on the channel is organized into uniform slots whose size equals the frame transmission time. Some central clock or other technique is needed to synchronize all stations. Transmission is permitted to begin only at a slot boundary. Thus frames that do overlap will do so totally. This increases the maximum utilization of the system to about 37 percent.

Both ALOHA and slotted ALOHA exhibit poor utilization. Both fail to take advantage of one of the key properties of both packet radio and LANs, which is that propagation delay between stations is usually very small compared to frame transmission time. Consider the following observations. If the station-to-station propagation time is large compared to the frame transmission time, then, after a station launches a frame, it will be a long time before other stations know about it. During that time, one of the other stations may transmit a frame; the two frames may interfere with each other and neither gets through. Indeed, if the distances are great enough, many stations may begin transmitting, one after the other, and none of their frames get through unscathed. Suppose, however, that the propagation time is small compared to frame transmission time. In that case, when a station launches a frame, all the other stations know it almost immediately. So if they had any sense, they would not try transmitting until the first station was done. Collisions would be rare since they would occur only when two stations began to transmit almost simultaneously. Another way to look at it is that a short delay time provides the stations with better feedback about the state of the network; this information can be used to improve efficiency.

The foregoing observations led to the development of carrier sense multiple access (CSMA). With CSMA, a station wishing to transmit first listens to the medium to determine if another transmission is in progress (carrier sense). If the medium is in use, the station must wait. If the medium is idle, the station may transmit. It may happen that two or more stations attempt to transmit at about the same time. If this happens, there will be a collision; the data from both transmissions will be garbled and not received successfully. To account for this, a station waits for an acknowledgment a reasonable amount of time after transmitting, taking into account the maximum round-trip propagation delay and the fact that the acknowledging station must also contend for the channel in order to respond. If there is no acknowledgment, the station assumes that a collision has occurred and retransmits.

One can see how this strategy would be effective for networks in which the average frame transmission time is much longer than the propagation time. Collisions can occur only when more than one user begins transmitting with a short time (the period of the propagation delay). If a station begins to transmit a frame and there are no collisions during the time it takes for the leading edge of the packet to propagate to the farthest station, there will be no collision for this frame since all other stations are now aware of the transmission.

The maximum utilization achievable using CSMA can far exceed that of ALOHA or slotted ALOHA. The maximum utilization depends on the length of the frame and on the propagation time; the longer the frames or the shorter the propagation time, the higher the utilization. This subject is explored in Chapter 13.

With CSMA, an algorithm is needed to specify what a station should do if the medium is found busy. Three approaches are depicted in Figure 6.1. One algorithm is *nonpersistent CSMA*. A station wishing to transmit listens to the medium and obeys the following rules:

1. If the medium is idle, transmit; otherwise, go to step 2.
2. If the medium is busy, wait an amount of time drawn from a probability distribution (the retransmission delay) and repeat step 1.

The use of random delays reduces the probability of collisions. To see this, consider that two stations become ready to transmit at about the same time while another transmission is in progress; if both stations delay the same amount of time before trying again, they will both attempt to transmit at about the same time. A problem with this approach is that capacity is wasted because the medium will generally remain idle following the end of a transmission even if there are one or more stations waiting to transmit.

To avoid idle channel time, the *1-persistent protocol* can be used. A station wishing to transmit listens to the medium and obeys the following rules:

1. If the medium is idle, transmit; otherwise, go to step 2.
2. If the medium is busy, continue to listen until the channel is sensed idle; then transmit immediately.

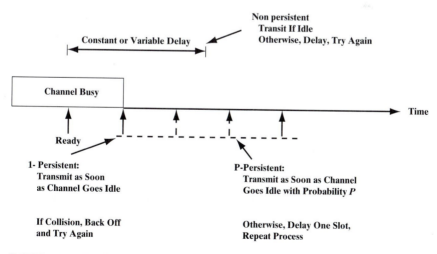

FIGURE 6.1   CSMA Persistence and Backoff

Whereas nonpersistent stations are deferential, 1-persistent stations are selfish. If two or more stations are waiting to transmit, a collision is guaranteed. Things get sorted out only after the collision.

A compromise that attempts to reduce collisions, like nonpersistent, and reduce idle time, like 1-persistent, is *p-persistent*. The rules are:

1. If the medium is idle, transmit with probability p and delay one time unit with probability $(1 - p)$. The time unit is typically equal to the maximum propagation delay.
2. If the medium is busy, continue to listen until the channel is idle and repeat step 1.
3. If transmission is delayed one time unit, repeat step 1.

The question arises as to what is an effective value of p. The main problem to avoid is one of instability under heavy load. Consider the case in which n stations have frames to send while a transmission is taking place. At the end of the transmission, the expected number of stations that will attempt to transmit is equal to the number of stations ready to transmit times the probability of transmitting, or np. If np is greater than 1, on average multiple stations will attempt to transmit and there will be a collision. What is more, as soon as all these stations realize that there transmission suffered a collision, they will be back again, almost guaranteeing more collisions. Worse yet, these retries will compete with new transmissions from other stations, further increasing the probability of collision. Eventually, all stations will be trying to send, causing continuous collisions, with throughput dropping to zero. To avoid this catastrophe, np must be less than 1 for the expected peaks of n; therefore, if a heavy load is expected to occur with some regularity, p must be small. However, as p is made smaller, stations must wait longer to attempt transmission. At low loads, this can result in very long delays. For example, if only a single station desires to transmit, the expected number of iterations of step 1, above, is $1/p$ (see Problem 6.6). Thus, if $p = 0.1$, at low load, a station will wait an average of 9 time units before transmitting on an idle line!

Description of CSMA/CD.   Although more efficient than ALOHA or slotted ALOHA, CSMA still has one glaring inefficiency. When two frames collide, the medium remains unusable for the duration of transmission of both damaged frames. For long frames, compared to propagation time, the amount of wasted capacity can be considerable. This waste can be reduced if a station continues to listen to the medium while transmitting. This leads to the following rules for CSMA/CD:

1. If the medium is idle, transmit; otherwise, go to step 2.
2. If the medium is busy, continue to listen until the channel is idle, then transmit immediately.

3. If a collision is detected during transmission, transmit a brief jamming signal to assure that all stations know that there has been a collision and then cease transmission.

4. After transmitting the jamming signal, wait a random amount of time, then attempt to transmit again (repeat from step 1).

Figure 6.2 illustrates the technique for a baseband bus. At time t_0, station A begins transmitting a packet addressed to D. At t_1, both B and C are ready to transmit. B senses a transmission and so defers. C, however, is still unaware of A's transmission and begins its own transmission. When A's

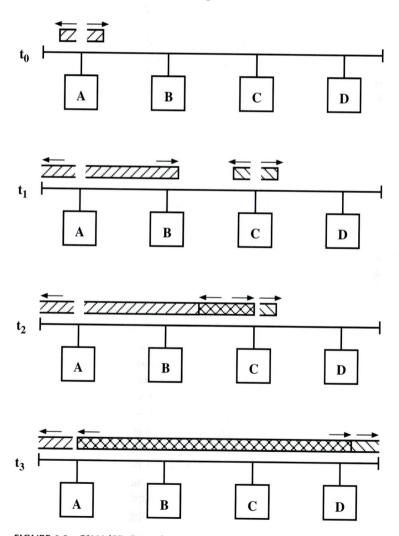

FIGURE 6.2   CSMA/CD Operation

transmission reaches C, at t_2, C detects the collision and ceases transmission. The effect of the collision propagates back to A, where it is detected some time later, t_3, at which time A ceases transmission.

With CSMA/CD, the amount of wasted capacity is reduced to the time it takes to detect a collision. Question: How long does that take? Let us consider first the case of a baseband bus and consider two stations as far apart as possible. For example, in Figure 6.2, suppose that station A begins a transmission and that just before that transmission reaches D, D is ready to transmit. Since D is not yet aware of A's transmission, it begins to transmit. A collision occurs almost immediately and is recognized by D. However, the collision must propagate all the way back to A before A is aware of the collision. By this line of reasoning, we conclude that the amount of time that it takes to detect a collision is no greater than twice the end-to-end propagation delay. For a broadband bus, the delay is even longer. Figure 6.3 shows a dual-cable system. This time, the worst case occurs for two stations as close together as possible and as far as possible from the headend. In this case, the maximum time to detect a collision is four times the propagation delay from an end of the cable to the headend.

An important rule followed in most CSMA/CD systems, including the IEEE standard, is that frames should be long enough to allow collision detection prior to the end of transmission. If shorter frames are used, collision detection does not occur, and CSMA/CD exhibits the same performance as that of the less efficient CSMA protocol.

Now let us look at a few details of CSMA/CD. First, which persistence algorithm should we use: non-, 1-, or p-? You may be surprised to learn that the most common choice is 1-persistent. It is used by Ethernet and in the IEEE 802 standard. Recall that both nonpersistent and p-persistent have performance problems. In the nonpersistent case, capacity is wasted because the medium will generally remain idle following the end of a transmission even if there are stations waiting to send. In the p-persistent case, p must be set low enough to avoid instability, with the result of sometimes atrocious delays under light load. The 1-persistent algorithm, which means, after all, that $p = 1$, would seem to be even more unstable than p-persistent due to the greed of the stations. What saves the day is that the wasted time due to collisions is mercifully short (if the frames are long relative to propagation delay!), and with random backoff, the two stations involved in a collision are unlikely to collide on their next tries. To ensure that backoff maintains stability, IEEE 802 and Ethernet use a technique known as binary exponential backoff. A station will attempt to transmit repeatedly in the face of repeated collisions, but after each collision, the mean value of the random delay is doubled. After 16 unsuccessful attempts, the station gives up and reports an error.

The beauty of the 1-persistent algorithm with binary exponential backoff is that it is efficient over a wide range of loads. At low loads, 1-persistence

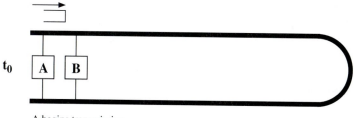

t_0

A begins transmission.

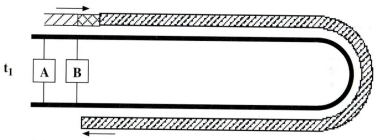

t_1

B begins transmission just before leading edge of A's packet arrives at B's receiver
B almost immediately detects A's transmission and ceases its own transmission.

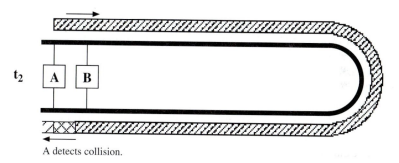

t_2

A detects collision.

FIGURE 6.3   Broadband Collision Detection Timing

guarantees that a station can seize the channel as soon as it goes idle, in contrast to the non- and p-persistent schemes. At high loads, it is at least as stable as the other techniques. However, one unfortunate effect of the backoff algorithm is that it has a last-in, first-out effect; stations with no or few collisions will have a chance to transmit before stations that have waited longer.

Although the implementation of CSMA/CD is substantially the same for baseband and broadband, there are differences. One example is the means for performing carrier sense. For baseband systems using Manchester encoding, carrier is conveniently sensed by detecting the presence of transitions on the channel. Strictly speaking, there is no carrier to sense digital signaling; the term was borrowed from the radio lexicon. With broadband, carrier sense is indeed performed. The station's receiver listens for the presence of a carrier on the outbound channel.

Collision detection also differs for the two systems. In a baseband system, a collision should produce substantially higher voltage swings than those produced by a single transmitter. Accordingly, Ethernet and the IEEE standard dictate that a transmitting transceiver will detect a collision if the signal on the cable at the transceiver exceeds the maximum that could be produced by the transceiver alone. Because a transmitted signal attenuates as it propagates, there is a potential problem with collision detection. If two stations far apart are transmitting, each station will receive a greatly attenuated signal from the other. The signal strength could be so small that when it is added to the transmitted signal at the transceiver, the combined signal does not exceed the CD threshold. For this reason, among others, IEEE 802 restricts the maximum length of cable to 500 meters. Because frames may cross repeater boundaries, collisions must cross as well. Hence if a repeater detects a collision on either cable, it must transmit a jamming signal on the other side. Since the collision may not involve a transmission from the repeater, the CD threshold is different for a nontransmitting transceiver: a collision is detected if the signal strength exceeds that which could be produced by two transceiver outputs in the worst case.

A much simpler collision detection scheme is possible with the twisted-pair star-wiring approach (Figure 3.16). In this case, collision detection is based on logic rather than sensing voltage magnitudes. For any hub, if there is activity (signal) on more than one input, a collision is assumed. A special signal called the *collision presence* signal is generated. This signal is generated and sent out as long as activity is sensed on any of the input lines. This signal is interpreted by every node as an occurrence of collision. Figure 6.4 gives examples of the operation of a star-wired system with and without collisions. In the first example, a frame transmitted from station *A* propagates up to HHUB and is eventually received by all stations in the network. In the second example, a collision is detected by *A*'s IHUB. The collision presence signal propagates up to HHUB and is rebroadcast down to all hubs and stations. The third example shows the result of a three-way collision.

There are several possible approaches to collision detection in broadband systems. The most common of these is to perform a bit-by-bit comparison between transmitted and received data. When a station transmits on the inbound channel, it begins to receive its own transmission on the outbound channel after a propagation delay to the headend and back. In the IEEE 802.3 specification, the bits up through the last bit of the source address field of the transmitted and received signals are compared, and a

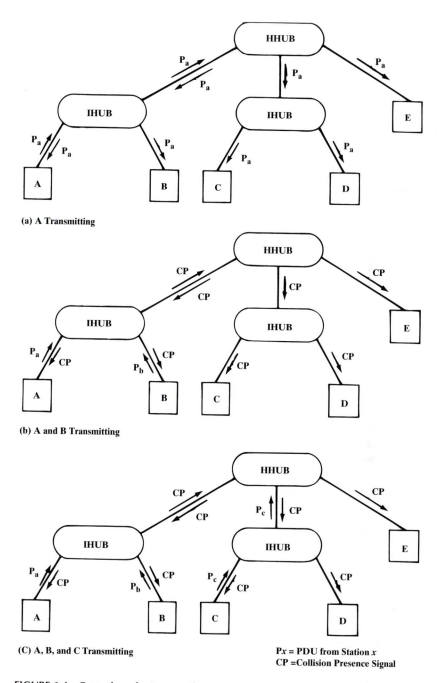

(a) A Transmitting

(b) A and B Transmitting

(C) A, B, and C Transmitting

Px = PDU from Station x
CP =Collision Presence Signal

FIGURE 6.4   Operation of a Two-Level Star-Wired CSMA/CD Configuration

collision is assumed if they differ. There are several problems with this approach. The most serious is the danger that differences in signal level between colliding signals will cause the receiver to treat the weaker signal as noise and fail to detect a collision. The cable system, with its taps, splitters, and amplifiers, must be carefully tuned so that attenuation effects and differences in transmitter signal strength do not cause this problem. Another problem for dual-cable systems is that a station must simultaneously transmit and receive on the same frequency. Its two RF modems must be carefully shielded to prevent crosstalk.

An alternative approach for broadband is to perform the CD function at the headend. This is most appropriate for the split system, which has an active component at the headend anyway. This reduces the tuning problem to one of making sure that all stations produce approximately the same signal level at the headend. The headend would detect collisions by looking for garbled data or higher-than-expected signal strength.

MAC Frame.   Figure 6.5 depicts the frame format for the 802.3 protocol. It consists of the following fields:

- *Preamble:* a 7-octet pattern of alternating zeros and ones used by the receiver to establish bit synchronization.
- *Start frame delimiter:* the sequence 10101011, which indicates the actual start of the frame and enables the receiver to locate the first bit of the rest of the frame.
- *Destination address (DA):* specifies the station(s) for which the frame is intended. It may be a unique physical address, a group address, or a global address. The choice of 16- or 48-bit address length is an implementation decision and must be the same for all stations on a particular LAN.
- *Source address (SA):* specifies the station that sent the frame.
- *Length:* length of LLC data field.
- *LLC data:* data unit supplied by LLC.
- *Pad:* octets added to ensure that the frame is long enough for proper CD operation.
- *Frame check sequence (FCS):* a 32-bit cyclic redundancy check, based on all fields except preamble, SFD, and FCS.

IEEE 802.3 Physical Layer Specifications

The IEEE 802.3 committee has been the most active in defining alternative physical configurations. This is both good and bad. On the good side, the standard has been responsive to evolving technology. On the bad side, the customer, not to mention the potential vendor, is faced with a bewildering

Octets	7	1	2 or 6	2 or 6	2	≥ 0	≥ 0	4
	Preamble	SFD	DA	SA	Length	LLC data	Pad	FCS

SFD = start frame delimiter
DA = destination address
SA = source address
FCS = frame check sequence

FIGURE 6.5   IEEE 802.3 Frame Format

array of options. However, the committee has been at pains to ensure that the various options can be easily integrated into a configuration that satisfies a variety of needs. Thus the user that has a complex set of requirements may find the flexibility and variety of the 802.3 standard to be an asset.

To distinguish the various implementations that are available, the committee has developed a concise notation:

<data rate in Mbps><signaling method><maximum segment length in hundreds of meters>

The defined alternatives are[1]:

- 10BASE5
- 10BASE2
- 10BASE-T
- 10BROAD36
- 10BASE-F

Note that 10BASE-T and 10-BASE-F do not quite follow the notation: "T" stands for twisted pair and "F" stands for optical fiber. Table 6.1 summarizes these options. In addition to these alternatives, there are several versions that operate at 100 Mbps; these are covered in Chapter 7. We examine each of these in turn.

Medium Access Unit.   The IEEE 802.3 standard anticipates that it may be desirable to locate stations some distance from their actual attachment point to the medium. A common configuration would place a minimum of electronics at the point of attachment to the medium, and the bulk of the hardware and software at the station. That portion that is colocated with the tap is referred to in the standard as the **medium attachment unit** (MAU).

The specification assumes that the MAU performs the following functions:

- Transmit signals on the medium
- Receive signals from the medium

[1]There is also a 1BASE-T alternative that defines a 1-Mbps twisted-pair system using a star topology. This is considered obsolete, although it is contained in the most recent version of the standard.

TABLE 6.1   IEEE 802.3 10-Mbps Physical Layer Medium Alternatives

	10BASE5	10BASE2	10BASE-T	10BROAD36	10BASE-FP
Transmission medium	Coaxial cable (50 ohm)	Coaxial cable (50 ohm)	Unshielded twisted pair	Coaxial cable (75 ohm)	850-nm optical fiber pair
Signaling technique	Baseband (Manchester)	Baseband (Manchester)	Baseband (Manchester)	Broadband (DPSK)	Manchester/on–off
Topology	Bus	Bus	Star	Bus/tree	Star
Maximum segment length (m)	500	185	100	1800	500
Nodes per segment	100	30	—	—	33
Cable diameter (mm)	10	5	0.4–0.6	0.4–1.0	62.5/125 µm

- Recognize the presence of a signal on the medium
- Recognize a collision

When the MAU is not physically integrated with the remainder of the 802.3 logic, the two are joined by a set of twisted-pair cables referred to as the **attachment unit interface** (AUI). There is one twisted pair for transmission in each direction, and several pairs for control signals.

10BASE5 Medium Specification.   10BASE5 is the original 802.3 medium specification (the only one included in the original 1985 IEEE/ANSI standard) and is based on Ethernet. 10BASE5 specifies the use of 50-ohm coaxial cable. This is a special-purpose coaxial cable that is generally used for baseband bus LANs in preference to the more common CATV 75-ohm cable. For digital signals, the 50-ohm cable suffers less intense reflections from the insertion capacitance of the taps and provides better immunity against low-frequency noise.

The data rate for 10BASE5 is 10 Mbps, using Manchester digital signaling.[2] With these parameters, the maximum length of a cable segment is set at 500 meters. The length of the network can be extended by the use of repeaters. In essence, a repeater consists of two MAUs joined together and connected to two different segments of cable. A repeater passes digital signals in both directions between the two segments that it connects, amplifying and regenerating the signals as they pass through. A repeater is transparent to the MAC level; as it does no buffering, it does not isolate one segment from another. So, for example, if two stations on different segments attempt to transmit at the same time, their transmissions will collide. To avoid looping, only one path of segments and repeaters is allowed between any two stations. The standard allows a maximum of four repeaters in the path between any two stations, extending the effective length of the medium to 2.5 km. Figure 3.5 is an example of a LAN with three segments and two repeaters.

In a baseband system, a collision should produce substantially higher voltage swings than those produced by a single transmitter. Accordingly, the standard specifies that a transmitting MAU will detect a collision if the signal on the cable exceeds the maximum that could be produced by the transmitter alone.

10BASE2 Medium Specification.   To provide a lower-cost system than 10BASE5 for personal computer LANs, 10BASE2 was added. As with 10BASE5, this specification uses 50-ohm coaxial cable and Manchester signaling at a data rate of 10 Mbps. The key difference is that 10BASE2 uses a thinner cable. This cable, which is used in products such as public address

---

[2]See Chapter 2 for a discussion of digital signaling.

systems, is more flexible. This makes it easier to bend around corners and bring to a workstation cabinet rather than installing the cable in the wall and having to provide a drop cable to the station.

The use of thinner cable results in costs savings in two ways. First, the thinner cable is cheaper. Second, the electronics is simpler since there is no need for transmitters and receivers between the station and the cable across a drop cable. That is, the MAU is integrated with the station, and there is no attachment unit interface. On the other hand, the thinner cable supports fewer taps over a shorter distance than the 10BASE5 cable.

Because they have the same data rate, it is possible to mix 10BASE5 and 10BASE2 segments in the same network by using a repeater that conforms to 10BASE5 on one side and 10BASE2 on the other side. The only restriction is that a 10BASE2 segment should not be used to bridge two 10BASE5 segments because a "backbone" segment should be as resistant to noise as the segments it connects.

10BASE-T Medium Specification.   By sacrificing some distance, it is possible to develop a 10-Mbps LAN using the unshielded twisted-pair medium. Such wire is often found prewired in office buildings as excess telephone cable and can be used for LANs. Such an approach is specified in the latest physical medium addition to the 802.3 family, the 10BASE-T specification.

The 10BASE-T specification defines a star-shaped topology. A simple system consists of a number of stations connected to a central point, referred to as a multiport repeater, via two twisted pairs. The central point accepts input on any one line and repeats it on all of the other lines.

Stations attach to the multiport repeater via a point-to-point link. Ordinarily, the link consists of two unshielded twisted pairs. The data rate is 10 Mbps using Manchester encoding. Because of the high data rate and the poor transmission qualities of unshielded twisted pair, the length of a link is limited to 100 meters. As an alternative, an optical fiber link may be used. In this case, the maximum length is 500 meters.

Figure 6.6 shows a sample configuration for 10BASE-T. Note that the connection between one repeater and the next is a link that appears the same as an ordinary station link. In fact, the repeater makes no distinction between a station and another repeater. All multiport repeaters function in the same manner, and indeed function in the same manner as an ordinary repeater on a 10BASE5 or 10BASE2 system:

- A valid signal appearing on any input is repeated on all other links.
- If two inputs occur, causing a collision, a collision enforcement signal is transmitted on all links.
- If a collision enforcement signal is detected on any input, it is repeated on all other links.

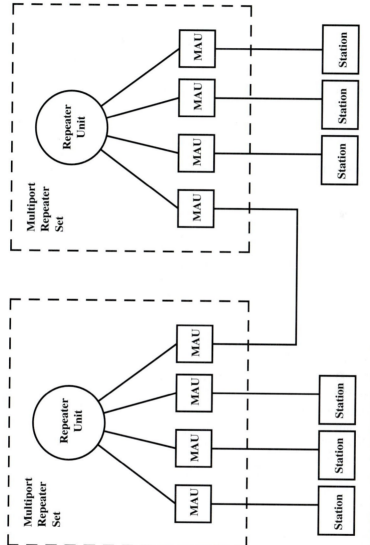

FIGURE 6.6   Simple 10BASE-T Configuration

189

One advantage of the use of repeaters and the use of a data rate of 10 Mbps is that the 10BASE-T system can be mixed with 10BASE2 and 10BASE5 systems. All that is required is that the medium access unit (MAU) conform to the appropriate specification. Figure 6.7 shows a configuration that containing four 10BASE-T systems and one 10BASE5 system.

Table 6.2 summarizes the allowable connections. The maximum transmission path permitted between any two stations is five segments and four repeater sets. A segment is either a point-to-point link segment, or a coaxial cable 10BASE5 or 10BASE2 segment. The maximum number of coaxial cable segments in a path is three.

10BROAD36 Medium Specification.   The 10BROAD36 specification is the only 802.3 specification for broadband. The medium employed is the standard 75-ohm CATV coaxial cable. Either a dual- or split-cable configuration is allowed. The maximum length of an individual segment, emanating from the headend, is 1800 meters; this results in a maximum end-to-end span of 3600 meters. A data rate of 10 Mbps is provided.

Before each MAC frame is transmitted, it goes through a scrambling algorithm.[3] This gives the data a pseudorandom nature that helps the receiver extract bit-timing information. It also improves the spectral characteristics of the signal, giving it a more uniform power distribution, as opposed to the potentially strong discrete spectral lines in nonscrambled data. The scrambled data are then modulated onto an analog carrier using differential phase-shift keying (DPSK). In ordinary PSK, a binary zero is represented by a carrier with a particular phase, and a binary one is represented by a carrier with the opposite phase (180° difference). DPSK makes use of differential encoding, in which a change of phase occurs when a zero occurs, and there is no change of phase when a one occurs. The advantage of differential encoding is that it is easier for the receiver to detect a change in phase than to determine the phase itself. The characteristics of the modulation process are specified so that the resulting 10 Mbps signal fits into a 14-MHz bandwidth.

For broadband collision detection, we can take advantage of the fact that there is a delay between a station's transmission and its reception of its own transmission. In essence, the station does a bit-by-bit comparison of the transmitted and received scrambled bits up through the last bit of the source address. A mismatch indicates a collision.

A station detecting a collision generates a constant-amplitude signal, known as the **collision enforcement signal,** on a dedicated band to notify all stations on the network. This collision enforcement is necessary because signals from different stations on the broadband cable system may be received at different power levels. As an example of the problem, consider

[3]Scrambling is discussed in Appendix 3C.

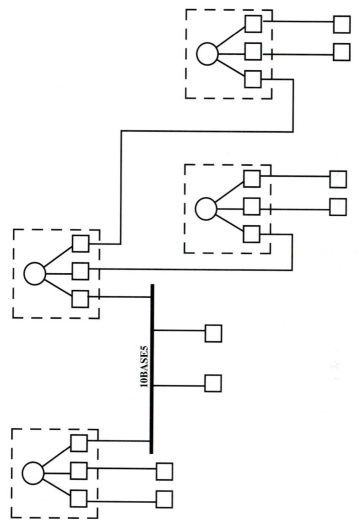

10BASE5

FIGURE 6.7   Mixed 10BASE-T and 10BASE5 Configuration

TABLE 6.2   Allowable Connections to a 10BASE-T Multiport Repeater

Transmission Medium	Number of Attached Devices	Maximum Length (m)
Two unshielded twisted pairs	2	100
Two optical fiber cables	2	500
Coaxial cable		
10BASE5	30	185
10BASE2	100	500

that *A* and *B* are transmitting and that *A*'s signals are received by both *A* and *B* at a significantly higher power levels than *B*'s signals. At both modems, the frame from *A* is demodulated error free; the overlapping signal from *B* appears as a small amount of noise. *A* does not detect the collision and therefore assumes that its frame reached the destination. *B* detects the collision by means of the bit-by-bit comparison and uses the collision enforcement signal to notify *A*.

Each 14-MHz data channel is provided with a dedicated 4-MHz collision enforcement channel. Thus, on a dual-cable system, each channel requires 18 MHz, and on a split-cable system, each channel requires 36 MHz.

10BASE-F Medium Specification.   The 10BASE-F specification was added to IEEE 802.3 in 1993 to enable users to take advantage of the distance and transmission characteristics available with the use of optical fiber. The standard actually contains three specifications:

- *10-BASE-FP (passive):* a passive-star topology for interconnecting stations and repeaters with up to 1 km per segment
- *10-BASE-FL (link):* defines a point-to-point link that can be used to connect stations or repeaters at up to 2 km
- *10-BASE-FB (backbone):* defines a point-to-point link that can be used to connect repeaters at up to 2 km

All three of these specifications make use of a pair of optical fibers for each transmission link, one for transmission in each direction. In all cases, the signaling scheme involves the use of Manchester encoding. Each Manchester signal element is then converted to an optical signal element, with the presence of light corresponding to high and the absence of light corresponding to low. Thus a 10-Mbps Manchester bit stream actually requires 20 Mbps on the fiber.

The 10-BASE-FP defines a passive-star system that can support up to 33 stations attached to a central passive star, of the type described in Chapter 3. 10-BASE-FL and 10-BASE-FP define point-to-point connections that can be used to extend the length of a network. The key difference between the two is that 10-BASE-FP makes use of synchronous retransmission. With synchronous signaling, an optical signal coming into a repeater is retimed with a local clock and retransmitted. With conventional asynchronous signaling, used with 10-BASE-FL, no such retiming takes place, so that any timing distortions are propagated through a series of repeaters. As a result, 10BASE-FB can be used to cascade up to 15 repeaters in sequence to achieve greater length.

6.2

TOKEN BUS

The IEEE 802.4 standard is designed to be applicable not only in office environments but also in factory and other industrial environments and in military environments. The standard makes use of the bus and tree topologies.

IEEE 802.4 Medium Access Control

The medium access control protocol for IEEE 802.4 is token bus. We first look at the basic token-bus MAC protocol, then at the optional priority mechanism that may be included with the protocol. This is followed by a description of the IEEE 802.4 MAC frame.

MAC Protocol.   For token bus, the stations on the bus or tree form a logical ring; that is, the stations are assigned logical positions in an ordered sequence, with the last member of the sequence followed by the first. Each station knows the identity of the station preceding and following it. The physical ordering of the stations on the bus is irrelevant and independent of the logical ordering.

A control frame known as the **token** regulates the right of access. The token contains a destination address. The station possessing the token is granted control of the medium for a specified time. The station may transmit one or more frames and may poll stations and receive responses. When the station is finished, or time has expired, it passes the token on to the next station in logical sequence. This station now has permission to transmit. Hence normal operation consists of alternating data transfer and token transfer phases. In addition, non-token-using stations are allowed on the bus. These stations can only respond to polls or requests for acknowledgment. The ring is created and maintained in such a way that the stations are linked in numerically descending order of station address, except that the station with the lowest address passes the token to the station with the highest address in the logical ring.

Figure 6.8 gives an example.[4] At any given time, a certain number of stations are active on the network and may receive frames. A certain number of these stations are part of the logical ring. The ordering within the logical ring is as follows: Each participating station knows the address of its predecessor (the station from which it receives the token), referred to as the *previous station* (PS). It knows its successor (the station to which it sends the token), referred to as the *next station* (NS). The PS and NS addresses are determined dynamically to maintain a single logical ring, in a manner described later in this section. The logical ring is created and maintained in such a way that the stations are logically ordered in numerically descending order of MAC address, except that the station with the lowest address is followed by the station with the highest address. In this example, stations 60, 50, 30, and 10, in that order, are part of the logical ring. Station 60 will pass the token to station 50, which passes it to station 30, which passes to station 10, which passes the token to station 60.

Figure 6.9 shows a portion of the operation of this configuration. At t_0, station 10 passes the token. Since the current ordering dictates that the next station in logical sequence is station 60, the destination address portion of the token transmitted by station 10 is 60. The token is seen by all of the other stations on the LAN, but it is ignored by all but station 60, whose address matches that in the token (t_1). Once station 60 has received the token, it is free to transmit a data frame. In this example it transmits a data frame addressed to station 20 (t_2). Note that station 20 need not be part of the logical ring to receive frames. However, it cannot initiate any transmissions of its own. Once station 60 has completed its data transmission, it issues a token addressed to the next station on the logical ring, in this case station 50 (t_3).

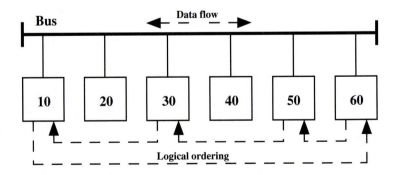

FIGURE 6.8   Token Bus Configuration

[4]The figure shows the numerical addresses in physical order on the bus; this is not required in the standard.

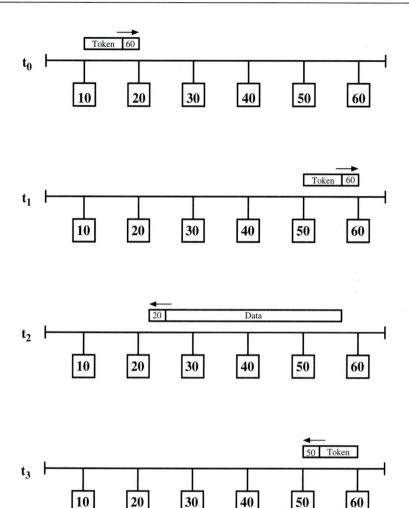

FIGURE 6.9   Token Bus Operation

This scheme requires considerable maintenance. These functions, at a minimum, must be performed by one or more stations:

- *Addition to ring.* Periodically, nonparticipating stations must be granted the opportunity to join the logical ring.
- *Deletion from ring.* A station can remove itself from the logical ring.
- *Ring initialization.* When the network is started, some cooperative procedure is needed to sort out who goes first, who goes second, and so on.
- *Token recovery.* If the token is lost due to a transmission error or station failure, some means of recovery is needed.

In the remainder of this subsection the approach taken for these functions in the 802.4 standard is described briefly.

To accomplish **addition to ring,** each station in the logical ring has the responsibility, periodically of granting an opportunity for new station to enter the ring. There are two variations on this process, depending on a station's position in the logical ring. First, consider a station other than the one with the lowest address (e.g., any station other than 10 in Figure 6.8). While holding the token, the station issues a *solicit-successor* frame, inviting stations with an address between itself and the next station in logical sequence to demand entrance. The transmitting station then waits for one response window (equal to twice the end-to-end propagation delay of the medium). One of four events can occur:

1. *No response.* The station passes the token to its successor as usual.
2. *One response.* One station issues a *set-successor* frame. The token holder sets its successor station to be the responding station and transmits the token to it; the requester sets its linkages accordingly and proceeds.
3. *Multiple responses.* If more than one station demands to enter the ring, the token holder will detect a garbled response. This conflict is resolved by an address-based contention scheme. The token holder transmits a *resolve-contention* frame and waits four response windows. Each demander can respond in one of these windows based on the first 2 bits of its address. If a demander hears anything before its window comes up, it refrains from demanding. If the token holder receives a valid set-successor frame, it proceeds as in step 2. Otherwise, it tries again, and only those stations that responded the first time are allowed to respond this time, based on the second pair of bits in their address. This process continues until a valid set-successor frame is received, no response is received, or the end of the address bits is reached. In the latter two cases, the token holder gives up and passes the token.
4. *Invalid response.* If the token holder receives a frame other than a set successor, it assumes that some other station thinks it holds the token. To avoid conflict, the station reverts to a listen state.

Now consider the case of the station in the logical ring with the lowest address (e.g., station 10 in Figure 6.8). In this case the procedure begins with the station sending a *solicit-successor-2* frame and waiting two response windows. Stations with an address less than that of the token holder may respond with a set-successor frame in the first response window. A station with an address greater than that of the token holder's current successor must wait for one response window. If it hears nothing, it may respond; otherwise, it may not respond to this invitation. The remainder of the procedure follows the sequence listed above.

Deletion of a station is a much simpler process than addition. If a station wishes to drop out of the logical ring, it waits until it receives the token and then sends a set-successor frame to its predecessor containing the address of its successor. This causes the predecessor station to update its NS variable. The token holder then sends the token as usual to its successor. On the next token rotation, the former predecessor of the exited station sends the token to the former successor of the exited station. Every time that a station receives a token, it updates its PS variable to equal the MAC address of the sending station. Thus the exited station is spliced out of the logical ring. For example, in Figure 6.8, station 50 can exit the ring by sending a set-successor frame to station 60 with an address of 30. The next time that station 60 gets the token, it will pass it on to station 30.

If a LAN has just been activated, or if the token has been lost, there will be no activity since there is no token. When one or more stations detect a lack of activity of duration longer than a timeout value, **ring initialization** is triggered. A detecting station will issue a *claim-token* frame. Contending claimants are resolved as follows. Any station issuing a claim-token frame pads the data field to be 0, 2, 4, or 6 times the length that would be transmitted in one response window, based on the first 2 bits of its address. After transmitting, a claimant listens to the medium and if it hears anything, drops its claim (some other station has transmitted a longer claim-token frame). Otherwise, it tries again, using the second pair of its address bits. When all address bits have been used, a station that succeeds on the last iteration considers itself the token holder. The ring can now be rebuilt by the station addition process described earlier.

The need for **token recovery** occurs in a number of circumstances, listed in Table 6.3. First, the token itself may be lost or damaged; in that case the logical ring initialization procedure discussed earlier is triggered. Next, while holding the token, a node may hear a frame indicating that another node has the token. If so, it immediately drops the token and reverts to the listener mode. In this way the number of token holders immediately drops to 1 or 0, thus overcoming the multiple-token problem. Finally, the need for token recovery may occur during the token-passing process. When the current token holder *(A)* issues a token frame, its successor *(B)* should, upon

TABLE 6.3 Token Bus Error Handling

Condition	Action
No token	Initialize after timeout
Multiple tokens	Defer/drop to 1 or 0 tokens
Unaccepted token	Retry
Failed station	*who-follows* procedure
Failed receiver	Drop out of ring

receipt, immediately issue a data or token frame. Therefore, after sending a token, *A* will listen for one slot time to make sure that its successor is active. The following sequence of events occurs:

1. If *B* is active, *A* will hear a valid frame and revert to listener mode.
2. If *A* does not hear a valid frame, it reissues the token to *B* a second time.
3. If *A* still does not hear a valid frame after two tries, it assumes that *B* has failed and issues a *who-follows* frame asking for the identity of the station that follows *B*. *A* should get back a set-successor frame from *B*'s successor. If so, *A* updates its NS variable and issues a token (back to step 1).
4. If *A* gets no response to its who-follows frame, it tries a second time.
5. If *A* gets no response to its second who-follows frame, it issues a solicit-successor frame with the full address range (every station is invited to respond). If this process succeeds, a two-station ring is established.
6. If two attempts of step 5 fail, *A* assumes that some major fault has occurred (e.g., all other stations have left the logical ring, the medium has failed, or *A*'s own receiver has failed). At this point, if *A* has any more data to send, it sends those data and tries passing the token again. It then ceases transmission and listens to the bus.

Token Bus Priority. As an option, 802.4 allows for the use of *classes of service* that provide a mechanism of prioritizing access to the bus. Four classes of service are defined, in descending order of priority: 6, 4, 2, 0. Any station may have data to send in one or more of these classes. The object is to allocate bus capacity to the higher-priority frames and only send lower-priority frames when there is sufficient capacity. To explain the algorithm, let us define the following variables:

THT = token holding time; the maximum time that a station can
         hold the token to transmit class 6 data

$\text{TRT}i$ = token rotation time for class i ($i = 4, 2, 0$); the maximum time
        that a token can take to circulate and still permit class i
        transmission

When a station receives the token, it can transmit classes of data according to the following rules (Figure 6.10). First, the station may transmit class 6 data for a time THT. Hence for an *N*-station ring, during one circulation of the token, the maximum amount of time available for class 6 transmission is $N \times$ THT. Next, after transmitting class 6 data, or if there were no class 6 data to transmit, the station may transmit class 4 data only if the amount of time for the last circulation of the token (including any class 6 data just sent) is less than TRT4. Class 2 and class 0 data are then handled in the same way as class 4.

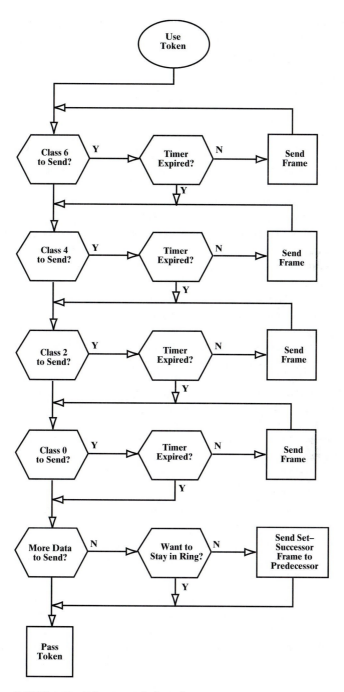

FIGURE 6.10   Token Bus Priority Scheme

This scheme, within limits, gives preference to frames of higher priority. Specifically, it guarantees that class 6 data may have a certain portion of the capacity, with any excess capacity utilized for classes 4, 2, and 0 in descending order of preference. Two cases are possible. If $N \times$ THT is greater than MAX[TRT4, TRT2, TRT0], the maximum possible token circulation time is $N \times$ THT, and class 6 data may occupy the entire cycle to the exclusion of the other classes. If $N \times$ THT is less than MAX[TRT4, TRT2, TRT0], the maximum circulation time is MAX[TRT4, TRT2, TRT0], and class 6 data are guaranteed $N \times$ THT amount of that time. This analysis ignores the time it takes to transmit the token and any other overhead, such as the reaction time at a station upon receipt of a token. However, these overhead quantities will generally be small compared to data transmission time.

Figure 6.11, which is adapted from one in[JAYA87] , illustrates the average behavior of the 802.4 capacity-allocation scheme. That is, the plots ignore temporary load fluctuations, instead depicting the steady-state performance. For convenience, we assume that TRT4 > TRT2 > TRT0 and that the load generated in each class of data is the same.

Figure 6.11a depicts the first case ($N \times$ THT > TRT4). At very low loads, the token circulation time is very short, and all of the data offered in all four classes are transmitted. As the load increases, the average token circulation time reaches TRT0. There is then a range, as indicated in the figure, in which the load continues to increase but the token circulation time remains at TRT0. In this range, the other classes of data increase their throughput at the expense of class 0 data, whose throughput declines. At some point, the load is such that the token circulation time equals TRT0, but

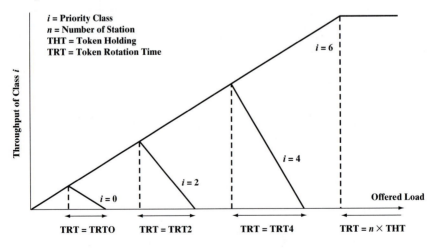

(a) Case I : $n \times$ THT > TRT4

FIGURE 6.11   Throughput of Token Bus Priority Classes

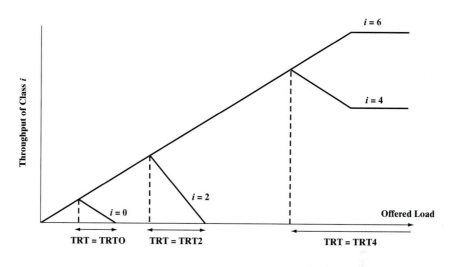

(b) Case IIa: (TRT4/2) < n × THT < TRT4

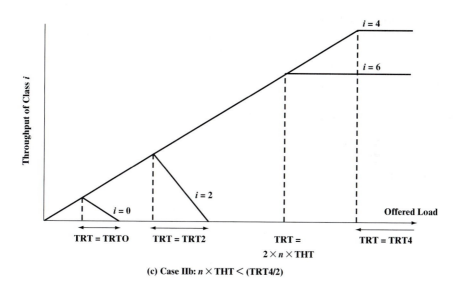

(c) Case IIb: n × THT < (TRT4/2)

FIGURE 6.11   (Cont.)

the amount of transmission in classes 2, 4, and 6 uses up all of that time and no class 0 data can be transmitted. Further increase in offered load results in renewed increase in the token circulation time. The same pattern repeats for class 2 and class 4 data. There is a period when the load increases at a constant token circulation time of TRT2, and during that period, class 2 data is gradually crowded out. Class 4 data are similarly crowded out at a higher level of load. Finally, a situation is reached in which only class 6 data are being transmitted, and the token circulation time stabilizes at $N \times$ THT.

For the second case just mentioned ($N \times$ THT < TRT4), we need to examine two subcases. Figure 6.11b shows the case in which (TRT4/2) < ($N \times$ THT) < TRT4. As before, with increasing load, class 0 and class 2 traffic are eliminated and the token circulation time increases. At some point the increasing load drives the token circulation time to TRT4. Using our simple example, when this point is reached, approximately half of the load is class 4 data and the other half is class 6. But since $N \times$ THT > TRT4/2, if the load on the network continues to increase, the portion of the load that is class 6 traffic will also increase. This will cause a corresponding decrease in class 4 traffic. Eventually, a point is reached at which all of the allowable class 6 traffic is being handled during each token circulation. This will take an amount of time $N \times$ THT and still leave some time left over for class 4 data. Thereafter, the total token circulation time remains stable at TRT4.

Finally, Figure 6.11c shows the case in which $N \times$ THT < TRT4/2. As before, increasing load eliminates class 0 and class 2 traffic. A point is reached at which the token circulation time is $2 \times N \times$ THT, with half of the traffic being class 4 and half being class 6. This is a maximum throughput-per-token circulation for class 6. However, the amount of class 4 data can continue to increase until the token circulation time is TRT4.

Figure 6.12 is a simplified example of a four-station logical ring with THT = 610 and TRT4 = TRT2 = TRT0 = 1600. Time is measured in *octet times*. Station 9 always transmits three class 6 frames of 128 octets each. Stations 7 and 5 send as many lower-priority frames as possible, of lengths 400 and 356 octets, respectively. Station 1 transmits class 6 frames of 305 octets each. Initially, station 1 has two frames to transmit each time it gets the token, and later has only one frame to send per token possession. We assume that the time to pass the token is 19 octet times. In the figure, there are two columns of numbers under each station. The value in the left-hand column is the token circulation time observed at that station for the previous rotation of the token. The right-hand value is the number of frames that station transmits. Each row represents one rotation of the token.

The example begins after a period during which no data frames have been sent, so that the token has been rotating as rapidly as possible; thus each station measures a token circulation time of 76. In the first rotation, station 9 transmits all of its class 6 frames. When station 7 receives the token, it measures a rotation time of 460 since it last received the token (3×128) + (4×19). Thus it is able to send three of its frames before its TRT is exhausted. Station 5 measures a rotation time of 1660 (3×400) + (3×128) + (4×19) and thus is prevented from sending any data. Finally, station 1 sends two class 6 frames.

Note that rotations 5 through 7 repeat rotations 2 through 4, showing a stable bandwidth allocation: stations 1 and 9 use 69 percent of the band-

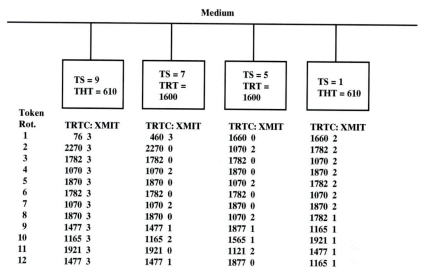

FIGURE 6.12   Operation of a Multiclass Token Bus Protocol

width for class 6 data and stations 5 and 7 share equally the remaining bandwidth for lower-priority data. Starting on the eighth rotation, station 1 reduces its use of the LAN. This reduces the bandwidth used for class 6 data to 52 percent, and lower-priority data are allowed to fill in the unused bandwidth.

CSMA/CD versus Token Bus.   At present, CSMA/CD and token bus are the two principal contenders for medium access control technique on bus/tree topologies. Table 6.4 attempts to summarize the pros and cons of the two techniques. A brief discussion follows.

TABLE 6.4   CSMA/CD versus Token Bus

Advantages	Disadvantages
CSMA/CD	
Simple algorithm	Collision detection requirement
Widely used	Fault diagnosis problems
Fair access	Minimum packet size
Good performance at low to medium load	Poor performance under very heavy load
	Biased to long transmissions
Token Bus	
Excellent throughput performance	Complex algorithm
Tolerates large dynamic range	Unproven technology
Regulated access	

Let us look at CSMA/CD first. On the positive side, the algorithm is simple; good news for the VLSI folks, and also good news for the user, in terms of cost and reliability. The protocol has been widely used for a long time, which also leads to favorable cost and reliability. The protocol provides fair access—all stations have an equal chance at the bandwidth; good if you require only fair access. As we shall see in Chapter 9, CSMA/CD exhibits quite good delay and throughput performance, at least up to a certain load, around 5 Mbps under some typical conditions.

There are, unfortunately, quite a few "cons" for CSMA/CD. From an engineering perspective, the most critical problem is the collision detection requirement. In order to detect collisions, the differences in signal strength from any pair of stations at any point on the cable must be small; this is no easy task to achieve. Other undesirable implications flow from the CD requirement. Since collisions are allowed, it is difficult for diagnostic equipment to distinguish expected errors from those induced by noise or faults. Also, CD imposes a minimum frame size, which is wasteful of bandwidth in situations where there are a lot of short messages, such as may be produced in highly interactive environments. There are some performance problems as well. For certain data rates and frame sizes, CSMA/CD performs poorly as load increases. Also, the protocol is biased toward long transmissions.

For token bus, perhaps its greatest positive feature is its excellent throughput performance. Throughput increases as the data rate increases and levels off but does not decline as the medium saturates. Further, this performance does not degrade as the cable length increases. A second "pro" for token bus is that, because stations need not detect collisions, a rather large dynamic range is possible. All that is required is that each station's signal be strong enough to be heard at all points on the cable; there are no special requirements related to relative signal strength.

Another strength of token bus is that access to the medium can be regulated. If fair access is desired, token bus can provide this as well as CSMA/CD. Indeed, at high loads, token bus may be fairer; it avoids the last-in, first-out phenomenon mentioned earlier. If priorities are required, as they may be in an operational or real-time environment, these can be accommodated. Token bus can also guarantee a certain bandwidth; this may be necessary for certain types of data, such as voice, digital video, and telemetry.

An advertised advantage of token bus is that it is deterministic; that is, there is a known upper bound to the amount of time any station must wait before transmitting. This upper bound is known because each station in the logical ring can hold the token only for a specified time. In contrast, with CSMA/CD, the delay time can be expressed only statistically. Furthermore, since every attempt to transmit under CSMA/CD can in principle produce a collision, there is a possibility that a station could be shut out indefinitely.

For process control and other real-time applications, this nondeterministic behavior is undesirable. Alas, in the real world, there is always a finite possibility of transmission error, which can cause a lost token. This adds a statistical component to token bus.

The main disadvantage of token bus is its complexity. The reader who made it through the description above can have no doubt that this is a complex algorithm. A second disadvantage is the overhead involved. Under lightly loaded conditions, a station may have to wait through many fruitless token passes for a turn.

Which to choose? That is left as an exercise to the reader, based on requirements and the relative costs prevailing at the time. The decision is also influenced by the baseband versus broadband debate. Both must be considered together when comparing vendors.

MAC Frame.   Figure 6.13 depicts the frame format for the 802.4 protocol. It consists of the following fields:

- *Preamble:* a pattern of one or more octets used by the receiver to establish bit synchronization.
- *Start delimiter (SD):* indicates start of frame. The SD consists of signaling patterns that are distinguishable from data. It is coded as follows: NNONNOOO, where N is a nondata symbol. The actual form of a nondata symbol depends on the signal encoding on the medium.
- *Frame control (FC):* the first 2 bits indicate whether this is a control frame or an LLC data frame. Control frames are used to manage the token bus protocol; one example is the token. For a control frame, the remaining 6 bits of the FC field indicate the identity of the control frame. For a frame containing LLC data, 3 bits of the FC field indicate

Octets	≥ 1	1	1	2 or 6	2 or 6	≥ 0	4	1
	Preamble	SD	FC	DA	SA	Data unit	FCS	ED

SD = start delimiter
FC = frame control
DA = destination address
SA = source address
FCS = frame check sequence
ED = end delimiter

(a) Frame

0	0	C	C	C	C	C	C

CCCCCC = type of control frame
(b) Frame control field for control frame

0	1	M	M	M	P	P	P

MMM = request_with_no_response,
        request_with_response, or response
PPP = priority bits
(c) Frame control field for data frame

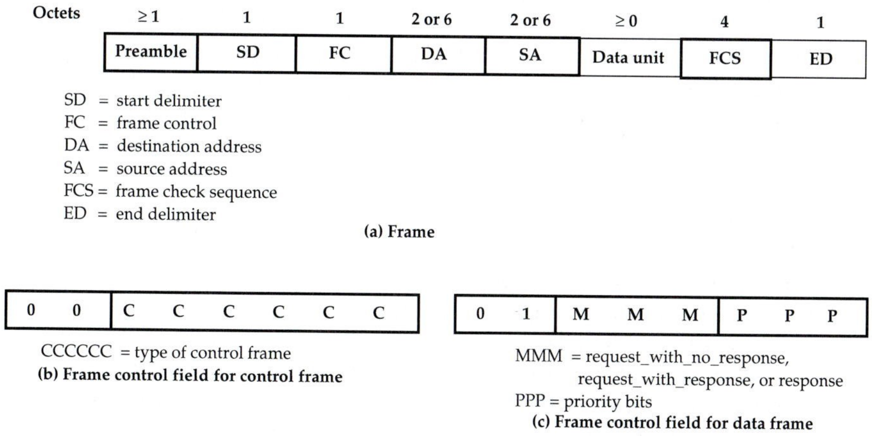

FIGURE 6.13   IEEE 802.4 Frame Format

whether this is a request_with_no_response frame (the default case), a request_with_response frame, or a response frame.

- *Destination address (DA):* as with 802.3.
- *Source address (SA):* as with 802.3.
- *Data unit:* contains LLC data unit or information related to a control operation.
- *Frame check sequence (FCS):* as with 802.3.
- *End delimiter (ED):* indicates end of frame.

IEEE 802.4 Physical Layer Specifications

The 802.4 standard specifies four alternative physical media, whose characteristics are listed in Table 6.5. Two of the alternatives use an analog transmission scheme known as carrierband. In contrast to broadband, with carrierband the entire spectrum of the cable is devoted to a single transmission path for the analog signals; frequency-division multiplexing is not used. Typically, a carrierband LAN has the following characteristics. Bidirectional transmission, using a bus topology, is employed. Hence there can be no amplifiers, and there is no need for a headend. Although the entire spectrum is used, most of the signal energy is concentrated at relatively low frequencies. This is an advantage because attenuation is less at lower frequencies.

Because the cable is dedicated to a single task, it is not necessary to take care that the modem output be confined to a narrow bandwidth. Energy can spread over the entire spectrum. As a result, the electronics are simple and relatively inexpensive.

Phase-Continuous Carrierband.   The lowest-cost alternative provided in 802.4 is the 1-Mbps phase-continuous carrierband, which uses a form of frequency-shift keying (FSK) in which the transition between signaling frequencies is accomplished by a continuous change of frequency, as opposed to the discontinuous replacement of one frequency by another. This type of FSK results in a tighter bandwidth and improved transmission and reception efficiency. To further improve reception, the digital data to be transmitted are first encoded using Manchester encoding. The high and low levels of the Manchester code are then passed through a modem at 6.25 and 3.75 MHz, respectively. This specification is intended to provide a low-cost system that can be installed with flexible or semirigid cable. A variety of older cables, already installed in buildings, can be used.

Phase-Coherent Carrierband.   The other carrierband technique standardized by 802.4 is phase-coherent FSK, at data rates of 5 and 10 Mbps. This is a form of FSK in which the two signaling frequencies are integrally related to the data rate. The scheme is called phase-coherent because the

TABLE 6.5   IEEE 802.4 Physical Layer Medium Alternatives

Parameter	Phase-Continuous Carrier Band		Phase-Coherent Carrier Band		Broadband			Optical Fiber
Data rate (Mbps)	1		5	10	1	5	10	5, 10, 20
Bandwidth	NA		NA	NA	1.5 MHz	6 MHz	12 MHz	270 nm
Center frequency	5 MHz		7.5 MHz	15 MHz	—	—		800–910 nm
Modulation	Manchester/ phase continuous FSK		Phase coherent FSK		Multilevel duobinary AM/PSK			On–off
Topology	Omnidirectional bus		Omnidirectional bus		Directional bus (tree)			Active or passive star
Transmission medium	Coaxial cable (75 ohm)		Coaxial cable (75 ohm)		Coaxial cable (75 ohm)			Optical fiber
Scrambling	No		No		Yes			No

zero-crossing points are in phase at the beginning and end of each bit time.

A binary one is represented by a frequency equal to the data rate, and a binary zero is represented by a frequency equal to twice the data rate. Thus for the 5-Mbps data rate, the two frequencies are 5 and 10 MHz, and for the 10-Mbps data rate, the two frequencies are 10 and 20 MHz. The phase-coherent scheme is intermediate in expense between a phase-continuous system and a broadband system. When implemented with semirigid coaxial cable, this system may be converted to broadband by making relatively simple hardware changes.

Broadband.   The broadband specification allows for data rates of 1, 5, and 10 Mbps, with bandwidths of 1.5, 6, and 12 MHz, respectively. The standard recommends the use of a single-cable system with a headend frequency translator. Dual cable is also permitted.

The modulation scheme used for the broadband specification is known as duobinary AM/PSK modulation. In this scheme, data are precoded and signaled as pulses in which both the amplitude and phase may vary. The nature of the encoding is such that receivers can demodulate the modulated signal without having to recover the phase of the signal. In essence, the PSK component of the modulation is used to reduce the signal bandwidth, not to carry data. As with the 802.3 10BROAD36 specification, the 802.4 broadband specification includes the use of scrambling.

Optical Fiber.   The most recent addition to the IEEE 802.4 physical layer standard is an optical fiber specification. Three data rates are specified: 5, 10, and 20 Mbps. In keeping with standard practice for optical fiber systems, the bandwidth and carrier are specified in terms of wavelength instead of frequency. For all three data rates, the bandwidth is 270 nm and the center wavelength is between 800 and 910 nm.

The encoding technique used for 802.4 optical fiber is a form of amplitude-shift keying (ASK) known as intensity modulation. Normally, with intensity modulation a binary one is encoded as a pulse of light and a binary zero is encoded as the absence of light. Because a long string of zeros or ones could result in loss of synchronization, the approach in 802.4 is first to encode the binary data to guarantee the presence of transitions and then to present the encoded data to the optical source for transmission. The precoding technique that is used is Manchester. Thus a binary zero is transmitted as a pulse of light (H) followed by the absence of a pulse (L), in uniform time slots; and a binary one is transmitted as the absence of a pulse (L) followed by a pulse (H). Note that this doubles the effective signaling rate. Thus the data rates of 5, 10, and 20 Mbps require optical signaling rates of 10, 20, and 40 Mbaud (one baud = one signal element per second).

The 802.4 optical fiber specification can be used with any topology that is logically a bus. That is, a transmission from any one station is received by all other stations, and if two stations transmit at the same time, a collision occurs. At the present time, a simple bus system is impractical because of the high cost of low-loss optical taps. Instead, the standard recommends the use of active or passive stars.

For both the active and passive stars, each station attaches to a central node via two optical fibers, one for transmission in each direction. The active star operates in the same fashion as the star topologies used for 802.3. That is, a transmission on any one input fiber to the central node is retransmitted on all output fibers.

The passive-star system is based on the use of a passive-star coupler. The passive-star coupler is fabricated by fusing together a number of optical fibers. The transmit fibers from all of the stations enter the coupler on one side, and all of the receive fibers exit on the other side. Any light input to one of the fibers on one side of the coupler will be divided equally among, and output through, all the fibers on the other side.

6.3

TOKEN RING

The IEEE 802.5 standard states that is intended for use in commercial and light industrial environments. Use in home or heavy industrial environments, although not precluded, is not considered within the scope of the standard. These environments are identical to those specified for IEEE 802.3.

IEEE 802.5 Medium Access Control

MAC Protocol.   The token ring technique is based on the use of a small frame, called a *token*, that circulates when all stations are idle. A station wishing to transmit must wait until it detects a token passing by. It then seizes the token by changing one bit in the token, which transforms it from a token to a start-of-frame sequence for a data frame. The station then appends and transmits the remainder of the fields needed to construct a data frame.

When a station seizes a token and begins to transmit a data frame, there is no token on the ring, so other stations wishing to transmit must wait. The frame on the ring will make a round trip and be absorbed by the transmitting station. The transmitting station will insert a new token on the ring when both of the following conditions have been met:

- The station has completed transmission of its frame.
- The leading edge of the transmitted frame has returned (after a complete circulation of the ring) to the station.

If the bit length of the ring is less than the frame length, the first condition implies the second. If not, a station could release a free token after it has finished transmitting but before it begins to receive its own transmission; the second condition is not strictly necessary and is relaxed under certain circumstances. The advantage of imposing the second condition is that it ensures that only one data frame at a time may be on the ring and only one station at a time may be transmitting, simplifying error recovery procedures.

Once the new token has been inserted on the ring, the next station downstream with data to send will be able to seize the token and transmit. Figure 9.9 illustrates the technique. In the example, *A* sends a packet to *C*, which receives it and then sends its own packets to *A* and *D*.

Note that under lightly loaded conditions, there is some inefficiency with token ring since a station must wait for the token to come around before transmitting. However, under heavy loads, which is when it matters, the ring functions in a round-robin fashion, which is both efficient and fair. To see this, consider the configuration in Figure 6.14. After station *A* transmits, it releases a token. The first station with an opportunity to transmit is *D*. If *D* transmits, it then releases a token and *C* has the next opportunity, and so on.

The principal advantage of token ring is the flexible control over access that it provides. In the simple scheme just described, the access is fair. As we shall see, schemes can be used to regulate access to provide for priority and guaranteed bandwidth services. The principal disadvantage of token ring is the requirement for token maintenance. Loss of the token prevents further utilization of the ring. Duplication of the token can also disrupt ring operation. One station must be selected as a monitor to ensure that exactly one token is on the ring and to reinsert a free token if necessary.

MAC Frame.   Figure 6.15 depicts the frame format for the 802.5 protocol. It consists of the following fields:

- *Starting delimiter (SD):* indicates start of frame. The SD consists of signaling patterns that are distinguishable from data. It is coded as follows: JK0JK000, where J and K are nondata symbols. The actual form of a nondata symbol depends on the signal encoding on the medium.
- *Access control (AC):* has the format PPPTMRRR, where PPP and RRR are 3-bit priority and reservation variables, and M is the monitor bit; their use is explained below. T indicates whether this is a token or data frame. In the case of a token frame, the only remaining field is ED.
- *Frame control (FC):* indicates whether this is an LLC data frame. If not, bits in this field control operation of the token ring MAC protocol.
- *Destination address (DA):* as with 802.3.
- *Source address (SA):* as with 802.3.

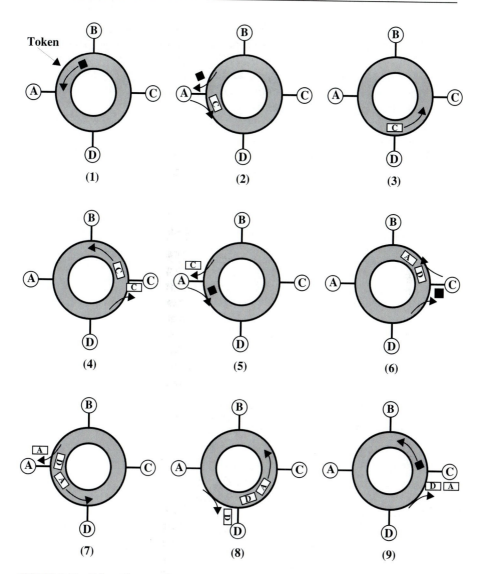

FIGURE 6.14   Token Ring Operation

- *Data unit:* contains LLC data unit.

- *Frame check sequence (FCS):* as with 802.3.

- *End delimiter (ED):* contains the error detection bit (E), which is set if any repeater detects an error, and the intermediate bit (I), which is used to indicate that this is a frame other than the final one of a multiple frame transmission.

- *Frame status (FS):* contains the address recognized (A) and frame copied (C) bits, whose use is explained below. Because the A and C bits are outside the scope of the FCS, they are duplicated to provide a redundancy check to detect erroneous settings.

We can now restate the token ring algorithm for the case when a single priority is used. In this case, the priority and reservation bits are set to zero. A station wishing to transmit waits until a token goes by, as indicated by a token bit of 0 in the AC field. The station seizes the token by setting the token bit to 1. The SD and AC fields of the received token now function as the first two fields of the outgoing frame. The station transmits one or more frames, continuing until either its supply of frames is exhausted or a token-holding timer expires. When the AC field of the last transmitted frame returns, the station sets the token bit to 0 and appends an ED field, resulting in the insertion of a new token on the ring.

Stations in the receive mode listen to the ring. Each station can check passing frames for errors and set the E bit to 1 if an error is detected. If a station detects its own MAC address, it sets the A bit to 1; it may also copy the frame, setting the C bit to 1. This allows the originating station to differentiate three results of a frame transmission:

- Destination station nonexistent or not active (A = 0, C = 0)
- Destination station exists but frame not copied (A = 1, C = 0)
- Frame received (A = 1, C = 1)

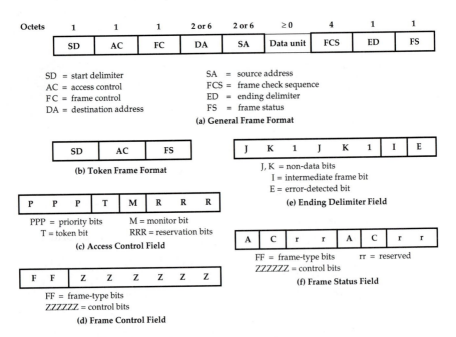

FIGURE 6.15   IEEE 802.5 Frame Format

Token Ring Priority.   The 802.5 standard includes a specification for an optional priority mechanism. Eight levels of priority are supported by providing two 3-bit fields in each data frame and token: a priority field and a reservation field. To explain the algorithm, let us define the following variables:

P_f = priority of frame to be transmitted by station

P_s = service priority: priority of current token

P_r = value of P_s as contained in the last token received by this station

R_s = reservation value in current token

R_r = highest reservation value in the frames received by this station during the last token rotation

The scheme works as follows:

1. A station wishing to transmit must wait for a token with $P_s \leq P_f$.
2. While waiting, a station may reserve a future token at its priority level (P_f). If a data frame goes by and if the reservation field is less than its priority $(R_s < P_f)$, the station may set the reservation field of the frame to its priority $(R_s \leftarrow P_f)$. If a token frame goes by and if $(R_s < P_f$ and $P_f < P_s)$, the station sets the reservation field of the frame to its priority $(R_s \leftarrow P_f)$. This has the effect of preempting any lower-priority reservation.
3. When a station seizes a token, it sets the token bit to 1 to start a data frame, sets the reservation field of the data frame to 0, and leaves the priority field unchanged (the same as that of the incoming token frame).
4. Following transmission of one or more data frames, a station issues a new token with the priority and reservation fields set as indicated in Table 6.6.

The effect of the foregoing steps is to sort the competing claims and allow the waiting transmission of highest priority to seize the token as soon as possible. A moment's reflection reveals that, as stated, the algorithm has a ratchet effect on priority, driving it to the highest used level and keeping it there. To avoid this, a station that raises the priority (issues a token that has a higher priority than the token that it received) has the responsibility of later lowering the priority to its previous level. Therefore, a station that raises the priority must remember both the old and the new priorities and downgrade the priority of the token at the appropriate time. In essence, each station is responsible for assuring that no token circulates indefinitely because its priority is too high. By remembering the priority of earlier transmissions, a station can detect this condition and downgrade the priority to a previous, lower priority or reservation.

To implement the downgrading mechanism, two stacks are maintained by each station, one for reservations and one for priorities:

S_x = stack used to store new values of token priority

S_r = stack used to store old values of token priority

The reason that stacks rather than scalar variables are required is that the priority can be raised a number of times by one or more stations. The successive raises must be unwound in the reverse order.

To summarize: A station having a higher-priority frame to transmit than the current frame can reserve the next token for its priority level as the frame passes by. When the next token is issued, it will be at the reserved priority level. Stations of lower priority cannot seize the token, so it passes to the reserving station or an intermediate station with data to send of equal or higher priority than the reserved priority level. The station that upgraded the priority level is responsible for downgrading it to its former level when all higher-priority stations are finished. When that station sees a token at the higher priority after it has transmitted, it can assume that there

TABLE 6.6 Actions Performed by the Token Holder to Implement the Priority Scheme [VALE92]

Condition	Action
Frame available AND $P_s \leq P_f$	Send frame
(Frame not available OR THT expired) AND $P_r \geq$ MAX $[R_r, P_f]$	Send token with: $P_s \leftarrow P_f$ $R_s \leftarrow$ MAX $[R_r, P_f]$
(Frame not available OR THT expired) AND $P_r <$ MAX $[R_r, P_f]$ AND $P_r > S_x$	Send token with: $P_s \leftarrow$ MAX $[R_r, P_f]$ $R_s \leftarrow 0$ Push $S_r \leftarrow P_r$ Push $S_x \leftarrow P_s$
(Frame not available OR THT expired) AND $P_r <$ MAX $[R_r, P_f]$ AND $P_r = S_x$	Send token with: $P_s \leftarrow$ MAX $[R_r, P_f]$ $R_s \leftarrow 0$ Pop S_x Push $S_x \leftarrow P_s$
(Frame not available OR frame available and $P_f < S_x$) AND $P_s = S_x$ AND $R_r > S_r$	Send token with: $P_s \leftarrow R_r$ $R_s \leftarrow 0$ Pop S_x Push $S_x \leftarrow P_s$
(Frame not available OR frame available and $P_f < S_x$) AND $P_s = S_x$ AND $R_r \leq S_r$	Send token with: $P_s \leftarrow R_r$ $R_s \leftarrow 0$ Pop S_r Pop S_x

is no more higher-priority traffic waiting, and it downgrades the token before passing it on.

Figure 6.16 is an example. The following events occur:

(a) *A* is transmitting a data frame to *B* at priority 0. When the frame has completed a circuit of the ring and returns to *A*, *A* will issue a token frame. However, as the data frame passes *D*, *D* makes a reservation at priority 3 by setting the reservation field to 3.

(b) *A* issues a token with the priority field set to 3.

(c) If neither *B* nor *C* has data of priority 3 or greater to send, they cannot seize the token. The token circulates to *D*, which seizes the token and issues a data frame.

(d) After *D*'s data frame returns to *D*, *D* issues a new token at the same priority as the token that it received: priority 3.

(e) *A* sees a token at the priority level that it used to last issue a token. It therefore seizes the token even if it has no data to send.

(f) *A* issues a token at the previous priority level: priority 0.

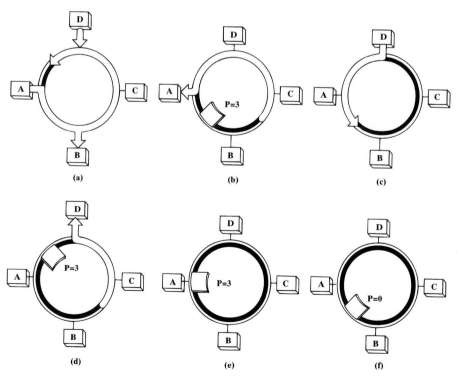

FIGURE 6.16   Token Ring Priority Scheme

Note that after *A* has issued a priority 3 token, any station with data of priority 3 or greater may seize the token. Suppose that at this point station *C* now has priority 4 data to send. *C* will seize the token, transmit its data frame, and reissue a priority 3 token, which is then seized by *D*. By the time that a priority 3 token arrives at *A*, all intervening stations with data of priority 3 or greater to send will have had the opportunity. It is now appropriate, therefore, for *A* to downgrade the token.

Token Maintenance.   To overcome various error conditions, one station is designated as the active monitor. The active monitor periodically issues an active-monitor-present control frame to assure other stations that there is an active monitor on the ring. To detect a lost-token condition, the monitor uses a valid-frame timer that is greater than the time required to traverse the ring completely. The timer is reset after every valid token or data frame. If the time expires, the monitor issues a priority 0 token. To detect a persistently circulating data frame, the monitor sets the monitor bit to 1 on any passing data frame the first time it goes by. If it sees a data frame with the monitor bit already set, it knows that the transmitting station failed to absorb the frame. The monitor absorbs the frame and transmits a priority 0 token. The same strategy is used to detect a failure in the priority mechanism: No token should circulate completely around the ring at a constant nonzero priority level. Finally, if the active monitor detects evidence of another active monitor, it immediately goes into standby monitor status.

All of the active stations on the ring cooperate to provide each station with a continuous update on the identity of its upstream neighbor. Each station periodically issues a standby-monitor-present (SMP) frame. Its downstream neighbor absorbs this frame, notes its sending address, and after a pause, sends its own SMP frame. The absence of SMP frames can be used in fault isolation.

Early Token Release.   When a station issues a frame, if the bit length of the ring is less than that of the frame, the leading edge of the transmitted frame will return to the transmitting station before it has completed transmission; in this case, the station may issue a token as soon as it has finished frame transmission. If the frame is shorter than the bit length of the ring, then after a station has completed transmission of a frame, it must wait until the leading edge of the frame returns before issuing a token. In the latter case, some of the potential capacity of the ring is unused.

To allow for more efficient ring utilization, an early token release (ETR) option has been added to the 802.5 standard. ETR allows a transmitting station to release a token as soon as it completes frame transmission, whether or not the frame header has returned to the station. The priority used for a token released prior to receipt of the previous frame header is the priority of the most recently received frame.

One effect of ETR is that access delay for priority traffic may increase when the ring is heavily loaded with short frames. Since a station must issue a token before it can read the reservation bits of the frame that it just transmitted, the station will not respond to reservations. Thus the priority mechanism is at least partially disabled. Stations that implement ETR are compatible and interoperable with those that do not.

IEEE 802.5 Physical Layer Specification

The 802.5 standard (Table 6.7) specifies the use of shielded twisted pair with data rates of 4 and 16 Mbps using Differential Manchester encoding. An earlier specification of a 1-Mbps system has been dropped from the most recent edition of the standard. A recent addition to the standard is the use of unshielded twisted pair at 4 Mbps.

TABLE 6.7   IEEE 802.5 Physical Layer Medium Specification

	Transmission Medium	
	Shielded Twisted Pair	**Unshielded Twisted Pair**
Data rate (Mbps)	4 or 16	4
Maximum number of repeaters	250	72
Maximum length between repeaters	Not specified	Not specified

6.4

RECOMMENDED READING

[VALE92] provides a detailed technical treatment of all of the standards discussed in this chapter.

[HEGE93] and [BIRD94] cover CSMA/CD and token ring LANs, respectively, in some depth.

BIRD94   Bird, D. *Token Ring Network Design*. Reading, MA: Addison-Wesley, 1994.

HEGE93   Hegering, H., and Lapple, A. *Ethernet: Building a Communications Infrastructure*. Reading, MA: Addison-Wesley, 1993.

VALE92   Valenzano, A., DeMartini, C., and Ciminiera, L. *MAP and TOP Communications: Standards and Applications*. Reading, MA: Addison-Wesley, 1992.

6.5

PROBLEMS

6.1 A disadvantage of the contention approach for LANs is the capacity wasted due to multiple stations attempting to access the channel at the same time. Suppose that time is divided into discrete slots with each of N stations attempting to transmit with probability p during each slot. What fraction of slots are wasted due to multiple simultaneous transmission attempts?

6.2 A simple medium access control protocol would be to use a fixed assignment time-division multiplexing (TDM) scheme, as described in Section 2.1. Each station is assigned one time slot per cycle for transmission. For the bus and tree, the length of each slot is the time to transmit 100 bits plus the end-to-end propagation delay. For the ring, assume a delay of one bit time per station, and assume that a round-robin assignment is used. Stations monitor all time slots for reception. Assume a propagation time of 2×10^8 m/sec. What are the limitations, in terms of number of stations and throughput per station, for:

a. A 1-km, 10-Mbps baseband bus?
b. A 1-km (headend to farthest point), 10-Mbps broadband bus?
c. A 10-Mbps broadband tree consisting of a 0.5-km trunk emanating from the headend and five 0.1-km branches from the trunk at the following points: 0.05 km, 0.15 km, 0.25 km, 0.35 km, 0.45 km?
d. A 10-Mbps ring with a total length of 1 km?
e. A 10-Mbps ring with a length of 0.1 km between repeaters?
f. Compute throughput for all of the above for 10 and 100 stations.

6.3 Consider two stations on a baseband bus at a distance of 1 km from each other. Let the data rate be 1 Mbps, the frame length be 100 bits, and the propagation velocity be 2×10^8 m/s. Assume that each station generates frames at an average rate of 1000 frames per second. For the ALOHA protocol, if one station begins to transmit a frame at time t, with is the probability of collision? Repeat for slotted ALOHA. Repeat for ALOHA and slotted ALOHA at 10 Mbps.

6.4 Repeat Problem 6.3 for a broadband bus. Assume that the two stations are 1 km apart and that one is very near the headend.

6.5 For a p-persistent CSMA, what is the probability that the next transmission after a successful transmission will be successful for $np = 0.1$, 1.0, and 10?

6.6 For p-persistent CSMA, consider the following situation. A station is ready to transmit and is listening to the current transmission. No other station is ready to transmit and there will be no other transmission for an indefinite period. If the time unit used in the protocol is T, show that the average number of iterations of step 1 of the protocol is $1/p$ and that therefore the expected time that the station will have to wait after the current transmission is

$$T\left(\frac{1}{p} - 1\right)$$

Hint: Use the equality $\sum_{i=1}^{\infty} iX^{i-1} = \dfrac{1}{(1 - X)^2}$

6.7 The binary exponential backoff algorithm is defined by IEEE 802 as follows: "The delay is an integral multiple of slot time. The number of slot times to delay before the nth retransmission attempt is chosen as a uniformly distributed random integer r in the range $0 < r < 2^K$, where $K = \min(n, 10)$." Slot time is roughly twice the round-trip propagation delay. Assume that two stations always have a frame to send. After a collision, what is the mean number of retransmission attempts before one station retransmits successfully? What is the answer if three stations always have frames to send?

6.8 IEEE 802.4 refers to the token bus service class scheme as a bandwidth (capacity) allocation scheme rather than a priority scheme. A priority scheme would provide that all frames of higher priority would be transmitted before any lower-priority frame would be allowed on the bus. Show by counterexample that the 802.4 scheme is not a priority scheme.

6.9 Write a program to implement the token ring priority mechanism.

6.10 For a token ring LAN, suppose that the destination station removes the data frame and immediately sends a short acknowledgment frame to the sender rather than letting the original frame return to sender. How will this affect performance?

6.11 If the token ring active monitor fails, it is possible that two stations will time out and claim that status. Suggest an algorithm for overcoming this problem.

6.12 Compare the token bus service class scheme with the token ring priority scheme. What are the relative pros and cons? Is it possible, with appropriate parameter settings, to achieve the same behavior from both?

6.13 Another medium access control technique for rings is the slotted ring. A number of fixed-length slots circulate continuously on the ring. Each slot contains a leading bit to designate the slot as empty or full. A station wishing to transmit waits until an empty slot arrives, marks the slot full, and inserts a frame of data as the slot goes by. The full slot makes a complete round trip, to be marked empty again by the station that marked it full. In what sense are the slotted ring and token ring protocols the complement of each other?

6.14 Consider a slotted ring of length 10 km with a data rate of 10 Mbps and 500 repeaters, each of which introduces a 1-bit delay. Each slot contains room for one source address byte, one destination address byte, two data bytes, and five control bits for a total length of 37 bits. How many slots are on the ring?

7

High-Speed Ethernet-Like LANs

In this chapter we examine two schemes standardized by the IEEE 802 committee that provide a 100-Mbps data rate over short distances. The 100BASE-T specification provides for a star-wired network using the IEEE 802.3 CSMA/CD MAC protocol and frame format. The IEEE 802.12 100VG-AnyLAN specification defines a hierarchical star-wire topology and uses a new priority-based MAC protocol; it supports both IEEE 802.3 and IEEE 802.5 frame formats.

The intent of both of these approaches is to provide a significant increase in data rate over the traditional Ethernet scheme (and over token ring in the case of IEEE 802.12) with minimal cost and minimal impact on existing networks. In the case of 100BASE-T, since both the frame format and the MAC protocol are unchanged, networking software currently running on 10-Mbps Ethernet should run unchanged on the higher-speed network. The same protocol analysis and management tools used on 10-Mbps Ethernet should adapt easily to the higher-speed network. In the case of 100VG-AnyLAN, the MAC protocol changes but the MAC frame formats do not; this should minimize transition difficulties. Table 7.1 provides a brief overview of the chief attributes of these two schemes.

TABLE 7.1   Attributes of 100BASE-T and 100VG-AnyLAN

	100BASE-T	100VG-AnyLAN
Number of stations	1024	Unspecified
Access method	CSMA/CD	Round robin
Frame size	1500 bytes	1500 or 4500 bytes
Extent	210 m	2.5 km
Topology	Star wired	Hierarchical star

7.1

100BASE-T

100BASE-T is a set of specifications developed by the IEEE 802.3 committee to provide a low-cost, Ethernet-compatible LAN operating at 100 Mbps. The committee defined a number of alternatives to be used with different transmission media.

Figure 7.1 shows the terminology used in labeling the specifications and indicates the media used. All of the 100BASE-T options use the IEEE 802.3 MAC protocol and frame format. 100BASE-X refers to a set of options that use the physical medium specifications originally defined for fiber distributed data interface (FDDI; covered in Chapter 8). All of the 100BASE-X schemes use two physical links between nodes; one for transmission and one for reception. 100BASE-TX makes use of shielded twisted pair (STP) or high-quality (category 5) unshielded twisted pair (UTP). 100BASE-FX uses optical fiber.

In many buildings, any of the 100BASE-X options require the installation of new cable. For such cases, 100BASE-T4 defines a lower-cost alternative that can use category 3, voice-grade UTP in addition to the higher-quality category 5 UTP.[1] To achieve the 100-Mbps data rate over lower-quality cable, 100BASE-T4 dictates the use of four twisted-pair lines between nodes, with the data transmission making use of three pairs in one direction at a time.

For all of the 100BASE-T options, the topology is similar to that of 10BASE-T, namely a star-wire topology. Table 7.2 summarizes key characteristics of the 100BASE-T options.

100BASE-X

For all of the transmission media specified under 100BASE-X, a unidirectional data rate of 100 Mbps is achieved transmitting over a single link (sin-

---

[1]See Chapter 3 for a discussion of category 3 and category 5 cable.

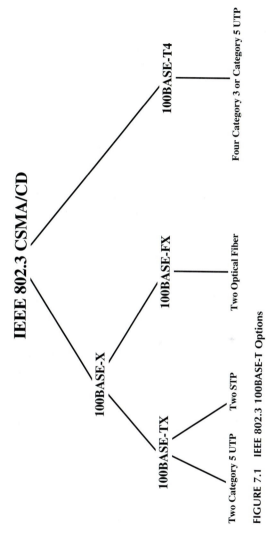

FIGURE 7.1   IEEE 802.3 100BASE-T Options

TABLE 7.2   IEEE 802.3 100BASE-T Physical Layer Medium Alternatives

	100BASE-TX	100BASE-TX	100BASE-FX	100BASE-T4
Transmission medium	Two pair, STP	Two pair, category 5 UTP	Two optical fibers	Four pair, category 3, 4, or 5 UTP
Signaling technique	4B5B, NRZI	4B5B, NRZI	4B5B, NRZI	8B6T, NRZ
Data rate	100 Mbps	100 Mbps	100 Mbps	100 Mbps
Maximum segment length	100 m	100 m	100 m	100 m
Network span	200 m	200 m	400 m	200 m

gle twisted pair, single optical fiber). For all of these media, an efficient and effective signal encoding scheme is required.

The basis of the encoding scheme is one originally defined for FDDI, and can be referred to as 4B/5B-NRZI. To understand the significance of this choice, first consider the simple alternative of a NRZ (nonreturn to zero) coding scheme. With NRZ, one signal state represents binary one and one signal state represents binary zero. The disadvantage of this approach is its lack of synchronization. Since transitions on the medium are unpredictable, there is no way for the receiver to synchronize its clock to the transmitter. The solution to this problem is first to encode the binary data to guarantee the presence of transitions and then to present the encoded data to the optical source for transmission. For example, the data could first be encoded using Manchester encoding. The disadvantage of this approach is that the efficiency is only 50 percent. That is, because there can be as many as two transitions per bit time, a signaling rate of 200 million signal elements per second (200 Mbaud) is needed to achieve a data rate of 100 Mbps. This represents an unnecessary cost and technical burden.

To achieve greater efficiency, the 100BASE-X standard specifies the use of a code referred to as 4B/5B. In this scheme, encoding is done 4 bits at a time; each 4 bits of data are encoded into a symbol with five *code bits,* and a set of five code bits is known as a code group. In effect, each set of 4 bits is encoded as 5 bits. The efficiency is thus raised to 80 percent; 100 Mbps is achieved with 125 Mbaud.

To ensure synchronization, there is a second stage of encoding: Each code group of the 4B/5B stream is treated as a binary value and encoded using nonreturn to zero inverted (NRZI), as shown in Figure 2.5. In this code, a binary 1 is represented with a transition at the beginning of the bit interval and a binary 0 is represented with no transition at the beginning of the bit interval; there are no other transitions. The advantage of NRZI is that it employs differential encoding. Recall from Chapter 3 that in differential encoding, the signal is decoded by comparing the polarity of adjacent signal elements rather than the absolute value of a signal element. A benefit of this scheme is that it is generally more reliable to detect a transition in the presence of noise and distortion than to compare a value to a threshold.

Now we are in a position to describe the 4B/5B code and to understand the selections that were made. Table 7.3 shows the symbol encoding used in 100BASE-X. Each 5-bit code group pattern is shown, together with its NRZI realization. Since we are encoding 4 bits with a 5-bit pattern, only 16 of the 32 possible patterns are needed for data encoding. The codes selected to represent the 16 4-bit data blocks are such that a transition is present at least twice for each 5-code group code. No more than three zeros in a row are allowed across one or more code groups.

The 100BASE-X encoding scheme can be summarized as follows:

TABLE 7.3   4B/5B Code Groups

Data Input (4 bits)	Code Group (5 bits)	NRZI Pattern	Interpretation
0000	11110		Data 0
0001	01001		Data 1
0010	10100		Data 2
0011	10101		Data 3
0100	01010		Data 4
0101	01011		Data 5
0110	01110		Data 6
0111	01111		Data 7
1000	10010		Data 8
1001	10011		Data 9
1010	10110		Data A
1011	10111		Data B
1100	11010		Data C

TABLE 7.3   4B/5B Code Groups (cont.)

Data Input (4 bits)	Code Group (5 bits)	NRZI Pattern	Interpretation
1101	11011		Data D
1110	11100		Data E
1111	11101		Data F
	11111		Idle
	11000		Start of stream delimiter, part 1
	10001		Start of stream delimiter, part 2
	01101		End of stream delimiter, part 1
	00111		End of stream delimiter, part 2
	00100		Transmit error
	Other		Invalid codes

1. A simple NRZ encoding is rejected because it does not provide synchronization; a string of ones or zeros will have no transitions.
2. The data to be transmitted must first be encoded to assure transitions. The 4B/5B code is chosen over Manchester because it is more efficient.
3. The 4B/5B code is further encoded using NRZI so that the resulting differential signal will improve reception reliability.
4. The specific 5-bit patterns chosen for the encoding of the sixteen 4-bit data patterns are chosen to guarantee no more than three zeros in a row to provide for adequate synchronization.

Those code groups not used to represent data are either declared invalid or assigned special meaning as control symbols. These assignments are listed in Table 7.3. The nondata symbols fall into the following categories:

- *Idle.* The idle code group is transmitted between data transmission sequences. It consists of a constant flow of binary ones, which in NRZI comes out as a continuous alternation between the two signal levels. This continuous fill pattern establishes and maintains synchronization and is used in the CSMA/CD protocol to indicate that the shared medium is idle.
- *Start-of-stream delimiter.* This is used to delineate the starting boundary of a data transmission sequence; consists of two different code groups.
- *End-of-stream delimiter.* This is used to terminate normal data transmission sequences; consists of two different code groups.
- *Transmit error.* This code group is interpreted as a signaling error. The normal use of this indicator is for repeaters to propagate received errors.

The 100BASE-X designation includes two physical medium specifications, one for twisted pair, known as 100BASE-TX, and one for optical fiber, known as 100-BASE-FX.

100BASE-TX. 100BASE-TX makes use of two pairs of twisted-pair cables, one pair used for transmission and one for reception. Both STP and category 5 UTP are allowed. For transmission over twisted pair, the 4B/5B signal is subject to further encoding to achieve desirable transmission characteristics. The following steps are involved:

1. *NRZI-to-NRZ conversion.* The 4B/5B NRZI signal of the basic 100BASE-X is converted back to NRZ.
2. *Scrambling.* The bit stream is scrambled to produce a more uniform spectrum distribution for the next stage.
3. *Encoder.* The scrambled bit stream is encoded using a scheme known as MLT-3.
4. *Driver.* The resulting encoding is transmitted.

The effect of the MLT-3 scheme is to concentrate most of the energy in the transmitted signal below 30 MHz, which reduces radiated emissions. This in turn reduces problems due to interference.

The MLT-3 encoding produces an output that has a transition for every binary 1 and that uses three levels: a positive voltage (+V), a negative voltage (−V), and no voltage (0). The encoding rules are best explained with reference to the encoder state diagram shown in Figure 7.2:

1. If the next input bit is zero, the next output value is the same as the preceding value.
2. If the next input bit is 1, then the next output value involves a transition:

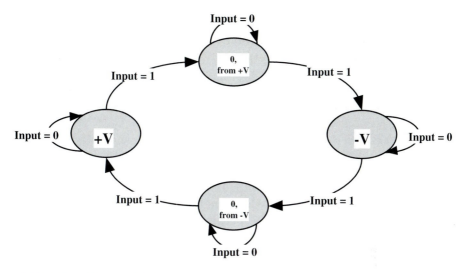

FIGURE 7.2   MLT-3 Encoder State Diagram

 a. If the preceding output value was either +V or −V, the next output value is zero.

 b. If the preceding output value was zero, the next output value is nonzero, and that output is of the opposite sign to the last nonzero output.

Figure 7.3 provides an example. Every time there is a input of 1, there is a transition. The occurrences of +V and −V alternate.

100BASE-FX. 100BASE-FX makes use of two optical fibers, one for transmission and one for reception. With 100BASE-FX, a means is needed to convert the 4B/5B-NRZI code groups stream into optical signals. The technique used is known as intensity modulation. A binary 1 is represented by a burst or pulse of light; a binary 0 is represented by either the absence of a light pulse or a light pulse at very low intensity.

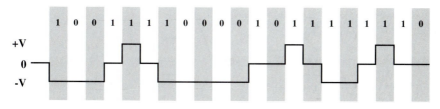

FIGURE 7.3   Example of MLT-3 Encoding

100BASE-T4

100BASE-T4 is designed to produce a 100-Mbps data rate over lower-quality category 3 cable, thus taking advantage of the large installed base of category 3 cable in office buildings. The specification also indicates that the use of category 5 cable is optional. 100BASE-T4 does not transmit a continuous signal between packets, which makes it useful in battery-powered applications.

For 100BASE-T4 using voice-grade category 3 cable, it is not reasonable to expect to achieve 100 Mbps on a single twisted pair. Instead, 100BASE-T4 specifies that the data stream to be transmitted is split up into three separate data streams, each with an effective data rate of 33⅓. Mbps. Figure 7.4 shows the manner in which the four twisted pairs are used and contrasts this with the 100BASE-X specification. For 100BASE-T4, data are transmitted using pairs labeled D1, D3, and D4. Data are received on pairs

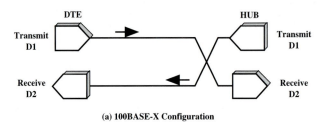

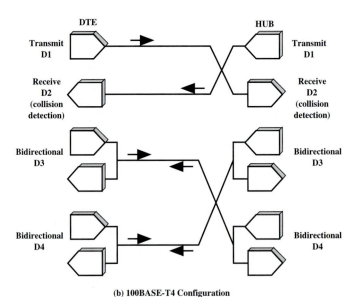

FIGURE 7.4   100BASE-T Use of Wire Pairs

D2, D3, and D4. Thus pairs D3 and D4 must be configured for bidirectional transmission. Pair D2, which is dedicated to reception, is also used for collision detection.

As with 100BASE-X, a simple NRZ encoding scheme is not used for 100BASE-T4. This would require a signaling rate of 33 Mbps on each twisted pair and does not provide synchronization. Instead, a ternary signaling scheme is used. With ternary signaling, each signal element can take on one of three values (positive voltage, negative voltage, zero voltage). A pure ternary code is one in which the full information-carry capacity of the ternary signal is exploited. However, pure ternary is not attractive for the same reasons that a pure binary (NRZ) code is rejected: the lack of synchronization. However, there are schemes, referred to as *block-coding methods*, which approach the efficiency of ternary and overcome this disadvantage. A new block coding scheme known as 8B6T is used for 100BASE-T4.

With 8B6T the data to be transmitted are handled in 8-bit blocks. Each block of 8 bits is mapped into a code group of six ternary symbols. The stream of code groups is then transmitted in round-robin fashion across the three output channels (Figure 7.5). Thus the ternary transmission rate on each output channel is

$$\frac{6}{8} \times 33\frac{1}{3} = 25 \text{ Mbaud}$$

Table 7.4 shows a portion of the 8B6T code table; the full table maps all possible 8-bit patterns into a unique code group of six ternary symbols. The mapping was chosen with two requirements in mind: synchronization and dc balance. For synchronization, the codes were chosen to maximize the average number of transitions per code group. The second requirement is to maintain dc balance, so that the average voltage on the line is zero. For this purpose all of the code groups selected have either an equal number of positive and negative symbols or an excess of one positive symbol. To maintain balance, a dc balancing algorithm is used. In essence, this algorithm monitors the cumulative weight of all the code groups transmitted on a single

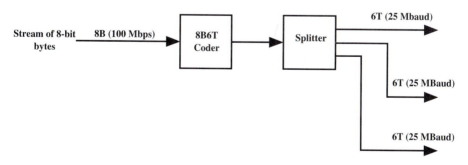

FIGURE 7.5   8B6T Transmission Scheme

TABLE 7.4   Portion of 8B6T Code Table

Data Octet	6T Code Group	Data Octet	6T Code Group	Data Octet	6T Code Group	Data Octet	6T Code Group
00	+−00+−	10	+0+−−0	20	00−++−	30	+−00−+
01	0+−+−0	11	++0−0−	21	−−+00+	31	0+−−+0
02	+−0+−0	12	+0+−0−	22	++−0+−	32	+−0−+0
03	−0++−0	13	0++−0−	23	++−0−+	33	−0+−+0
04	−0+0+−	14	0++−−0	24	00+0−+	34	−0+0−+
05	0+−−0+	15	++00−−	25	00+0+−	35	0+−+0−
06	+−0−0+	16	+0+0−−	26	00−00+	36	+−0+0−
07	−0+−0+	17	0++0−−	27	−−+++−	37	−0++0−
08	−+00+−	18	0+−0+−	28	−0−++0	38	−+00−+
09	0−++−0	19	0+−0−+	29	−−0+0+	39	0−+−+0
0A	−+0+−0	1A	0+−++−	2A	−0−+0+	3A	−+0−+0
0B	+0−+−0	1B	0+−00+	2B	0−−+0+	3B	+0−−+0
0C	+0−0+−	1C	0−+00+	2C	0−−++0	3C	+0−0−+
0D	0−+−0+	1D	0−+++−	2D	−−00++	3D	0−++0−
0E	−+0−0+	1E	0−+0−+	2E	−0−0++	3E	−+0+0−
0F	+0−−0+	1F	0−+0+−	2F	0−−0++	3F	+0−+0−

pair. Each code group has a weight of 0 or 1. To maintain balance, the algorithm may negate a transmitted code group (change all + symbols to − symbols and all − symbols to + symbols), so that the cumulative weight at the conclusion of each code group is always either 0 or 1.

Configuration and Operation

In its simplest form, a 100BASE-T network is configured in a star-wire topology, with all stations connected directly to a central point referred to as a multiport repeater. In this configuration, the repeater has the responsibility for detecting collisions rather than the attached stations. The repeater functions as follows:

- A valid signal appearing on any single input is repeated on all output links.
- If two inputs occur at the same time, a jam signal is transmitted on all links.

Thus the star-wire topology functions logically in the same manner as a bus topology CSMA/CD network: a transmission by any one station is received by all stations; if the transmissions of two stations overlap, a collision occurs, which is detected by all stations.

The term *collision domain* is used to define a single CSMA/CD network. This means that if two stations transmit at the same time, a collision will occur. Stations separated by a simple multiport repeater are within the same collision domain, whereas stations separated by a bridge are in different collision domains. Figure 7.6 illustrates this difference. The bridge operates in a store-and-forward fashion and therefore participates in two CSMA/CD algorithms, one for each of the two collision domains that it connects.

The 100BASE-T standard defines two types of repeaters. A class I repeater can support unlike physical media segments, such as 100BASE-T4 and 100BASE-TX. In this case there is likely to be increased internal delay in the repeater to handle the conversion from one signaling scheme to another. Therefore, only a single class I repeater is used in a collision domain. A class I repeater is limited to a single physical media type, and two class II repeaters may be used in a single collision domain (Figure 7.7).

Figure 7.7 is drawn to suggest that the connection between two class II repeaters appears the same as an ordinary station link to each repeater. The repeater makes no distinction between a station and another repeater. Similarly, Figure 7.6 indicates that a bridge is treated the same as any other station from the perspective of the repeater. Table 7.5 lists the allowable distances for various collision domains.

Full-Duplex Operation

A traditional Ethernet is half-duplex: A station can either transmit or receive a frame, but it cannot do both simultaneously. With full-duplex operation, a station can transmit and receive simultaneously. If a 100-Mbps Ethernet ran in full-duplex mode, the theoretical transfer rate would become 200 Mbps.

Several changes are needed to operate in full-duplex mode. The attached stations must have full-duplex rather than half-duplex adapter cards. The central point in the star wire cannot be a simple multiport repeater but must be some sort of switched hub, such as a bridge. In this case each station constitutes a separate collision domain. In fact, there are no collisions and the CSMA/CD algorithm is no longer needed. Full-duplex operation is currently not part of the 100-BASE-T standard but is under consideration. However, a number of vendors offer a full-duplex Ethernet scheme.

Auto-Negotiation

Auto-negotiation is an optional capability of the 100BASE-T standard that enables two devices connected to the same link to exchange information

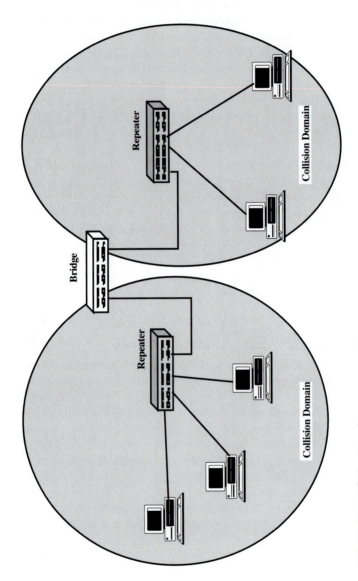

FIGURE 7.6   Collision Domains

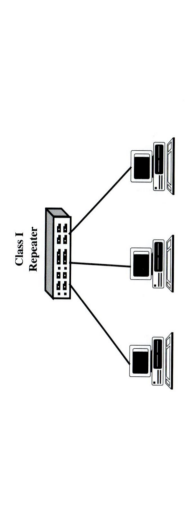

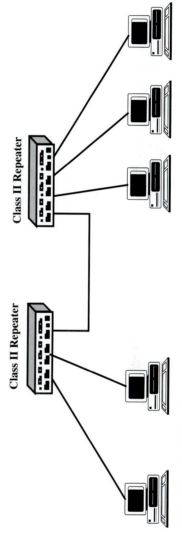

FIGURE 7.7   100BASE-T Repeater Types

TABLE 7.5   Maximum Collision Domain (meters)

Repeater Type	Copper	Copper and Fiber[a]	Fiber
DTE-DTE	100	NA	400
One Class I repeater	200	230	240
One Class II repeater	200	285	318
Two Class II repeaters	205 (200 category 3)	212	226

[a]Mixed copper and fiber assumes a 100-meter copper link.

about their capabilities. At a minimum it enables a device to indicate whether it operates at 100 or 10 Mbps. This capability makes it possible to implement a hub that support a mixture of devices that conform to the various 100BASE-T and the 10BASE-T medium options.

Auto-negotiation is performed by passing information encapsulated within a burst of closely separated pulses known as *link integrity pulses*. The pulses are defined such that a 10BASE-T receiver will recognize these as part of a normal link maintenance procedure but not respond. Similarly, a 100BASE-T receiver that does not implement auto-negotiation will recognize the pulse burst as a link maintenance signal. The pulse burst is transmitted only during idle times on the link and does not interfere with normal traffic.

The pulse burst consists of 33 pulse positions. The 17 odd-numbered pulse positions contain a link pulse. Each of the 16 even-numbered pulse positions contains either a pulse to represent binary 1 or no pulse to represent binary 0. Thus a 16-bit code word is embedded in the pulse burst. The code word consists of the following fields:

- *Selector field (5 bits):* used to identify the type of message being sent. One value identifies an IEEE 802.3 message type. Most of the other values are reserved for future use.
- *Technology ability field (8 bits):* indicates which medium technologies this device is capable of supporting.
- *Remote fault bit:* if set, indicates to the link partner that a fault condition has occurred.
- *Acknowledge bit:* if set, indicates that a device has received its link partner's code word successfully.
- *Next page bit:* if set, indicates that another code word will follow this one. The next code word may provide supplemental information that is proprietary or that has been defined in IEEE 802.3. For example, if the remote fault bit is set, the next code word could contain information about the fault.

Each of the 8 bits of the technology ability field indicates a separate technology that may be supported. Currently, five different technologies are defined and the remaining 3 bits are reserved for future technologies. The five technologies are assigned the following priorities, from highest to lowest:

- 100BASE-TX full duplex
- 100BASE-T4
- 100BASE-TX
- 10BASE-T full duplex
- 10BASE-T

The highest common supported technology is the one that will be used in subsequent exchanges between the two devices. An example of the use of this feature is the following. A station is equipped with an IEEE 802.3 interface that can automatically be configured to run at 10 or 100 Mbps. Initially, the device is connected to a repeater that conforms to 10BASE-T. Upon initialization, the device generates a pulse burst but receives only normal 10BASE-T link maintenance signals in response. The device therefore configures itself for 10-Mbps operation. Later, the repeater is replaced with a 100-Mbps repeater. When this repeater is powered up, it sends a pulse burst to each attached device, advertising its capabilities. The attached device can then acknowledge this code word and reconfigure itself automatically for 100-Mbps operation.

7.2

100VG-ANYLAN

Like 100BASE-T, 100VG-AnyLAN[2] is intended to be a 100-Mbps extension to the 10-Mbps Ethernet and to support IEEE 802.3 frame types. It also provides compatibility with IEEE 802.5 token ring frames. 100VG-AnyLAN is designed to operate efficiently over category 3 cable as well as category 5 cable. 100VG-AnyLAN uses a new MAC scheme known as demand priority to determine the order in which nodes share the network. Since this specification does not use CSMA/CD, it has been standardized under a new working group, IEEE 802.12, rather than remain in the 802.3 working group.

Topology

The topology for a 100VG-AnyLAN network is hierarchical star. The simplest configuration consists of a single central hub and a number of attached devices. More complex arrangements are possible, in which there is a single

---

[2]VG, voice grade; AnyLAN, support for multiple LAN frame types.

root hub, with one or more subordinate level 2 hubs; a level 2 hub can have additional subordinate hubs at level 3, and so on, to an arbitrary depth.

Figure 7.8 shows an example configuration with two levels. The root hub supports two level 2 hubs. In addition, there is an end system attached directly to the root hub as well as an Ethernet switch and an Ethernet bridge. Both the Ethernet switch and the bridge are each treated as a single end system for purposes of access control. The hub is responsible for handling the 802.3 frames and converting between 802.3 and 802.5 frame formats if necessary (not necessary in this example).

Medium Access Control

The MAC algorithm for 802.12 is a round-robin scheme with two priority levels. We first describe the algorithm for a single-hub network and then discuss the general case.

Single-Hub Network.   When a station wishes to transmit a frame, it first issues a request to the central hub and then awaits permission from the hub to transmit. A station must designate each request as normal priority or high priority.

The central hub continually scans all of its ports for a request in round-robin fashion. Thus an n-port hub looks for a request first on port 1, then port 2, and so on, up to port n. The scanning process then begins again at port 1. The hub maintains two pointers: a high-priority pointer and a normal-priority pointer. During one complete cycle, the hub grants each high-priority request in the order in which the requests are encountered. If at any time there are no pending high-priority requests, the hub will grant any normal-priority requests that it encounters.

Figure 7.9 gives an example. The sequence of events is as follows.

1. The hub sets both pointers to port 1 and begins scanning. The first request encountered is a low-priority request from port 2. The hub grants this request and updates the low-priority pointer to port 3.

2. Port 2 transmits a low-priority frame. The hub receives this frame and retransmits it. During this period, two high-priority requests are generated.

3. Once the frame from port 2 is transmitted, the hub begins granting high-priority requests in round-robin order, beginning with port 1 and followed by port 5. The high-priority pointer is set to port 6.

4. After the high-priority frame from port 5 completes, there are no outstanding high-priority requests and the hub turns to the normal-priority requests. Four requests have arrived since the last low-priority frame was transmitted: from ports 2, 7, 3, and 6. Since the normal-priority pointer is set to port 3, these requests will be granted in the order 3, 6, 7, 2 if no other requests intervene.

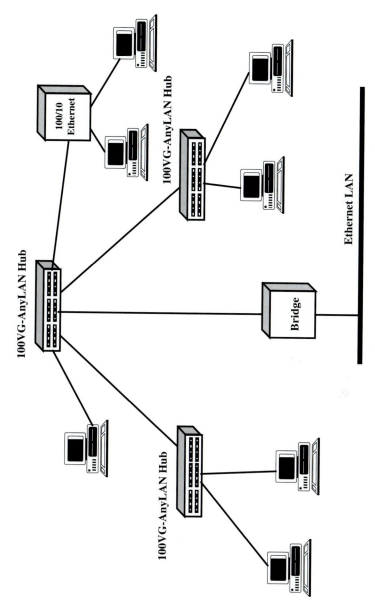

FIGURE 7.8 Example 100VG-AnyLAN Configuration

239

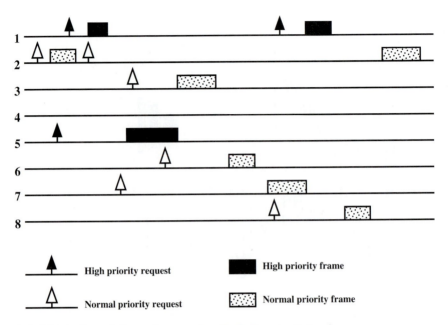

FIGURE 7.9   Example Frame Sequence in a Single-Repeater Network

5. The frames from ports 3, 6, and 7 are transmitted in turn. During the transmission of frame 7, a high-priority request arrives from port 1 and a normal-priority request arrives from port 8. The hub sets the normal-priority pointer to port 8.

6. Since high-priority requests take precedence, port 1 is granted access next.

7. After the frame from port 1 is transmitted, the hub has two outstanding normal-priority requests. The request from port 2 has been waiting the longest. However, port 8 is next in round-robin order to be satisfied, so its request is granted, followed by that of port 2.

Figure 7.10 is a logical representation of the scanning algorithm. We can view the process as involving two circular buffers, each with one position for each port. When a high-priority request is generated by port k, that request is placed in position k in the high-priority buffer. Similarly, a normal-priority request is placed in the normal-priority buffer. As long as the high-priority buffer is not empty, the high-priority pointer scans the buffer and honors each request that it encounters. When the high-priority buffer is empty, the normal-priority pointer scans its buffer granting requests. Finally, if a request remains in the normal-priority buffer for an extended period (default: 500 ms), it is moved to the corresponding position in the high-priority buffer.

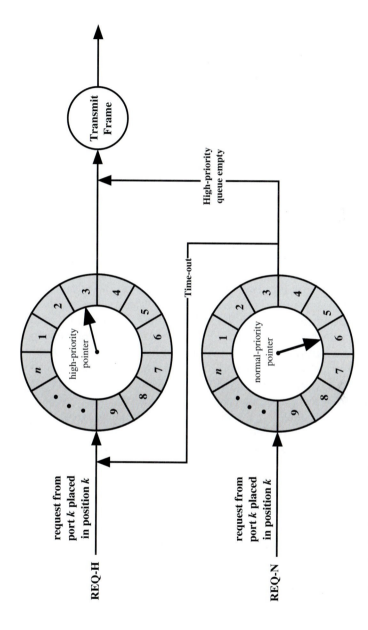

FIGURE 7.10   100VG-AnyLAN Priority Scheme

Hierarchical Network.   In a hierarchical network all the end-system ports on all hubs are treated as a single set of ports for purposes of the round-robin algorithm. The hubs are configured to cooperate in scanning the ports in the proper order. Put another way, the set of hubs are treated logically as a single hub.

Figure 7.11 indicates port ordering in a hierarchical network. The order is generated by walking a tree representation of the network, in which the branches under each node in the tree are arranged in increasing order from left to right. With this convention, the port order is generated by traversing the tree in what is referred to as preorder traversal, which is defined recursively as follows:

1. Visit the root.
2. Traverse the subtrees from left to right.

This method of traversal is also known as a depth-first search of the tree.

Let us now consider the mechanics of medium access and frame transmission in a hierarchical network. There are a number of contingencies to consider. First consider the behavior of the root hub. This hub performs the high-priority and normal-priority round-robin algorithms for all directly attached devices. Thus, if there are one or more pending high-priority requests, the hub grants these requests in round-robin fashion. If there are no pending high-priority requests, the hub grants any normal-priority requests in round-robin fashion. When a request is granted by the root hub to a directly attached end system, that system may immediately transmit a frame. When a request is granted by the root hub to a directly attached level 2 hub, control passes to the level 2 hub. The level 2 hub then proceeds to execute its own round-robin algorithms.

Any end system that is ready to transmit sends a request signal to the hub to which it attaches. If the end system is attached directly to the root hub, the request is conveyed directly to the root hub. If the end system is attached to a lower-level hub, the request is transmitted directly to that hub. If that hub does not currently have control of the round-robin algorithm, it passes the request up to the next higher-level hub. Eventually, all requests that are not granted at a lower level are passed up to the root hub.

The scheme described so far does enforce a round-robin discipline among all attached stations, but two refinements are needed. First, a preemption mechanism is needed. This is best explained by an example. Consider the following sequence of events:

1. Suppose that the root hub (R) in Figure 7.11 is in control and that there are no high-priority requests pending anywhere in the network. However, stations 5-1, 5-2, and 5-3 have all issued normal-priority requests, causing hub B to issue a normal-priority request to R.
2. R will eventually grant this request, passing control to B.

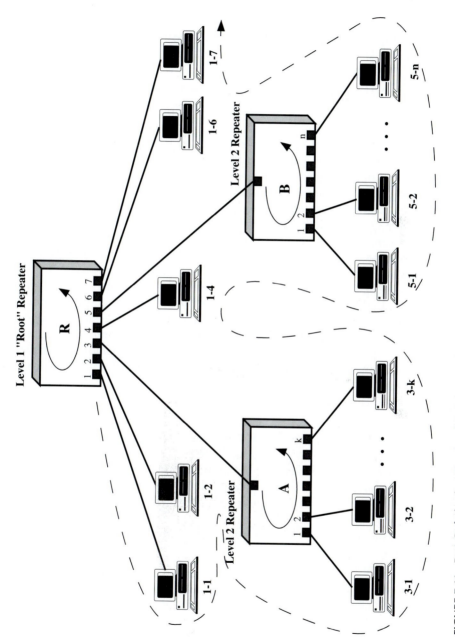

FIGURE 7.11 Port Ordering in a Two-Level IEEE 802.12 Network

3. B then proceeds to honor its outstanding requests one at a time.

4. While B is honoring its first normal-priority request, station 1-6 issues a high-priority request.

5. In response to the request from 1-6, R issues a preempt signal to B. This tells B to relinquish control after the completion of the current transmission.

6. R grants the request of 1-6 and then continues its round-robin algorithm.

The second refinement is a mechanism to prevent a nonroot hub from retaining control indefinitely. To see the problem, suppose that B in Figure 7.11 has a high-priority request pending from 5-1. After receiving control from R, B grants the request to 5-1. Meanwhile, other stations subordinate to B issue high-priority requests. B could continue in round-robin fashion to honor all of these requests. If additional requests arrive from other subordinates of B during these other transmissions, B would be able to continue granting requests indefinitely even though there are other high-priority requests pending elsewhere in the network. To prevent this kind of lockup, a subordinate hub may only retain control for a signal round-robin cycle through all of its ports.

The IEEE 802.12 MAC algorithm is quite effective. When multiple stations offer high loads, the protocol behaves much like a token ring protocol, with network access rotating among all high-priority requesters, followed by low-priority requesters when there are no outstanding high-priority requests. At low load, the protocol behaves in a fashion similar to CSMA/CD under low load: A single requester gains medium access almost immediately.

Frame Transmission. In a network consisting of a single hub and attached stations, the procedure for frame transmission is quite simple. When a station has been granted access, it transmits a frame to the central hub. If the destination address in the frame refers to a single destination station, the hub retransmits that frame to just that destination. If the frame has a multicast or broadcast destination address, the hub retransmits the frame on all ports except the incoming port.

In a hierarchical network, the foregoing procedure is generalized. For example, consider a transmission from station 3-1 in Figure 7.11. The following are the possible outcomes:

1. If the frame has a multicast or broadcast destination address, *A* retransmits the frame to all of its subordinate stations and also retransmits the frame up to R. R will in turn retransmit the frame out through all of its ports except the port to *A* (port 3). When *B* receives the frame, it retransmits the frame on all of its subordinate ports. Thus the frame is transmitted exactly once on each subordinate port of each repeater.

2. If the frame is addressed to one of the other stations directly attached to A, then A retransmits the frame just to that destination station.

3. If the frame is addressed to a station other than one of its subordinate stations, A retransmits the frame only upward to the root. If the frame is addressed to one of the stations directly attached to R (1-1, 1-2, 1-4, 1-6, 1-7), R retransmits the frame only to that station; otherwise, R retransmits the frame downward to all directly attached hubs except A.

A hub needs to know the MAC address of all directly attached subordinate stations but does not need to know the MAC address of any other end systems. This simplifies the configuration task and the routing algorithm.

Physical Level

The current version of IEEE 801.12 calls for the use of four-pair unshielded twisted pair (UTP) using category 3, 4, or 5 cable. Future versions will also support two-pair category 5 UTP, shielded twisted pair, and fiber optic cabling.

Signal Encoding.   A key objective of the 100VG-AnyLAN effort is to be able to achieve 100 Mbps over short distances using ordinary voice-grade (category 3) cabling. The advantage of this is that in many existing buildings, there is an abundance of voice-grade cabling and very little else. Thus, if this cabling can be used, installation costs are minimized.

With present technology, a data rate of 100 Mbps over one or two category 3 pairs is impractical. To meet the objective, 100VG-AnyLAN specifies a novel encoding scheme that involves using four pairs to transmit data in a half-duplex mode. Specifically, a MAC frame is divided into 5-bit chunks (quintets) and each successive chunk is transmitted over a different channel in round-robin fashion. Thus to achieve a data rate of 100 Mbps, a data rate of only 25 Mbps is needed on each channel.

To ensure adequate transitions on each line for synchronization, an encoding scheme known as 5B6B is used. The 5B6B scheme is based on the same strategy as the 4B/5B scheme described in Section 7.1. In this case, each group of 5 input bits is mapped into a set of 6 output bits. Thus for an effective data rate of 25 Mbps, a signaling rate of 30 Mbaud is required.

With the 5B6B scheme, there are 32 possible 5-bit inputs. Ideally, we would like to assign to each 5-bit input a 6-bit code that has an equal number of ones and zeros. This would maintain a dc balance of zero. However, only 20 6-bit code words have three ones and zeros. These codes are assigned to 20 of the input patterns. For the remaining 12 input patterns, two code words are assigned, one with four zeros and two ones (mode 2) and one with two zeros and four ones (mode 4). Successive instances of any of these 24 unbalanced code words must alternate between mode 2 and mode 4 output to maintain balance. If, during reception, a station or repeater receives two of the same type of unbalanced words in a row (with any number of intervening balanced words), the receiver knows that a transmission error has occurred and will ask for a retransmission of the data.

Table 7.6 shows the complete 5B6B encoding scheme. There is a unique output code word for 12 of the input patterns. For the rest, the transmitter keeps track of whether the last unbalanced transmitted word was mode 2 or mode 4 and transmits the appropriate output code word to maintain balance.

Figure 7.12 depicts the 100VG-AnyLAN transmission scheme. Data from the MAC layer can be viewed as a stream of octets. The bits from this stream are taken five at a time to form a stream of quintets that are then passed down to the four transmission channels in round-robin fashion. Next, each quintet passes through a simple scrambling algorithm to increase the number of transitions between 0 and 1 and to improve the signal spectrum (see Appendix 3C). At this point it might be possible simply to transmit the data using NRZ. However, even with the scrambling, the further step of 5B6B encoding is used to ensure synchronization and also to maintain dc balance.

TABLE 7.6　5B6B Encoding Table

Input Quintet	Mode 2 Output	Mode 4 Output	Input Quintet	Mode 2 Output	Mode 4 Output
00000	001100	110011	10000	000101	111010
00001	101100	101100	10001	100101	100101
00010	100010	101110	10010	001001	110110
00011	001101	001101	10011	010110	010110
00100	001010	110101	10100	111000	111000
00101	010101	010101	10101	011000	100111
00110	001110	001110	10110	011001	011001
00111	001011	001011	10111	100001	011110
01000	000111	000111	11000	110001	110001
01001	100011	100011	11001	101010	101010
01010	100110	100110	11010	010100	101011
01011	000110	111001	11011	110100	110100
01100	101000	010111	11100	011100	011100
01101	011010	011010	11101	010011	010011
01110	100100	100100	11110	010010	101101
01111	101001	101001	11111	110010	110010

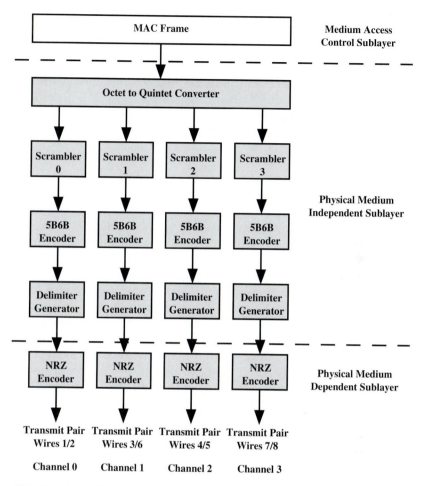

FIGURE 7.12   100VG-AnyLAN Data Transmission Scheme

Since the MAC frame is being divided among four channels, the beginning and ending of a MAC frame must be delimited on each of the channels, which is the purpose of the delimiter generators. Finally, NRZ transmission is used on each channel.

The transmission scheme just described defines a half-duplex form of operation; that is, all four wire pairs are used to transmit in one direction at a time. In addition, a full-duplex form of operation is used to exchange simple control signals. The control signals are defined as a combination of two tones, referred to as tone 1 and tone 2. Tone 1 is generated by transmitting an alternating pattern of 16 ones followed by 16 zeros at a rate of 30 Mbaud using NRZ; tone 2 is an alternating pattern of eight ones followed by eight zeros. With full-duplex operation, two wire pairs are available for transmission in each direction. Hence each end of the link can transmit one of two tones on each of two lines, for a total of four different control indicators.

Table 7.7 lists the definition for the tone combinations transmitted by the hub and the node. A link training request indicates to the node or hub that link initialization is being requested. During link initialization, the two sides exchange basic configuration information is control frames. The remainder of the indicators are explained in the following subsection.

Data Frame Transfer. When an end node transmits a frame, the sequence of operations begins and ends with the end node and the hub in an idle state with respect to their link. Figure 7.13 illustrates this sequence. The initiating node first issues a request indicator to the hub, indicating a normal or high-priority request. When the hub is prepared to honor the request, based on the IEEE 802.12 MAC algorithm, the hub acknowledges the request by ceasing to transmit tones on the two wire pairs that it uses for control indicators. This silence is interpreted by the end node as permission to transmit. The end node then begins to transmit a frame using all four wire pairs. Once the hub has determined how to route the frame, it issues an incoming indicator over each link that will be used to retransmit the frame. An end node that receives the incoming indicator acknowledges that it is ready to receive by ceasing to transmit tones. The hub can then retransmit the frame to the destination end node. Note from the figure that retransmission may begin before the entire frame is received at the hub. Once the hub reads the MAC destination address it can make its routing decision and begin retransmitting without waiting for the entire frame to arrive. This greatly enhances the efficiency of the scheme.

TABLE 7.7 100VG-AnyLAN Tone Definitions

Tone Pattern Transmitted	Meaning Received by the:	
	Node	**Hub**
1–1	Idle	Idle
1–2	Incoming data packet	Normal priority request
2–1	Reserved	High priority request
2–2	Link training request	Link training request

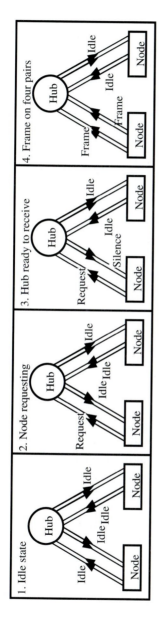
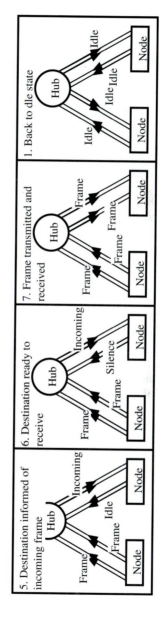

FIGURE 7.13   Transfer of a Data Frame

249

7.3

RECOMMENDED READING

[SPUR95] contains a concise summary of the specifications for 100BASE-T, including configuration guidelines for a single segment of each media type, as well as guidelines for building multisegment Ethernets using a variety of media types. [WATS95], [BARI94], and [ALBR94] provide good technical summaries of 100VG-AnyLAN. [MCMU94] contains several papers discussing and comparing 100BASE-T and 100VG-AnyLAN.

ALBR94   Albrecht, A., et al. "An Overview of IEEE 802.12 Demand Priority." *Proceedings, IEEE GlobeCom,* 1994.

BARI94   Barilovits, S., and Kadambi, J. "100VG-AnyLAN: Network Operation and Real-Time Capabilities." *Proceedings, 19th Conference on Local Computer Networks,* October 1994.

MCMU94   McMullen, M. (editor). *Networks 2000.* San Francisco: Miller Freeman, 1994.

SPUR95   Spurgeon, C. *Quick Reference Guide to Ethernet.* Austin, TX: Harris Park Press, 1995.

WATS95   Watson, G., et al. "The Demand Priority MAC Protocol." *IEEE Network,* January/February 1995.

7.4

PROBLEMS

7.1 With 8B6T coding, the effective data rate on a single channel is 33 Mbps with a signaling rate of 25 Mbaud. If a pure ternary scheme were used, what is the effective data rate for a signaling rate of 25 Mbaud?

7.2 With 8B6T coding, the dc algorithm sometimes negates all of the ternary symbols in a code group. How does the receiver recognize this condition? How does the receiver discriminate between a negated code group and one that has not been negated? For example, the code group for data byte 00 is +−00+− and the code group for data byte 38 is the negation of that, namely −+00−+.

7.3 Draw the MLT decoder state diagram that corresponds to the encoder state diagram of Figure 7.2.

7.4 For the bit stream 0101110, sketch the waveforms for NRZ, NRZI, Manchester, Differential Manchester, and MLT-3.

7.5 Consider the priority order in the technology ability field used in the 100BASE-T auto-negotiation scheme. Justify the order in which items appear in that table (i.e., explain the relative priority of the alternatives).

7.6 Consider a 100VG-AnyLAN network shown in Figure 7.11, and suppose that requests are issued in the following order:

1-2(N), 3-8(N), 1-1(H), 1-2(N), 5-1(N), 3-6(H), 1-4(N), 5-2(N), 1-1(H)

Generate a timing diagram similar to that of Figure 7.9 that shows the transmission sequence of the requests noted above. Assume that all frames are of equal length and that requests arrive at a uniform rate of one per 0.5 frame times.

7.7 Fill in all the values for the 5B6B decoding table whose outline is shown below.

Received Sextet	Mode 2 Output Quintet	Mode 4 Output Quintet
000000		
•		
•		
•		
111111		

7.8 The algorithm for routing frames through a 100VG-AnyLAN network was described in Section 7.2 using the specific example of Figure 7.11. State the algorithm in general terms for a root hub and for a nonroot hub.

7.9 For 100VG-AnyLAN, if we view the signal patterns of tone 1 and tone 2 as square waves, what is the effective frequency of the two tones?

Fiber Distributed Data Interface

The ANSI-accredited standards committee ASC X3T9.5 is responsible for the development of the fiber distributed data interface (FDDI) standards. The bulk of the FDDI work has been standardized by both ANSI and in the ISO 9314 series. FDDI fulfills both a LAN and a MAN role. FDDI is a token ring scheme, similar to the IEEE 802.5 specification. There are several differences that are designed to accommodate the higher data rate (100 Mbps) of FDDI. Table 8.1 summarizes the key differences. Some of these are at the MAC layer and some are at the physical layer.

8.1

FDDI MAC PROTOCOL

The MAC protocol is best explained after an examination of the frame format.

MAC Frame

Figure 8.1 depicts the frame format for the FDDI protocol. The standard defines the contents of this format in terms of symbols, with each data symbol corresponding to 4 data bits. Symbols are used because at the physical

TABLE 8.1 Comparison of FDDI and IEEE 802.5 Token Ring

	FDDI	IEEE 802.5
Transmission medium	Optical fiber Shielded twisted pair Unshielded twisted pair	Shielded twisted pair Unshielded twisted pair
Data rate	100 Mbps	4 or 16 Mbps
Signaling rate	125 Mbaud	8 or 32 Mbaud
Maximum frame size	4500 bytes	4500 bytes (4 Mbps) 18,000 bytes (16 Mbps)
Reliability specification	Yes	No
Signal encoding	4B/5B (optical fiber) MLT (twisted pair)	Differential Manchester
Clocking	Distributed	Centralized
Capacity allocation	Timed token rotation	Priority and reservation bits
Token release	Release after transmit	Release after receive Release after transmit (option)

layer, data are encoded in 4-bit chunks. However, MAC entities in fact must deal with individual bits, so the discussion that follows sometimes refers to 4-bit symbols and sometime to bits. A frame other than a token frame consists of the following fields:

- *Preamble:* synchronizes the frame with each station's clock. The originator of the frame uses a field of 16 idle symbols (64 bits); subsequent repeating stations may change the length of the field consistent with clocking requirements. The idle symbol is a nondata fill pattern. The actual form of a nondata symbol depends on the signal encoding on the medium.
- *Starting delimiter (SD):* indicates start of frame. It is coded as JK, where J and K are nondata symbols.
- *Frame control (FC):* has the bit format CLFFZZZZ, where C indicates whether this is a synchronous or an asynchronous frame (explained below); L indicates the use of 16- or 48-bit addresses; FF indicates whether this is an LLC, MAC control, or reserved frame. For a control frame, the remaining 4 bits indicate the type of control frame. Table 8.2 lists the formats defined in the standard; some of these are self-explanatory; others will be explained as the discussion proceeds.
- *Destination address (DA):* specifies the station(s) for which the frame is intended. It may be a unique physical address, a multicast-group address, or a broadcast address. The ring may contain a mixture of 16- and 48-bit address lengths.

Bits	64	8	8	16 or 48	16 or 48	≥ 0	32	4	1
	Preamble	SD	FC	DA	SA	Info	FCS	ED	FS

SD = starting delimiter
FC = frame control
DA = destination address
SA = source address
FCS = frame check sequence
ED = ending delimiter
FS = frame status

(a) General Frame Format

Preamble	SD	FC	FS

(b) Token Frame Format

FIGURE 8.1   FDDI Frame Formats

- *Source address (SA):* specifies the station that sent the frame.
- *Information:* contains LLC data unit or information related to a control operation.
- *Frame check sequence (FCS):* a 32-bit cyclic redundancy check, based on the FC, DA, SA, and information fields.
- *Ending delimiter (ED):* contains a nondata symbol (T) and marks the end of the frame, except for the FS field.
- *Frame status (FS):* contains the error detected (E), address recognized (A), and frame copied (F) indicators. Each indicator is represent by a symbol, which is R for "reset" or "false" and S for "set" or "true."

A token frame consists of the following fields:

- *Preamble:* as above
- *Starting delimiter:* as above
- *Frame control (FC):* has the bit format 10000000 or 11000000 to indicate that this is a token
- *Ending delimiter (ED):* contains a pair of nondata symbols (T) that terminate the token frame

A comparison with the 802.5 frame (Figure 6.15) shows that the two are quite similar. The FDDI frame includes a preamble to aid in clocking, which is more demanding at the higher data rate. Both 16- and 48-bit addresses are allowed in the same network with FDDI; this is more flexible than the scheme used on all the 802 standards. Finally, there are some differences in the control bits. For example, FDDI does not include priority and reservation bits; capacity allocation is handled in a different way, as described below.

TABLE 8.2   FDDI Frame Control Field

Type	CLFF ZZZZ	Description
Void	0X00 0000	Logically not a frame; ignored
Nonrestricted token	1000 0000	For synchronous and nonrestricted asynchronous transmission
Restricted token	1100 0000	For synchronous and restricted asynchronous transmission
MAC Frames		
MAC	1L00 0001 to 1L00 1111	Range of values reserved for MAC control frames
Beacon	1L00 0010	Indicates serious ring failure
Claim	1L00 0011	Used to determine which station creates a new token and initializes the ring
Station Management Frames		
Station management	0L00 0001 to 0L00 1111	Range of values reserved for station management frames
Next station addressing	0L00 1111	Used in station management
LLC Frames		
Asynchronous	0L01 rPPP	Asynchronous transmission at priority PPP
Synchronous	1L01 rrrr	Synchronous transmission
Reserved Frames		
Reserved for implementer	CL10 r000 to CL10 r111	Implementation-dependent
Reserved for future standardization	CL11 rrrr	To be used in future version of standard

MAC Protocol

The basic (without capacity allocation) FDDI MAC protocol is fundamentally the same as IEEE 802.5 There are two key differences:

1. In FDDI, a station waiting for a token seizes the token by aborting (failing to repeat) the token transmission as soon as the token frame is recognized. After the captured token is completely received, the station begins transmitting one or more data frames. The 802.5 technique of flipping a bit to convert a token to the start of a data frame was considered impractical because of the high data rate of FDDI.

2. In FDDI, a station that has been transmitting data frames releases a new token as soon as it completes data frame transmission, even if it has not begun to receive its own transmission. This is the same technique as the early token release option of 802.5. Again, because of the high data rate, it would be too inefficient to require the station to wait for its frame to return, as in normal 802.5 operation.

Figure 8.2 gives an example of ring operation. After station *A* has seized the token, it transmits frame F1 and immediately transmits a new token. F1 is addressed to station *C*, which copies it as it circulates past. The frame eventually returns to *A*, which absorbs it. Meanwhile, *B* seizes the token issued by *A* and transmits F2 followed by a token. This action could be repeated any number of times, so that at any one time, there may be multiple frames circulating the ring. Each station is responsible for absorbing its own frames based on the source address field.

A further word should be said about the frame status (FS) field. Each station can check passing bits for errors and can set the E indicator if an error is detected. If a station detects its own address, it sets the A indicator; it may also copy the frame, setting the C indicator. This allows the originating station, when it absorbs a frame that it previously transmitted, to differentiate three conditions:

- Station nonexistent/nonactive
- Station active but frame not copied
- Frame copied

When a frame is absorbed, the status indicators (E, A, C) in the FS field may be examined to determine the result of the transmission. However, if an error or failure-to-receive condition is discovered, the MAC protocol entity does not attempt to retransmit the frame but reports the condition to LLC. It is the responsibility of LLC or some higher-layer protocol to take corrective action.

Capacity Allocation

As with IEEE 802.5, FDDI provides a capacity allocation scheme.

Requirements. The priority scheme used in 802.5 will not work in FDDI, as a station will often issue a token before its own transmitted frame returns. Hence the use of a reservation field is not effective. Furthermore, the FDDI standard is intended to provide for greater control over the capacity of the network than 802.5 to meet the requirements for a high-speed LAN. Specifically, the FDDI capacity allocation scheme seeks to accommodate the following requirements:

- Support for a mixture of stream and bursty traffic
- Support for multiframe dialogue

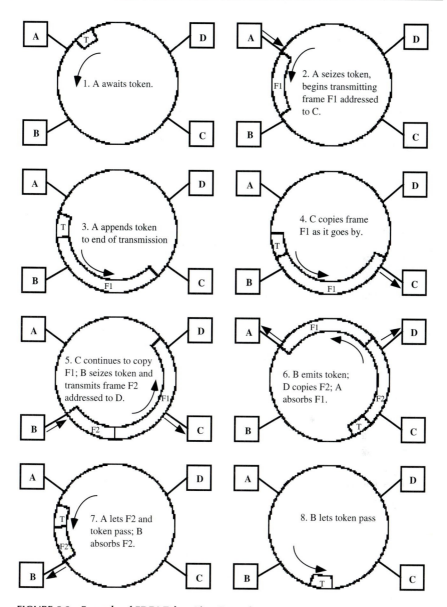

FIGURE 8.2   Example of FDDI Token Ring Operation

With respect to the first requirement, a high-capacity LAN would be expected to support a large number of devices or to act as a backbone for a number of other LANs. In either case, the LAN would be expected to support a wide variety of traffic types. For example, some of the stations may generate short, bursty traffic with modest throughput requirements but a need for a short delay time. Other stations may generate long streams of traffic that require high throughput, but they may be able to tolerate moderate delays prior to the start of transmission.

With respect to the second requirement, there may sometime be a need to dedicate a fixed fraction or all of the capacity of the LAN to a single application. This permits a long sequence of data frames and acknowledgments to be interchanged. An example of the utility of this feature is a read or write to a high-performance disk. Without the ability to maintain a constant high-data-rate flow over the LAN, only one sector of the disk could be accessed per revolution—an unacceptable performance.

Synchronous Traffic.   To accommodate the requirement to support a mixture of stream and bursty traffic, FDDI defines two types of traffic: synchronous and asynchronous. Each station is allocated a portion of the total capacity (the portion may be zero); the frames that it transmits during this time are referred to as synchronous frames. Any capacity that is not allocated or that is allocated but not used is available for the transmission of additional frames, referred to as asynchronous frames.

The scheme works as follows. A **target token rotation time** (TTRT) is defined; each station stores the same value for TTRT. Some or all stations may be provided a **synchronous allocation** (SA$_i$), which may vary among stations. The allocations must be such that

$$\text{DMax} + \text{FMax} + \text{Token Time} + \sum \text{SA}_i \leq \text{TTRT}$$

where

$$\text{SA}_i = \text{synchronous allocation for station } i$$
$$\text{DMax} = \text{propagation time for one complete circuit of the ring}$$
$$\text{FMax} = \text{time required to transmit a maximum-length frame (4500}$$
$$\text{octets)}$$
$$\text{TokenTime} = \text{time required to transmit a token}$$

The assignment of values for SA$_i$ is by means of a station management protocol involving the exchange of station management frames. The protocol assures that the equation above is satisfied. Initially, each station has a zero allocation and it must request a change in the allocation. Support for synchronous allocation is optional; a station that does not support synchronous allocation may only transmit asynchronous traffic.

All stations have the same value of TTRT and a separately assigned value of SA$_i$. In addition, several variables that are required for the operation of the capacity-allocation algorithm are maintained at each station:

- Token-rotation timer (TRT)
- Token-holding timer (THT)
- Late counter (LC)

Each station is initialized with TRT set equal to TTRT and LC set to zero.[1] When the timer is enabled, TRT begins to count down. If a token is received before TRT expires, TRT is reset to TTRT. If TRT counts down to 0 before a token is received, LC is incremented to 1 and TRT is reset to TTRT and again begins to count down. IF TRT expires a second time before receiving a token, LC is incremented to 2, the token is considered lost, and a claim process (described below) is initiated. Thus LC records the number of times, if any, that TRT has expired since the token was last received at that station. The token is considered to arrive early if TRT has not expired since the station received the token, that is, if LC = 0.

When a station receives the token, its actions will depend on whether the token is early or late. If the token is early, the station saves the remaining time from TRT in THT, resets TRT, and enables TRT:

THT ← TRT

TRT ← TTRT

Enable TRT

The station can then transmit according to the following rules:

1. It may transmit synchronous frames for a time SA_i.
2. After transmitting synchronous frames, or if there were no synchronous frames to transmit, THT is enabled. The station may begin transmission of asynchronous frames as long as THT > 0.

If a station receives a token and the token is late, LC is set to zero and TRT continues to run. The station can then transmit synchronous frames for a time SA_i. The station may not transmit any asynchronous frames.

This scheme is designed to assure that the time between successive sightings of a token is on the order of TTRT or less. Of this time, a given amount is always available for synchronous traffic and any excess capacity is available for asynchronous traffic. Because of random fluctuations in traffic, the actual token circulation time may exceed TTRT, as demonstrated below.

The FDDI algorithm is similar to the 802.4 algorithm with only two classes of data, 6 and 4. Synchronous data corresponds to class 6, and the value of SA_i in FDDI corresponds to the token holding time in 802.4. TTRT corresponds to TRT4. Since the sum of the SA_i (all the synchronous allocations) must be less than or equal to TTRT, the FDDI restrictions correspond to case IIa in Figure 6.11.

Figure 8.3 illustrates the use of the station variables in FDDI by displaying the values of TRT, THT, and LC for a particular station. In this example, the TTRT is 100 milliseconds (ms). The station's synchronous capacity allocation, SA_i, is 30 ms. The following events occur:

---

[1]*Note:* All timer values in the standard are negative numbers with counters counting up to zero. For clarity, the discussion uses positive numbers.

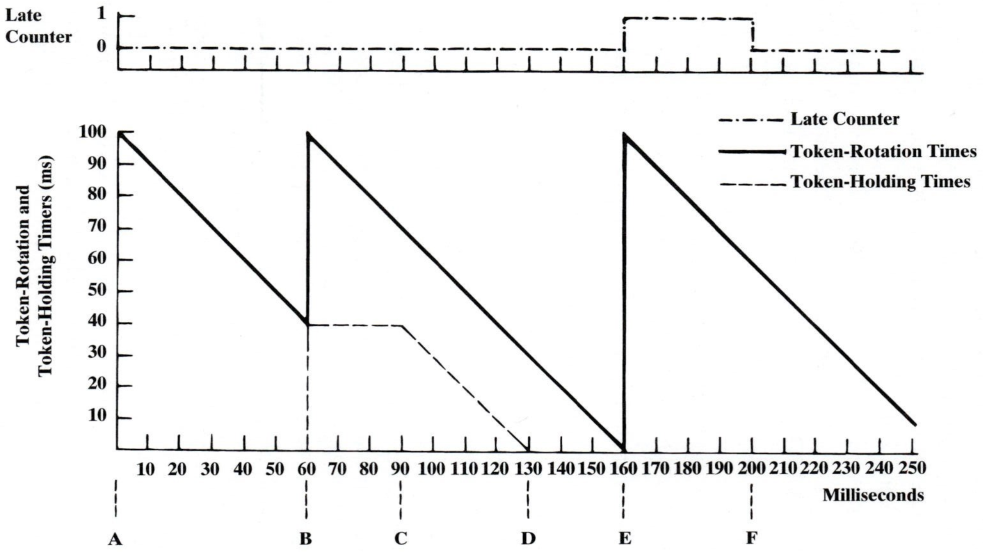

FIGURE 8.3   FDDI Capacity Allocation Example [MCCO88]

A. A token arrives early. The station has no frames to send. TRT is set to TTRT (100 ms) and begins to count down. The station allows the token to go by.

B. The token returns 60 ms later. Since TRT = 40 and LC = 0, the token is early. The station sets THT ← TRT and TRT ← TTRT, so that THT = 40 and TRT = 100. TRT is enabled immediately. The station has synchronous data to transmit and begins to do so.

C. After 30 ms, the station has consumed its synchronous allocation. It has asynchronous data to transmit, so it enables THT and begins transmitting.

D. THT expires, and the station must cease transmission of asynchronous frames. The station issues a token.

E. TRT expires. The station increments LC to 1 and resets TRT to 100.

F. The token arrives. Since LC is 1, the token is late, and no asynchronous data may be transmitted. At this point, the station also has no synchronous data to transmit. LC is reset to 0 and the token is allowed to go by.

Figure 8.4 provides a simplified example of a four-station ring. The following assumptions are made:

1. Traffic consists of fixed-length frames.
2. TTRT = 100 frame times.
3. SA_i = 20 frame times for each station.
4. Each station is always prepared to send its full synchronous allocation as many asynchronous frames as possible.

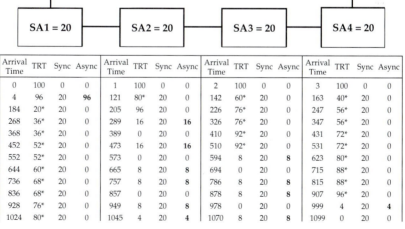

Arrival Time	TRT	Sync	Async	Arrival Time	TRT	Sync	Async	Arrival Time	TRT	Sync	Async	Arrival Time	TRT	Sync	Async
0	100	0	0	1	100	0	0	2	100	0	0	3	100	0	0
4	96	20	96	121	80*	20	0	142	60*	20	0	163	40*	20	0
184	20*	20	0	205	96	20	0	226	76*	20	0	247	56*	20	0
268	36*	20	0	289	16	20	16	326	76*	20	0	347	56*	20	0
368	36*	20	0	389	0	20	0	410	92*	20	0	431	72*	20	0
452	52*	20	0	473	16	20	16	510	92*	20	0	531	72*	20	0
552	52*	20	0	573	0	20	0	594	8	20	8	623	80*	20	0
644	60*	20	0	665	8	20	8	694	0	20	0	715	88*	20	0
736	68*	20	0	757	8	20	8	786	8	20	8	815	88*	20	0
836	68*	20	0	857	0	20	0	878	8	20	8	907	96*	20	0
928	76*	20	0	949	8	20	8	978	0	20	0	999	4	20	4
1024	80*	20	0	1045	4	20	4	1070	8	20	8	1099	0	20	0

* LC = 1; otherwise LC = 0

FIGURE 8.4   Operation of FDDI Capacity Allocation Scheme

5. The total overhead during one complete token circulation is four frame times (one frame time per station).

One row of the table corresponds to one circulation of the token. For each station the token arrival time is shown, followed by the value of TRT at the time of arrival, followed by the number of synchronous and asynchronous frames transmitted while the station holds the token.

The example begins after a period during which no data frames have been sent, so that the token has been circulating as rapidly as possible (four frame times). Thus, when station 1 receives the token at time 4, it measures a circulation time of 4 (its TRT = 96). It is therefore able to send not only its 20 synchronous frames but also 96 asynchronous frames; recall that THT is not enabled until after the station has sent its synchronous frames. Station 2 experiences a circulation time of 120 (20 frames + 96 frames + 4 overhead frames) but is nevertheless entitled to transmit its 20 synchronous frames. Note that if each station continues to transmit its maximum allowable synchronous frames, the circulation time surges to 180 (at time 184) but soon stabilizes at approximately 100. With a total synchronous utilization of 80 and an overhead of four frame times, there is an average capacity of 16 frame times available for asynchronous transmission. Note that if all stations always have a full backlog of asynchronous traffic, the opportunity to transmit asynchronous frames is distributed among them.

This example demonstrates that the synchronous allocation does not always provide a guaranteed fraction of capacity $SA_i/TTRT$. Rather, the fraction of capacity available to a station for synchronous transmission during any token circulation is SA_i/τ, where τ is the actual circulation time. As we have seen, τ can exceed TTRT. It can be shown that τ tends, in the steady state, to approach TTRT and has an upper bound of $2 \times$ TTRT [JOHN87].

Asynchronous Traffic.   Asynchronous traffic can be further subdivided into eight levels of priority. Each station has a set of eight threshold values, T_Pr(1), ..., T_Pr(8), such that T_Pr(i) = maximum time that a token can take to circulate and still permit priority i frames to be transmitted. Rule 2 on p. 259 is revised as follows:

2. After transmitting synchronous frames, or if there were no synchronous frames to transmit, THT is enabled and begins to run from its set value. The station may transmit asynchronous data of priority i only as long as THT > T_Pr(i). The maximum value of any of the T_Pr(i) must be no greater than TTRT.

This scheme is essentially the one used in the 802.4 token bus standard (Figure 6.10).

The rules above satisfy the requirement for support for both stream and bursty traffic and, with the use of priorities, provide a great deal of flex-

ibility. In addition, FDDI provides a mechanism that satisfies the requirements for dedicated multiframe traffic mentioned earlier. When a station
wishes to enter an extended dialogue, it may gain control of all the unallo-
cated (asynchronous) capacity on the ring by using a restricted token. The
station captures a nonrestricted token, transmits the first frame of the dialogue to the destination station, then issues a restricted token. Only the station that received the last frame may transmit asynchronous frames using
the restricted token. The two stations may then exchange data frames and
restricted tokens for an extended period, during which no other station may
transmit asynchronous frames. The standard assumes that restricted transmission is predetermined not to violate the TTRT limitation, and it does not
mandate the use of THT during this mode. Synchronous frames may be
transmitted by any station upon capture of either type of token.

Figure 8.5 depicts the complete FDDI capacity allocation scheme,
and Figure 8.6 summarizes the relationship among the various types of
traffic.

Ring Monitoring

The responsibility for monitoring the functioning of the token ring algorithm is distributed among all stations on the ring. Each station monitors
the ring for invalid conditions requiring ring initialization. Invalid conditions include an extended period of inactivity or incorrect activity (e.g., per-
sistent data frame). To detect the latter condition, each station keeps track of
how long it has been since it last saw a valid token. If this time exceeds 2 ×
TTRT, an error condition is assumed.

Three processes are involved in error detection and correction:

- Claim token process
- Initialization process
- Beacon process

Two MAC control frames are used: the beacon frame and the claim frame
(Table 8.2).

Claim Token Process.   A station will detect the need for initialization of
the ring by observing the lack of token; as explained above, this event
occurs when the station sets LC to 2. Any station detecting a lost token initiates the claim token process by issuing a sequence of claim frames. The
purpose of the claim token process is to negotiate the value to be assigned
to TTRT and to resolve contention among stations attempting to initialize
the ring. Each claiming station sends a continuous stream of claim frames.
The information field of the claim frame contains the station's bid for the
value of TTRT. Each claiming station inspects incoming claim frames and
either defers (ceases to transmit its own claim frames and just repeats

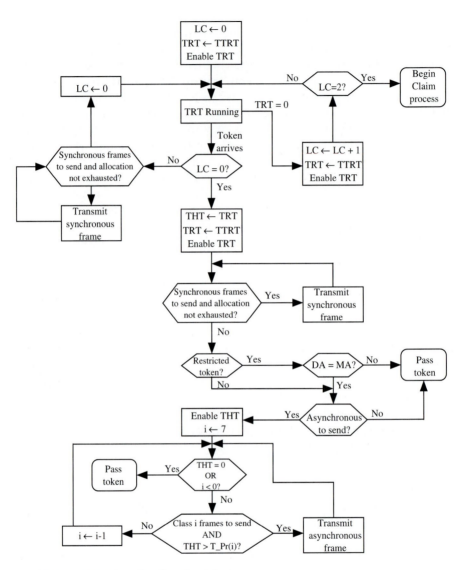

FIGURE 8.5 FDDI Capacity Allocation Scheme

incoming frames) or not (continues to transmit its own claim frames and absorbs incoming frames), according to the following arbitration hierarchy:

- The frame with the lower TTRT has precedence.
- Given equal values of TTRT, a frame with a 48-bit address has precedence over a frame with a 16-bit address.
- Given equal values of TTRT and equal address lengths, the frame with the address of larger numerical value has precedence.

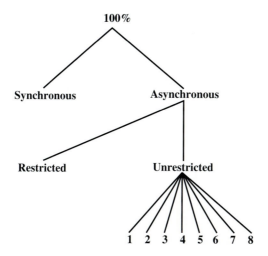

FIGURE 8.6   FDDI Capacity Allocation Categories

The process completes when one station receives its own claim frame, which has made a complete circuit of the ring without being preempted. At this point, the ring is filled with that station's claim frames and all other stations have yielded. All stations store the value of TTRT contained in the latest claim frame to be received. The result is that the smallest requested value for TTRT is stored by all stations and will be used to allocate capacity.

The motivation for given precedence to the lowest TTRT value is to make the LAN responsive to time-critical applications. If we define ring latency (RL) as the total overhead during one complete token circulation, ring utilization can be expressed as

$$\frac{TTRT - RL}{TTRT}$$

Low values of TTRT will provide a low guaranteed response time for synchronous traffic and thus support real-time applications. High values of TTRT allow very high ring use under heavy loads.

Initialization Process.   The station that has won the claim token process is responsible for initializing the ring. All the stations on the ring recognize the initialization process as a result of having seen one or more claim frames. The initializing station issues a nonrestricted token. On the first circulation of the token, it may not be captured. Rather, each station uses the appearance of the token for transition from an initialization state to an operational state, and to reset its TRT. Figure 8.7 illustrates the ring initialization process.

Beacon Process.   The beacon frame is used to isolate a serious ring failure such as a break in the ring. For example, when a station is attempting the

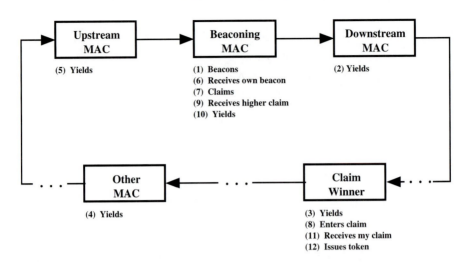

FIGURE 8.7   Normal FDDI Ring Initialization

claim token process, it will eventually time out if it does not come to a resolution (winning or losing), and enter the beacon process. Upon entering
the beacon process, a station continuously transmits beacon frames. A station always yields to a beacon frame received from an upstream station.
Consequently, if the logical break persists, the beacon frames of the station
immediately downstream from the break will normally be propagated. If a
station in the beacon process receives its own beacon frames, it assumes that
the ring has been restored, and it initiates the claim token process.

8.2

FDDI PHYSICAL LAYER SPECIFICATION

The FDDI physical layer specification details the encoding scheme and
transmission medium characteristics for both optical fiber and twisted-pair
media. It also includes considerations of timing jitter and station and FDDI
network configurations.

Optical Fiber FDDI

As the name suggests, the original FDDI specification defined a ring LAN
using an optical fiber medium. The standard includes a data encoding
scheme and a physical medium specification.

Data Encoding.   As is the case with the IEEE 802.4 optical fiber specification, the FDDI data encoding scheme is based on the use of intensity modulation. In the case of 802.4, the data to be transmitted are precoded in Man-

chester form before being submitted to the intensity modulation process, in order to provide transitions for synchronization. The disadvantage of this approach is that the efficiency is only 50 percent. That is, because there can be as many as two transitions per bit time, a signaling rate of 200 million signal elements per second (200 Mbaud) is needed to achieve a data rate of 100 Mbps. At the high data rate of FDDI, this represents an unnecessary cost and technical burden.

To achieve greater efficiency, the FDDI standard specifies the use of the 4B/5B code described in Chapter 7 for 100BASE-T. In this scheme, encoding is done 4 bits at a time; each 4 bits of data are encoded into a symbol with five *cells,* such that each cell contains a single signal element (presence or absence of light). In effect, each set of 4 bits is encoded as 5 bits. The efficiency is thus raised to 80 percent: 100 Mbps is achieved with 125 Mbaud. As in 100BASE-T, each cell of the 4B/5B stream is treated as a binary value and encoded using nonreturn to zero inverted (NRZI).

Table 8.3 shows the symbol encoding used in FDDI, which differs somewhat from the assignments used in 100BASE-T (Table 7.3). Since we are encoding 4 bits with a 5-bit pattern, only 16 of the 32 possible patterns are needed for data encoding. The codes selected to represent the 16 4-bit data blocks are such that a transition is present at least twice for each five-cell code. Given an NRZI format, no more than three zeros in a row are allowed.

The FDDI encoding scheme can be summarized as follows:

1. A simple intensity modulation encoding is rejected because it does not provide synchronization; a string of ones or zeros will have no transitions.
2. The data to be transmitted must first be encoded to assure transitions. The 4B/5B code is chosen over Manchester because it is more efficient.
3. The 4B/5B code is further encoded using NRZI so that the resulting differential signal will improve reception reliability.
4. The specific 5-bit patterns chosen for the encoding of the 16 4-bit data patterns are chosen to guarantee no more than three zeros in a row to provide for adequate synchronization.

Only 16 of the 32 possible cell patterns are required to represent the input data. The remaining cell patterns are either declared invalid or assigned special meaning as control symbols. These assignments are listed in Table 8.3. The nondata symbols fall into the following categories:

- *Line state symbols.* Q indicates the absence of any transitions and loss of clock recovery ability. Halt indicates a forced logical break in activity while maintaining dc balance and clock recovery. I indicates normal condition between frame and token transmissions. The I symbols are used in frame absorption. When a frame returns to the originating

TABLE 8.3   4B/5B Code

Code Group	Symbol	Assignment
Line State Symbols		
00000	Q	Quiet
11111	I	Idle
00100	H	Halt
Starting Delimiter		
11000	J	First of sequential SD pair
10001	K	Second of sequential SD pair
Data Symbols		
11110	0	0000
01001	1	0001
10100	2	0010
10101	3	0011
01010	4	0100
01011	5	0101
01110	6	0110
01111	7	0111
10010	8	1000
10011	9	1001
10110	A	1010
10111	B	1011
11010	C	1100
11011	D	1101
11100	E	1110
11101	F	1111

TABLE 8.3 4B/5B Code (cont.)

Code Group	Symbol	Assignment
Ending Delimiter		
01101	T	Used to terminate the data stream
Control Indicators		
00111	R	Denoting logical ZERO (reset)
11001	S	Denoting logical ONE (set)
Invalid Code Assignments		
00001	V or H	Violation or Halt
00010	V or H	Violation or Halt
00011	V	Violation
00101	V	Violation
00110	V	Violation
01000	V or H	Violation or Halt
01100	V	Violation
10000	V or H	Violation or Halt

station, it is stripped by that station by transmitting I's immediately following its recognition (following the source address field), instead of repeating the frame. Similarly, a token is absorbed by a station by transmitting I's after determining that the incoming frame is a token.

- *Starting delimiter.* The starting delimiter field consists of a J and K symbol pair and is used to designate the beginning of a frame.
- *Ending delimiter.* The ending delimiter field consists of one or two T symbols and is used to designate the end of the frame, except for the frame status field, if present.
- *Control indicators.* The R and S symbols are used in the frame status field to indicate the presence or absence of a condition, as explained in Section 10.2.
- *Invalid code assignments.* The remaining symbol codes are designated as violation (V) symbols, some of which may be recognized as an off-alignment H symbols.

Fiber Medium Specification.   The FDDI standard specifies an optical fiber ring with a data rate of 100 Mbps, using the NRZI-4B/5B encoding scheme described previously. The wavelength specified for data transmission is 1300 nm.

The original specification specifies the use of multimode fiber transmission. Although today's long-distance networks rely primarily on single-mode fiber, that technology generally requires the use of lasers as light sources rather than the cheaper and less-powerful light-emitting diodes (LEDs), which are adequate for FDDI requirements. The dimensions of the fiber cable are specified in terms of the diameter of the core of the fiber and the outer diameter of the cladding layer that surrounds the core. The combination specified in the standard is 62.5/125 μm. The standard lists as alternatives 50/125, 82/125, and 100/140 μm. In general, smaller diameters offer higher potential bandwidths but also higher connector loss.

More recently, two additional fiber medium specifications have been added (Table 8.4). The single-mode fiber specification can be used to configure much longer links between repeaters. The low-cost fiber specification provides lower-cost optical fiber connections for lengths up to 500 meters. The main savings is achieved by relaxing some of the specifications for the optical transceivers.

Twisted-Pair FDDI

The FDDI standard specifies a twisted pair ring with a data rate of 100 Mbps. The signaling scheme that is used is the MLT-3 scheme described for 100BASE-TX in Chapter 7. In this scheme the 4B/5B NRZI signal is converted back to NRZ, scrambled with a stream cipher that distributes

TABLE 8.4   FDDI Optical Fiber Medium Alternatives

	Multimode Fiber	Single-Mode Fiber	Low-Cost Fiber
Light source	LED	Laser	LED
Wavelength	1300 nm	1300 nm	1300 nm
Maximum distance between repeaters	2 km	40–60 km	500 m
Cable size (core/cladding)	62.5/125 μm	8–10/125 μm	62.5/125 μm

the energy for radiated emissions reduction, and then encoded using MLT-3.

Two twisted-pair media are specified: 100-ohm category 5 unshielded twisted pair[2] and 150-ohm shielded twisted pair. In both cases, the maximum distance between repeaters is 100 meters. The twisted-pair specification provides a low-cost alternative that can be used over short distances employing wiring that may already be preinstalled.

Timing Jitter

In a ring LAN, an important concern has to do with the ability to keep all of the repeaters around the ring synchronized. In essence, each repeater recovers clocking information from incoming signals by means of the transitions imposed by the encoding scheme (e.g., differential Manchester in 802.5 and 4B/5B in FDDI). As data circulate around the ring, each repeater receives the data and recovers the clocking. The clocking enables the receiver to maintain bit synchronization so that it samples the incoming stream once per bit time. This clock recovery will deviate in a random fashion from the timing of the transmitter due to signal impairments in transmission and imperfections in the receiver circuitry. In addition, the repeater must either use the recovered clock information for its own transmissions or maintain its own clock. In the former case, the reception difficulties just mentioned cause clock deviation. In the latter case, there may be drift between clocks in adjacent repeaters. All of these problems result in timing errors that are referred to as **timing jitter.**

As each repeater receives incoming data, it issues a clean signal with no distortion. However, the timing error is not eliminated. The cumulative effect of the jitter is to cause the bit latency or "bit length" of the ring to vary. However, unless the latency of the ring remains constant, bits will be dropped (not retransmitted) as the latency of the ring decreases, or added as the latency increases.

The approach taken by FDDI for dealing with timing jitter is to use a distributed clocking scheme with elastic buffers. Each repeater uses its own autonomous clock to transmit bits from its MAC layer onto the ring. For repeating incoming data, a buffer is imposed between the receiver and the transmitter. Data are clocked into the buffer at the clock rate recovered from the incoming stream but are clocked out of the buffer at the station's own clock rate. The buffer has a capacity of 10 bits and expands and contracts as needed. At any time, the buffer contains a certain number of bits. As bits come in, they are placed in the buffer and thus experience a delay equal to the time it takes to transmit the bits ahead of it in the buffer. If the received signal is slightly faster than the repeater's clock, the buffer will expand to

---

[2]See Chapter 2 for a discussion of category 5 unshielded twisted pair.

avoid dropping bits. If the received signal is slow, the buffer will contract to avoid adding bits to the repeated bit stream.

The buffer in each repeater is initialized to its center position each time that it begins to receive a frame, during the preamble that begins the frame. This increases or decreases the length of the preamble, initially transmitted as 16 symbols, as it proceeds around the ring. Because the stability of the transmitter clock is specified as 0.005 percent, a buffer of 10 bits allows transmission of frames 4500 octets in length without overrunning or underrunning the limits of the buffer.

Station and FDDI Network Configurations

Each FDDI station is composed of logical entities that conform to the FDDI standards. The role of a given station depends on the number of entities it has. Networks with different physical topologies may be constructed, depending on the types of stations used.

Dual Ring.   To enhance the reliability of an FDDI ring, the standard provides for the construction of a dual ring, as illustrated in Figure 8.8. Stations participating in a dual ring are connected to their neighbors by two links that transmit in opposite directions. This creates two rings: a primary ring, and a secondary ring on which data may circulate in the opposite direction. Under normal conditions, the secondary ring is idle. When a link failure occurs, the

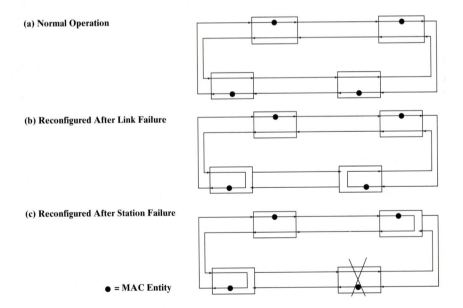

(a) Normal Operation

(b) Reconfigured After Link Failure

(c) Reconfigured After Station Failure

● = MAC Entity

FIGURE 8.8   FDDI Dual-Ring Operation

stations on either side of the link reconfigure as shown in Figure 8.8b. This isolates the link fault and restores a closed ring. In this figure, a dark dot represents a MAC attachment within the station. Thus, in the counter direction, signals may be merely repeated, while the MAC protocol is involved only in the primary direction. As an option, a station may contain two MAC entities and therefore execute that MAC protocol in both directions.

Should a station fail, as shown in Figure 8.8c, the stations on either side reconfigure to eliminate the failed station and both links to that station.

Station Types.   The type of station just described is only one of four station types defined in the FDDI standard (Table 8.5). The use of four different station types allows for the creation of complex topologies and for designs with high levels of reliability.

As just described, the dual attachment station (DAS) can be used to construct a dual ring. In some cases this dual ring will constitute the entire FDDI LAN. In other cases the dual ring can serve as the trunk ring for a more complex topology. In its most general form, the topology that can be achieved with FDDI is referred to as a *dual ring of trees*.

Figure 8.9 is an example that shows the use of all four station types. The main trunk is a dual ring consisting only of stations that are capable of supporting the two rings. Some of these stations are DASs, whose function is to provide an attachment point for end-user stations. Others are dual attachment concentrators (DACs), which participate in the dual ring and may support an end-user station. In addition, each DAC may support stations that attach to a single ring. Each DAC therefore serves as the root of a tree. Single attachment stations (SASs) may attach to the DAC by means of a single ring. The SAS connection does not provide the reliability of the dual-ring configuration available to the DAS. However, FDDI constrains the topology so that an SAS must attach to a concentrator. In the event of a failure of the SAS or its connection to the concentrator, the concentrator may isolate the SAS. Therefore, the reliability of the dual ring is maintained. To achieve a tree structure of depth greater than two, single attachment concentrators (SACs) may be used. An SAC may attach to a DAC or another SAC and may support one or more SASs.

It is important to note that even with an elaborate tree structure, an FDDI configuration still maintains a ring topology. Figure 8.10 shows the circulation path for a simple configuration of a dual ring of two stations, one of which is a DAC. Note that the six stations form a single ring around which a single token will circulate. In addition, a secondary ring is available for reliability that encompasses the DASs and DACs.

Figure 8.11 illustrates the architecture of the various station types. A SAS has one physical layer protocol (PMD, PHY) and one MAC entity. A DAS has two PMD and PHY entities and one or two MAC entities. Finally, both types of concentrators have a similar architecture. Each consists of

TABLE 8.5 FDDI Station Types

Station Type	Definition	Connects to:
Dual attachment (DAS)	Has two pairs of PHY and PMD entities and one or more MAC entities; participates in the trunk dual ring	DAS, DAC
Dual attachment concentrator (DAC)	A DAS with additional PHY and PMD entities beyond those required for attachment to the dual ring; the additional entities permit attachment of additional stations that are logically part of the ring but are physically isolated from the trunk ring	DAS, DAC, SAC, SAS
Single attachment station (SAS)	Has one each PHY, PMD, and MAC entities, and therefore cannot be attached into the trunk ring, but must be attached by a concentrator	DAC, SAC
Single attachment concentrator (SAC)	A SAS with additional PHY and PMD entities beyond those required for attachment to a concentrator; the additional entities permit attachment of additional stations in a tree-structured fashion	DAC, SAC, SAS

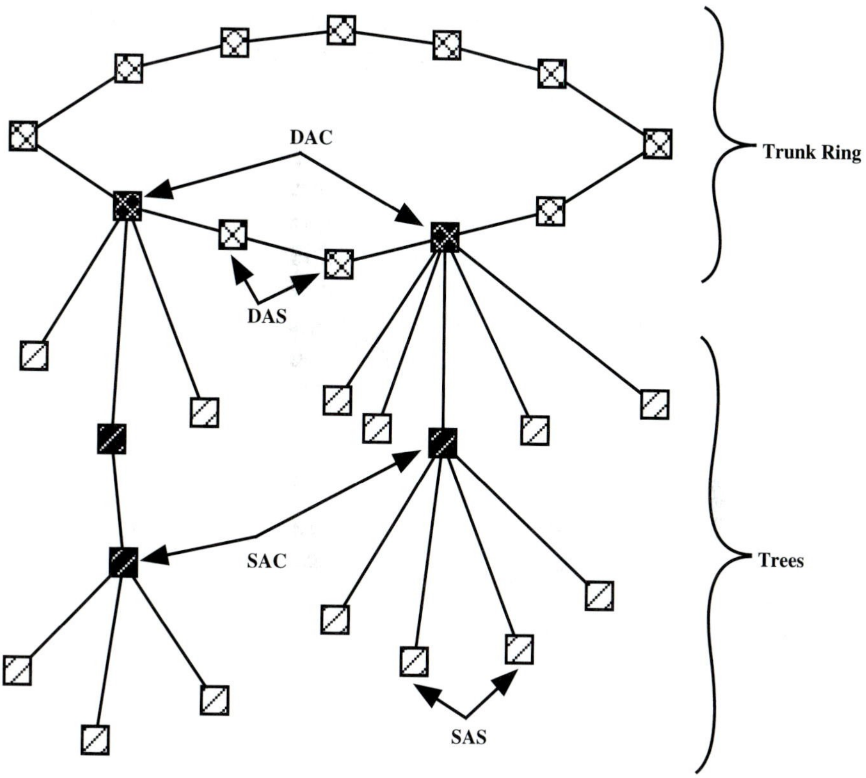

FIGURE 8.9   General FDDI Topology

multiple PMD and PHY entities, with an optional MAC entity. In the case of the SAC, there are at least two sets of physical layer entities: one for connection to a master and at least one for the connection of slaves. In the case of a DAC, there are at least three sets: one for primary connection to the dual ring, one for secondary connection to the dual ring, and at least one for connection of slaves. For both kinds of concentrators, there needs to be something equivalent to a configuration switch that can switch physical layer entity pairs (PMD, PHY) into and out of the ring.

Port Types.   The FDDI standard specifies connection rules to ensure against the construction of illegal topologies. These rules are expressed in terms of allowable connections between port types. Table 8.6 defines the four port types and Figure 8.12 illustrates their use.

FDDI Topologies.   The definition of four station types allows for the creation of a wide variety of topologies. The following are of particular interest:

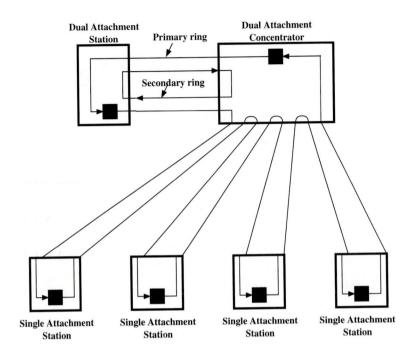

FIGURE 8.10   Star-Shaped Ring

- *Stand-alone concentrator with attached stations.* This consists of a single concentrator and its attached stations. Such a configuration could be used to connect multiple high-performance devices in a workgroup or multiple LANs, with each FDDI station being a bridge.
- *Dual ring.* This consists of a set of DASs connected to form a single dual ring. This topology is useful when there are a limited number of users. It could also be used to interconnect departmental LANs, with each FDDI station being a bridge.
- *Tree of concentrators.* This is a good choice for interconnecting large groups of user devices. Concentrators are wired in a hierarchical star arrangement with one concentrator serving as the root of the tree. This topology provides great flexibility for adding and removing concentrators and stations or changing their location without disrupting the LAN.
- *Dual ring of trees.* This is the most elaborate and flexible topology. Key stations can be incorporated into the dual ring for maximum availability, and the tree structure provides the flexibility described in the preceding item.

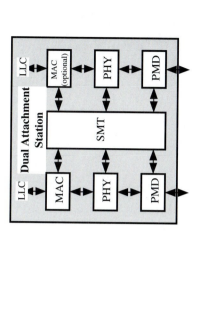

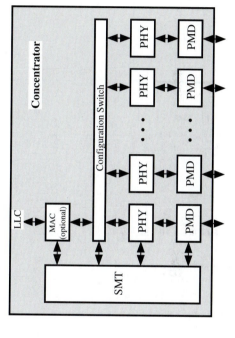

FIGURE 8.11   FDDI Station Architecture

277

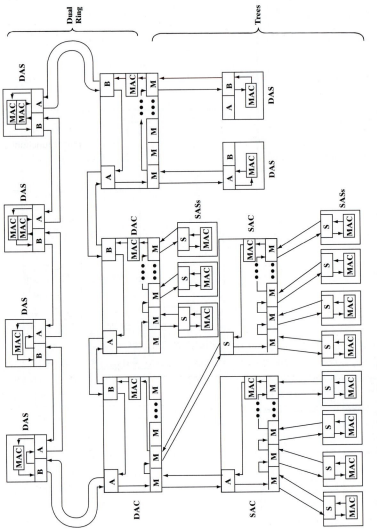

FIGURE 8.12 Ring-of-Trees Topology

TABLE 8.6   FDDI Port Types[a]

Port Type	Definition	Part of:
Port A	Connects to the incoming primary ring and the outgoing secondary ring of a dual ring	DAS, DAC
Port B	Connects to the outgoing primary ring and the incoming secondary ring of a dual ring	DAS, DAC
Port M (master)	Connects a concentrator to an SAS, DAS, or another concentrator	DAC, SAC
Port S (slave)	Connects an SAS or SAC to a concentrator	SAS, SAC

[a]When a DAS is used in a tree configuration (not part of the dual ring), port B functions as a slave port and connects to port M of a concentrator (DAC, SAC); port A is not used.

Dual Homing.   We have so far described the use of DACs and DASs in the dual ring, with SACs and SASs in the tree elements below the dual ring. This arrangement provides redundancy for the dual-ring stations only. In addition, the FDDI standard allows redundant paths in tree topologies as well as in the dual ring, by using DACs and DASs in the tree portion. The concept is referred to as dual homing.

Figure 8.13 illustrates a simple case of dual homing. A DAC or DAS is cascaded from two DACs that are part of the dual ring. Initially, the B port of the slave station and the corresponding M port of the master station are active, with the A port of the slave and the corresponding M port of another master station are set up as backup links. The backup links are shown in Figure 8.13 as dashed lines. The backup connection (port A) becomes active only if the primary connection (port B) fails.

Optical Bypass.   An additional degree of reliability can be provided by the use of an optical bypass switch, which can be installed in any DAC or DAS. The switch bypasses the station's receiver and transmitter connections so that the optical signal from the preceding station is passed directly to the next station. Bypassing can be activated by the station itself, a neighboring station, or a human operator. It can be activated automatically at the loss of power at the station or by means of a network control function.

However, optical bypass switches have a power penalty that may cause the maximum allowable loss between stations to be exceeded. Thus only a limited number of stations in the dual ring can be equipped with such devices. Figure 8.14 shows the logical position of an optical bypass switch in the physical layer block diagram.

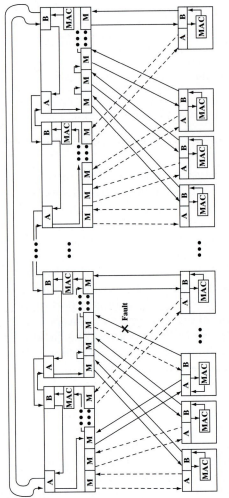

FIGURE 8.13 Concentrator Tree with Dual Homed Stations

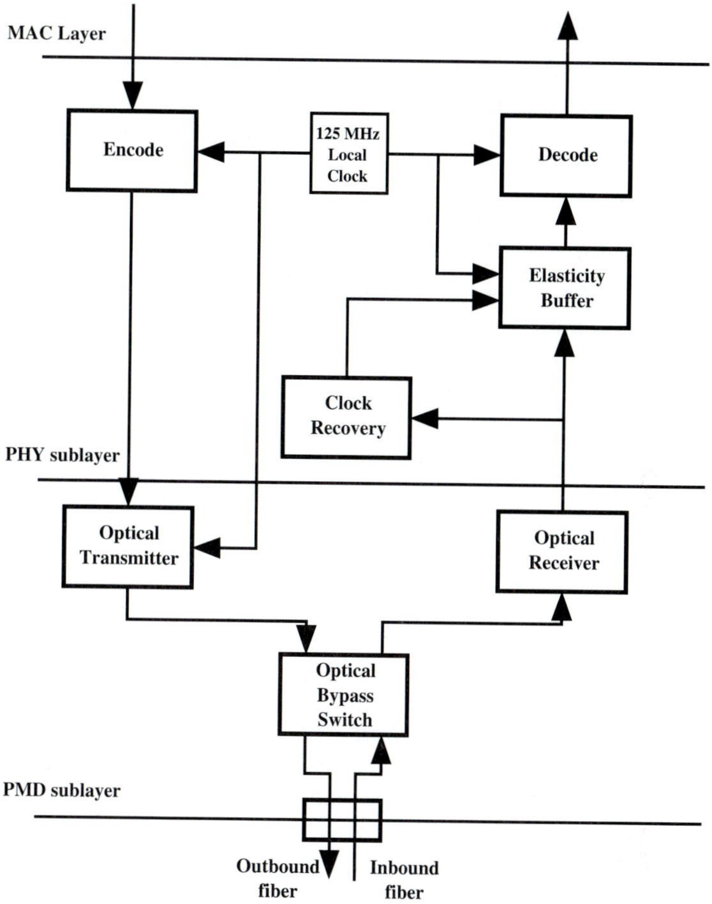

FIGURE 8.14   FDDI Physical Layer Block Diagram

8.3

FDDI STATION MANAGEMENT

The FDDI station management (SMT) specification defines three major functions:

- Connection management (CMT)
- Ring management (RMT)
- SMT frame services

Connection Management

Connection management is concerned with the insertion of stations onto the ring and removal of stations from the ring. This involves establishing or terminating a physical link between adjacent ports and the connection of ports to MAC entities. Connection management can be considered as comprising three subcomponents:

- Entity coordination management
- Physical connection management
- Configuration management

Entity Coordination Management. Entity coordination management (ECM) is responsible for the media interface to the FDDI ring, including the coordination of the activity of all the ports and the optional optical bypass switch associated with that station. For example, ECM coordinates the trace function, which is part of ring management.

Physical Connection Management. Physical connection management provides for managing the point-to-point physical links between adjacent PHY/PMD pairs. This includes initializing the link and testing the quality of the link (referred to as link confidence). Initialization is accomplished by signaling between the adjacent ports. One port transmits a continuous stream of symbols until the neighbor responds with another stream of symbols. PCM sequences through a number of these request–response exchanges to communicate the following information:

- Port type (A, B, M, S)
- Willingness to establish a link
- Duration of the link confidence test performed
- Availability of the MAC entity for a link confidence test
- Outcome of the link confidence test
- Availability of the MAC for a local loop test
- Intent to place a MAC in the connection if established

Once the connection has been verified, configuration management is invoked.

Configuration Management. Configuration management provides for configuring PHY and MAC entities within a node. Essentially, configuration management is concerned with the internal organization of the station entities and may be thought of as controlling a configuration switch (Figure 8.11) which implements the desired interconnections.

Ring Management

Ring management receives status information from media access control (MAC) and from connection management. Services provided by ring management include:

- Stuck beacon detection
- Resolution of problems through the trace process
- Detection of duplicate addresses

Stuck Beacon Detection.   As discussed in Section 10.2, a beacon is a MAC control frame used to isolate a serious ring failure such as a break in the ring. A stuck beacon indicates that a station is locked into sending continuous beacon frames. As described previously, a station that suspects a ring failure will transmit a continuous stream of beacons. Eventually, it should receive either a beacon from an upstream station or its own beacon. If neither event occurs, the station will continue to transmit its own beacon indefinitely, a condition known as a stuck beacon.

A stuck-beacon timer under the control of ring management measures the duration of beacon transmission. If a time limit is exceeded, ring management initiates a stuck-beacon recovery procedure. The procedure begins with the transmission of a *directed beacon,* with a group address of all stations that implement ring management, and which informs the ring of the stuck condition. The directed beacons are sent for a sufficiently long time to assure that they are seen by all the MACs. After the directed beacons are sent and the stuck-beacon condition is still unresolved, a trace function is initiated.

Trace Function.   The trace function uses PHY signaling of symbol streams to recover from a stuck beacon condition. The result of the directed beacon is to localize the fault to the beaconing MAC and its nearest upstream neighbor.

Duplicate Address Detection.   If two or more MAC entities have the same address, the ring cannot function properly. Duplicate address detection is performed during ring initialization and consists of monitoring the ring for conditions that indicate that duplicate addresses are present.

If two or more MACs have the same address, at least one of the MACs will experience one of the following conditions:

- Receive its own beacon while issuing claim frames for longer than the maximum delay of the FDDI ring (DMax). This indicates that the other duplicate is sending beacon frames while this duplicate is sending claim frames.

- Receive its own claim frames while issuing beacon frames for longer than DMax. This indicates that the other duplicate is sending claim frames while this duplicate is sending beacon frames.
- Receive its own claim frames for a period of time greater than DMax after having "won" the claim-token contest. This indicates that the other duplicate is sending claim frames while this duplicate has stopped claiming and issued a token.
- Receive its own claim frame with a different value of TTRT. This indicates that duplicates with different requested TTRT values are both claiming.

When a station detects the duplicate address condition, it can respond by changing its MAC address, configuring the MAC to lose the claim process and disabling its LLC services, or removing the MAC from the ring.

SMT Frame Services

The frame services portion of SMT deals with the management of the station after the ring has achieved an operational state. These services are implemented by a set of SMT frames. Table 8.7 lists the frames and Figure 8.15 illustrates the frame format. The frames are:

- *Neighborhood information frame:* used to transmit its own address and basic station descriptor to downstream neighbors. Each station issues the frame periodically using next station addressing (NSA). NSA is a special addressing mode that permits a station to send a frame to the next station in the token path without knowing the address of that station.
- *Station information frame:* used to request and supply a station's configuration and operating information.
- *Echo frame:* used for SMT-to-SMT loopback testing.
- *Resource allocation frame:* intended to support a variety of network policies for the allocation of resources. A typical use is the allocation of synchronous bandwidth to the stations within a ring.
- *Request denied frame:* issued in response to an unsupported optional frame class or type request or unsupported version ID.
- *Status report frame:* used by stations to announce station status periodically, which may be of interest to the manager of an FDDI ring.
- *Parameter management frame:* provides the means for remote management of station attributes via the parameter management protocol.
- *Extended service frame:* user-defined frame that extends or exercises new SMT services.

TABLE 8.7   FDDI SMT Frames

Frame Class	Abbreviation	Frame Types in Class
Neighbor information	NIF	Announcement, Request, Response

Station information
  Configuration
  Operation
	SIF	
		Request,[a] Response
		Request,[a] Response

Echo	ECF	Request,[a] Response
Resource allocation	RAF	Announcement, Request, Response
Request denied	RDF	Response
Status report	SRF	Announcement[a]

Parameter management
  Get PMF
  Change PMF
  Add PMF
  Remove PMF
	PMF	
		Request,[a] Response[a]
		Request,[a] Response[a]
		Request,[a] Response[a]
		Request,[a] Response[a]

Extended service	ESF	Announcement,[a] Request,[a] Response[a]

[a]Optional.

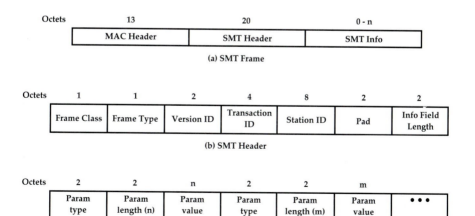

(a) SMT Frame

(b) SMT Header

(c) SMT Info Field

FIGURE 8.15   SMT Frame Format

8.4

RECOMMENDED READING

Two detailed accounts of FDDI are [MILL95] and [SHAH94]. The former provides more detail on physical layer issues, while the latter has more coverage of the MAC protocol. [KESS92] also provides good technical coverage of FDDI.

KESS92   Kessler, G., and Train, D. *Metropolitan Area Networks: Concepts, Standards, and Services.* New York: McGraw-Hill, 1992.

MILL95   Mills, A. *Understanding FDDI.* Englewood Cliffs, NJ: Prentice Hall, 1995.

SHAH94   Shah, A., and Ramakrishnan, G. *FDDI: A High-Speed Network.* Englewood Cliffs, NJ: Prentice Hall, 1994.

8.5

PROBLEMS

8.1 Compare the capacity allocation schemes of token bus, 803.5 token ring, and FDDI. What are the relative pros and cons?

8.2 Rework the example of Figure 8.4 using a TTRT of 12 frames and assume that no station ever has more than eight asynchronous frames to send.

Fibre Channel

As the speed and memory capacity of personal computers, workstations, and servers have grown, and as applications have become ever more complex with greater reliance on graphics and video, the requirement for greater speed in delivering data to the processor has grown. This requirement affects two methods of data communications with the processor: I/O channel and network communications.

An I/O channel is a direct point-to-point or multipoint communications link, predominantly hardware based and designed for high speed over very short distances. The I/O channel transfers data between a buffer at the source device and a buffer at the destination device, moving only the user contents from one device to another, without regard to the format or meaning of the data. The logic associated with the channel typically provides the minimum control necessary to manage the transfer plus hardware error detection. I/O channels, typically manage transfers between processors and peripheral devices, such as disks, graphics equipment, CD-ROMs, and video I/O devices.

A *network* is a collection of interconnected access points with a software protocol structure that enables communication. The network typically allows many different types of data transfer, using software to implement the networking protocols and to provide flow control, error detection, and error recovery. As we have discussed in this book, networks typically manage transfers between end systems over local, metropolitan, or wide-area distances.

Fibre Channel is designed to combine the best features of both technologies: the simplicity and speed of channel communications with the flexibility and interconnectivity that characterize protocol-based network communications. This fusion of approaches allows system designers to combine traditional peripheral connection, host-to-host internetworking, loosely coupled processor clustering, and multimedia applications in a single multiprotocol interface. The types of channel-oriented facilities incorporated into the Fibre Channel protocol architecture include:

- Data-type qualifiers for routing frame payload into particular interface buffers
- Link-level constructs associated with individual I/O operations
- Protocol interface specifications to allow support of existing I/O channel architectures, such as the Small Computer System Interface (SCSI)

The types of network-oriented facilities incorporated into the Fibre Channel protocol architecture include:

- Full multiplexing of traffic between multiple destinations
- Peer-to-peer connectivity between any pair of ports on a Fibre Channel network
- Capabilities for internetworking to other connection technologies

Depending on the needs of the application, either channel or networking approaches can be used for any data transfer.

This chapter begins with an overview of the layered Fibre Channel protocol architecture. The remainder of the chapter provides details for Fibre Channel layers.

9.1

FIBRE CHANNEL ARCHITECTURE

The Fibre Channel is designed to provide a common, efficient transport system so that a variety of devices and applications can be supported through a single port type. The Fibre Channel Association, which is the industry consortium promoting Fibre Channel, lists the following ambitious requirements that Fibre Channel is intended to satisfy [FCA94]:

- Full duplex links with two fibers per link
- Performance from 100 to 800 Mbps on a single link (200 to 1600 Mbps per link)

- Support for distances up to 10 km
- Small connectors
- High-capacity utilization with distance insensitivity
- Greater connectivity than that of existing multidrop channels
- Broad availability (i.e., standard components)
- Support for multiple cost/performance levels, from small systems to supercomputers
- Ability to carry multiple existing interface command sets for existing channel and network protocols

The solution was to develop a simple generic transport mechanism based on point-to-point links and a switching network. This underlying infrastructure supports a simple encoding and framing scheme that in turn supports a variety of channel and network protocols.

The Fibre Channel standard makes use of a number of terms not found in other networking standards or that have special meaning in the context of Fibre Channel. For convenience, Table 9.1 lists some of the more important terms and their definitions.

Fibre Channel Elements

The key elements of a Fibre Channel network are the end systems, called *nodes,* and the network itself, which consists of one or more switching elements. The collection of switching elements is referred to as a *fabric.* These elements are interconnected by point-to-point links between ports on the individual nodes and switches. Communication consists of the transmission of frames across the point-to-point links.

Figure 9.1 illustrates these basic elements. Each node includes three or more ports, called N_Ports, for interconnection. Similarly, each fabric switching element includes one or more ports, called F_Ports. Interconnection is by means of bidirectional links between ports. Any node can communicate with any other node connected to the same fabric using the services of the fabric. All routing of frames between N_Ports is done by the fabric. Frames may be buffered within the fabric, making it possible for different nodes to connect to the fabric at different data rates.

A fabric can be implemented as a single fabric element, as depicted in Figure 9.1, or as a more general network of fabric elements, as shown in Figure 9.2. In either case the fabric is responsible for buffering and routing frames between source and destination nodes.

The Fibre Channel network is quite different from the other LANs that we have examined so far. Fibre Channel is more like a traditional circuit-switched or packet-switched network, in contrast to the typical

TABLE 9.1   Fibre Channel Terms

Dedicated connection
A communicating circuit guaranteed and retained by the fabric for two given N_Ports.

Datagram
Refers to the class 3 Fibre Channel service that allows data to be sent rapidly to multiple devices attached to the fabric, with no confirmation of receipt.

Exchange
The basic mechanism that transfers information, consisting of one or more related nonconcurrent sequences in one or both directions.

Fabric
The entity that interconnects various N_Ports attached to it and handles the routing of frames.

Frame
A set of transmitted bits that define a basic transport element.

Intermix
A mode of service that reserves the full Fibre Channel capacity for a dedicated (class 1) connection but also allows connectionless (class 2 and class 3) traffic to share the link if the bandwidth is available.

Node
A collection of one or more N_Ports.

Operation
A set of one or more, possibly concurrent, exchanges that is associated with a logical construct above the FC-2 layer.

Originator
The logical function associated with an N_Port that initiates an exchange.

Port
The hardware entity within a node that performs data communications over a Fibre Channel link. An N_Port is a port at the end-system end of a link; an F_Port is an access point of the fabric.

Responder
The logical function in an N_Port responsible for supporting an exchange initiated by an originator.

Sequence
A set of one or more data frames with a common sequence ID, transmitted unidirectionally from one N_Port to another N_Port, with a corresponding response, if applicable, transmitted in response to each data frame.

shared-medium LAN. Thus Fibre Channel need not be concerned with medium access control (MAC) issues. Because it is based on a switching network, the Fibre Channel scales easily in terms of N_Ports, data rate, and distance covered. This approach provides great flexibility. Fibre Channel can readily accommodate new transmission media and data rates by

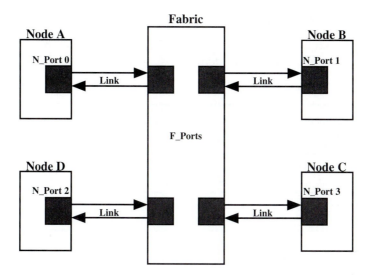

FIGURE 9.1   Fibre Channel Port Types

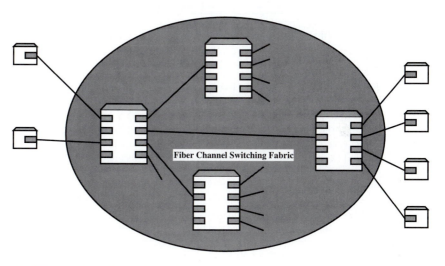

FIGURE 9.2   Fibre Channel Network

adding new switches and F_Ports to an existing fabric. Thus an existing investment is not lost with an upgrade to new technologies and equipment. Further, as we shall see, the layered protocol architecture accommodates existing I/O interface and networking protocols, preserving the preexisting investment.

Fibre Channel Protocol Architecture

The Fibre Channel standard is organized into five levels. These are illustrated in Figure 9.3, with brief definitions in Table 9.2. Each level defines a

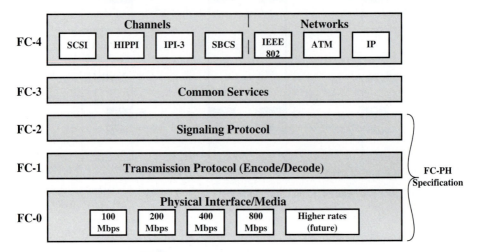

FIGURE 9.3   Fibre Channel Levels

TABLE 9.2   Fibre Channel Levels

FC-O   Physical media
• Optical cable with laser or LED transmitters for long distance transmissions
• Copper coaxial cable for highest speeds over short distances
• Shielded twisted pair for lower speeds over short distances

FC-1   Byte synchronization and encoding
• 8B/10B encoding/decoding scheme provides balance, is simple to implement, and
  provides useful error-detection capability
• Special code character maintains byte and word alignment

FC-2   Actual transport mechanism
• Framing protocol and flow control between N_Ports
• Three classes of service between ports

FC-3   Common services layer
• Port-related services
• Services across two or more ports in a node

FC-4   Upper layer protocols
• Supports a variety of channel and network protocols

function or set of related functions. The standard does not dictate a correspondence between levels and actual implementations, with a specific interface between adjacent levels. Rather, the standard refers to the level as a "document artifice" used to group related functions.

Levels FC-0 through FC-2 of the Fibre Channel hierarchy are currently defined in a standard referred to as Fibre Channel Physical and Signaling Interface (FC-PH). Currently, there is no final standard for FC-3. At level FC-4, individual standards have been produced for mapping a variety of channel and network protocols onto lower levels.

We briefly examine each of these levels in turn in the remainder of this section, and then look in more detail at the lowest three levels in the remainder of the chapter.

Physical Interface and Media.   Fibre Channel level FC-0 allows a variety of physical media and data rates; this is one of the strengths of the specification. Currently, data rates ranging from 100 to 800 Mbps per fiber are defined. The physical media are optical fiber, coaxial cable, and shielded twisted pair. Depending on the data rate and medium involved, maximum distances for individual point-to-point links range from 50 meters to 10 km.

Transmission Protocol.   FC-1, the transmission protocol level, defines the signal encoding technique used for transmission and for synchronization across the point-to-point link. The encoding scheme used is 8B/10B, in which each 8 bits of data from level FC-2 is converted into 10 bits for transmission. This scheme has a philosophy similar to that of the 4B/5B scheme used for FDDI, discussed in Chapter 8. The 8B/10B scheme was developed and patented by IBM for use in their 200-Mbaud ESCON interconnect system. The 8B/10B scheme is more powerful than 4B/5B in terms of transmission characteristics and error detection capability.

Framing Protocol.   Level FC-2, referred to as the framing protocol level, deals with the transmission of data between N_Ports in the form of frames. Among the concepts defined at this level:

- Node and N_Port and their identifiers
- Topologies
- Classes of service provided by the fabric
- Segmentation of data into frames and reassembly
- Grouping of frames into logical entities called sequences and exchanges
- Sequencing, flow control, and error control

Common Services.   FC-3 provides a set of services that are common across multiple N_Ports of a node. The functions so far defined in the draft FC-3 documents include:

- *Striping:* makes use of multiple N_Ports in parallel to transmit a single information unit across multiple links simultaneously. This achieves higher aggregate throughput. A probable use is for transferring large data sets in real time, as in video-imaging applications.
- *Hunt groups:* a set of associated N_Ports at a single node. This set is assigned an alias identifier that allows any frame sent to this alias to be routed to any available N_Port within the set. This may decrease latency by decreasing the chance of waiting for a busy N_Port.
- *Multicast:* delivers a transmission to multiple destinations. This includes sending to all N_Ports on a fabric (broadcast) or to a subset of the N_Ports on a fabric.

Mapping.   FC-4 defines the mapping of various channel and network protocols to FC-PH. I/O channel interfaces include:

- *Small computer system interface (SCSI):* a widely used high-speed interface typically implemented on personal computers, workstations, and servers.[1] SCSI is used to support high-capacity and high-data-rate devices, such as disks and graphics and video equipment.
- *High-performance parallel interface (HIPPI):* a high-speed channel standard used primarily for mainframe/supercomputer environments. At one time, HIPPI and extensions to HIPPI were viewed as a possible general-purpose high-speed LAN solution, but HIPPI has been superseded by Fibre Channel.

Network interfaces include:

- *IEEE 802:* frames map onto Fibre Channel frames
- *Asynchronous transfer mode:* both a wide-area and a local area technology, discussed in Chapter 10
- *Internet protocol (IP):* described in Chapter 15

The FC-4 mapping protocols make use of the FC-PH capabilities to transfer upper-layer protocol (ULP) information. Each FC-4 specification defines the formats and procedures for ULP.

---

[1]See [STAL96] for a detailed discussion of SCSI.

9.2

PHYSICAL MEDIA AND TOPOLOGIES

One of the major strengths of the Fibre Channel standard is that it provides a range of options for the physical medium, the data rate on that medium, and the topology of the network. These areas are explored in this section.

Transmission Media

Table 9.3 summarizes the options that are available under Fibre Channel for physical transmission medium and data rate. Each entry specifies the maximum point-to-point link distance (between ports) that is defined for a given transmission medium at a given data rate. These media may be mixed in an overall configuration. For example, a single-mode optical link could be used to connect switches in different buildings, with multimode optical links used for vertical distribution inside, and shielded twisted pair or coaxial cable links to individual workstations.

The FC-0 standard includes a compact notation, or nomenclature, for designating the combination of options that define a specific transmission medium operating at a specific data rate. Figure 9.4 illustrates this nomenclature. For example, the designation 100-SM-LL-L indicates a long link operating at 100 MBps over each single-mode fiber using a long-wavelength laser transmitter. Figure 9.4 not only illustrates this notation but summarizes the options that are currently available in the standard. Let us examine the options in more detail.

Optical Fiber Transmission Media.   FC-0 specifies both single-mode and multimode optical fiber alternatives. For the single-mode case, specifica-

TABLE 9.3   Maximum Distance for Fibre Channel Media Types

	800 Mbps	400 Mbps	200 Mbps	100 Mbps
Single-mode fiber	10 km	10 km	10 km	—
50-μm multimode fiber	0.5 km	1 km	2 km	10 km
62.5-μm multimode fiber	175 m	350 m	1500 m	1500 m
Video coaxial cable	25 m	50 m	75 m	100 m
Miniature coaxial cable	10 m	15 m	25 m	35 m
Shielded twisted pair	—	—	50 m	100 m

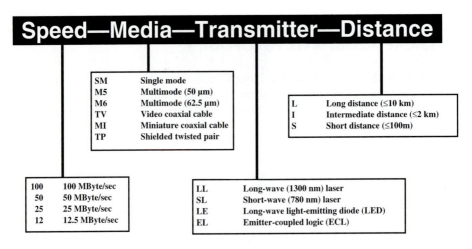

FIGURE 9.4   FC-0 Nomenclature

tions are provided for optical fiber that will operate at up to 800 Mbps and distances up to 10 km. The differences among the various single-mode options deal primarily with the spectral characteristics of the signal produced by the transmitter.

There are a number of options for multimode fiber. These include the use of 62.5- and 50-μm-diameter fiber and the use of a wavelength of 780 or 1300 nm. For a given data rate, greater distances can be achieved with the 50-μm fiber. For a given diameter fiber, greater data rates can be achieved with the 1300-nm wavelength (see Table 9.3).

Coaxial Cable Transmission Media.   Coaxial cable provides a lower-cost alternative to optical fiber when long distances are not required. The two types of coaxial cable that are specified, video and miniature, are both 75-ohm cables. The video coaxial cable is what is referred to as RG 6/U type or RG 59/U type. These are flexible cables, generally used as drop cables, with an outside diameter of 0.332 and 0.242 inch, respectively. The miniature coaxial cable has an outside diameter of 0.1 inch. The thinner the cable, the more attenuation is experienced and consequently, the lower the data rate and/or shorter the distance that can be supported.

Shielded Twisted-Pair Transmission Media.   The final media specified in FC-0 are two types of 150-ohm shielded twisted pair; these are the type 1 and type 2 cable defined in EIA 568. These cables can only be used over very short distances and at only the 100- and 200-Mbps data rates. Type 1 consists of two twisted pairs enclosed in a metallic shield and covered in an appropriate sheath. Type 2 contains four twisted pairs packaged similarly; typically, two of the twisted pairs are for data transmission and two are for voice transmission.

Topologies

The most general topology supported by Fibre Channel is referred to as a fabric or switched topology. This is an arbitrary topology that includes at least one switch to interconnect a number of N_Ports, as shown in Figure 9.5a. The fabric topology may also consist of a number of switches forming a switched network, with some or all of these switches also supporting end nodes (Figure 9.2).

Routing in the fabric topology is transparent to the nodes. Each port in the configuration has a unique address. When data from a node are transmitted into the fabric, the edge switch to which the node is attached uses the destination port address in the incoming data frame to determine the destination port location. The switch then either delivers the frame to another node attached to the same switch or transfers the frame to an adjacent switch to begin the routing of the frame to a remote destination.

The fabric topology provides scaleability of capacity: As additional ports are added, the aggregate capacity of the network increases, thus minimizing congestion and contention and increasing throughput. The fabric is protocol independent and largely distance insensitive. The technology of the switch itself and of the transmission links connecting the switch to nodes may be changed without affecting the overall configuration. Another advantage of the fabric topology is that the burden on nodes is minimized. An individual Fibre Channel node (end system) is only responsible for managing a simple point-to-point connection between itself and the fabric; the fabric is responsible for routing between N_Ports and error detection.

In addition to the fabric topology, the Fibre Channel standard defines two other topologies. With the point-to-point topology (Figure 9.5b) there are only two N_Ports, and these are directly connected, with no intervening fabric switches. In this case there is no routing. Finally, the arbitrated loop topology (Figure 9.5c) is a simple, low-cost topology for connecting up to 126 nodes in a loop. The ports on an arbitrated loop must contain the functions of both N_Ports and F_Ports; these are called NL_Ports. The arbitrated loop operates in a manner roughly equivalent to the token ring protocols that we have seen. Each port sees all frames and passes and ignores those not addressed to itself. There is a token acquisition protocol to control access to the loop.

The fabric and arbitrated loop topologies may be combined in one configuration to optimize the cost of the configuration. In this case, one of the nodes on the arbitrated loop must be a fabric-loop (FL_Port) node so that it participates in routing with the other switches in the fabric configuration.

The type of topology need not be configured manually by a network manager. Rather, the type of topology is discovered early in the link initialization process.

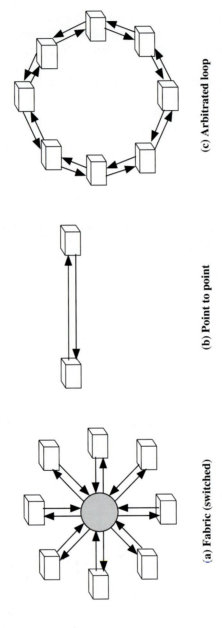

(a) Fabric (switched)

(b) Point to point

(c) Arbitrated loop

FIGURE 9.5   Basic Fibre Channel Topologies

9.3

DATA ENCODING

The FC-1 level defines the encoding scheme used for transmitting data over Fibre Channel links. The code chosen is the 8B/10B transmission code, originally developed by IBM [WIDM83]. The developers of this code list the following advantages:

- Can be implemented with relatively simple and reliable transceivers at low cost
- Is well-balanced, with minimal deviation from the occurrence of an equal number of 1 and 0 bits across any sequence
- Provides good transition density for easier clock recovery
- Provides useful error detection capability

The 8B/10B code is an example of the more general mBnB code, in which *m* binary source bits are mapped into *n* binary bits for transmission. Redundancy is built into the code to provide the desired transmission features by making *n* > *m*. Figure 9.6 illustrates the operation of this code. The code actually combines two other codes, a 5B/6B code and a 3B/4B code. The use of these two codes is simply an artifact that simplifies the definition of the mapping and the implementation: The mapping could have been defined directly as an 8B/10B code. In any case, a mapping is defined that transports each of the possible 8-bit source blocks into a 10-bit code block. There is also a function called *disparity control*. In essence, this function keeps track of the excess of zeros over ones or ones over zeros. If there is an excess in either direction, this is referred to as a disparity. If there is a disparity, and if the current code block would add to that disparity, the disparity control block complements the 10-bit code block. This has the effect of either eliminating the disparity or at least moving it in the opposite direction of the current disparity.

The encoding mechanism also includes a control line input, K, which indicates whether the lines A through H are data or control bits. In the latter case, a special nondata 10-bit block is generated. A total of 12 of these nondata blocks are defined as valid in the standard. These are used for synchronization and other FC-1-level control purposes.

9.4

FRAMING PROTOCOL

The FC-2 framing protocol level defines the rules for the exchange of higher-layer information between nodes. FC-2 specifies types of frames, procedures for their exchange, and formats. FC-2 is similar to the data link

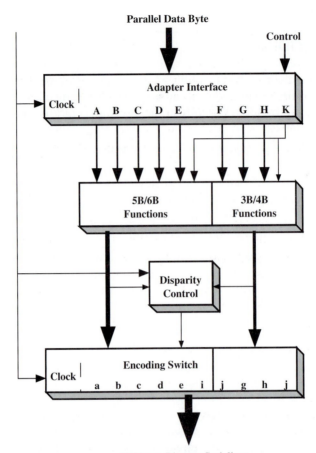

FIGURE 9.6   8B/10B Encoding [FCA94]

layer functions of the OSI model. FC-2 is a complex protocol, incorporating many features and a number of options. The main elements of this level are surveyed in this section.

Classes of Service

As with the IEEE 802.2 logical link control (LLC), the FC-2 level of Fibre Channel defines a number of different classes of service. These classes are determined by the way communication is established between two ports and on the flow control and error control features of the communications channel. The following classes have been defined:

- Class 1 service: dedicated connection
- Class 2 service: multiplex

- Class 3 service: datagram
- Intermix service

Class 1 Service.   Class 1 service provides a dedicated path through the fabric, much as is done in a circuit-switched network. Thus the path appears to the end systems to behave like a dedicated point-to-point link. Within the fabric, the connection is established before data transfer can occur. This dedicated connection is not available for other traffic.

Class 1 service provides a guaranteed data rate between the two communicating ports and also guarantees delivery of frames in the order in which they are transmitted.

A class 1 connection is requested by an N_Port by transmitting a frame containing a special start-of-frame delimiter referred to as SOFc1. This alerts the fabric that a connection is requested. The fabric allocates a circuit between the requesting N_Port and the destination N_Port. The destination N_Port can then transmit an ACK indicating its acceptance of the connection to the requesting N_Port.

Class 1 service is useful when the connection setup time is short relative to the data transmission time. It is especially useful if large blocks of data are to be transmitted or if various throughput data rates are required.

Class 2 Service.   Class 2 service is called *frame multiplex* and is also referred to as a *frame-switched service*. Class 2 service is analogous to the acknowledged connectionless LLC service. There is no dedicated physical or logical connection. However, notification of delivery of frames is guaranteed by means of acknowledgments from the receiving port. If delivery cannot be made due to congestion, a busy response is returned and the sender tries again. The busy response indicates that the sender does not have to wait for a long timeout period to expire but may retransmit in a shorter period of time. If delivery fails due to a link error, notification is not guaranteed since the source address in the nondelivered frame may not be valid. Class 2 service does not guarantee to deliver frames in the order in which they are transmitted; each frame may take a different path through the fabric.

As with traditional packet-switching and frame relay networks, the path between two N_Ports using class 2 service is not dedicated, allowing more efficient use of network capacity. Data frames from a number of sources can be multiplexed over the same links within the fabric and can be delivered over the same link to a given destination port. As an example, this service is useful for data transfers to and from a mass-storage system shared among a number of workstations.

Class 3 Service.   As with class 2, class 3 is a connectionless service that allows data to be sent rapidly to multiple devices attached to the fabric.

Class 3 service gives no notification of receipt and is hence referred to as a datagram service.

Intermix Service.   Intermix is an option of class 1 service that allows interleaving of class 2 and class 3 frames during an established class 1 dedicated connection. Class 2 and class 3 frames may be interchanged between the two connected N_Ports or between either of the connected N_Ports and other N_Ports. While a class 1 connection guarantees throughput for class 1 frames up to a maximum data rate, this entire capacity may not always be used. In that case the excess capacity may be allocated to class 2 and class 3 traffic.

Frames, Sequences, and Exchanges

FC-2 provides more than just a simple frame delivery mechanism. Instead, the standard defines a hierarchy of building blocks that support upper-level functions in a natural fashion. Figure 9.7 suggests this hierarchy. At any given node, FC-2 may offer a number of different classes of service. Each class of service may be provided by one or more N_Ports. FC-2 also defines a number of basic protocols, or procedures, used to implement a service at a port. These include procedures for setting up a connection, for transferring data, and for terminating a connection. Each of these procedures is defined as part of an exchange of information between N_Ports. An exchange consists of one or more unidirectional sequences, and each sequence consists of one or more frames.

Frames.   All traffic between N_Ports over Fibre Channel is in the form of a stream of frames. There are two categories of frames: Data frames transfer higher-level information between source and destination N_Ports; link control frames are used to manage frame transfer and to provide some control for FC-2 class 1 and class 2 services. In general, link control frames are used to indicate receipt or loss of a frame, to provide flow control functions, and to indicate when a destination N_Port or the fabric is busy.

Three types of data frames have been defined:

- *FC-4 device data:* used to transfer higher-layer data units from supported FC-4 protocols, such as IEEE 802, SCSI, and IP
- *FC-4 video data:* transferred by an N_Port directly to or from a video buffer without first directing them to an intermediate storage location
- *Link data:* used to transfer link application information between N_Ports; supports a control function of a higher level, such as the transmission of abort sequences, echo, and termination of class 1 connections

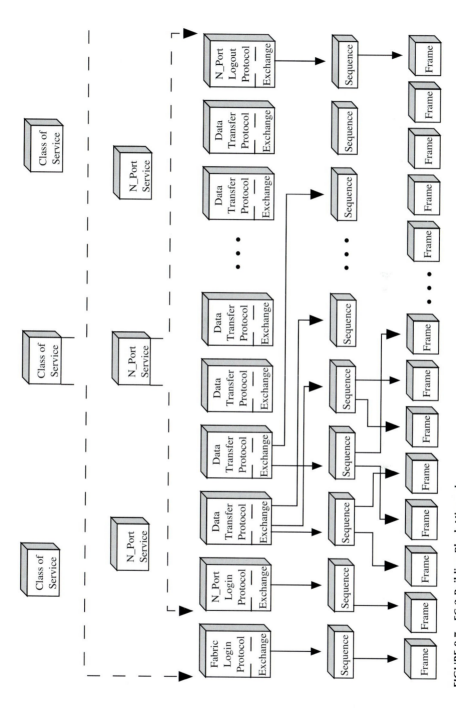

FIGURE 9.7 FC-2 Building-Block Hierarchy

The three types of link control frames are:

- *Link continue (acknowledge):* used in various Fibre Channel sliding-window flow control mechanisms to report successful delivery (flow control is described later in this section)
- *Link response:* used in various Fibre Channel sliding-window flow control mechanisms to report unsuccessful delivery
- *Link command:* a reset command used to reinitialize the sliding-window credit scheme

Sequences. In Fibre Channel, a maximum frame size for each direction is negotiated between two communicating ports and between the communicating ports and the fabric. However, this frame size is transparent to the higher-layer user of FC-2. FC-2 places no limit on the size of the unit of transfer, called a *sequence,* which must be negotiated at a higher layer. FC-2 converts a sequence into a set of one or more data frames transmitted unidirectionally from one N_Port to another N_Port, with corresponding link control frames, if needed, transmitted in response. FC-2 performs two functions related to sequences: segmentation and reassembly, and error control.

On transmission, FC-2 accepts a sequence of data and segments this into one or more data frames. Each data frame includes a sequence identifier in its header that uniquely identifies the frame as part of a particular sequence. Each frame also includes a sequence count that numbers the frames within a sequence so that they may be reassembled by FC-2 at the receiving port.

The sequence also serves as the recovery boundary at the FC-2 level. When an error is detected, FC-2 identifies the sequence containing the error and enables that sequence and any subsequent sequence to be retransmitted.

Exchanges. The exchange is a mechanism for organizing multiple sequences into a higher-level construct for the convenience of applications. For example, in the Fibre Channel standard for SCSI support, the various command, data transfer, and response sequences associated with an individual disk operation are grouped into a single exchange; this allows the SCSI logic to treat all the transport functions of the operation as a single atomic unit for tracking and error recovery.

An exchange may involve either the unidirectional or bidirectional transfer of sequences. It is composed of one or more non-concurrent sequences. Figure 9.8 shows a typical example of an exchange. In this case, it consists of a command to write some data, followed by the data transfer, followed by the completion status of the operation. Each phase (command, data transfer, status) is a separate sequence.

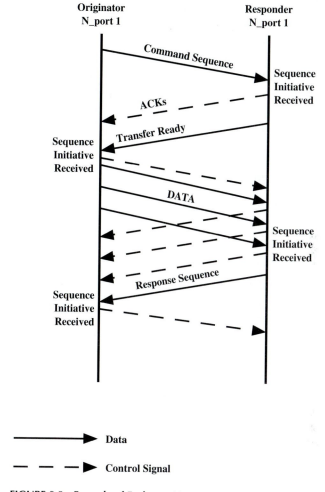

FIGURE 9.8   Example of Exchange Usage

The restriction to nonconcurrent sequences means that within a given exchange, only a single sequence may be active at any one time. However, sequences from different exchanges may be concurrently active.

Protocols.   An exchange is associated with a protocol tied to a service for higher levels. Some of these protocols are specific to the higher-layer service. In addition, there are some common protocols defined in Fibre Channel that may be used by any higher-level application. These include:

- *Fabric login.* This protocol is executed upon initialization of an N_Port. It enables the N_Port to exchange operational and configuration information with the fabric. The information exchanged includes the address assigned to the N_Port, classes of service supported, and credit for buffer-to-buffer flow control (described later in this section).

- *N_Port login.* Before performing data transfer, the N_Port interchanges its service parameters with those of another N_Port. Service parameters include amount of buffer space available for data transfer, total number of concurrent sequences that the N_Port can support as a recipient, and supported service classes.

- *Data transfer.* This defines the transfer of upper-layer protocol data between N_Ports.

- *N_Port logout.* This is used to terminate a connection to another N_Port. This request may be used to free up resources at the two N_Ports.

Flow Control

Fibre Channel provides a complex array of frame types and procedures for controlling the flow of frames through the fabric. Two categories of flow control are supported:

- *End-to-end flow control:* used between two communicating N_Ports. Each of the two N_Ports in a communication provides credit for a certain number of frames. This is the only type of flow control available on dedicated connections after the first frame.

- *Buffer-to-buffer flow control:* used between two ports connected by a single point-to-point link. This type of flow control regulates traffic between an N_Port and the F_Port to which it is attached.

Key to the operation of both flow control mechanisms is the concept of credit. Prior to communication between two N_Ports (end to end) and between two adjacent ports (buffer to buffer), each communicating port is allocated a credit during the initialization procedure. The transmitting port limits the number of outstanding unacknowledged frames to the allocated credit of each type and adjusts the credit according to the responses received. The mechanism used is a Credit_Count. This count is initially 0 and is increased by one for each data frame transmitted and decreased by one for each acknowledgment of a data frame. The count represents the number of outstanding data frames that have not been acknowledged and is not permitted to exceed the corresponding maximum credit negotiated at login.

End-to-End Flow Control.   End-to-end flow control paces the flow of frames between N_Ports. Since the flow control mechanism requires some form of acknowledgment, the end-to-end flow control can only be used in class 1 and class 2. A number of different control frames are used to enforce end-to-end flow control. Table 9.4 indicates which frames are relevant to which class and, for class 1 service, which frames are used to respond to an SOFc1 data frame (which initiates a dedicated connection) and which frames are used to respond to all other data frames. Figure 9.9a illustrates the relationship among these frames.

As Figure 9.9a indicates, flow control is activated by the flow of class 1 or class 2 data frames from the initiator of a sequence of frames to the sequence recipient. The available Credit_Count begins at 0 and is incremented by one for each transmission. Three types of ACK frames can be returned from the receiving N_Port:

- *ACK_1:* acknowledges an individual data frame; the sequence initiator decrements Credit_Count by 1.
- *ACK_N:* acknowledges one or more data frames; the sequence initiator decrements Credit_Count by the amount indicated in the control frame.
- *ACK_0:* acknowledges an entire sequence; the sequence initiator decrements Credit_Count by the number of frames in the sequence.

TABLE 9.4   Flow Control Mechanisms[a]

Flow Control Mechanism	Class 1		Class 2	Class 3
	With SOFc1	Without SOFc1		
R_RDY primitive signal	Yes	No	Yes	Yes
ACK_1	Yes	Yes	Yes	No
ACK_N	Yes	Yes	Yes	No
ACK_0	Yes	One per sequence	One per sequence	No
F_BSY (data frame)	Yes	No	Yes	No
F_BSY (link control frame)	No	No	Yes	No
F-RJT	No	Yes	Yes	No
P_BSY	No	Yes	Yes	No
P_RJT	Yes	Yes	Yes	No

[a]Shaded, buffer-to-buffer credit; unshaded, end-to-end credit.

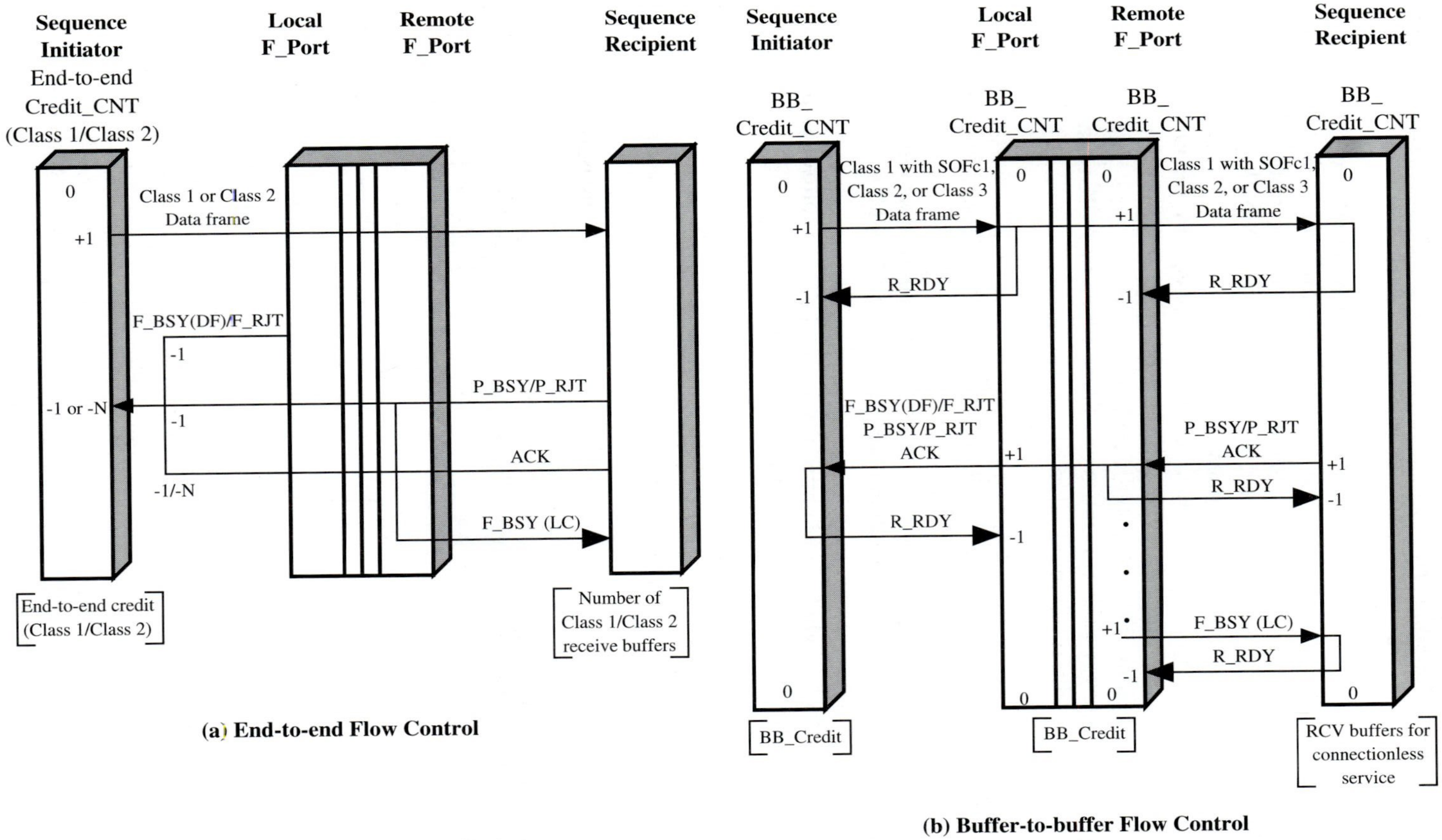

(a) End-to-end Flow Control

(b) Buffer-to-buffer Flow Control

FIGURE 9.9 Fibre Channel Flow Control Models

These acknowledgment types cannot be mixed. For example, if ACK_1 is used, every frame must be acknowledged by an individual ACK_1 frame, and if ACK_0 is used, no other acknowledgment frames may be used during the transfer of the sequence acknowledged by the ACK_0.

In addition, busy and reject control frames are used to regulate flow. The F_BSY control frame indicates that the fabric is temporarily occupied with other link activity and the fabric is unable to deliver a frame. Similarly, the P_BSY control frame indicates the destination port is temporarily unable to accept a frame. When an N_Port receives a busy response, it retransmits the data frame up to a predefined retry limit. An F_BSY can also be issued by an F_Port in response to a link control frame.

As with the busy control frames, the F_RJT and P_RJT reject control frames indicate that delivery of a data frame is being denied. In the case of a reject, however, the entire sequence containing the rejected frame is aborted. Depending on the reason for the reject, the sequence initiator may or may not be able to try to resend the entire sequence.

Buffer-to-Buffer Flow Control.   Buffer-to-buffer flow control is a local, link control mechanism between ports connected by a point-to-point link. This mechanism is applicable to class 2 and class 3 service. It is also applicable to the initial frame used in setting up a connection for class 1 service (SOFc1 frame). Otherwise, buffer-to-buffer flow control is not used for class 1 service, since class 1 service provides a transparent circuit-switched type of connection between N_Ports.

As Table 9.4 indicates, a single type of control signal, the R_RDY primitive signal, is used for buffer-to-buffer flow control. Its use is illustrated in Figure 9.9b. The upper part of the figure indicates the use of R_RDY to regulate the flow of data frames. As before, the sequence initiator maintains a Credit_Count, which is incremented by one for each transmitted frame, up to the maximum credit allocated for this link. The R_RDY indicates that an interface buffer is available for further frame reception. The sequence initiator decrements its Credit_Count for each R_RDY received. The lower part of Figure 9.9b indicates that the R_RDY is also used to acknowledge receipt of control frames across the link.

Frame Format

Figure 9.10 illustrates the basic Fibre Channel frame format. Let us consider each of the fields in turn.

Start-of-Frame Delimiter.   The start-of-frame (SOF) delimiter includes nondata symbols to assure recognition of the beginning of a new frame. There are actually a number of different SOF delimiters, depending on the class of service and type of frame (Table 9.5). The SOF connect frame is used

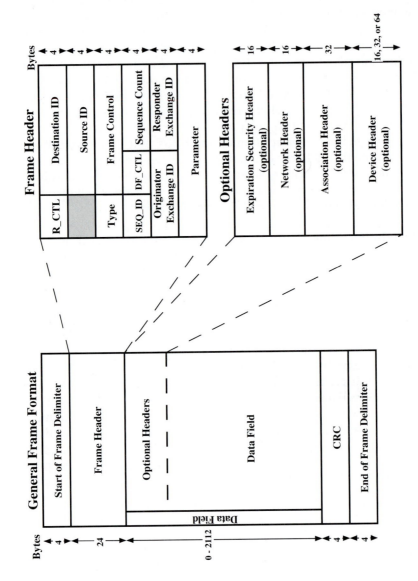

FIGURE 9.10 Fibre Channel Frame Format

Frame Header

Bytes

R_CTL	Destination ID	4
	Source ID	4
Type	Frame Control	4
SEQ_ID	DF_CTL	Sequence Count	4
Originator Exchange ID	Responder Exchange ID	4
Parameter		4

Optional Headers

Expiration Security Header (optional)	16
Network Header (optional)	16
Association Header (optional)	32
Device Header (optional)	16, 32, or 64

General Frame Format

Bytes

Start of Frame Delimiter	4
Frame Header	24
Optional Headers	
Data Field	0 - 2112
Data Field	
CRC	4
End of Frame Delimiter	4

TABLE 9.5 Frame Delimiters

Type	Delimiter Name	Abbreviation
Start-of-frame delimiter	SOF Connect class 1	SOFc1
	SOF Initiate class 1	SOFi1
	SOF Normal class 1	SOFn1
	SOF Initiate class 2	SOFi2
	SOF Normal class 2	SOFn2
	SOF Initiate class 3	SOFi3
	SOF Normal class 3	SOFn3
	SOF Fabric	SOFf
End-of-frame delimiter	EOF Terminate	EOFt
	EOF Disconnect-Terminate (class 1)	EOFdt
	EOF Abort	EOFa
	EOF Normal	EOFn
	EOF Disconnect-Terminate Invalid (class 1)	EOFdti
	EOF Normal-Invalid	EOFni

to request a class 1 connection; this frame may also include a data field. The SOF initiate delimiter indicates that this is the first frame of a sequence (except SOFc1); all other data frames in a sequence are indicated by SOF normal. The SOF fabric is used for frames within a fabric.

Frame Header. The frame header contains the bulk of the control information needed to manage the FC-2 protocol. It consists of the following fields:

- *Routing control (R_CTL):* consists of a 4-bit routing subfield and a 4-bit information category subfield. The routing subfield indicates the type of frame (e.g., device data, video data, link control), and the information category subfield indicates the type of data contained in the frame (e.g., solicited/unsolicited data, solicited/unsolicited control).
- *Destination identifier:* the address of the destination N_Port or F_Port.
- *Source identifier:* the address of the source N_Port or F_Port.
- *Type:* when R_CTL indicates that this is an FC-4 frame, identifies the specific FC-4 frame type (e.g., SCSI, IEEE 802, IP).
- *Frame control:* contains control information relating to frame content. For example, this field indicates whether the frame is from the exchange originator, whether it is part of the first or last sequence of an exchange, and whether this is part of an original sequence transmission or a sequence retransmission.
- *Sequence ID:* a unique identifier associated with all of the frames of a given sequence.
- *Data field control (DF_CTL):* specifies the presence or absence of each of the four optional headers at the beginning of the data field for device data or video data frames.
- *Sequence count:* a unique sequence number associated with each data frame in a sequence. The first frame of a sequence has sequence count = 0. This sequence number is used in the flow control mechanism and for segmentation and reassembly.
- *Originator exchange identifier:* a unique identifier assigned by the originator of an exchange. It is present in all frames transmitted by the originator and responder as part of the exchange.
- *Responder exchange identifier:* a unique identifier assigned by the responder of an exchange. It is present in all frames transmitted by the responder as part of the exchange.
- *Parameter:* for link control frames, carries information specific to the individual link control frame. For data frames, this field may be used by the upper layer protocol to specify the offset of the data in this frame relative to a base address meaningful to the upper-layer protocol.

The R_CTL and Type fields together provide the receiving N_Port with the necessary information for routing each incoming frame to the appropriate upper-layer protocol or other service at the destination.

Fibre Channel uses a 24-bit address to identify each port uniquely. This address has three components: domain, area, and port. This enables an easily managed hierarchical address structure for use by the fabric. Figure 9.11 illustrates the Fibre Channel addressing scheme.

Data Field.   The data field, if present, contains user data that is a multiple of 4 bytes in length up to a maximum of 2112 bytes. The data field includes an optional payload and zero or more of the following optional headers:

- *Expiration security header:* includes an expiration time and security-related information that is beyond the scope of the FC-PH standard.
- *Network header:* may be used by a bridge or gateway node that interfaces to an external network. It includes an 8-byte network destination address and an 8-byte network source address.
- *Association header:* may be used to identify a specific process or group of processes within a node associated with an exchange. Both originator and responder identifiers are included.
- *Device header:* determined by a level above FC-2.

CRC Field.   The 32-bit cyclic redundancy check (CRC) is calculated on the basis of the frame header and data fields. The algorithm is the same used for FDDI and IEEE 802.

End-of-Frame Delimiter.   The end-of-frame (EOF) delimiter indicates the end of the frame transmission. The EOF may be modified by an intervening fabric element to indicate that the frame is invalid or that the frame content was corrupted and this transmission is truncated. Table 9.5 indicates the possible values of the EOF delimiter.

For a valid frame, there are three possible EOF values. EOFt indicates the successful completion of a sequence. EOFdt is used with class 1 service to indicate that this frame is terminating a logical connection. EOFn indicates successful transmission of frames other than those covered by EOFt and EOFdt. If the frame content is invalid (e.g., code violation or CRC error), EOFni replaces the EOFn or EOFt that was present before the invalid condition was detected, and EOFdti replaces EOFdt. Finally, EOFa terminates a frame that is partial due to a malfunction in a link facility during transmission.

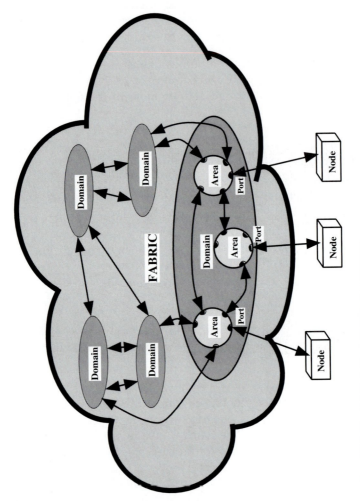

FIGURE 9.11 Fabric Address Partitioning [FCA94]

314

9.5

RECOMMENDED READING

The most comprehensive description of Fibre Channel is [STEP95]. This book provides a detailed technical treatment of each layer of the Fibre Channel architecture. A shorter but worthwhile treatment is [FCA94], which is a 50-page book from the Fibre Channel Association, an industry consortium formed to promote the Fibre Channel. [WALF95] describes the development of specific Fibre Channel Profiles, which are high-level design specifications that define specific combinations of Fibre Channel options for use in specific applications and environments.

FCA94   Fibre Channel Association. *Fibre Channel: Connection to the Future.* Austin, TX: Fibre Channel Association, 1994.

STEP95   Stephens, G., and Dedek, J. *Fiber Channel.* Menlo Park, CA: Ancot Corporation, 1995.

WALF95   Walford, P., and Frymoyer, E. "Providing Interoperable High-Speed Connections with Fiber Channel Technology." *ConneXions,* March 1995.

9.6

PROBLEMS

9.1 Describe the application of each of the entries in Table 9.4; that is, explain when each control frame is used and what its effect is.

9.2 For end-to-end flow control, what adjustment, if any, does the sequence initiator make to its Credit_Count upon receipt of each of the following frames?

   a. F_BSY

   b. F_RJT

   c. P_BSY

   d. P_RJT

ATM LANs

The capacity and throughput demands placed on local area networks continue to increase, for two reasons:

1. Organizations are relying more heavily on networking as more and more computer-based equipment is used, including workstations, personal computers, and servers. In particular, the emphasis on client–server computing has increased the total network traffic in a typical local installation.
2. The speed and capacity of attached systems has increased dramatically, allowing the introduction of applications, such as multimedia and graphics, that greatly increase the traffic generated by devices attached to local area networks.

Not so long ago, 10 Mbps seemed ample, even extravagant, for handling local demand. With the proliferation of inexpensive, high-performance workstations and other devices, this is no longer the case. It is not uncommon to have as few as five users on a single Ethernet; indeed, many Ethernets have just one user, with the various users lashed together by switches, intelligent hubs, bridges, and routers.

Of course, dividing the workload among a number of small LANs does not eliminate the problem. There is still the need for some sort of backbone to tie all of the equipment together and to provide a data path from each device to every other device. Solutions such as FDDI and Fibre Channel address this problem. However, there is another solution, known as the ATM LAN, that seems likely to become a major factor in local area networking. The ATM LAN is based on the asynchronous transfer mode (ATM) technology used in broadband ISDN and other wide-area networks. The ATM LAN approach has several important strengths:

1. The ATM technology provides an open-ended growth path for supporting attached devices. ATM is not constrained to a particular physical medium or data rate. A dedicated data rate between workstations of 155 Mbps is practical today. As demand increases and prices continue to drop, ATM LANs will be able to support devices at dedicated speeds, which are standardized for ATM, of 622 Mbps, 2.5 Gbps, and above.

2. ATM is becoming the technology of choice for wide-area networking. ATM can therefore be used effectively to integrate LAN and WAN configurations.

We begin this chapter with an overview of ATM protocols and architecture. Next, we look at some of the configurations possible for an ATM LAN. Finally, the concept of ATM LAN emulation is explored.

10.1
ASYNCHRONOUS TRANSFER MODE

Asynchronous transfer mode (ATM), also known as *cell relay*, is in some ways similar to packet switching using X.25 and to frame relay. Like packet switching and frame relay, ATM involves the transfer of data in discrete chunks. Also, like packet switching and frame relay, ATM allows multiple logical connections to be multiplexed over a single physical interface. In the case of ATM, the information flow on each logical connection is organized into fixed-size packets called *cells*.

ATM is a streamlined protocol with minimal error and flow control capabilities. This reduces the overhead of processing ATM cells and reduces the number of overhead bits required with each cell, thus enabling ATM to operate at high data rates. Further, the use of fixed-size cells simplifies the processing required at each ATM node, again supporting the use of ATM at high data rates.

ATM Protocol Architecture

The standards issued for ATM by ITU-T are based on the protocol architecture shown in Figure 10.1, which illustrates the basic architecture for

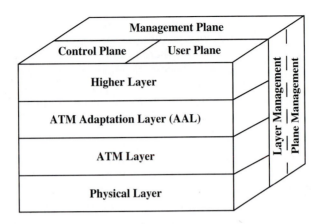

FIGURE 10.1 ATM Protocol Reference Model

an interface between user and network. As usual, the physical layer involves the specification of a transmission medium and a signal encoding scheme. The data rates specified at the physical layer include 155.52 Mbps and 622.08 Mbps. Other data rates, both higher and lower, are possible.

Two layers of the protocol architecture relate to ATM functions. There is an ATM layer common to all services that provides packet transfer capabilities, and an ATM adaptation layer (AAL) that is service dependent. The ATM layer defines the transmission of data in fixed-size cells and also defines the use of logical connections. The use of ATM creates the need for an adaptation layer to support information transfer protocols not based on ATM. The AAL maps higher-layer information into ATM cells to be transported over an ATM network, then collects information from ATM cells for delivery to higher layers.

The protocol reference model makes reference to three separate planes:

- *User plane:* provides for user information transfer, along with associated controls (e.g., flow control, error control)
- *Control plane:* performs call control and connection control functions
- *Management plane:* includes plane management, which performs management functions related to a system as a whole and provides coordination between all the planes, and layer management, which performs management functions relating to resources and parameters residing in its protocol entities

The remainder of this section provides an overview of the ATM and AAL layers.

ATM Logical Connections

Logical connections in ATM are referred to as *virtual channel connections* (VCCs). A VCC is analogous to a virtual circuit in X.25; it is the basic unit of switching in an ATM network. A VCC is set up between two end users through the network and a variable-rate, full-duplex flow of fixed-size cells is exchanged over the connection. VCCs are also used for user–network exchange (control signaling) and network–network exchange (network management and routing).

For ATM, a second sublayer of processing has been introduced that deals with the concept of virtual path (Figure 10.2). A virtual path connection (VPC) is a bundle of VCCs that have the same endpoints. Thus all of the cells flowing over all of the VCCs in a single VPC are switched together.

The virtual path concept was developed in response to a trend in high-speed networking in which the control cost of the network is becoming an increasingly higher proportion of the overall network cost. The virtual path technique helps contain the control cost by grouping connections sharing common paths through the network into a single unit. Network management actions can then be applied to a small number of groups of connections instead of a large number of individual connections.

Several advantages can be listed for the use of virtual paths:

- *Simplified network architecture.* Network transport functions can be separated into those related to an individual logical connection (virtual channel) and those related to a group of logical connections (virtual path).

- *Increased network performance and reliability.* The network deals with fewer, aggregated entities.

- *Reduced processing and short connection setup time.* Much of the work is done when the virtual path is set up. By reserving capacity on a virtual path connection in anticipation of later call arrivals, new virtual channel connections can be established by executing simple control functions at the endpoints of the virtual path connection; no call processing is required at transit nodes. Thus the addition of new virtual channels to an existing virtual path involves minimal processing.

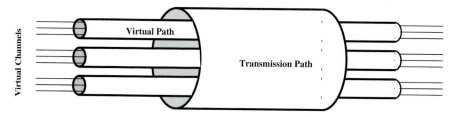

FIGURE 10.2   ATM Connection Relationships

- *Enhanced network services.* The virtual path is used internal to the network but is also visible to the end user. Thus the user may define closed user groups or closed networks of virtual channel bundles.

Figure 10.3 suggests in a general way the call establishment process using virtual channels and virtual paths. The process of setting up a virtual path connection is decoupled from the process of setting up an individual virtual channel connection:

- The virtual path control mechanisms include calculating routes, allocating capacity, and storing connection state information.
- For an individual virtual channel setup, control involves checking that there is a virtual path connection to the required destination node with sufficient available capacity to support the virtual channel, with the

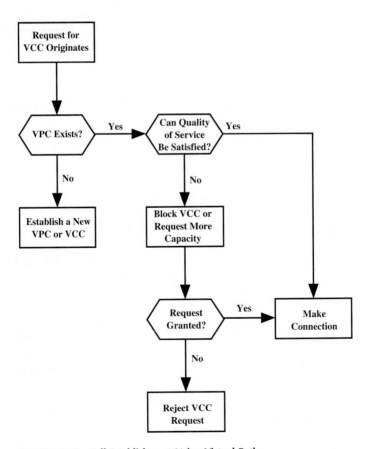

FIGURE 10.3   Call Establishment Using Virtual Paths

appropriate quality of service, and then storing the required state information (virtual channel/virtual path mapping).

The terminology of virtual paths and virtual channels used in the standard is a bit confusing and is summarized in Table 10.1.

Virtual Channel Connection Uses.   The endpoints of a VCC may be end users, network entities, or an end user and a network entity. In all cases, cell sequence integrity is preserved within a VCC; that is, cells are delivered in

TABLE 10.1   Virtual Path/Virtual Connection Terminology

Term	Definition
Virtual channel (VC)	A generic term used to describe unidirectional transport of ATM cells associated by a common unique identifier value.
Virtual channel link	A means of unidirectional transport of ATM cells between a point where a VCI value is assigned and the point where that value is translated or terminated.
Virtual channel identifier (VCI)	Identifies a particular VC link for a given VPC.
Virtual channel connection (VCC)	A concatenation of VC links that extends between two points where the adaptation layer is accessed. VCCs are provided for the purpose of user–user, user–network, or network–network information transfer. Cell sequence integrity is preserved for cells belonging to the same VCC.
Virtual path	A generic term used to describe unidirectional transport of ATM cells belonging to virtual channels that are associated by a common unique identifier value.
Virtual path link	A group of VC links, identified by a common value of VPI, between a point where a VPI value is assigned and the point where that value is translated or terminated.
Virtual path identifier (VPI)	Identifies a particular VP link.
Virtual path connection (VPC)	A concatenation of VP links that extends between the point where the VCI values are assigned and the point where those values are translated or removed (i.e., extending the length of a bundle of VC links that share the same VPI). VPCs are provided for the purpose of user–user, user–network, or network–network information transfer.

the same order in which they are sent. Let us consider examples of the three uses of a VCC:

- *Between end users:* can be used to carry end-to-end user data; can also be used to carry control signaling between end users, as explained below. A VPC between end users provides them with an overall capacity; the VCC organization of the VPC is up to the two end users, provided that the set of VCCs does not exceed the VPC capacity.
- *Between an end user and a network entity:* used for user-to-network control signaling, as discussed below. A user-to-network VPC can be used to aggregate traffic from an end user to a network exchange or network server.
- *Between two network entities:* used for network traffic management and routing functions. A network-to-network VPC can be used to define a common route for the exchange of network management information.

Virtual Path/Virtual Channel Characteristics.   ITU-T Recommendation I.150 lists the following as characteristics of virtual channel connections:

- *Quality of service.* A user of a VCC is provided with a quality of service specified by parameters such as cell loss ratio (ratio of cells lost to cells transmitted) and cell delay variation.
- *Switched and semipermanent virtual channel connections.* Both switched connections, which require call-control signaling, and dedicated channels can be provided.
- *Cell sequence integrity.* The sequence of transmitted cells within a VCC is preserved.
- *Traffic parameter negotiation and usage monitoring.* Traffic parameters can be negotiated between a user and the network for each VCC. The input of cells to the VCC is monitored by the network to ensure that the negotiated parameters are not violated.

The types of traffic parameters that can be negotiated include average rate, peak rate, burstiness, and peak duration. The network may need a number of strategies to deal with congestion and to manage existing and requested VCCs. At the crudest level, the network may simply deny new requests for VCCs to prevent congestion. Additionally, cells may be discarded if negotiated parameters are violated or if congestion becomes severe. In an extreme situation, existing connections might be terminated.

I.150 also lists characteristics of VPCs. The first four characteristics listed are identical to those for VCCs. That is, quality of service, switched and semipermanent VPCs, cell sequence integrity, and traffic parameter negotiation and usage monitoring are all also characteristics of a VPC. There are a number of reasons for this duplication. First, this provides some flexibility in how the network service manages the requirements placed upon it. Second, the network must be concerned with the overall requirements for a VPC, and within a VPC, may negotiate the establishment of virtual channels with given characteristics. Finally, once a VPC is set up, it is possible for the end users to negotiate the creation of new VCCs. The VPC characteristics impose a discipline on the choices that the end users may make.

In addition, a fifth characteristic is listed for VPCs:

- *Virtual channel identifier restriction within a VPC.* One or more virtual channel identifiers, or numbers, may not be available to the user of the VPC, but may be reserved for network use. Examples include VCCs used for network management.

Control Signaling.   In ATM, a mechanism is needed for the establishment and release of VPC and VCCs. The exchange of information involved in this process, referred to as *control signaling,* takes place on separate connections from those that are being managed.

For VCCs, I.150 specifies four methods for providing an establishment/release facility. One or a combination of these methods will be used in any particular network:

1. **Semipermanent VCCs** may be used for user-to-user exchange. In this case, no control signaling is required.
2. If there is no preestablished call control signaling channel, one must be set up. For that purpose, a control signaling exchange must take place between the user and the network on some channel. Hence we need a permanent channel, probably of low data rate, that can be used to set up VCCs that can be used for call control. Such a channel is called a **meta-signaling channel,** since the channel is used to set up signaling channels.
3. The meta-signaling channel can be used to set up a VCC between the user and the network for call control signaling. This **user-to-network signaling virtual channel** can then be used to set up VCCs to carry user data.
4. The meta-signaling channel can also be used to set up a **user-to-user signaling virtual channel.** Such a channel must be set up within a preestablished VPC. It can then be used to allow the two end users, without network intervention, to establish and release user-to-user VCCs to carry user data.

For VPCs, three methods are defined in I.150:

1. A VPC can be established on a **semipermanent** basis by prior agreement. In this case, no control signaling is required.

2. VPC establishment/release may be **customer controlled.** In this case the customer uses a signaling VCC to request the VPC from the network.

3. VPC establishment/release may be **network controlled.** In this case the network establishes a VPC for its own convenience. The path may be network to network, user to network, or user to user.

ATM Cells

The asynchronous transfer mode makes use of fixed-size cells, consisting of a 5-octet header and a 48-octet information field. There are several advantages to the use of small, fixed-size cells. First, the use of small cells may reduce queuing delay for a high-priority cell, since it waits less if it arrives slightly behind a lower-priority cell that has gained access to a resource (e.g., the transmitter). Second, it appears that fixed-size cells can be switched more efficiently, which is important for the very high data rates of ATM. With fixed-size cells it is easier to implement the switching mechanism in hardware.

Header Format.   Figure 10.4a shows the header format at the user–network interface. Figure 10.4b shows the cell header format internal to the network. Internal to the network, the generic flow control field, which performs end-to-end functions, is not retained. Instead, the virtual path identifier field is expanded from 8 bits to 12 bits. This allows support for an expanded number of VPCs internal to the network, to include those supporting subscribers and those required for network management.

The **generic flow control** (GFC) field can be used for control of cell flow at the local user–network interface. The details of its application are a subject for further study. The field could be used to assist the customer in controlling the flow of traffic for different qualities of service. One candidate for the use of this field is a multiple-priority level indicator to control the flow of information in a service-dependent manner. In any case, the GFC mechanism is used to alleviate short-term overload conditions in the network.

The **virtual path identifier** (VPI) constitutes a routing field for the network. It is 8 bits at the user–network interface and 12 bits at the network–network interface, allowing for more virtual paths to be supported within the network. The **virtual channel identifier** (VCI) is used for routing to and from the end user. Thus it functions much as a service access point.

The **payload type** field indicates the type of information in the information field. Table 10.2 shows the interpretation of the PT bits. A value of 0 in the first bit indicates user information, that is, information from the next-higher layer. In this case the second bit indicates whether congestion has been experienced; the third bit, known as the ATM-user-to-ATM-user

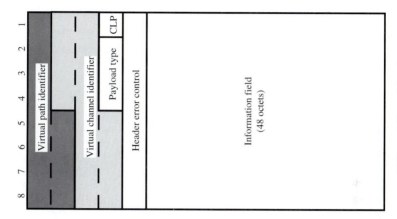

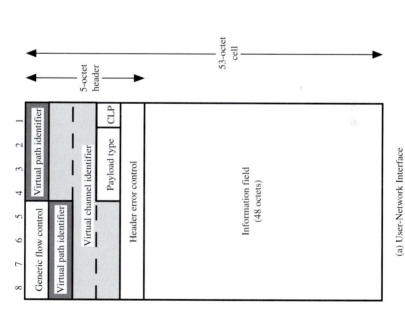

(a) User-Network Interface

(b) Network-Network Interface

FIGURE 10.4   ATM Cell Format

TABLE 10.2   Payload Type Field Coding

PT Coding	Interpretation[a]
0 0 0	User data cell, AAU = 0, congestion not experienced
0 0 1	User data cell, AAU = 1, congestion not experienced
0 1 0	User data cell, AAU = 0, congestion experienced
0 1 1	User data cell, AAU = 1, congestion experienced
1 0 0	OAM F5 segment associated cell
1 0 1	OAM F5 end-to-end associated cell
1 1 0	Resource management cell
1 1 1	Reserved for future function

[a]AAU, ATM user to ATM user indication.

(AAU) indication bit is a 1-bit field that can be used to convey information between end users. A value of 1 in the first bit indicates that this cell carries network management or maintenance information. This indication allows the insertion of network-management cells onto a user's VCC without affecting user's data. Thus it can provide in-band control information.

The **cell loss priority** (CLP) is used to provide guidance to the network in the event of congestion. A value of 0 indicates a cell of relatively higher priority, which should not be discarded unless no other alternative is available. A value of 1 indicates that this cell is subject to discard within the network. The user might employ this field so that extra information may be inserted into the network, with a CLP of 1, and delivered to the destination if the network is not congested. The network may set this field to 1 for any data cell that is in violation of a agreement between the user and the network concerning traffic parameters. In this case the switch that does the setting realizes that the cell exceeds the agreed traffic parameters but that the switch is capable of handling the cell. At a later point in the network, if congestion is encountered, this cell has been marked for discard in preference to cells that fall within agreed traffic limits.

Header Error Control.   Each ATM cell includes an 8-bit header error control field (HEC) that is calculated based on the remaining 32 bits of the header. The polynomial used to generate the code is $X^8 + X^2 + X + 1$. In most existing protocols that include an error control field, such as MAC protocols, the data that serve as input to the error code calculation are in general much longer than the size of the resulting error code. This allows for error detection. In the case of ATM, the input to the calculation is only 32 bits, compared to 8 bits for the code. The fact that the input is relatively short allows the code to be used not only for error detection but, in some cases, for actual error correction. This is because there is sufficient redundancy in the code to recover from certain error patterns.

Figure 10.5 depicts the operation of the HEC algorithm at the receiver. At initialization, the receiver's error correction algorithm is in the default mode for single-bit error correction. As each cell is received, HEC calculation and comparison are performed. As long as no errors are detected, the receiver remains in error correction mode. When an error is detected, the receiver will correct the error if it is a single-bit error or will detect that a multibit error has occurred. In either case, the receiver now moves to detection mode. In this mode, no attempt is made to correct errors. The reason for this change is a recognition that a noise burst or other event might cause a sequence of errors, a condition for which the HEC is insufficient for error correction. The receiver remains in detection mode as long as errored cells are received. When a header is examined and found not to be in error, the receiver switches back to correction mode. The flowchart of Figure 10.6 shows the consequence of errors in the cell header.

The error protection function provides both recovery from single-bit header errors and a low probability of the delivery of cells with errored headers under bursty error conditions. The error characteristics of fiber-based transmission systems appear to be a mix of single-bit errors and relatively large burst errors. For some transmission systems, the error correction capability, which is more time consuming, might not be invoked. Figure 10.7, based on one in ITU-T I.432, indicates how random bit errors affect the probability of occurrence of discarded cells and valid cells with errored headers when HEC is employed.

ATM Adaptation Layer

AAL Services.   ITU-T I.362 lists the following general examples of services provided by AAL:

- Handling of transmission errors
- Segmentation and reassembly, to enable larger blocks of data to be carried in the information field of ATM cells

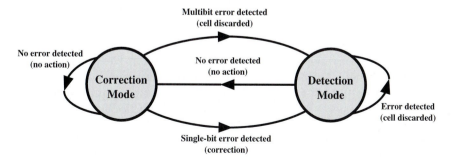

FIGURE 10.5   HEC Operation at Receiver

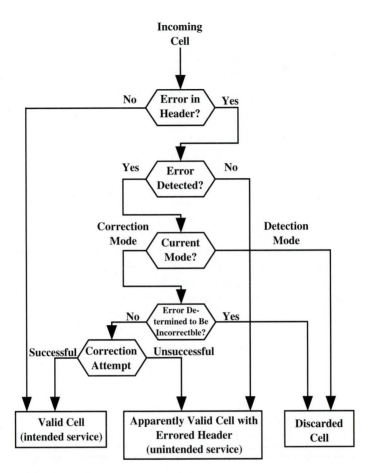

FIGURE 10.6   Effect of Error in Cell Header

- Handling of lost and misinserted cell conditions
- Flow control and timing control

    To minimize the number of different AAL protocols that must be specified to meet a variety of needs, ITU-T has defined four classes of service that cover a broad range of requirements (Figure 10.8). The classification is based on whether a timing relationship must be maintained between source and destination, whether the application requires a constant bit rate, and whether the transfer is connection-oriented or connectionless. An example of a class A service is circuit emulation. In this case, a constant bit rate, which requires the maintenance of a timing relation, is used, and the transfer is connection oriented. An example of class B service is variable-bit-rate video, such as might be used in a videoconference. Here the application is

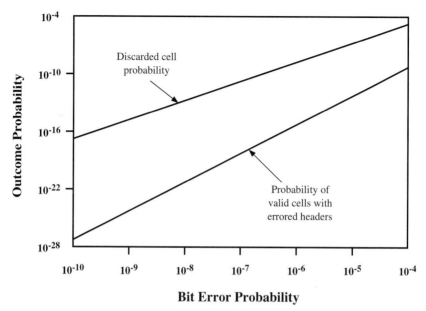

FIGURE 10.7   Impact of Random Bit Errors on HEC Performance

	Class A	Class B	Class C	Class D
Timing relation between souce and destination	Required		Not required	
Bit rate	Constant	Variable		
Connection mode	Connection-oriented			Connectionless
AAL Protocol	Type 1	Type 2	Type 3/4,Type 5	Type 3/4

FIGURE 10.8   Service Classification for AAL

connection oriented and timing is important, but the bit rate varies depending on the amount of activity in the scene. Classes C and D correspond to data transfer applications. In both cases the bit rate may vary and no particular timing relationship is required; differences in data rate are handled by the end systems using buffers. The data transfer may be either connection oriented (class C) or connectionless (class D).

AAL Protocols.   To support these various classes of service, a set of protocols at the AAL level are defined. The AAL layer is organized in two logical sublayers: the convergence sublayer (CS) and the segmentation and reassembly sublayer (SAR). The convergence sublayer provides the functions needed to support specific applications using AAL. Each AAL user attaches to AAL at a service access point (SAP), which is simply the address of the application. This sublayer is thus service dependent.

The segmentation and reassembly sublayer is responsible for packaging information received from CS into cells for transmission and for unpacking the information at the other end. As we have seen, at the ATM layer, each cell consists of a 5-octet header and a 48-octet information field. Thus SAR must pack any SAR headers and trailers plus CS information into 48-octet blocks.

Initially, ITU-T defined one protocol type for each class of service, called type 1 through type 4. Actually, each protocol type consists of two protocols, one at the CS sublayer and one at the SAR sublayer. More recently, types 3 and 4 were merged, with the result being defined as type 3/4, and a new type, type 5, was defined. Figure 10.8 shows which services are supported by which types. In all of these cases, a block of data from a higher layer is encapsulated into a PDU at the CS sublayer. In fact, this sublayer is referred to as the common part convergence sublayer (CPCS), leaving open the possibility that additional, specialized functions may be performed at the CS level. The CPCS PDU is then passed to the SAR sublayer, where it is broken up into payload blocks. Each payload block can fit into an SAR-PDU, which has a total length of 48 octets. Each 48-octet SAR-PDU fits into a single ATM cell. Figure 10.9 shows the formats of the protocol data units (PDUs) at the SAR level except for type 2, which has not yet been defined.

The protocol type with most relevance to ATM LANs is type 5. This protocol was introduced to provide a streamlined transport facility for higher-layer protocols that are connection oriented. If it is assumed that the higher layer takes care of connection management and that the ATM layer produces minimal errors, most of the fields in the SAR and CPCS PDUs are not necessary. For example, with connection-oriented service, the MID field is not necessary: The VCI/VPI is available for cell-by-cell multiplexing, and the higher layer supports message-by-message multiplexing.

Type 5 was introduced to:

- Reduce protocol processing overhead
- Reduce transmission overhead
- Ensure adaptability to existing transport protocols

To understand the operation of type 5, let us begin with the CPCS level. The CPCS-PDU (Figure 10.10) includes a trailer with the following fields:

- *CPCS user-to-user indication (1 octet):* used to transfer user-to-user information transparently.
- *Cyclic redundancy check (4 octets):* used to detect bit errors in the CPCS-PDU.

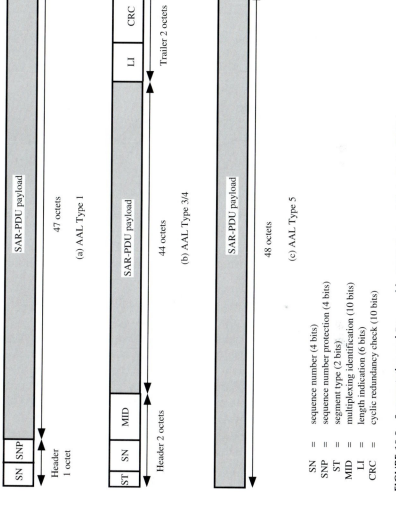

FIGURE 10.9 Segmentation and Reassembly (SAR) Protocol Data Units (PDUs)

SN = sequence number (4 bits)
SNP = sequence number protection (4 bits)
ST = segment type (2 bits)
MID = multiplexing identification (10 bits)
LI = length indication (6 bits)
CRC = cyclic redundancy check (10 bits)

(a) AAL Type 1

Header
1 octet

47 octets

SAR-PDU payload

SN SNP

(b) AAL Type 3/4

Header 2 octets

44 octets

Trailer 2 octets

SAR-PDU payload

ST SN MID

LI CRC

(c) AAL Type 5

48 octets

SAR-PDU payload

331

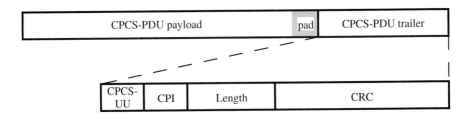

CPCS-UU   =   CPCS user-to-user indication (1 octet)
CPI   =   common part indicator (1 octet)
Length   =   length of CPCS-PDU payload (2 octets)
CRC   =   cyclic redundancy check (4 octets)

FIGURE 10.10   AAL Type 5 CPCS-PDU

- *Common part indicator (1 octet):* indicates the interpretation of the remaining fields in the CPCS-PDU header. Currently, only one interpretation is defined.
- *Length (2 octets):* length of the CPCS-PDU payload field.

The payload from the next-higher layer is padded out so that the entire CPCS-PDU is a multiple of 48 octets.

The SAR-PDU consists simply of 48 octets of payload, carrying a portion of the CPCS-PDU. The lack of protocol overhead has several implications:

1. Because there is no sequence number, the receiver must assume that all SAR-PDUs arrive in the proper order for reassembly. The CRC field in the CPCS-PDU is intended to verify that.
2. The lack of MID field means that it is not possible to interleave cells from different CPCS-PDUs. Therefore, each successive SAR-PDU carries a portion of the current CPCS-PDU or the first block of the next CPCS-PDU. To distinguish between these two cases, the ATM user-to-user indication (AAU) bit in the payload type field of the ATM cell header is used (Figure 10.4). A CPCS-PDU consists of zero or more consecutive SAR-PDUs, with AAU set to 0 followed immediately by an SAR-PDU with AAU set to 1.
3. The lack of an LI field means that there is no way for the SAR entity to distinguish between CPCS-PDU octets and filler in the last SAR-PDU. Therefore, there is no way for the SAR entity to find the CPCS-PDU trailer in the last SAR-PDU. To avoid this situation, it is required that the CPCS-PDU payload be padded out so that the last bit of the CPCS-trailer occurs as the last bit of the final SAR-PDU.

Figure 10.11 shows an example of AAL 5 transmission. The CPCS-PDU, including padding and trailer, is divided into 48-octet blocks. Each block is transmitted in a single ATM cell.

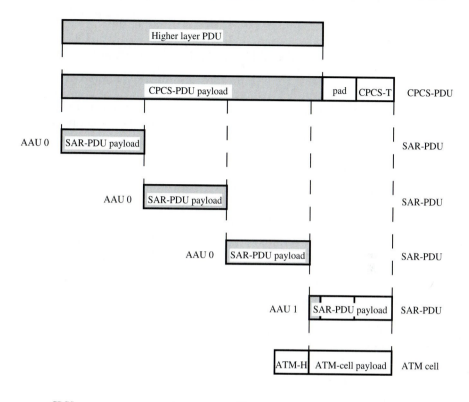

CPCS   =   common part convergence sublayer
SAR   =   segmentation and reassembly
PDU   =   protocol data unit
CPCS-T   =   CPCS trailer
ATM-H   =   ATM header
AAU   =   ATM-user-to-ATM-user indication bit

FIGURE 10.11   Example of AAL 5 Transmission

10.2

ATM LAN ARCHITECTURE

A document on customer premises networks jointly prepared by Apple, Bellcore, Sun, and Xerox [ABSX92] identifies three generations of LANs:

- *First generation:* typified by the CSMA/CD and token ring LANs. The first generation provided terminal-to-host connectivity and supported client–server architectures at moderate data rates.
- *Second generation:* typified by FDDI. The second generation responds to the need for backbone LANs and for support of high-performance workstations.

- *Third generation:* typified by ATM LANs. The third generation is designed to provide the aggregate throughputs and real-time transport guarantees that are needed for multimedia applications.

Typical requirements for a third-generation LAN include:

1. Support multiple, guaranteed classes of service. A live video application, for example, may require a guaranteed 2-Mbps connection for acceptable performance, while a file transfer program can utilize a "background" class of service.
2. Provide scaleable throughput that is capable of growing both per host capacity (to enable applications that require large volumes of data in and out of a single host) and aggregate capacity (to enable installations to grow from a few to several hundred high-performance hosts).
3. Facilitate the interworking between LAN and WAN technology.

ATM is ideally suited to these requirements. Using virtual paths and virtual channels, multiple classes of service are easily accommodated, either in a preconfigured fashion (permanent connections) or on demand (switched connections). ATM is easily scaleable by adding more ATM switching nodes and using higher (or lower) data rates for attached devices. Finally, with the increasing acceptance of cell-based transport for wide-area networking, the use of ATM for a premises network enables seamless integration of LANs and WANs.

The term *ATM LAN* has been used by vendors and researchers to apply to a variety of configurations. At the very least, an ATM LAN implies the use of ATM as a data transport protocol somewhere within the local premises. Among the possible types of ATM LANs:

- *Gateway to ATM WAN.* An ATM switch acts as a router and traffic concentrator for linking a premises network complex to an ATM WAN.
- *Backbone ATM switch.* Either a single ATM switch or a local network of ATM switches interconnect other LANs.
- *Workgroup ATM.* High-performance multimedia workstations and other end systems connect directly to an ATM switch.

These are all "pure" configurations. In practice, a mixture of two or all three of these types of networks is used to create an ATM LAN.

Figure 10.12 shows an example of a backbone ATM LAN that includes links to the outside world. In this example, the local ATM network consists of four switches interconnected with high-speed point-to-point links running at the standardized ATM rates of 155 and 622 Mbps. On the premises, there are three other LANs, each of which has a direct connection to one of the ATM switches. The data rate from an ATM switch to an attached LAN conforms to the native data rate of that LAN. For example, the connection

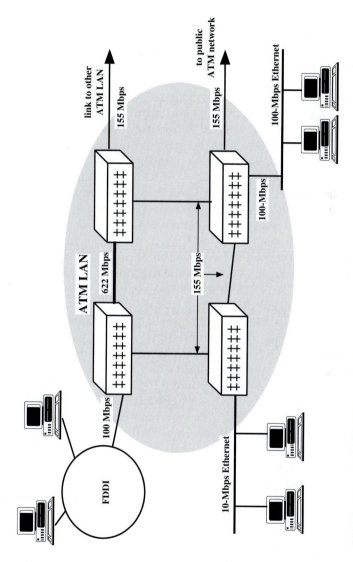

FIGURE 10.12 Example ATM LAN Configuration

335

to the FDDI network is at 100 Mbps. Thus the switch must include some buffering and speed conversion capability to map the data rate from the attached LAN to an ATM data rate. The ATM switch must also perform some sort of protocol conversion from the MAC protocol used on the attached LAN to the ATM cell stream used on the ATM network. A simple approach is for each ATM switch that attaches to a LAN to function as a bridge or router.[1]

An ATM LAN configuration such as that shown in Figure 10.12 provides a relatively painless method for inserting a high-speed backbone into a local environment. As the on-site demand rises, it is a simple matter to increase the capacity of the backbone by adding more switches, increasing the throughput of each switch, and increasing the data rate of the trunks between switches. With this strategy, the load on individual LANs within the premises can be increased and the number of LANs can grow.

However, this simple backbone ATM LAN does not address all of the needs for local communications. In particular, in the simple backbone configuration, the end systems (workstations, servers, etc.) remain attached to shared-media LANs with the limitations on data rate imposed by the shared medium.

A more advanced and more powerful approach is to use ATM technology in a hub. Figure 10.13 suggests the capabilities that can be provided with this approach. Each ATM hub includes a number of ports that operate at different data rates and use different protocols. Typically, such a hub consists of a number of rack-mounted modules, with each module containing ports of a given data rate and protocol.

The key difference between the ATM hub shown in Figure 10.13 and the ATM nodes depicted in Figure 10.12 is the way in which individual end systems are handled. Notice that in the ATM hub, each end system has a dedicated point-to-point link to the hub. Each end system includes the communications hardware and software to interface to a particular type of LAN, but in each case, the LAN contains only two devices: the end system and the hub! For example, each device attached to a 10-Mbps Ethernet port operates using the CSMA/CD protocol at 10 Mbps. However, since each end system has its own dedicated line, the effect is that each system has its own dedicated 10-Mbps Ethernet. Therefore, each end system can operate at close to the maximum 10-Mbps data rate.

The use of a configuration such as that of either Figure 10.12 or 10.13 has the advantage that existing LAN installations and LAN hardware, so-called legacy LANs, can continue to be used while ATM technology is introduced. The disadvantage is that the use of such a mixed-protocol environment requires the implementation of some sort of protocol conversion

---

[1]The functionality of bridges and routers is discussed briefly in Chapter 4 and is examined in depth in Chapters 14 and 15.

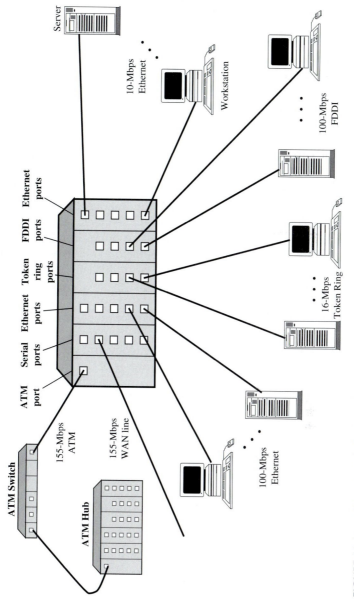

FIGURE 10.13   ATM LAN Hub Configuration

337

capability, a topic that is explored in Section 10.3. A simpler approach, but one that requires that end systems be equipped with ATM capability, is to implement a "pure" ATM LAN.

Figure 10.14 illustrates the configuration of a single node in a pure ATM LAN and also suggests a means of implementing the ATM switch. In this case, each end system connects directly to an ATM switch at a standardized ATM data rate, such as 155 Mbps.

The switching matrix shown in Figure 10.14 is typical of some products currently on the market. Each element has two inputs and two outputs, and each stage consists of a bank of switching elements. When a transmission comes in to the first stage of the device, a switching element chooses randomly to pass it through one of its two outputs. The output of the first stage becomes the input to the second, and so on. This process ensures that transmissions are evenly distributed throughout the switching matrix, reducing the chance that transmissions will be blocked.

Typically, each switching element has a buffer large enough to hold a few ATM cells. Cells can be buffered both to avoid congestion and to be duplicated for multicasting. In the case of multicasting, the switching element checks to see if it needs to copy a cell. If so, the element passes a copy of the cell through both of its outputs.

Mention should be made of the overlapping areas of application of ATM LANs and Fibre Channel. Both use fiber optics as their primary delivery medium. Both rely on switching technology and both sport open-ended data rates well above 100 Mbps. The emphasis of the ATM LAN is on high-speed, timely delivery and seamless integration with wide-area ATM networks. The emphasis of Fibre Channel is on high speed, moving large amounts of data efficiently, and integration of I/O channel and network support. Within a building or campus environment, the two technologies are competitive.

10.3

ATM LAN EMULATION

One issue that was not addressed in our discussion of Section 10.2 has to do with the interoperability of end systems on a variety of interconnected LANs. End systems attached directly to one of the legacy LANs implement the MAC layer appropriate to that type of LAN. End systems attached directly to an ATM network implement the ATM and AAL protocols. As a result, there are three areas of compatibility to consider:

1. Interaction between an end system on an ATM network and an end system on a legacy LAN.

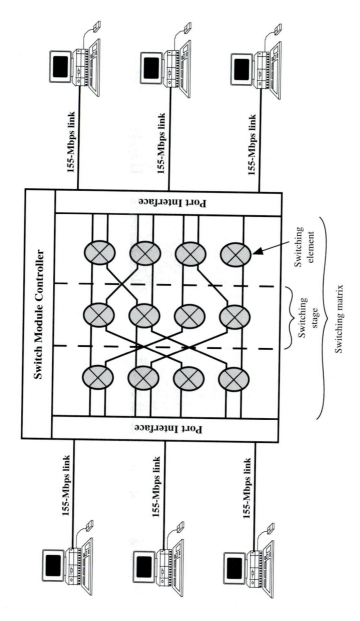

FIGURE 10.14 LAN Based on an ATM Switch

339

2. Interaction between an end system on a legacy LAN and an end system on another legacy LAN of the same type (e.g., two IEEE 802.3 networks).

3. Interaction between an end system on a legacy LAN and an end system on another legacy LAN of a different type (e.g., an IEEE 802.3 network and an IEEE 802.5 network).

The most general solution to this problem is the router, which was introduced in Chapter 4 and is discussed in detail in Chapter 15. In essence, the router operates at the level of the Internet Protocol (IP). All of the end systems implement IP, and all networks are interconnected with routers. If data are to travel beyond the scope of an individual LAN, it is directed to the local router. There, the LLC and MAC layers are stripped off, and the IP PDU is routed across one or more other networks to the destination LAN, where the appropriate LLC and MAC layers are invoked. Similarly, if one or both of the end systems is attached directly to an ATM network, the AAL and ATM layers are stripped off or added to an IP PDU.

Although this approach is effective, it introduces a certain amount of processing overhead and delay at each router. In very large internetworks, these delays can become substantial. Networks of 1000 routers are increasingly common, and networks of as many as 10,000 routers have been installed [LANG95]. A technique that exploits the efficiency of ATM and that reduces the number of routers required is desired.

Another way to approach the problem is to convert all end systems to operate directly on ATM. In this case, there is a seamless technology used throughout any network, including local and wide-area components. However, with millions of Ethernet and token ring nodes installed on today's shared-media LANs, most organizations simply cannot afford a one-shot upgrade of all systems to ATM. In addition, although the cost of ATM interface cards is dropping, Ethernet and token ring interfaces remain cheaper for the time being.

In response to this need, the ATM Forum[2] has created a specification for the coexistence of legacy LANs and ATM LANs, known as ATM LAN

---

[2]The ATM Forum is a nonprofit international industry consortium, which is playing a crucial role in the development of ATM standards. In the ITU and the constituent member bodies from the participating countries, the process of developing standards is characterized by wide participation by government, users, and industry representatives, and by consensus decision making. This process can be quite time consuming. While ITU-T has streamlined its efforts, the delays involved in developing standards is particularly significant in the area of ATM technology. Because of the strong level of interest in ATM, the ATM Forum was created with the goal of accelerating the development of ATM standards. The ATM Forum has seen more active participation from computing vendors than has been the case in ITU-T. Because the forum works on the basis of majority rule rather than consensus, it has been able to move rapidly to define some of the needed details for the implementation of ATM. This effort, in turn, has fed into the ITU-T standardization effort.

emulation [ATM95]. The objective on ATM LAN emulation is to enable existing shared-media LAN nodes to interoperate across an ATM network and to interoperate with devices that connect directly to ATM switches.

Figure 10.15 illustrates the type of configuration that can be constructed using ATM LAN emulation. In its present form, the ATM specification satisfies two of the three requirements listed earlier; namely, ATM LAN emulation defines the following:

1. The way in which end systems on two separate LANs of the same type (same MAC layer) can exchange MAC frames across the ATM network
2. The way in which an end system on a LAN can interoperate with an end system emulating the same LAN type and attached directly to an ATM switch

The specification does not as yet address interoperability between end systems on different LANs with different MAC protocols.

Protocol Architecture

Figure 10.16 indicates the protocol architecture involved in ATM LAN emulation. In this case we are looking at the interaction of an ATM-attached system with an end system attached to a legacy LAN. Note that the end system attached to a legacy LAN is unaffected: It is able to use the ordinary repertoire of protocols, including the MAC protocol specific to this LAN and LLC running on top of MAC. Thus the end system runs TCP/IP over LLC and various application-level protocols on top of that; the various application-level protocols are unaware that there is an ATM network underneath.

As was discussed in Chapter 4, it is possible to link two LANs that employ the same MAC protocol[3] using a bridge. If a bridge is attached to two LANs, a MAC address space that spans both LANs may be used, with a unique MAC address for each attached system. If a MAC frame transmitted on one LAN is addressed to a system on the other LAN, the bridge picks up the MAC frame from the first LAN and retransmits it on the second LAN. This process is transparent to the end systems, which can function as though they are all connected to the same LAN.

In Figure 10.16, the bridge logic must be augmented by the capability of converting MAC frames to and from ATM cells. This is one of the key functions of the LAN emulation module. The ATM Forum specification calls for making use of AAL 5 to segment MAC frames into ATM cells and to

---

[3]Actually, a form of bridge can be used between dissimilar LANs. This is discussed in Chapter 14 but need not be considered at this point in the discussion.

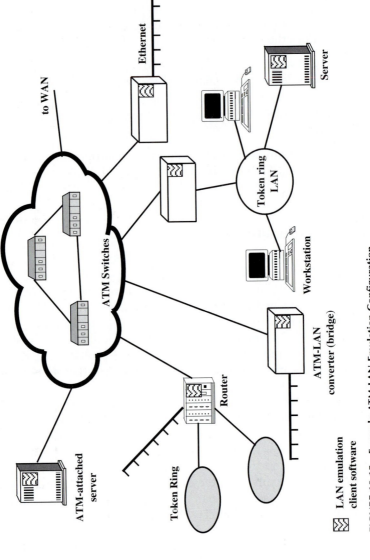

FIGURE 10.15   Example ATM LAN Emulation Configuration

to WAN

Ethernet

ATM Switches

Token ring
LAN

Server

Workstation

ATM-attached
server

ATM-LAN
converter (bridge)

Router

Token Ring

▨ LAN emulation
client software

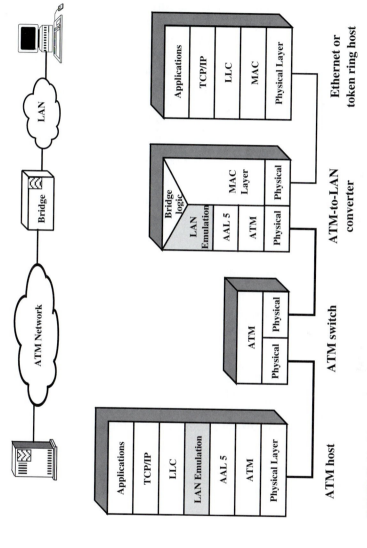

FIGURE 10.16   LAN Emulation Protocol Architecture

343

reassemble incoming ATM cells into MAC frames. For outgoing ATM cells, the ATM-to-LAN converter connects in the usual fashion to an ATM switch as part of an ATM network.

Figure 10.16 shows the case in which a host on a legacy LAN is exchanging data with a host attached directly to an ATM network. To accommodate this exchange, the ATM host must include a LAN emulation module that accepts MAC frames from AAL and passes the contents up to an LLC layer. Thus the host is indeed emulating a LAN since it can receive and transmit MAC frames in the same format as the distant legacy LAN. From the point of view of end systems on the legacy LAN, the ATM host is just another end system with a MAC address. The entire LAN emulation process is transparent to existing systems implementing LLC and MAC.

Emulated LANs

With the protocol architecture just described, it is possible to set up a number of logically independent *emulated LANs*. An emulated LAN supports a single MAC protocol, of which two types are currently defined: Ethernet/IEEE 802.3 and IEEE 802.5 (token ring). An emulated LAN consists of some combination of the following:

- End systems on one or more legacy LANs
- End systems attached directly to an ATM switch

Each end system on an emulated LAN must have a unique MAC address. Data interchange between end systems on the same emulated LAN involves the use of the MAC protocol and is transparent to the upper layers. That is, it appears to LLC that all of the end systems on an emulated LAN are on the same shared-medium LAN. Communication between end systems on different emulated LANs is possible only through routers or bridges. Note that the bridges or routers have to reassemble the cells into packets and chop them up into cells to send them to another emulated LAN.

LAN Emulation Clients and Servers

The discussion so far leaves out a number of issues that must be addressed, including the following:

1. Devices attached directly to ATM switches and ATM-to-LAN converter systems have ATM-based addresses. How are translations made between these addresses and MAC addresses?
2. ATM makes use of a connection-oriented protocol involving virtual channels and virtual paths. How can the connectionless LAN MAC protocol be supported over this connection-oriented framework?

3. Multicasting and broadcasting on a shared-medium LAN is easily achieved. How is this capability carried over into the ATM environment?

To address these issues, the ATM Forum developed a capability based on a client–server approach, which is discussed next.

ATM LAN emulation requires two types of components: clients and servers. Clients operate on behalf of devices that are attached to legacy LANs and that use MAC addresses. A client is responsible for adding its MAC entities into the overall configuration and for dealing with the tasks associated with translating between MAC addresses and ATM addresses. Typically, a client would be provided in a router, an ATM-attached server (see Figure 10.15), or perhaps in an ATM switch that connects directly to one of the above (referred to as an *edge switch*). Servers are responsible for integrating MAC entities into the overall configuration and for managing all of the associated tasks, such as finding addresses and emulating broadcasting. Servers may be implemented in separate components or in ATM switches. Each emulated LAN consists of one or more clients and a single LAN emulation service.

The LAN emulation service in fact comprises three types of servers, which perform separate tasks: the LAN Emulation Configuration Server (LECS), the LAN Emulation Server (LES), and the Broadcast and Unknown Server (BUS). The reason for breaking the server up into three modules is that a manager may decide to have more of one kind of server than another, for efficient operation, and may decide to distribute the servers physically to minimize the communications burden. Table 10.3 provides a brief definition of the three types of server and of the client.

Figure 10.17 indicates the way in which clients and the three types of servers interact. The client can establish virtual channel connections, called *control connections*, to the LECS and the LES. The link to the LECS is used by an LEC to gain entrance to an emulated LAN and to locate an LES. The LES is responsible for registering new clients and their MAC addresses into an emulated LAN and for mapping between MAC addresses and ATM addresses.

Once a client and its end systems have joined an emulated LAN, most of the work is done across virtual channel connections called data connections. MAC frames, segmented into ATM cells, are transmitted via data connections between end systems on the same emulated LAN. For a unicast transmission, a virtual channel connection is set up between two clients; this is the protocol setup illustrated in Figure 10.16. Finally, the data connection between a client and a BUS carries transmissions intended for broadcast or multicast and also is used to handle transmissions in which the sending client does not know the address of the receiving client.

LAN Emulation Scenario

To clarify the concepts involved in LAN emulation, let us follow a typical sequence of events.

TABLE 10.3   LAN Emulation Client and Servers

Entity	Description
LAN emulation client (LEC)	Sets up control connections to LAN emulation servers; sets up data connections to other clients; maps MAC addresses to ATM addresses
LAN emulation configuration server (LECS)	Assists client in selecting an LES
LAN emulation server (LES)	Performs initial address mapping; accepts clients
Broadcast and unknown server (BUS)	Performs multicasting

Initialization.   To join an emulated LAN, a client must begin by obtaining the ATM address of the LAN emulation server (LES) for that emulated LAN. Typically, the way in which this is done is that the client establishes a virtual channel connection to the LAN emulation configuration server (LECS).

There are three possible techniques by which the client can discover the LECS ATM address so that it can perform initialization:

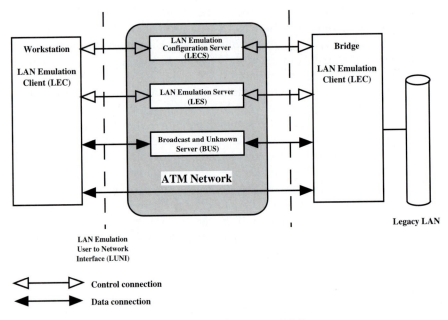

FIGURE 10.17   LAN Emulation Client Connections across LUNI

1. The client can use a network management procedure defined as part of the ATM Forum's interim local management interface (ILMI). This procedure takes place between the client and ILMI software in the associated ATM switch. If the ILMI software has the LECS address for the requested emulated LAN, it provides that address to the client. The client then establishes a virtual channel connection to the LECS.

2. If the ILMI procedure fails, the client tries a predefined address listed in the specification, known as the *well-known address*. This address is supposed to correspond to an LECS on any ATM network that conforms to the ATM Forum specification. The client uses this address to establish a virtual channel connection to the LECS.

3. If the well-known address fails, the client tries the well-known *virtual path identifier/virtual channel identifier* defined in the ATM Forum specification. When the ATM network is configured, the network manager can establish this permanent virtual path/virtual channel.

Configuration.   Once a connection is established between the client and the LECS, the client can engage in a dialogue with the LECS. Based upon its own policies, configuration database, and information provided by the client, the LECS assigns the client to a particular emulated LAN service by giving the client the LES's ATM address. The LECS returns to the client information about the emulated LAN, including MAC protocol, maximum frame size, and the name of the emulated LAN. The name may be something defined by the configuration manager to be meaningful in defining logical workgroups (e.g., finance, personnel).

Joining.   The client now has the information it needs to join an emulated LAN. It proceeds by setting up a control connection to the LES. The client then issues a JOIN REQUEST to the LES, which includes the client's ATM address, its MAC address, LAN type, maximum frame size, a client identifier, and a proxy indication. The latter parameter indicates whether this client corresponds to an end system attached directly to an ATM switch or is a LAN-to-ATM converter supporting end systems on a legacy LAN. If the LES is prepared to accept this client, it sends back a JOIN RESPONSE indicating acceptance. Otherwise, it sends back a join response indicating rejection.

Registration and BUS Initialization.   Once a client has joined an emulated LAN, it goes through a registration procedure. If the client is a proxy for a number of end systems on a legacy LAN, it sends a list of all MAC addresses on the legacy LAN that are to be part of this emulated LAN to the LES. Next, the client sends a request to the LES for the ATM address of the BUS. This address functions as the broadcast address for the emulated LAN and is used when a MAC frame is to be broadcast to all stations on the emulated LAN. The client then sets up a data connection to the BUS.

Data Transfer.　Once a client is registered, it is able to send and receive MAC frames. First, consider the sending of MAC frames. In the case of an end system attached to an ATM switch, the end system generates its own MAC frames for transmission to one or more other end systems on the emulated LAN. In the case of a proxy client, it functions as a bridge that receives MAC frames from end systems on its legacy LAN and then transmits those MAC frames. In both cases, an outgoing MAC frame must be segmented into ATM cells and transmitted over a virtual channel. There are three cases to consider:

- Unicast MAC frame, ATM address known
- Unicast MAC frame, address unknown
- Multicast or broadcast MAC frame

If the client knows the ATM address of the unicast frame, it checks whether it has a virtual data connection already established to the destination client. If so, it sends the frame over that connection (as a series of ATM cells). Otherwise, it uses ATM signaling to set up the connection and then sends the frame.

If the address is unknown, the sending client performs two actions. First, the client sends the frame to the BUS over the data connection that it maintains with the BUS. The BUS, in turn, either transmits the frame to the intended MAC destination or else broadcasts the frame to all MAC destinations on the emulated LAN. In the latter case, the intended destination will recognize its MAC address and accept the frame. Second, the client attempts to learn the ATM address for this MAC for future reference. It does this by sending an LE_ARP_REQUEST (LAN emulation address resolution protocol request) command to the LES; the command includes the MAC address for which an ATM address is desired. If the LES knows the ATM address, it returns the address to the client in an LE_ARP_RESPONSE. Otherwise, the LES holds the request while it attempts to learn the ATM address. The LES sends out its own LE_ARP_REQUEST to all clients on the emulated LAN. The client that represents the MAC address in question will return its ATM address to the LES, which can then send that address back to the original requesting client.

Finally, if the MAC frame is a multicast or broadcast frame, the sending client transmits the frame to the BUS over the virtual data connection it has to the BUS. The bus then replicates that frame and sends it over virtual data connections to all of the clients on the emulated LAN.

LAN Emulation Frame Formats

LAN emulation makes use of two types of frame formats: data frame formats used over data connections between clients and between a client and the BUS, and control frame formats over control connections between clients and the LES and LECS. Figure 10.18 shows the data frame formats. One format is defined for an IEEE 802.3 emulated LAN and one for an IEEE 802.5 emulated LAN; recall that all of the end systems on a single emulated LAN must use the same MAC protocol.

In each case, the data frame format is derived from the MAC frame format. Let us consider the case of IEEE 802.3 first. When a client receives an LLC PDU from the next-higher layer (see Figure 10.16), it constructs a

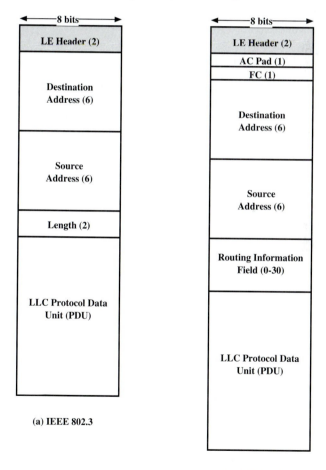

(a) IEEE 802.3

(b) IEEE 802.5

FIGURE 10.18   LAN Emulation Data Frame Formats

MAC frame for transmission. This frame has the same format as an ordinary MAC frame, with the following exceptions. First, the closing frame check sequence (FCS) field is omitted; this eliminates unnecessary overhead. Second, an LE header is added. This 16-bit header contains the client identifier. When this frame is received by the destination client, the LE header is stripped off. If the destination client is an ATM-attached system, it strips off the remaining MAC fields and passes the LLC information up. If the destination client is an ATM-to-LAN converter attached to an IEEE 802.3 LAN, it strips off the LE header, adds an FCS field to the MAC frame, and transmits the MAC frame on the LAN.

The description for the IEEE 802.5 MAC frame is similar. Again, an LE header is added. In this case, the last three fields in the frame are stripped off: frame check sequence (FCS), ending delimiter (ED), and frame status (FS). Again, these fields are restored if the frame is ultimately retransmitted on a token ring LAN.[4]

Figure 10.19 shows the general control frame format. It consists of the following fields:

- *Marker:* always X"FF00", indicating a control frame
- *Protocol:* always X"01", indicating ATM LAN Emulation protocol
- *Version:* always X"01", indicating version 1
- *Op-code:* control frame type; examples: LE_CONFIGURE_REQUEST and LE_ARP_REQUEST
- *Status:* set to zero in requests; used in responses; examples: invalid request parameters; duplicate ATM address; invalid LAN destination
- *Transaction ID:* arbitrary value assigned by requester and used by responder so that requester can discriminate among responses to different outstanding requests
- *Requester-LECID:* identifier of the requester
- *Flags:* modifiers to certain requests
- *Source-LAN-destination*
- *Target-LAN-destination*
- *Source-ATM-address:* ATM address of sender
- *LAN type:* IEEE 802.3 or IEEE 802.5
- *Max frame size:* maximum frame size allowed on this emulated LAN or maximum frame size that this client will accept
- *Number TLVs:* number of type-length-value entries
- *ELAN name size:* Number of bytes of ELAN name field
- *Target-ATM-address:* ATM address of receiver

[4]The routing information field was not described in Chapter 6. This field is present when bridges are used, and is discussed in Chapter 14.

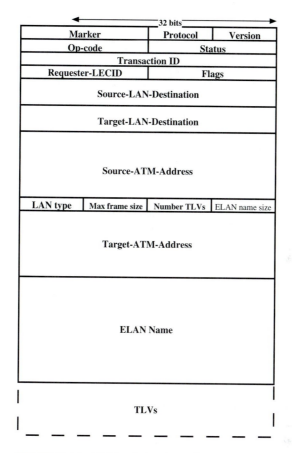

←——————32 bits——————→

Marker		Protocol	Version
Op-code		Status	
Transaction ID			
Requester-LECID		Flags	
Source-LAN-Destination			
Target-LAN-Destination			
Source-ATM-Address			

LAN type	Max frame size	Number TLVs	ELAN name size

Target-ATM-Address

ELAN Name

TLVs

FIGURE 10.19   LAN Emulation Control Frame

- *ELAN name:* name assigned to this emulated LAN
- *TLVs:* a series of parameters specific to a given op code, each consisting of a type (identifies parameter), length (length of value in bytes), and value (value of parameter)

10.4

RECOMMENDED READING

[KAVA95], [NEWM94], and [BIAG93] are good survey articles on LAN ATM architecture and configurations. LAN emulation is explained in [TRUO95] and [JEFF94]. [STAL95a] covers ATM protocols, architecture, and traffic control techniques. Other worthwhile treatments of ATM include [HAND94], [PRYC93], and [MCDY95].

BIAG93   Biagioni, E., Cooper, E., and Sansom, R. "Designing a Practical ATM LAN." *IEEE Network*, March 1993.

HAND94   Handel, R., Huber, N., and Schroder, S. *ATM Networks: Concepts, Protocols, Applications.* Reading, MA: Addison-Wesley, 1994.

JEFF94   Jeffries, R. "ATM LAN Emulation: The Inside Story." *Data Communications,* September 21, 1994.

KAVA95   Kavak, N. "Data Communication in ATM Networks." *IEEE Network,* May/June 1995.

MCDY95   McDysan, D., and Spohn, D. *ATM: Theory and Application.* New York: McGraw-Hill, 1995.

NEWM94   Newman, P. "ATM Local Area Networks." *IEEE Communications Magazine,* March 1994.

PRYC93   Prycker, M. *Asynchronous Transfer Mode: Solutions for Broadband ISDN.* New York: Ellis Horwood, 1993.

STAL95a   Stallings, W. *ISDN and Broadband ISDN, with Frame Relay and ATM, 3rd ed.* Englewood Cliffs, NJ: Prentice Hall, 1995.

TRUO95   Truong, H., et al. "LAN Emulation on an ATM Network." *IEEE Communications Magazine,* May 1995.

10.5

PROBLEMS

10.1 One method of transmitting ATM cells is as a continuous stream of cells, with no framing imposed; therefore, the transmission is simply a stream of bits, with all bits being part of cells. Since there is no external frame, some other form of synchronization is needed. This can be achieved using the HEC function. The requirement is to assure that the receiver knows the beginning and ending cell boundaries and does not drift with respect to the sender. Draw a state diagram for the use of the HEC to achieve cell synchronization, and explain its functionality.

10.2 Although ATM does not include any end-to-end error detection and control functions on the user data, it is provided with a HEC field to detect and correct header errors. Let us consider the value of this feature. Suppose that the bit error rate of the transmission system is B. If errors are uniformly distributed, the probability of an error in the header is

$$\frac{h}{h+i} \times B$$

and the probability of error in the data field is

$$\frac{i}{h+i} \times B$$

where h is the number of bits in the header and i is the number of bits in the data field.

a. Suppose that errors in the header are not detected and not corrected. In that case a header error may result in a misrouting of the cell to the wrong destination; therefore, i bits will arrive at an incorrect destination, and i bits will not arrive at the correct destination. What is the overall bit error rate $B1$? Find an expression for the multiplication effect on the bit error rate: $M1 = B1/B$.

b. Now suppose that header errors are detected but not corrected. In that case i bits will not arrive at the correct destination. What is the overall bit error rate $B2$? Find an expression for the multiplication effect on the bit error rate: $M2 = B2/B$.

c. Now suppose that header errors are detected and corrected. What is the overall bit error rate $B3$? Find an expression for the multiplication effect on the bit error rate: $M3 = B3/B$.

d. Plot $M1$, $M2$, and $M3$ as a function of header length, for $i = 48 \times 8 = 384$ bits. Comment on the results.

10.3 One key design decision for ATM was whether to use fixed- or variable-length cells. Let us consider this decision from the point of view of efficiency. We can define transmission efficiency as

$$N = \frac{\text{number of information octets}}{\text{number of information octets} + \text{number of overhead octets}}$$

a. Consider the use of fixed-length packets. In this case the overhead consists of the header octets. Define:

L = data field size of the cell in octets
H = header size of the cell in octets
X = number of information octets to be transmitted as a single message

Derive an expression for N. (*Hint:* The expression will need to use the operator $\lceil \bullet \rceil$, where $\lceil Y \rceil$ is the smallest integer greater than or equal to Y.)

b. If cells have variable length, overhead is determined by the header, plus the flags to delimit the cells or an additional length field in the header. Let Hv = additional overhead octets required to enable the use of variable-length cells. Derive an expression for N in terms of X, H, and Hv.

c. Let $L = 48$, $H = 5$, and $Hv = 2$. Plot N versus message size for fixed- and variable-length cells. Comment on the results.

10.4 Another key design decision for ATM is the size of the data field for fixed-size cells. Let us consider this decision from the point of view of efficiency and delay.

a. Assume that an extended transmission takes place, so that all cells are completely filled. Derive an expression for the efficiency N as a function of H and L.

b. Packetization delay is the delay introduced into a transmission stream by the need to buffer bits until an entire packet is filled before transmission. Derive an expression for this delay as a function of L and the data rate R of the source.

c. Common data rates for voice coding are 32 and 64 kbps. Plot packetization delay as a function of L for these two data rates; use a left-hand y axis with a maximum value of 2 ms. On the same graph, plot transmission efficiency as a function of L; use a right-hand y axis with a maximum value of 100 percent. Comment on the results.

10.5 Suppose that AAL 5 is being used and that the receiver is in an idle state (no incoming cells). Then a block of user data is transmitted as a sequence of SAR-PDUs.

a. Suppose that a single bit error occurs in one of the SAR-PDUs. What happens at the receiving end?

b. Suppose that one of the cells with AAU = 0 is lost. What happens at the receiving end?

c. Suppose that one of the cells with AAU = 1 is lost. What happens at the receiving end?

10.6 Draw a figure similar to Figure 10.16 that shows the protocol architecture for the interconnection of two end systems on separate LANs (with the same MAC protocol) across an ATM switch.

Wireless LANs

In just the past few years, wireless LANs have come to occupy a significant niche in the local area network market. Increasingly, organizations are finding that wireless LANs are an indispensable adjunct to traditional wired LANs, to satisfy requirements for mobility, relocation, ad hoc networking, and coverage of locations difficult to wire.

This chapter provides a survey of wireless LANs. We begin with an overview that looks at the motivations for using wireless LANs and summarizes the various approaches in current use. Then we look at the standards being developed by IEEE 802. The remaining three sections examine in more detail the three principal types of wireless LANs, classified according to transmission technology: infrared, spread spectrum, and narrowband microwave.

11.1

OVERVIEW

As the name suggests, a wireless LAN is one that makes use of a wireless transmission medium. Until relatively recently, wireless LANs were little used. The reasons for this included high prices, low data rates, occupational safety concerns, and licensing requirements. As these problems have been addressed, the popularity of wireless LANs has grown rapidly. In this section we look first at the requirements for and advantages of wireless LANs, and then preview the key approaches to wireless LAN implementation.

Wireless LANs Applications

[PAHL95a] lists four application areas for wireless LANs: LAN extension, cross-building interconnect, nomadic access, and ad hoc networks. Let us consider each of these in turn.

LAN Extension.   Early wireless LAN products, introduced in the late 1980s, were marketed as substitutes for traditional wired LANs. A wireless LAN saves the cost of the installation of LAN cabling and eases the task of relocation and other modifications to network structure. However, this motivation for wireless LANs was overtaken by events. First, as awareness of the need for LANs became greater, architects designed new buildings to include extensive prewiring for data applications. Second, with advances in data transmission technology, there is an increasing reliance on twisted-pair cabling for LANs, in particular category 3 unshielded twisted pair. Most older buildings are already wired with an abundance of category 3 cable. Thus the use of a wireless LAN to replace wired LANs has not happened to any great extent.

However, in a number of environments, there is a role for the wireless LAN as an alternative to a wired LAN. Examples include buildings with large open areas, such as manufacturing plants, stock exchange trading floors, and warehouses; historical buildings with insufficient twisted pair and where drilling holes for new wiring is prohibited; and small offices where installation and maintenance of wired LANs is not economical. In all of these cases, a wireless LAN provides an effective and more attractive alternative. In most of these cases, an organization will also have a wired LAN to support servers and some stationary workstations. For example, a manufacturing facility typically has an office area that is separate from the factory floor but which must be linked to it for networking purposes. Therefore, typically, a wireless LAN will be linked into a wired LAN on the same premises. Thus this application area is referred to as LAN extension.

Figure 11.1 indicates a simple wireless LAN configuration that is typical of many environments. There is a backbone wired LAN, such as Ethernet, that supports servers, workstations, and one or more bridges or routers to link with other networks. In addition, there is a control module (CM) that acts as an interface to a wireless LAN. The control module includes either bridge or router functionality to link the wireless LAN to the backbone. In addition, it includes some sort of access control logic, such as a polling or token-passing scheme, to regulate the access from the end systems. Note

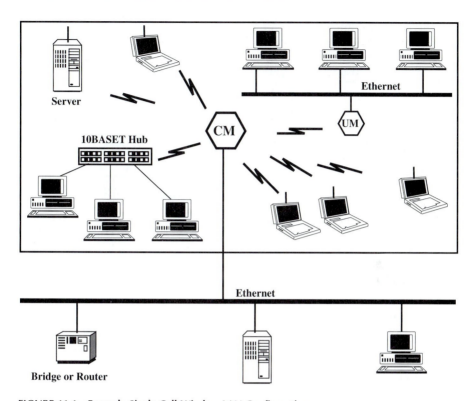

FIGURE 11.1   Example Single-Cell Wireless LAN Configuration

that some of the end systems are stand-alone devices such as a workstation or a server. In addition, hubs or other user modules (UM) that control a number of stations off a wired LAN may also be part of the wireless LAN configuration.

The configuration of Figure 11.1 can be referred to as a single-cell wireless LAN; all of the wireless end systems are within range of a single control module. Another common configuration, suggested by Figure 11.2, is a multiple-cell wireless LAN. In this case there are multiple control modules interconnected by a wired LAN. Each control module supports a number of wireless end systems within its transmission range. For example, with an infrared LAN, transmission is limited to a single room; therefore, one cell is needed for each room in an office building that requires wireless support.

Cross-Building Interconnect.   Another use of wireless LAN technology is to connect LANs in nearby buildings, be they wired or wireless LANs. In this case a point-to-point wireless link is used between two buildings. The devices so connected are typically bridges or routers. This single point-to-

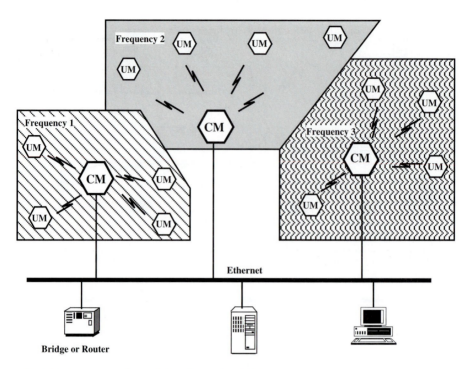

FIGURE 11.2   **Example Multiple-Cell Wireless LAN Configuration**

point link is not a LAN per se, but it is usual to include this application under the heading of wireless LAN.

Nomadic Access.   Nomadic access provides a wireless link between a LAN hub and a mobile data terminal equipped with an antenna, such as a laptop computer or notepad computer. One example of the utility of such a connection is to enable an employee returning from a trip to transfer data from a personal portable computer to a server in the office. Nomadic access is also useful in an extended environment such as a campus or a business operating out of a cluster of buildings. In both of these cases, users may move around with their portable computers and may wish access to the servers on a wired LAN from various locations.

Ad Hoc Networking.   An ad hoc network is a peer-to-peer network (no centralized server) set up temporarily to meet some immediate need. For example, a group of employees, each with a laptop or palmtop computer may convene in a conference room for a business or classroom meeting. The employees link their computers in a temporary network just for the duration of the meeting. Figure 11.3 suggests the differences between an ad hoc

High-speed Backbone Wired LAN

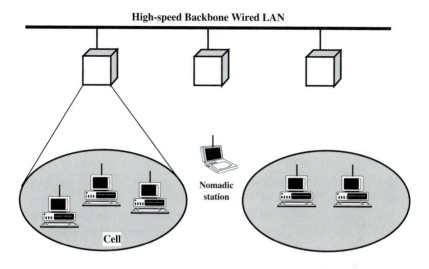

(a) Infrastructure Wireless LAN

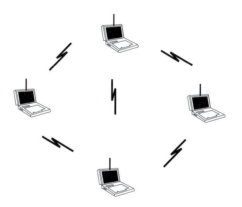

(b) Ad hoc LAN

FIGURE 11.3   Wireless LAN Configurations

wireless LAN and a wireless LAN that supports LAN extension and nomadic access requirements. In the former case, the wireless LAN forms a stationary infrastructure consisting of one or more cells with a control module for each cell. Within a cell, there may be a number of stationary end systems. Nomadic stations can move from one cell to another. In contrast, there is no infrastructure for an ad hoc network. Rather, a peer collection of stations within range of each other may dynamically configure themselves into a temporary network.

Wireless LAN Requirements

A wireless LAN must meet the same sort of requirements typical of any LAN, including high capacity, ability to cover short distances, full connectivity among attached stations, and broadcast capability. In addition, there are a number of requirements specific to the wireless LAN environment. The following are among the most important requirements for wireless LANs:

- *Throughput.* The medium access control protocol should make as efficient use as possible of the wireless medium to maximize capacity.
- *Number of nodes.* Wireless LANs may need to support hundreds of nodes across multiple cells [CHEN94].
- *Connection to backbone LAN.* In most cases, interconnection with stations on a wired backbone LAN is required. For infrastructure wireless LANs, this is easily accomplished through the use of control modules that connect to both types of LANs. There may also need to be accommodation for mobile users and ad hoc wireless networks.
- *Service area.* A typical coverage area for a wireless LAN may be up to 300 to 1000 ft in diameter.
- *Battery power consumption.* Mobile workers use battery-powered workstations that need to have a long battery life when used with wireless adapters. This suggests that a MAC protocol that requires mobile nodes to monitor access points constantly or engage in frequent handshakes with a base station is inappropriate.
- *Transmission robustness and security.* Unless properly designed, a wireless LAN may be interference prone and easily eavesdropped. The design of a wireless LAN must permit reliable transmission even in a noisy environment and should provide some level of security from eavesdropping.
- *Collocated network operation.* As wireless LANs become more popular, it is quite likely for two or more wireless LANs to operate in the same area or in some area where interference between the LANs is possible. Such interference may thwart the normal operation of a MAC algorithm and may allow unauthorized access to a particular LAN.
- *License-free operation.* Users would prefer to buy and operate wireless LAN products without having to secure a license for the frequency band used by the LAN.
- *Handoff/roaming.* The MAC protocol used in the wireless LAN should enable mobile stations to move from one cell to another.
- *Dynamic configuration.* The MAC addressing and network management aspects of the LAN should permit dynamic and automated addition, deletion, and relocation of end systems without disruption to other users.

It is instructive to compare wireless LANs to wired LANs and mobile data networks using Kiviat graphs,[1] as shown in Figure 11.4.

Wireless LAN Technology

Wireless LANs are generally categorized according to the transmission technique that is used. All current wireless LAN products fall into one of the following categories:

- *Infrared (IR) LANs.* An individual cell of an IR LAN is limited to a single room, since infrared light does not penetrate opaque walls.
- *Spread spectrum LANs.* This type of LAN makes use of spread spectrum transmission technology. In most cases these LANs operate in the ISM (industrial, scientific, and medical) bands, so no FCC licensing is required for their use in the United States.
- *Narrowband microwave.* These LANs operate at microwave frequencies but do not use spread spectrum. Some of these products operate at frequencies that require FCC licensing; others use one of the unlicensed ISM bands.

Table 11.1 summarizes some of the key characteristics of these three technologies; the details are explored in the next three sections.

11.2

INFRARED LANS

Optical wireless communication in the infrared portion of the spectrum is commonplace in most homes, being used for a variety of remote control devices. More recently, attention has turned to the use of infrared technology to construct wireless LANs. In this section we begin with an comparison of the characteristics of infrared LANs with those of radio LANs and then look at some of the details of infrared LANs.

Strengths and Weaknesses

The two competing transmission media for wireless LANs are microwave radio, using either spread spectrum or narrowband transmission, and infrared. Infrared (IR) offers a number of significant advantages over the

---

[1]A Kiviat graph provides a pictorial means of comparing systems along multiple variables. The variables are laid out at equal angular intervals. A given system is defined by one point on each variable; these points are connected to yield a shape that is characteristic of that system. This technique was first applied to wireless data networks in [PAHL95b].

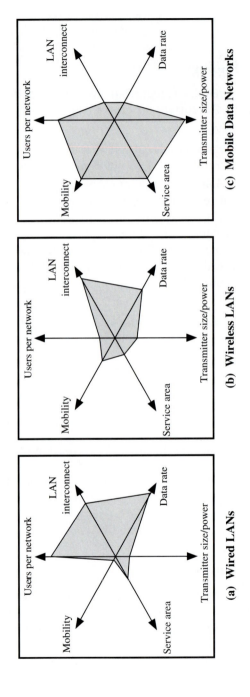

(a) Wired LANs

(b) Wireless LANs

(c) Mobile Data Networks

FIGURE 11.4 Kiviat Graphs for Data Networks

TABLE 11.1 Comparison of Wireless LAN Technologies

	Infrared		Spread Spectrum		Radio
	Diffused Infrared	Directed Beam Infrared	Frequency Hopping	Direct Sequence	Narrowband Microwave
Data rate (Mbps)	1–4	10	1–3	2–20	5–10
Mobility	Stationary/mobile	Stationary with LOS	Mobile	Stationary/mobile	
Range (ft)	50–200	80	100–300	100–800	40–130
Detectability	Negligible		Little		Some
Wavelength/ frequency	λ–800–900 nm		ISM bands: 902–928 MHz 2.4–2.4835 GHz 5.725–5.85 GHz		18.825–19.205 GHz or ISM band
Modulation technique	OOK		GFSK	QPSK	FS/QPSK
Radiated power	NA		<1W		25 mW
Access method	CSMA	Token ring, CSMA	CSMA		Reservation ALOHA, CSMA
License required	No		No		Yes unless ISM

microwave radio approaches. First, the spectrum for infrared is virtually unlimited, which presents the possibility of achieving extremely high data rates. The IR spectrum is unregulated worldwide, which is not true of some portions of the microwave spectrum.

In addition, infrared shares some properties of visible light that make it attractive for certain types of LAN configurations. Infrared light is diffusely reflected by light-colored objects; thus it is possible to use ceiling reflection to achieve coverage of an entire room. Infrared light does not penetrate walls or other opaque objects. This has two advantages: (1) IR communications can be secured against eavesdropping more easily than can microwave, and (2) a separate IR installation can be operated in every room in a building without interference, enabling the construction of very large infrared LANs.

Another strength of infrared is that the equipment is relatively inexpensive and simple. Infrared data transmission typically uses intensity modulation, so that IR receivers need to detect only the amplitude of optical signals, whereas most microwave receivers must detect frequency or phase.

The IR medium also exhibits some drawbacks. Many indoor environments experience rather intense IR background radiation, from sunlight and indoor lighting. This ambient radiation appears as noise in an IR receiver, requiring the use of higher-power transmitters than would otherwise be required and limiting the range. However, increases in transmitter power are limited by concerns of eye safety and excessive power consumption.

Transmission Techniques

There are three alternative transmission techniques commonly used for IR data transmission: the transmitted signal can be focused and aimed (as in a remote TV control), it can be radiated omnidirectionally, or it can be reflected from a light-colored ceiling.

Directed-Beam Infrared. Directed-beam IR can be used to create point-to-point links. In this mode the range depends on the emitted power and on the degree of focusing. A focused IR data link can have a range of kilometers. Such ranges are not needed for constructing indoor wireless LANs. However, an IR link can be used for cross-building interconnect between bridges or routers located in building within a line of sight of each other. One indoor use of point-to-point IR links is to set up a token-ring LAN (Figure 11.5). A set of IR transceivers can be set up so that data circulate around them in a ring configuration. Each transceiver supports a workstation or a hub of stations, with the hub providing a bridging function.

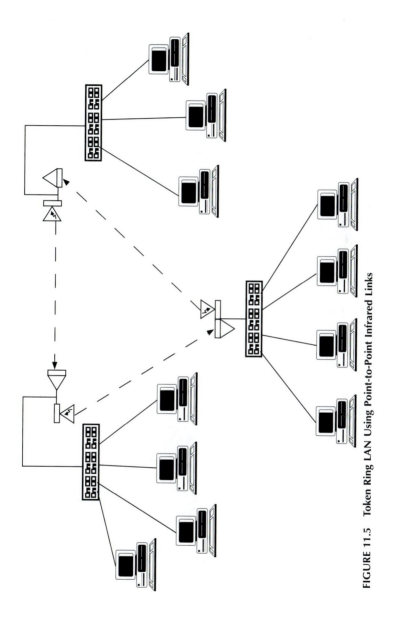

FIGURE 11.5   Token Ring LAN Using Point-to-Point Infrared Links

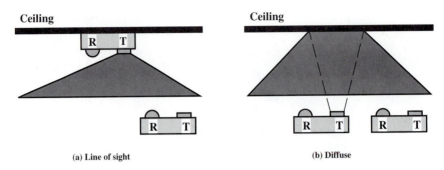

FIGURE 11.6   Configurations for Diffused Infrared LANs

Ominidirectional.   An omnidirectional configuration involves a single base station that is within line of sight of all other stations on the LAN. Typically, this station is mounted on the ceiling (Figure 11.6a). The base station acts as a multiport repeater similar to the type we saw for 10BASE-T and 100BASE-T. The ceiling transmitter broadcasts an omnidirectional signal that can be received by all of the other IR transceivers in the area. These other transceivers transmit a directional beam aimed at the ceiling base unit.

Diffused.   In this configuration, all of the IR transmitters are focused and aimed at a point on a diffusely reflecting ceiling (Figure 11.6b). IR radiation striking the ceiling is reradiated omnidirectionally and picked up by all of the receivers in the area. Figure 11.7 shows a typical configuration for a wireless IR LAN installation. There are a number of ceiling-mounted base

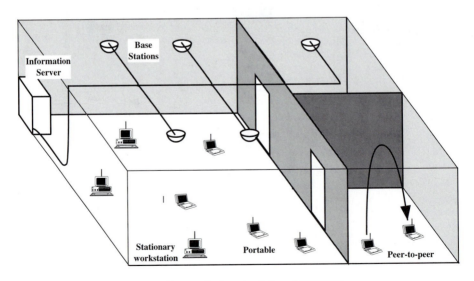

FIGURE 11.7   Network of Portable Terminals Using Infrared [BARR94]

stations, one to a room. Each station provides connectivity for a number of stationary and mobile workstations in its area. Using ceiling wiring, the base stations are all connected back to an server that can act as an access point to a wired LAN or a WAN. In addition, there may be conference rooms without a base station where ad hoc networks may be set up.

11.3

SPREAD SPECTRUM LANS

Currently, the most popular type of wireless LAN uses spread spectrum techniques. We provide an overview of spread spectrum technology and then examine spread spectrum LAN configurations.

Spread Spectrum Communications

The spread spectrum technique was developed initially for military and intelligence requirements. The essential idea is to spread the information signal over a wider bandwidth in order to make jamming and interception more difficult. The first type of spread spectrum developed is known as *frequency hopping*.[2] A more recent version is direct-sequence spread spectrum. Both of these techniques are used in wireless LAN products.

Figure 11.8 highlights the key characteristics of any spread spectrum system. Input is fed into a channel encoder that produces an analog signal with a relatively narrow bandwidth around some center frequency. This signal is further modulated using a sequence of seemingly random digits known as a *pseudorandom sequence*. The effect of this modulation is to increase significantly the bandwidth (spread the spectrum) of the signal to be transmitted. On the receiving end, the same digit sequence is used to

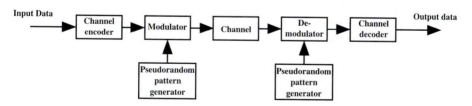

FIGURE 11.8   General Model of Spread Spectrum Digital Communication System

[2]Spread spectrum (using frequency hopping) was invented, believe it or not, by Hollywood screen siren Hedy Lamarr in 1940 at the age of 26. She and a partner who later joined her effort were granted a patent in 1942 (U.S. Patent 2,292,387; 11 August 1942). Lamarr considered this her contribution to the war effort and never profited from her invention. For an interesting account, see [MEEK90].

demodulate the spread spectrum signal. Finally, the signal is fed into a channel decoder to recover the data.

A comment about pseudorandom numbers is in order. These numbers are generated by an algorithm using an initial value called the *seed*. The algorithm is deterministic and therefore produces sequences of numbers that are not statistically random. However, if the algorithm is good, the resulting sequences will pass many reasonable tests of randomness. Such numbers are often referred to as *pseudorandom numbers*.[3] The important point is that unless you know the algorithm and the seed, it is impractical to predict the sequence. Hence only a receiver that shares this information with a transmitter will be able to decode the signal successfully.

Frequency Hopping.   Under this scheme the signal is broadcast over a seemingly random series of radio frequencies, hopping from frequency to frequency at split-second intervals. A receiver, hopping between frequencies in synchronization with the transmitter, picks up the message. Would-be eavesdroppers hear only unintelligible blips. Attempts to jam the signal succeed only at knocking out a few bits of it.

Figure 11.9 shows an example of a frequency-hopping signal for transmitting two 5-bit words of data. In this case, each bit is represented by a single frequency. It is also possible to use the same frequency for multiple bits, changing frequency less often. In either case the signal at any given time is not actually a constant frequency but data modulated around a given center frequency. Thus, in the figure, the first bit is represented in some encoding scheme that centers around frequency f_4.

A typical block diagram for a frequency-hopping system is shown in Figure 11.10. For transmission, binary data are fed into a modulator using a digital-to-analog encoding scheme, such as frequency-shift keying (FSK) or binary phase-shift keying (BPSK). The resulting signal is centered around a base frequency. A pseudorandom number source serves as an index into a table of frequencies. At each successive interval, a new frequency is selected from the table. This frequency is then modulated by the signal produced from the initial modulator to produce a new signal with the same shape but now centered on the frequency chosen from the table.

On reception, the spread spectrum signal is demodulated using the same sequence of table-derived frequencies and then demodulated to produce the output data. For example, if FSK is employed, the modulator selects one of two frequencies, say f_0 or f_1, corresponding to the transmission of binary 0 or 1. The resulting binary FSK signal is translated in frequency by an amount determined by the output sequence from the pseudorandom number generator. Thus if the frequency selected at time i is f_i, the signal at time i is either $f_i + f_0$ or $f_i + f_1$.

[3]See [STAL95b] for a more detailed discussion of pseudorandom numbers.

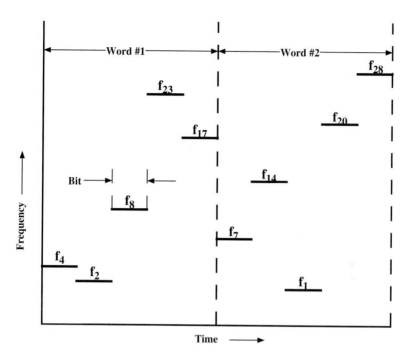

FIGURE 11.9   Example of a Frequency-Hopped Signal

Direct Sequence.   Under this scheme, each bit in the original signal is represented by multiple bits in the transmitted signal, known as a *chipping code*. The chipping code spreads the signal across a wider frequency band in direct proportion to the number of bits used. Therefore, a 10-bit chipping code spreads the signal across a frequency band that is 10 times greater than a 1-bit chipping code.

One technique with direct-sequence spread spectrum is to combine the digital information stream with the pseudorandom bit stream using an exclusive-OR. Figure 11.11 shows an example. Note that an information bit of 1 inverts the pseudorandom bits in the combination, while an information bit of 0 causes the pseudorandom bits to be transmitted without inversion. The combination bit stream has the data rate of the original pseudorandom sequence, so it has a wider bandwidth than the information stream. In this example the pseudorandom bit stream is clocked at four times the information rate.

Figure 11.12 shows a typical direct-sequence implementation. In this case the information stream and the pseudorandom stream are both converted to analog signals and then combined, rather than performing the exclusive-or of the two streams and then modulating. The spectrum spread-

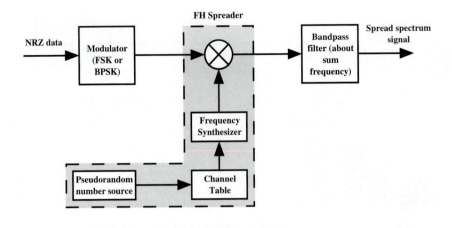

(a) Transmitter

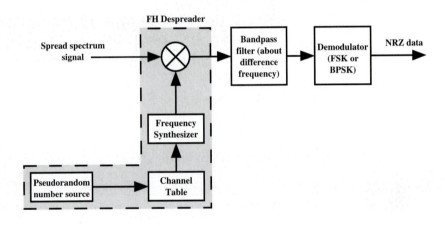

(b) Receiver

FIGURE 11.10   Frequency-Hopping Spread Spectrum System

ing achieved by the direct-sequence technique is easily determined (Figure 11.13). In our example the information signal has a bit width of T_b, which is equivalent to a data rate of $1/T_b$. In that case the spectrum of the signal, depending on encoding technique, is roughly $2/T_b$. Similarly, the spectrum of the pseudorandom signal is $2/T_c$. Figure 11.13c shows the resulting spectrum spreading. The amount of spreading that is achieved is a direct result of the data rate of the pseudorandom stream. This is shown in Figure 11.14, where the pseudorandom data rates a, b, and c, which are progressively higher, produce spectrums A, B, and C.

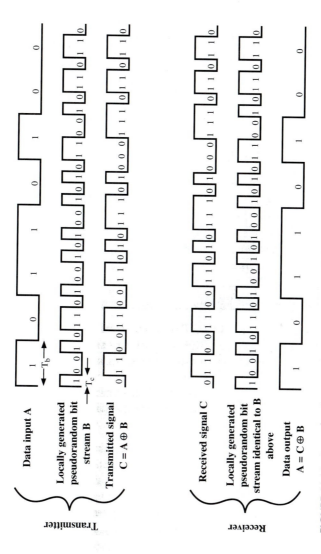

FIGURE 11.11   Example of Direct Sequence Spread Spectrum

371

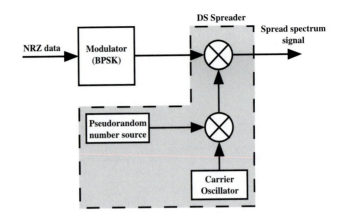

(a) Transmitter

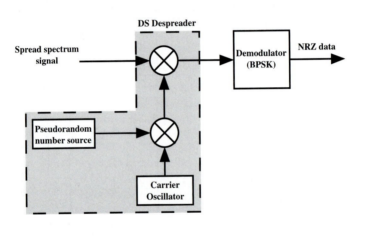

(b) Receiver

FIGURE 11.12   **Direct Sequence Spread Spectrum System**

Spread Spectrum LAN Design

Configuration.   Except for quite small offices, a spread spectrum wireless LAN makes use of a multiple-cell arrangement, as was illustrated in Figure 11.2. Adjacent cells make use of different center frequency within the same band to avoid interference. Within a given cell, the topology can be either hub or peer to peer. The hub topology is indicated in Figure 11.2. In a hub topology, the hub is typically mounted on the ceiling and connected to a backbone-wired LAN to provide connectivity to stations attached to the

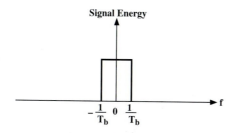

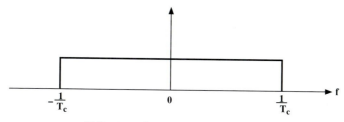

(a) Spectrum of data signal

(b) Spectrum of pseudorandom signal

(c) Spectrum of combined signal

FIGURE 11.13   Spectrum of a Direct Sequence Spread Spectrum Signal

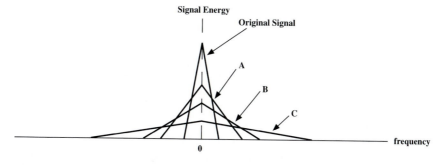

FIGURE 11.14   Distribution of Power of Different Direct Sequence Rates

wired LAN and to stations that are part of wireless LANs in other cells. The hub may also control access, as in the IEEE 802.11 point coordination function. The hub may also control access by acting as a multiport repeater with functionality similar to that of the multiport repeaters of 10BASE-T and 100BASE-T. In this case all stations in the cell transmit only to the hub and receive only from the hub. Alternatively, and regardless of access control mechanism, each station may broadcast using an omnidirectional antenna so that all other stations in the cell may receive; this corresponds to a logical bus configuration. One other potential function of a hub is automatic handoff of mobile stations. At any time, a number of stations are dynamically assigned to a given hub based on proximity. When the hub senses a weakening signal, it can hand off automatically to the nearest adjacent hub.

A peer-to-peer topology is one in which there is no hub. A MAC algorithm such as CSMA is used to control access. This topology is appropriate for ad hoc LANs.

Transmission Issues.   A desirable, though not necessary characteristic of a wireless LAN is that it be usable without having to go through a licensing procedure. The licensing regulations differ from one country to another, which complicates this objective. Within the United States, the Federal Communications Commission (FCC) has authorized two unlicensed applications within the ISM band: spread spectrum systems, which can operate at up to 1 watt, and very low power systems, which can operate at up to 0.5 watt. Since this band was opened up by the FCC, its use for spread spectrum wireless LANs has become popular.

In the United States, three microwave bands have been set aside for unlicensed spread spectrum use: 902 to 928 MHz (915-MHz band), 2.4 to 2.4835 GHz (2.4-GHz band), and 5.725 to 5.825 GHz (5.8-GHz band). Of these, the 2.4 GHz is also used in this manner in Europe and Japan. The higher the frequency, the higher the potential bandwidth, so the three bands are of increasing order of attractiveness from a capacity point of view. In addition, the potential for interference must be considered. There are a number of devices that operate at around 900 MHz, including cordless telephones, wireless microphones, and amateur radio. There are fewer devices operating at 2.4 GHz; one notable example is the microwave oven, which tends to have greater leakage of radiation with increasing age. At present there is little competition at the 5.8-GHz band; however, the higher the frequency band, in general, the more expensive the equipment.

Because a spread spectrum system makes use of considerable bandwidth, compared to a narrowband system, it operates at a correspondingly lower data rate. Most spread spectrum wireless LANs are limited to 1 to 3 Mbps. With complex and rather expensive circuitry, some LAN vendors have managed to achieve data rates of 10 to 20 Mbps in the highest ISM band (5.8 GHz).

11.4

NARROWBAND MICROWAVE LANs

The term *narrowband microwave* refers to the use of a microwave radio-frequency band for signal transmission, with a relatively narrow bandwidth, just wide enough to accommodate the signal. Until recently, all narrowband microwave LAN products have used a licensed microwave band. More recently, at least one vendor has produced a LAN product in the ISM band.

Licensed Narrowband RF

Microwave radio frequencies usable for voice, data, and video transmission are licensed and coordinated within specific geographic areas to avoid potential interference between systems. Within the United States, licensing is controlled by the FCC. Each geographic area has a radius of 17.5 miles and can contain five licenses, with each license covering two frequencies. Motorola holds 600 licenses (1200 frequencies) in the 18-GHz range that cover all metropolitan areas with populations of 30,000 or more.

A narrowband scheme typically makes use of the cell configuration illustrated in Figure 11.2. Adjacent cells use nonoverlapping frequency bands within the overall 18-GHz band. In the United States, since Motorola controls the frequency band, it can assure that independent LANs in nearby geographical locations do not interfere with one another. To provide security from eavesdropping, all transmissions are encrypted.

One advantage of a licensed narrowband LAN is that it guarantees interference-free communication. Unlike an unlicensed spectrum such as ISM, a licensed spectrum gives the license holder a legal right to an interference-free data communications channel. Users of an ISM-band LAN are at risk of interference disrupting their communications, for which they may not have a legal remedy.

Unlicensed Narrowband RF

In 1995, RadioLAN became the first vendor to introduce a narrowband wireless LAN using the unlicensed ISM spectrum. This spectrum can be used for narrowband transmission at low power (0.5 watt or less). The RadioLAN product operates at 10 Mbps in the 5.8-GHz band. The product has a range of 150 feet in a semiopen office and 300 feet in open offices.

The RadioLAN product makes use of a peer-to-peer configuration with an interesting feature. As a substitute for a stationary hub, the Radio-

LAN product automatically elects one node as the Dynamic Master, based on parameters such as location, interference, and signal strength. The identity of the master can change automatically as conditions change. The LAN also includes a dynamic relay function, which allows each station to act as a repeater to move data between stations that are out of range of each other.

11.5

WIRELESS LAN STANDARDS

Work on wireless LANs within the IEEE 802 committee began in 1987 within the IEEE 802.4 group. The initial interest was in developing an ISM-based wireless LAN using the equivalent of a token-passing bus MAC protocol. After some work it was decided that token bus was not suitable for controlling a radio medium without causing inefficient use of the radio-frequency spectrum. IEEE 802 then decided in 1990 to form a new working group, IEEE 802.11, specifically devoted to wireless LANs, with a charter to develop a MAC protocol and physical medium specification. As of this writing, the work of IEEE 802.11 is still in draft form.

The terminology and some of the specific features of 802.11 are unique to this standard and are not reflected in all commercial products. However, it is useful to be familiar with the standard since its features are representative of the wireless LAN capabilities required. Figure 11.15 indicates the model developed by the 802.11 working group. The smallest building block of a wireless LAN is a basic service set (BSS), which consists of some num-

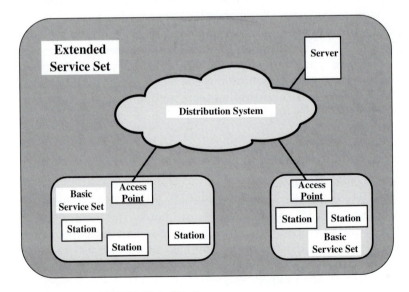

FIGURE 11.15   IEEE 802.11 Architecture

ber of stations executing the same MAC protocol and competing for access to the same shared medium. A basic service set may be isolated or it may connect to a backbone distribution system through an access point. The access point functions as a bridge. The MAC protocol may be fully distributed or controlled by a central coordination function housed in the access point. The basic service set generally corresponds to what is referred to as a cell in the literature.

An extended service set (ESS) consists of two or more basic service sets interconnected by a distribution system. Typically, the distribution system is a wired backbone LAN. The extended service set appears as a single logical LAN to the logical link control (LLC) level.

The standard defines three types of stations based on mobility:

- *No transition.* A station of this type is either stationary or moves only within the direct communication range of the communicating stations of a single BSS.

- *BSS transition.* This is defined as a station movement from one BSS to another BSS within the same ESS. In this case, delivery of data to the station requires that the addressing capability be able to recognize the new location of the station.

- *ESS transition.* This is defined as a station movement from a BSS in one ESS to a BSS within another ESS. This case is supported only in the sense that the station can move. Maintenance of upper-layer connections supported by 802.11 cannot be guaranteed. In fact, disruption of service is likely to occur.

IEEE 802.11 Services

IEEE 802.11 defines a number of services that need to be provided by the wireless LAN to provide functionality equivalent to that which is inherent to wired LANs. These services are:

- *Association:* establishes an initial association between a station and an access point. Before a station can transmit or receive frames on a wireless LAN, its identity and address must be known. For this purpose a station must establish an association with an access point within a particular BSS. The access point can then communicate this information to other access points within the ESS to facilitate routing and delivery of addressed frames.

- *Reassociation:* enables an established association to be transferred from one access point to another, allowing a mobile station to move from one BSS to another.

- *Disassociation:* a notification from either a station or an access point that an existing association is terminated. A station should give this notification before leaving an ESS or shutting down. However, the MAC management facility protects itself against stations that disappear without notification.

- *Authentication:* used to establish the identity of stations to each other. In a wired LAN it is generally assumed that access to a physical connection conveys authority to connect to the LAN. This is not a valid assumption for a wireless LAN, in which connectivity is achieved simply by having an attached antenna that is properly tuned. The authentication service is used by stations to establish their identity with stations with which they wish to communicate. The standards do not mandate any particular authentication scheme, which could range from relatively unsecure handshaking to public-key encryption schemes.

- *Privacy:* used to prevent the contents of messages from being read by other than the intended recipient. The standard provides for the optional use of encryption to assure privacy.

Physical Medium Specification

Three physical media are defined in the current 802.11 standard:

- Infrared at 1 and 2 Mbps operating at a wavelength between 850 and 950 nm.
- Direct-sequence spread spectrum operating in the 2.4-GHz ISM band. Up to seven channels, each with a data rate of 1 or 2 Mbps, can be used.
- Frequency-hopping spread spectrum operating in the 2.4-GHz ISM band. The details of this option are for further study.

Medium Access Control

The 802.11 working group considered two types of proposals for a MAC algorithm: distributed access protocols which, like Ethernet, distributed the decision to transmit over all the nodes using a carrier-sense mechanism; and centralized access protocols, which involve regulation of transmission by a centralized decision maker. A distributed access protocol makes sense of an ad hoc network of peer workstations and may also be attractive in other wireless LAN configurations that consist primarily of bursty traffic. A centralized access protocol is natural for configurations in which a number of wireless stations are interconnected with each other and some sort of base station that attaches to a backbone-wired LAN; it is especially useful if some of the data are time sensitive or high priority.

The end result of the 802.11 is a MAC algorithm called DFWMAC (distributed foundation wireless MAC) that provides a distributed access control mechanism with an optional centralized control built on top of that. Figure 11.16 illustrates the architecture. The lower sublayer of the MAC layer is the distributed coordination function (DCF). DCF uses a contention algorithm to provide access to all traffic. Ordinary asynchronous traffic uses DCF directly. The point coordination function (PCF) is a centralized MAC algorithm used to provide contention-free service. PCF is built on top of DCF and exploits features of DCF to assure access for its users. Let us consider these two sublayers in turn.

Distributed Coordination Function.   The DCF sublayer makes use of a simple CSMA algorithm. If a station has a MAC frame to transmit, it listens to the medium. If the medium is idle, the station may transmit; otherwise, the station must wait until the current transmission is complete before transmitting. The DCF does not include a collision detection function (i.e., CSMA/CD) because collision detection is not practical on a wireless network. The dynamic range of the signals on the medium is very large, so that a transmitting station cannot effectively distinguish incoming weak signals from noise and the effects of its own transmission.

To ensure smooth and fair functioning of this algorithm, DCF includes a set of delays that amounts to a priority scheme. Let us start by considering a single delay known as an interframe space (IFS). In fact, there are three different IFS values, but the algorithm is best explained by initially ignoring this detail. Using an IFS, the rules for CSMA access are as follows:

1. A station with a frame to transmit senses the medium. If the medium is idle, it waits to see if the medium remains idle for a time equal to IFS. If so, the station may transmit immediately.

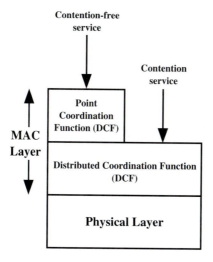

FIGURE 11.16   IEEE 802.11 Protocol Architecture

2. If the medium is busy (either because the station initially finds the medium busy or because the medium becomes busy during the IFS idle time), the station defers transmission and continues to monitor the medium until the current transmission is over.

3. Once the current transmission is over, the station delays another IFS. If the medium remains idle for this period, the station backs off using a binary exponential backoff scheme and again senses the medium. If the medium is still idle, the station may transmit.

As with Ethernet, the binary exponential backoff provides a means of handling a heavy load. If a station attempts to transmit and finds the medium busy, it backs off a certain amount and tries again. Repeated failed attempts to transmit result in longer and longer backoff times.

The scheme described above is refined for DCF to provide priority-based access by the simple expedient of using three values for IFS:

- *SIFS (short IFS):* the shortest IFS, used for all immediate response actions, as explained below
- *PIFS (point coordination function IFS):* a midlength IFS, used by the centralized controller in the PCF scheme when issuing polls
- *DIFS (distributed coordination function IFS):* the longest IFS, used as a minimum delay for asynchronous frames contending for access

Figure 11.17a illustrates the use of these time values. Consider first the SIFS. Any station using SIFS to determine transmission opportunity has, in effect, the highest priority, because it will always gain access in preference to a station waiting an amount of time equal to PIFS or DIFS. The SIFS is used in the following circumstances:

- Acknowledgment *(ACK)*. When a station receives a frame addressed only to itself (not multicast or broadcast) it responds with an ACK frame after waiting only for an SIFS gap. This has two desirable effects. First, since collision detection is not used, the likelihood of collisions is greater than with CSMA/CD, and the MAC-level ACK provides for efficient collision recovery. Second, the SIFS can be used to provide efficient delivery of an LLC protocol data unit (PDU) that requires multiple MAC frames. In this case, the following scenario occurs. A station with a multiframe LLC PDU to transmit sends out the MAC frames one at a time. Each frame is acknowledged after SIFS by the recipient. When the source receives an ACK, it immediately (after SIFS) sends the next frame in the sequence. The result is that once a station has contended for the channel, it will maintain control of the channel until it has sent all of the fragments of an LLC PDU.

- *Clear to send (CTS).* A station can ensure that its data frame will get through by first issuing a small request to send (RTS) frame. The sta-

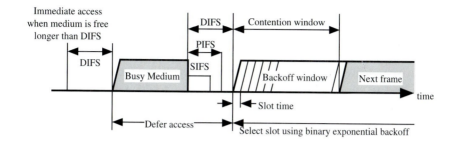

(a) Basic Access Method

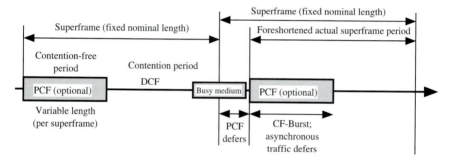

(b) PCF Superframe Construction

FIGURE 11.17   IEEE 802.11 MAC Timing

tion to which this frame is addressed should respond immediately with a CTS frame if it is ready to receive. All other stations receive the RTS and defer using the medium until they see a corresponding CTS or until a timeout occurs.

- *Poll response.* This is explained in the discussion of PCF, below.

The next-longest IFS interval is the PIFS. This is used by the centralized controller in issuing polls and takes precedence over normal contention traffic. However, those frames transmitted using SIFS have precedence over a PCF poll. Finally, the DIFS interval is used for all ordinary asynchronous traffic.

Point Coordination Function.   PCF is an alternative access method implemented on top of the DCF. The operation consists of polling with the centralized polling master (point coordinator). The point coordinator makes use of PIFS when issuing polls. Because PIFS is smaller than DIFS, the point coordinator can seize the medium and lock out all asynchronous traffic while it issues polls and receives responses.

As an extreme, consider the following possible scenario. A wireless network is configured so that a number of stations with time-sensitive traffic are controlled by the point coordinator while remaining traffic contends for access using CSMA. The point coordinator could issue polls in a round-robin fashion to all stations configured for polling. When a poll is issued, the polled station may respond using SIFS. If the point coordinator receives a response, it issues another poll using PIFS. If no response is received during the expected turnaround time, the coordinator issues a poll.

If the discipline of the preceding paragraph were implemented, the point coordinator would lock out all asynchronous traffic by repeatedly issuing polls. To prevent this, an interval known as the *superframe* is defined. During the first part of this interval, the point coordinator issues polls in a round-robin fashion to all stations configured for polling. The point coordinator then idles for the remainder of the superframe, allowing a contention period for asynchronous access.

Figure 11.17b illustrates the use of the superframe. At the beginning of a superframe, the point coordinator may optionally seize control and issues polls for a give period of time. This interval varies because of the variable frame size issued by responding stations. The remainder of the superframe is available for contention-based access. At the end of the superframe interval, the point coordinator contends for access to the medium using PIFS. If the medium is idle, the point coordinator gains immediate access and a full superframe period follows. However, the medium may be busy at the end of a superframe. In this case, the point coordinator must wait until the medium is idle to gain access; this results in a foreshortened superframe period for the next cycle.

11.6

RECOMMENDED READING

[PAHL95a] and [BANT94] are excellent survey articles on wireless LANs. Two book-length treatments are noteworthy: [SANT94] focuses on the technology of wireless LAN components and on signal encoding techniques; [DAVI95] deals with applications for wireless LANs as well as configuration and management issues. Good coverage of wireless LANs can also be found in the following books on wireless networking in general: [PAHL95b] provides thorough coverage of signal transmission and medium access technologies; [BATE94] is a less technical but broad survey of the various wireless network technologies and configurations; [MULL95] looks at wireless network applications and products.

BANT94 Bantz, D., and Bauchot, F. "Wireless LAN Design Alternatives." *IEEE Network*, March/April 1994.

BATE94 Bates, B. *Wireless Networked Communications*. New York: McGraw-Hill, 1994.

DAVI95 Davis, P., and McGuffin, C. *Wireless Local Area Networks*. New York: McGraw-Hill, 1995.

MULL95 Muller, N. *Wireless Data Networking*. Boston: Artech House, 1995.

PAHL95a Pahlavan, K., Probert, T., and Chase, M. "Trends in Local Wireless Networks." *IEEE Communications Magazine*, March 1995.

PAHL95b Pahlavan, K., and Levesque, A. *Wireless Information Networks*. New York: Wiley, 1995.

SANT94 Santamaria, A., and Lopez-Hernandez, F. (editors). *Wireless LAN Systems*. Boston: Artech House, 1994.

11.7

PROBLEMS

11.1 By far the most widely used technique for pseudorandom number generation is the linear congruential method. The algorithm is parameterized with four numbers, as follows:

m	modulus	$m > 0$
a	multiplier	$0 \leq a < m$
c	increment	$0 \leq c < m$
X_0	starting value, or seed	$0 \leq X_0 < m$

The sequence of pseudorandom numbers $\{X_n\}$ is obtained via the following iterative equation:

$$X_{n+1} = (aX_n + c) \bmod m$$

If m, a, c, and X_0 are integers, this technique will produce a sequence of integers with each integer in the range $0 \leq X_n < m$. An essential characteristic of a pseudorandom number generator is that the sequence generated appears random. Although the sequence is not random, because it is generated deterministically, there is a variety of statistical tests that can be used to assess the degree to which a sequence exhibits randomness. Another desirable characteristic is that the function should be a full-period generating function. That is, the function should generate all the numbers between 0 and m before repeating.

With the linear congruential algorithm, a choice of parameters that provides a full period does not necessarily provide good randomization. For example, consider the two generators

$$X_{n+1} = (6X_n) \bmod 13$$
$$X_{n+1} = (7X_n) \bmod 13$$

Write out the two sequences to show that both are full period. Which one appears more random to you?

11.2 We would like *m* to be very large, so that there is the potential for producing a long series of distinct random numbers. A common criterion is that *m* be nearly equal to the maximum representable nonnegative integer for a given computer. Thus a value of *m* near or equal to 2^{31} is typically chosen. Many experts recommend a value of $2^{31} - 1$. You may wonder why one should not simply use 2^{31}, since the latter number can be represented with no additional bits and the mod operation should be easier to perform. In general, the modulus $2^k - 1$ is preferable to 2^k. Why is this so?

11.3 In any use of pseudorandom numbers, whether for encryption, simulation, or statistical design, it is dangerous to trust blindly the random number generator that happens to be available in your computer's system library. [PARK88] found that many contemporary textbooks and programming packages make use of flawed algorithms for pseudorandom number generation. This exercise will enable you to test your system.

The test is based on a theorem attributed to Ernesto Cesaro (see [KNUT81] for a proof), which states that the probability is $6/\pi^2$ that the greatest common divisor of two randomly chosen integers is 1. Use this theorem in a program to determine statistically the value of π. The main program should call three subprograms: the random number generator from the system library to generate the random integers, a subprogram to calculate the greatest common divisor of two integers using Euclid's algorithm, and a subprogram that calculates square roots. If the latter two programs are not available, you will have to write them as well. The main program should loop through a large number of random numbers to give an estimate of the probability referenced above. From this it is a simple matter to solve for your estimate of π.

If the result is close to 3.14, congratulations! If not, the result is probably low, usually a value of around 2.7. Why would such an inferior result be obtained?

11.4 The IEEE 802.11 MAC standards combines polling and CSMA. Initially, a token bus protocol was considered and then rejected. Suggest reasons why a token bus protocol is not optimal for a wireless LAN.

11.5 Explain the rationale for the IEEE 802.11 RTS/CTS mechanism.

CHAPTER

12

Distributed Queue
Dual Bus

Among the newest networking standards are those for metropolitan area networks (MANs). Although the IEEE 802.6 committee was chartered in 1982, it was only after a number of false starts that the committee has defined a technical approach to MANs that has achieved widespread support. The result is the IEEE 802.6 standard, which has been adopted by ANSI.

As the name suggests, a MAN occupies a middle ground between local area networks (LANs) and wide-area networks (WANs). Interest in MANs has come about as the result of recognition that the traditional point-to-point and switched network techniques used in WANs may be inadequate for the growing needs of organizations. While broadband ISDN, with ATM, holds out promise for meeting a wide range of high-speed needs, there is a requirement now for both private and public networks that provide high capacity at low costs over a large area. The high-speed shared-medium approach of the LAN standards provides a number of benefits that can be realized on a metropolitan scale.

A useful way to view the 802.6 MAN standard is that it is an adaptation of the features of both LANs and wide-area ATM and is well suited to the metropolitan area. Some of the key characteristics of the 802.6 MAN are as follows:

- *High speed.* The 802.6 MAN offers a variety of speeds. The initial standard specifies 44.7 Mbps. Work is ongoing on speeds ranging from

1.544 to 155 Mbps. These rates overlap the range of the IEEE 802 LANs and wide-area ATM.

- *Shared medium.* Like IEEE 802 LANs, the 802.6 MAN uses a shared medium with much greater capacity than that of the attached devices. This allows support of bursty, asynchronous traffic as well as isochronous traffic.
- *Support for LLC.* The 802.6 standards has been designed to support data traffic under unacknowledged connectionless 802.2 LLC.
- *Addressing.* 802.6 stations must be able to recognize the 48- and 16-bit addresses used by the other 802 LAN standards. In addition, the 60-bit ITU-T format is an option; this enables ISDN compatibility.
- *Fixed-length packets.* Unlike the 802 LANs, and like ATM, 802.6 uses a fixed-length packet. For compatibility with ATM, the same 53-octet cell (called a slot in 802.6) with a 48-octet payload is used. The fixed-length format provides effective and efficient support for small and large packets (the latter handled by segmentation) and for isochronous data.
- *Dual bus.* The most obvious difference between 802.6 and 802 LANs is the use in 802.6 of two separate buses, both of which carry data at the same time.

The IEEE 802.6 standard is referred to as the *distributed queue dual bus* (DQDB) *subnetwork* standard. The term *DQDB* refers to the topology and access control technique employed, and the term *subnetwork* suggests that a single DQDB network will be a component in a collection of networks to provide a service.

Figure 12.1, based on one in IEEE 802.6, suggests the use of DQDB subnetworks. A subnetwork or set of subnetworks can be used as a public network controlled by a Bell operating company or other public provider, or as a private backbone network covering a building or set of buildings for a given user. To support services across a metropolitan area, a single DQDB network may range from a few kilometers to more than 50 km in extent. Subnetworks can operate at a variety of data rates.

DQDB subnetworks can be connected by bridges or routers. The links between a pair of bridges or routers can be point to point, or a network such as a packet-switched network, a circuit-switched network, or ISDN.

12.1

TOPOLOGY

The topology chosen for the 802.6 MAN was in large part dictated by the assumption that the medium for the MAN would be optical fiber. Optical fiber provides the high data rates needed for the MAN application. On the

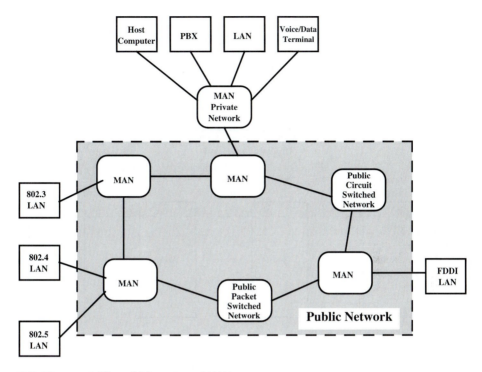

FIGURE 12.1   Public and Private Use of MANs

other hand, optical fiber as a shared medium presents a number of problems. In particular, the use of multiple optical fiber taps on a medium introduces significant losses and limits the range of the medium and the number of devices that can be supported.

Two approaches are possible to deal with the problems of optical fiber. One approach is the ring topology, which involves a set of point-to-point links between stations. This is the approach taken by FDDI. Another approach, which has been studied for many years, is the use of a dual-bus architecture. This is the approach taken by IEEE 802.6.

The dual-bus approach allows the use of unidirectional taps rather than bidirectional taps. A unidirectional tap is technically more feasible for optical fiber. Figure 12.2a shows the dual-bus topology using unidirectional taps. Each node attaches to both buses and has both transmit and receive taps on each bus. On each bus, a station may transmit only to those stations downstream from it. By using both buses, a station may transmit to and receive from all other stations. A given node, however, must know which bus to use to transmit to another node; if not, all data would have to be sent out on both buses. Transmissions on the two buses

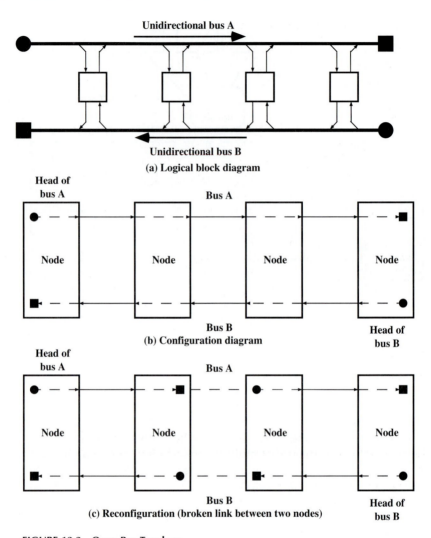

FIGURE 12.2   Open Bus Topology

are independent; thus the effective data rate of a DQDB network is twice the data rate of the bus.

For clarity in our discussion, we use the following terminology (not part of the 802.6 standard): upstream(A) refers to upstream on bus A; downstream(A) refers to downstream on bus A. The node that is upstream(A) of all other nodes is designated head of bus A, or head(A). Upstream(B), downstream(B), and head(B) have the obvious corresponding meanings.

Synchronization and Timing

Transmission on each bus consists of a steady stream of fixed-size slots with a length of 53 octets. Nodes read and copy data from the slots; they also gain access to the subnetwork by writing to the slots. Head(A) is responsible for generating the slots on bus A, while head(B) is responsible for generating the slots on bus B. The slot-generation function is indicated by a solid circle in Figure 12.2b; the bus termination function is indicated by a solid square.

Operation of the subnetwork is controlled by a 125-μs clock. The timing interval was chosen to provide support for isochronous services; it reflects the 8-kHz public networking frequency required by voice services. The slot generators in head(A) and head(B) transmit multiple slots to the shared medium every 125 μs; the number of slots generated per clock cycle depend on the physical data rate.

Under normal conditions, the 125-μs timing is provided by a single source. If the DQDB subnetwork is connected to a public telecommunications network, the timing may be provided by that network. Indeed, if the subnetwork is supporting certain isochronous services and is connected to a public network, it may be required that the timing be derived from the public network. The alternative source of timing is a node within the DQDB subnetwork. One node would be designated for this purpose.

Looped Bus Topology

The topology depicted in Figure 12.2a is, for self-evident reasons, referred to as an *open bus topology*. There is an alternative topology, depicted in Figure 12.3a, known as the *looped bus topology*. In this topology the nodes are attached to the two buses to form two closed loops. The head(A) and head(B) roles are both played by the same node. Note that the looped bus topology resembles a dual-ring topology. The two are different, however, since the head(A,B) node does not repeat incoming transmissions on the corresponding outgoing link.

Reconfiguration

The DQDB subnetwork includes a reconfiguration capability in the event of the failure of a link or node. This feature is particularly effective in the case of the looped bus topology, since full connectivity can be maintained. Figure 12.3c shows the effect of the loss of a link on the looped bus topology. The head(A) and head(B) functions migrate from the original head(A,B) node to the two nodes adjacent to the fault. The result is a fully connected open bus topology. If a node adjacent to a break is not capable of perform-

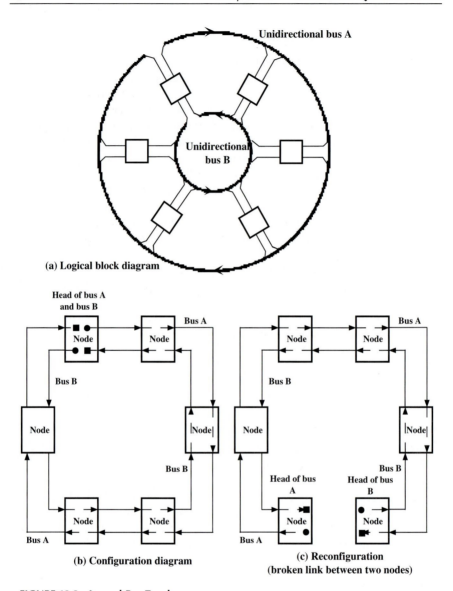

(a) Logical block diagram

(b) Configuration diagram

(c) Reconfiguration
(broken link between two nodes)

FIGURE 12.3   Looped Bus Topology

ing the head-of-bus functions, the node on the side of the fault that is nearest the fault and capable of performing the head-of-bus functions is designated as the head of one of the buses. The nodes that are passed over thus
become isolated from the subnetwork. When a fault occurs on an open bus
topology, the best that can be done is to reconfigure as two separate open
bus subnetworks, as shown in Figure 12.2c.

12.2

PROTOCOL ARCHITECTURE

Figure 12.4 depicts the protocol architecture of the IEEE 802.6 DQDB standard. As with the IEEE 802 LAN standards, the DQDB standard is divided into three layers. The upper layer corresponds to the upper portion of the OSI data link layer. In the case of the 802 LAN standards, this is the *LLC layer*. In the case of 802.6, a number of different protocols can be supported at this layer.

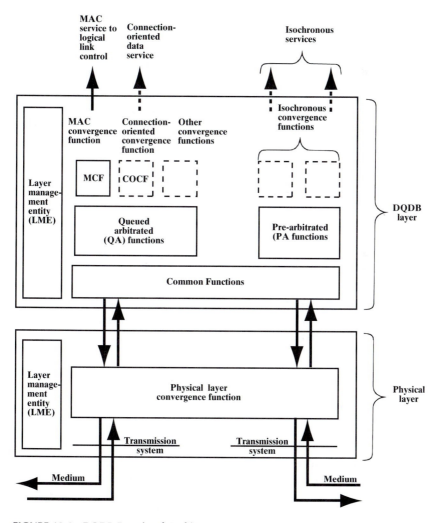

FIGURE 12.4   DQDB Functional Architecture

The middle layer of 802.6 is referred to as the *DQDB layer*. This corresponds roughly with the MAC layer of the 802 LAN standards and, as with the MAC layer, regulates access to the shared medium. It corresponds to the lower portion of the OSI data link layer.

The lowest layer of the 802.6 architecture is, of course, the *physical layer*. This layer is defined to support a variety of physical transmission schemes.

DQDB Services

The layer above the DQDB layer is not part of the 802.6 protocol architecture as such. Rather, it serves to define the services that an 802.6 subnetwork must support. Three types of services have been defined so far: connectionless service, connection-oriented data service, and isochronous services. Convergence functions within the DQDB layer adapt the underlying medium access service to provide a specific service to the user.

The **connectionless data service** provides support for connectionless communication via the LLC type 1 protocol (see Chapter 5). The connectionless media access service supports the transport of frames up to a length of 9188 octets. Transmission is in the form of fixed-length 52-octet segments. Accordingly, the service must include a segmentation and reassembly function.

The **connection-oriented service** supports the transport of 52-octet segments between nodes sharing a virtual channel connection. Thus, as with the connectionless service, segmentation and reassembly are required. The control signaling required to establish, maintain, and clear a connection are outside the scope of the current 802.6 standard.

The **isochronous service** provides support for users that require a constant interarrival time; this is in effect a circuit-switched service. The service is provided over a logical isochronous connection. The term *isochronous* refers to the use of regularly repeating time slots. The control signaling required to establish, maintain, and clear a connection are outside the scope of the current 802.6 standard.

DQDB Layer

The DQDB layer can be viewed as being organized into three sublayers:

- Common functions
- Arbitrated functions
- Convergence functions

Common Functions. The common functions module deals with the relay of slots in the two directions and provides a common platform for asynchronous and isochronous services. In addition to the basic transmission and reception of slots, the common functions module is responsible for head-of-bus, configuration control, and MID page allocation functions.

The **head-of-bus function** is performed only by the one or two nodes designated as head of bus. It includes generating and transmitting slots. Each slot is a formatted data unit. Included in the header is a bit to indicate the type of slot; this is marked by the head-of-bus function to indicate whether this is a slot for isochronous data or asynchronous data. In the former case, the head also inserts the virtual channel identifier into the slot header.

The **configuration control function** is involved in the initialization of the subnetwork and its reconfiguration after a failure. An example of a configuration control function is the activation and deactivation of the head-of-bus functions at appropriate nodes during the process of reconfiguration.

The **MID page allocation function** participates in a distributed protocol with all nodes on the subnetwork to control the allocation of message ID values to nodes. The message ID is used in the segmentation and reassembly function, as described in Section 12.4.

Arbitrated Functions.   The arbitrated functions are responsible for medium access control. There are two functions, corresponding to the two kinds of slots carried on the bus. All slots on the bus are 53 octets in length, consisting of a 1-octet access control field and a 52-octet segment. The two types of slots generated on the network are queued arbitrated (QA) and pre-arbitrated (PA) slots.

PA slots are used to carry isochronous data. The **PA function** provides access control for the connection-oriented transfer over a guaranteed bandwidth channel of octets which form part of an isochronous octet stream. The PA function assumes the previous establishment of a connection. As a result of connection establishment, the PA function will be informed of the virtual channel ID (VCI) associated with this connection. The VCI is part of the access control field and is generated by the head-of-bus function. An isochronous connection may involve all of the segment octets in a slot; alternatively, a single segment may be shared by more than one isochronous connection. In the latter case, the PA will be informed of the VCI and the offset of the octets to be used for reading and writing within the multiple-user PA segment payload.

QA slots are used to carry isochronous data. The **QA function** provides access control for asynchronous data transfer of 48-octet segment payloads. The QA function accepts the segment payloads from a convergence function and adds the appropriate segment header to form a segment. A distributed reservation scheme known as *distributed queuing* is used to provide medium access control. The MAC protocol is used to gain access to an available QA slot.

Convergence Functions.   The DQDB layer is intended to provide a range of services. For each service, a convergence function is needed to map the data stream of the DQDB user into the 53-octet transmission scheme of the DQDB layer. The concept is the same as that of the ATM adaptation layer (AAL) described in Chapter 10. Three services have been identified so far:

- *Connectionless data transfer.* The standard fully specifies the convergence function to support the connectionless MAC data service to LLC.
- *Isochronous service.* The standard gives guidelines for the provision of an isochronous service.
- *Connection-oriented data service.* The convergence function for this service is under study.

The **MAC convergence function** (MCF) adapts the connectionless MAC service to the QA function. The key task here is one of segmentation and reassembly. MAC service units of a length up to 9188 octets must be transmitted in a sequence of slots. The MCF transmit process involves encapsulating the LLC PDU (MAC SDU) to form an initial MAC PDU (IMPDU). The IMPDU is segmented into segmentation units of 44 octets, each of which is carried in a QA slot. The segmentation and reassembly protocol is described in Section 12.4.

The **isochronous convergence function** (ICF) adapts an isochronous octet-based service to the guaranteed-bandwidth octet-based service of the PA function. The ICF is analogous to the isochronous MAC service of FDDI-II. The primary function of the ICF is buffering to allow for instantaneous rate differences between the PA service and the isochronous service provided. This is because the PA function guarantees the average arrival and transmission rate of isochronous services but cannot guarantee that octets will be supplied at regular fixed intervals. The buffering ensures that a fixed interarrival time can be maintained.

A **connection-oriented convergence function** (COCF) is mentioned in the standard but not defined. The COCF would use the QA slots and the same segmentation and reassembly procedures as the MCF.

Physical Layer

The DQDB layer is independent of the physical layer. Therefore, a variety of DQDB networks can be implemented using the same access layer but operating at different data rates over different transmission systems. The following transmission systems are referenced in the standard:

- *ANSI DS1:* transmits at 1.544 Mbps over a metallic medium
- *ANSI DS3:* transmits at 44.736 Mbps over coaxial cable or optical fiber
- *ITU-T G.703:* transmits at 2.048 Mbps over a metallic medium

- *ITU-T G.751:* transmits at 34.368 and 139.264 Mbps over a metallic medium
- *ANSI SONET (ITU-T SDH):* transmits data at 155.52 Mbps and above over single-mode optical fiber

For each transmission system, a physical layer convergence protocol is used to provide a consistent physical layer service to the DQDB layer.

12.3

DISTRIBUTED QUEUE ACCESS PROTOCOL

Access to QA slots on the DQDB medium is provided by the distributed queue access protocol. Although the basic mechanism of this protocol at any one node is straightforward, the resulting distributed activity is complex. In addition, the basic protocol is augmented by two features designed to optimize the protocol: bandwidth balancing and priorities. We begin with a general description of the basic protocol. This is followed by a more detailed discussion of the protocol mechanism and a worked-out example. Bandwidth balancing and priorities are covered in the final two subsections.

In discussing the distributed queue protocol, we need to remember that there are actually two media: bus A and bus B. Since the access control mechanisms are exactly the same with respect to bus A and bus B, we generally confine ourselves to a discussion of access control of bus A, unless otherwise noted.

Description of the Basic Protocol

The distributed queue access protocol is a *distributed reservation* scheme. The two words suggest the key characteristics of the protocol:

- *Reservation.* For most reservation schemes, including this one, time on the medium is divided into slots, much as with synchronous TDM. A node wishing to transmit reserves a future slot.
- *Distributed.* To accommodate changing requirements, the reservation scheme must be dynamic. That is, nodes make reservation requests when they have data to send. The function of granting requests can be either centralized at a single node or distributed. In the latter case, the network nodes collectively determine the order in which slots are granted.

The distributed reservation scheme for the DQDB subnetwork must take into account the nature of the topology. The essence of the protocol can be summarized as follows. Node X wishes to transmit a block of data to node Y. X must choose the bus on which Y is downstream from X. Let us assume that the bus is A; that is, Y is downstream(A) from X. For X to transmit a block of data in a slot to Y, it must use an available block coming from upstream(A). If the upstream(A) stations monopolize the medium, X is prevented from transmitting. Therefore, X's reservation request must be made to its upstream(A) peers. This requires the use of bus B, since those stations upstream(A) from X are also downstream(B) from X and capable of receiving a reservation request from X on bus B.

The protocol requires that each station defer its own need to transmit to the needs of its downstream peers. As long as one or more downstream peers have an outstanding reservation request, a station will refrain from transmitting, allowing unused slots to continue downstream. The key requirement for the protocol, then, is a mechanism by which each station can keep track of the requests of all of its downstream peers.

The actual behavior of a node will depend on its position on the bus. The four positions of significance (with respect to bus A) are illustrated in Figure 12.5, which shows a DQDB subnetwork with N nodes. Consider first **node (N-1),** which is head(B). This node has no downstream(A) nodes and therefore does not transmit data on bus A and does not need to make reservations on bus B. The only data transfer activity for node (N-1) on bus A is reception. The node reads all passing slots. Any QA slot with a destination address matching node (N-1) is copied.

Now consider the node closest to head(B), which in this case is labeled **node (N-2).** Whenever this node needs to transmit a segment of data, it issues a request on bus B for an available slot on bus A. This is actually done by setting a request bit in a passing slot. Although node (N-2) makes reservations on bus B, it never receives any reservation requests on bus B: its only upstream(B) peer is node (N-1), which does not issue requests on bus B. On bus A, node (N-2) receives segments of data addressed to it. In addition, when node (N-2) has data to send and has issued a request, it may transmit its segment of data in the first free slot that passes. One bit in the slot indicates whether the slot is free or busy.

A third node whose position is important is head(A), which is labeled **node 0** in the figure. As the head of bus A, this node is responsible for generating the stream of slots on bus A. Thus there will be no QA slots on bus A with data addressed to this node, and all QA slots originate as free slots. When this node has data to send to any other node, it can simply insert that data in the next QA slot that it generates. Because there are no upstream(B) peers of node 0, it has no need to issue requests.

However, head(A) is responsible for seeing that outstanding requests plus its own needs are satisfied in a round-robin, or first-come-first-served basis. To do this, node 0 must keep a running count of how many requests have arrived on bus B that have not yet been satisfied. Table 12.1a summarizes the required behavior. Head(A) keeps track of the number of out-

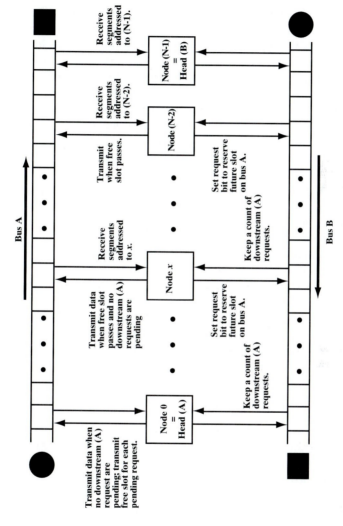

FIGURE 12.5 Basic Operation of the Distributed Queue Protocol (data transmission on bus A)

397

standing requests, which is simply the difference between incoming QA slots with a request and outgoing QA slots that are free. If head(A) has a segment of data to send at time T, it must wait until it has satisfied all of the requests outstanding at that time by issuing free QA slots. Once it has satisfied all those requests, it may transmit its own segment. Meanwhile, head(A) must keep track of additional requests that arrive after time T. To distinguish between requests that arrive before and after time T, they are referred to as preceding and following requests, respectively, in Table 12.1.

One way to visualize this operation is to think of it in terms of tickets. Each time that a request arrives, head(A) generates a ticket. Each time that head(A) issues a free QA slot, it discards the oldest ticket. When the node has its own data to send, it generates a ticket on its behalf and places it on the bottom of the stack. As additional tickets are generated by arriving requests, these are placed on the bottom of the stack. When head(A)'s ticket reaches the top of the stack, head(A) can issue a busy QA slot containing its data.

Finally, Figure 12.5 depicts the behavior of a node other than the three already discussed, labeled **node x.** Like node (N-2), whenever node *x* needs to transmit a segment of data, it issues a request on bus B for an available slot on bus A. In addition, like node 0, node *x* must keep a count of requests that pass by on bus B so that its own requests are handled fairly. On bus A, node *x* receives segments of data addressed to it. To enforce a round-robin discipline, node *x* must keep track of incoming requests that precede and follow its own request, in a manner similar to the behavior of node 0. When node *x* has data to send and has issued a request, it may transmit its segment of data in a passing free slot only after all preceding requests have been satisfied. Table 12.1b, which is quite similar to Table 12.1a, summarizes the rules of behavior for node *x*.

Counter Mechanism

The DQDB protocol described can be described in terms of a distributed collection of FIFO queues. At each node, a queue is formed for each bus. For each request read in a passing slot, the node inserts one item in the queue. When the node itself issues a request, it adds an item to the queue for itself. When its own item is at the top of the queue, the node may transmit in the next free QA slot. A node may only have one item for itself in each queue (one for each bus) at any time.

This queuing mechanism can simply be implemented with a pair of counters for each queue, as illustrated in Figure 12.6, which shows the counters used for transmission on bus A; a corresponding pair of counters are used by the same node for transmission on bus B. When the node is not ready to send, it keeps track of requests on bus B from its downstream(A) neighbors in a request count. Each time a request is observed (request bit is

TABLE 12.1 Behavior of Nodes in Figure 12.6

(a) Behavior of Head(A)

At instant of time when it is ready to issue the next QA slot on bus A

	No preceding requests outstanding	One or more preceding requests outstanding
Head(A) has no data to send	Issue a free QA slot (busy bit set to zero).	Issue a free QA slot and reduce by one the count of preceding requests.
Head(A) has a segment of QA data to send	Issue a QA slot containing the data (busy bit set to one; destination address and data inserted); following requests, if any, now become preceding requests.	Issue a free QA slot and reduce by one the count of preceding requests.

(b) Behavior of Node x

At instant of time when it observes a free QA slot on bus A

	No preceding requests outstanding	One or more preceding requests outstanding
Node x has no data to send	Let free slot pass.	Let free slot pass and reduce by one the count of preceding requests.
Node has a segment of QA data to send and has previously issued a request on bus B	Set the busy bit to one on the passing slot and insert data; following requests, if any, now become preceding requests.	Let free slot pass and reduce by one the count of preceding requests.

TABLE 12.1 Behavior of Nodes in Figure 12.6 (continued)

	At instant of time when it receives the next QA slot on bus B	
	Incoming slot contains a request	Incoming slot does not contain a request
Head(A) has no data to send	Add 1 to count of preceding requests	—
Head(A) has a segment of QA data to send	Add 1 to count of following requests	—

	At instant of time when it observes a QA slot on bus B	
	Incoming slot contains a request	Incoming slot does not contain a request
Node x does not have an outstanding request	Add 1 to count of preceding requests	—
Node x has a segment of QA data to send and has already issued a request for that segment	Add 1 to count of following requests	—
Node x has a segment of QA data to send and has not yet issued a request for that segment	Add 1 to count of preceding requests	Insert request into passing slot (set request bit to 1)

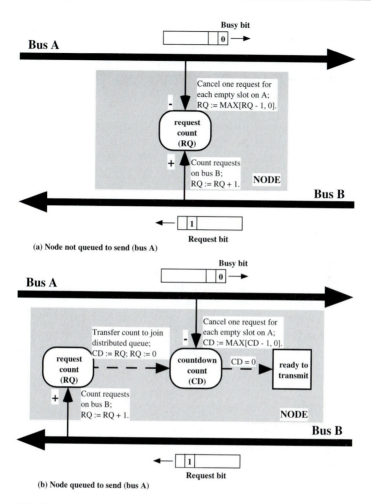

FIGURE 12.6   Request and Countdown Counter Operation

set), the count is increased by 1; each time that a free slot passes on bus A, the count is decremented by 1 to a minimum count of 0.

At any time, the value of RQ represents the unmet need for free QA slots by the node's downstream(A) peers. The node is obligated to let this number of free slots pass before itself using a QA slot to transmit. Therefore, when the node does have data to transmit on bus, it issues a request on bus B as soon as possible. The earliest opportunity will be the first slot to pass in which the request bit has not yet been set. Of course, while waiting for the opportunity to set the request bit, the node must continue to count passing requests in RQ. When the node does set the request bit on a passing slot on bus B, it immediately transfers the current value of RQ to a countdown count (CD) and resets RQ to 0. The node then decrements CD until it reaches 0, at which time the node may transmit on bus A in the next free QA slot. Meanwhile, the node counts new requests on bus B in RQ. The effect of the above is to maintain a single FIFO queue into which the node may insert its own request.

Note that the queue formation is such that a slot is never wasted on the subnetwork if there is a segment queued for it. This is so since the CD count in the queued nodes represents the number of segments queued ahead. Since at any point in time one segment must have queued first, at least one node is guaranteed to have a CD count of zero. It is that node that will access the next passing free QA slot.

This is a remarkably effective protocol. Under conditions of light load, the value of CD will be small or zero and free QA slots will be frequent. Thus, with a light load, delay is negligible, a property shared by CSMA/CD protocols. Under heavy loads, virtually every free QA slot will be utilized by one of the waiting nodes. Thus, with a heavy load, efficiency approaches 100 percent, a property shared by token bus and token ring protocols. This combination of quick access under light load and predictable queuing under heavy load makes the protocol suitable for a MAN of high data rate that will carry a mix of bursty traffic (e.g., interactive use) and more sustained streamlike traffic (e.g., file transfers).

Simple Example

Figure 12.7, adapted from an example in the 802.6 document, provides a simple example of the operation of the basic protocol. The example is limited to transmission of data on bus A; none of the nodes is a head-of-bus node.

The example starts at a point when there are no outstanding requests. At that point, all nodes have an RQ value of 0. Then the following events occur:

a. Node E issues a request on bus B by changing the busy bit in a passing slot from 0 to 1. Each downstream(B) node (nodes A through D) increments its RQ counter. At the same time, node E transfers it RQ count to its CD count. In this case the count is 0, so node E can transmit on bus A as soon as it sees a free QA slot.

b. Node B issues a request on bus B. The node transfers the value of RQ, which is 1, to CD and sets RQ to 0. This node will have to wait until one free QA slot passes on bus A before gaining access. Node A sees the request bit that has been set and increments its RQ value to 2.

c. Node C issues a request on bus B. C sets its CD value to 1 and its RQ value to 0. Node B increments its RQ value to 1. Note that B's CD

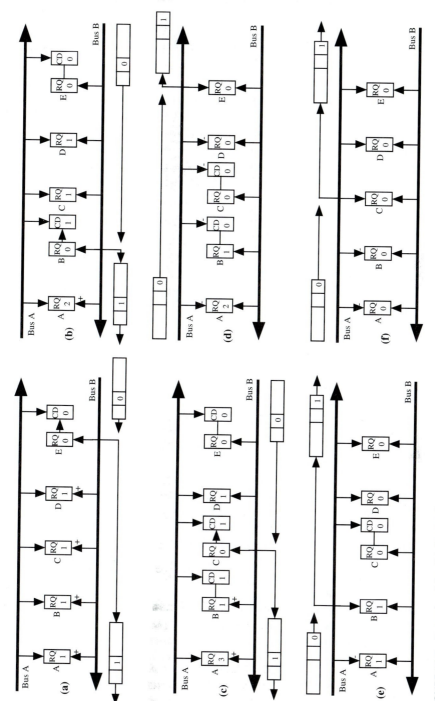

FIGURE 12.7 Example of the QA Protocol

value is unchanged; the arrival of new requests after B has issued its own request does not affect the timing of B's access to bus A. Node A increments its RQ to 3.

d. A free QA slot passes down bus A. Nodes A and D decrement their RQ counts. Nodes B and C decrement their CD counts. Node E has a CD of 0 and so can seize the free slot by changing the busy bit from 0 to 1 and inserting a QA segment.

e. Another free QA slot passes down bus A. Node A decrements its RQ count. Both nodes B and C are eligible to seize the free slot. However, the free slot passes node B first, which uses it to transmit a QA segment.

f. Node C uses the next passing free slot to transmit. The system returns to its original state, in which all nodes have an RQ value of 0.

Note that the three requests are satisfied in the order issued. Thus the behavior of the network as a whole is that of a FIFO queue.

Priority Distributed Queuing

The distributed queuing protocol supports three levels of priority. Priority access control is absolute in that QA segments with a higher priority will always gain access ahead of segments at all lower levels. This is achieved by operating separate distributed queues for each level of priority.

Several refinements need to be made to the access method described so far to support priority. Each segment includes 3 request bits, one for each level of priority. A node wishing to transmit on bus A at a particular priority level sets the appropriate bit on the next slot on bus B for which that bit is 0. To keep track of these requests, each node must maintain six RQ counters, one for each priority level in each direction, and six CD counters.

Operation of the RQ and CD counters is specified in such a way as to achieve absolute priority. We need to consider the two cases of a request pending and no request pending by a node at a particular priority level for one of the buses. First, let us consider the case of a node that has no requests pending at a given priority level for bus A; the same description will also apply to bus B. The RQ count operating at that priority level will count requests at the same and higher priority levels. Thus the RQ count records all queued segments at equal and higher priorities. As before, the RQ count is decremented for each passing QA slot on bus B.

Now suppose that the node has a QA segment queued at a particular priority level for bus A. In our original definition of the CD count, this variable is decremented with passing QA slots on one bus and unaffected by traffic on the other bus. To account for priorities, we continue to decrement CD with every passing free QA slot on one bus, but increment CD for every request on the other bus that is of higher priority. This allows the higher-priority segments to claim access ahead of segments already queued. To avoid double counting, the RQ count is incremented only for requests of the same priority level; the higher-priority requests are already being counted in the CD count.

At the present time, use of the priority levels is unspecified in the standard. The standard dictates that connectionless data segments (carry LLC PDUs) must operate at the lowest priority level (level 0). It is possible that control signaling messages or connection-oriented data might be assigned to one of the two higher priority levels; this is a matter for further study.

Bandwidth Balancing

A problem can arise in the access control mechanism so far described under conditions of heady load and a network of large extent. To understand the problem, which is one of bandwidth unfairness, we first need to clarify the relationship between data that a node needs to send, the use of requests, and the use of free slots. This relationship is illustrated in Figure 12.8, taken from the 802.6 document. The relationship concerns data generated at a node to be transmitted in QA segments. The DQDB user (i.e., LLC) provides service data units to the DQDB layer. Each block of arriving data is broken up into one or more segments and placed in a FIFO segment queue awaiting transmission. There are six such queues, one for each of three levels of priority on each of the two buses.

The figure shows the relationships for one of the six segment queues. A segment transmit queue is used to hold a segment that is awaiting a free slot on the bus. When a segment is transferred from the segment queue to the transmit queue, a request needs to be issued on the other bus. It may not be possible to issue the request immediately, since the node must wait for a passing slot in which the corresponding request bit has not yet been set. Therefore, a request queue is needed, which holds the requests until they can be issued. Each time that an empty request bit on a passing slot is set, one item is removed from the request queue.

The DQDB protocol dictates that once a node has issued a request for a free QA slot, it cannot issue another request until the first one is satisfied. To enforce this, the transmit queue can hold only one segment. If there is a segment in the transmit queue, it may be issued when the corresponding CD count is zero and an empty QA slot passes. If there is no segment in the transmit queue, one item from the segment queue may be transferred to the transmit queue, accompanied by the insertion of an entry in the request queue.

We are now in a position to explain the bandwidth unfairness problem, using an example in [HAHN90]. Consider two nodes that are transmitting very long messages on bus A; call the upstream(A) node 1 and the downstream(A) node 2, and assume that no other nodes require access to bus A. Define the following:

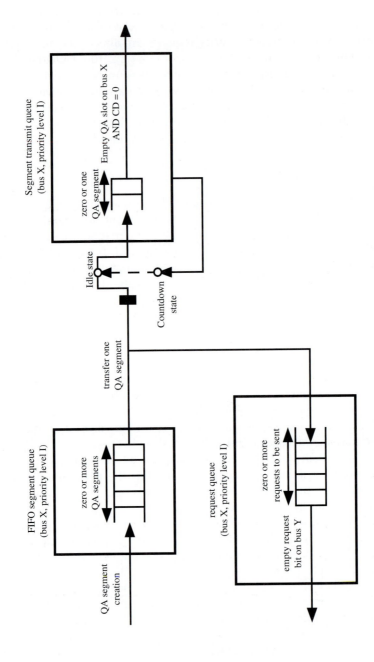

FIGURE 12.8 Relationship between QA Segment Queue, Request Queue, and Segment Transmit Queue

D = number of slots in transit between nodes 1 and 2, obviously a direct function of the physical length of the medium between the two nodes; assume an integer value

Δ = difference in the arrival times of the messages from DQDB users to the DQDB entities; that is,

= (time that the first segment is placed in the segment queue of node 2) – (time that the first segment is placed in the segment queue of node 1)

$c(\Delta)$ = a function that clips its argument to the range $[-D, D]$

P = number of requests plus idle slots circulating between the two nodes

Once both nodes have received messages from their users (both nodes have begun filling their segment queues), node 1 leaves slots idle only in response to requests from node 2. Therefore, once node 2 begins to receive QA slots from node 1, the only idle slots node 2 receives are in response to its earlier requests. Each idle slot received by node 2 results in a segment being transmitted, a new segment being placed in the transmit queue, and a request being issued on bus B. Therefore, the value of P is constant; let us refer to these conserved entities as *permits*. This quantity determines the throughput of the downstream node. We can express P as follows:

$$P = 1 + D - c(\Delta)$$

To verify this equation, consider two extreme cases. First, assume that a message arrives from node 1's user more than D time units before node 2 has a message to send ($\Delta \geq D$). In that case node 1 will fill the bus with data and will allow a free slot to pass only when it receives a request from node 2. When node 2 is ready to transmit, it must issue a request to wait for that request to reach node 1 and for a free slot to return. In this instance, there is only one permit in the network: $P = 1$. At the other extreme is the case of $\Delta \leq -D$. Initially, only node 2 is active. It inserts its first segment in the transmit queue and sends its first reservation request. The first segment is transmitted immediately in a free slot. The node continues to transmit segments and issue requests in this fashion. By the time node 1 is ready to transmit, bus B is already carrying D requests. In the time that it takes for node 1's first segment to reach node 2, node 2 injects another D requests, so that $P \approx 2D$.

Now define the following quantities:

γ_1 = steady-state throughput of node 1 (in segments per slot time)
γ_2 = steady-state throughput of node 2 (in segments per slot time)
Q = average value of CD at node 1

Note that at any instant in time, permits can be stored in the request channel (bus B between nodes 1 and 2), the data channel (bus A between nodes 1 and 2), and in the counter CD at node 1. Some thought should convince you that the following relationships hold:

$$\gamma_1 + \gamma_2 = 1$$
$$\gamma_1 = 1/Q$$
$$\gamma_2 = P/T$$
$$T = 2D + Q$$

Solving these equations, we have:

$$\gamma_1 = \frac{2}{2 - D - c(\Delta) + \sqrt{[D - c(\Delta) + 2]^2 + 4Dc(\Delta)}}$$
$$\gamma_2 = 1 - \gamma_1$$

Note that if the nodes are very close together ($D \approx 0$) or if they start transmitting at about the same ($\Delta \approx 0$), each node gets about half of the capacity. However, if D is very large (large network) and the downstream node starts later, its predicted throughput rate is only about $1/2D$. Node 1 also suffers a penalty if it starts later, although not as great; its worst-case rate is approximately $1/\sqrt{2D}$.

As [HAHN90] points out, one way of explaining the bandwidth unfairness phenomenon of DQDB is that the protocol pushes the system too hard. In its attempt to use every single slot on the bus, the protocol causes request queues to build up in the nodes that never recede. The refinement proposed in the paper and subsequently adopted by IEEE 802.6 "leaks" some bandwidth to prevent the hogging of bandwidth in overload situations. The technique is known as **bandwidth balancing.**

In ordinary DQDB, a node may transmit a segment when its CD count is zero and the current QA slot is free. Bandwidth balancing permits the node to transmit only a fraction α of that time. This is achieved by artificially incrementing RQ after every β segments transmitted; thus $\alpha = \beta/(1 - \beta)$. This forces the node to send an extra free slot downstream after using β free slots. For example, if $\alpha = 0.9$ ($\beta = 9$), then after every nine QA segments transmitted, the node lets an extra slot pass. To implement this scheme, one more counter, called the *trigger counter,* is needed for each direction at each node. The trigger counter is incremented by one every time a QA segment is transmitted. When the counter equals β, it is set to 0 and RQ is incremented by one.

The parameter β, called the *bandwidth balancing modulus,* or BWB_MOD, in the standard must be set in each node. The value may be set between 0 and 64, with a default value of 8. A value of 0 disables the bandwidth balancing function.

The standard recommends that bandwidth balancing be enabled for a bus that spans a distance that is greater than the effective length of one 53-octet slot, which is approximately the following:

2 km at 44.376 Mbps (DS3 rate)

546 m at 155.520 Mbps (STM-1 rate)

137 m at 622.080 Mbps (STM-4 rate)

State Machine Description

The IEEE 802.6 standard contains a state machine description of the distributed queue access protocol which helps to clarify the mechanism. Figure 12.9 is adapted from a figure in the standard. It shows the state machine for a station for one priority level X (X = A or B; Y = the other bus) and one priority level I (I = 0,1,2). Each node has six such state machines operating simultaneously. There are two states: A node is in the idle state when it has no QA segments to send; a node is in the countdown state when it has a QA segment to send.

First consider the **idle state.** Three internal events can occur. If data arrive from the DQDB user at priority level I intended for a downstream(X) node, the node transitions to the countdown state. The node performs several actions as part of the transition:

- It informs the other two bus X state machines within the node of this internal request with a signal, SELF_REQ_I.
- It transfers the value of its request count (RQ_I) to its countdown count (CD_I) and clears RQ_I.
- It queues a request signal for bus Y.

Another internal event is the arrival of a SELF_REQ_J signal from one of the other bus X state machines. If the priority of the internal request is greater than I, then RQ_I must be incremented by 1 to give that request priority. The final internal event occurs when the bandwidth balancing counter (BWB_MOD) for bus X is reset to 0. This is depicted as a signal, BWB_reset_X, sent to each bus X state machine. The resulting action is to increment RQ_I.

Two external events affect the machine in the idle state. When an empty QA slot passes on bus X, RQ_I is decremented by 1 to a minimum value of 0. If a slot passes on bus Y with the priority J bit set (REQ_J), and J ≥ I, then RQ_I is incremented by 1.

In the **countdown state,** external events related to the Y bus affect the machine. If a slot passes on bus Y with the REQ_J set, and J > I, then CD_I is incremented by 1. If a slot passes on bus Y with the REQ_I set, then RQ_I is incremented by 1. These actions keeps the machine's request queued properly.

There are also two significant internal events. One is the arrival of a SELF_REQ_J signal from one of the other bus X state machines. If J > I, then CD_I is incremented, so that a new internal request of higher priority gets preference over a waiting QA segment of lower priority. The other internal event is the arrival of a BWB_reset_X signal. Again, this causes CD_I to be incremented: bandwidth balancing takes precedence over waiting QA segments.

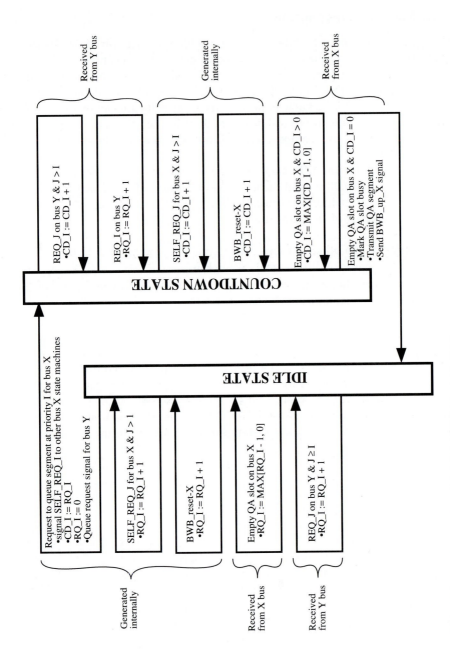

FIGURE 12.9   State Machine Description of Counter Mechanism

Finally, two external events related to bus X affect the machine in the countdown state. If an empty QA slot passes and CD_I is greater than 0, then CD_I is decremented by 1 to a minimum value of 0. If an empty QA slot passes and CD_I is equal to 0, the node transitions to the idle state. The node performs several actions as part of the transition:

- Mark the passing QA slot as busy by setting the busy bit to 1.
- Begin transmitting its QA segment in the QA slot.
- Cause the BWB_MOD counter for bus X to be incremented (modulo its maximum value) by issuing a BWB_up_X signal.

12.4
DQDB PROTOCOL DATA UNITS

A rather complex set of protocol data unit formats is used to support the DQDB layer functions. Table 12.2 lists the five PDU types and indicates their relationship to each other and the DQDB sublayer that is responsible for generating and reading each type.

Slot

As we have already discussed, the basic unit of transfer on a DQDB subnetwork is the 53-octet slot. The slot consists of a 1-octet header and a 52-octet segment; its format is shown in Figure 12.10a. The slot header, referred to as the *access control field*, contains the bits that control slot access. The fields are:

- *Busy:* indicates whether the slot contains information or is free.
- *Slot type:* indicates whether this is a QA slot or a PA slot. The combination of busy bit and slot-type bit is referred to as the *slot access control field*, with the assignments indicated in Table 12.3a.
- *Previous slot reserved:* indicates whether or not the segment in the previous slot may be cleared. This bit is set by a node when the slot immediately preceding contained a QA segment destined only for that node. The use of this bit is for further study.
- *Reserved:* set to 00; reserved for future use.
- *Request:* three request bits for the three priority levels.

Segment

Each slot contains a 52-octet segment, which may be either a QA segment or a PA segment. Both types of segments consist of a 4-octet header followed

TABLE 12.2 IEEE 802.6 PDU Formats

PDU	Relative Position[a]	Sublayer	Description
Slot	Contains a QA segment, a PA segment, or isochronous data	Common functions	Basic unit of data transfer
QA segment	Contained in a slot; carries a DMPDU	Queued arbitrated (QA) functions	Used to carry a portion of a MAC service data unit or other SDU
PA segment	Contained in a slot	Pre-arbitrated (PA) functions	Used to carry isochronous service octets
Initial MAC protocol data unit (IMPDU)	Carried in a sequence of DMPDUs	MAC convergence function (MCF)	Contains a MAC service data unit
Derived MAC protocol data unit (DMPDU)	Carries a portion of a IMPDU; contained in a QA segment	MAC convergence function (MCF)	A sequence of DMPDUs carries a single IMPDU

[a]See Figure 11.12.

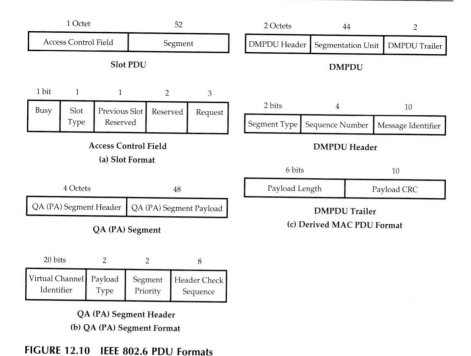

FIGURE 12.10   IEEE 802.6 PDU Formats

by a 48-octet segment payload. The QA and PA segment headers have the identical format, with some differences in interpretation of the fields. The formats are shown in Figure 12.10b. The header fields are:

- *Virtual channel identifier:* identifies the virtual channel, or logical connection, to which the segment belongs. The VCI value of all ones corresponds to the connectionless MAC service. Other nonzero VCI values are available for use for the connection-oriented data service and isochronous services.

- *Payload type:* indicates the nature of the data to be transferred. The field could be used by DQDB subnetworks interconnected via bridges, where this value could differentiate between user data and network signaling and management data. The default value for both PA and QA segments is 00; all other values are for further study.

- *Segment priority:* reserved for future use with multiport bridges. A multiport bridge is one that connects three or more subnetworks.

- *Header check sequence:* covers the segment header and is used for the detection of errors and the correction of single-bit errors. It uses the same polynomial code as for ATM ($X^8 + X^2 + X + 1$). The operation of the error control mechanism, shown in Figure 12.11, is almost identical to that specified for ATM (Figure 10.5). The only difference is that when the HCS decoder is in the correction state, there is a probability

TABLE 12.3 Coding of Some IEEE 802.6 PDU Fields

(a) Slot Access Control Field

BUSY	SL_TYPE	Slot State
0	0	Empty QA slot
0	1	Reserved
1	0	Busy QA slot
1	1	PA slot

(b) Address Type Subfield

ADDRESS_TYPE	MSAP Address Structure
0010	16 bit
1000	48 bit
1100	Individual 60 bit, publicly administered
1101	Individual 60 bit, privately administered
1110	Group 60 bit, publicly administered
1111	Group 60 bit, privately administered
All other codes	Reserved for future standardization

(c) Protocol Identification (PI) Field

PI Range	Protocol Entity
1	LLC
48–63	Available for use by local administration
Other values	Reserved for future standardization by IEEE 802.6

(d) Quality of Service: Delay (QOS_DELAY)

Priority Requested	QOS_DELAY Subfield	Relative Delay Requested
7	1 1 1	Shortest
6	1 1 0	
5	1 0 1	
4	1 0 0	
3	0 1 1	
2	0 1 0	
1	0 0 1	
0	0 0 0	Longest

(e) DMPDU Segment_Type Field

Segment_Type	DMPDU Type
00	Continuation of message (COM)
01	End of message (EOM)
10	Beginning of message (BOM)
11	Single-segment message (SSM)

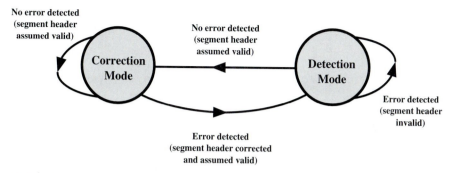

No error detected
(segment header
assumed valid)

No error detected
(segment header
assumed valid)

Correction
Mode

Detection
Mode

Error detected
(segment header
invalid)

Error detected
(segment header corrected
and assumed valid)

FIGURE 12.11 HCS Operation at Receiver

that multiple-bit errors will be corrected as if they were single-bit errors, allowing an errored header to pass as valid.

Transfer of MAC Service Data Units

The DQDB layer provides the MAC service by accepting MAC service data units (LLC PDUs) from a DQDB user and transmitting each to a destination DQDB user. Since the QA segment format limits the protocol to a segment payload of 48 octets, it is clear that a segmentation and reassembly function must be performed. The approach that is taken to this function is depicted in Figure 12.12. An arriving MAC SDU is encapsulated into an initial MAC PDU (IMPDU), which includes an IMPDU header and trailer plus the entire MAC SDU. This IMPDU is then segmented into 44-octet *segmentation units*, each of which can be fit into a derived MAC PDU (DMPDU). The DMPDU includes the 44-octet segmentation unit plus a header and trailer, for a total length of 48 octets. Thus each 48-octet DMPDU fits into a single QA segment, which in turn fits into a single QA slot.

Initial MAC Protocol Data Unit. A MAC SDU is transferred within an IMPDU. An IMPDU is transferred between peer MAC convergence function protocol entities. The format of an IMPDU is shown in Figure 12.13. The IMPDU is constructed by adding the following major elements to a variable-length MAC SDU, which is stored in the INFO field:

- *Common PDU header:* carried in all DQDB layer PDUs supporting frame-based bursty data services.
- *MCP header:* specific to the MAC convergence protocol, and therefore specific to the transfer of a MAC SDU.
- *Header extension:* provides the optional capability to convey additional IMPDU protocol control information that may be standardized in the future. An example of its use would be to convey service-provider-specific information in cases where this protocol is used to access the services of a public network.

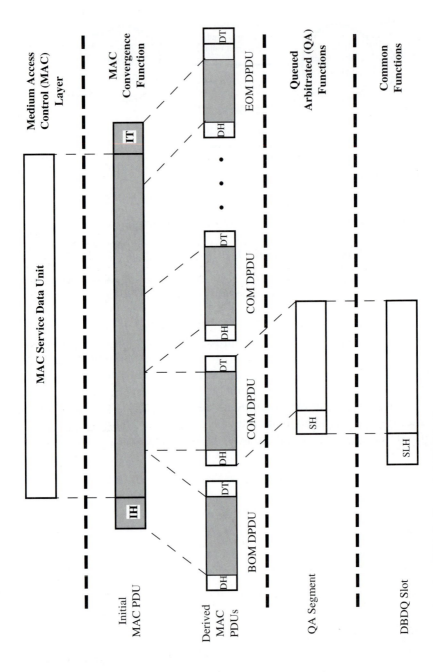

FIGURE 12.12 PDUs for Support of MAC Service

416

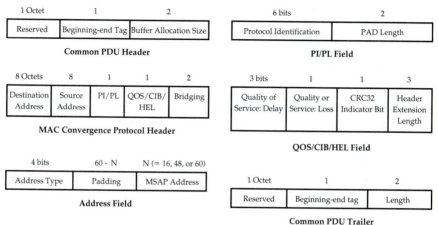

IMPDU Header						
Common PDU Header	MAC Convergence Protocol Header	Header Extension	INFO	PAD	CRC 32	Common PDU Trailer
4 Ocets	20	+	*	#	!	4

+ = In the range 0 to 20 octets inclusive, in steps of 4 octets
* = Contains the MAC SDU; up to and including 9188 octets
# = 0, 1, 2, or 3 octets, as needed to make the total length of the INFO plus PAD fields an integral multiple of 4 octets
! = absent (0 octets) or present (4 octets)

IMPDU

| 1 Octet | 1 | 2 |
| Reserved | Beginning-end Tag | Buffer Allocation Size |

Common PDU Header

| 6 bits | 2 |
| Protocol Identification | PAD Length |

PI/PL Field

| 8 Octets | 8 | 1 | 1 | 2 |
| Destination Address | Source Address | PI/PL | QOS/CIB/ HEL | Bridging |

MAC Convergence Protocol Header

| 3 bits | 1 | 1 | 3 |
| Quality of Service: Delay | Quality or Service: Loss | CRC32 Indicator Bit | Header Extension Length |

QOS/CIB/HEL Field

| 4 bits | 60 - N | N (= 16, 48, or 60) |
| Address Type | Padding | MSAP Address |

Address Field

| 1 Octet | 1 | 2 |
| Reserved | Beginning-end tag | Length |

Common PDU Trailer

FIGURE 12.13   Initial MAC PDU Format

- *PAD:* contains the minimum number of octets so that the total length of the INFO field plus the PAD field is an integral multiple of four octets.
- *CRC 32:* provides the optional capability for including a 32-bit CRC, calculated over all the fields of the MCP header, the header extension field, the INFO field, and the PAD field.
- *Common PDU trailer:* carried in all DQDB layer PDUs supporting frame-based bursty data services.

The **common PDU header** consists of three fields:

- *Reserved:* reserved for future use.
- *Beginning-end tag:* an 8-bit sequence number associated with an IMPDU, and incremented by one (modulo 256) for successive IMPDUs sent by the node. This value is used in segmentation and reassembly, explained below.
- *Buffer allocation size:* the total length of the IMPDU, exclusive of the common PDU header and trailer. This alerts the receiver to buffer space requirements. Again, this value is used in segmentation and reassembly.

The **MCP header** consists of the following fields:

- *Destination address:* the MAC address of the destination node.
- *Source address:* the MAC address of the source node.
- *PI/PL:* the Protocol identification subfield that identifies the MAC service user to which the INFO field is to be sent. Valid values for this field are shown in Table 12.3c. The pad length subfield indicates the length of the PAD field in the IMPDU.
- *QOS/CIB/HEL:* the QOS delay subfield that indicates the requested quality of service for an IMDPU with respect to delay in accessing the subnetwork. The value is based on the priority requested by the MAC user, and the coding is shown in Table 12.3d. The QOS loss bit is currently reserved. It may be used for congestion control at bridges by indicating which IMPDUs are eligible for discard. The CRC32 indicator bit indicates the presence or absence of the CRC32 field in the IMPDU. The header extension length subfield gives the length of the header extension field in the IMPDU, in units of 4 octets.
- *Bridging:* reserved for future use for MAC-level bridging. One use for this field would be a hop count: after an IMPDU has passed through a given number of bridges, it would be discarded.

The two address fields have the format shown in Figure 12.13. The first 4 bits indicate the address type, with the values indicated in Table 12.3b. Support for 48-bit addresses is mandatory. Support for 16-bit addresses is optional. Both of these address types conform to the MAC address format for IEEE 802. Support is also optional for 60-bit addresses, which may be publicly administered (local MAN operator) or privately administered.

The **common PDU trailer** contains the same information in the same format as the common PDU header. The same value is inserted into the beginning–end tag field in both header and trailer, and the same value is inserted in the buffer allocation size and length fields.

Derived MAC Protocol Data Unit.   As Figure 12.13 illustrates, an IMPDU is segmented into one or more DMPDUs. Each DMPDU carries a 44-octet portion of the IMPDU, known as a **segmentation unit.** In addition, each DMPDU has a header and trailer.

The **DMPDU header** contains the following fields:

- *Segment type.* There are four types of DMPDUs. A single sequence message (SSM) contains an entire IMPDU. If the IMPDU is segmented into two or more DMPDUs (Figure 12.13), the first DMPDU is the beginning of message (BOM), the last DMPDU is the end of message (EOM), and any intermediate DMPDUs are continuations of message (COM). The coding is shown in Table 12.3e.

- *Sequence number.* This is used in reassembling an IMPDU to verify that all of the DMPDU segmentation units have been received and concatenated properly. A value of the sequence number is set at BOM and incremented for each successive COM and the EOM for a single IMPDU.
- *Message identifier.* This is a unique identifier associated with the set of DMPDUs that carries a single IMPDU. Again, this number is needed to ensure proper reassembly.

The **DMPDU trailer** contains the following fields:

- *Payload length:* indicates the number of octets from the IMPDU that occupy the segmentation unit of the DMPDU. The number has a value between 4 and 44 octets, in multiples of 4. The value will always be 44 for BOM and COM DMPDUs. It is a lower number in an SSM if the IMPDU is less than 44 octets in length. It is a lower number in an EOM if the length of the IMPDU is not an integer multiple of 44 octets in length, necessitating the use of a partially filled EOM.
- *Payload CRC:* a 10-bit CRC on the entire DMPDU.

12.5

PHYSICAL LAYER CONVERGENCE PROCEDURE FOR DS3

The physical layer convergence procedure (PLCP) adapts the services of the transmission system to provide a uniform, generic physical layer service to the DQDB layer. The PLCP maps DQDB timing information, slot octets, and management information octets into a format that is suitable for transfer by the associated transmission system. A different PLCP is needed for each transmission system.

The first PLCP that was standardized by IEEE 802.6 is for the DS3 transmission system. DS3 was chosen because it is the only commonly used signal in North America with adequate bandwidth for the services being defined. The DS3 PLCP frame format is defined for use over the standard public network and can be extended into the customer's premises.

DS3

The DS3 signal is one of the most difficult formats for adaption. Unlike SONET, DS1, and most other signaling schemes, DS3 is not based on a 125-μs frame duration. The DS3 signal operates at a data rate of 44.736 Mbps and provides a frame duration that is nominally 106.4 μs. Its payload is typically quantized into nibbles (one nibble = 4 bits) due to the nature of the format.

Table 12.4 lists the key characteristics of DS3. The DS3 frame of 595 octets is divided into seven subframes of 680 bits each. Each subframe in turn consist of eight blocks of 85 bits. The first bit in each block is for management and framing purposes; the remaining 84 bits, or 21 nibbles, is the payload. Since one bit in 85 is overhead, the nominal information rate is $(84/85) \times 44.736$ Mbps = 44.21 Mbps.

PLCP Frame Format

To accommodate DQDB, which uses 125-μs timing. You can observe that the DS3 signal contains exactly 699 octets over a 125-μs period, which is an integral number of octets. However, the actual payload available from DS3 is at a rate of 44.21 Mbps, which yields 690.78 octets, or 1381.56 nibbles, over a 125-μs frame. The PCLP must find a way of mapping the 53-octet slots into this DS3 payload. We must therefore assume a frame size of 690 octets, with bit stuffing used to smooth out the frame size to the actual transmission rate.

If we work with the numbers of Table 12.4, we can design a frame to hold the maximum number of DQDB slots. Each slot is 53 octets. The highest multiple of 53 octets that will fit into a frame of 690 octets is 13. However, with $53 \times 13 = 689$ octets, this leaves virtually no capacity for framing and management information. Accordingly, the PCLP frame for DS3 includes 12 DQDB slots, for a total payload of 636 octets.

Figure 12.14 shows the resulting frame format. The format can be depicted as 12 rows of 57 octets, with the last row containing a trailer of 13 or 14 nibbles. The first two columns (A1, A2) are used to provide slot delineation. Each A1 octet has the bit pattern 11110110 and each A2 octet has the bit pattern 00101000. These codes are the same used in the ITU-T synchronous digital hierarchy (SDH) recommendations G.707-9.

TABLE 12.4   Construction of DQDB PLCP Frame for DS3

	DS3	DQDB PLCP
Frame size	595 octets	690–691 octets
Frame time	106.4 μs	125 μs
Signaling rate	44.736 Mbps	44.21 Mbps
Overhead	56 bits/frame	54.5–55 octets
Payload size	588 octets	636 octets
Payload data rate	44.21 Mbps	40.704 Mbps

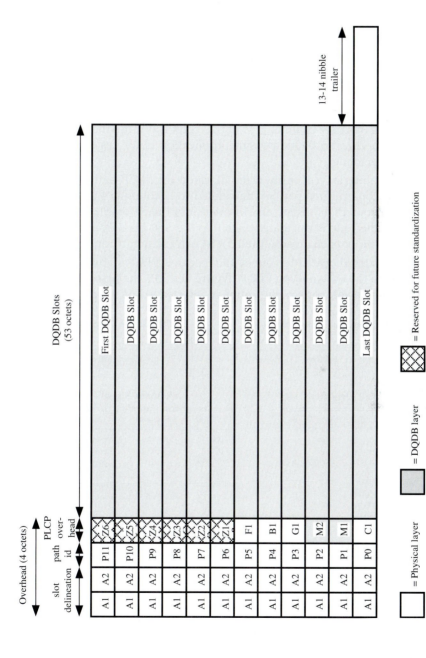

FIGURE 12.14 PLCP Frame Format for DS3 Transmission

421

The third column (P11-P0) identifies the PCLP overhead octets of the fourth column. That is, each P_i uniquely identifies one row of the PLCP and therefore uniquely identifies one of the octets from the fourth column. Figure 12.15a shows the convention used. The first 6 bits of octet P_i are set to the binary value of *i*. The seventh bit is reserved, and the eighth bit provides odd parity.

The fourth column is referred to as PLCP *path overhead*. The following octets make up the column:

- *Z6-Z1:* reserved for future use.
- *F1:* a 64-kbps user channel. Use of this octet is outside the scope of the PLCP specification. One possible application is for assisting maintenance personnel.
- *B1:* a bit-interleaved parity octet allocated for PLCP path error monitoring. Longitudinal parity is calculated over columns 4 through 57 of the previous PLCP frame and inserted into the B1 octet of the current frame. The code is calculated such that the first bit is even parity over the first bit of each octet in the 12×54 octet structure, and so on.
- *G1:* an octet allocated to convey the received PLCP status and performance to the transmitting PLCP (Figure 12.15b). The first 4 bits, the far end block error, convey the count of interleaved-bit blocks that have

Path Overhead Identifier Octet Format

6 bits	1	1
Path Overhead Label	Reserved	Parity

Path Status Format

4 bits	1	3
Far End Block Error	Yellow Signal	Link Status Signal

Path Overhead Identifier Codes

P11	001011	0	0
P10	001010	0	1
P9	001001	0	1
P8	001000	0	0
P7	000111	0	0
P6	000110	0	1
P5	000101	0	1
P4	000100	0	0
P3	000011	0	1
P2	000010	0	0
P1	000001	0	0
P0	000000	0	1

(a) Path Identifier Octet (P11-P0)

Link Status Signal Codes

LSS Code	LSS Name	Link Status
000	Connected	Received link connected
011	rx_link_dn	Received link down, no input or forced down
110	rx_link_up	Received link up

(b) Path Status Octet (G1)

Cycle/Stuff Counter Codes

C1 Code	Frame Phase of Cycle	Trailer Link
11111111	1	13
00000000	2	14
01100110	3 (no stuff)	13
10011001	3 (stuff)	14

(c) Cycle/Stuff Counter (C1)

FIGURE 12.15   Format and Coding of Some PLCP Frame Octets

been detected to be in error by the B1 code in the preceding frame. The yellow signal bit alerts the transmitting PLCP that a received failure indication has been declared along the PLCP path. When the failure has ceased, the bit is reset to zero on subsequent frames. The link status signal is used to communicate information about the status of the transmission link between the two adjacent PLCP entities.

- *M2-M1:* provided for the transport of DQDB layer management information octets and are not processed by the PLCP sublayer.

- *C1:* used to guide a nibble-stuffing function to maintain alignment and synchronization between the PLCP frame and the DS3 frame. As indicated in Figure 12.14, each PLCP frame ends with 13 or 14 nibbles. Frame transmission is organized into groups of three frames. The first frame in the group always ends with 13 nibbles; the second frame ends in 14 nibbles; and the third frame ends in either 13 or 14 nibbles as timing needs dictate. The C1 code (Figure 12.15c) indicates which phase of the three-frame cycle this frame is and, if it is the third frame, whether or not the 14th nibble is added.

Use of DS3 Frames to Carry PLCP Payload

Figure 12.16 illustrates the DS3 frame format and the way in which its payload nibbles are used to carry PLCP frames. Note that the PLCP frame "floats" inside the DS3 frame structure: There is no relationship between the start of the PLCP frame and the start of the DS3 frame.

12.6

RECOMMENDED READING

[KESS92] provides good technical coverage of DQDB.

KESS92   Kessler, G., and Train, D. *Metropolitan Area Networks: Concepts, Standards, and Services.* New York: McGraw-Hill, 1992.

12.7

PROBLEMS

12.1 Assess CSMA/CD, token bus, and the DQDB scheme as MAC algorithms for a MAN. Justify the assertion that DQDB is best suited to the requirements of a bus-based MAN.

12.2 How many slots are spread out on the DQDB bus in each direction for a 30-km bus running at 150 Mbps?

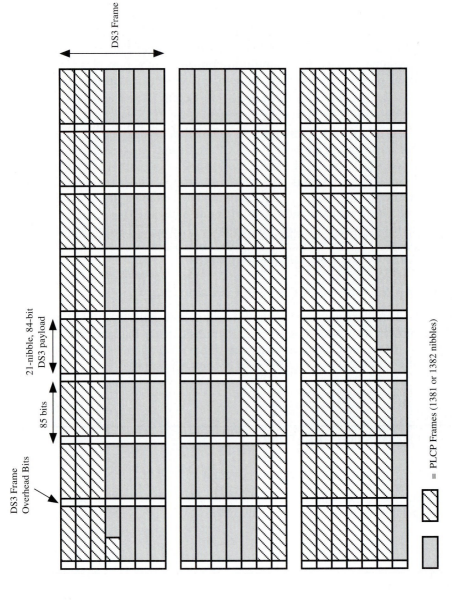

Figure 12.16 Use of DS3 Frames to Carry PLCP Payload [BRAN90]

DS3 Frame

21-nibble, 84-bit
DS3 payload

85 bits

DS3 Frame
Overhead Bits

= PLCP Frames (1381 or 1382 nibbles)

12.3 Suppose that two nodes are randomly placed on a bus; that is, each is placed independently and the position of each is chosen from a uniform distribution over the length of the bus. For a bus of length L, show that the expected distance between the two nodes is $\frac{1}{3}$.

12.4 The bandwidth balancing technique is one method of overcoming the unfairness of the DQDB protocol. Another proposed solution is referred to as reservation request control (RRC). The basic idea of RRC is to prevent unfair access to request bits. This is accomplished by providing downstream nodes with information about the number of upstream nodes, and allowing each node to have multiple outstanding requests for the same bus and priority level. If a node knows that there are N upstream (A) nodes that need access to bus A, it may send a request on the first available slot on bus B and then must defer to the N upstream (A) nodes by allowing N slots available for sending requests to pass on bus B before it tries to send its next request. In this case, each upstream (A) node can use one of these slots to send a request.

  a. Suggest a dynamic means of implementing RRC dynamically that allows the node to consider only the upstream nodes that may want to send rather than the physical total of all upstream nodes.

  b. Compare RRC with bandwidth balancing, in terms of fairness and in terms of efficient use of the medium.

LAN/MAN Performance

This chapter has two objectives:

1. To give the reader some insight into the factors that affect performance and the relative performance of various local network schemes
2. To present analytic techniques that can be used for network sizing and to obtain first approximations of network performance

It is beyond the scope of this book to derive analytic expressions for all of the performance measures presented; that would require an entire book on local network performance. Further, this chapter can only sketch the techniques that would be useful to the analyst in approximating performance; for deeper study, references to appropriate literature are provided.

This chapter begins by presenting some of the key performance considerations for LANs and MANs; the section serves to put the techniques and results presented subsequently into perspective. Separate sections present results for LAN and MAN systems.

13.1

LAN/MAN PERFORMANCE CONSIDERATIONS

The key characteristics of the LAN that structure the way its performance is analyzed are that there is a shared access medium, requiring a medium access control protocol, and that packet switching is used. MANs share these characteristics. It follows that the basic performance considerations, and the approaches to performance analysis, will be the same for both. With the above points in mind, this section explores these basic considerations. The section begins by defining the basic measures of performance, then looks at the key parameter for determining LAN/MAN performance, known affectionately to devotees as a. Having been introduced to a, the reader is in a position to appreciate the interrelationship of the various factors that affect LAN/MAN performance, which is the final topic.

The results that exist for the portion of performance within the local network boundary are summarized in subsequent sections. As we shall see, these results are best organized in terms of the medium access control protocol.

Measures of Performance

Three measures of LAN and MAN performance are commonly used:

D: the delay that occurs between the time a packet or frame is ready for transmission from a node, and the completion of successful transmission

S: the throughput of the local network; the total rate of data being transmitted between nodes (carried load)

U: the utilization of the local network medium; the fraction of total capacity being used

These measures concern themselves with performance within the local network. How they relate to the overall performance of the network and attached devices is discussed later.

The parameter S is often normalized and expressed as a fraction of capacity. For example, if over a period of 1 s, the sum of the successful data transfers between nodes is 1 Mb on a 10-Mbps channel, then $S = 0.1$. Thus S can also be interpreted as utilization. The analysis is commonly done in terms of the total number of bits transferred, including overhead (headers, trailers) bits; the calculations are a bit easier, and this approach isolates performance effects due to the local network alone. One must work backward from this to determine effective throughput.

Results for S and D are generally plotted as a function of the offered load G, which is the actual load or traffic demand presented to the local network. Note that S and G differ. S is the normalized rate of data packets successfully transmitted; G is the total number of packets offered to the network; it includes control packets, such as tokens, and collisions, which are destroyed packets that must be retransmitted. G, too, is often expressed as a fraction of capacity. Intuitively, we would expect D to increase with G: the more traffic competing for transmission time, the longer the delay for any individual transmission. S should also increase with G, up to some saturation point, beyond which the network cannot handle more load.

Figure 13.1 shows the ideal situation: channel utilization increases to accommodate load up to an offered load equal to the full capacity of the system; then utilization remains at 100 percent. Of course, any overhead or inefficiency will cause performance to fall short of the goal. The depiction of S versus G is a reasonable one from the point of view of the network itself. It shows the behavior of the system based on the actual load on it. But from the point of view of the user or the attached device, it may seem strange. Why? Because the offered load includes not only original transmissions but also acknowledgments and, in the case of errors or collisions, retransmissions. The user may want to know the throughput and the delay characteristics as a function of the device-generated data to be put through the system—the input load. Or if the network is the focus, the analyst may want to know what the offered load is, given the input load. We will return to this discussion later.

The reader may also wonder about the importance of U. D and S are certainly of interest, but the efficiency or utilization of the channel may seem of minor importance. After all, local networks are advertised as having very high bandwidth and low cost compared to long-haul networks. Although it is true that utilization is of less importance for local compared

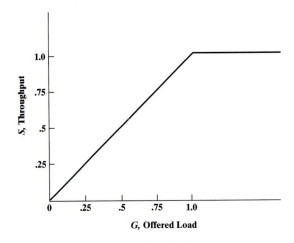

FIGURE 13.1   Ideal Channel Utilization

to long-haul links, it is still worth considering. Local network capacity is not free, and demand has a tendency to expand to fill available capacity.

In summary, we have introduced two additional parameters:

1. *G:* the offered load to the local network; the total rate of data presented to the network for transmission
2. *I:* the input load; the rate of data generated by the stations attached to the local network

Table 13.1 is a very simplified example to show the relationship among these parameters. Here we assume a network with a capacity of $C = 1000$ frames per second. For simplicity, I, S, and G are expressed in frames per second. It is assumed that 1 percent of all transmitted frames are lost and must be repeated. Thus at an input $I = 100$ frames per second, on the average 1 frame per second will be repeated. Thus $S = 100$ and $G = 101$. Assume that the input load arrives in batches, once per second. Hence, on average, with $I = 100$, $D = 0.0505$ s. The utilization is defined as $S/C = 0.1$.

The next two entries are easily seen to be correct. Note that for $I = 990$, the entire capacity of the system is being used ($G = 1000$). If I increases beyond this point, the system cannot keep up. Only 1000 frames per second will be transmitted. Thus S remains at 990 and U at 0.99. But G and D grow without bound as more and more backlog accumulates; there is no steady-state value. This pattern will become familiar as the chapter proceeds.

Effect of Propagation Delay and Transmission Rate

Recall from Figure 1.1 that local networks are distinguished from wide-area networks on the one hand, and multiprocessor systems on the other, by the data rate (R) employed and the distance (d) of the communications path. In fact, it is the product of these two terms, $R \times d$, that can be used to character-

TABLE 13.1   Example of Relationships Among LAN/MAN Measures of Performance[a,b]

I	S	G	D	U
100	100	101	0.0505	0.1
500	500	505	0.2525	0.5
990	990	1000	0.5	0.99
2000	990	—	—	0.99

[a]Capacity: 1000 frames/s.

[b]*I* input load (frames per second); *S*, throughput (frames per second); *G*, offered load (frames per second;) *D*, delay (seconds); *U*, utilization (fraction of capacity).

ize local networks. Furthermore, as we shall see, this term, or cousins of it, is the single most important parameter for determining the performance of a local network. We shall see that a network's performance will be the same, for example, for both a 100-Mbps, 1 km-bus and a 10-Mbps, 10-km bus.

A good way to visualize the meaning of $R \times d$ is to divide it by the propagation velocity of the medium, which is nearly constant among most media of interest. A good approximation for propagation velocity is about two-thirds of the speed of light, or 2×10^8 m/s. A dimensional analysis of the formula

$$\frac{Rd}{V}$$

shows this to be equal to the length of the transmission medium in bits, that is, the number of bits that may be in transit between two nodes at any one time.

We can see that this does indeed distinguish local networks from multiprocessor and long-haul networks. Within a multiprocessor system, there are generally only a few bits in transit. For example, the latest IBM I/O channel offering operates at up to 24 Mbps over a distance of up to 120 m, which yields at most about 15 bits. Processor-to-processor communication within a single computer will typically involve fewer bits than that in transit. On the other hand, the bit length of a long-haul network can be hundreds of thousands of bits. In between, we have local networks. Several examples: a 500-m Ethernet system (10 Mbps) has a bit length of 25; a typical 5-km broadband LAN (5 Mbps) is about 250 bits long.

A useful way of looking at this is to consider the length of the medium as compared to the typical frame transmitted. Multiprocessor systems have very short bit lengths compared to frame length; long-haul nets have very long ones. Local networks generally are shorter than a frame up to about the same order of magnitude as a frame.

Intuitively, one can see that this will make a difference. Compare local networks to multiprocessor computers. Relatively speaking, things happen almost simultaneously in a multiprocessor system; when one component begins to transmit, the others know it almost immediately. For local networks, the relative time gap leads to all kinds of complications in the medium access control protocols, as we have seen. Compare long-haul networks to local networks. To have any hope of efficiency, the long-haul link must allow multiple frames to be in transit simultaneously. This places specific requirements on the link-layer protocol, which must deal with a sequence of outstanding frames waiting to be acknowledged. LAN and MAN protocol generally allow only one frame to be in transit at a time, or at the most a few for some ring protocols. Again, this affects the access protocol.

The length of the medium, expressed in bits, compared to the length of the typical frame is usually denoted by *a*:

$$a = \frac{\text{length of data path (in bits)}}{\text{length of frame}}$$

Some manipulation shows that

$$a = \frac{Rd}{VL}$$

where L is the length of the frame. But d/V is the propagation time on the medium (worst case), and L/B is the time it takes a transmitter to get an entire frame out onto the medium. So

$$a = \frac{\text{propagation time}}{\text{transmission time}}$$

Typical values of a range from about 0.01 to 0.1 for LANs and 0.01 to over 1 for MANs. Table 13.2 gives some sample values for a bus topology. In computing a, keep in mind that the maximum propagation time on a broadband network is double the length of the longest path from the head-end, plus the delay, if any, at the headend. For baseband bus and ring networks, repeater delays must be included in propagation time.

The parameter a determines an upper bound on the utilization of a local network. Consider a perfectly efficient access mechanism that allows only one transmission at a time. As soon as one transmission is over, another node begins transmitting. Furthermore, the transmission is pure data—no overhead bits. (*Note:* These conditions are very close to being met in a digital switch but not, alas, in LANs and MANs.) What is the maximum possible utilization of the network? It can be expressed as the ratio of total throughput of the system to the capacity or bandwidth:

$$U = \frac{\text{throughput}}{R} = \frac{L/(\text{propagation} + \text{transmission time})}{R} \qquad (13.1)$$

$$= \frac{L/(d/V + L/R)}{R} = \frac{1}{1 + a}$$

So, utilization varies inversely with a. This can be grasped intuitively by studying Figure 13.2. This figure shows a baseband bus with two stations as far apart as possible (worst case) that take turns sending frames. If we normalize time such that the frame transmission time = 1, then a = propagation time. The sequence of events can be expressed as follows:

1. A station begins transmission at t_0.
2. Reception begins at $t_0 + a$.
3. Transmission is completed at $t_0 + 1$.
4. Reception ends at $t_0 + 1 + a$.
5. The other station begins transmitting.

Event 2 occurs *after* event 3 if $a > 1.0$. In any case, the total time for one "turn" is $1 + a$, but the transmission time is only 1, for a utilization of $1/(1 + a)$.

TABLE 13.2   Values of *a*

Data Rate (Mbps)	Packet Size (bits)	Cable Length (km)	*a*
1	100	1	0.05
1	1,000	10	0.05
1	100	10	0.5
10	100	1	0.5
10	1,000	1	0.05
10	1,000	10	0.5
10	10,000	10	0.05
50	10,000	1	0.025
50	100	1	2.5

The same effect can be seen to apply to a ring network in Figure 13.3. Here we assume that one station transmits and then waits to receive its own transmission before any other station transmits. The identical sequence of events outlined above applies.

Equation (13.1) is plotted in Figure 13.4. The implications for throughput are shown in Figure 13.5. As offered load increases, throughput remains equal to offered load up to the full capacity of the network [when $S = G = 1/(1 + a)$], and then remains at $S = 1/(1 + a)$ as load increases.

So we can say that an upper bound on the utilization or efficiency of a LAN or MAN is $1/(1 + a)$, regardless of the medium access protocol used. Two caveats: First, this assumes that the maximum propagation time is incurred on each transmission. Second, it assumes that only one transmission may occur at a time. These assumptions are not always true; nevertheless, the formula $1/(1 + a)$ is usually a valid upper bound, because the overhead of the medium access protocol more than makes up for the lack of validity of these assumptions.

The overhead is unavoidable. Frames must include address and synchronization bits. There is administrative overhead for controlling the protocol. In addition, there are forms of overhead peculiar to one or more of the protocols. We highlight these briefly for the most important protocols:

- *Contention protocols (ALOHA, S-ALOHA, CSMA, CSMA/CD):* time wasted due to collisions; need for acknowledgment frames. S-ALOHA requires that slot size equals transmission plus maximum propagation time.
- *Token bus:* time waiting for token if logically intervening stations have no data to send; token transmission; acknowledgment frames.
- *Token ring:* time waiting for token if intervening stations have no data to send.

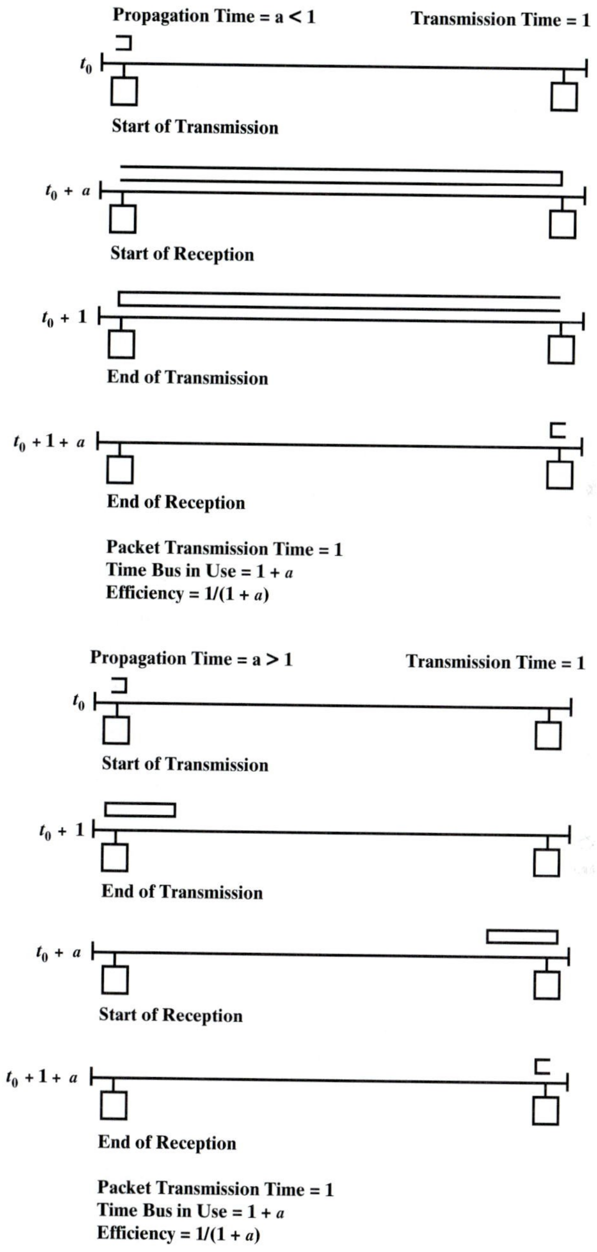

Propagation Time = a < 1   Transmission Time = 1

t_0

Start of Transmission

$t_0 + a$

Start of Reception

$t_0 + 1$

End of Transmission

$t_0 + 1 + a$

End of Reception

Packet Transmission Time = 1
Time Bus in Use = 1 + a
Efficiency = 1/(1 + a)

Propagation Time = a > 1   Transmission Time = 1

t_0

Start of Transmission

$t_0 + 1$

End of Transmission

$t_0 + a$

Start of Reception

$t_0 + 1 + a$

End of Reception

Packet Transmission Time = 1
Time Bus in Use = 1 + a
Efficiency = 1/(1 + a)

FIGURE 13.2   Effect of a on Utilization: Baseband Bus

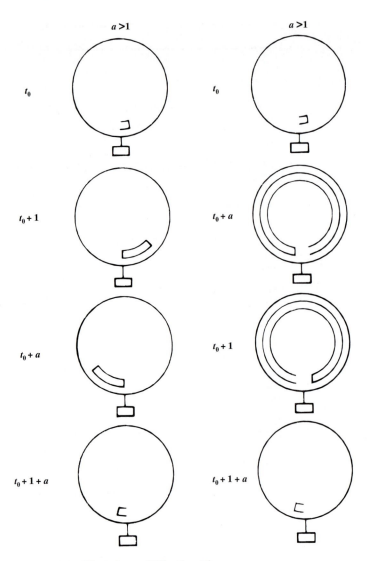

FIGURE 13.3 Effect of *a* on Utilization: Ring

- *Explicit reservation:* reservation transmission, acknowledgments.
- *Implicit reservation:* overhead of protocol used to establish reservation, acknowledgments.

There are two distinct effects here. One is that the efficiency or utilization of a channel decreases as *a* increases. This, of course, affects throughput. The other effect is that the overhead attributable to a protocol wastes bandwidth and hence reduces effective utilization and effective

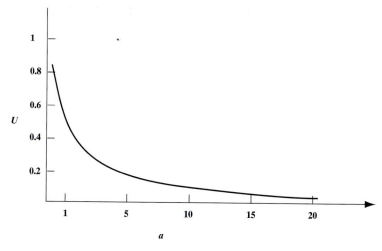

FIGURE 13.4   Utilization as a Function of *a*

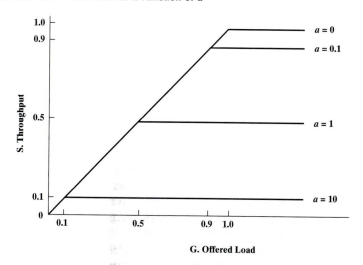

FIGURE 13.5   Effect of *a* on Throughput

throughput. By and large, we can think of these two effects as independent and additive. However, we shall see that, for contention protocols, there is a strong interaction such that the overhead of these protocols increases as a function of *a*.

In any case it would seem desirable to keep *a* as low as possible. Looking back to the defining formula, for a fixed network, *a* can be reduced by increasing frame size. This will be useful only if the length of messages produced by a station is an integral multiple of the frame size (excluding overhead bits). Otherwise, the large frame size is itself a source of waste. Furthermore, a large frame size increases the delay for other stations. This leads us to the next topic: the various factors that affect LAN/MAN performance.

Factors That Affect Performance

We list here those factors that affect the performance of a LAN or a MAN. We are concerned here with that part which is independent of the attached devices—those factors that are exclusively under the control of the local network designer. The chief factors are:

- Capacity
- Propagation delay
- Number of bits per frame
- Local network protocols
- Offered load
- Number of stations

The first three terms have already been discussed; they determine the value of a.

Next are the local network protocols: physical, medium access, and link. The physical layer is not likely to be much of a factor; generally, it can keep up with transmissions and receptions with little delay. The link layer will add some overhead bits to each frame and some administrative overhead, such as virtual circuit management and acknowledgments. This leaves the medium access layer, which can have a significant effect on network performance. Sections 13.2 and 13.3 are devoted to this topic.

We can think of the first three factors listed above as characterizing the network; they are generally treated as constants or givens. The local network protocol is the focus of the design effort—the choice that must be made. The next two factors, offered load and the number of stations, concerned with determining performance as a function of these two variables. Note that these two variables must be treated separately. Certainly, it is true that for a fixed offered load per station, the total offered load increases as the number of stations increases. The same increase could be achieved by keeping the number of stations fixed but increasing the offered load per station. However, as we shall see, the network performance will be different for these two cases.

One factor that was not listed above: the error rate of the channel. An error in a frame transmission necessitates a retransmission. Because the error rates on local networks are so low, this is not likely to be a significant factor.

13.2

LAN PERFORMANCE

A considerable amount of work has been done on the analysis of the performance of various LAN protocols for bus/tree and ring. This section is limited to summarizing the results for the protocols discussed in Chapter 5, those protocols that are most common for LANs.

We begin by presenting an easily used technique for quickly establishing bounds on performance. Often, this back-of-the-envelope approach is adequate for system sizing.

Next, a comparison of the three protocols standardized by IEEE 802 (CSMA/CD, token bus, token ring) is presented. These three protocols are likely to dominate the market and an insight into their comparative performance is needed.

We then look more closely at contention protocols and devote more time here to the derivation of results. This process should give the reader a feeling for the assumptions that must be made and the limitations of the results. More time is spent on the contention protocols because we wish to understand their inherent instability. As we shall see, the basis of this instability is a positive feedback mechanism that behaves poorly under heavy load.

Bounds on Performance

The purpose of this section is to present a remarkably simple technique for determining bounds on the performance of a LAN. Although a considerable amount of work has been done on developing detailed analytic and simulation models of the performance of various LAN protocols, much of this work is suspect because of the restrictive assumptions made. Furthermore, even if the models were valid, they provide a level of resolution not needed by the local network designer.

A common-sense argument should clarify this point. In any LAN or MAN, there are three regions of operation, based on the magnitude of the offered load:

1. A region of low delay through the network, where the capacity is more than adequate to handle the load offered.

2. A region of high delay, where the network becomes a bottleneck. In this region, relatively more time is spent controlling access to the network and less in actual data transmission compared to the low-delay region.

3. A region of unbounded delay, where the offered load exceeds the total capacity of the system.

This last region is easily identified. For example, consider the following network:

- Capacity = 1 Mbps
- Number of stations = 1000
- Frame size = 1000 bits

If, on average, each station generates data at a rate exceeding 1 frame per second, then the total offered load exceeds 1 Mbps. The delay at each station will build up and up without bound.

The third region is clearly to be avoided. But almost always, the designer will wish to avoid the second region as well. The second region implies an inefficient use to the network. Further, a sudden surge of data while in the second region would cause corresponding increases in the already high delay. In the first region, the network is not a bottleneck, and will contribute typically only a small amount to the end-to-end delay.

Thus the crucial question is: What region will the network operate in, based on projected load and network characteristics? The third region is easily identified and avoided; it is the boundary between the first two regions that must be identified. If the network operates below that boundary, it should not cause a communications bottleneck. If it operates above the boundary, there is reason for concern and perhaps redesign. Now, the issue is: How precisely do we need to know the boundary? The load on the network will vary over time and can only be estimated. Because the load estimates are unlikely to be precise, it is not necessary to know exactly where that boundary is. If a good approximation for the boundary can be developed, then the network can be sized so that the estimated load is well below the boundary. In the example just described, the estimated load is 1 Mbps. If the capacity of the LAN is such that the boundary is approximately 4 Mbps, the designer can be reasonably sure that the network will not be a bottleneck.

With the above points in mind, we present a technique for estimating performance bounds, based on the approach taken by the IEEE 802 committee [STUC85]. To begin, let us ignore the medium access control protocol and develop bounds for throughput and delay as a function of the number of active stations. Four quantities are needed:

T_{idle} = the mean time that a station is idle between transmission attempts: the station has no messages awaiting transmission

T_{msg} = the time required to transmit a message once medium access is gained

T_{delay} = the mean delay from the time a station has a packet to transmit until completion of transmission; includes queueing time and transmission time

THRU = mean total throughput on the network of messages per unit time

We assume that there are N active stations, each with the same load-generating requirements. To find an upper bound on total throughput, consider the ideal case in which there is no queueing delay: each station transmits when it is ready. Hence each station alternates between idle and transmission with a throughput of $1/(T_{idle} + T_{msg})$. The maximum possible throughput is just the summation of the throughputs of all N stations:

$$\text{THRU} \leq \frac{N}{T_{idle} + T_{msg}} \tag{13.2}$$

This upper bound increases as N increases, but is reasonable only up to the point of raw capacity of the network, which can be expressed

$$\text{THRU} \leq \frac{1}{T_{msg}} \tag{13.3}$$

The breakpoint between these two bounds occurs at

$$\frac{N}{T_{idle} + T_{msg}} = \frac{1}{T_{msg}} \tag{13.4}$$

$$N = \frac{T_{idle} + T_{msg}}{T_{msg}}$$

This breakpoint defines two regions of operation. With the number of stations below the breakpoint, the system is not generating enough load to utilize fully system capacity. However, above the breakpoint, the network is saturated: it is fully utilized and is not able to satisfy the demands of the attached stations.

To see the reasonableness of this breakpoint, consider that the capacity of the network is $1/T_{msg}$. For example, if it takes 1 µs to transmit a message, the data rate is 10^6 messages per second. The amount of traffic being generated by N stations is $N/(T_{idle} + T_{msg})$. If the traffic exceeds the network's capacity, messages get backlogged and delay increases. Note also that traffic increases either by increasing the number of stations (N) or increasing the rate at which stations transmit messages (reduce T_{idle}).

These same considerations allow us to place a lower bound on delay. Clearly,

$$T_{delay} \geq T_{msg} \tag{13.5}$$

Now, consider that at any load the following relationship holds:

$$\text{THRU} = \frac{N}{T_{idle} + T_{delay}} \tag{13.6}$$

since $1/(T_{idle} + T_{delay})$ is the throughput of each station. Combining (13.3) and (13.6) we have

$$T_{delay} \geq NT_{msg} - T_{idle}$$

The breakpoint calculation, combining (13.5) and the equation above, yields the same result as before (see Figure 13.6). Keep in mind that these bounds are asymptotes of the true delay and throughput curves. The breakpoint delimits two regions. Below the breakpoint, capacity is underutilized and delay is low. Above the breakpoint, capacity saturates and delay blows up. In actuality, the changes are gradual rather than abrupt.

Bounds on the other side are easily found. The delay would be maximized if all N stations had a message to transmit simultaneously:

$$T_{\text{delay}} \leq NT_{\text{msg}}$$

Combining with (13.6) gives us

$$\text{THRU} \geq \frac{N}{T_{\text{idle}} + NT_{\text{msg}}}$$

These bounds give one a rough idea of the behavior of a system. They allow one to do a simple back-of-the-envelope calculation to determine if a proposed system is within reasonable bounds. If the answer is no, much analysis and grief may be saved. If yes, the analyst must dig deeper.

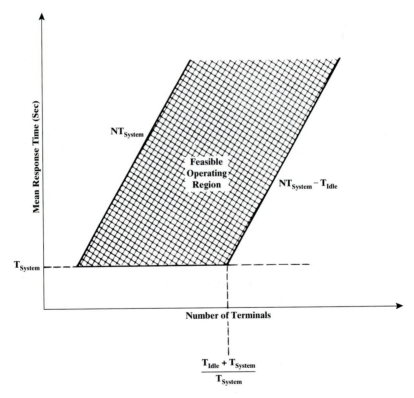

FIGURE 13.6   Feasible Operating Region, Zero-Overhead System

Two examples should clarify the use of these equations. First, consider a workstation attached to a 1-Mbps local network that generates, on average, three messages per minute, with messages averaging 500 bits. With message transmission time equal to 500 µs, the mean idle time is 20 s. The breakpoint number of stations is, roughly,

$$N = \frac{20}{500 \times 10^{-6}} = 40,000 \text{ stations}$$

If the number of stations is much less than this, say 1000, congestion should not be a problem. If it is much more, say 100,000, congestion may be a problem.

Second, consider a set of stations that generates PCM digitized voice packets on a 10-Mbps local network. Data are generated at the rate of 64 kbps. For 0.1-s packets, we have a transmission time per packet of 640 µs. Thus

$$N = \frac{0.1}{640 \times 10^{-6}} = 156 \text{ stations}$$

Generally, we would not expect all voice stations (telephones) to be active at one time; perhaps one-fourth is a reasonable estimate, so the breakpoint is around 600 stations.

Note that in both these examples, we have very quickly arrived at a first-order sizing of the system with no knowledge of the protocol. All that is needed is the load generated per station and the capacity of the network.

The calculations above are based on a system with no overhead. They provide bounds for a system with perfect scheduling. One way to account for overhead is to replace T_{msg} with T_{sys}, where the latter quantity includes an estimate of the overhead per packet. This is done in Figure 9.6.

A more accurate though still rough handle on performance can be had by considering the protocol involved. We develop the results for token passing. This protocol, for bus or ring, has the following characteristics:

- Stations are given the opportunity to transmit in a fixed cyclical sequence.
- At each opportunity, a station may transmit one message.
- Frames may be of fixed or variable length.
- Preemption is not allowed.

Some additional terms are needed:

$R(K)$ = mean throughput rate (messages/second) of station K
T_{over} = total overhead (seconds) in one cycle of the N stations
C = duration (seconds) of a cycle
$UTIL(K)$ = utilization of the network due to station K

Let us begin by assuming that each station always has messages to transmit; the system is never idle. The fraction of time that the network is busy handling requests from station K is just

$$\text{UTIL}(K) = R(K)T_{\text{msg}}(K)$$

To keep up with the work, the system must not be presented with a load greater than its capacity:

$$\sum_{K=1}^{N} \text{UTIL}(K) = \sum_{K=1}^{N} R(K)T_{\text{msg}}(K) \le 1$$

Now consider the overhead in the system, which is the time during a cycle required to pass the token and perform other maintenance functions. Clearly,

$$C = T_{\text{over}} + \sum_{K=1}^{N} T_{\text{msg}}(K)$$

From this we can deduce that

$$R(K) = \frac{1}{C} = \frac{1}{T_{\text{over}} + \sum_{K=1}^{N} T_{\text{msg}}(K)}$$

Now, let us assume that the medium is always busy but that some stations may be idle. This line of reasoning will lead us to the desired bounds on throughput and delay. Since we assume that the network is never idle, the fraction of time the system spends on overhead and transmission must sum to unity:

$$\frac{T_{\text{over}}}{C} + \sum_{K=1}^{N} R(K)T_{\text{msg}}(K) = 1$$

Thus

$$C = \frac{T_{\text{over}}}{1 - \sum_{K=1}^{N} R(K)T_{\text{msg}}(K)}$$

Note that the duration of a cycle is proportional to the overhead; doubling the mean overhead time should double the cycle time for a fixed load. This result may not be intuitively obvious; the reader is advised to work out a few examples.

With C known, we can place an upper bound on the throughput of any one source:

$$R(J) \le \frac{1}{C} = \frac{1 - \sum_{K=1}^{N} R(K)T_{\text{msg}}(K)}{T_{\text{over}}} \tag{13.7}$$

Now let us assume that all sources are identical: $R(K) = R$, $T_{msg}(K) = T_{msg}$. Then (13.7) reduces to

$$R \le \frac{1 - NRT_{msg}}{T_{over}}$$

Solving for R yields

$$R < \frac{1}{T_{over} + NT_{msg}}$$

But, by definition, $R = 1/(T_{delay} + T_{idle})$, so we can express

$$T_{delay} = \frac{1}{R} - T_{idle}$$

$$T_{delay} \ge T_{over} + NT_{msg} - T_{idle}$$

In practice, T_{over} may consist of some fixed amount of time C_0 for each cycle plus an amount C_1 for each station that receives the token. These numbers will differ for token ring and token bus:

$$T_{delay} \ge C_0 + N(T_{msg} + C_1) - T_{idle}$$

We also have the inequality of (9.5) and can solve for the breakpoint:

$$N = \frac{T_{msg} + T_{idle} - C_0}{T_{msg} + C_1} \tag{13.8}$$

Figure 13.7 depicts the delay-station plot, showing the two regions. Note that the slope of the line in the heavily loaded region is $T_{msg} + C_1$.

A similar analysis can be carried out for CSMA/CD. Figure 13.8 is a comparison developed in [STUC85]. The absolute positions of the various policies depend on specific assumptions about overhead and, in the case of CSMA/CD, the value of a. But the relative positions are generally true: under lightly loaded conditions CSMA/CD has a shorter delay time, but the protocol breaks down more rapidly under increasing load.

Comparative Performance of Token Passing and CSMA/CD

The purpose of this section is to give the reader some insight into the relative performance of the most important LAN protocols: CSMA/CD, token bus, and token ring. We begin with simplified models that highlight the main points of comparison. Following this, a careful analysis performed by the IEEE 802 committee is reported.

For the models, we assume a local network with N active stations. Our purpose is to estimate the maximum throughput achievable on the LAN. For this purpose, we assume that each station is always prepared to send a frame.

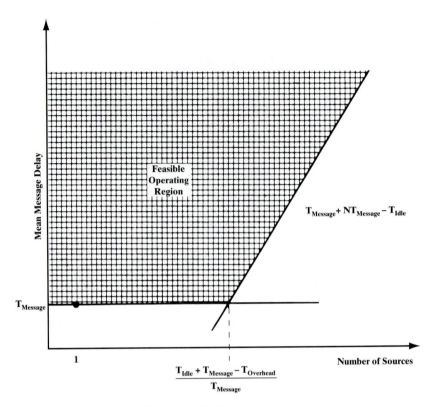

FIGURE 13.7   **Bounds on Token-Passing Performance**

First, let us consider token ring. Time on the ring will alternate between data frame transmission and token passing. Refer to a single instance of a data frame followed by a token as a cycle and define:

C average time for one cycle
DF average time to transmit a data frame
TF average time to pass a token

It should be clear that the average cycle rate is just $1/C = 1/(DF + TF)$. Intuitively,

$$S = \frac{DF}{DF + TF} \tag{13.9}$$

That is, the throughput, normalized to system capacity, is just the fraction of time that is spent transmitting data.

Refer now to Figure 13.3; time is normalized such that frame transmission time equals 1 and propagation time equals a. For the case of $a < 1$, a station transmits a frame at time t_0, receives the leading edge of its own frame at $t_0 + a$, and completes transmission at $t_0 + 1$. The station then emits

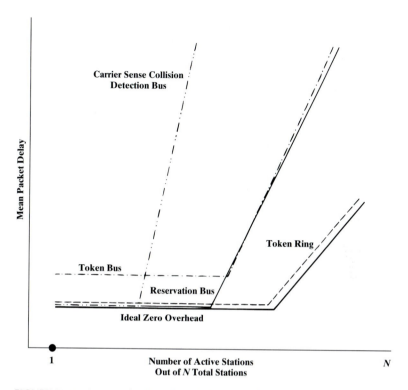

FIGURE 13.8   Comparative Bounds on LAN Protocols

a token, which takes time a/N to reach the next station (assuming equally spaced stations). Thus one cycle takes $1 + a/N$ and the transmission time is 1. So $S = 1/(1 + a/N)$.

For $a > 1$, the reasoning is slightly different. A station transmits at t_0, completes transmission at $t_0 + 1$, and receives the leading edge of its frame at $t_0 + a$. At that point, it is free to emit a token, which takes a time a/N to reach the next station. The cycle time is therefore $a + a/N$ and $S = 1/[a(1 + 1/N)]$. Summarizing, we have

$$\text{Token: } S = \begin{cases} \dfrac{1}{1 + a/N} & a < 1 \\[2mm] \dfrac{1}{a(1 + 1/N)} & a > 1 \end{cases} \tag{13.10}$$

The reasoning above applies equally well to token bus, where we assume that the logical ordering is the same as the physical ordering and that token-passing time is therefore a/N.

Consider time on the medium to be organized into slots whose length is twice the end-to-end propagation delay. This is a convenient way to view the activity on the medium; the slot time is the maximum time, from the start of transmission, required to detect a collision. Again, assume that there are N active stations, each generating the same load. Clearly, if each station always has a packet to transmit, it does, so there will be nothing but collisions on the line. Therefore, we assume that each station restrains itself to transmitting during an available slot with probability p.

Time on the medium consists of two types of intervals. First is a transmission interval, which lasts $1/2a$ slots. Second is a contention interval, which is a sequence of slots with either a collision or no transmission in each slot. The throughput is just the proportion of time spent in transmission intervals [similar to the reasoning for equation (13.1)].

To determine the average length of a contention interval, we begin by computing A, the probability that exactly one station attempts a transmission in a slot and therefore acquires the medium. This is just the binomial probability that any one station attempts to transmit and the others do not:

$$A = \left(\frac{N}{1}\right)p^1(1-p)^{N-1}$$

$$= Np(1-p)^{N-1}$$

This function takes on a maximum over p when $p = 1/N$:

$$A = \left(1 - \frac{1}{N}\right)^{N-1}$$

Why are we interested in the maximum? Well, we want to calculate the maximum throughput of the medium. It should be clear that this will be achieved if we maximize the probability of successful seizure of the medium. During periods of heavy usage, a station should restrain its offered load to $1/N$. (This assumes that each station knows the value of N; in order to derive an expression for maximum possible throughput, we live with this assumption.) On the other hand, during periods of light usage, maximum utilization cannot be achieved because G is too low; this region is not of interest here.

Now we can estimate the mean length of a contention interval, w, in slots:

$$E[w] = \sum_{i=1}^{\infty} i \cdot \Pr\ [i \text{ slots in a row with a collision or no}$$

transmission followed by a slot with one transmission]

$$= \sum_{i=1}^{\infty} i\,(1-A)^i A$$

The summation converges to

$$E[w] = \frac{1-A}{A}$$

We can now determine the maximum utilization, which is just the length of a transmission interval as a proportion of a cycle consisting of a transmission and a contention interval.

$$\text{CSMA/CD: } S = \frac{1/2a}{1/2a + \dfrac{1-A}{A}} = \frac{1}{1 + 2a \dfrac{1-A}{A}} \tag{13.11}$$

Figure 13.9 shows normalized throughput as a function of a for various values of N and for both token passing and CSMA/CD. For both protocols, throughput declines as a increases. This is to be expected. But the dramatic difference between the two protocols is seen in Figure 13.10, which shows throughput as a function of N. Token-passing performance actually improves as a function of N, because less time is spent in token passing. Conversely, the performance of CSMA/CD decreases because of the increased likelihood of collision.

It is interesting to note the asymptomatic value of S as N increases. For token:

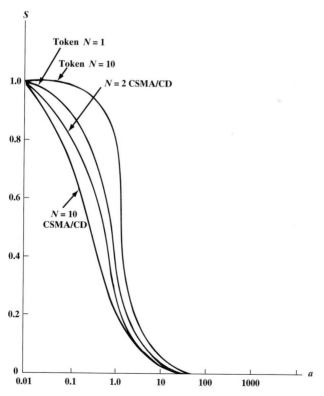

FIGURE 13.9   **Throughput as a Function of _a_ for Token Passing and CSMA/CD**

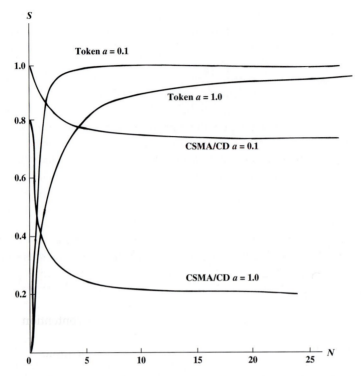

FIGURE 13.10 **Throughput as a Function of *N* for Token Passing and CSMA/CD**

$$\text{Token: } \lim_{N \to \infty} S = \begin{cases} 1 & a < 1 \\ \dfrac{1}{a} & a > 1 \end{cases}$$

For CSMA/CD, we need to know that $\lim_{N \to \infty}(1 - 1/N)^{N-1} = 1/e$. Then

$$\text{CSMA/CD: } \lim_{N \to \infty} S = \frac{1}{1 + 3.44a}$$

Continuing this example, it is relatively easy to derive an expression for delay for token passing. Once a station (station 1) transmits, it must wait for the following events to occur before it can transmit again:

- Station 1 transmits token to station 2.
- Station 2 transmits data frame.
- Station 2 transmits token to station 3.
- Station transmits data frame.

-
-
-
-

- Station $N - 1$ transmits token to station N.
- Station N transmits data frame.
- Station N transmits token to station 1.

Thus the delay consists of $(N - 1)$ cycles plus a/N, the token passing time. We have

$$\text{Token: } D = \begin{cases} N + a - 1 & a < 1 \\ aN & a > 1 \end{cases} \qquad (13.12)$$

Thus, delay increases linearly with load, and for a fixed number of stations delay is constant and finite even if all stations always have something to send. The delay for CSMA/CD is more difficult to express and depends on the exact nature of the protocol (persistence, retry policy). In general, we can say that the delay grows without bound as the system becomes saturated. As N increases, there are more collisions and longer contention intervals. Individual frames must make more attempts to achieve successful transmission. We explore this behavior further in the next station.

We now report the results of a deeper analysis done for the IEEE 802 committee [STUC85]. The analysis is based on considering not only mean values but second moments of delay and message length. Two cases of message arrival statistics are employed. In the first, only 1 station out of 100 has messages to transmit and is always ready to transmit. In such a case, one would hope that the network would not be the bottleneck, but could easily keep up with one station. In the second case, 100 stations out of 100 always have messages to transmit. This represents an extreme of congestion and one would expect that the network may be a bottleneck.

The results are shown in Figure 13.11. It shows the actual data transmission rate versus the transmission speed on a 2-km bus. Note that the abscissa is not offered load but the actual capacity of the medium. The 1 station or 100 stations provide enough input to utilize the network fully. Hence these plots are a measure of maximum potential utilization. Three systems are examined: token ring with a 1-bit latency per station, token bus, and CSMA/CD. The analysis yields the following conclusions:

- For the given parameters, the smaller the mean frame length, the greater the difference in maximum mean throughput rate between token passing and CSMA/CD. This reflects the strong dependence of CSMA/CD on a.
- Token ring is the least sensitive to workload.

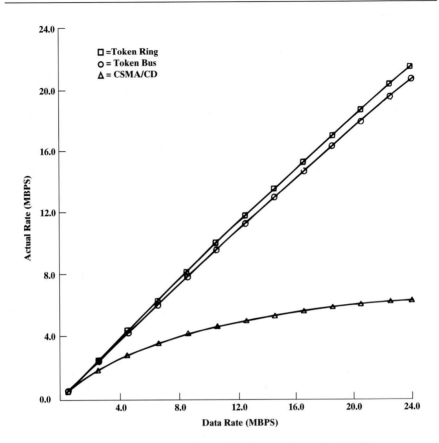

FIGURE 13.11A   Maximum Potential Data Rate for LAN Protocols; 2000 bits per packet, 100 stations active out of 100 stations total

- CSMA/CD offers the shortest delay under light load, while it is most sensitive under heavy load to the workload.

Note also that in the case of a single station transmitting, token bus is significantly less efficient than the other two protocols. This is so because the assumption is made that the propagation delay is longer than for token ring, and that the delay in token processing is greater than for token ring.

Another phenomenon of interest is seen most clearly in Figure 13.11b. For a CSMA/CD system under these conditions, the maximum effective throughput at 5 Mbps is only about 1.25 Mbps. If the expected load is, say, 0.75 Mbps, this configuration may be perfectly adequate. If, however, the load is expected to grow to 2 Mbps, raising the network data rate to 10 Mbps or even 20 Mbps will not accommodate the increase! The same conclusion, less precisely, can be drawn from the model presented at the beginning of this section.

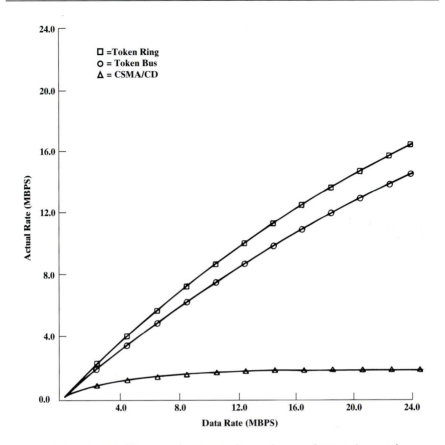

FIGURE 13.11B   500 bits per packet, 100 stations active out of 100 stations total

As with all the other results presented in this chapter, these depend on the nature of the assumptions made and do not reflect accurately the nature of the real-world load. Nevertheless, they show in a striking manner the nature of the instability of CSMA/CD and the ability of token ring and token bus to continue to perform well in the face of overload conditions.

Behavior of Contention Protocols

The preceding section revealed that CSMA/CD performs less well than token passing under increasing load or increasing a. This is characteristic of all contention protocols. In this section we explore this subject in more detail for the interested reader. To do this, we present results based on the assumption that there is an infinite number of stations. This may strike the reader as an absurd tactic, but, in fact, it leads to analytically tractable equations that are, up to a point, very close to reality. We will define that point shortly. For now, we state the infinite-source assumption precisely: there is an infinite

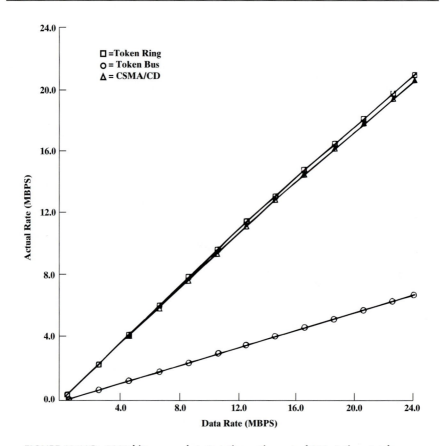

FIGURE 13.11C   2000 bits per packet, 1 station active out of 100 stations total

number of stations, each generating an infinitely small rate of frames such that the total number of frames generated per unit of time is finite.

The following additional assumptions are made:

1. All frames are of constant length. In general, such frames give better average throughput and delay performance than do variable-length frames. In some analyses, an exponential distribution of frame length is used.
2. The channel is noise-free.
3. Frames do not collect at individual stations; that is, a station transmits each frame before the next arrives, hence $I = S$. This assumption weakens at higher loads, where stations are faced with increasing delays for each packet.

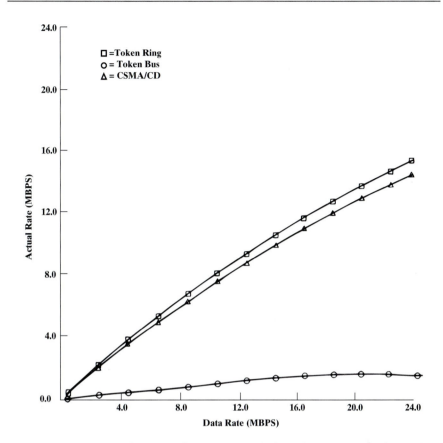

FIGURE 13.11D   500 bits per packet, 1 station active out of 100 stations total

4. G, the offered load, is Poisson distributed.
5. For CSMA/CD, no time is lost for carrier sense and collision detection.

These assumptions do not accurately reflect any actual system. For example, higher-order moments or even the entire probability distribution of frame length or G may be needed for accurate results. These assumptions do provide analytic tractability, enabling the development of closed-form expressions for performance. Thus they provide a common basis for comparing a number of protocols and they allow the development of results that give insight into the behavior of systems. In the following discussion, we shall cite simulation and measurement studies that indicate that these insights are valid.

Let us look first at the simplest contention protocol, pure ALOHA. Traffic, of course, is generated at so many frames per second. It is convenient to normalize this to the frame transmission time; then we can view S

as the number of frames generated per frame time. Since the capacity of the channel is one frame per frame time, S also has the usual meaning of throughput as a fraction of capacity.

The total traffic on the channel will consist of new frames plus frames that must be retransmitted because of collision:

$$G = S$$
$$+ \text{(number of retransmitted frames per frame transmission time)}$$

Now, a frame must be retransmitted if it suffers a collision. Thus we can express the rate of retransmissions as $G \cdot \Pr$ [individual frame suffers a collision]. Note that we must use G rather than S in this expression. To determine the probability of collision, consider as a worst case two stations, A and B, as far apart as possible on a bus (i.e., a normalized distance a, as in Figure 13.2). A frame transmitted by station A will suffer a collision if B begins transmission prior to A but within a time $1 + a$ of the beginning of A's transmission, or if B begins transmission after A within a time period $1 + a$ of the beginning of A's transmission. Thus the vulnerable period is of length $2(1 + a)$.

We have assumed that G is Poisson distributed. For a Poisson process with rate λ, the probability of an arrival in a period of time t is $1 - e^{-\lambda t}$. Thus the probability of an arrival during the vulnerable period is $1 - e^{-2(1 + a)G}$. Therefore, we have

$$G = S + G[1 - e^{-2(1 + a)G}]$$

So

$$\text{ALOHA: } S = Ge^{-2(1 + a)G} \qquad (13.13)$$

This derivation assumes that G is Poisson, which is not the case even for I Poisson. However, studies indicate that this is a good approximation [SCHW77]. Also, deeper analysis indicates that the infinite population assumption results closely approximate finite population results at reasonably small numbers—say, 50 or more stations [KLEI76]. This is also true for CSMA and CSMA/CD systems [TOBA80, TOBA82].

Another way of deriving (13.13) is to note that S/G is the fraction of offered frames transmitted successfully, which is just the probability that for each frame, no additional frames arrive during the vulnerable period, which is $e^{-2(1 + a)G}$.

Throughput for slotted ALOHA is also easily calculated. All frames begin transmission on a slot boundary. Thus the number of frames transmitted during a slot time is equal to the number that was generated during the previous slot and awaits transmission. To avoid collisions between frames in adjacent slots, the slot length must equal frame transmission time plus propagation delay (i.e., $1 + a$). Thus the probability that an individual frame suffers collision is $1 - e^{-(1 + a)G}$. Thus we have

$$\text{S-ALOHA: } S = Ge^{-(1+a)G} \qquad (13.14)$$

Differentiating (13.13) and (13.14) with respect to G, the maximum possible values for S are $1/[2e(1 + a)$ and $1/[e(1 + a)]$, respectively. These results differ from those reported in many accounts of local network performance, which ignore a and have $S = Ge^{-2G}$ for ALOHA and $S = Ge^{-G}$ for slotted ALOHA. The discrepancy arises because these formulas were originally derived for satellite channels, for which they are valid, but are often compared with CSMA-type protocols derived for local networks. The results that correspond to $a = 0$ are plotted in Figure 13.12. For small values of $a(a \leq 0.01)$, these figures are adequate; but for comparison with CSMA protocols, equations (13.13) and (13.14) should be used.

Figure 13.12 provides insight into the nature of the instability problem with contention protocols. As offered load increases, so does throughput until, beyond its maximum value, throughput actually declines as G increases. This is because there is an increased frequency of collisions: more frames are offered, but fewer successfully escape collision. Worse, this situation may persist even if the input to the system drops to zero! Consider: For high G, virtually all offered frames are retransmissions and virtually none get through. So, even if no new frames are generated, the system will remain occupied in an unsuccessful attempt to clear the backlog; the effective capacity of the system is virtually zero. Thus, even in a moderately loaded system, a temporary burst of work could move the network into the high-collision region permanently. This type of instability is not possible with the noncontention protocols.

Delay is more difficult to calculate, but the following reasoning gives a good approximation. We define delay as the time interval from when a node is ready to transmit a frame until when it is successfully received. This delay is simply the sum of queueing delay, propagation delay, and trans-

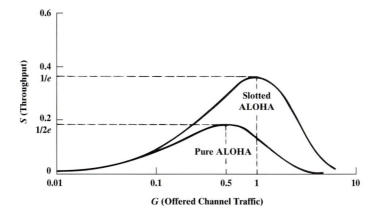

FIGURE 13.12   Performance of ALOHA, S-ALOHA with $a = 0$

mission time. In ALOHA, the queueing delay is 0; that is, a node transmits immediately when it has a frame to transmit. However, because of collisions, we may consider the queueing delay time to be the total time consumed prior to successful transmission (i.e., the total time spent in unsuccessful transmissions). To get at this, we need to know the expected number of transmissions per frame. A little thought shows that this is simply G/S. So the expected number of retransmissions per frame is just $G/S - 1 = e^{2(1 + a)G} - 1$. The delay D can then be expressed as

$$D = [e^{2(1 + a)G} - 1]\delta + a + 1$$

where δ is the average delay for one transmission. A common algorithm used for ALOHA is to retransmit after a time selected from a uniform distribution of from 1 to K frame-transmission times. This minimizes repeated collisions. The average delay is then $(K + 1)/2$. To this, we must add the amount of time a station must wait to determine that its frame was unsuccessful. This is just the time it would take to complete a transmission $(1 + a)$ plus the time it would take for the receiver to generate an acknowledgment (w) plus the propagation time for the acknowledgment to reach the station (a). For simplicity, we assume that acknowledgment packets do not suffer collisions. Thus:

$$\text{ALOHA: } D = [e^{2(1 + a)G} - 1]\left(1 + 2a + w + \frac{K + 1}{2}\right) + a + 1 \qquad (13.15)$$

For S-ALOHA, a similar reasoning obtains. The main difference now is that there is a delay, averaging half a slot time between the time a node is ready to send a frame and the time the next slot begins:

$$\text{S-ALOHA: } D = [e^{(1 + a)G} - 1]\left(1 + 2a + w + \frac{K + 1}{2}\right) + 1.5a + 1.5 \qquad (13.16)$$

These formulas confirm the instability of contention-based protocols under heavy load. As the rate of new frames increases, so does the number of collisions. We can see that both the number of collisions and the average delay grow exponentially with G. Thus there is not only a trade-off between throughput (S) and delay (D), but a third factor enters the trade-off: stability. Figure 13.13 illustrates this point. Figure 13.13a shows that delay increases exponentially with offered load. But Figure 13.13b is perhaps more meaningful. It shows that delay increases with throughput up to the maximum possible throughput. Beyond that point, although throughput declines because of increased numbers of collisions, the delay continues to rise.

It is worth pondering Figures 13.12 and 13.13 to get a better feeling for the behavior of contention channels. Recall that we mentioned that both S and G are derived parameters, and what we would really like to estimate is the actual traffic generated by network devices, the input load I. As long as

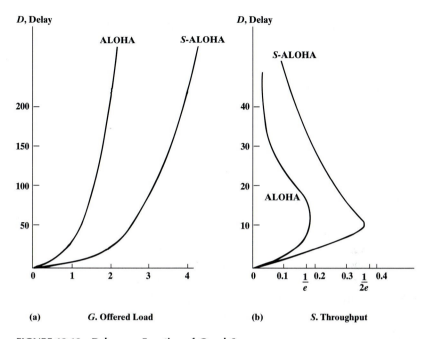

FIGURE 13.13   Delay as a Function of G and S

the input load is less than the maximum potential throughput, $Max_G(S)$, then $I = S$. That is, the throughput of the system equals the input load. Therefore, all frames get through. However, if $I > Max_G(S)$, Figures 13.12 and 13.13 no longer apply. The system cannot transmit frames as fast as they arrive. The result: If I remains above the threshold indefinitely, D goes to infinity, S goes to zero, and G grows without bound.

Figure 13.13b shows that, for a given value of S, there are two possible values of D. How can this be? In both cases, $I = S$, and the system is transmitting all input frames. The explanation is as follows: as the input, $I = S$, approaches the saturation point, the stochastic nature of the input will eventually lead to a period of a high rate of collisions, resulting in decreased throughput and higher frame delays.

Finally, we mention that these results depend critically on the assumptions made. For example, if there is only one station transmitting, then the achievable throughput is 1.0, not 0.18 or 0.37. Indeed, with a single user at a high data rate and a set of other users at very low data rates, utilization approaching 1 can be achieved. However, the delay encountered by the other users is significantly longer than in the homogeneous case. In general, the more unbalanced the source rates, the higher the throughput [KLEI76].

We now turn to the CSMA protocols. A similar line of reasoning can be used to derive closed-form analytic results as is done with ALOHA and S-ALOHA. For derivations, see [BERT92, KLEI76, and SCHW77].

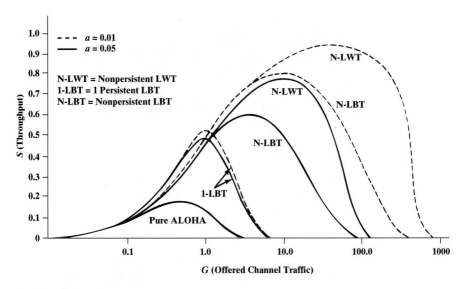

FIGURE 13.14   Throughput for Various Contention Protocols

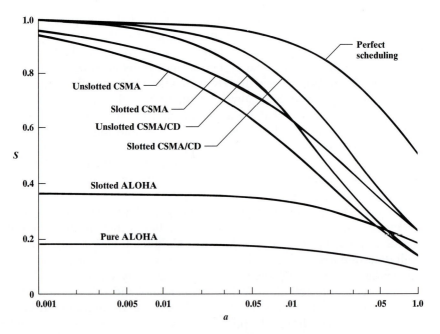

FIGURE 13.15   Maximum Channel Utilization for Various Contention Protocols

Figure 13.14 compares the various contention protocols for $a = 0.01$ and 0.05. Note the dramatic improvement in throughput of the various CSMA schemes over ALOHA. Also note the decline in performance for increased a. This is seen more clearly in Figure 13.15. As expected, the performance of all CSMA schemes declines with increasing a since the period of vulnerability grows. For high enough values of a, say 0.5 to 1.0, the slotted protocols approach S-ALOHA, and the unslotted protocols approach ALOHA. At these values, neither the carrier sense nor the collision detection is of much use. Thus the distributed reservation protocol for MANs in Chapter 12 does not suffer by using S-ALOHA rather than CSMA to contend for reservations.

Figure 13.16 shows delay as a function of throughput. As can be seen, CSMA/CD offers significant delay and throughput improvements over CSMA at $a = 0.05$. As a increases, these protocols converge with each other and with S-ALOHA.

One of the critical assumptions used in deriving all these results is that the number of sources is infinite. The validity of the assumption can be seen in Figure 13.10. Note that for small values of a, the efficiency of the system with a finite number of stations differs little from that achieved as the number of stations grows to infinity. For larger values of a, the differences are more marked. The figure shows that the infinite-population assumption underestimates efficiency but is still a good approximation.

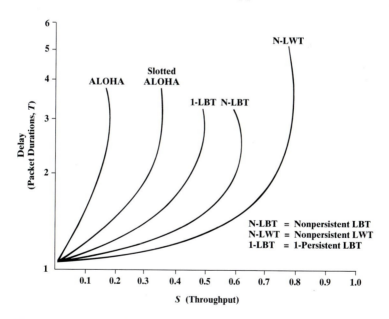

FIGURE 13.16   Delay for Various Contention Protocols

A second assumption that is unrealistic is that of fixed frame sizes. While a local network could enforce fixed frame sizes, this is clearly inefficient if the messages are of variable length. One common situation is to have one long frame size for file transfer and a shorter size for interactive traffic and acknowledgments. Now, as frame length decreases, *a* increases, so if all frames were short, then the utilization would be less than if all frames were long. Presumably, with a mixture of the two traffic types, the efficiency would be somewhere in between. The analysis also showed that only a small percentage of longer frames is sufficient to achieve close to the higher throughput of the case of long frames only. However, this increased throughput is to the detriment of the throughput and delay characteristics of the shorter frames. In effect, they are crowded out.

A final point about the foregoing derivations: all represent analytic models of local network performance. Greater validity can be achieved through simulation, where some of the assumptions may be relaxed, and through actual performance measurement. In general, these efforts tend to confirm the validity of the analytic models. Although not entirely accurate, these models provide a good feel for the behavior of the network.

13.3

MAN PERFORMANCE

There has been considerably less material published on MAN performance than on LAN performance. The principles, of course, remain the same. In this section we look at some of the key performance aspects of FDDI and DQDB and at a comparative study of the two protocols.

FDDI Performance

One of the key performance factors for FDDI is TTRT, the target token rotation time. Recall from Chapter 8 that this parameter, negotiated among all participating stations, defines the expected time between successive sighting of a token by a station when the ring is busy. Since this parameter is set by user action, it is important to understand its effect on performance.

The FDDI standard specifies a number of rules for the selection of TTRT:

1. The token rotation time can be as high as twice the TTRT. Thus a station with synchronous data to transmit may suffer a delay of up to 2 × TTRT. Therefore, a station requiring a guaranteed response time should request a TTRT value of one-half the required response time.

2. Each station has a parameter T_Min, which is the minimum value of TTRT that may be requested. T_Min may be set by station manage-

ment (see Chapter 11) dynamically or may be configured as a default value. The maximum default value of T_Min is 4 ms. That is, if stations are configured with a default value of T_Min, that value may not exceed 4 ms.

3. Each station has a parameter T_Max, which is the maximum value of TTRT that may be requested. T_Max may be set by station management (see Chapter 8) dynamically or may be configured as a default value. The minimum default value of T_Min in basic mode is 165 ms, and the minimum default value in hybrid mode is 670 ms.

Within these constraints, TTRT should be chosen to optimize performance. We now consider some aspects of the effect of TTRT on performance. A simple analytic model for the effect of TTRT has been reported in [JAIN91]. In what follows, we summarize the derivation of this model and the key results.

Consider an FDDI ring with the following parameters:

D = ring latency; total time for a token to circulate the ring in the absence of data traffic

N = number of stations on the ring

T = the negotiated value of TTRT

We will show that the following equations hold:

$$U = \frac{N \times (\text{TTRT} - D)}{(N \times \text{TTRT}) + D} \tag{13.17}$$

$$\text{maximum access delay} = (N - 1) \times \text{TTRT} + 2D \tag{13.18}$$

Let us first demonstrate that this relationship holds for a ring with three stations. Figure 13.17 shows the ring and illustrates a sequence of events. Time proceeds vertically down the page. The token is shown as a thick horizontal line, and a frame transmission is indicated by a thick line along the time axis. We assume that, initially, all three stations are idle until $t + D$, when the three stations suddenly have a large number of asynchronous frames to send. The sequence of events is as follows:

1. $t = 0$. Station S_1 sees the token and resets its token rotation time (TRT). Since the station has no data to send, it does not capture the token, which proceeds around the ring.
2. $t = t_{12}$. Station S_2 resets its TRT and allows the token to pass.
3. $t = t_{13}$. Station S_3 resets its TRT and allows the token to pass.
4. $t = D$. Station S_1 captures the token. Its value of TRT is D, so it can hold the token and transmit data for a time $T - \text{TRT} = T - D$.
5. $t = T$. The token holding timer THT expires at S_1 and it issues a token.

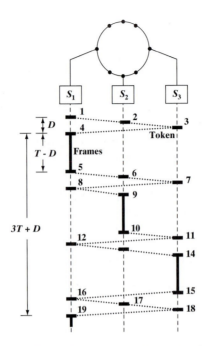

FIGURE 13.17   Sequence of Events for Three-Station FDDI Network

6. $t = T + t_{12}$. Station S_2 observes the token. The elapsed time since its last sighting is T, so it is unable to transmit any asynchronous frames. The token is allowed to pass.

7. $t = T + t_{13}$. Station S_3 must also allow the token to pass.

8. $t = T + D$. Station S_1 must also allow the token to pass.

9. $t = T + D + t_{12}$. Station S_1 captures the token. Its value of TRT is D, so it can hold the token and transmit data for a time $T - \text{TRT} = T - D$.

10. $t = T + D + t_{12} + (T - D) = 2T + t_{12}$. The token holding timer THT expires at S_1 and it issues a token.

The remainder of the steps are easily followed. The illustration ends at $t = 3T + D$. We can see that the system goes through a cycle in which each station can transmit for a total time of $T - D$, and the total elapsed time is $3T + D$. As long as each station has unlimited asynchronous frames to transmit, the cycle will repeat. During each cycle, the total time spent transmitting is $3(T - D)$. During each cycle, each station waits for an interval of $2T + 2D$ after releasing the token. This interval is the maximum access delay; it will be less at lower loads. Thus, for a ring with three active stations, the efficiency and maximum access delay under heavy load are

$$U = \frac{3 \times (T - D)}{(3 \times T) + D}$$

maximum access delay $= (3 - 1) \times T + 2D$

The analysis above can be generalized to N stations. Equations (13.17) and (13.18) can be used to compute the utilization and maximum access delay for any FDDI ring configuration. For example, consider a ring with 16 stations and a total fiber length of 20 km. Light travels along fiber at a speed of 5.085 μs/km, and a typical repeater delay is 1 μs. The ring latency can therefore be calculated as follows:

$$D = (20 \times 5.085) + (16 \times 1) = 0.12 \text{ ms}$$

Assuming a TTRT of 5 ms and all 16 stations active, we have

$$U = \frac{16 \times (5 - 0.12)}{(16 \times 5) + 0.12} = 0.975$$

maximum access delay $= (16 - 1) \times 5 + 2 \times 0.12 = 75.24 \text{ ms}$

Figure 13.18 shows the effect of TTRT on utilization. Three configurations are considered:

- *Typical:* consists of 20 single attachment stations (SASs) on a 4-km ring. This would be sufficient to interconnect a number of LANs and com-

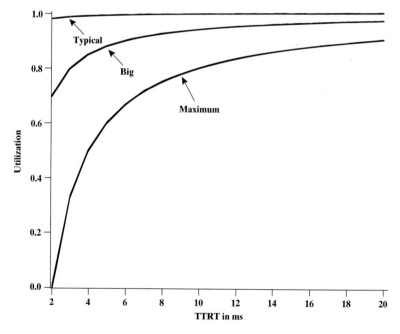

FIGURE 13.18   FDDI Utilization as a Function of TTRT

puters in a single office building. The ring latency for this configuration is about 0.04 ms.

- *Big:* consists of 100 SASs on a 100-km ring. The ring latency for this configuration is about 0.6 ms.
- *Maximum:* consists of 500 dual-attachment, dual-MAC stations (one MAC entity in each direction) on a 200-km ring. The ring latency for this configuration is about 2 ms.

The figure shows that efficiency is low at values close to ring latency and increases as TTRT increases. This is intuitively reasonable: If TTRT is very small, then on many token circulations, many of the stations will have to let the token pass. Note also that beyond a certain point, increases in TTRT bring very little increase in utilization. Of course, as might also be expected, as the utilization of the ring increases, there is increasing congestion and queuing delays for stations to transmit. This effect is shown in Figure 13.19. Thus there is a trade-off in setting TTRT between efficient utilization of the ring and minimizing delay to active stations.

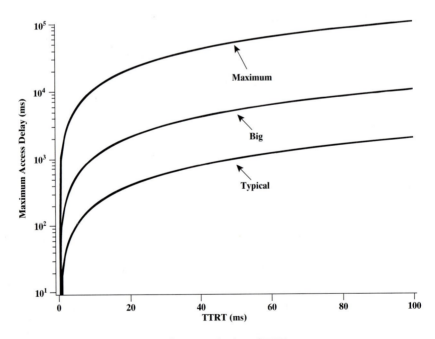

FIGURE 13.19 FDDI Access Delay as a Function of TTRT

DQDB Performance

As with FDDI, there is a key user-settable parameter in DQDB that has a significant effect on performance: the bandwidth balancing modulus. Recall from Chapter 12 that a node without bandwidth balancing may use an empty QA slot if it has placed a reservation and there are no downstream reservations in line ahead of it. With bandwidth balancing, after every BWB_MOD QA segment transmitted, a node must let an extra free QA slot pass, where BWB_MOD is the bandwidth balancing modulus.

To get a feel for the effect of BWB_MOD on performance, let us consider the following set of conditions, which yield maximum subnetwork throughput:

- No station has any PA traffic.
- Every station has QA traffic ready to transmit at all times.
- All QA segments have the same priority.
- All nodes have the same value for BWB_MOD.

Define

γ = throughput of any one node
N = number of nodes
β = value of BWB_MOD

Recall that the maximum throughput of a node is limited by $\beta/(1 + \beta)$. We can express the throughput of a node as the amount of capacity not used by the other nodes, subject to the limitation. Therefore,

$$\gamma = \frac{\beta}{1 + \beta} \times [1 - (N - 1) \times \gamma]$$

Solving for γ gives

$$\gamma = \frac{1}{N + (1/\beta)}$$

Thus the total normalized throughput, or utilization, for a bus with N stations is

$$U = \frac{N}{N + (1/\beta)}$$

Figure 13.20 plots utilization as a function of the number of stations for various values of BWB_MOD. The smaller the value of BWB_MOD, the greater the number of slots that each station will let pass unused. Accordingly, the smaller the value of BWB_MOD, the lower the utilization. On the other hand, increasing the number of stations increases utilization, since there is an increased opportunity for passed slots to be used downstream.

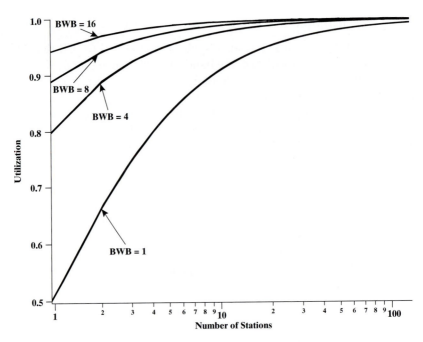

FIGURE 13.20   Effect of Bandwidth Balancing on DQDB Utilization

Comparative Performance of FDDI and DQDB

As yet, little work has been reported on comparing the performance of FDDI and DQDB. As the figures of this section suggest, both schemes are capable of achieving very high levels of utilization. This is important because the high speed and large extent of these networks make efficient utilization difficult to achieve. One of the clearest analyses that has been published is reported in [DRAV91]. Similar but less detailed results are reported in [BURR94, GHAN91].

Figure 13.21 shows the results reported in [DRAV91]. The figures assume a mixed application environment of interactive and bulk file transfer applications, with all stations uniformly loaded with 20 percent of the load from the file transfer application. A distinction is made between short packets generated by interactive applications and long packets generated by file transfer. In the case of FDDI, a short packet is transferred in a short frame; a long packet is transferred in one or a very few large frames. In the case of DQDB, a short packet is carried in a single QA slot; a long packet requires a number of QA slots. The figure yields several interesting results:

- DQDB provides much less delay for short packets for both network sizes. This is because, with multiple QA segments, a node must wait

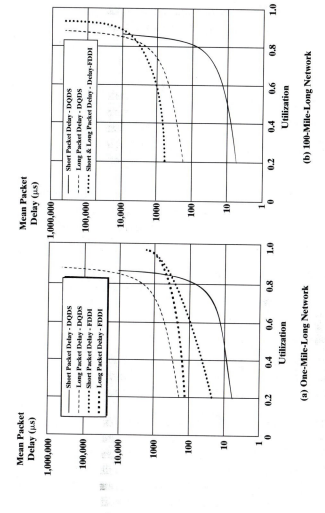

FIGURE 13.21   Delay for FDDI and DQDB

467

until one segment is transmitted before reserving for the next segment and then must wait for a free slot after all intervening downstream reservations have been satisfied.

- Utilization above about 80 percent causes long queuing delays for all DQDB traffic, whereas a small FDDI network can sustain higher utilization.

- DQDB appears to be better suited to interactive traffic, whereas FDDI is better suited to bulk traffic.

13.4

RECOMMENDED READING

Books with rigorous treatments of LAN/MAN performance include [STUC85], [HAMM86], [SPRA91], and [BERT92].

BERT92 Bertsekas, D., and Gallager, R. *Data Networks*. Englewood Cliffs, NJ: Prentice Hall, 1992.

HAMM86 Hammond, J., and O'Reilly, P. *Performance Analysis of Local Computer Networks*. Reading, MA: Addison-Wesley, 1986.

SPRA91 Spragins, J., Hammond, J., and Pawlikowski, K. *Telecommunications Protocols and Design*. Reading, MA: Addison-Wesley, 1991.

STUC85 Stuck, B., and Arthurs, E. *A Computer Communications Network Performance Analysis Primer*. Englewood Cliffs, NJ: Prentice Hall, 1985.

13.5

PROBLEMS

13.1 Equation (13.1) is valid for token ring and baseband bus. Determine an equivalent expression for:
a. Broadband bus
b. Broadband tree (use several different configurations)

13.2 Develop a display similar to Figure 13.6 that shows throughput as a function of N.

13.3 Derive equations similar to (13.10) and (13.11) for the case where there are two types of frames, one 10 times as long as the other, that are transmitted with equal probability by each station.

13.4 Consider a 10-Mbps, 1-km bus, with N stations and frame size = F. Determine throughput and delay for token bus and throughput for CSMA/CD:

      a. $N = 10, F = 1000$
      b. $N = 100, F = 1000$
      c. $N = 10, F = 10,000$
      d. $N = 100, F = 10,000$

13.5 Compare equations (13.1), (13.10), and (13.11). Under what circumstances does the throughput for the latter two equations exceed the theoretical maximum of (13.1)? Explain.

13.6 For the graphs in Figure 13.11, determine a and comment on the results.

13.7 Demonstrate that the number of stations and offered load affect performance independently for the following protocols.
    a. CSMA/CD
    b. Collision avoidance
    c. Token bus
    d. Token ring

13.8 Consider an S-ALOHA system with a finite number of stations N and $a = 0$. The offered load from each station is G_1, the throughput S_i. Derive an equation for S as a function of G_i. Assume that the G_is are identical; what is the equation for S? Verify that this approaches Ge^{-G} as $N \to \infty$. Above what value of N is the difference negligible?

13.9 Demonstrate that CSMA/CD is biased toward long transmissions.

13.10 Show that, for $a = 0$, the following relationship holds for 1-persistent CSMA

$$S = \frac{G(1 + G)e^{-G}}{G + e^{-G}}$$

13.11 The performance of CSMA/CD depends on whether the collision detection is performed at the same site as the transmission (baseband) or at a time later whose average is a (broadband). What would you expect the relative performance to be?

13.12 Let $T_{msg}(K) = 0.1$ s and $T_{over} = 0.1$ s for a 50-station token system. Assume that all stations always have something to transmit. Compute C, $R(K)$, and UTIL(K). What is the percentage of overhead? Now let $T_{over} = 0.2$. What is the percentage of overhead?

13.13 Consider the conditions extant at the end of Problem 13.12. Assume that individual stations may be busy or idle. What is the cycle time C? Now halve the overhead ($T_{over} = 0.1$). What is the cycle time C?

13.14 For equation (13.7), let the number of stations be two. Plot $R(2)$ versus $R(1)$ and show the admissible mean throughput rates. Interpret the result in terms of relative static priority policies.

13.15 Do an asymptotic breakpoint analysis for CSMA/CD.

13.16 Equations (13.10) and (13.12) are valid for token ring and for token baseband bus. What are equivalent equations for broadband bus?

13.17 What is the equivalent equation to (13.11) for broadband CSMA/CD?

13.18 For equations (13.17) and (13.18), consider the special cases of one active station ($N = 1$) and a large number of active stations (N approaches ∞). Discuss the resulting equations.

CHAPTER
14

Bridges

In most cases a LAN or MAN is not an isolated entity. An organization may have more than one type of LAN at a given site to satisfy a spectrum of needs. An organization may have multiple LANs of the same type at a given site to accommodate performance or security requirements. And an organization may have LANs and possibly MANs at various sites and need them to be interconnected for central control of distributed information exchange.

Table 14.1 lists some commonly used terms relating to the interconnection of networks, or internetworking. From a user's point of view, an interconnected set of networks may appear simply as a larger network. However, if each constituent network retains its identity and special mechanisms are needed for communicating across multiple networks, the entire configuration is often referred to as an **internet,** and each of the constituent networks as a **subnetwork.**

Each constituent subnetwork in an internet supports communication among the devices attached to that subnetwork; these devices are referred to as **end systems** (ESs). In addition, subnetworks are connected by devices referred to in the ISO documents as **intermediate systems** (ISs).[1] ISs provide a communications path and perform the necessary relaying and routing functions so that data can be exchanged between devices attached to different subnetworks in the internet.

---

[1]The term *gateway* is sometimes used to refer to an IS or to a particular kind of IS. Because of the lack of consistency in the use of this term, we avoid it.

TABLE 14.1   **Internetworking Terms**

Communication Network
A facility that provides a data transfer service among stations attached to the network.

Internet
A collection of communication networks interconnected by bridges and/or routers.

Subnetwork
Refers to a constituent network of an internet. This avoids ambiguity since the entire internet, from a user's point of view, is a single network.

End System (ES)
A device attached to one of the subnetworks of an internet that is used to support end-user applications or services.

Intermediate System (IS)
A device used to connect two subnetworks and permit communication between end systems attached to different subnetworks.

Bridge
An IS used to connect two LANs that use similar LAN protocols. The bridge acts as an address filter, picking up packets from one LAN that are intended for a destination on another LAN and passing those packets on. The bridge does not modify the contents of the packets and does not add anything to the packet. The bridge operates at layer 2 of the OSI model.

Router
A device used to connect two subnetworks that may or may not be similar. The router employs an internet protocol present in each router and each end system of the network. The router operates at layer 3 of the OSI model.

Two types of ISs of particular interest are bridges and routers. The differences between them have to do with the types of protocols used for the internetworking logic. In essence, a **bridge** operates at layer 2 of the open systems interconnection (OSI) 7-layer architecture and acts as a relay of frames between like networks. A **router** operates at layer 3 of the OSI architecture and routes packets between potentially dissimilar networks. Both the bridge and the router assume that the same upper-layer protocols are in use. In this chapter we examine the protocol architecture and functionality of bridges. Chapter 15 is devoted to routers.

14.1

BRIDGE OPERATION

Functions of a Bridge

The simplest of the internetworking devices is the bridge. This device is designed for use between local area networks (LANs) that use identical protocols for the physical and medium access layers (e.g., all conforming to

IEEE 802.3 or all conforming to FDDI). Because the devices all use the same protocols, the amount of processing required at the bridge is minimal. The concept of a bridge was introduced in Chapter 4.

Figure 14.1, which repeats Figure 4.8, illustrates the operation of a bridge between two LANs, *A* and *B*. The bridge performs the following functions:

- Read all frames transmitted on *A,* and accept those addressed to stations on *B.*
- Using the medium access control protocol for *B*, retransmit the frames onto *B.*
- Do the same for *B-to-A* traffic.

The bridge provides an extension to the LAN that requires no modification to the communications software in the stations attached to the LANs. It appears to all stations on the two (or more) LANs that there is a single LAN on which each station has a unique address. The station uses that unique address and need not explicitly discriminate between stations on the same LAN and stations on other LANs; the bridge takes care of that.

The bridge encompasses only layers 1 and 2 of the OSI model. In effect, the bridge operates as a layer 2 relay. Layers 3 and above must be identical in the two end systems for successful end-to-end communications.

Since the bridge is used in a situation in which all of the LANs have the same characteristics, the reader may ask why not simply have one large LAN. Depending on circumstance, there are several reasons for the use of multiple LANs connected by bridges:

- *Reliability.* The danger in connecting all data processing devices in an organization to one network is that a fault on the network may disable communication for all devices. By using bridges, the network can be partitioned into self-contained units.
- *Performance.* In general, performance on a LAN or MAN declines with an increase in the number of devices or the length of the medium. A number of smaller LANs will often give improved performance if devices can be clustered so that *intranetwork* traffic significantly exceeds *internetwork* traffic.
- *Security.* The establishment of multiple LANs may improve security of communications. It is desirable to keep different types of traffic (e.g., accounting, personnel, strategic planning) that have different security needs on physically separate media. At the same time, the different types of users with different levels of security need to communicate through controlled and monitored mechanisms. This topic is explored further in Chapter 12.

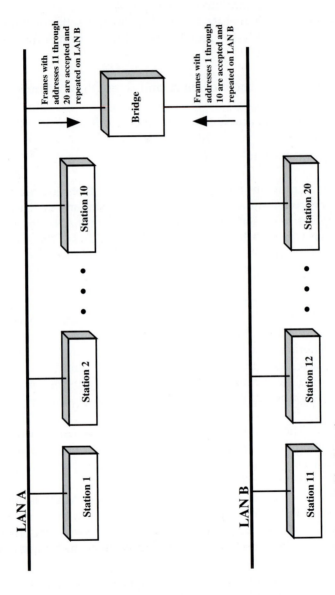

FIGURE 14.1 Bridge Operation

474

- *Geography.* Clearly, two separate LANs are needed to support devices clustered in two geographically distant locations. Even in the case of two buildings separated by a highway, it may be far easier to use a microwave bridge link than to attempt to string coaxial cable between the two buildings. In the case of widely separated networks, two "half bridges" are needed (see Figures 14.3 and 14.4, below).

The description above has applied to the simplest sort of bridge. More sophisticated bridges can be used in more complex collections of LANs. These would include additional functions, such as:

- Each bridge can maintain status information on other bridges, together with the cost and number of bridge-to-bridge hops required to reach each network. This information may be updated by periodic exchanges of information among bridges. This allows the bridges to perform a dynamic routing function.
- A control mechanism can manage frame buffers in each bridge to overcome congestion. Under saturation conditions, the bridge can give precedence to en-route packets over new packets just entering the internet from an attached LAN, thus preserving the investment in line bandwidth and processing time already made in the enroute frame.

Bridge Protocol Architecture

The IEEE 802.1D specification defines the protocol architecture for MAC bridges. In addition, the standard suggest formats for a globally administered set of MAC station addresses across multiple homogeneous LANs. In this subsection we examine the protocol architecture of these bridges. Within the 802 architecture, the endpoint or station address is designated at the MAC level. At the LLC level, only an SAP address is specified. Thus it is at the MAC level that a bridge can function. Figure 14.2 shows the simplest case, which consists of two LANs connected by a single bridge. The LANs employ the same MAC and LLC protocols. The bridge operates as described previously. A MAC frame whose destination is not on the immediate LAN is captured by the bridge, buffered briefly, and then transmitted on the other LAN. As far as the LLC layer is concerned, there is a dialogue between peer LLC entities in the two endpoint stations. The bridge need not contain an LLC layer since it is merely serving to relay the MAC frames.

Figure 14.2b indicates the way in which data is encapsulated using a bridge. Data are provided by some user to LLC. The LLC entity appends a header and passes the resulting data unit to the MAC entity, which appends a header and a trailer to form a MAC frame. On the basis of the destination MAC address in the frame, it is captured by the bridge. The bridge does not strip off the MAC fields; its function is to relay the MAC frame intact to the

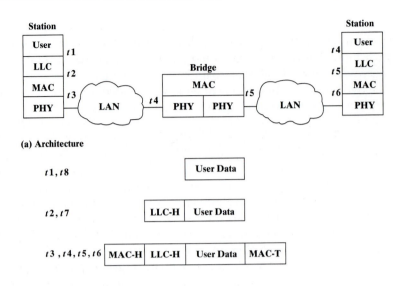

(a) Architecture

$t1, t8$ | User Data |

$t2, t7$ | LLC-H | User Data |

$t3, t4, t5, t6$ | MAC-H | LLC-H | User Data | MAC-T |

(b) Operation

FIGURE 14.2   Connection of Two LANs by a Bridge

destination LAN. Thus the frame is deposited on the destination LAN and captured by the destination station.

The concept of a MAC relay bridge is not limited to the use of a single bridge to connect two nearby LANs. If the LANs are some distance apart, they can be connected by two bridges that are in turn connected by a communications facility. For example, Figure 14.3 shows the case of two bridges connected by a point-to-point link. In this case, when a bridge captures a

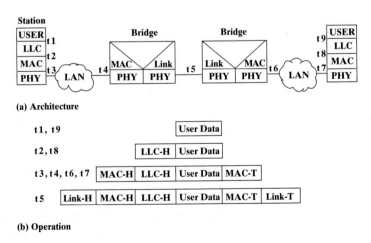

(a) Architecture

$t1, t9$ | User Data |

$t2, t8$ | LLC-H | User Data |

$t3, t4, t6, t7$ | MAC-H | LLC-H | User Data | MAC-T |

$t5$ | Link-H | MAC-H | LLC-H | User Data | MAC-T | Link-T |

(b) Operation

FIGURE 14.3   Bridge over a Point-to-Point Link

MAC frame, it appends a link-layer (e.g., HDLC) header and trailer to transmit the MAC frame across the link to the other bridge. The target bridge strips off these link fields and transmits the original, unmodified MAC frame to the destination station.

The intervening communications facility can even be a network, such as a wide-area packet-switching network, as illustrated in Figure 14.4. In this case the bridge is somewhat more complicated, although it performs the same function of relaying MAC frames. The connection between bridges is via an X.25 virtual circuit. Again, the two LLC entities in the end systems have a direct logical relationship with no intervening LLC entities. Thus in this situation, the X.25 packet layer is operating below an 802 LLC layer. As before, a MAC frame is passed intact between the endpoints. When the bridge on the source LAN receives the frame, it appends an X.25 packet layer header and an X.25 link-layer header and trailer and sends the data to the DCE (packet-switching node) to which it attaches. The DCE strips off the link-layer fields and sends the X.25 packet through the network to another DCE. The target DCE appends the link-layer field and sends this to the target bridge. The target bridge strips off all the X.25 fields and transmits the original unmodified MAC frame to the destination endpoint.

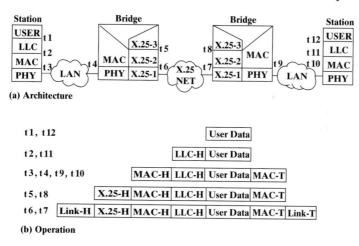

FIGURE 14.4   Bridge over an X.25 Network

14.2

ROUTING WITH BRIDGES

In the configuration of Figure 14.1, the bridge makes the decision to relay a frame on the basis of destination MAC address. In a more complex configuration, the bridge must also make a routing decision. Consider the configuration of Figure 14.5. Suppose that station 1 transmits a frame on LAN A intended for station 5. The frame will be read by both bridges 101 and 102. For each bridge the station addressed is not on a LAN to which the bridge is attached. Therefore, each bridge must make a decision as to whether or not to retransmit the frame on its other LAN, in order to move it closer to its intended destination. In this case, bridge 101 should repeat the frame on LAN B, whereas bridge 102 should refrain from retransmitting the frame. Once the frame has been transmitted on LAN B, it will be picked up by both bridges 103 and 104. Again, each must decide whether or not to forward the frame. In this case, bridge 104 should retransmit the frame on LAN E, where it will be received by the destination, station 5.

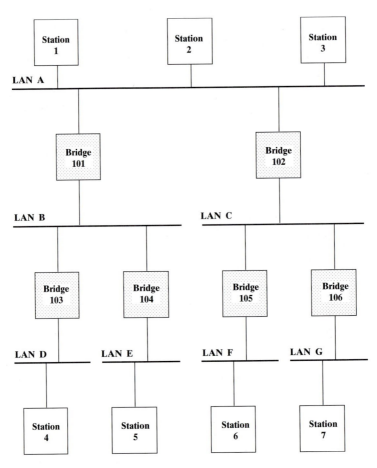

FIGURE 14.5   Internet Configuration of Bridges and LANs

Thus we see that in the general case, the bridge must be equipped with a routing capability. When a bridge receives a frame, it must decide whether or not to forward it. If the bridge is attached to two or more networks, it must decide whether or not to forward the frame, and if so, on which LAN the frame should be transmitted.

The routing decision may not always be a simple one. In Figure 14.6, bridge 107 is added to the previous configuration, directly linking LAN A and LAN E. Such an addition may be made to provide for higher overall internet availability. In this case, if station 1 transmits a frame on LAN A intended for station 5 on LAN E, either bridge 101 or bridge 107 could forward the frame. It would appear preferable for bridge 107 to forward the frame, since it will involve only one "hop," whereas if the frame travels through bridge 101, it must suffer two hops. Another consideration is that there may be changes in the configuration. For example, bridge 107 may fail, in which case subsequent frames from station 1 to station 5 should go through bridge 101. So we can say that the routing capability must take into account the topology of the internet configuration and may need to be altered dynamically.

Figure 14.6 suggests that a bridge knows the identity of each station on each LAN. In a large configuration, such an arrangement is unwieldy. Furthermore, as stations are added to and dropped from LANs, all directories of station location must be updated. It would facilitate the development of a routing capability if all MAC-level addresses were in the form of a network part and a station part. For example, the IEEE 802.5 standard suggests that 16-bit MAC addresses consist of a 7-bit LAN number and an 8-bit station number, and that 48-bit addresses consist of a 14-bit LAN number and a 32-bit station number.[2] In the remainder of this discussion, we assume that all MAC addresses include a LAN number and that routing is based on the use of that portion of the address only.

A variety of routing strategies have been proposed and implemented in recent years. The simplest, and most common strategy, is **fixed routing.** This strategy is suitable for small internets and for internets that are relatively stable. More recently, two groups within the IEEE 802 committee developed specifications for routing strategies. The IEEE 802.1 group has issued a standard for routing based on the use of a **spanning tree algorithm.** The token ring committee, IEEE 802.5, has issued its own specification, referred to as **source routing.** We examine these three strategies in turn.

---

[2]The remaining bit in the 16-bit format is used to indicate whether this is a group or individual address. Of the two remaining bits in the 48-bit format, one is used to indicate whether this is a group or individual address, and the other is used to indicate whether this is a locally or globally administered address.

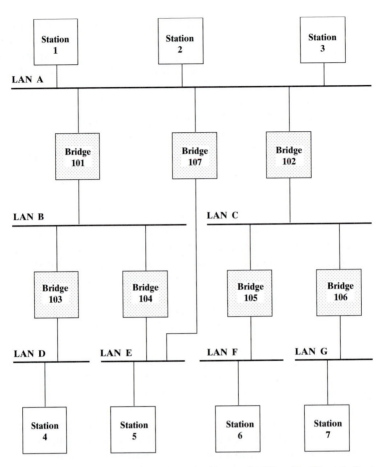

FIGURE 14.6   **Internet Configuration of Bridges and LANs, with Alternate Routes**

Fixed Routing

For fixed routing, a route is selected for each source–destination pair of LANs in the internet. If alternate routes are available between two LANs, then typically the route with the least number of hops is selected. The routes are fixed, or at least only change when there is a change in the topology of the internet.

Figure 14.7 suggests how fixed routing might be implemented. A central routing matrix is created, to be stored perhaps at a network control center. The matrix shows for each source–destination pair of LANs the identity of the first bridge on the route. So, for example, the route from LAN E to LAN F begins by going through bridge 107 to LAN A. Again consulting the matrix, the route from LAN A to LAN F goes through bridge 102 to LAN C. Finally, the route from LAN C to LAN F is directly through bridge 105. Thus

Central Routing Matrix
Destination LAN

Source LAN	A	B	C	D	E	F	G
A	–	101	102	101	107	102	102
B	101	–	101	103	104	101	101
C	102	102	–	102	102	105	106
D	103	103	103	–	103	103	103
E	107	104	107	104	–	107	107
F	105	105	105	105	105	–	105
G	106	106	106	106	106	106	–

Bridge 101 Table

From LAN A		From LAN B	
Dest.	Next	Dest.	Next
B	B	A	A
C	–	C	A
D	B	D	–
E	–	E	–
F	–	F	A
G	–	G	A

Bridge 102 Table

From LAN A		From LAN C	
Dest.	Next	Dest.	Next
B	–	A	A
C	C	B	A
D	–	D	A
E	–	E	A
F	C	F	–
G	C	G	–

Bridge 103 Table

From LAN B		From LAN D	
Dest.	Next	Dest.	Next
A	–	A	B
C	–	B	B
D	D	C	B
E	–	E	B
F	–	F	B
G	–	G	B

Bridge 104 Table

From LAN B		From LAN E	
Dest.	Next	Dest.	Next
A	–	A	–
C	–	B	B
D	–	C	–
E	E	D	B
F	–	F	–
G	–	G	–

Bridge 105 Table

From LAN C		From LAN F	
Dest.	Next	Dest.	Next
A	–	A	C
B	–	B	C
D	–	C	C
E	–	D	C
F	F	E	C
G	–	G	C

Bridge 106 Table

From LAN C		From LAN G	
Dest.	Next	Dest.	Next
A	–	A	C
B	–	B	C
D	–	C	C
E	–	D	C
F	–	E	C
G	G	F	C

Bridge 107 Table

From LAN A		From LAN E	
Dest.	Next	Dest.	Next
B	–	A	A
C	–	B	–
D	–	C	A
E	E	D	–
F	–	F	A
G	–	G	A

FIGURE 14.7   Fixed Routing (Using Figure 14.6)

the complete route from LAN E to LAN F is bridge 107, LAN A, bridge 102, LAN C, bridge 105.

From this overall matrix, routing tables can be developed and stored at each bridge. Each bridge needs one table for each LAN to which it attaches. The information for each table is derived from a single row of the matrix. For example, bridge 105 has two tables, one for frames arriving from LAN C and one for frames arriving from LAN F. For each possible destination MAC address, the table shows the identity of the LAN to which the bridge should forward the frame. The table labeled "From LAN C" is derived from the row labeled C in the routing matrix. Every entry in that row that contains bridge number 105 results in an entry in the corresponding table in bridge 105.

Once the directories have been established, routing is a simple matter. A bridge copies each incoming frame on each of its LANs. If the destination MAC address corresponds to an entry in its routing table, the frame is retransmitted on the appropriate LAN.

The fixed routing strategy is widely used in commercially available products. It is the advantage of simplicity and minimal processing requirements. However, in a complex internet, in which bridges may be dynamically added and in which failures must be allowed for, this strategy is too limited. In the next two sections, we cover more powerful alternatives.

14.3

SPANNING TREE ROUTING

The IEEE 802.1 committee has developed a bridge routing approach referred to as the transparent bridge. The distinguishing characteristics of this standard are:

- It is intended for use in interconnecting not just LANs with the same MAC protocol but also dissimilar LANs that satisfy any of the MAC standards (802.3, 802.4, 802.5)—hence the term *transparent*.
- The routing mechanism is a technique referred to as the spanning tree algorithm.

We look first at the basic operation of the transparent bridge and then in more detail at the three key aspects of bridge operation: frame forwarding, address learning, and spanning tree calculation.

Basic Operation

So far we have discussed the bridge as a device that relays frames from one LAN to another. In the case of the 802.1 transparent bridge, we need to be more careful and more explicit in describing the way in which this is done. The transparent bridge must be capable of relaying a MAC frame from one type of LAN to another. However, as we know (see Figures 6.5, 6.13, and 6.15), the MAC formats for the various 802 LANs differ. Accordingly, it is not possible simply to pick up a frame from one LAN and place it down, unaltered, on another LAN. If the two LANs use different MAC protocols, the bridge must map the contents of the incoming frame into an outbound frame that conforms to the frame format for the outbound LAN.

Figure 14.8a, taken from the standard, indicates the bridge architecture that supports this mapping. Each bridge attachment to a LAN is referred to as a **port.** A bridge with N ports will have N MAC entities; thus the bridge has N MAC addresses, one for each port. Each MAC entity conforms to the relevant MAC standard and behaves in the normal manner with one exception: The MAC entity will capture all frames, not just those addressed to the bridge itself. Incoming MAC frames fall into three categories:

- *Frames addressed to this bridge.* These include bridge protocol data units (BPDUs) that are part of the spanning tree algorithm described later, and management frames. All such frames are passed to higher-layer entities within the bridge using the standard MAC service for that MAC protocol.

- *Control frames.* These are handled as part of the MAC protocol. Examples include tokens and frames involved in the maintenance of the token bus and token ring protocols. These frames are handled by the MAC entity without reference to any higher layer.

- *User data frames.* These are frames containing LLC information. The LLC information is handed to the MAC relay entity using an internal sublayer service. If a capture frame is to be forwarded onto another LAN, the LLC information is handed down to the appropriate MAC relay entity, again using the internal sublayer service.

The internal sublayer service is defined in the usual way, as a set of primitives and parameters. Figure 14.9 shows this service definition, and Table 14.2 defines the parameters. The operation implied by these definitions is as follows: An incoming frame is disassembled, and the LLC information field plus the values of some of the other fields are passed up to a MAC relay entity. This information is then passed down to the MAC entity for the outgoing LAN, and the MAC frame is reconstructed. Because the frame is disassembled and then reconstructed, the format can be altered to allow a bridge to function between two different types of LANs.

Several parameters in the service definition deserve additional comment. Only frames with a frame_type of user_data_frame will be relayed by a bridge between dissimilar LANs. MAC-specific frames may be relayed for a bridge between two similar LANs; this would allow certain MAC-specific management functions to be implemented. The mac_action parameter is only relevant to IEEE 802.4, which has a special feature that allows for a request/response type of exchange of MAC frames.

The user_priority and access_priority parameters relate to the problem of how to handle priorities. In the case of IEEE 802.3, priority is not sup-

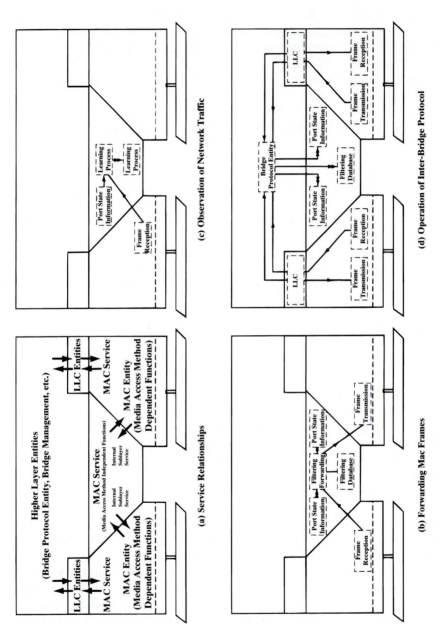

(a) Service Relationships

(b) Forwarding Mac Frames

(c) Observation of Network Traffic

(d) Operation of Inter-Bridge Protocol

FIGURE 14.8   IEEE 802.1D Bridge Architecture

484

M_UNITDATA.indication   (M_UNITDATA.request   (
                         frame_type   frame_type
                         mac_action   mac_action
                         destination_address   destination_address
                         source_address   source_address
                         mac_service_data_unit   mac_service_data_unit
                         user_priority   user_priority
                         frame_check_sequence   access_priority
)   frame_check_sequence
)

FIGURE 14.9   IEEE 802.1D MAC Bridge Internal Sublayer Service Primitives

TABLE 14.2   Definition of IEEE 802.1D MAC Bridge Internal
Sublayer Service Parameters

Parameter	Definition
frame_type	Type of frame: value is user_data_frame, mac_specific_frame, or reserved_frame
mac_action	If the value of the frame_type parameter is user_data_frame, the mac_action parameter is request_with_response, request_with_no_response, or response
destination_address	Address of destination MAC entity or group of MAC entities
source_address	Address of the source MAC entity that initiated transmission of the mac_service_data_unit
mac_service_data_unit	Service user data. For a user data frame, this is provided by the source LLC
user_priority	Priority requested by the originating service user
access_priority	Priority to be used by the local MAC service provider to convey the request
frame_check_sequence	Frame check sequence value of the incoming frame

ported. Both IEEE 802.4 and IEEE 802.5 support eight levels of priority.[3] The user_priority value provided to the MAC layer entity in an MA_UNIT-DATA.indication is derived from the incoming MAC frame; in the case of an incoming 802.3 frame, no priority value is available and a value of *unspecified* is used. The user_priority value issued to a MAC entity in an MA_UNITDATA.request is to be placed in the outbound MAC frame for 802.4 and 802.5. The access_priority refers to the priority used by a bridge

---

[3]In fact, as we have seen, 802.4 supports four classes of access: classes 6, 4, 2, and 0. However, 3 bits are reserved in the frame control field for priority. These are mapped into access classes as follows: access class 6 = priority 7 and 6; class 4 = priority class 5 and 4; class 2 = priority class 3 and 2; class 0 = priority class 1 and 0.

MAC entity to access a LAN for frame transmission. We may not want the access priority to be equal to the user priority for several reasons:

- A frame that must go through a bridge has already suffered more delay than a frame that does not have to go through a bridge; therefore, we may wish to give such a frame a higher access priority than the user priority requested.
- It is important that the bridge not become a bottleneck. Therefore, we may wish to give all frames being transmitted by a bridge a relatively high priority.

In considering user priority and access priority, we can group the alternatives into three cases:

- *Outbound LAN = 802.3.* Priorities are not used to transmit 802.3 MAC frames, and the frame itself has no priority field. Therefore, any inbound priority is ignored, and there is no access priority.
- *Outbound LAN = 802.4 or 802.5; inbound LAN = 802.4 or 802.5.* The priority field in the outbound MAC frame is set equal to the priority field in the inbound MAC frame; the value is communicated from inbound to outbound via the user_priority parameter. The access priority used on the outbound LAN can either be set to the user_priority value or to a default access_priority value.
- *Outbound LAN = 802.4 or 802.5; inbound LAN = 802.3.* The priority field in the outbound frame is set to a default user_priority value. The access priority used on the outbound LAN is set to a default access_priority value.

The frame_check_sequence value provided to the MAC layer entity in an MA_UNITDATA.indication is derived from the incoming MAC frame. If the outbound LAN is the same type as the inbound LAN, the outbound MAC frame will be the same as the inbound MAC frame, and the FCS can be reused.

Table 14.3 summarizes these relationships, plus one other that is significant. One concern relates to the maximum frame size limitation on the various networks. In the case of 802.3, the maximum size is 1518 octets. For 802.4, it is 8191 octets. For 802.5, the maximum frame size may not exceed the token holding time; for the default value of 10 ms, this results in a maximum frame size of 5000 octets at 4 Mbps and 20,000 octets at 16 Mbps. If the outbound LAN does not support a frame size large enough to handle an inbound frame, that frame must be discarded.

Frame Forwarding

In this scheme, a bridge maintains a **filtering database,** which is based on MAC address (Figure 14.9b). Each entry consists of a MAC individual or

TABLE 14.3 MAC-Dependent Bridge Actions

Source LAN	Destination LAN		
	IEEE 802.3	**IEEE 802.4**	**IEEE 802.5**
IEEE 802.3		Calculate frame check sequence Set default user priority Use default access priority	Calculate frame check sequence. Set default user priority. Use default access priority.
IEEE 802.4	Discard frame if too long Calculate frame check sequence Discard user priority	Use user priority of inbound frame Use user priority or default access priority for access.	Discard frame if too long. Calculate frame check sequence. Use user priority of inbound frame. Use user priority or default access priority for access.
IEEE 802.5	Discard frame if too long Calculate frame check sequence Discard user priority	Discard frame if too long. Calculate frame check sequence. Use user priority of inbound frame. Use user priority or default access priority for access.	Use user priority of inbound frame. Use user priority or default access priority for access.

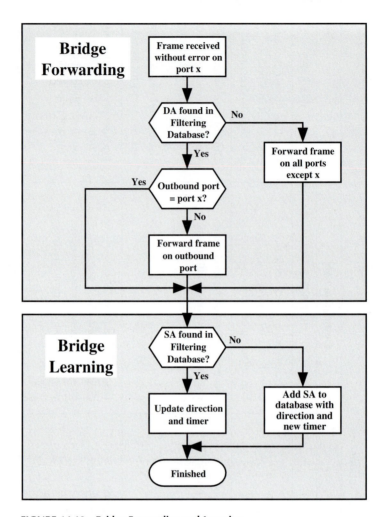

FIGURE 14.10   Bridge Forwarding and Learning

group address, a port number, and an aging time (described below). We can interpret this in the following fashion. A station is listed with a given port number if it is on the "same side" of the bridge as the port. For example, for bridge 102 of Figure 14.5, stations on LANs C, F, and G are on the same side of the bridge as the LAN A port, and stations on LANs A, B, D, and E are on the same side of the bridge as the LAN C port. When a frame is received on any port, the bridge must decide whether that frame is to be forwarded through the bridge and out through one of the bridge's other ports. Suppose that a bridge receives a MAC frame on port x. The following rules are applied (Figure 14.10):

1. Search the forwarding database to determine if the MAC address is listed for any port except port x.
2. If the destination MAC address is not found, flood the frame by sending it out on all ports except the port by which it arrived.
3. If the destination address is in the forwarding database for some port $y \neq x$, then determine whether port y is in a blocking or forwarding state. For reasons explained below, a port may sometimes be blocked, which prevents it from receiving or transmitting frames.
4. If port y is not blocked, transmit the frame through port y onto the LAN to which that port attaches.

Rule 2 is needed because of the dynamic nature of the filtering database. When a bridge is initialized, the database is empty. Since the bridge does not know where to send the frame, it floods the frame onto all of its LANs except the LAN on which the frame arrives. As the bridge gains information, the flooding activity subsides.

Address Learning

The scheme described above is based on the use of a filtering database that indicates the direction, from the bridge, of each destination station. This information can be preloaded into the bridge, as in static routing. However, an effective automatic mechanism for learning the direction of each station is desirable. A simple scheme for acquiring this information is based on the use of the source address field in each MAC frame (Figures 14.8c and 14.10).

When a frame arrives on a particular port, it clearly has come from the direction of the incoming LAN. The source address field of the frame indicates the source station. Thus a bridge can update its filtering database for that MAC address. To allow for changes in topology, each entry in the database is equipped with an aging timer. When a new entry is added to the database, its timer is set; the recommended default value is 300 seconds. If the timer expires, the entry is eliminated from the database, since the corresponding direction information may no longer be valid. Each time a frame is received, its source address is checked against the database. If the entry is already in the database, the entry is updated (the direction may have changed) and the timer is reset. If the entry is not in the database, a new entry is created, with its own timer.

The discussion above indicated that the individual entries in the database are station addresses. If a two-level address structure (LAN number, station number) is used, only LAN addresses need to be entered in the database. Both schemes work the same. The only difference is that the use of station addresses requires a much larger database than the use of LAN addresses. Note from Figure 14.10 that the bridge learning process is applied to all frames, not just those that are forwarded.

Spanning Tree Algorithm

The address learning mechanism described above is effective if the topology of the internet is a tree, that is, if there are no alternate routes in the network. The existence of alternate routes means that there is a closed loop. For example, in Figure 14.6, the following is a closed loop: LAN A, bridge 101, LAN B, bridge 104, LAN E, bridge 107, LAN A.

To see the problem created by a closed loop, consider Figure 14.11. At time t_0, station A transmits a frame addressed to station B. The frame is captured by both bridges. Each bridge updates its database to indicate that station A is in the direction of LAN X and retransmits the frame on LAN Y. Say that bridge α retransmits at time t_1 and bridge β a short time later, t_2. Thus B will receive two copies of the frame. Furthermore, each bridge will receive the other's transmission on LAN Y. Note that each transmission is a MAC frame with a source address of A and a destination address of B. Thus each bridge will update its database to indicate that station A is in the direction of LAN Y. Neither bridge is now capable of forwarding a frame addressed to station A.

But the problem is potentially more serious. Assume that the two bridges do not yet know of the existence of station B. In this case we have the following scenario. A transmits a frame addressed to B. Each bridge captures the frame. Then, each bridge, because it does not have information about B, automatically retransmits a copy of the frame on LAN Y. The frame transmitted by bridge α is captured by station B *and* by bridge β. Because

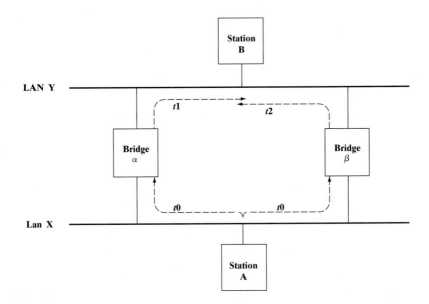

FIGURE 14.11   Loop of Bridges

bridge β does not know where B is, it takes this frame and retransmits it on LAN X. Similarly, bridge α receives bridge β's transmission on LAN Y and retransmits the frame on LAN X. There are now two frames on LAN X that will be picked up for retransmission on LAN Y. This process repeats indefinitely.

To overcome this problem, a simple result from graph theory is used: For any connected graph consisting of nodes and edges connecting pairs of nodes, there is a spanning tree of edges that maintains the connectivity of the graph but contains no closed loops. In terms of internets, each LAN corresponds to a graph node, and each bridge corresponds to a graph edge. Thus, in Figure 14.6, the removal of one (and only one) of bridges 107, 101, and 104 results in a spanning tree. What is desired is to develop a simple algorithm by which the bridges of the internet can exchange sufficient information to derive a spanning tree automatically (without user intervention). The algorithm must be dynamic. That is, when a topology change occurs, the bridges must be able to discover this fact and derive a new spanning tree automatically.

The algorithm is based on the use of the following:

1. Each bridge is assigned a unique identifier; in essence, the identifier consists of a MAC address for the bridge plus a priority level.
2. There is a special group MAC address that means "all bridges on this LAN." When a MAC frame is transmitted with the group address in the destination address field, all of the bridges on the LAN will capture that frame and interpret it as a frame addressed to itself.
3. Each port of a bridge is uniquely identified within the bridge, with a "port identifier."

With this information established, the bridges are able to exchange routing information in order to determine a spanning tree of the internet. We explain the operation of the algorithm using Figures 14.12 and 14.13 as an example. The following concepts are needed in the creation of the spanning tree:

- *Root bridge.* The bridge with the lowest value of bridge identifier is chosen to be the root of the spanning tree.
- *Path cost.* Associated with each port on each bridge is a path cost, which is the cost of transmitting a frame onto a LAN through that port. A path between two stations will pass through zero or more bridges. At each bridge, the cost of transmission is added to give a total cost for a particular path. In the simplest case, all path costs would be assigned a value of 1; thus the cost of a path would simply be a count of the number of bridges along the path. Alternatively, costs could be assigned in inverse proportion to the data rate of the corresponding LAN or any other criterion chosen by the network manager.

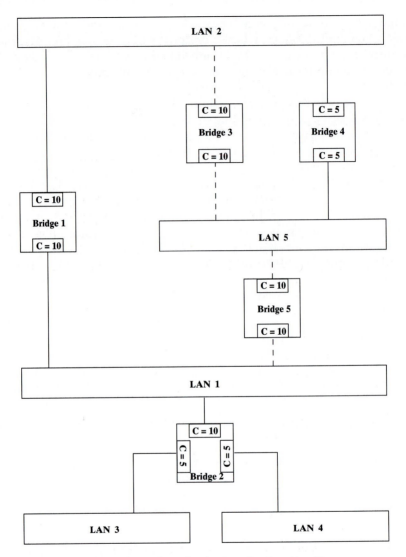

FIGURE 14.12   Example Configuration for Spanning Tree Algorithm

- *Root port.* Each bridge discovers the first hop on the minimum-cost path to the root bridge. The port used for that hop is labeled the root port. When the cost is equal for two ports, the lower port number is selected so that a unique spanning tree is constructed.
- *Root path cost.* For each bridge, the cost of the path to the root bridge with minimum cost (the path that starts at the root port) is the root path cost for that bridge.

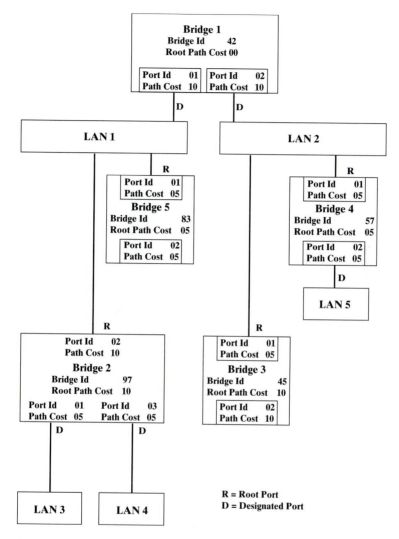

FIGURE 14.13   Spanning Tree for Configuration of Figure 14.12

- *Designated bridge, designated port.* On each LAN, one bridge is chosen to be the designated bridge. This is the bridge on that LAN that provides the minimum cost path to the root bridge. This is the only bridge allowed to forward frames to and from the LAN for which it is the designated bridge. The port of the designated bridge that attaches the bridge to the LAN is the designated port. For all LANs to which the root bridge is attached, the root bridge is the designated bridge. All internet traffic to and from the LAN passes through the designated port.

In general terms, the spanning tree is constructed in the following fashion:

1. Determine the root bridge.
2. Determine the root port on all other bridges.
3. Determine the designated port on each LAN. This will be the port with the minimum root path cost. In the case of two or more bridges with the same root path cost, the highest-priority bridge is chosen as the designated bridge. If the designated bridge has two or more ports attached to this LAN, the port with the lowest value of port identifier is chosen.

By this process, when two LANs are directly connected by more than one bridge, all of the bridges but one are eliminated. This cuts any loops that involve two LANs. It can be demonstrated that this process also eliminates all loops involving more than two LANs and that connectivity is preserved. Thus this process discovers a spanning tree for the given internet. In our example the solid lines indicate the bridge ports that participate in the spanning tree.

The steps outlined above require that the bridges exchange information (Figure 14.8d). The information is exchanged in the form of bridge protocol data units (BPDUs). A BPDU transmitted by one bridge is addressed to and received by all of the other bridges on the same LAN. Each BPDU contains the following information:

- The identifier of this bridge and the port on this bridge
- The identifier of the bridge that this bridge considers to be the root
- The root path cost for this bridge

To begin, all bridges consider themselves to be the root bridge. Each bridge will broadcast a BPDU on each of its LANs that asserts this fact. On any given LAN, only one claimant will have the lowest-valued identifier and will maintain its belief. Over time, as BPDUs propagate, the identity of the lowest-valued bridge identifier throughout the internet will be known to all bridges. The root bridge will regularly broadcast the fact that it is the root bridge on all of the LANs to which it is attached. This allows the bridges on those LANs to determine their root port and the fact that they are directly connected to the root bridge. Each of these bridges in turn broadcasts a BPDU on the other LANs to which it is attached (all LANs except the one on its root port), indicating that it is one hop away from the root bridge. This activity is propagated throughout the internet. Every time that a bridge receives a BPDU, it transmits BPDUs indicating the identity of the root bridge and the number of hops to reach the root bridge. On any LAN, the bridge claiming to be the one that is closest to the root becomes the designated bridge.

We can trace some of this activity with the configuration of Figure 14.12. At startup time, bridges 1, 3, and 4 all transmit BPDUs on LAN 2 claiming to be the root bridge. When bridge 3 receives the transmission from bridge 1, it recognize a superior claimant and defers. Bridge 3 has also received a claiming BPDU from bridge 5 via LAN 5. Bridge 3 recognizes that bridge 1 has a superior claim to be the root bridge; it therefore assigns its LAN 2 port to be its root port and sets the root path cost to 10. By similar actions, bridge 4 ends up with a root path cost of 5 via LAN 2; bridge 5 has a root path cost of 5 via LAN 1; and bridge 2 has a root path cost of 10 via LAN 1.

Now consider the assignment of designated bridges. On LAN 5, all three bridges transmit BPDUs attempting to assert a claim to be designated bridge. Bridge 3 defers because it receives BPDUs from the other bridges that have a lower root path cost. Bridges 4 and 5 have the same root path cost, but bridge 4 has the higher priority and therefore becomes the designated bridge.

The results of all this activity are shown in Figure 14.13. Only the designated bridge on each LAN is allowed to forward frames. All of the ports on all of the other bridges are placed in a blocking state. After the spanning tree is established, bridges continue periodically to exchange BPDUs to be able to react to any change in topology, cost assignments, or priority assignment. Any time that a bridge receives a BPDU on a port it makes two assessments:

1. If the BPDU arrives on a port that is considered the designated port, does the transmitting port have a better claim to be the designated port?
2. Should this port be my root port?

The behavior of the bridges can be explained more precisely with reference to the state transition diagram of Figure 14.14. When a bridge is initialized or when a bridge must participate in a change of configuration, all of its ports are placed in a listening state. For each port an associated timer is initialized to a value called *forward delay*. This timer is allowed to run down as long as no information is received to indicate that this port should be blocked from transmitting and receiving MAC frames. In the listening state, the spanning tree protocol information is received and transmitted, but station traffic is not forwarded to or from the bridge port, and MAC frames that arrive are not submitted to the learning process.

Once the forwarding timer expires, the bridge port transitions to the learning state, and the timer is reinitialized to the value of the forward delay parameter. Behavior in the learning state is exactly as in the listening state, with the exception that frames are submitted to the learning process.

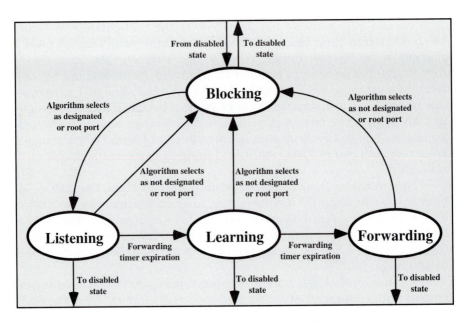

FIGURE 14.14 Spanning Tree State Transition Diagram for a Bridge Port

Once the forward delay timer expires a second time, the bridge port moves to the forwarding state. This means that this port is part of the spanning tree and will accept frames to be forwarded through the bridge and will transmit frames out of the bridge as appropriate.

If at any time, the bridge receives configuration information that indicates that this port should not be part of the spanning tree, the port is put in the blocking state. A future change in topology will move the port back to the listening state. The motivation for this apparently complex process is to account for the propagation delays in communicating configuration information among the bridges. To move a state directly from a block state to a forwarding state risks having temporary data loops and the duplication and misordering of frames. Time is needed for new information to be received by all bridges and for other bridges to reply to inferior protocol information before starting to forward frames.

Bridge Protocol Data Units

The 802.1D standard defines two bridge protocol data units: the configuration BPDU and the topology change notification BPDU. Figure 14.15 illustrates the formats. The **configuration BPDU** consists of the following fields:

- *Protocol identifier (2 octets):* identifies the spanning tree algorithm and protocol defined by 802.1. The value is all zeros.
- *Protocol version identifier (1 octet):* identifies the version of this standard.

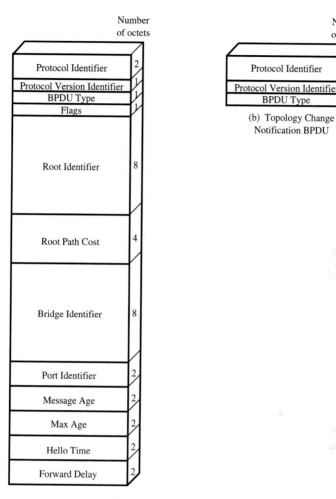

(a) Configuration BPDU

(b) Topology Change
Notification BPDU

FIGURE 14.15   Bridge Protocol Data Units

- *BPDU type (1 octet):* the type of BPDU. For the configuration BPDU, the value is all zeros.
- *Flags (1 octet):* consists of the Topology Change flag (bit 1 of octet 5) and the topology change acknowledgment flag (bit 8 of octet 5). The use of these flags is explained below.
- *Root identifier (8 octets):* the unique bridge identifier of the bridge assumed to be the root by the bridge transmitting this BPDU. This parameter is conveyed to enable all bridges to agree on the root.
- *Root path cost (4 octets):* the cost of the path from the transmitting bridge to the bridge identified by the root identifier above. This para-

meter is conveyed to enable a bridge to decide which of the bridges attached to the LAN on which this BPDU has been received offers the lowest-cost path to the root for that LAN.

- *Bridge identifier (8 octets):* the unique identifier of the bridge transmitting this BPDU. This parameter is conveyed to enable a bridge to decide, in the case of a LAN to which two or more bridges are attached and which offer equal cost paths to the root, which of the bridges should be selected as the designated bridge for that LAN.
- *Port identifier (2 octets):* the identifier of the port transmitting this BPDU. This identifier uniquely identifies a port on the transmitting bridge.
- *Message age (2 octets):* the age of the configuration message, which is the time since the generation of the configuration BPDU by the root which instigated the generation of this configuration BPDU. This parameter is conveyed to enable a bridge to discard information whose age exceeds the maximum age.
- *Maximum age (2 octets):* a timeout value to be used by all bridges in the internet. The value is set by the root. This parameter is conveyed to ensure that each bridge has a consistent value against which to test the age of stored configuration information.
- *Hello time (2 octets):* the time interval between the generation of configuration BPDUs by the root. This parameter is not directly used in the spanning tree algorithm but is conveyed to facilitate the monitoring of protocol performance by management functions.
- *Forward delay (2 octets):* a timeout value to be used by all bridges. The value is set by the root. This parameter is conveyed to ensure that each bridge uses a consistent value for the forward delay timer when transferring the state of a port to the forwarding state. This parameter is also used as the timeout value for aging filtering database dynamic entries following changes in active topology.

The transmission of configuration BPDUs is triggered by the root (or a bridge that temporarily considers itself to be the root). The root will periodically (once every hello time) issue a configuration BPDU on all LANs to which it is attached. A bridge that receives a configuration BPDU on what it decides is its root port passes that information on to all the LANs for which it believes itself to be the designated bridge. Thus, in a stable configuration, generation of a configuration BPDU by the root causes a cascade of configuration BPDUs throughout the spanning tree. This collection of BPDU transmissions is referred to as a **configuration message.**

A bridge may decide that it must change the topology of the spanning tree. For example, in Figure 14.13, if bridge 4 fails, it would cease to transmit configuration BPDUs as part of the periodic configuration messages.

Bridge 3 would time out bridge 4 as the designated bridge on LAN 2 once the maximum age timer expires, and enter the listening state. Eventually, the port on LAN 2 of bridge 3 would enter the forwarding state. At this point, bridge 3 must notify the root of a change in topology. This is done by transmitting a **topology change notification BPDU** on the root port of the bridge. This BPDU consists merely of a protocol identifier, protocol version identifier, and a BPDU type field with a code for this type of 10000000.

The intent is to communicate the topology change notification to the root. This is done by, in effect, relaying the change notification up the spanning tree to the root. To assure reliable delivery of the notification, the transmitting bridge will repeat the topology change notification BPDU until it receives an acknowledgment from the designated bridge for that LAN. The acknowledgment is carried in a configuration BPDU (topology change acknowledgment flag). The designated bridge passes the notification to, or toward, the root using the same procedure.

When the root receives such a notification, or changes the topology itself (e.g., if a new root is declared), it will set the topology change flag in all configuration messages transmitted for some time. This time is such that all bridges will receive one or more configuration messages. While this flag is set, bridges use the value of forwarding delay to age out entries in the filtering database. When the flag is reset again, the bridges revert to using a filtering timer, which, typically, is much longer. It is desirable to shorten the aging time during this period of reconfiguration because, after a topology change, stations may be in a new direction with respect to the bridge. Since a bridge must endure a wait of at least two forwarding times (see Figure 14.14) to transition from listening to forwarding, this will allow enough time for frames currently en route to be delivered or eliminated by timeout.

14.4

SOURCE ROUTING

The IEEE 802.5 committee has developed a bridge routing approach referred to as *source routing*. With this approach, the sending station determines the route that the frame will follow and includes the routing information with the frame; bridges read the routing information to determine if they should forward the frame.

Basic Operation

The basic operation of the algorithm can be described with reference to the configuration of Figure 14.16. A frame from station X can reach station Z by either of the following routes:

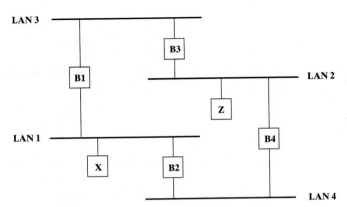

(a) Configuration

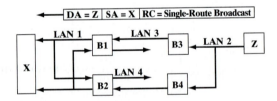

(b) Single-Route Broadcast Request

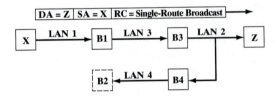

(c) All-Routes Broadcast Response

FIGURE 14.16   Route Discovery Example

- LAN 1, bridge B1, LAN 3, bridge B3, LAN 2
- LAN 1, bridge B2, LAN 4, bridge B4, LAN 2

Station X may choose one of these two routes and place the information, in the form of a sequence of LAN and bridge identifiers, in the frame to be transmitted. When a bridge receives a frame, it will forward that frame if the bridge is on the designated route; all other frames are discarded. In this case, if the first route above is specified, bridges B1 and B3 will forward the frame; if the second route is specified, bridges B2 and B4 will forward the frame.

Note that with this scheme, bridges need not maintain routing tables. The bridge makes the decision whether or not to forward a frame solely on the basis of the routing information contained in the frame. All that is required is that the bridge know its own unique identifier and the identifier of each LAN to which it is attached. The responsibility for designing the route falls to the source station.

For this scheme to work, there must be a mechanism by which a station can determine a route to any destination station. Before dealing with this issue, we need to discuss various types of routing directives.

Routing Directives and Addressing Modes

The source routing scheme developed by the IEEE 802.5 committee includes four different types of routing directives. Each frame that is transmitted includes an indicator of the type of routing desired. The four directive types are:

- *Null.* No routing is desired. In this case, the frame can only be delivered to stations on the same LAN as the source station.
- *Nonbroadcast.* The frame includes a route, consisting of a sequence of LAN numbers and bridge numbers that defines a unique route from the source station to the destination station. Only bridges on that route forward the frame, and only a single copy of the frame is delivered to the destination station.
- *All-routes broadcast.* The frame will reach each LAN of the internet by all possible routes. Thus each bridge will forward each frame once to each of its ports in a direction away from the source node and multiple copies of the frame may appear on a LAN. The destination station will receive one copy of the frame for each possible route through the network.
- *Single-route broadcast.* Regardless of the destination address of the frame, the frame will appear once, and only once, on each LAN in the internet. For this effect to be achieved, the frame is forwarded by all bridges that are on a spanning tree (with the source node as the root) of the internet. The destination station receives a single copy of the frame.

Let us first examine the potential application of each of these four types of routing and then examine the mechanisms that may be employed to achieve them. First, consider null routing. In this case the bridges that share the LAN with the source station are told not to forward the frame. This will be done if the intended destination is on the same LAN as the source station. Nonbroadcast routing is used when the two stations are not on the same LAN and the source station knows a route that can be used to reach the destination station. Only the bridges on that route will forward the frame.

The remaining two types of routing can be used by the source to discover a route to the destination. For example, the source station can use all-routes broadcasting to send a request frame to the intended destination. The destination returns a response frame, using nonbroadcast routing, on each of the routes followed by the incoming request frame. The source station can pick one of these routes and send future frames on that route. Alternatively, the source station could use single-route broadcasting to send a single request frame to the destination station. The destination station could send its response frame via all-routes broadcasting. The incoming frames would reveal all of the possible routes to the destination station, and the source station could pick one of these for future transmissions. Finally, single-route broadcasting could be used for group addressing, as discussed below.

Now consider the mechanisms for implementing these various routing directives. Each frame must include an indicator of which of the four types of routing is required. For null routing, the frame is ignored by the bridge. For nonbroadcast routing, the frame includes an ordered list of LAN numbers and bridge numbers. When a bridge receives a nonbroadcast frame, it forwards the frame only if the routing information contains the sequence LAN i, Bridge x, LAN j, where

> LAN i = LAN from which the frame arrived
> Bridge x = this bridge
> LAN j = another LAN to which this bridge is attached

For all-routes broadcasting, the source station marks the frame for this type of routing but includes no routing information. Each bridge that forwards the frame will add its bridge number and the outgoing LAN number to the frame's routing information field. Thus, when the frame reaches its destination, it will include a sequenced list of all LANs and bridges visited. To prevent the endless repetition and looping of frames, a bridge obeys the following rule. When an all-routes broadcast frame is received, the bridge examines the routing information field. If the field contains the number of a LAN to which the bridge is attached, the bridge will refrain from forwarding the frame on that LAN. Put the other way, the bridge will only forward the frame to a LAN that the frame has not already visited.

Finally, for single-route broadcasting, a spanning tree of the internet must be developed. This can either be done automatically, as in the 802.1 specification, or manually. In either case, as with the 802.1 strategy, one bridge on each LAN is the designated bridge for that LAN and is the only one that forwards single-route frames.

It is worth noting the relationship between addressing mode and routing directive. Recall from Chapter 4 that there are three types of MAC addresses:

- *Individual.* The address specifies a unique destination station.
- *Group.* The address specifies a group of destination addresses; this is also referred to as multicast.

- *All-stations.* The addresses specifies all stations that are capable of receiving this frame; this is also referred to as *broadcast*. We will refrain from using the latter term since it is also used in the source routing terminology.

In the case of a single, isolated LAN, group and all-stations addresses refer to stations on the same LAN as the source station. In an internet it may be desirable to transmit a frame to multiple stations on multiple LANs. Indeed, since a set of LANs interconnected by bridges should appear to the user as a single LAN, the ability to do group and all-stations addressing across the entire internet is mandatory.

Table 14.4 summarizes the relationship between routing specification and addressing mode. If no routing is specified, all addresses refer only to the immediate LAN. If nonbroadcast routing is specified, addresses may refer to any station on any LAN visited on the nonbroadcast route. From an addressing point of view, this combination is not generally useful for group and all-stations addressing. If either the all-routes or single-route specification is included in a frame, all stations on the internet can be addressed. Thus the total internet acts a single network from the point of view of MAC addresses. Since less traffic is generated by the single-route specification, this is to be preferred for group and all-stations addressing. Note also that the single-route mechanism in source routing is equivalent to the 802.1 spanning tree approach. Thus the latter supports both group and all-stations addressing.

Route Discovery and Selection

With source routing, bridges are relieved of the burden of storing and using routing information. Thus the burden falls on the stations that wish to transmit frames. Clearly, some mechanism is needed by which the source stations can know the route to each destination for which frames are to be sent. Three strategies suggest themselves.

1. Manually load the information into each station. This is simple and effective but has several drawbacks. First, any time that the configuration is changed, the routing information at all stations must be updated. Second, this approach does not provide for automatic adjustment in the face of the failure of a bridge or LAN.
2. One station on a LAN can query other stations on the same LAN for routing information about distant stations. This approach may reduce the overall amount of routing messages that must be transmitted compared to option 3 below. However, at least one station on each LAN must have the needed routing information, so this is not a complete solution.

TABLE 14.4 Effects of Various Combinations of Addressing and Source Routing

Addressing Mode	Routing Specification			
	No Routing	Nonbroadcast	All Routes	Single Route
Individual	Received by station if it is on the same LAN	Received by station if it is on one of the LANs on the route	Received by station if it is on any LAN	Received by station if it is on any LAN
Group	Received by all group members on the same LAN	Received by all group members on all LANs visited on this route	Received by all group members on all LANs	Received by all group members on all LANs
All stations	Received by all stations on the same LAN	Received by all stations on all LANs visited on this route	Received by all stations on all LANs	Received by all stations on all LANs

3. When a station needs to learn the route to a destination station, it engages in a dynamic route discovery procedure.

Option 3 is the most flexible and the one that is specified by IEEE 802.5. As was mentioned earlier, two approaches are possible. The source station can transmit an all-routes request frame to the destination. Thus all possible routes to the destination are discovered. The destination station can send back a nonbroadcast response on each of the discovered routes, allowing the source to choose which route to follow in subsequently transmitting the frame. This approach generates quite a bit of both forward and backward traffic and requires the destination station to receive and transmit a number of frames. An alternative is for the source station to transmit a single-route request frame. Only one copy of this frame will reach the destination. The destination responds with an all-routes response frame, which generates all possible routes back to the source. Again, the source can choose among these alternative routes.

Figure 14.16 illustrates the latter approach. Assume that the spanning tree that has been chosen for this internet consists of bridges B1, B3, and B4. In this example, station X wishes to discover a route to station Z. Station X issues a single-route request frame. Bridge B2 is not on the spanning tree and so does not forward the frame. The other bridges do forward the frame and it reaches station Z. Note that bridge B4 forwards the frame to LAN 4, although this is not necessary; it is simply an effect of the spanning tree mechanism. When Z receives this frame, it responds with an all-routes frame. Two messages reach X: one on the path LAN 2, B3, LAN 3, B1, LAN 1, and the other on the path LAN 2, B4, LAN 4, B2, LAN 1. Note that frame that arrived by the latter route is received by bridge B1 and forwarded onto LAN 3. However, when bridge B3 receives this frame, it sees in the routing information field that the frame has already visited LAN 2; therefore, it does not forward the frame. A similar fate occurs for the frame that follows the first route and is forwarded by bridge B2.

Once a collection of routes has been discovered, the source station needs to select one of the routes. The obvious criterion would be to select the minimum-hop route. Alternatively, a minimum-cost route could be selected, where the cost of a network is inversely proportional to its data rate. In either case, if two or more routes are equivalent by the chosen criterion, there are several alternatives:

1. Choose the route corresponding to the response message that arrives first. One may assume that that particular route is less congested than the others since the frame on that route arrived earliest.
2. Choose randomly. This should have the effect, over time, of leveling the load among the various bridges.

Another point to consider is how often to update a route. Routes should certainly be changed in response to network failures and perhaps should be changed in response to network congestion. If connection-oriented logical link control is used (see Chapter 5), one possibility is to rediscover the route with each new connection. Another alternative, which works with either connection-oriented or connectionless service, is to associate a timer with each selected route and rediscover the route when its time expires.

Frame Format

With source routing, changes must be made to the MAC frame format. Figure 14.17 shows the frame format specified by the 802.5 source routing document. Recall that the first bit of the destination address indicates whether the address is an individual or a group address. Clearly, a source address must always be an individual address. To accommodate source routing, this

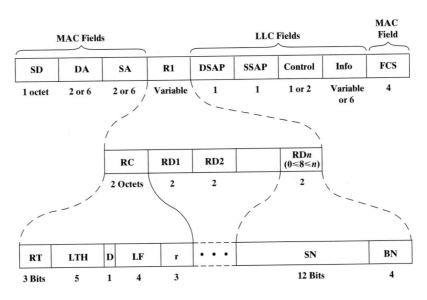

SD = Starting delimiter
DA = Destination (MAC) address
SA = Source (MAS) address
RI = Routing information
DSAP = Destination (LLC) service access point
SSAP = Source (LLC) service access point
Control = LLC control
Info = User information
FCS = Frame check sequence

RI = Routing information
RC = Routing control
RD*i* = Route designator *i*
RT = Routing type
LTH = Length
D = Direction
LF = Largest frame
r = Reserved
SN = Segment number
BN = Bridge number

FIGURE 14.17   Source Routing Formats

bit becomes the routing information indicator (RII). The RII bit is set to 0 to indicate null routing and to 1 to indicate that routing information is present in the frame. In the latter case, a new field is added to the MAC frame, the routing information field, which consists of a routing control field followed by from 0 to 14 route designation fields. The routing control field consists of the following subfields:

- *Routing type (3 bits):* indicates the type of routing directive (none, non-broadcast, all-routes, single-route)
- *Length (5 bits):* indicates the length of the routing information control field, in octets
- *Direction (1 bit):* indicates to a bridge whether the frame is traveling from the originating station to the target, or vice versa. Its use allows the list of route designation fields to appear in the same order for frames traveling in both directions along the route.
- *Largest frame (4 bits):* specifies the largest size of the MAC information field that may be transmitted on this route. This field is encoded to indicate certain common sizes. For example, 0011 indicates a maximum size of 1500 octets, which corresponds to the IEEE 802.3 CSMA/CD and Ethernet limitations; 0111 indicates 4472 octets, which corresponds to FDDI. When a bridge receives a frame, it updates this field if the specified size exceeds what the bridge can handle or its adjoining LANs allow. In this way, the route discovery process also discovers the maximum frame size that can be handled on a particular route.

The remainder of the routing information field consists of a sequence of route designators, each designator corresponding to one hop. The route designator consists of a 12-bit segment number (LAN number) and a 4-bit bridge number.

Spanning Tree versus Source Routing

In this subsection a brief comparison of the two approaches to bridge routing is provided.

The spanning tree approach requires no addition to the station logic and no changes to MAC frame format. Thus it preserves full transparency. That is, a collection of LANs interconnected by bridges using spanning tree routing behaves, from the station's point of view, as a single LAN. The principal drawback of this approach is that it limits the use of redundant bridges to a standby role for availability. Only designated bridges forward frames and other bridges are unused until a designated bridge fails. Thus redundant bridges cannot be used to share the traffic load, which would provide load leveling and perhaps improved throughput.

Source routing requires additional station logic (route discovery, route selection, insertion of the routing information field in the MAC frame) and changes to the MAC frame format. Thus this method is not fully transparent. However, source routing does permit the selection of an optimal route for each source–destination pair, and permits all bridges to participate in frame forwarding, thus leveling the load. Furthermore, this method requires additional bits to be added to each frame that traverses more than one LAN, increasing the traffic burden.

The other concern relating to source routing is the magnitude of the effect of the route discovery algorithm. We will illustrate the concern with an example, which uses the configuration of Figure 14.18. The shaded bridges in the configuration are assumed to be the designated bridges if the spanning tree approach is used. Using the spanning tree approach, a frame sent from H2 to H1 will traverse 2 bridges and 3 LANs; only one copy of the frame will arrive at H1. In the source routing case, the route from H1 to H2 must first be discovered. Using single-route broadcasting, a request frame is sent from H2 to H1. H1 responds with an all-routes frame. When B0, B1, and B3 receive the frame, each of them will try to forward it further to LANs it has not passed through. The original response frame will then be fabricated to multiple copies on other LANs. Specifically, four copies will be transmitted on LAN 2, five on LAN 3, and six on LAN 4, for a total of 16 transmissions of the frame (including the initial transmission on LAN 1). The result of this effort will be a route through B3 which is shorter than the spanning tree route through B2 and B1.

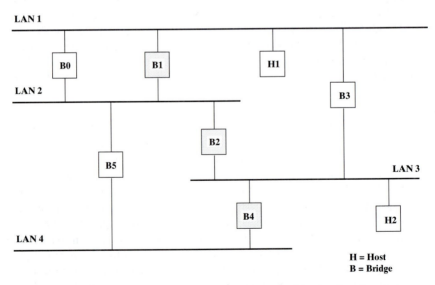

FIGURE 14.18   Internet Configuration for Comparison of Bridge Routing Approaches [ZHAN88]

Thus, while the source routing method may produce shorter routes and provide load leveling, the source discovery algorithm is very resource intensive. Even for this small example, 16 transmissions were required. In general, the number of frame copies transmitted for route discovery is on the order of $O(N^M)$, where N is the average number of bridges on each LAN and M the number of LANs in the configuration [ZHAN88]. For example, a configuration consisting of 12 LANs with an average of 2 bridges per LAN, which is still a modest configuration, would generate on the order of $2^{12} = 4096$ frames for each route discovery.

In summary, source routing offers certain advantages in route selection at the cost of additional station logic, frame overhead, and considerable traffic overhead. In most situations the spanning tree approach should prove adequate and avoids the disadvantages of the source routing approach.

Source Routing Transparent

The transparent bridge standard is available on many IEEE 802.3 and 802.4 products, while the source routing bridge standard is widely available on 802.5 products. While both types of bridges have advantages and disadvantages, a key problem with both is that they are incompatible. To allow the interconnection of LANs by a mixture of transparent and source routing bridges, a new standard has been developed by the 802.5 committee, referred to as the SRT (source routing transparent) technique.

The key to the operation of an SRT bridge is the RII bit in the MAC source address field. Recall that this bit is set to 1 by a source station to indicate that routing is desired and to 0 to indicate that no routing is to be performed (i.e., the frame should not be picked up by a source routing bridge). This bit is not used by stations that are supported by transparent bridges. As the name implies, the transparent bridge approach is transparent to the end stations. Thus the RII bit is always set to 0 by a station that is not participating in source routing.

Figure 14.19 indicates how the RII bit is used by an SRT bridge. All passing user data frames are observed by the bridge. If RII = 1, the frame is handled by source routing logic; if RII = 0, the frame is handled by transparent bridge logic.

So much for the basic frame forwarding logic. The difficult design problems associated with SRT bridging have to do with how routes are established. For transparent bridging, a spanning tree must be developed among all of the bridges. For source routing, a spanning tree must also be developed. The requirement for SRT operation is that the bridge must permit both transparent and source routing stations to participate within the same spanning tree. Since the SRT bridge includes transparent bridge logic, it can interoperate with pure transparent bridges to create the spanning tree.

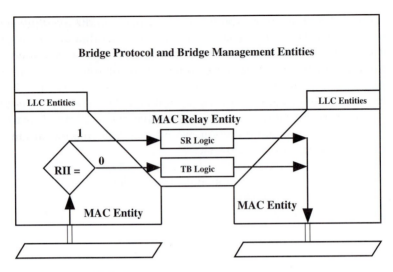

FIGURE 14.19   SRT Bridge Logic

Thus we can have a collection of LANs interconnected by a mixture of transparent bridges and SRT bridges. However, pure source routing bridges could not be incorporated into such a configuration, because they are incapable of passing transparent frames.

14.5

RECOMMENDED READING

The definitive study of the topics in this chapter is [PERL92]. [BERT92], and [SPRA91] examine the performance implications of transparent bridging and source routing.

BERT92   Bertsekas, D., and Gallager, R. *Data Networks*. Englewood Cliffs, NJ: Prentice Hall, 1992.

PERL92   Perlman, R. *Interconnections: Bridges and Routers*. Reading, MA: Addison-Wesley, 1992.

SPRA91   Spragins, J., Hammond, J., and Pawlikowski, K. *Telecommunications Protocols and Design*. Reading, MA.: Addison-Wesley, 1991.

14.6

PROBLEMS

14.1 Consider a token-passing LAN configured as a single network with N stations or two subnetworks, each with $N/2$ stations, connected by a bridge. Assume no delay at the bridge other than medium access delay. Do a breakpoint analysis of the type described in Chapter 13 to show the relative delay characteristics of the two configurations as a function of the percentage of internetwork traffic.

14.2 Recall that the token ring MAC protocol specifies that the A and C bits may be set by a station on the ring to indicate address recognized and frame copied, respectively. This information is then available to the source station when the frame returns after circulating around the ring. If a bridge captures a frame and forwards it, should it set the A and C bits or not? Make a case for each policy.

Internetworking and Routers

The bridge is only applicable to a configuration involving a single type of LAN. Of course, in many cases, an organization will need access to devices on a variety of networks. For example, an organization may have a tiered LAN architecture, with different types of LANs used for different purposes within an organization. There may also need to be access to devices on a wide-area network. Examples of the latter are a public information source or data base for query and transaction applications and a customer or supplier computer for transferring ordering information.

A general-purpose device that can be used to connect dissimilar networks and that operates at layer 3 of the OSI model is known as a *router*. We begin this chapter by looking at the requirements that must be satisfied by the router to support internetworking. Next, the internet protocol (IP), part of the TCP/IP protocol suite, is examined. Finally, the issue of internetwork routing is explored.

15.1

INTERNETWORKING

Internetworking is achieved by using intermediate systems, or routers, to interconnect a number of independent networks. Essential functions that the router must perform include:

1. Provide a link between networks.
2. Provide for the routing and delivery of data between processes on end systems attached to different networks.
3. Provide these functions in such a way as to not require modifications of the networking architecture of any of the attached subnetworks.

Point three means that the router must accommodate a number of differences among networks, such as:

- *Addressing schemes.* The networks may use different schemes for assigning addresses to devices. For example, an IEEE 802 LAN uses either 16-bit or 48-bit binary addresses for each attached device; an X.25 public packet-switching network uses 12-digit decimal addresses (encoded as four bits per digit for a 48-bit address). Some form of global network addressing must be provided, as well as a directory service.

- *Maximum packet sizes.* Packets from one network may have to be broken into smaller pieces to be transmitted on another network, a process known as *segmentation*. For example, Ethernet imposes a maximum packet size of 1500 bytes; a maximum packet size of 1000 bytes is common on X.25 networks. A packet that is transmitted on an Ethernet system and picked up by a router for retransmission on an X.25 network may have to segment the incoming packet into two smaller ones.

- *Interfaces.* The hardware and software interfaces to various networks differ. The concept of a router must be independent of these differences.

- *Reliability.* Various network services may provide anything from a reliable end-to-end virtual circuit to an unreliable service. The operation of the routers should not depend on an assumption of network reliability.

The foregoing requirements are best satisfied by a protocol, referred to as an *internetworking protocol,* that is implemented in all end systems and routers. In the remainder of this section we examine the protocol architecture and design issues related to an internetworking protocol. In the next section we look at the most widely used internetworking protocol, the internet protocol (IP).

Protocol Architecture

Router operation depends on the use of an internetworking protocol. Figure 15.1 depicts a typical example using IP, in which two LANs are interconnected by a X.25 packet-switched WAN. The figure depicts the operation of the internet protocol for data exchange between host A on one LAN (subnetwork 1) and host B on another departmental LAN (subnetwork 2) through the WAN. The figure shows the format of the data unit at each stage. The end systems and routers must all share a common internet protocol. In addition, the end systems must share the same protocols above IP. The intermediate routers need only implement up through IP.

The IP at A receives blocks of data to be sent to B from the higher layers of software in A. IP attaches a header specifying, among other things, the global internet address of B. That address is logically in two parts: network identifier and end system identifier. The result is called an *internet protocol data unit,* or simply a *datagram.* The datagram is then encapsulated with the LAN protocol and sent to the router, which strips off the LAN fields to read the IP header. The router then encapsulates the datagram with the X.25 protocol fields and transmits it across the WAN to another router. This router strips off the X.25 fields and recovers the datagram, which it then wraps in LAN fields appropriate to LAN 2 and sends it to B.

Let us now look at this example in more detail. End system A has a datagram to transmit to end system B; the datagram includes the internet address of B. The IP module in A recognizes that the destination (B) is on another subnetwork. So the first step is to send the data to a router, in this case router X. To do this, IP passes the datagram down to the next-lower layer (in this case LLC) with instructions to send it to router X. LLC in turn passes this information down to the MAC layer, which inserts the MAC-level address of router X into the MAC header. Thus the block of data transmitted onto LAN 1 includes data from a layer or layer above TCP, plus a TCP header, an IP header, an LLC header, and a MAC header and trailer.

Next, the packet travels through subnetwork 1 to router X. The router removes MAC and LLC fields and analyzes the IP header to determine the ultimate destination of the data, in this case B. The router must now make a routing decision. There are three possibilities:

1. The destination station Y is connected directly to one of the subnetworks to which the router is attached. In this case the router sends the datagram directly to the destination.

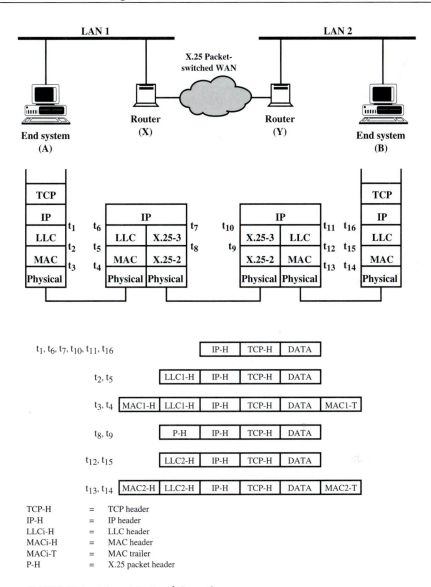

FIGURE 15.1   Internet Protocol Operation

2. To reach the destination, one or more additional routers must be traversed. In this case a routing decision must be made: To which router should the datagram be sent? In both cases the IP module in the router sends the datagram down to the next-lower layer with the destination subnetwork address. Please note that we are speaking here of a lower-layer address that refers to this network.

3. The router does not know the destination address. In this case the router returns an error message to the source of the datagram.

In this example the data must pass through router *Y* before reaching the destination. So router *X* constructs a new packet by appending an X.25 header, containing the address of router *Y*, to the IP data unit. When this packet arrives at router *Y*, the packet header is stripped off. The router determines that this IP data unit is destined for *B*, which is connected directly to a network to which this router is attached. The router therefore creates a frame with a destination address of *B* and sends it out onto LAN 2. The data finally arrive at *B*, where the LAN and IP headers can be stripped off.

At each router, before the data can be forwarded, the router may need to segment the data unit to accommodate a smaller maximum packet size limitation on the outgoing network. The data unit is split into two or more segments, each of which becomes an independent IP data unit. Each new data unit is wrapped in a lower-layer packet and queued for transmission. The router may also limit the length of its queue for each network to which is attaches so as to avoid having a slow network penalize a faster one. Once the queue limit is reached, additional data units are simply dropped.

The process described above continues through as many routers as it takes for the data unit to reach its destination. As with a router, the destination end system recovers the IP data unit from its network wrapping. If segmentation has occurred, the IP module in the destination end system buffers the incoming data until the entire original data field can be reassembled. This block of data is then passed to a higher layer in the end system.

This service offered by the internet protocol is an unreliable one. That is, the internet protocol does not guarantee that all data will be delivered or that the data that are delivered will arrive in the proper order. It is the responsibility of the next-higher layer (e.g., TCP) to recover from any errors that occur. This approach provides for a great deal of flexibility.

With the internet protocol approach, each unit of data is passed from router to router in an attempt to get from source to destination. Since delivery is not guaranteed, there is no particular reliability requirement on any of the subnetworks. Thus the protocol will work with any combination of subnetwork types. Since the sequence of delivery is not guaranteed, successive data units can follow different paths through the internet. This allows the protocol to react to congestion and failure in the internet by changing routes.

Design Issues

With that brief sketch of the operation of an IP-controlled internet, we can now go back and examine some design issues in greater detail. These are:

- Addressing
- Routing
- Datagram lifetime
- Segmentation and reassembly

Addressing.   To transfer data from one end system to another end system, there must be some way of uniquely identifying the destination ES. Thus, with each ES, we must be able to associate a unique identifier, or address. This address will allow ESs and ISs to perform the routing function properly.

In the OSI environment, this unique address is typically equated to a **network service access point** (NSAP). An NSAP uniquely identifies a ES within the internet. A ES may have more than one NSAP, but each is unique to that particular system. A network layer address may also refer to the network protocol entity itself. The latter is appropriate in an intermediate system, which does not support upper layers via an NSAP. In the case of an IS, the network layer address is called a **network entity title** (NET).

Both NSAPs and NETs provide an unambiguous global internet address. Frequently, this address is in the form of *(network, host)*, where the parameter *network* identifies a particular subnetwork and the parameter *host* identifies a particular ES attached to that subnetwork.

Figure 15.2 suggests that another level of addressing is needed. Each subnetwork must maintain a unique address for each ES attached to that subnetwork. This allows the subnetwork to route data units through the subnetwork and deliver them to the intended ES. Such an address is referred to as a **subnetwork point of attachment** (SNPA) address.

It would appear convenient for the *host* parameter in the global address to be identical to the SNPA for that ES. Unfortunately, this may not always be practical. Different networks use different addressing formats and different address lengths. Furthermore, an ES may enjoy more than one attachment point into the same network. Accordingly, we must assume that the *host* parameter has global significance and that the SNPA has significance only within a particular subnetwork. In this case the internetworking facility must translate from the global address to the locally significant address to route data units.

Routing.   Routing is generally accomplished by maintaining a routing table in each end system and router that gives, for each possible destination network, the next router to which the internet datagram should be sent.

The routing table may be static or dynamic. A static table, however, could contain alternate routes if a router is unavailable. A dynamic table is more flexible in responding to both error and congestion conditions. In the Internet, for example, when a router goes down, all of its neighbors will send out a status report, allowing other routers and stations to update their

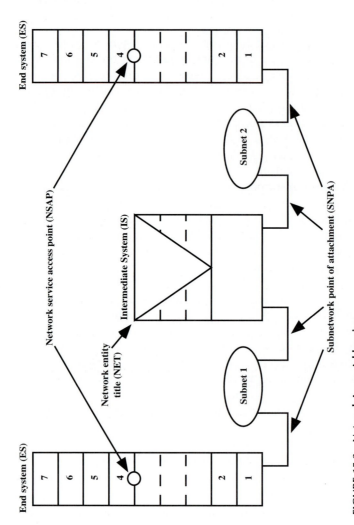

FIGURE 15.2   Network-Layer Addressing

518

routing tables. A similar scheme can be used to control congestion. This latter is particularly important because of the mismatch in capacity between local and wide-area networks. Section 15.3 discusses routing protocols.

Routing tables may also be used to support other internetworking services, such as security and priority. For example, individual networks might be classified to handle data up to a given security classification. The routing mechanism must assure that data of a given security level is not allowed to pass through networks not cleared to handle such data.

Another routing technique is source routing. The source station specifies the route by including a sequential list of routers in the datagram. This, again, could be useful for security or priority requirements.

Finally, we mention a service related to routing: route recording. To record a route, each router appends its internet address to a list of addresses in the datagram. This feature is useful for testing and debugging purposes.

Datagram Lifetime.   If dynamic or alternate routing is used, the potential exists for a datagram or some of its segments to circulate indefinitely through the internet. For example, if there are sudden, significant shifts in internet traffic, the datagram might be diverted first one way and then another to avoid areas of congestion. Additionally, there might be a flaw in the routing tables of the various routers that causes the datagram to stay inside the network. These problems place an undesirable burden on the internet. To avoid these problems, each datagram can be marked with a lifetime. Once the lifetime expires, the datagram is discarded.

A simple way to implement lifetime is to use a hop count. Each time that a datagram passes through a router, the count is decremented. Alternatively, the lifetime could be a true measure of time. This requires that the routers must somehow know how long it has taken for the datagram to traverse the last network, so as to know by how much to decrement the lifetime field. The advantage of using a true measure of time is that it can be used in the reassembly algorithm, which is described next.

Segmentation and Reassembly.   Individual subnetworks within an internet may specify different maximum packet sizes. It would be inefficient and unwieldy to try to dictate uniform packet size across networks. Thus routers may need to segment incoming datagrams into smaller pieces before transmitting on to the next subnetwork.

If datagrams can be segmented (perhaps more than once) in the course of their travels, the question arises as to where they should be reassembled. The easiest solution is to have reassembly performed at the destination only. The principal disadvantage of this approach is that packets can only get smaller as data move through the internet. This may impair the efficiency of some networks. On the other hand, if intermediate router reassembly is allowed, the following disadvantages result:

1. Large buffers are required at routers, and there is the risk that all of the buffer space will be used up storing partial datagrams.
2. All fragments of a datagram must pass through the same gateway. This inhibits the use of dynamic routing.

In IP, datagram segments are reassembled at the destination end system. The IP segmentation technique uses the following fields in the IP header:

- Data unit identifier (ID)
- Data length
- Offset
- More flag

The *ID* is a means of uniquely identifying an end-system-originated datagram. In IP it consists of the source and destination addresses, an identifier of the protocol layer that generated the data (e.g., TCP), and a sequence number supplied by that protocol layer. The *data length* is the length of the user data field in octets, and the *offset* is the position of a segment of user data in the data field of the original datagram, in multiples of 64 bits.

The source end system creates a datagram with a *data length* equal to the entire length of the data field, with offset = 0, and a *more flag* set to 0 (false). To segment a long datagram, an IP module in a router performs the following tasks:

1. Create two new datagrams and copy the header fields of the incoming datagram into both.
2. Divide the incoming user data field into two approximately equal portions along a 64-bit boundary, placing one portion in each new datagram. The first portion must be a multiple of 64 bits.
3. Set the *data length* of the first new datagram to the length of the inserted data, and set *more flag* to 1 (true). The offset field is unchanged.
4. Set the *data length* of the second new datagram to the length of the inserted data, and add the length of the first data portion divided by 8 to the offset field. The *more flag* remains the same.

Table 15.1 gives an example. The procedure can easily be generalized to an *n*-way split.

To reassemble a datagram, there must be sufficient buffer space at the reassembly point. As segments with the same ID arrive, their data fields are inserted in the proper position in the buffer until the entire data field is reassembled, which is achieved when a contiguous set of data exists starting with an *offset* of zero and ending with data from a segment with a false *more flag*.

TABLE 15.1   Segmentation Example

Original Datagram	First Segment	Second Segment
Data length = 472	Data length = 240	Data length = 232
Segment offset = 0	Segment offset = 0	Segment offset = 30
More = 0	More = 1	More = 0

One eventuality that must be dealt with is that one or more of the segments may not get through: the IP service does not guarantee delivery. Some means is needed to decide to abandon a reassembly effort to free up buffer space. Two approaches are commonly used. First, assign a reassembly lifetime to the first segment to arrive. This is a local, real-time clock assigned by the reassembly function and decremented while the segments of the original datagram are being buffered. If the time expires prior to complete reassembly, the received segments are discarded. A second approach is to make use of the datagram lifetime, which is part of the header of each incoming segment. The lifetime field continues to be decremented by the reassembly function; as with the first approach, if the lifetime expires prior to complete reassembly, the received segments are discarded.

15.2

INTERNET PROTOCOL

The internet protocol (IP), part of the TCP/IP protocol suite, is the most widely used internetworking protocol. It is functionally similar to the ISO standard connectionless network protocol (CLNP). As with any protocol standard, IP is specified in two parts:

- The interface with a higher layer (e.g., TCP), specifying the services that IP provides
- The actual protocol format and mechanisms

IP Services

IP provides two service primitives at the interface to the next-higher layer (Figure 15.3). The send primitive is used to request transmission of a data unit. The deliver primitive is used by IP to notify a user of the arrival of a data unit. The parameters associated with the two primitives are:

- *Source address:* internetwork address of sending IP entity
- *Destination address:* internetwork address of destination IP entity
- *Protocol:* recipient protocol entity (an IP user)

```
Send   (                              Deliver   (
        Source address                          Source address
        Destination address                     Destination address
        Protocol                                Protocol
        Type of service indicators              Type of service indicators
        Identifier
        Don't fragment identifier
        Time to live
        Data length                             Data length
        Option data                             Option data
        Data                                    Data
        )                                       )
```

FIGURE 15.3   IP Service Primitives and Parameters

- *Type of service indicators:* used to specify the treatment of the data unit in its transmission through component networks
- *Identifier:* used in combination with the source and destination addresses and user protocol to identify the data unit uniquely; needed for reassembly and error reporting
- *Don't fragment identifier:* indicates whether IP can segment (called fragment in the standard) data to accomplish delivery
- *Time to live:* measured in network hops
- *Data length:* length of data being transmitted
- *Option data:* options requested by the IP user
- *Data:* user data to be transmitted

Note that the *identifier, don't fragment identifier,* and *time to live* parameters are present in the send primitive but not in the deliver primitive. These three parameters provide instructions to IP that are not of concern to the recipient IP user.

The sending IP user includes the *type of service* parameter to request a particular quality of service. The user may specify one or more of the options listed in Table 15.2. This parameter can be used to guide routing decisions. For example, if a router has several alternative choices for the next hop in routing a datagram, it may choose a network with higher data rate if the high throughput option has been selected. This parameter is also passed down to the network access protocol for use over individual networks if possible. For example, if a precedence level is selected and if the subnetwork supports precedence or priority levels, the precedence level will be mapped onto the network level for this hop.

The options parameter allows for future extensibility and for inclusion of parameters that are usually not invoked. The currently defined options are:

- *Security:* allows a security label to be attached to a datagram.
- *Source routing:* a sequenced list of router addresses that specifies the route to be followed; may be strict (only identified routers may be visited) or loose (other intermediate routers may be visited)

TABLE 15.2 IP Service Quality Options

Option	Definition
Precedence	A measure of a datagram's relative importance. Eight levels of precedence are used. IP will attempt to provide preferential treatment for higher precedence datagrams.
Reliability	One of two levels may be specified: normal or high. A high value indicates a request that attempts be made to minimize the likelihood that this datagram will be lost or damaged.
Delay	One of two levels may be specified: normal or low. A low value indicates a request to minimize the delay that this datagram will experience.
Throughput	One of two levels may be specified: normal or high. A high value indicates a request to maximize the throughput for this datagram.

- *Route recording:* a field allocated to record the sequence of routers visited by the datagram
- *Stream identification:* names reserved resources used for stream service; provides special handling for volatile periodic traffic (e.g., voice)
- *Timestamping:* the source IP entity and some or all intermediate routers that add a timestamp (precision to milliseconds) to the data unit as it goes by

IP Protocol

The protocol between IP entities is best described with reference to the IP datagram format, shown in Figure 15.4. The fields are:

- *Version (4 bits):* indicates version number, to allow evolution of the protocol.
- *Internet header length (4 bits):* length of header in 32-bit words. The minimum value is five, for a minimum header length of 20 octets.
- *Type of service (8 bits):* specifies reliability, precedence, delay, and throughput parameters.
- *Total length (16 bits):* total datagram length, in octets.
- *Identifier (16 bits):* a sequence number that, together with the source address, destination address, and user protocol, is intended to identify a datagram uniquely. Thus the identifier should be unique for the datagram's source address, destination address, and user protocol for the time during which the datagram will remain in the internet.
- *Flags (3 bits):* only two of the bits are currently defined. The More bit is used for segmentation (fragmentation) and reassembly, as previously explained. The Don't Fragment bit prohibits fragmentation when set.

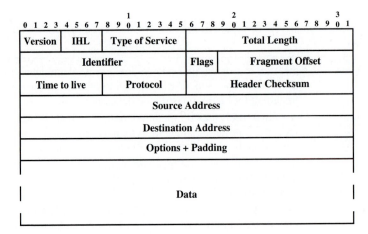

FIGURE 15.4   Internet Protocol (IP) Format

This bit may be useful if it is known that the destination does not have the capability to reassemble segments. However, if this bit is set, the datagram will be discarded if it exceeds the maximum size of an en route subnetwork. Therefore, if the bit is set, it may be advisable to use source routing to avoid subnetworks with small maximum packet size.

- *Fragment offset (13 bits):* indicates where in the original datagram this fragment belongs, measured in 64-bit units. This implies that fragments other than the last fragment must contain a data field that is a multiple of 64 bits in length.
- *Time to live (8 bits):* measured in router hops.
- *Protocol (8 bits):* indicates the next-higher-level protocol that is to receive the data field at the destination.
- *Header checksum (16 bits):* an error-detecting code applied to the header only. Since some header fields may change during transit (e.g., time to live, segmentation-related fields), this is reverified and recomputed at each router. The checksum field is the 16-bit one's-complement addition of all 16-bit words in the header. For purposes of computation, the checksum field is itself initialized to a value of zero.
- *Source address (32 bits):* coded to allow a variable allocation of bits to specify the network and the end system attached to the specified network (7 and 24 bits, 14 and 16 bits, or 21 and 8 bits).
- *Destination address (32 bits):* as above.
- *Options (variable):* encodes the options requested by the sending user.
- *Padding (variable):* used to ensure that the datagram header is a multiple of 32 bits in length.

- *Data (variable):* must be an integer multiple of 8 bits in length. The maximum length of the datagram (data field plus header) is 65,535 octets.

It should be clear how the IP services specified in the Send and Deliver primitives map into the fields of the IP datagram.

15.3

ROUTING

The routers in an internet are responsible for receiving and forwarding packets through the interconnected set of subnetworks. Each router makes routing decisions based on knowledge of the topology and conditions of the internet. In a simple internet, a fixed routing scheme is possible. In more complex internets, a degree of dynamic cooperation is needed among the routers. In particular, the router must avoid portions of the network that have failed and should avoid portions of the network that are congested. To make such dynamic routing decisions, routers exchange routing information using a special routing protocol for that purpose. Information is needed about the status of the internet, in terms of which networks can be reached by which routes, and the delay characteristics of various routes.

In considering the routing function of routers, it is important to distinguish two concepts:

- *Routing information:* information about the topology and delays of the internet
- *Routing algorithm:* the algorithm used to make a routing decision for a particular datagram, based on current routing information

There is another way to partition the problem that is useful from the point of view both of allocating routing functions properly and effective standardization. This is to partition the routing function into:

- Routing between end systems (ESs) and routers
- Routing between routers

The reason for the partition is that there are fundamental differences between what an ES must know to route a packet and what a router must know. In the case of an ES, it must first know whether the destination ES is on the same subnet. If so, data can be delivered directly using the subnetwork access protocol. If not, the ES must forward the data to a router attached to the same subnetwork. If there is more than one such router, it is simply a matter of choosing one. The router forwards datagrams on behalf of other systems and needs to have some idea of the overall topology of the network in order to make a global routing decision. In this section we look at an example of an ES-to-router and router-to-router protocol.

Autonomous Systems

In order to proceed in our discussion of router–router protocols, we need to introduce the concept of an **autonomous system.** An autonomous system is an internet connected by homogeneous routers; generally the routers are under the administrative control of a single entity. An **interior router protocol** (IRP) passes routing information between routers within an autonomous system. The protocol used within the autonomous system does not need to be implemented outside the system. This flexibility allows IRPs to be custom tailored to specific applications and requirements.

It may happen, however, that an internet will be constructed of more than one autonomous system. For example, all of the LANs at a site, such as an office complex or campus, could be linked by routers to form an autonomous system. This system might be linked through a wide-area network to other autonomous systems. The situation is illustrated in Figure 15.5. In this case the routing algorithms and routing tables used by routers in different autonomous systems may differ. Nevertheless, the routers in one autonomous system need at least a minimal level of information concerning networks outside the system that can be reached. The protocol used to pass routing information between routers in different autonomous systems is referred to as an **exterior router protocol** (ERP).

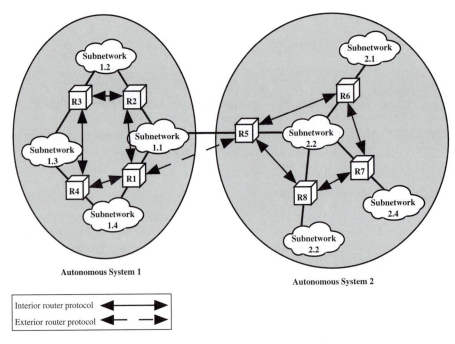

FIGURE 15.5   **Application of Exterior and Interior Routing Protocols**

We can expect that an ERP will need to pass less information and be simpler than an IRP, for the following reason. If a datagram is to be transferred from a host in one autonomous system to a host in another autonomous system, a router in the first system need only determine the target autonomous system and devise a route to get into that target system. Once the datagram enters the target autonomous system, the routers within that system can cooperate to finally deliver the datagram.

Border Gateway Protocol

The *border gateway protocol* (BGP)[1] was developed for use in conjunction with internets that employ the TCP/IP protocol suite, although the concepts are applicable to any internet. BGP has become the standardized exterior router protocol for the Internet.

Functions.   BGP was designed to allow routers, called gateways in the standard, in different autonomous systems (ASs) to cooperate in the exchange of routing information. The protocol operates in terms of messages, which are sent over TCP connections. The repertoire of messages is summarized in Table 15.3.

Three functional procedures are involved in BGP:

- Neighbor acquisition
- Neighbor reachability
- Network reachability

Two routers are considered to be neighbors if they are attached to the same subnetwork. If the two routers are in different autonomous systems, they may wish to exchange routing information. For this purpose it is first necessary to perform **neighbor acquisition.** The term *neighbor* refers to two routers that share the same subnetwork. In essence, neighbor acquisition occurs when two neighboring routers in different autonomous systems agree to exchange routing information on a regular basis. A formal acquisi-

TABLE 15.3   BGP-4 Messages

Message	Definition
Open	Used to open a neighbor relationship with another router
Update	Used to (1) transmit information about a single route and/or (2) to list multiple routes to be withdrawn
Keepalive	Used to (1) acknowledge an Open message and (2) periodically confirm the neighbor relationship
Notification	Send when an error condition is detected

[1]*A Border Gateway Protocol 4 (BGP-4)*, RFC 1771, March 1995.

tion procedure is needed since one of the routers may not wish to participate. For example, the router may be overburdened and not want to be responsible for traffic coming in from outside the system. In the neighbor acquisition process, one router sends a request message to the other, which may either accept or refuse the offer. The protocol does not address the issue of how one router knows the address or even the existence of another router, nor how it decides that it needs to exchange routing information with that particular router. These issues must be dealt with at configuration time or by active intervention of a network manager.

To perform neighbor acquisition, one router sends an Open message to another. If the target router accepts the request, it returns a Keepalive message in response.

Once a neighbor relationship is established, the **neighbor reachability** procedure is used to maintain the relationship. Each partner needs to be assured that the other partner still exists and is still engaged in the neighbor relationship. For this purpose, the two routers periodically issue Keepalive messages to each other.

The final procedure specified by BGP is **network reachability.** Each router maintains a database of the subnetworks that it can reach and the preferred route for reaching that subnetwork. Whenever a change is made to this database, the router issues an Update message that is broadcast to all other routers implementing BGP. By the broadcasting of these Update messages, all of the BGP routers can build up and maintain routing information.

BGP Messages.   Figure 15.6 illustrates the formats of all of the BGP messages, and Table 15.4 defines the fields. Each message begins with a 19-octet header containing three fields, as indicated by the shaded portion of each message in the figure. To acquire a neighbor, a router first opens a TCP connection to the neighbor router of interest. It then sends an Open message. This message identifies the AS to which the sender belongs and provides the IP address of the router. It also includes a Hold Time parameter, which indicates the number of seconds that the sender proposes for the value of the Hold Timer. If the recipient is prepared to open a neighbor relationship, it calculates a value of Hold Timer that is the minimum of its Hold Time and the Hold Time in the Open message. This calculated value is the maximum number of seconds that may elapse between the receipt of successive Keepalive and/or Update messages by the sender.

The Keepalive message consists simply of the header. Each router issues these messages to each of its peers often enough to prevent the Hold Time from expiring.

The Update message communicates two types of information:

1. Information about a single route through the internet. This information is available to be added to the database of any recipient router.

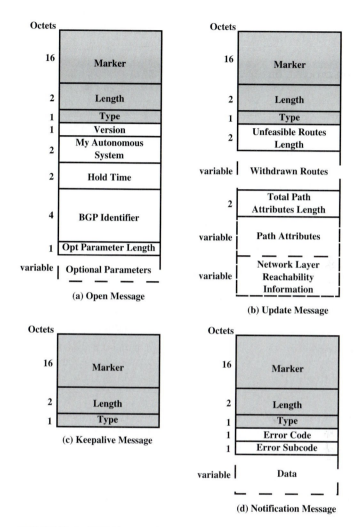

FIGURE 15.6   BGP Message Formats

2. A list of routes previously advertised by this router that are being withdrawn.

An Update message may contain one or both types of information. Let us consider the first type of information first. Information about a single route through the network involves three fields: the network layer reachability information (NLRI) field, the total path attributes length field, and the path attributes field. The NLRI field consists of a list of identifiers of subnetworks that can be reached by this route. Each subnetwork is identified by its IP address, which is actually a portion of a full IP address. Recall that an IP address is a 32-bit quantity of the form {network, end system}.

TABLE 15.4 BGP Message Fields

Field	Description
Header	
Marker	Reserved for authentication. The sender may insert a value in this field that would be used as part of an authentication mechanism to enable the recipient to verify the identity of the sender.
Length	Length of message in octets.
Type	Type of message: Open, Update, Notification, Keepalive.
Open Message	
Version	BGP protocol version.
My AS	Identifier of autonomous system of sender.
Hold Time	Proposed value of Hold Timer.
BGP Identifier	IP address identifying the BGP sender.
Optional Parameter Length	Length of the Optional Parameter field in octets.
Optional Parameters	List of optional parameters; Authentication Information is the only parameter defined in BGP-4.
Update Message	
Unfeasible Routes Length	Length of the Withdrawn Routes field in octets.
Withdrawn Routes	List of IP address prefixes for routes being withdrawn from service.
Total Path Attribute Length	Length of the Path Attributes field in octets.
Path Attributes	Sequence of path attributes.
Network Layer Reachability Information	List of IP address prefixes.
Notification	
Error code	Indicates type of notification.
Error subcode	Provides additional information about the reported error.
Data	Contains diagnostic information related to the notification.

The left-hand or prefix portion of this quantity identifies a particular sub-network.

The path attributes field contains a list of attributes that apply to this particular route. The following are the defined attributes:

- *Origin:* indicates whether this information was generated by an interior router protocol (e.g., OSPF) or an exterior router protocol (in particular, BGP).
- *AS_Path:* a list of the ASs that are traversed for this route.
- *Next_Hop:* the IP address of the border router that should be used as the next hop to the destinations listed in the NLRI field.
- *Multi_Exit_Disc:* used to communicate some information about routes internal to an AS. This is described later in this section.
- *Local_Pref:* used by a router to inform other routers within the same AS of its degree of preference for a particular route. It has no significance to routers in other ASs.
- *Atomic_Aggregate, Aggregator:* implement the concept of route aggregation. In essence, an internet and its corresponding address space can be organized hierarchically, or as a tree. In this case, subnetwork addresses are structured in two or more parts. All of the subnetworks of a given subtree share a common partial internet address. Using this common partial address, the amount of information that must be communicated in NLRI can be reduced significantly.

The AS_Path attribute actually serves two purposes. Because it lists the ASs that a datagram must traverse if it follows this route, the AS_Path information enables a router to perform policy routing. That is, a router may decide to avoid a particular path, to avoid transiting a particular AS. For example, information that is confidential may be limited to certain kinds of ASs. Or, a router may have information about the performance or quality of the portion of the internet that is included in an AS that leads the router to avoid that AS. Examples of performance or quality metrics include link speed, capacity, tendency to become congested, and overall quality of operation. Another criterion that could be used is minimizing the number of transit ASs.

The reader may wonder about the purpose of the Next_Hop attribute. The requesting router will necessarily want to know which networks are reachable via the responding router, but why provide information about other routers? This is best explained with reference to Figure 15.5. In this example, router R1 in autonomous system 1 and router R5 in autonomous system 2 implement BGP and acquire a neighbor relationship. R1 issues Update messages to R5 indicating which networks it could reach and the distances (network hops) involved. R1 also provides the same information on behalf of R2. That is, R1 tells R5 what networks are reachable via R2. In this example, R2 does not implement BGP. Typically, most of the routers in an autonomous system will not implement BGP. Only a few routers will be assigned responsibility for communicating with routers in other autonomous systems. A final point: R1 is in possession of the necessary information about R2, since R1 and R2 share an interior router protocol (IRP).

The second type of update information is the withdrawal of one or more routes. In each case the route is identified by the IP address of the destination subnetwork.

Finally, the Notification Message is sent when an error condition is detected. The following errors may be reported:

- *Message header error:* includes authentication and syntax errors.
- *Open message error:* includes syntax errors and options not recognized in an Open message. This message can also be used to indicate that a proposed Hold Time in an Open message is unacceptable.
- *Update message error:* includes syntax and validity errors in an Update message.
- *Hold timer expired:* if the sending router has not received successive Keepalive and/or Update and/or Notification messages within the Hold Time period, this error is communicated and the connection is closed.
- *Finite state machine error:* includes any procedural error.
- *Cease:* used by a router to close a connection with another router in the absence of any other error.

BGP Routing Information Exchange.   The essence of BGP is the exchange of routing information among participating routers in multiple ASs. This process can be quite complex. In what follows we provide a simplified overview.

Let us consider router R1 in autonomous system A (AS1) in Figure 15.5. To begin, a router that implements BGP will also implement an internal routing protocol such as OSPF. Using OSPF, R1 can exchange routing information with other routers within AS1 and build up a picture of the topology of the subnetworks and routers in AS1 and construct a routing table. Next, R1 can issue an Update message to R5 in AS2. The Update message could include the following:

- *AS_Path:* the identity of AS1
- *Next_Hop:* the IP address of R1
- *NLRI:* a list of all of the subnetworks in AS1

This message informs R5 that all of the subnetworks listed in NLRI are reachable via R1 and that the only autonomous system traversed is AS1.

Suppose now that R5 also has a neighbor relationship with another router in another autonomous system, say R9 in AS3. R5 will forward the information just received from R1 to R9 in a new Update message. This message includes the following:

- *AS_Path:* the list of identifiers {AS2, AS1}
- *Next_Hop:* the IP address of R5
- *NLRI:* a list of all of the subnetworks in AS1

This message informs R9 that all of the subnetworks listed in NLRI are reachable via R5 and that the autonomous systems traversed are AS2 and AS1. R9 must now decide if this is its preferred route to the subnetworks listed. It may have knowledge of an alternate route to some or all of these subnetworks that it prefers for reasons of performance or some other policy metric. If R9 decides that the route provided in R5's update message is preferable, R9 incorporates that routing information into its routing database and forwards this new routing information to other neighbors. This new message will include an AS_Path field of {AS1, AS2, AS3}.

In this fashion, routing update information is propagated through the larger internet, consisting of a number of interconnected autonomous systems. The AS_Path field is used to assure that such messages do not circulate indefinitely: If an Update message is received by a router in an AS that is included in the AS_Path field, that router will not forward the update information to other routers, preventing looping of messages.

The preceding discussion leaves out several details that are summarized briefly here. Routers within the same AS, called *internal neighbors,* may exchange BGP information. In this case the sending router does not add the identifier of the common AS to the AS_Path field. When a router has selected a preferred route to an external destination, it transmits this route to all of its internal neighbors. Each of these routers then decides if the new route is preferred, in which case the new route is added to its database and a new Update message goes out.

When there are multiple entry points into an AS that are available to a border router in another AS, the Multi_Exit_Disc attribute may be used to choose among them. This attribute contains a number that reflects some internal metric for reaching destinations within an AS. For example, suppose in Figure 15.5 that both R1 and R2 implemented BGP and both had a neighbor relationship with R5. Each provides an Update message to R5 for subnetwork 1.3 that includes a routing metric used internal to AS1, such as a routing metric associated with the OSPF internal router protocol. R5 could then use these two metrics as the basis of choosing between the two routes.

Open Shortest Path First (OSPF) Protocol

The open shortest path first (OSPF) protocol is widely used as an interior router protocol in TCP/IP networks.[2] OSPF uses what is known as a *link state routing algorithm*. Each router maintains descriptions of the state of its local links to subnetworks, and from time to time transmits updated state information to all of the routers of which is aware. Every router receiving an update packet must acknowledge it to the sender. Such updates produce a minimum of routing traffic because the link descriptions are small and rarely need to be sent.

OSPF computes a route through the internet that incurs the least cost based on a user-configurable metric of cost. The user can configure the cost to express a function of delay, data rate, dollar cost, or other factors. OSPF is able to equalize loads over multiple equal-cost paths.

Internet Topology.   Each router maintains a database that reflects the known topology of the autonomous system of which it is a part. The topology is expressed as a directed graph. The graph consists of:

- Vertices, or nodes, of two types
  —Router
  —Network, which is in turn of two types
    - Transit if it can carry data that neither originate nor terminate on an end system attached to this network
    - Stub, if it is not a transit network
- Edges of two types
  —A graph edge connects two router vertices when the corresponding routers are connected to each other by a direct point-to-point link.
  —A graph edge connects a router vertex to a network vertex when the router is directly connected to the network.

Figure 15.7 shows an example of an autonomous system, and Figure 15.8 is the resulting directed graph. The mapping is straightforward:

- Two routers joined by a point-to-point link are represented in the graph as being directly connected by a pair of edges, one in each direction (e.g., routers 6 and 10).
- When multiple routers are attached to a network (such as a LAN or packet-switching network), the directed graph shows all routers bi-directionally connected to the network vertex (e.g., routers 1, 2, 3, and 4 all connect to network 3).

[2]*OSPF Version 2*, RFC 1583, March 1994.

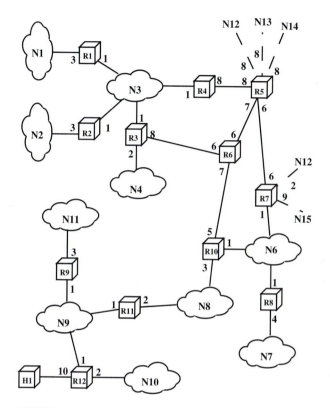

FIGURE 15.7   Sample Autonomous System

- If a single router is attached to a network, the network will appear in the graph as a stub connection (e.g., network 7).
- An end system, called a *host*, can be directly connected to a router, in which case it is depicted in the corresponding graph (e.g., host 1).
- If a router is connected to other autonomous systems, the path cost to each network in the other system must be obtained by some exterior routing protocol (ERP). Each such network is represented on the graph by a stub and an edge to the router with the known path cost (e.g., networks 12 through 15).

A cost is associated with the output side of each router interface. This cost is configurable by the system administrator. Arcs on the graph are labeled with the cost of the corresponding router output interface. Arcs having no labeled cost have a cost of zero. Note that arcs leading from networks to routers always have a cost of zero.

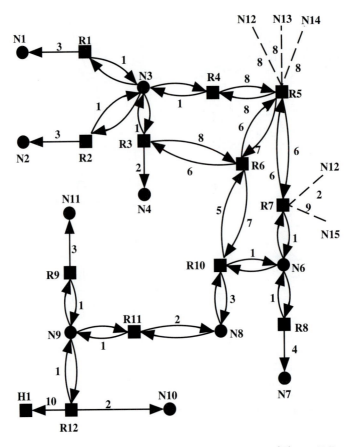

FIGURE 15.8   Directed Graph of Autonomous System of Figure 15.7

A database corresponding to the directed graph is maintained by each router. It is pieced together from link state messages from other routers in the internet. Using an algorithm explained in the next subsection, a router calculates the least-cost path to all destination networks. The results for router 6 of Figure 15.7 are shown as a tree in Figure 15.9, with R6 as the root of the tree. The tree gives the entire route to any destination network or host. However, only the next hop to the destination is used in the forwarding process. The resulting routing table for router 6 is shown in Table 15.5. The table includes entries for routers advertising external routes (routers 5 and 7). For external networks whose identity is known, entries are also provided.

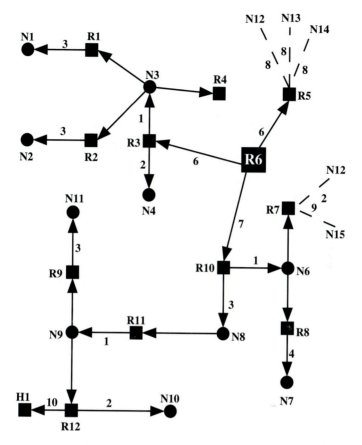

FIGURE 15.9   SPF Tree for Router R6

Least-Cost Routing Algorithm.   The hop costs are used as input to the path calculation routine. Each router maintains an information base containing the topology and hop costs of each link. This information is used to perform what is referred to as a *least-cost routing algorithm*, which can be stated simply as follows:

> Given a network of nodes connected by bidirectional links, where each link has a cost associated with it in each direction, define the cost of a path between two nodes as the sum of the costs of the links traversed. For each pair of nodes, find the path with the least cost.

TABLE 15.5   Routing Table for RT6

Destination	Next Hop	Distance
N1	RT3	10
N2	RT3	10
N3	RT3	7
N4	RT3	8
N6	RT10	8
N7	RT10	12
N8	RT10	10
N9	RT10	11
N10	RT10	13
N11	RT10	14
H1	RT10	21
RT5	RT5	6
RT7	RT10	8
N12	RT10	10
N13	RT5	14
N14	RT5	14
N15	RT10	17

The algorithm used in OSPF was originally proposed by Dijkstra [DIJK59]. It enables each router to find the least-cost route to every other router and network of interest. The algorithm can be stated as: Find the shortest paths from a given source node to all other nodes, by developing the paths in order of increasing path length. The algorithm proceeds in stages. By the kth stage, the shortest paths to the k nodes closest to (least cost away from) the source node have been determined; these nodes are in a set M. At stage $(k + 1)$, that node not in M that has the shortest path from the source node is added to M. As each node is added to M, its path from the source is defined. The algorithm can be formally described as follows. Define:

N = set of nodes in the network

s = source node

M = set of nodes so far incorporated by the algorithm

d_{ij} = link cost from node i to node j; $d_{ii} = 0$; $d_{ij} = \infty$ if the two nodes are not directly connected; $d_{ij} \geq 0$ if the two nodes are directly connected

D_n = cost of the least-cost path from node s to node n that is currently known to the algorithm

The algorithm has three steps; steps 2 and 3 are repeated until $M = N$. That is, steps 2 and 3 are repeated until final paths have been assigned to all nodes in the network:

1. Initialize:

   $M = \{s\}$ i.e., set of nodes incorporated is only the source node

   $D_n = d_{sn}$ for $n \neq s$ i.e., initial path costs to neighboring nodes are simply the link costs

2. Find the neighboring node not in M that has the least-cost path from node s and incorporate that node into M: This can be expressed as:

$$\text{Find } w \notin M \text{ such that } D_w = \min_{j \in M} D_j; D_w = \min_{j \in M} D_j.$$

   Add w to M.

3. Update least-cost paths:

$$D_n = \min[D_n, D_w + d_{wn}] \text{ for all } n \notin M$$

   If the latter term is the minimum, the path from s to n is now the path from s to w concatenated with the link from w to n.

One iteration of steps 2 and 3 adds one new node to M and defines the least-cost path from s to that node. That path passes only through nodes that are in M. To see this, consider the following line of reasoning. After k iterations, there are k nodes in M, and the least-cost path from s to each of these nodes has been defined. Now consider all possible paths from s to nodes not in M. Among those paths, there is one of least cost that passes exclusively through nodes in M (see Problem 15.9), ending with a direct link from some node in M to a node not in M. This node is added to M and the associated path is defined as the least-cost path for that node.

Table 15.6 shows the result of applying this algorithm to Figure 15.10, using $s = 1$. Note that at each step the path to each node plus the total cost of that path is generated. After the final iteration, the least-cost path to each node and the cost of that path has been developed. The same procedure can be used with node 2 as source node, and so on. Figure 15.11 illustrates the results.

TABLE 15.6 Example of OSPF Least-Cost Routing Algorithm

Iteration	M	D_2	Path	D_3	Path	D_4	Path	D_5	Path	D_6	Path
1	{1}	2	1–2	5	1–3	1	1–4	∞	—	∞	—
2	{1, 4}	2	1–2	4	1–4–3	1	1–4	2	1–4–5	∞	—
3	{1, 2, 4}	2	1–2	4	1–4–3	1	1–4	2	1–4–5	∞	—
4	{1, 2, 4, 5}	2	1–2	3	1–4–5–3	1	1–4	2	1–4–5	4	1–4–5–6
5	{1, 2, 3, 4, 5}	2	1–2	3	1–4–5–3	1	1–4	2	1–4–5	4	1–4–5–6
6	{1, 2, 3, 4, 5, 6}	2	1–2	3	1–4–5–3	1	1–4	2	1–4–5	4	1–4–5–6

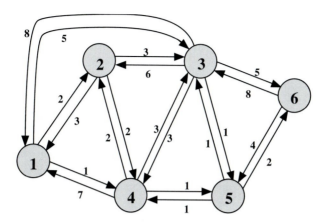

FIGURE 15.10   Example Directed Graph

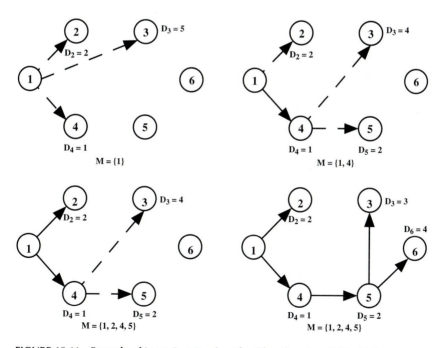

FIGURE 15.11   Example of Least-Cost Routing Algorithm (based on Table 15.6)

15.4

RECOMMENDED READING

Good coverage of internetworking and IP can be found in [COME95], [FEIT93], and [BLAC95]. Detailed coverage of OSPF and other routing algorithms is provided by [HUIT95]; these topics are also treated in [STEE95] and [PERL92].

BLAC95 Black, U. *TCP/IP & Related Protocols*. New York: McGraw-Hill, 1995.

COME95 Comer, D. *Internetworking with TCP/IP*, Volume I: *Principles, Protocols, and Architecture*. Englewood Cliffs, NJ: Prentice Hall, 1995.

FEIT93 Feit, S. *TCP/IP: Architecture, Protocols, and Implementation*. New York: McGraw-Hill, 1993.

HUIT95 Huitema, C. *Routing in the Internet*. Englewood Cliffs, NJ: Prentice Hall, 1995.

PERL92 Perlman, R. *Interconnections: Bridges and Routers*. Reading, MA: Addison-Wesley, 1992.

STEE95 Steenstrup, M. *Routing in Communications Networks*. Englewood Cliffs, NJ: Prentice Hall, 1995.

15.5

PROBLEMS

15.1 Would the spanning tree approach be good for an internet including routers?

15.2 What is the header overhead in the IP protocol?

15.3 Describe some circumstances where it might be desirable to use source routing rather than let the routers make the routing decision.

15.4 Because of segmentation, an IP datagram can arrive in several pieces, not necessarily in the correct order. The IP entity at the receiving end system must accumulate these segments until the original datagram is reconstituted.

a. Consider that the IP entity creates a buffer for assembling the data field in the original datagram. As assembly proceeds, the buffer will contain blocks of data and "holes" between the data blocks. Describe an algorithm for reassembly based on this concept.

b. For the algorithm in part (a), it is necessary to keep track of the holes. Describe a simple mechanism for doing this.

15.5 What are the pros and cons of intermediate reassembly of IP datagrams versus reassembly at the destination?

15.6 The IP checksum needs to be recalculated at routers because of changes to the IP header, such as the lifetime field. It is possible to recalculate the checksum from scratch. Suggest a procedure that involves less calculation. *Hint:* Suppose that the value in octet k is changed by Z = new_value − old_value; consider the effect of this change on the checksum.

15.7 An IP datagram is to be segmented. Which options in the option field need to be copied into the header of each segment, and which need only be retained in the first segment?

15.8 In the discussion of IP, it was mentioned that the *identifier, don't fragment identifier,* and *time to live* parameters are present in the Send primitive but not in the Deliver primitive because they are only of concern to IP. For each of these primitives indicate whether it is of concern to the IP entity in the source, the IP entities in any intermediate routers, and the IP entity in the destination end systems. Justify your answer.

15.9 In the discussion of the OSPF routing algorithm, it is asserted that at each iteration, a new node is added to M and that the least-cost path for that node passes only through nodes already in M. Demonstrate that this is true. *Hint:* Begin at the beginning. Show that the first node added to M must have a direct link to the source node. Then show that the second node added to M must either have a direct link to the source node or a direct link to the first node added to M, and so on. Remember that all link costs are assumed nonnegative.

15.10 In step 3 of the OSPF routing algorithm, the least-cost path values are only updated for nodes not yet in M. Is it not possible that a lower-cost path could be found to a node already in M? If so demonstrate by example; if not, prove why not.

15.11 Generate a least-cost route to all other nodes for nodes 2 through 6 of Figure 15.10. Display the results as in Table 15.6.

APPENDIX 15A

TRANSMISSION CONTROL PROTOCOL

To fully understand the operation of IP, it is useful to have a brief overview of transmission control protocol (TCP). For most applications that make use of the TCP/IP protocol suite, the application relies on TCP to assure reliable delivery of data; TCP in turn relies on IP to handle addressing and routing chores.

We begin with a discussion of one of the central mechanisms of TCP: flow control. The functionality of TCP is then summarized by discussing the elements in the TCP header.

TCP Flow Control

As with most protocols that provide flow control, TCP uses a form of sliding-window mechanism. It differs from the mechanism used in many other protocols, such as LLC, HDLC, and X.25, in that it decouples acknowledgment of received data units from the granting of permission to send additional data units.

The flow control mechanism used by TCP[3] is known as a credit-allocation scheme. For this scheme, each individual octet of data that is transmitted is considered to have a sequence number. When a TCP entity sends a block of data, or protocol data unit (PDU), it includes the sequence number of the first octet in the PDU data field. A TCP entity acknowledges an incoming PDU with a message of the form (SN i, W j), with the following interpretation:

- All octets through sequence number (SN) $i - 1$ are acknowledged; the next expected octet has sequence number i.
- Permission is granted to send an additional window (W) of j octets of data, that is, the j octets corresponding to sequence numbers i through $i + j - 1$.

Figure 15.12 illustrates the mechanism (compare Figure 5.5). For simplicity, we show data flow in one direction only and assume that only one octet of data is sent in each PDU and that the octets are numbered sequentially modulo 8. Initially, through the connection establishment process, the sending and receiving sequence numbers are synchronized and A is granted an initial credit allocation of 7. After sending octets with sequence numbers corresponding to 0, 1, and 2, A has shrunk its window to a size of 4. Following receipt of these data units, B acknowledges receipt of numbers 0, 1, and 2, and issues a credit of 5. This means that A can send octets 3, 4, 5, 6, and 7. However, by the time that B's message has arrived at A, A has already sent octets 3 and 4 (which was permissible under the initial allocation). Thus A's remaining credit at this point is only 3 (numbers 5, 6, and 7). As the exchange proceeds, A advances the trailing edge of its window each time that it transmits, and advances the leading edge only when it is granted credit.

The credit allocation mechanism is quite flexible. For example, consider that the last message issued by B was (SN i, W j) and that the last octet of data received by B was octet number $i - 1$. Then:

- To increase credit to an amount k ($k > j$) when no additional data has arrived, B issues (SN i, W k).
- To acknowledge an incoming PDU containing m octets of data ($m < j$) without granting additional credit, B issues (SN $i + m$, W $j - m$).

---

[3]This same mechanism is used in the ISO standard reliable transport protocol, known as TP4.

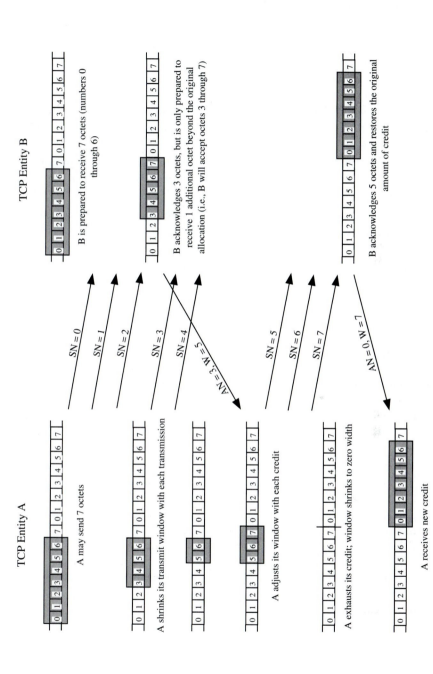

FIGURE 15.12   Example of Credit Allocation Mechanism

545

TCP PDU Format

TCP uses a single type of PDU format, called a TCP segment, shown in Figure 15.13. Because one header must support all protocol mechanisms, it is rather large. The fields of the header are:

- *Source port (16 bits):* identifies source service access point, or port.
- *Destination port (16 bits):* identifies destination port.
- *Sequence number (32 bits):* sequence number of the first data octet in this segment.
- *Acknowledgment number (32 bits):* a piggybacked acknowledgment. It contains the sequence number of the next data octet that the TCP entity expects to receive.
- *Data offset (4 bits):* length of the header, in units of 32-bit words. Equivalently, the position of the start of the data field relative to the start of the segment.
- *Flags (6 bits):* a set of 1-bit indicators:

    URG   Urgent pointer field significant
    ACK   Acknowledgment field significant
    PSH   Push function; this instructs the receiver to deliver all of the data received so far to the applications
    RST   Reset the connection
    SYN   Synchronize the sequence numbers, and open a TCP connection
    FIN   No more data from sender; ready to close the connection

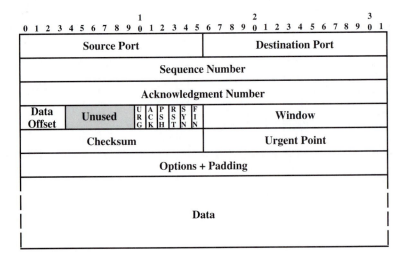

FIGURE 15.13   **Transmission Control Protocol (TCP) Format**

- *Window (16 bits):* credit allocation in octets. Value is the number of data octets, beginning with the one indicated in the acknowledgment field, that the sender is willing to accept.
- *Checksum (16 bits):* the 16-bit one's-complement addition of all 16-bit words in the segment plus a pseudoheader (described below). For purposes of computation, the checksum field is itself initialized to a value of zero.
- *Urgent pointer (16 bits):* points to the octet following the urgent data. This indicates to the receiver that all the data in this PDU, up to this point, should be considered urgent and be delivered to the application as soon as possible.
- *Options (variable):* at present, only one option is defined, which specifies the maximum segment size that will be accepted.

Several of the fields in the TCP header warrant further elaboration. The *source port* and *destination port* specify the sending and receiving users of TCP. As with IP, there are a number of common users of TCP that have been assigned numbers. These numbers should be reserved for that purpose in any implementation. Other port numbers must be arranged by agreement between communicating parties.

The *sequence number* and *acknowledgment number* are bound to octets rather than to entire segments. For example, if a segment contains sequence number 1000 and includes 600 octets of data, the sequence number refers to the first octet in the data field; the next segment in logical order will have sequence number 1600. Thus TCP is logically stream oriented: It accepts a stream of octets from the user, groups them into segments as it sees fit, and numbers each octet in the stream.

The *checksum* field applies to the entire segment plus a *pseudoheader* prefixed to the header at the time of calculation (at both transmission and reception). The pseudoheader includes the following fields from the IP header: source and destination internet address and protocol, plus a segment length field. By including the pseudoheader, TCP protects itself from misdelivery by IP. That is, if IP delivers a segment to the wrong host, even if the segment contains no bit errors, the receiving TCP entity will detect the delivery error.

The reader may feel that some items are missing from the TCP header, and that is indeed the case. TCP is designed specifically to work with IP. Hence some user parameters are passed down by TCP to IP for inclusion in the IP header. The relevant ones are:

- Precedence (a 3-bit field)
- Normal-delay/low-delay
- Normal-throughput/high-throughput
- Normal-reliability/high-reliability
- Security (an 11-bit field)

Network Management

Networks and distributed processing systems are of critical and growing importance in enterprises of all sorts. The trend is toward larger, more complex networks supporting more applications and more users. As these networks grow in scale, two facts become painfully evident:

- The network and its associated resources and distributed applications become indispensable to the organization.
- More things can go wrong, disabling the network or a portion of the network or degrading performance to an unacceptable level.

A large network cannot be put together and managed by human effort alone. The complexity of such a system dictates the use of automated network management tools. The urgency of the need for such tools is increased, and the difficulty of supplying such tools is also increased, if the network includes equipment from multiple vendors.

Of course, the foregoing comments apply to the total networking facilities of an organization, including local area networks (LANs) and wide-area networks (WANs). However, LANs are the core of any organization's networking strategy and must be the focus of any network management program.

In this chapter we provide an overview of a very big and complex subject: network management, with a special emphasis on LAN/MAN management. Specifically, we focus on the hardware and software tools, and organized systems of such tools, that aid the human network manager in this difficult task.

We begin by looking at the requirements for network management. This should give some idea of the scope of the task to be accomplished. To manage a network, it is fundamental that one know something about the current status and behavior of that network. For either LAN management alone, or for a combined LAN/WAN environment, what is needed is a network management system that includes a comprehensive set of data gathering and control tools and that is integrated with the network hardware and software. We look at the general architecture of a network management system and then examine the most widely used standardized software package for supporting network management: SNMP.

Then we look at the special requirements for LAN management and the tools that have been developed for that purpose. This is followed by an introduction to the LAN/MAN management standards developed by IEEE 802. These standards provide a set of tools and a framework for management, to be supplemented by specific logic for each type of network.

16.1

NETWORK MANAGEMENT REQUIREMENTS

Table 16.1 lists key areas of network management as suggested by the International Organization for Standardization (ISO). These categories provide a useful way of organizing our discussion of requirements.

Fault Management

Overview.   To maintain proper operation of a complex network, care must be taken that systems as a whole, and each essential component individually, are in proper working order. When a fault occurs, it is important, as rapidly as possible, to:

- Determine exactly where the fault is.
- Isolate the rest of the network from the failure so that it can continue to function without interference.
- Reconfigure or modify the network is such a way as to minimize the impact of operation without the failed component or components.
- Repair or replace the failed components to restore the network to its initial state.

TABLE 16.1   OSI Management Functional Areas

Area	Description
Fault management	The facilities that enable the detection, isolation, and correction of abnormal operation of the OSI environment
Accounting management	The facilities that enable charges to be established for the use of managed objects and costs to be identified for the use of those managed objects
Configuration and name management	The facilities that exercise control over, identify, collect data from, and provide data to managed objects for the purpose of assisting in providing for continuous operation of interconnection services
Performance management	The facilities needed to evaluate the behavior of managed objects and the effectiveness of communication activities
Security management	Addresses those aspects of OSI security essential to operate OSI network management correctly and to protect managed objects

Central to the definition of fault management is the fundamental concept of a fault. Faults are to be distinguished from errors. A **fault** is an abnormal condition that requires management attention (or action) to repair. A fault is usually indicated by failure to operate correctly or by excessive errors. For example, if a communications line is physically cut, no signals can get through. Or a crimp in the cable may cause wild distortions so that there is a persistently high bit error rate. Certain errors (e.g., a single bit error on a communication line) may occur occasionally and are not normally considered to be faults. It is usually possible to compensate for errors using the error control mechanisms of the various protocols.

User Requirements. Users expect fast and reliable problem resolution. Most end users will tolerate occasional outages. When these infrequent outages do occur, however, the user generally expects to receive immediate notification and expects that the problem will be corrected almost immediately. To provide this level of fault resolution requires very rapid and reliable fault detection and diagnostic management functions. The impact and duration of faults can also be minimized by the use of redundant components and alternate communication routes, to give the network a degree of "fault tolerance." The fault management capability itself should be redundant to increase network reliability.

Users expect to be kept informed of the network status, including both scheduled and unscheduled disruptive maintenance. Users expect reassurance of correct network operation through mechanisms that use confidence tests or analyze dumps, logs, alerts, or statistics.

After correcting a fault and restoring a system to its full operational state, the fault management service must ensure that the problem is truly resolved and that no new problems are introduced. This requirement is called *problem tracking and control*.

As with other areas of network management, fault management should have minimal effect on network performance.

Accounting Management

Overview.   In many enterprise networks, individual divisions or cost centers, or even individual project accounts, are charged for the use of network services. These are internal accounting procedures rather than actual cash transfers, but they are important to the participating users nevertheless. Furthermore, even if no such internal charging is employed, the network manager needs to be able to track the use of network resources by user or user class for a number of reasons, including:

- A user or group of users may be abusing their access privileges and burdening the network at the expense of other users.
- Users may be making inefficient use of the network, and the network manager can assist in changing procedures to improve performance.
- The network manager is in a better position to plan for network growth if user activity is known in sufficient detail.

User Requirements.   The network manager needs to be able to specify the kinds of accounting information to be recorded at various nodes, the desired interval between sending the recorded information to higher-level management nodes, and the algorithms to be used in calculating the charging. Accounting reports should be generated under network manager control.

In order to limit access to accounting information, the accounting facility must provide the capability to verify users' authorization to access and manipulate that information.

Configuration and Name Management

Overview.   Modern data communication networks are composed of individual components and logical subsystems (e.g., the device driver in an operating system) that can be configured to perform many different applications. The same device, for example, can be configured to act either as a router or as an end system node or both. Once it is decided how a device is to be used, the configuration manager can choose the appropriate software and set of attributes and values (e.g., a transport layer retransmission timer) for that device.

Configuration management is concerned with initializing a network and gracefully shutting down part or all of the network. It is also concerned with maintaining, adding, and updating the relationships among components and the status of components themselves during network operation.

User Requirements.   Startup and shutdown operations on a network are the specific responsibilities of configuration management. It is often desirable for these operations on certain components to be performed unattended (e.g., starting or shutting down a network interface unit).

The network manager needs the capability to identify initially the components that comprise the network and to define the desired connectivity of these components. Those who regularly configure a network with the same or a similar set of resource attributes need ways to define and modify default attributes and to load these predefined sets of attributes into the specified network components. The network manager needs the capability to change the connectivity of network components when users' needs change. Reconfiguration of a network is often desired in response to performance evaluation or in support of network upgrade, fault recovery, or security checks.

Users often need to, or want to, be informed of the status of network resources and components. Therefore, when changes in configuration occur, users should be notified of these changes. Configuration reports can be generated either on some routine periodic basis or in response to a request for such a report. Before reconfiguration, users often want to inquire about the upcoming status of resources and their attributes.

Network managers usually want only authorized users (operators) to manage and control network operation (e.g., software distribution and updating).

Performance Management

Overview.   Modern data communications networks are composed of many and varied components, which must intercommunicate and share data and resources. In some cases it is critical to the effectiveness of an application that the communication over the network be within certain performance limits.

Performance management of a computer network comprises two broad functional categories: monitoring and controlling. Monitoring is the function that tracks activities on the network. The controlling function enables performance management to make adjustments to improve network performance. Some of the performance issues of concern to the network manager:

- What is the level of capacity utilization?
- Is there excessive traffic?
- Has throughput been reduced to unacceptable levels?
- Are there bottlenecks?
- Is response time increasing?

To deal with these concerns, the network manager must focus on some initial set of resources to be monitored in order to assess performance levels. This includes associating appropriate metrics and values with relevant network resources as indicators of different levels of performance. For example, what count of retransmissions on a transport connection is considered to be a performance problem requiring attention? Performance management, therefore, must monitor many resources to provide information in determining network operating level. By collecting this information, analyzing it, and then using the resultant analysis as feedback to the prescribed set of values, the network manger can become more and more adept at recognizing situations indicative of present or impending performance degradation.

User Requirements.   Before using a network for a particular application, a user may want to know such things as the average and worst-case response times and the reliability of network services. Thus performance must be known in sufficient detail to assess specific user queries. End users expect network services to be managed in such a way as consistently to afford their applications good response time.

Network managers need performance statistics to help them plan, manage, and maintain large networks. Performance statistics can be used to recognize potential bottlenecks before they cause problems to the end users. Appropriate corrective action can then be taken. This action can take the form of changing routing tables to balance or redistribute traffic load during times of peak use or when a bottleneck is identified by a rapidly growing load in one area. Over the long term, capacity planning based on such performance information can indicate the proper decisions to make, for example, with regard to expansion of lines in that area.

Security Management

Overview.   Security management is concerned with generating, distributing, and storing encryption keys. Passwords and other authorization or access control information must be maintained and distributed. Security management is also concerned with monitoring and controlling access to computer networks and access to all or part of the network management information obtained from the network nodes. Logs are an important security tool, and therefore, security management is very much involved with the collection, storage, and examination of audit records and security logs, as well as with the enabling and disabling of these logging facilities.

User Requirements.   Security management provides facilities for protection of network resources and user information. Network security facilities should be available for authorized users only. Users want to know that the proper security policies are in force and effective and that the management of security facilities is itself secure.

16.2
NETWORK MANAGEMENT SYSTEMS

A network management system is a collection of tools for network monitoring and control that is integrated in the following senses:

- A single operator interface with a powerful but user-friendly set of commands for performing most or all network management tasks.
- A minimal amount of separate equipment. That is, most of the hardware and software required for network management is incorporated into the existing user equipment.

A network management system consists of incremental hardware and software additions implemented among existing network components. The software used in accomplishing the network management tasks resides in the host computers and communications processors (e.g., front-end processors, terminal cluster controllers, bridges, routers). A network management system is designed to view the entire network as a unified architecture, with addresses and labels assigned to each point and the specific attributes of each element and link known to the system. The active elements of the network provide regular feedback of status information to the network control center.

Figure 16.1 suggests the architecture of a network management system. Each network node contains a collection of software devoted to the network management task, referred to in the diagram as a network management entity (NME). Each NME performs the following tasks:

- Collect statistics on communications and network-related activities.
- Store statistics locally.

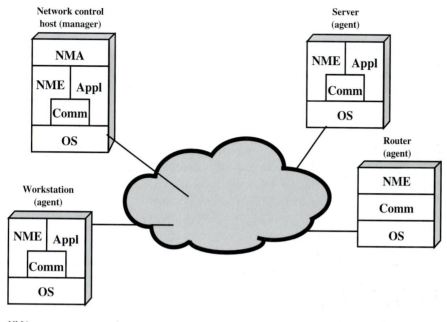

NMA	=	network management application
NME	=	network management entity
Appl	=	application
Comm	=	communications software
OS	=	operating system

FIGURE 16.1   Elements of a Network Management System

- Respond to commands from the network control center, including commands to:
  1. Transmit collected statistics to the network control center.
  2. Change a parameter (e.g., a timer used in a transport protocol).
  3. Provide status information (e.g., parameter values, active links).
  4. Generate artificial traffic to perform a test.

At least one host in the network is designated as the network control host, or **manager.** In addition to the NME software, the network control host includes a collection of software called the network management application (NMA). The NMA includes an operator interface to allow an authorized user to manage the network. The NMA responds to user commands by displaying information and/or by issuing commands to NMEs throughout the network. This communication is carried out using an application-level network management protocol that employs the communications architecture in the same fashion as any other distributed application.

Each other node in the network that is part of the network management system includes a NME and, for purposes of network management, is referred to as an **agent.** Agents include end systems that support user applications as well as nodes that provide a communications service, such as front-end processors, cluster controllers, bridges, and routers.

Several observations are in order:

1. Since the network management software relies on the host operating system and on the communications architecture, most offerings to date are designed for use on a single vendor's equipment. As was mentioned, standards in this area are still evolving. However, recent years have seen the emergence of standardized network management systems designed to manage a multiple-vendor network.

2. As depicted in Figure 16.1, the network control host communicates with and controls the NMEs in other systems.

3. For maintaining high availability of the network management function, two or more network control hosts are used. In normal operation, one of the centers is idle or simply collecting statistics, while the other is used for control. If the primary network control host fails, the backup system can be used.

16.3

SIMPLE NETWORK MANAGEMENT PROTOCOL

Simple network management protocol (SNMP) was developed for use as a network management tool for networks and internetworks operating TCP/IP. It has since been expanded for use in all types of networking environments. The term *simple network management protocol* (SNMP) is actually used to refer to a collection of specifications for network management that include the protocol itself, the definition of a database, and associated concepts.

Basic Concepts

Network Management Architecture.   The model of network management that is used for SNMP includes the following key elements:

- Management station
- Management agent
- Management information base
- Network management protocol

The **management station** is typically a stand-alone device, but may be a capability implemented on a shared system. In either case, the management station serves as the interface for the human network manager into the network management system. The management station will have, at minimum:

- A set of management applications for data analysis, fault recovery, and so on
- An interface by which the network manager may monitor and control the network
- The capability of translating the network manager's requirements into the actual monitoring and control of remote elements in the network
- A database of information extracted from the MIBs of all the managed entities in the network

Only the last two elements are the subject of SNMP standardization.

The other active element in the network management system is the **management agent.** Key platforms, such as hosts, bridges, routers, and hubs, may be equipped with SNMP so that they may be managed from a management station. The management agent responds to requests for information from a management station, responds to requests for actions from the management station, and may asynchronously provide the management station with important but unsolicited information.

The means by which resources in the network may be managed is to represent these resources as objects. Each object is, essentially, a data variable that represents one aspect of the managed agent. The collection of objects is referred to as a **management information base** (MIB). The MIB functions as a collection of access points at the agent for the management station. These objects are standardized across systems of a particular class (e.g., bridges all support the same management objects). A management station performs the monitoring function by retrieving the value of MIB objects. A management station can cause an action to take place at an agent or can change the configuration settings of an agent by modifying the value of specific variables.

The management station and agents are linked by a **network management protocol.** The protocol used for the management of TCP/IP networks is the simple network management protocol (SNMP). This protocol includes the following key capabilities:

- *Get:* enables the management station to retrieve the value of objects at the agent
- *Set:* enables the management station to set the value of objects at the agent
- *Trap:* enables an agent to notify the management station of significant events

There are no specific guidelines in the standards as to the number of management stations or the ratio of management stations to agents. In general, it is prudent to have at least two systems capable of performing the management station function, to provide redundancy in case of failure. The other issue is the practical one of how many agents a single management station can handle. As long as SNMP remains relatively "simple," that number can be quite high, certainly in the hundreds.

Network Management Protocol Architecture. SNMP was designed to be an application-level protocol that is part of the TCP/IP protocol suite. As Figure 16.2 illustrates, SNMP is intended to operate over the user datagram protocol (UDP).[1] For a stand-alone management station, a manager process controls access to the central MIB at the management station and provides an interface to the network manager. The manager process achieves network management by using SNMP, which is implemented on top of UDP, IP, and the relevant network-dependent protocols (e.g., Ethernet, FDDI, X.25).

Each agent must also implement SNMP, UDP, and IP. In addition, there is an agent process that interprets the SNMP messages and controls the agent's MIB. For an agent device that supports other applications, such as FTP, TCP as well as UDP is required.

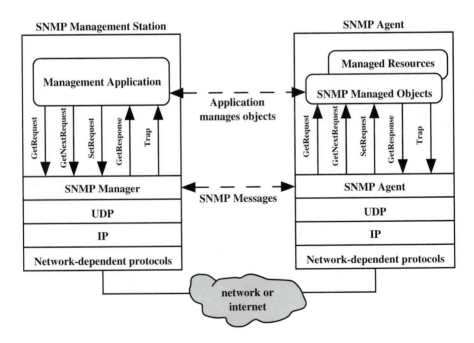

FIGURE 16.2   **Role of SNMP**

[1]See Appendix 16A for a description of UDP.

From a management station, three types of SNMP messages are issued on behalf of a management applications: GetRequest, GetNextRequest, and SetRequest. The first two are variations of the get function. All three messages are acknowledged by the agent in the form of a GetResponse message, which is passed up to the management application. In addition, an agent may issue a trap message in response to an event that affects the MIB and the underlying managed resources.

Because SNMP relies on UDP, which is a connectionless protocol, SNMP is itself connectionless. No ongoing connections are maintained between a management station and its agents. Instead, each exchange is a separate transaction between a management station and an agent.

Trap-Directed Polling.   If a management station is responsible for a large number of agents, and if each agent maintains a large number of objects, it becomes impractical for the management station to regularly poll all agents for all of their readable object data. Instead, SNMP and the associated MIB are designed to encourage the manager to use a technique referred to as trap-directed polling.

The recommended strategy is this. At initialization time, and perhaps at infrequent intervals, such as once a day, a management station can poll all of the agents it knows of for some key information, such as interface characteristics and perhaps some baseline performance statistics, such as average number of packets sent and received over each interface over a given period of time. Once this baseline is established, the management station refrains from polling. Instead, each agent is responsible for notifying the management station of any unusual event. Examples are the agent crashes and is rebooted, the failure of a link, or an overload condition as defined by the packet load crossing some threshold. These events are communicated in SNMP messages known as *traps*.

Once a management station is alerted to an exception condition, it may choose to take some action. At this point, the management station may direct polls to the agent reporting the event and perhaps to some nearby agents in order to diagnose any problem and to gain more specific information about the exception condition.

Trap-directed polling can result in substantial savings of network capacity and agent processing time. In essence, the network is not made to carry management information that the management station does not need, and agents are not made to respond to frequent requests for uninteresting information.

Proxies.   The use of SNMP requires that all agents, as well as management stations, must support UDP and IP. This limits direct management to such devices and excludes other devices, such as some bridges and modems, that do not support any part of the TCP/IP protocol suite. Further, there may be numerous small systems (personal computers, workstations, programmable controllers) that do implement TCP/IP to support their applications but for which it is not desirable to add the additional burden of SNMP, agent logic, and MIB maintenance.

To accommodate devices that do not implement SNMP, the concept of proxy was developed. In this scheme an SNMP agent acts as a proxy for one or more other devices; that is, the SNMP agent acts on behalf of the proxied devices.

Figure 16.3 indicates the type of protocol architecture that is often involved. The management station sends queries concerning a device to its proxy agent. The proxy agent converts each query into the management protocol that is used by the device. When a reply to a query is received by the agent, it passes that reply back to the management station. Similarly, if an event notification of some sort from the device is transmitted to the proxy, the proxy sends that on to the management station in the form of a trap message.

Protocol Specification

With SNMP, information is exchanged between a management station and an agent in the form of an SNMP message. Each message includes a version number, indicating the version of SNMP, a community name to be used for this exchange, and one of five types of protocol data units.[2] This structure is depicted in Figure 16.4, and the constituent fields are defined in Table 16.2. Note that the GetRequest, GetNextRequest, and SetRequest PDUs have the same format as the GetResponse PDU, with the error-status and error-index

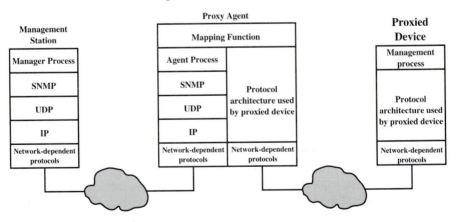

FIGURE 16.3　**Proxy Configuration**

[2]The terminology chosen by the SNMP developers is unfortunate. It is common practice to designate the overall block of information being transferred as a *protocol data unit*. In the case of SNMP, this term is used to refer to only a portion of the information transferred.

Version	Community	SNMP PDU

(a) SNMP Message

PDU type	request-id	0	0	variable-bindings

(b) GetRequest-PDU, GetNextRequest-PDU, and SetRequest-PDU

PDU type	request-id	error-status	error-index	variable-bindings

(c) GetResponse-PDU

PDU type	enterprise	agent-addr	generic-trap	specific-trap	time-stamp	variable-bindings

(d) Trap-PDU

name1	value1	name2	value2	• • •	namen	valuen

(e) Variable-bindings

FIGURE 16.4   SNMP Formats

fields always set to 0. This convention reduces by one the number of different PDU formats that the SNMP entity must deal with.

Figure 16.5 shows the timing relationship of the various PDUs. The GetRequest and GetNextRequest PDUs are both commands from a manager to retrieve data from an agent. The difference is that the GetRequest lists a specific variable or variables to be retrieved, while the GetNextRequest is used of traversing a tree-structured MIB. In both cases, the values, if available, are returned in a GetResponse PDU. The Set command is a command from a manager to update variables in an agent; in this case the GetResponse PDU provides an acknowledgment. Finally, the Trap PDU is a notification from an agent to a manager.

Transmission of an SNMP Message.   In principle, an SNMP entity performs the following actions to transmit one of the five PDU types to another SNMP entity.

1. The PDU is constructed.
2. This PDU is then passed to an authentication service, together with the source and destination transport addresses and a community name. The authentication service then performs any required transformations for this exchange, such as encryption or the inclusion of an authentication code, and returns the result. The community name is a value that indicates the context for this authentication procedure.
3. The protocol entity then constructs a message, consisting of a version field, the community name, and the result from action 2.

TABLE 16.2   SNMP Message Fields

Field	Description
version	SNMP version; RFC 1157 is version 1.
community	A pairing of an SNMP agent with some arbitrary set of SNMP application entities. The name of the community functions as a password to authenticate the SNMP message.
request-id	Used to distinguish among outstanding requests by providing each request with a unique ID.
error-status	Used to indicate that an exception occurred while processing a request. Values are: noError (0), tooBig (1), noSuchName (2), badValue (3), readOnly (4), genErr (5)
error-index	When error-status is nonzero, error-index may provide additional information by indicating which variable in a list caused the exception. A variable is an instance of a managed object.
variable-bindings	A list of variable names and corresponding values. In some cases (e.g., GetRequest-PDU), the values are null.
enterprise	Type of object generating trap; based on sysObjectID.
agent-addr	Address of object-generating trap.
generic-trap	Generic trap type. Values are: coldStart (0), warmStart (1), linkDown (2), linkUp (3), authenticationFailure (4), egpNeighborLoss (5), enterpriseSpecific (6).
specific-trap	Specific trap code.
time-stamp	Time elapsed between the last (re)initialization of the network entity and the generation of the trap; contains the value of sysUpTime.

4. This message is passed to the transport service.

In practice, authentication is not typically invoked.

Receipt of an SNMP Message.   In principle, an SNMP entity performs the following actions upon reception of an SNMP message.

1. It does a basic syntax-check of the message, and discards the message if it fails to parse.

2. It verifies the version number, and discards the message if there is a mismatch.

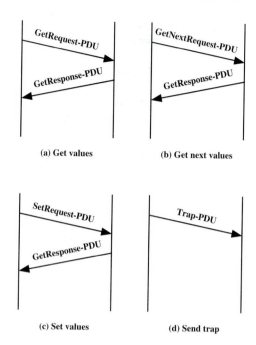

(a) Get values   (b) Get next values

(c) Set values   (d) Send trap

FIGURE 16.5   SNMP PDU Sequences

3. The protocol entity then passes the user name, the PDU portion of the message, and the source and destination transport addresses (supplied by the transport service that delivered the message) to an authentication service.
   a. If authentication fails, the authentication service signals the SNMP protocol entity, which generates a trap and discards the message.
   b. If authentication succeeds, the authentication service returns the PDU.
4. The protocol entity does a basic syntax-check of the PDU and discards the PDU if it fails to parse. Otherwise, using the named community, the appropriate SNMP access policy is selected and the PDU is processed accordingly.

In practice, the authentication service merely serves to verify that the community name authorizes receipt of messages from the source SNMP entity.

Variable Bindings.   All SNMP operations involve access to scalar objects. However, it is possible in SNMP to group a number of operations of the same type (get, set, trap) into a single message. Thus if a management station wants to get the values of all of the scalar objects in a particular group at a particular agent, it can send a single message requesting all values and get a single response listing all values. This technique can greatly reduce the communications burden of network management.

To implement multiple-object exchanges, all of the SNMP PDUs include a variable bindings field. This field consists of a sequence of references to object instances, together with the value of those objects. Some PDUs are concerned only with the name of the object instance (e.g., get operations). In this case, the value entries in the variable bindings field are ignored by the receiving protocol entity.

SNMPv2

SNMP has proliferated rapidly because it is what it claims to be: a simple tool for network management. SNMP provides a bare-bones set of functions that is easy to implement, relatively easy to use, and if used sensibly, that imposes minimal overhead on network operations. Essentially, the SNMP specification defines a syntax for representing management information and a protocol for retrieving and updating that information. The popularity of SNMP eventually caught up with it. Now that (human) managers are used to the level of control available with SNMP, they see its flaws and want more functionality. Among the most noteworthy areas needing improvement were support for decentralized network management strategies, efficient transfer of large blocks of data, and security. All of these areas are addressed in the next generation, version 2, known as SNMPv2. A draft set of standards for SNMPv2 were issued in 1993. These were subsequently withdrawn for an overhaul. At the time of this writing, the standards group for SNMPv2 is still contemplating substantial changes to the details of SNMPv2. Accordingly, this section provides a general overview of SNMPv2 functionality.

Decentralized Network Management.   In a traditional centralized network management scheme, one host in the configuration has the role of a network management station; there may be possibly one or two other management stations in a backup role. The remainder of the devices on the network contain agent software and a MIB, to allow monitoring and control from the management station. As networks grow in size and traffic load, such a centralized system is unworkable. Too much burden is placed on the management station, and there is too much traffic, with reports from every single agent having to wend their way across the entire network to headquarters. In such circumstances, a decentralized, distributed approach works best (e.g., Figure 16.6). In a decentralized network management scheme, there may be multiple top-level management stations, which might be referred to as *management servers*. Each such server might directly manage a portion of the total pool of agents. However, for many of the agents, the management server delegates responsibility to an intermediate manager. The intermediate manager plays the role of manager to monitor and control the agents under its responsibility. It also plays an agent role to provide information and accept control

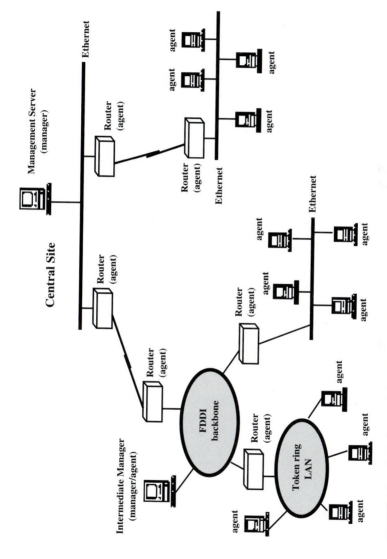

FIGURE 16.6   Example-Distributed Network Management Configuration

565

from a higher-level management server. This type of architecture spreads the processing burden and reduces total network traffic.

An essential element of a decentralized network management scheme is a powerful and flexible capability for cooperation among managers. To support manager-to-manager cooperation, SNMPv2 introduces two new features: an Inform command and a manager-to-manager MIB.

A manager uses the Inform command to send unsolicited information to another manager. For example, using the Inform command, a manager can notify another manager when some unusual event occurs, such as the loss of a physical link, or an excessive rate of traffic at some point in the network. Such unsolicited notifications provide an ideal tool for configuring a decentralized network management scheme. Higher-level managers need not concern themselves with the details of remote parts of the network; for example, when a local event that requires central attention occurs, the local manager can use the Inform command to alert the central manager. This ability for one manager to alert another is lacking in SNMP.

SNMPv2 also includes a manager-to-manager MIB, which defines tables that can be used to set up an event-reporting scheme. A manager can be configured to issue notifications when something unusual happens, such as a surge in local traffic, and line failure, and so on. The MIB specifies which events will trigger a notification, what information is to be provided in the notification, and which manager or managers are to receive the notification. The notification information is transmitted in an Inform command. The advantage of this scheme, which again is lacking in the original SNMP, is that it is an easy matter to configure a distributed network management strategy in which low-level management stations will deal with ordinary network management tasks and alert a higher-level management station when a predefined event occurs.

Data Transfer.   One of the concerns that users have had with the original SNMP is the amount of traffic that can be generated as managers communicate with agents. With SNMP, only a limited amount of data can be exchanged in a single transaction, thus frequently forcing management workstations and agents to generate multiple transactions. The result can be a heavy load on the network that can affect response time for end-user applications.

To streamline these exchanges, SNMPv2 adds a new command, the GetBulk command, and introduces an improved version of SNMP's Get command.

The GetBulk command targets the one area of information exchange capable of generating the most traffic: retrieval of tables. A table represents a related set of information about a resource (e.g., a router) or activity (e.g, the traffic over a TCP connection). It is organized as a collection of rows of variables, with each row having the same sequence of variables.

For example, each router in a configuration maintains a routing table with one row for each destination. The row is indexed by the destination address and includes a field for the next hop to take to get to the destination, and the amount of time since this routing information was last changed. All of the rows have the same format, with one row per destination.

With the original SNMP, it is possible to retrieve information from such a table only one row at a time. If a manager needs to see an entire routing table, for example, a tedious series of get/response transactions is needed, one for each row.

With the GetBulk command, the manager can retrieve the entire table with one transaction and even retrieve additional nontable information in that same transaction. For example, suppose that a manager wished to retrieve the entire routing table plus the variable sysUpTime, so that it could associate a system time with the retrieved table. The manager would issue a getBulk command that would list the variable sysUpTime and the variables that correspond to each field in the table, including destination, next hop, and age (see Figure 16.7). The command also includes two parameters: The nonrepeaters parameter indicates how many of the listed variables are to return just one value; in this case there is only one such variable, sysUpTime, so nonrepeaters is set to 1. The max-repetitions parameter indicates how many rows of the table are to be retrieved. If the manager knows the number, of rows, max-repetitions is set to that value. Otherwise, the manager makes an educated guess and, if necessary, issues additional Get-Bulk commands to get additional rows.

Another feature SNMPv2 offers to improve the efficiency of data transfer is the *nonatomic* Get command. Management stations in both SNMP and SNMPv2 use the Get command to obtain the value of one or more variables. In SNMP, if a Get command lists multiple variables, and if the agent is unable to return a value for even one of those variables, the entire command is rejected. If this happens, the manager must reissue the Get command with fewer variables. SNMPv2's nonatomic Get command allows partial results to be returned (hence the term *nonatomic*); that is, the agent will return those values that it can and ignore the rest of the variables in the command. Again, this improves efficiency by reducing the number of exchanges across the network.

Security Features.   The most substantial improvement SNMPv2 offers over the original SNMP is the addition of security features. This deals with one of the major concerns that users of SNMP have expressed: its lack of effective security. Specifically, users want to know that only authorized personnel are able to perform network management functions (e.g., disable/enable a line) and that only authorized personnel are able to read network management information (e.g., contents of a configuration file).

The three new security features provided by SNMPv2 are authentication, secrecy, and access control. Authentication enables an agent to verify that an incoming command is from an authorized manager and that the contents of the command have not been altered. To achieve this, each man-

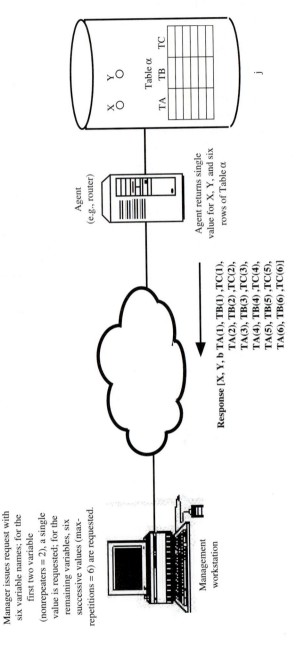

GetBulkRequest (nonrepeaters = 2, max-repetitions = 6, X, Y, TA, TB, TC)

Manager issues request with six variable names; for the first two variable (nonrepeaters = 2), a single value is requested; for the remaining variables, six successive values (max-repetitions = 6) are requested.

Table α

X Y
O O

TA TB TC

j

Agent (e.g., router)

Agent returns single value for X, Y, and six rows of Table α

Response [X, Y, b TA(1), TB(1) ,TC(1),
TA(2), TB(2) ,TC(2),
TA(3), TB(3) ,TC(3),
TA(4), TB(4) ,TC(4),
TA(5), TB(5) ,TC(5),
TA(6), TB(6) ,TC(6)]

Management workstation

FIGURE 16.7 GetBulkRequest Command

ager and agent that wish to communicate must share a secret key. The manager uses this key to calculate a message authentication code that is a function of the message to be transmitted and appends that code to the message. When the agent receives the message, it uses the same key and calculates the message authentication code once again. If the agent's version of the code matches the value appended to the incoming message, the agent knows that the message can only have originated from the authorized manager and that the message was not altered in transit.

The secrecy facility enables managers and agents to encrypt messages to prevent eavesdropping by third parties. Again, manager and agent share a secret key. In this case, if the two are configured to use the secrecy facility, all traffic between them is encrypted using the data encryption standard (DES).

Finally, the access control facility makes it possible to configure agents to provide different levels of access to different managers. Access can be limited in terms of the commands that the agent will accept from a given manager and also in terms of the portion of the agent's MIB that a given manager may access. The access control policy to be used by an agent for each manager must be preconfigured and essentially consists of a table that details the access privileges of the various authorized managers.

Figure 16.8 highlights the SNMPv2 security features.

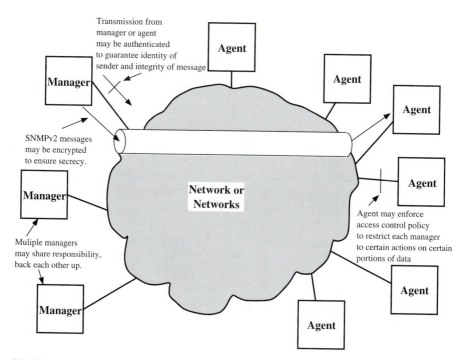

FIGURE 16.8   Features of SNMPv2 Security

16.4

LAN-SPECIFIC NETWORK MANAGEMENT

A LAN by itself seems a much more manageable network than one involving wide-area components. For one thing, the transmission technologies used are reduced in number. Also, everything is at hand; it is much easier to localize faults and to monitor everything, since it is all clustered together in a small area. Nevertheless, for a local network supporting a substantial amount of equipment, network management is required. In many cases, the LAN vendors provide many of the tools needed for network management in a package of hardware and software that can be optionally acquired with the network. In this section we give an overview of the types of capabilities typically found in such products.

Special Importance of LAN Management

Most LANs start out as a homogeneous set of equipment from a single networking vendor. At that time, they usually have one main application, such as multiuser accounting, desktop publishing, electronic mail, or host communications. But rapid growth breeds complexity. And, as users come to depend on the LAN, the network's applications expand.

Thus LANs evolve from being a nice extra to being a critical part of an organization's day-to-day operations. Downtime can cost a corporation dearly as work backs up. Slowdowns, due to increased server and network loads, can lead to wasted time as users wait for transactions to finish or customer accounts to be called up. Unfortunately, most users do not recognize the difficulties of managing LANs until serious problems are encountered. Networks are easy to install and deliver substantial benefits when their size and scope are limited. Network popularity, however, often outpaces users' understanding of network management and methods for spotting and identifying network problems.

The combination of larger size, more internetworking, and multivendor configurations can rapidly change a simple network into a maze that can leave all but the most sophisticated users stymied. Isolating problems and improving performance in complex and feature-laden networks is one of the major challenges in today's LAN environments.

LANs that were once small and easy to use become very easy to misuse when they grow to meet users' ever-expanding needs. For example, one naive user could utilize the wrong boot disk, containing last year's version of network drivers. This could have a catastrophic effect on hundreds of users in a large network installation. Another user innocently utilizing a workstation for a particular database application might discover that simply by exceeding some internal limit, the application unexpectedly starts to use all of the resources of the file server.

In yet another problem scenario, a network manager installs a file server, which should routinely send out a single packet regarding the health of the file server every 15 minutes. If a mistake is made in setting parameters, the server may send out a flood of packets, which can cause a service "brownout" due to retransmissions and broadcasts through the network. To the unsophisticated network manager, such a brownout has the same symptoms as those of a saturated network.

These problems are quite common, and in many instances, the network manager does not know the cause. A sophisticated and easy-to-use network control center can make the job of LAN management much easier.

LAN Network-Control Center

With many local area network (LAN) products, a network-control center (NCC) is provided. Typically, this is a separate dedicated microcomputer attached to the network through a network interface unit (NIU). All of the functions of a LAN network-control center involve observation, active control, or a combination of the two. They fall into three categories:

- Configuration functions
- Monitoring functions
- Fault isolation

Configuration Functions.   One of the principal functions of an NCC is to maintain a directory of names and addresses of resources available on the network. This allows users to set up connections by name. A resource may be any device or service: terminals, hosts, peripherals, application programs, or utility programs. For example, a user at a terminal who wishes to use the accounts payable package could request it with LOGON ACCOUNTS PAYABLE. Because the directory linking names with addresses can be altered, the manager, via the NCC, has the ability to move applications around (for load balancing or because a host is down). The directory is maintained at the NCC, but portions or all of it can also be downloaded to NIUs to reduce the network traffic required for directory lookup.

The NCC can also control the operation of the NIUs. The NCC could have the ability to shut down and start up NIUs and to set NIU parameters. For example, an NIU may be restricted to a certain set of NIUs or destination names that it can communicate with. This is a simple means of setting up a type of security scheme. Another example is to assign different priorities to different NIUs or different users.

Monitoring Functions.   In a typical LAN control center, monitoring functions fall into three categories: performance monitoring, network status, and accounting.

Table 16.3 lists the types of measurements reported in a typical LAN facility. These measurements can be used to answer a number of questions. Questions concerning possible errors or inefficiencies include:

- Is traffic evenly distributed among the network users or are there source–destination pairs with unusually heavy traffic?
- What is the percentage of each type of packet? Are some packet types of unusually high frequency, indicating an error or an inefficient protocol?
- What is the distribution of data packet sizes?
- What are the channel acquisition and communication delay distributions? Are these times excessive?
- Are collisions a factor in getting packets transmitted, indicating possible faulty hardware or protocols?
- What is the channel utilization and throughput?

These areas are of interest to the network manager. Other questions of concern have to do with response time and throughput by user class and determining how much growth the network can absorb before certain performance thresholds are crossed.

TABLE 16.3   Performance Measurement Reports

Name	Variables	Description
Host communication matrix	Source × destination	(Number, %) of (packets, data packets, data bytes)
Group communication matrix	Source × destination	As above, consolidated into address groups
Packet-type histogram	Packet type	(Number, %) of (packets, original packets) by type
Data packet-size histogram	Packet size	(Number, %) of data packets by data byte length
Throughput-utilization disttribution	Source	(Total bytes, data bytes) transmitted
Packet interarrival time histogram	Interarrival time	Time between consecutive carrier (network busy) signals
Channel acquisition delay histogram	NIU acquisition delay	(Number, %) of packets delayed at NIU by given amount
Communication delay histogram	Packet delay	Time from original packet ready at source to receipt
Collision count histogram	Number of collisions	Number of packets by number of collisions
Transmission count histogram	Number of transmissions	Number of packets by transmission attempts

Because of the broadcast nature of LANs, many of the measurements can be collected passively at the NCC, without perturbing the network. The NCC can be programmed to accept all packets, regardless of destination address. For a heavily loaded network, this may not be possible, and a sampling scheme must be used. In a LAN containing bridges, one collection point per segment is required.

However, not all information can be centrally collected by observing the traffic on the LAN. To get end-to-end measures, such as response time, would require knowing the time that a packet is generated by a host or terminal and the ability to identify the responding packet. This sort of measure requires some collection capability at the individual NIUs. From time to time, the NIUs can send the collected data to the NCC. Unfortunately, this technique increases the complexity of the NIU logic and imposes a communication overhead.

Another major area of NCC monitoring is that of network status. The NCC keeps track of which NIUs are currently activated and the connections that exist. This information is displayed to the network manager on request.

Finally, the NCC can support some accounting and billing functions. This can be done on either a device or user basis. The NCC could record the amount of traffic generated by a particular device or user and the resources that a device or user connected to and for how long.

Fault Isolation.   The NCC can continuously monitor the network to detect faults and, to the extent possible, narrow the fault down to a single component or small group of components. As an example, the NCC can periodically poll each LAN interface, requesting that it return a status packet. When an NIU fails to respond, the NCC reports the failure and also attempts to disable the NIU so that it does not interfere with the rest of the LAN.

16.5
RECOMMENDED READING

[STAL96b] provides a comprehensive and detailed examination of network management protocol standards, including SNMP and SNMPv2; the book also provides an overview of network management technology. [STAL93] contains reprints of key recent papers on network management technology and standards. One of the few textbooks on the subject of network management is [TERP92].

STAL96b   Stallings, W. *SNMP, SNMPv2, and RMON: Network Management*. Reading, MA: Addison-Wesley, 1996.

STAL93 Stallings, W. *Network Management.* Los Alamitos, CA: IEEE Computer Society Press, 1993.

TERP92 Terplan, K. *Communication Networks Management.* Englewood Cliffs, NJ: Prentice Hall, 1992.

16.6

PROBLEMS

16.1 List useful protocol-specific performance measures for the following protocols. Indicate whether collection can be centralized or must be distributed.
  a. Token bus
  b. Token ring
  c. DQDB

16.2 For centrally collected measurement data, there is a timing bias due to the propagation delay of the medium. Give examples of performance measures that are (are not) affected by this bias.

16.3 The original (version 1) specification of SNMP has the following definition of a data type known as Gauge:

> This application-wide type represents a non-negative integer, which may increase or decrease, but which latches at a maximum value. This standard specifies a maximum value of 2^{32-1} (4294967295 decimal) for gauges.

Unfortunately, the word *latch* is not defined and this resulted in two different interpretations. The SNMPv2 standard cleared up the ambiguity with the following definition:

> The value of a Gauge has its maximum value whenever the information being modeled is greater than or equal to that maximum value; if the information being modeled subsequently decreases below the maximum value, the Gauge also decreases.

  a. What is the alternative interpretation?
  b. Discuss the pros and cons of the two interpretations.

APPENDIX 16A

USER DATAGRAM PROTOCOL

In addition to TCP, there is one other transport-level protocol that is in common use as part of the TCP/IP protocol suite: the user datagram protocol

(UDP) specified in RFC 768. The UDP provides a connectionless service for application-level procedures. UDP does not guarantee delivery, preservation of sequence, or protection against duplication. UDP enables a procedure to send messages to other procedures with a minimum of protocol mechanism. SNMP makes use of UDP.

UDP sits on top of IP. Because it is connectionless, UDP has very little to do. Essentially, it adds a port addressing capability to IP. This is best seen by examining the UDP header, shown in Figure 16.9.

The header includes a source port and destination port, which identify the sending and receiving users of TCP. For example, port number 161 identifies an SNMP agent, and port number 162 identifies an SNMP manager. The length field contains the length in octets of the entire UDP segment, including header and data. The checksum is the same algorithm used for TCP and IP. It applies to the entire UDP segment plus a *pseudoheader* prefixed to the UDP header at the time of calculation. The pseudoheader includes the following fields from the IP header: source and destination internet address and protocol. By including the pseudoheader, UDP protects itself from misdelivery by IP. That is, if IP delivers a segment to the wrong host, even if the segment contains no bit errors, the receiving UDP entity will detect the delivery error. If an error is detected, the segment is discarded and no further action is taken.

The checksum field in UDP is optional. If it is not used, it is set to zero. However, it should be pointed out that the IP checksum applies only to the IP header and not to the IP data field, which in this case consists of the UDP header and the user data. Thus if no checksum calculation is performed by UDP, no check is made on the user data.

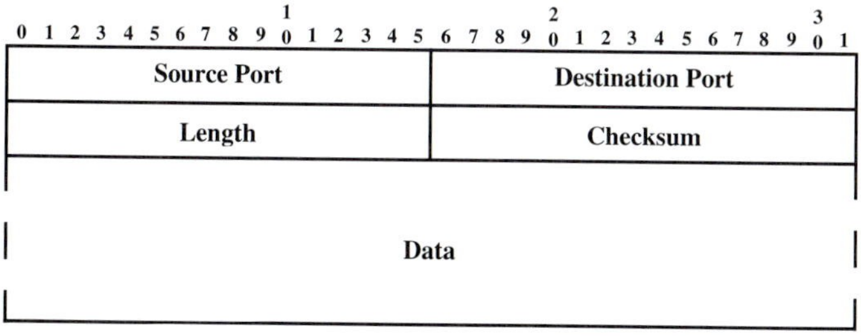

FIGURE 16.9   User Datagram Protocol (UDP) Format

Glossary

ALOHA. A medium access control technique for multiple access transmission media. A station transmits whenever it has data to send. Unacknowledged transmissions are repeated.

AMPLIFIER. An analog device designed to compensate for the loss in a section of transmission medium. It increases the signal strength of an analog signal over a range of frequencies.

ANS X3T9.5. A committee sponsored by the American National Standards Institute (ANSI) that is responsible for a variety of system interconnection standards. The committee has produced draft standards for high-speed coaxial cable bus and fiber optic ring local networks.

BANDWIDTH. Refers to a relative range of frequencies, that is, the difference between the highest and lowest frequencies transmitted. For example, the bandwidth of a TV channel is 6 MHz.

BASEBAND. Transmission of signals without modulation. In a baseband local network, digital signals (ones and zeros) are inserted directly onto the cable as voltage pulses. The entire spectrum of the cable is consumed by the signal. This scheme does not allow frequency-division multiplexing.

BRIDGE. A device used to link two or more homogeneous LANs or MANs. It accepts frames from attached networks addressed to devices on other networks, buffers them, and retransmits them in the direction of the other network. A bridge does not alter the frame content but acts merely as a relay. It operates at the MAC layer.

BROADBAND. The use of coaxial cable for providing data transfer by means of analog or radio-frequency signals. Digital signals are passed through a modem and transmitted over one of the frequency bands of the cable.

BUS. A topology in which stations are attached to a shared transmission medium. The transmission medium is a linear cable; transmissions propagate the length of the medium and are received by all stations.

CARRIERBAND. Same as *single-channel broadband*.

CATV. Community antenna television. CATV cable is used for broadband local networks.

CENTRALIZED BUS ARCHITECTURE. A bus topology in which the bus is very short and the links to attached devices are relatively much longer.

CENTREX. A voice and data-switching service that performs switching functions in the telephone company's central office as opposed to a digital PBX, which performs switching on the customer's premises.

CHEAPERNET. A baseband local area network that uses a thinner cable and less expensive components than Ethernet or the original IEEE 802.3 standard. Although the data rate is the same (10 Mbps), the network span and number of stations is less for Cheapernet.

CIRCUIT SWITCHING. A method of communicating in which a dedicated communications path is established between two devices through one or more intermediate switching nodes. Unlike packet switching, digital data are sent as a continuous stream of bits. Bandwidth is guaranteed, and delay is essentially limited to propagation time. The telephone system uses circuit switching.

COAXIAL CABLE. An electromagnetic transmission medium consisting of a center conductor and an outer, concentric conductor.

CODEC. Coder/decoder. Transforms analog voice into a digital bit stream (coder), and digital signals into analog voice (decoder), usually using pulse code modulation (PCM).

COLLISION. A condition in which two packets are being transmitted over a medium at the same time. Their interference makes both unintelligible.

CONTENTION. The condition when two or more stations attempt to use the same channel at the same time.

CRC. Cyclic redundancy check. A numeric value derived from the bits in a message. The transmitting station calculates a number that is attached to the message. The receiving station performs the same calculation. If the results differ, then one or more bits are in error.

CSMA. Carrier sense multiple access. A medium access control technique for multiple-access transmission media. A station wishing to transmit first senses the medium and transmits only if the medium is idle.

CSMA/CD. Carrier sense multiple access with collision detection. A refinement of CSMA in which a station ceases transmission if it detects a collision.

DATAGRAM. A packet-switching service in which packets (datagrams) are independently routed and may arrive out of order. The datagram is self-contained and carries a complete address. Delivery confirmation is provided by higher-level protocols.

DCE. Data circuit-terminating equipment. A generic name for network-owned devices that provide a network attachment point for user devices.

DIFFERENTIAL ENCODING. A means of encoding digital data on a digital signal such that the binary value is determined by a signal change rather than a signal level.

DIFFERENTIAL MANCHESTER ENCODING. A digital signaling technique in which there is a transition in the middle of each bit time to provide clocking. The encoding of a 0(1) is represented by the presence (absence) of a transition at the beginning of the bit period.

DIGITAL DATA SWITCH. A star topology local network using circuit switching. Usually refers to a system that handles only data but not voice.

DIGITAL PRIVATE BRANCH EXCHANGE. A local network based on the private branch exchange architecture. Provides an integrated voice/data switching service. *See also* PBX.

DTE. Data terminal equipment. A generic name for user-owned devices or stations that attach to a network.

DUAL CABLE. A type of broadband cable system in which two separate cables are used: one for transmission and one for reception.

ETHERNET. A 10-Mbps baseband local area network specification developed jointly by Xerox, Intel, and Digital Equipment. It is the forerunner of the IEEE 802.3 CSMA/CD standard.

FRAME. A group of bits that includes data plus one or more addresses. Generally refers to a link layer (layer 2) protocol.

FREQUENCY-AGILE MODEM. A modem used on some broadband systems that can shift frequencies in order to communicate with stations in different dedicated bands.

FREQUENCY-DIVISION MULTIPLEXING (FDM). A technique for combining multiple signals on one circuit by separating them in frequency.

FREQUENCY TRANSLATOR. In a split broadband cable system, an analog device at the headend that converts a block of inbound frequencies to a block of outbound frequencies.

FSK. Frequency-shift keying. A digital-to-analog modulation technique in which two different frequencies are used to represent ones and zeros.

GATEWAY. A device that connects two systems, especially if the two systems use different protocols. Recently, the term *gateway* has been reserved for the interconnection of networks at layer 7 of the OSI model.

GRADE OF SERVICE. For a circuit-switched system, the probability that, during a specified period of peak traffic, an offered call will fail to find an available circuit.

HEADEND. The endpoint of a broadband bus or tree network. Transmission from a station is toward the headend. Reception by a station is from the headend.

HIGH-SPEED LOCAL NETWORK (HSLN). A local network designed to provide high throughput between expensive, high-speed devices, such as mainframes and mass storage devices.

HIGHSPLIT.   A type of broadband cable system in which the available frequencies are split into two groups: one for transmission (5 to 174 MHz) and one for reception (232 to 400 MHz). Requires a frequency translator.

HOST.   The collection of hardware and software that attaches to a network and uses that network to provide interprocess communication and user services.

HYBRID LOCAL NETWORK.   An integrated local network consisting of more than one type of local network (LAN, HSLN, digital PBX).

IEEE 802.   A committee of IEEE organized to produce a LAN standard.

INBOUND PATH.   On a broadband LAN, the transmission path used by stations to transmit packets toward the headend.

INFRARED.   Electromagnetic waves whose frequency range is above that of microwave and below the visible spectrum: 3×10^{11} to 4×10^{14} Hz.

INJECTION LASER DIODE (ILD).   A solid-state device that works on the laser principle to produce a light source for optical fiber.

INTERNET.   A collection of packet-switched networks connected via gateways.

INTERNETWORKING.   Communication among devices across multiple networks.

LASER.   Electromagnetic source capable of producing infrared and visible light.

LIGHT-EMITTING DIODE (LED).   A solid-state device that emits light when a current is applied. Used as a light source for optical fiber.

LISTEN BEFORE TALK (LBT).   Same as carrier sense multiple access (CSMA).

LISTEN WHILE TALK (LWT).   Same as carrier sense multiple access with collision detection (CSMA/CD).

LOCAL AREA NETWORK (LAN).   A general-purpose local network that can serve a variety of devices. Typically used for terminals, microcomputers, and minicomputers.

LOCAL NETWORK.   A communications network that provides interconnection of a variety of data communicating devices within a small area.

MANCHESTER ENCODING.   A digital signaling technique in which there is a transition in the middle of each bit time. A 1 is encoded with a high level during the first half of the bit time; a 0 is encoded with a low level during the first half of the bit time.

MEDIUM ACCESS CONTROL (MAC).   For bus, tree, and ring topologies, the method of determining which device has access to the transmission medium at any time. CSMA/CD and token are common access methods.

MESSAGE SWITCHING.   A switching technique using a message store and forward system. No dedicated path is established. Rather, each message contains a destination address and is passed from source to destination through intermediate nodes. At each node, the entire message is received, stored briefly, and then passed on to the next node.

MICROWAVE.   Electromagnetic waves in the frequency range 1 to 30 GHz.

MIDSPLIT.   A type of broadband cable system in which the available frequencies are split into two groups: one for transmission (5 to 116 MHz) and one for reception (168 to 400 MHz). Requires a frequency translator.

MODEM.   Modulator/demodulator. Transforms a digital bit stream into an analog signal (modulator) and vice versa (demodulator). The analog signal may be sent over telephone lines, or could be radio frequencies or lightwaves.

NETWORK CONTROL CENTER.   The operator interface to software that observes and controls the activities in a network.

NETWORK INTERFACE UNIT.   A communications controller that attaches to a local network. It implements the local network protocols and provides an interface for device attachment.

NETWORK MANAGEMENT.   A set of human and automated tasks that support the creation, operation, and evolution of a network.

NONBLOCKING NETWORK.   A circuit-switched network in which there is always at least one available path between any pair of idle endpoints regardless of the number of endpoints already connected.

OPTICAL FIBER.   A thin filament of glass or other transparent material through which a signal-encoded light beam may be transmitted by means of total internal reflection.

OUTBOUND PATH.   On a broadband LAN, the transmission path used by stations to receive packets coming from the headend.

PACKET.   A group of bits that includes data plus source and destination addresses. Generally refers to a network layer (layer 3) protocol.

PACKET SWITCHING.   A method of transmitting messages through a communications network, in which long messages are subdivided into short packets. The packets are then transmitted as in message switching. Usually, packet switching is more efficient and rapid than message switching.

PASSIVE HEADEND.   A device that connects the two broadband cables of a dual-cable system. It does not provide frequency translation.

PASSIVE STAR.   A star-topology local network configuration in which the central switch or node is a passive device. Each station is connected to the central node by two links, one for transmit and one for receive. A signal input on one of the transmit links passes through the central node where it is split equally among and output to all of the receive links.

PBX.   Private branch exchange. A telephone exchange on the user's premises. Provides a switching facility for telephones on extension lines within the building and access to the public telephone network. May be manual (PMBX) or automatic (PABX).

PCM.   Pulse code modulation. A common method for digitizing voice. The data rate typically used for a single digitized voice channel is 64 kbps.

PROPAGATION DELAY.   The delay between the time a signal enters a channel and the time it is received.

PROTOCOL.   A set of rules governing the exchange of data between two entities.

REGISTER INSERTION RING.   A medium access control technique for rings. Each station contains a register that can temporarily hold a circulating packet. A station may transmit whenever there is a gap on the ring and, if necessary, may hold an oncoming packet until it has completed transmission.

REMODULATOR.   In a split broadband cable system, a digital device at the head-end that recovers the digital data from the inbound analog signal and then retransmits the data on the outbound frequency.

REPEATER.   A device that receives data on one communication link and transmits it, bit by bit, on another link as fast as it is received, without buffering. An integral part of the ring topology. Used to connect linear segments in a baseband bus local network.

RING.   A topology in which stations are attached to repeaters connected in a closed loop. Data are transmitted in one direction around the ring, and can be read by all attached stations.

RING WIRING CONCENTRATOR.   A site through which pass the links between repeaters, for all or a portion of a ring.

ROUTER.   A device used to link two or more networks. The router makes use of an internet protocol, which is a connectionless protocol operating at layer 3 of the OSI model.

SINGLE-CHANNEL BROADBAND.   A local network scheme in which the entire spectrum of the cable is devoted to a single transmission path; frequency-division multiplexing is not used. Also known as *carrierband*.

SLOTTED ALOHA.   A medium access control technique for multiple-access transmission media. The technique is the same as ALOHA, except that packets must be transmitted in well-defined time slots.

SLOTTED RING.   A medium access control technique for rings. The ring is divided into slots designated empty or full. A station may transmit when an empty slot goes by, by marking it full and inserting a packet into the slot.

SPACE-DIVISION SWITCHING.   A circuit-switching technique in which each connection through the switch takes a physically separate and dedicated path.

SPECTRUM.   Refers to an absolute range of frequencies. For example, the spectrum of CATV cable is now about 5 Hz to 400 MHz.

SPLITTER.   Analog device for dividing one input into two outputs and combining two outputs into one input. Used to achieve tree topology on broadband CATV networks.

STAR.   A topology in which all stations are connected to a central switch. Two stations communicate via circuit switching.

STAR WIRING.   A method of laying out the transmission medium that is installed for a local network. All cables are concentrated in a wiring closet, with a dedicated cable run from the closet to each device on the network.

STATISTICAL TIME-DIVISION MULTIPLEXING.   A method of TDM in which time slots on a shared transmission line are allocated to I/O channels on demand.

SUBSPLIT.   A type of broadband cable system in which the available frequencies are split into two groups: one for transmission (5 to 30 MHz) and one for reception (54 to 400 MHz). Requires a frequency translator.

SYNCHRONOUS TIME-DIVISION MULTIPLEXING.   A method of TDM in which time slots on a shared transmission line are assigned to I/O channels on a fixed, predetermined basis.

TAP.   An analog device that permits signals to be inserted or removed from a twisted pair of coax cable.

TDM BUS SWITCHING. A form of time-division switching in which time slots are used to transfer data over a shared bus between transmitter and receiver.

TERMINAL. A collection of hardware and possibly software that provides a direct user interface to a network.

TERMINATOR. An electrical resistance at the end of a cable that serves to absorb the signal on the line.

TIME-DIVISION MULTIPLEXING (TDM). A technique for combining multiple signals on one circuit by separating them in time.

TIME-DIVISION SWITCHING. A circuit-switching technique in which time slots in a time-multiplexed stream of data are manipulated to pass data from an input to an output.

TIME-MULTIPLEXED SWITCHING (TMS). A form of space-division switching in which each input line is a TDM stream. The switching configuration may change for each time slot.

TIME-SLOT INTERCHANGE (TSI). The interchange of time slots within a time-division multiplexed stream.

TIMING JITTER. Deviation of clock recovery that can occur when a receiver attempts to recover clocking as well as data from the received signal. The clock recovery will deviate in a random fashion from the transitions of the received signal.

TOKEN BUS. A medium access control technique for bus/tree. Stations form a logical ring, around which a token is passed. A station receiving the token may transmit data, and then must pass the token on to the next station in the ring.

TOKEN RING. A medium access control technique for rings. A token circulates around the ring. A station may transmit by seizing the token, inserting a packet onto the ring, and then retransmitting the token.

TOPOLOGY. The structure, consisting of paths and switches, that provides the communications interconnection among nodes of a network.

TRANSCEIVER. A device that both transmits and receives.

TRANSCEIVER CABLE. A twin-pair cable that connects the transceiver in a baseband coax LAN to the controller.

TRANSMISSION MEDIUM. The physical path between transmitters and receivers in a communications network.

TREE. A topology in which stations are attached to a shared transmission medium. The transmission medium is a branching cable emanating from a headend, with no closed circuits. Transmissions propagate throughout all branches of the tree and are received by all stations.

TWISTED PAIR. An electromagnetic transmission medium consisting of two insulated wires arranged in a regular spiral pattern.

VIRTUAL CIRCUIT. A packet-switching service in which a connection (virtual circuit) is established between two stations at the start of transmission. All packets follow the same route, need not carry a complete address, and arrive in sequence.

WIRING CLOSET. A specially designed closet used for wiring data and voice communication networks. The closet serves as a concentration point for the cabling that interconnects devices, and as a patching facility for adding and deleting devices from the network.

References

ABEY91   Abeysundara, B., and Kamal, A. "High-Speed Local Area Networks and Their Performance: A Survey." *ACM Computing Surveys,* June 1991.

ABSX92   Apple Computer, Bellcore, Sun Microsystems, and Xerox. *Network Compatible ATM for Local Network Applications, Version 1.01.* October 19, 1992 (available at parcftp.xerox.com/pub/latm).

ALBR94   Albrecht, A., et al. "An Overview of IEEE 802.12 Demand Priority." *Proceedings, IEEE GlobeCom,* 1994.

ATM95   ATM Forum. *LAN Emulation over ATM Specification, Version 1.0.* 1995.

BANT94   Bantz, D., and Bauchot, F. "Wireless LAN Design Alternatives." *IEEE Network,* March/April 1994.

BARI94   Barilovits, S., and Kadambi, J. "100VG-AnyLAN: Network Operation and Real-Time Capabilities." *Proceedings, 19th Conference on Local Computer Networks,* October 1994.

BARR94   Barry, J. *Wireless Infrared Communications.* Boston: Kluwer Academic Publishers, 1994.

BATE94   Bates, B. *Wireless Networked Communications.* New York: McGraw-Hill, 1994.

BERT92   Bertsekas, D., and Gallager, R. *Data Networks.* Englewood Cliffs, NJ: Prentice Hall, 1992.

BIAG93   Biagioni, E., Cooper, E., and Sansom, R. "Designing a Practical ATM LAN." *IEEE Network,* March 1993.

BIRD94   Bird, D. *Token Ring Network Design.* Reading, MA: Addison-Wesley, 1994.

BLAC95   Black, U. *TCP/IP & Related Protocols.* New York: McGraw-Hill, 1995.

BURR94   Burr, W., and Wakid, S. "A Comparison of FDDI Asynchronous Mode and DQDB Queue Arbitrated Mode Data Transmission for Metropolitan Area Networks." *IEEE Transactions on Communications,* February/March/April 1994.

CHEN94   Chen, K. "Medium Access Control for Wireless LANs for Mobile Computing." *IEEE Network,* September/October 1994.

COME95   Comer, D. *Internetworking with TCP/IP,* Volume I: *Principles, Protocols, and Architecture.* Englewood Cliffs, NJ: Prentice Hall, 1995.

COUC95   Couch, L. *Modern Communication Systems: Principles and Applications.* Englewood Cliffs, NJ: Prentice Hall, 1995.

DAVI95   Davis, P., and McGuffin, C. *Wireless Local Area Networks.* New York: McGraw-Hill, 1995.

DIJK59   Dijkstra, E. "A Note on Two Problems in Connection with Graphs." *Numerical Mathematics,* October 1959.

DRAV91   Dravida, S.; Rodrigues, M.; and Saksena, V. "Performance Comparison of High-Speed Multiple-Access Networks." *Proceedings of the International Teletraffic Congress,* June 1991.

ENG95   Eng, J. and Mollenaver, J. "IEEE Project 802.14: Standards for Digital Convergence." *IEEE Communications Magazine,* May 1995.

FCA94   Fibre Channel Association. *Fibre Channel: Connection to the Future.* Austin, TX: Fibre Channel Association, 1994.

FEIT93   Feit, S. *TCP/IP: Architecture, Protocols, and Implementation.* New York: McGraw-Hill, 1993.

GHAN91   Ghani, S., and Schwartz, M. "Comparison of DQDB and FDDI MAC Access Protocols." *Proceedings of the 16th Conference on Local Computer Networks,* October 1991.

HAHN90   Hahne, E., Choudhury, A., and Maxemchuk, N. "Improving the Fairness of Distributed-Queue-Dual-Bus Networks." *Proceedings, INFOCOM '90,* June 1990.

HAMM86   Hammond, J., and O'Reilly, P. *Performance Analysis of Local Computer Networks.* Reading, MA: Addison-Wesley, 1986.

HAND94   Handel, R., Huber, N., and Schroder, S. *ATM Networks: Concepts, Protocols, Applications.* Reading, MA: Addison-Wesley, 1994.

HEGE93   Hegering, H., and Lapple, A. *Ethernet: Building a Communications Infrastructure.* Reading, MA: Addison-Wesley, 1993.

HUIT95   Huitema, C. *Routing in the Internet.* Englewood Cliffs, NJ: Prentice Hall, 1995.

JAIN91   Jain, R. "Performance Analysis of FDDI Token Ring Networks: Effect of Parameters and Guidelines for Setting TTRR." *IEEE LTS,* May 1991.

JAYA87   Jayasumana, A. "Performance Analysis of Token Bus Priority Schemes." *Proceedings, INFOCOM '87,* 1987.

JEFF94   Jeffries, R. "ATM LAN Emulation: The Inside Story." *Data Communications,* September 21, 1994.

JOHN87 Johnson, M. "Proof That Timing Requirements of the FDDI Token Ring Protocol Are Satisfied." *IEEE Transactions on Communications,* June 1987.

KARO90 Karol, M., and Gitlin, R. "High-Performance Optical Local and Metropolitan Area Networks: Enhancements of FDDI and IEEE 802.6 DQDB." *IEEE Journal on Selected Areas in Communications,* October 1990.

KAVA95 Kavak, N. "Data Communication in ATM Networks." *IEEE Network,* May/June 1995.

KESS92 Kessler, G., and Train, D. *Metropolitan Area Networks: Concepts, Standards, and Services.* New York: McGraw-Hill, 1992.

KESS94 Kessler, G. "A Happy Union: IEEE 802.9." *LAN Magazine,* May 1994.

KLEI76 Kleinrock, L. *Queueing Systems,* Volume II: *Computer Applications.* New York: Wiley, 1976.

KNUT81 Knuth, D. *The Art of Computer Programming,* Volume 2: *Seminumerical Algorithms.* Reading, MA: Addison-Wesley, 1981.

LANG95 Lang, L. "Using Multilayer Switches to Connect Legacy LANs and the ATM Backbone." *Telecommunications,* March 1995.

MADR94 Madron, T. *Local Area Networks: New Technologies, Emerging Standards.* New York: Wiley, 1994.

MART94 Martin, J., Chapman, K., and Leben, J. *Local Area Networks: Architectures and Implementations.* Englewood Cliffs, NJ: Prentice Hall, 1994.

MCDY95 McDysan, D., and Spohn, D. *ATM: Theory and Application.* New York: McGraw-Hill, 1995.

MCEL93 McElroy, M. *The Corporate Cabling Guide.* Boston: Artech House, 1993.

MCMU94 McMullen, M. (editor). *Networks 2000.* San Francisco: Miller Freeman, 1994.

MEEK90 Meeks, F. "The Sound of Lamarr." *Forbes,* May 14, 1990.

MILL95 Mills, A. *Understanding FDDI.* Englewood Cliffs, NJ: Prentice Hall, 1995.

MULL95 Muller, N. *Wireless Data Networking.* Boston: Artech House, 1995.

NEWM88 Newman, R., Budrikis, Z., and Hullett, J. "The QPSX MAN." *IEEE Communications Magazine,* April 1988.

NEWM94 Newman, P. "ATM Local Area Networks." *IEEE Communications Magazine,* March 1994.

PAHL95a Pahlavan, K., Probert, T., and Chase, M. "Trends in Local Wireless Networks." *IEEE Communications Magazine,* March 1995.

PAHL95b Pahlavan, K., and Levesque, A. *Wireless Information Networks.* New York: Wiley, 1995.

PARK88 Park, S., and Miller, K. "Random Number Generators: Good Ones Are Hard to Find." *Communications of the ACM,* October 1988.

PERL92 Perlman, R. *Interconnections: Bridges and Routers.* Reading, MA: Addison-Wesley, 1992.

PRYC93 Prycker, M. *Asynchronous Transfer Mode: Solutions for Broadband ISDN.* New York: Ellis Horwood, 1993.

SADI95 Sadiku, M. *Metropolitan Area Networks.* Boca Raton, FL: CRC Press, 1995.

SANT94   Santamaria, A., and Lopez-Hernandez, F. (editors). *Wireless LAN Systems.* Boston: Artech House, 1994.

SCHW77   Schwartz, M. *Computer-Communication Network Design and Analysis.* Englewood Cliffs, NJ: Prentice Hall, 1977.

SEVC87   Sevcik, K., and Johnson, M. "Cycle Time Properties of the FDDI Token Ring Protocol." *IEEE Transactions on Software Engineering,* March 1987.

SHAH94   Shah, A., and Ramakrishnan, G. *FDDI: A High-Speed Network.* Englewood Cliffs, NJ: Prentice Hall, 1994.

SPRA91   Spragins, J., Hammond, J., and Pawlikowski, K. *Telecommunications Protocols and Design.* Reading, MA: Addison-Wesley, 1991.

SPUR95   Spurgeon, C. *Quick Reference Guide to Ethernet.* Austin, TX: Harris Park Press, 1995.

STAL93   Stallings, W. *Network Management.* Los Alamitos, CA: IEEE Computer Society Press, 1993.

STAL97   Stallings, W. *Data and Computer Communications, 5th ed.* Englewood Cliffs, NJ: Prentice Hall, 1997.

STAL95a   Stallings, W. *ISDN and Broadband ISDN, with Frame Relay and ATM, 3rd ed.* Englewood Cliffs, NJ: Prentice Hall, 1995.

STAL95b   Stallings, W. *Network and Internetwork Security: Principles and Practice.* Englewood Cliffs, NJ: Prentice Hall, 1995.

STAL96a   Stallings, W. *Computer Organization and Architecture, 4th ed.* Englewood Cliffs, NJ: Prentice Hall, 1996.

STAL96b   Stallings, W. *SNMP, SNMPv2, and RMON: Practical Network Management.* Reading, MA: Addison-Wesley, 1996.

STEE95   Steenstrup, M. *Routing in Communications Networks.* Englewood Cliffs, NJ: Prentice Hall, 1995.

STEP95   Stephens, G., and Dedek, J. *Fiber Channel.* Menlo Park, CA: Ancot Corporation, 1995.

STER93   Sterling, D. *Technician's Guide to Fiber Optics.* Albany, NY: Delmar Publications, 1993.

STUC85   Stuck, B., and Arthurs, E. *A Computer Communications Network Performance Analysis Primer.* Englewood Cliffs, NJ: Prentice Hall, 1985.

TANE88   Tanenbaum, A. *Computer Networks.* Englewood Cliffs, NJ: Prentice Hall, 1988.

TERP92   Terplan, K. *Communication Networks Management.* Englewood Cliffs, NJ: Prentice Hall, 1992.

TOBA80   Tobagi, F., and Hunt, V. "Performance Analysis of Carrier Sense Multiple Access with Collision Detection." *Computer Networks,* October/November 1980.

TOBA82   Tobagi, F. "Distributions of Packet Delay and Interdeparture Time in Slotted ALOHA and Carrier Sense Multiple Access." *Journal of the ACM,* October 1982.

TRUO95   Truong, H., et al. "LAN Emulation on an ATM Network." *IEEE Communications Magazine,* May 1995.

VALE92   Valenzano, A., DeMartini, C., and Ciminiera, L. *MAP and TOP Communications: Standards and Applications.* Reading, MA: Addison-Wesley, 1992.

VALK93   Valkenburg, M. *Reference Data for Engineers: Radio, Electronics, Computer, and Communications.* Carmel, IN: SAMS Publishing, 1993.

WALF95   Walford, P., and Frymoyer, E. "Providing Interoperable High-Speed Connections with Fiber Channel Technology." *ConneXions,* March 1995.

WATS95   Watson, G., et al. "The Demand Priority MAC Protocol." *IEEE Network,* January/February 1995.

WHIT92   White, G. *Internetworking and Addressing.* New York: McGraw-Hill, 1992.

WIDM83   Widmer, A., and Franaszek, P. "A DC-Balanced, Partitioned, 8B/10B Transmission Code." *IBM Journal of Research and Development,* September 1983.

YEN83   Yen, C., and Crawford, R. "Distribution and Equalization of Signal on Coaxial Cables Used in 10-Mbits Baseband Local Area Networks." *IEEE Transactions on Communications,* October 1983.

Index